Tort Law

'This is a comprehensive text which very much me … potential lawyers. The text really lives up to the se… …nes Tort Law in the real world with everyday scenarios leading to a … …ing of its function and purpose.

I also particularly like the use of practitioner interviews within the book; they provide valuable comments on their particular area of expertise.'

Lesley Lomax, Sheffield Hallam University

'An excellent book. It is comprehensive, very accessible and Frances Quinn brings a welcome new approach to the subject, making it ideal for any undergraduate course. This book must be considered by anyone teaching tort.'

Sean Curley, Principle Lecturer, University of Huddersfield.

Tort Law

Frances Quinn

PEARSON

Harlow, England • London • New York • Boston • San Francisco • Toronto • Sydney
Auckland • Singapore • Hong Kong • Tokyo • Seoul • Taipei • New Delhi
Cape Town • São Paulo • Mexico City • Madrid • Amsterdam • Munich • Paris • Milan

LIVINGLAW

Pearson Education Limited
Edinburgh Gate
Harlow
Essex CM20 2JE
England

and Associated Companies throughout the world

Visit us on the World Wide Web at:
www.pearson.com/uk

First published 2012

ISBN 978-1-4082-2265-2

British Library Cataloguing-in-Publication Data
A catalogue record for this book is available from the British Library

Library of Congress Cataloging-in-Publication Data
Quinn, Frances.
Tort law / Frances Quinn.
p. cm.
Includes bibliographical references and index.
ISBN 978-1-4082-2265-2 (pbk.)
1. Torts. 2. Negligence. I. Title.
K923.Q85 2012
346.03--dc23
2012006111

10 9 8 7 6 5 4 3 2 1
16 15 14 13 12

Typeset in 10.5/13pt Minion Pro by 35
Printed by Ashford Colour Press Ltd., Gosport

Brief contents

Contents

premium
mylawchamber
unrivalled support for legal education

Join over 5,000 students in succeeding with mylawchamber

Visit **www.mylawchamber.co.uk/quinntort** to access a wealth of tools to help you develop and test your knowledge of tort law, strengthening your understanding so you can excel.

The **Pearson eText** is a fully searchable, interactive version of *Tort Law*. You can make notes in it, highlight it, bookmark it, even link to online sources – helping you get more out of studying and revision. The Pearson eText is linked to the learning tools you'll find in MyLawChamber.

- Practice exam questions with guidance to hone your exam technique
- Annotated weblinks to help you read more widely around the subject and really impress your lecturers
- Glossary and key case flashcards to test yourself on legal terms, principles and definitions
- Legal newsfeed to help you read more widely, stay right up to date with the law and impress examiners
- Legal updates to help you stay up to date with the law and impress examiners
- Interactive 'You be the judge' questions

Case Navigator provides in-depth analysis of the leading cases in tort law, improving your case-reading skills and understanding of how the law is applied.

Use the access card at the back of the book to activate mylawchamber premium. Online purchase is also available at **www.mylawchamber.co.uk/register**.

Lecturers *Teach your course, your way.*

MyLawChamber is a powerful teaching tool which you can use to assess your students, and improve their understanding.

Make the interactive Pearson eText a 'live' teaching resource. You can annotate with your own commentary, add links to external sources, critique, or updates to the law and share with your students.

PEARSON mytest

Set quizzes and mini-assessments using the bank of over 450 multiple-choice questions to gauge your students' understanding.

Use Case Navigator, a case reading resource we offer in conjunction with LexisNexis, to assign student seminar work.

For information about teaching support materials, please contact your local Pearson sales consultant or visit **www.mylawchamber.co.uk**.

The regularly maintained mylawchamber premium site provides the following features:

- Search tool to help locate specific items of content.
- Online help and support to assist with website usage and troubleshooting.

Case Navigator access is included with your mylawchamber premium registration. The LexisNexis element of Case Navigator is only available to those who currently subscribe to LexisNexis Butterworths online.

Guided tour

Key points
Identify the essential elements of each chapter, aiding your core understanding of the chapter.

Key points In this chapter we will be looking

- How an occupier of premises can be liable for accidents that happen to people who have permission to be there, under the Occupiers' Liability Act 1957
- How an occupier of premises can be liable for accidents that happen to people without permission to be there, un Occupiers' Liability Act 1984
- How far it is possible to exclude ei type of liability
- Defences applicable under each Ac

People in the law
Read the interviews from people working in tort law and gain insight from their first hand work experience.

People in the law

Kevin Walker is Head of the Personal Injury department at solicitors Myers Lister Price in Manchester, and has wide experience of occupiers' liability cases.

What kinds of occupiers' liability cases do you deal with? There's a wide variety of this type of claim where an accident occurs on property or land owned by someone else. I deal with a lot of slip and trip claims – particularly those occurring in supermarkets, playground and play centre accidents, swimming pools, and have dealt with cases of people being injured by falling branches when they've been out walking.

In the majority of cases, injuries are relatively minor and the compensation tends to average somewhere between £5,000 and £10,000. I do have considerable experience of dealing with catastrophic injuries though and one such case I'm dealing with at the moment

Source: Kevin Walker (*text and photo*)

cases compared to a minor road traffic acciden

Law in action
Learn how the system works in practice through examples and problem scenarios found in the news.

Law in action The *Wilsher* case

Reading the official reports of the cases which make legal history sometimes tells you only half the story. In Martin Wilsher's case, it is often assumed that he lost his claim after the House of Lords case. In fact, the dispute still had some years left to run. The House of Lords ordered that the case should be retried, using the test for causation that they had outlined. They were not saying that he could not prove his case, only that the wrong test had been used in the original trial, so Martin's win there could not stand and the case needed to be looked at again using a different test of causation. However, this must have come as a huge blow for Martin's parents. By the time the case came to the House of Lords, Martin was 9, so their legal battle had already been

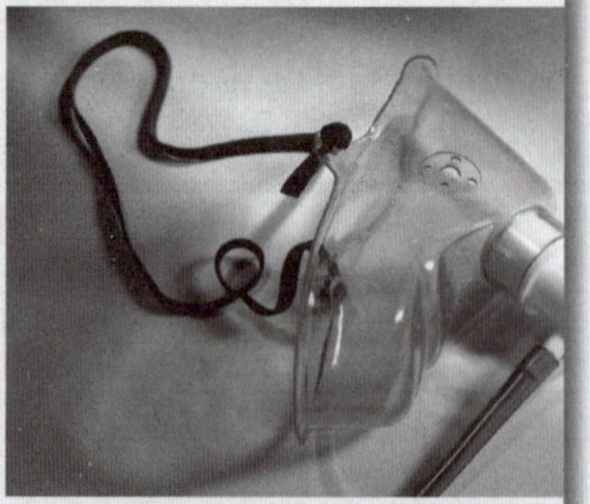

Source: Pearson Education Ltd/Jupiter Images/Brand X/Alamy

Case summary
Learn the essential facts, details of the case and the decision, all in these concise summaries, integrated into the text yet pulled out in the margins for easy reference.

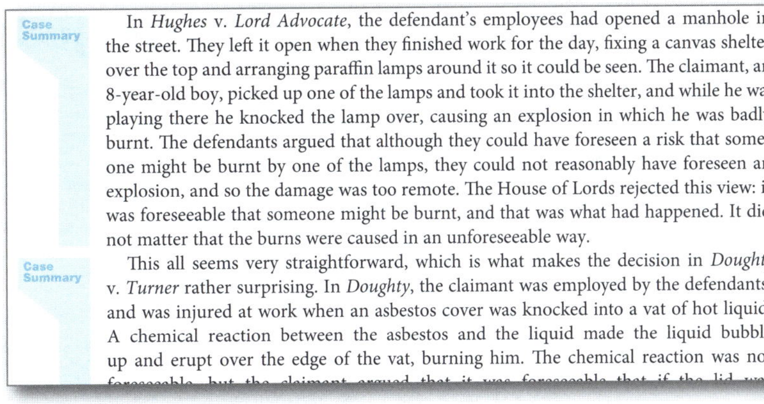

Case Summary

In *Hughes* v. *Lord Advocate*, the defendant's employees had opened a manhole in the street. They left it open when they finished work for the day, fixing a canvas shelter over the top and arranging paraffin lamps around it so it could be seen. The claimant, an 8-year-old boy, picked up one of the lamps and took it into the shelter, and while he was playing there he knocked the lamp over, causing an explosion in which he was badly burnt. The defendants argued that although they could have foreseen a risk that someone might be burnt by one of the lamps, they could not reasonably have foreseen an explosion, and so the damage was too remote. The House of Lords rejected this view: it was foreseeable that someone might be burnt, and that was what had happened. It did not matter that the burns were caused in an unforeseeable way.

Case Summary

This all seems very straightforward, which is what makes the decision in *Doughty* v. *Turner* rather surprising. In *Doughty*, the claimant was employed by the defendants, and was injured at work when an asbestos cover was knocked into a vat of hot liquid. A chemical reaction between the asbestos and the liquid made the liquid bubble up and erupt over the edge of the vat, burning him. The chemical reaction was not

Documenting the law
See real life tort law documents reproduced within the text to give you a sense of how the law looks and feels in practice.

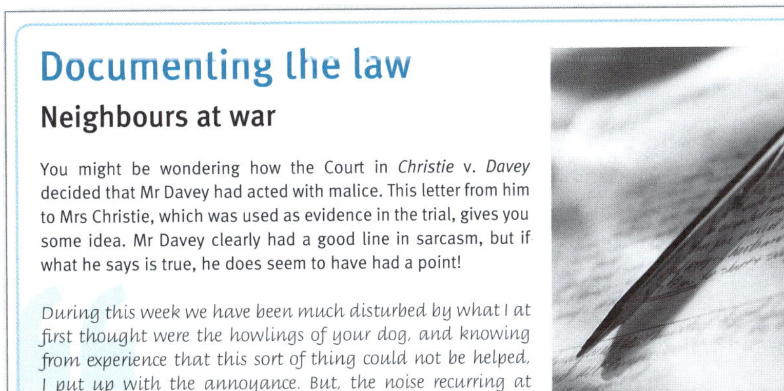

Documenting the law

Neighbours at war

You might be wondering how the Court in *Christie* v. *Davey* decided that Mr Davey had acted with malice. This letter from him to Mrs Christie, which was used as evidence in the trial, gives you some idea. Mr Davey clearly had a good line in sarcasm, but if what he says is true, he does seem to have had a point!

During this week we have been much disturbed by what I at first thought were the howlings of your dog, and knowing from experience that this sort of thing could not be helped, I put up with the annoyance. But, the noise recurring at

Key stats
Information about what is actually happening in the real world helps you to relate to the practical side of the law.

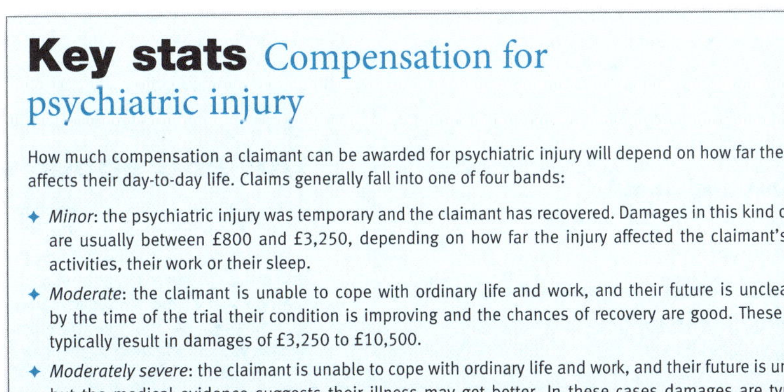

Key stats Compensation for psychiatric injury

How much compensation a claimant can be awarded for psychiatric injury will depend on how far the i affects their day-to-day life. Claims generally fall into one of four bands:

- *Minor*: the psychiatric injury was temporary and the claimant has recovered. Damages in this kind of are usually between £800 and £3,250, depending on how far the injury affected the claimant's activities, their work or their sleep.
- *Moderate*: the claimant is unable to cope with ordinary life and work, and their future is unclear by the time of the trial their condition is improving and the chances of recovery are good. These c typically result in damages of £3,250 to £10,500.
- *Moderately severe*: the claimant is unable to cope with ordinary life and work, and their future is un but the medical evidence suggests their illness may get better. In these cases damages are typ

Diagrams and **flowcharts**
These visual aids will make complex legal processes easier to follow and understand.

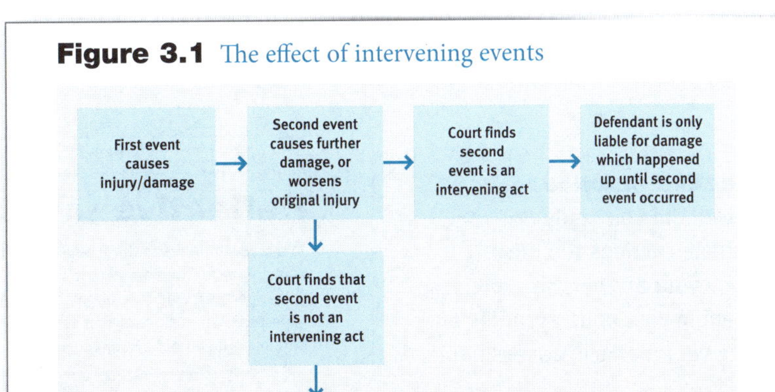

Figure 3.1 The effect of intervening events

You be the judge

Use your knowledge and apply it as you go to real life scenarios to fully test your understanding.

You be the judge

Q: Pat owns a farm, which once a year holds an open day for visitors to come and see how the farm works. Tina is one of the visitors, and particularly wants to see inside the dairy where Pat makes their cows' milk into yogurt. Pat explains that they cannot allow visitors inside the building because they have to keep the area scrupulously clean to avoid contaminating the yogurt. While Pat is talking to another visitor, Tina takes her chance and sneaks into the dairy. She trips on a loose flagstone and seriously injures her knee. Which of the Occupiers' Liability Acts would Tina's claim be judged under?

Source: Pearson Education Ltd/Imagestate/J Collection

A: The 1984 Act. Although Tina has permission to be on the farm, she clearly does not have permis to go into the dairy, so she is a non-visitor.

Writing and drafting

Put your knowledge of tort law into practice by completing the writing and drafting exercises contained throughout to enhance your practical legal skills and employability.

Writing and drafting

You are a solicitor and one of your clients is a large building firm. They are being sued by a woman who was injured when a plank of wood fell on her as she was passing a building that the company was working on. The person who dropped the plank is a temporary worker that the building firm call in now and then when they are short-staffed. They have always considered him to be self-employed, and they hope to avoid vicarious liability by proving that he is not their employee. Based on the cases discussed above, draw up a list of questions that you would ask the building firm in order to decide whether they may be able to avoid vicarious liability.

Out and about

Venture out and visit the suggested places or stay in and visit the websites to enhance your understanding of the areas covered.

Out and about

Gather together a range of newspapers (both tabloids and the more serious papers) and magazines. Bearing in mind everything you have read in this chapter so far, go through them, and see how many potentially defamatory stories and articles you can spot. Keep the examples you find, as you will use them again in an exercise in Chapter 17.

Source: Pearson Education Ltd/Photodisc/Photolink

Reflective practice

How well did you really do?
Use these sections to critically analyse your answers to exercises, deepening your understanding and raising your marks in assessments.

views, and make up your mind after you have heard both sides, not before.

Reflective practice

Take a few minutes to think about how this exercise went. What did you find difficult? Was it easy for the barristers to work out which points to make, or more difficult than you expected? Was the judge's decision easier or more difficult to make than you expected? What did you find worked well for you? Is there anything you would do differently if you did a similar exercise?

Summaries

Identify and recall the important cases and legal principles you need to aid revision and guarantee you go into assessments with confidence.

Summary

- Vicarious liability is a legal concept which makes employers liable for torts committed by their employees.
- Vicarious liability applies where:
  - the tortfeasor was an employee;
  - the tort was committed within the course of their employment.
- Tests for employee status include:
  - Does the employer control the employee's work?
  - Is the tortfeasor 'in business on their own account'?
  - Did the tortfeasor agree to provide work and skill in return for payment, and be subject to
- Employers can be liable in tort for crimi acts, if they are so closely connected wi job that it is fair to impose vicarious lia
- Vicarious liability can only arise if the employee was liable for a tort in the first place.
- Companies can be liable for torts comm by independent contractors if:
  - there is a non-delegable duty; or
  - the duty is delegable but the compa fails to take reasonable steps to find competent person or firm to do the w or to make sure it was done properly

Question and answer

Test and apply your knowledge of tort law by answering the questions provided using the guidance to help and structure your answers.

Question and answer*

Problem: John takes his son Kevin, aged 6, to the local park, which is owned by th A sign at the entrance to the park says 'Anytown Borough Council accepts n for injury or damage to property'. A little while after they arrive John needs to use the toilet, but the par are locked. He decides to find a convenient tree, but there are none nearby. He spots a fenced-off decides that looks private enough. The gate to the area is bolted and there is a sign saying 'Dange Enter', but John is desperate by now and goes in anyway. Just inside the gate is a deep hole conce sheet of wood. John falls into the hole, breaks his leg and smashes his expensive watch.

By now Kevin has fed all the bread they brought to the ducks, and he is wondering where his fat goes to look for him and comes across a bush with bright red berries. There is a sign saying that the it are poisonous and should not be eaten and a low fence around the bush. Despite the fence, the bu easy to reach and, as Kevin is feeling quite hungry by now, he picks a handful of the berries and eats becomes seriously ill.

Advise John about any claims he or Kevin may have against the council under the Occupiers' Lia 1957 and 1984.

You should allow yourself no more than 40 minutes to complete this task.

Essay: Critically examine the differences between the duty owed to visitors under the Occ Liability Act 1957, and the duty owed to non-visitors under the Occupiers' Liability Ac

This question should be answered in 40 minutes.

Further reading

Annotated references to journals and websites point you to that extra reading necessary to ensure you hit the higher marks.

Further reading and references

Better Regulation Taskforce (2004) *Better Routes to Redress*, London: Cabinet Office Publications.
This report looks at whether we really have a compensation culture, and gives suggestions for better ways to improve access to justice for those who have genuine claims. It has lots of useful background information on how the tort system works.

Cane, P. (2006) *Atiyah's Accidents, Compensation and the Law*, 7th edn, Cambridge: Cambridge University Press.
This book has been through many editions but still remains one of the best and most detailed explanations of the way the law treats personal

Harris, D., et al. (1984) *Compensatio Support for Illness and Injury* (The O Survey), Oxford: Clarendon Press.
Although it is now over 30 years old, this research still sheds useful light on the difficulties the tort system places in the way of claimants.

Morgan, J. (2004) 'Tort insurance ar incoherence', 67(3) MLR 384.
An interesting article on the impact of insu on decisions in tort cases. The author argu decisions influenced by insurance issues ha to incoherent rules.

National Audit Commission (2001) *H*

Preface

This is the second book in the Living Law series. As the name suggests, the aim of the series is to bring the subject of law alive, and show that it is a living, breathing subject that affects all sorts of people every single day – and not a dry, dusty collection of rules that only lawyers in wigs could possibly get interested in. Nowhere is that more true than in tort, an area of law that covers everything from footballers trying to conceal their extra-marital affairs, to patients suing for botched operations, neighbours spending tens of thousands of pounds fighting over a couple of inches of garden, and defective underpants causing itching where you would least want itching to occur. If you are interested in people, in how they relate to each other, and what is important to them, I don't think you can fail to be interested in this area of the law.

To help bring the law alive you will find special features throughout the chapters, looking at cases you may have heard about on the news, giving you insider knowledge about the way the law really works, and talking to people who work in the law about their jobs and the cases they are involved in. You will also find tasks and exercises that are designed to give you an insight into the skills a lawyer needs, from being able to research a subject, to explaining complex issues in a simple way, or developing a convincing argument and getting it across to other people. These are skills that will prove useful in almost any professional context, so they are well worth developing whether you want to be a lawyer or to use your degree in another field.

As well as bringing law alive, the Living Law series aims to make it accessible. All too often, law is seen as an impossibly difficult subject, full of incomprehensible language and horribly complicated concepts. It isn't – or at least it doesn't have to be. This book is written in clear, ordinary language, and where you need to know a technical term, or some legal jargon, you will find it explained there and then, and usually in the Glossary at the back as well. I've used everyday examples to explain legal concepts, so it's easy to understand what they are and how they apply, and throughout each chapter, you will find 'You be the judge' questions that you can use to test yourself, and fix what you have read in your mind.

What this book does not do, however, is 'dumb down' the subject by giving you only the very basics. It includes all the subjects that are usually covered on an undergraduate course, and as well as the legal rules that make up each tort, it looks at the issues and problems surrounding the law, so you have plenty of material to help you with essays and seminars. For those of you who want to delve even further into these areas, each chapter has a 'Further reading' section listing useful articles and books, and in particular those which not only have something interesting and useful to say but also manage to say it in language a normal human being can understand.

I hope you enjoy reading this book as much as I enjoyed writing it. If you have any comments about the book, or suggestions for features you would like to see in future editions, you can contact me via the **mylawchamber** site. I have aimed to state the law as it is on 1 October 2011, and regular updates will be posted on the **mylawchamber** site.

Good luck with your studies!

Frances Quinn
Tunbridge Wells
October 2011

Acknowledgements

Author's acknowledgements

Thank you to my editor throughout most of the process of writing this book, Zoe Botterill. Zoe came up with the idea for the Living Law series, and was a great source of advice and ideas, as well as being incredibly understanding when a series of small disasters pushed the deadline further and further back. Thank you, too, to my new editor, Cheryl Cheasley, for her encouragement during the final, slightly fraught weeks before the manuscript was finished, and to assistant editor Gabriella Playford for all her help and support throughout. And, of course, thanks to desk editor Anita Atkinson and copy-editor Barbara Massam for their attention to detail in the final stages, and for dealing so efficiently and patiently with a very tight schedule.

Thanks also to all the people who let me interview them for the 'People in the Law' feature, and generously shared their time, their expertise and their anecdotes.

Finally, thanks, as always, to my long-suffering husband, Mike Jeffree, for listening, cooking dinner even more often than usual, providing a regular supply of caramel macchiatos, and knowing when things had gone way beyond coffee and it was time to get the corkscrew out.

Publisher's acknowledgements

We are grateful to the following for permission to reproduce copyright material:

Text

Interview on page 19 from Marek Bednarczyk; Interview on page 52 from Muiris Lyons; Interview on page 76 from Ann-Marie Christie; Interview on page 118 from Wendy Wright; Interview on page 169 from Rawdon Crozier; Interview on page 187 from David Marshall; Interview on page 215 from Rosalind Coe; Interview on page 250 from Kevin Walker; Interview on page 280 from Gordon Hayward; Interview on page 355 from Matthew Wayman; Interview on page 404 from Gill Phillips; Form on page 520 from http://hmctsformfinder.justice.gov.uk/courtfinder/forms/n16a_e0407.pdf, Crown Copyright material is reproduced with permission under the terms of the Click-Use License; Form on pages 521–2 from http://hmctsfirnfubder.justice.gov.uk/HMCTS/GetForm.do?court_forms_id=841, Crown Copyright material is reproduced with permission under the terms of the Click-Use License

Picture Credits

The publisher would like to thank the following for their kind permission to reproduce their photographs:

Marek Bednarczyk: 19; **Ann-Marie Christie:** 76; **Rosalind Coe:** 215–216; **Rawdon Crozier:** 169; **Gordon Hayward:** 280; **Ingram Publishing:** 510; **David Marshall:** 187; **Muiris Lyons:** 52; **Pearson Education Ltd:** 81A Productions/Photolibrary 38, Blend Images/TIPS Images 449, Comstock Images 270, 430, Corbis 496, David Sanderson 179, Digital Stock 492, Fancy/Veer/Corbis 386, Image Source 182, 232, 506, Imagestate/John Foxx Collection 10, 37, 209, 241, 245, 350, 364, Jupiter Images/Brand X/Alamy 73, 83, Lord and Leverett 296, MIXA Co., Ltd 308, Nick Koudis/Photodisc 480, Pearson Education Asia Ltd/Coleman Yuen 219, 439, Photodisc 317, Photodisc/Cole Publishing Group/Kevin Sanchez 275, Photodisc/Cole Publishing Group/Michael Lamotte 206, Photodisc/Don Farrall 55, Photodisc/Don Tremain 114, Photodisc/Life File/Jeremy Hoare 383, Photodisc/Malcolm Fife 293, Photodisc/Michael Matisse 190, Photodisc/Neil Beer 150, Photodisc/Photolink 335, 399, Photodisc/Photolink/Kent Knudson 340, Photodisc/Photolink/R. Morley 163, Photodisc/C Squared Studios 168, Photodisc/Daisuke Morita 415, Photodisc/Greg Kuchik 474, Photodisc/Janis Christie 354, Photodisc/Steve Cole 457, Photos.com/Jupiterimages 11, Shenval/Alamy 139, Tudor Photography 3; **Gill Phillips:** 404; **Kevin Walker:** 250; **Matthew Wayman:** 355; **Wendy Wright:** 118

In some instances we have been unable to trace the owners of copyright material, and we would appreciate any information that would enable us to do so.

Table of cases

Case Navigator cases are highlighted in **bold**.

Table of statutes

Table of statutory instruments

Table of European legislation

Chapter 1
What is tort law?

Key points In this chapter we will be looking at:

- What a tort is
- What kinds of activity tort law covers
- How torts compare to crimes and breaches of contract
- How tort law is made
- Some practical issues in tort law
- Tort and fault
- The relationship between tort law and human rights law
- The way the tort system operates in personal injury cases

Introduction

Imagine a young man, who we will call James, is walking along the street one day, when he is run over by a car. The car is driven by Ted, who is talking on his mobile phone and not really concentrating on his driving. James suffers a serious head injury that permanently affects his powers of thinking and concentration and, as a result, he cannot go back to his well-paid job as a computer programmer. You probably know that dangerous driving is a criminal offence, so Ted may be prosecuted and, if convicted, fined or even sent to prison. But where does that leave James? Ted's carelessness has not only caused him serious pain and suffering but also financial loss, since at best he can only do a less well-paid job, and may even be unable to work at all. That is where tort law comes in. It offers a way for James to get compensation both for the pain and suffering, and for the financial loss, by suing Ted. Whereas the criminal law aims to punish wrongdoers on behalf of society, tort law aims to compensate the person who has suffered wrongdoing.

However, tort law does not only deal with car accidents, or even only with people who are physically injured. Just as there are lots of different crimes covering different types of activity and harm, there are lots of different torts too, covering a wide range of different situations where one person (or organisation) has caused harm to another or infringed their legal rights. Just to give a few examples, the tort of defamation can provide a remedy if a newspaper publishes something untrue about you that damages your reputation, the tort of nuisance can give you a claim if your neighbour keeps very smelly pigs and the smell means you cannot enjoy sitting out in your garden, and the tort of trespass to the person can help if a doctor operates on you without your permission.

This book looks at 13 of the most important torts, and each one provides a set of rules under which the person wronged can make a claim against the person who is alleged to have done wrong.

When a claim is made in tort, the person who has been wronged is known as the **claimant**, and the person alleged to have done wrong is known as the **defendant**. You may also see the person alleged to have done wrong referred to as the **tortfeasor**, an old term which simply means someone who has committed a tort. One other thing to remember when you are writing about tort is that if the claimant wins their case, the defendant is described as being 'liable' for the tort, rather than 'guilty of' it; the term 'guilty' is only used in criminal law.

Defining what a tort is

Academics have been trying for many years to pin down a precise definition of a tort, but it has proved quite difficult to come up with one description that covers every kind of tort. As already explained, a tort is a wrong committed by one party against another, but not every kind of wrong will be a tort. This is because the basis of tort law is that we all have interests which the law should protect. These include our own personal security, our physical health, our finances, our reputations and any property or land we own. Only a wrong that infringes one of the interests that the law protects will be a tort. For example, the tort of defamation protects against damage to reputation, the tort of nuisance protects interests in land, and the tort of trespass to the person protects personal security.

Where someone does wrong, but the harm caused does not relate to an interest protected by the law, there is no tort. For example, let's say that someone you know tells your boyfriend or girlfriend a secret about you that you did not want them to know and, because of this, your relationship breaks up. You would probably consider that what your friend did was a wrong against you, but your interest in keeping your boyfriend or girlfriend is not one that is protected by the law, so there is no tort.

This will probably seem quite a slippery concept at this stage, but don't worry, it will become clearer when we go on to look at the individual torts.

Out and about

Source: Pearson Education Ltd/Tudor Photography

Take a couple of newspapers – national or local – and go through them, looking for stories about people seeking compensation for a wrong that has been done to them. Many of these stories will concern torts (you will not usually see that word mentioned, but you may see the names of individual torts such as negligence, defamation, trespass or nuisance; if you're not sure, your tutor can help you pinpoint which cases are tort ones). In each case, identify the wrong that is alleged to have been done to the claimant, and then try to work out what right the law might be trying to protect (you can ignore employment tribunal cases as these involve employment law and not tort).

Elements of a tort

As a general (but only very general) rule, most torts consist of the following:

- There must be an act or **omission** by the defendant, or in other words, something they have done or failed to do.
- The claimant must have been caused harm, and this harm must be a type of harm that the law protects against.
- It must be possible to prove that the defendant's act or omission caused the harm.
- The defendant must be at fault in some way.

In the example of James and Ted that we looked at in the beginning of this chapter, the act was Ted hitting James with his car. This caused James physical injury and financial loss, which are both protected by the law of tort. The accident clearly caused the physical injury, and James will be able to get medical evidence to show that he cannot go back to his job and so prove that the accident also caused his financial loss. Finally, the accident was the fault of James, because he was driving without taking reasonable care.

There are, however, a few torts that do not fit this pattern, and these fall into two groups:

- torts committed without harm;
- torts committed without fault.

Torts committed without harm

While the vast majority of torts do require the defendant to have caused some kind of harm, there are a small number that can be committed merely by infringing the claimant's legal rights, even though nothing we would recognise as harm has been caused. For example, the tort of trespass imposes liability when someone enters land without permission, even if they cause no damage to the land or loss to the owner of the land. Torts that can be committed without harm are known as being '**actionable per se**'. The idea behind them is that there are some legal rights that are so important that the law should protect against any infringement of them, and the right to exclude others from your land, which would include your home, is one of these.

Torts committed without fault

When we talk about fault in tort, what we mean is either that the defendant deliberately acted wrongfully, or that there was something they could reasonably have been expected to do to prevent the harm they caused and they failed to do this. Most torts require the defendant to have been at fault, for the obvious reason that it seems fairer to expect someone to pay for harm they could reasonably have avoided, than for damage that was not their fault and which there was nothing they could do to prevent. However, you may be surprised to learn that there are torts which can be committed without the defendant being at fault in any way. These are known as **strict liability** torts. An example can be found in the Animals Act 1971, which states that someone who keeps an animal that is classified as a dangerous species under the Act is liable for any damage that animal does, even if there was nothing they should have done to prevent it. In some cases, a strict liability tort will include **defences**, which provide that despite the strict liability there are still some circumstances in which a defendant will not be liable. Under the Animals Act 1971, for example, the keeper of a dangerous animal will not be liable if the harm done was completely the fault of the claimant.

The reasoning behind strict liability varies, and we will look at this issue a little later in this chapter, under the heading 'Tort and the requirement of fault'.

Torts compared to other legal wrongs

Another way to get an idea of exactly what a tort is is to compare it to other legal wrongs that you will have studied or be studying, namely crimes and breaches of contract. If we look first at crimes, we can see that often crimes and torts will have a lot in common in that they involve one person doing harm to another. In fact, in many cases, a single act can be both a crime and a tort. We saw this in the example of James and Ted, where the same accident could make Ted guilty of the crime of dangerous driving and liable to James in tort.

In legal terms, the key difference is that a crime is considered to be committed against the state, which is why prosecutions are brought by the state in the name of the Queen, and why people convicted of crime are punished by the state in the form of fines, imprisonment and other penalties. A tort, on the other hand, is treated in law as a matter between the defendant and the claimant, and the aim is to compensate the claimant for the harm done rather than punish the wrongdoer. However, in practice there is some overlap between the two legal functions, in that the criminal courts can order compensation for crime victims, and that someone who has to pay huge **damages** in a tort case may well feel as though they have been punished, even if that is not the law's intention. Similarly, damages in a tort case are intended to act as a deterrent to wrongdoing, just as punishments in a criminal case are.

When we compare torts to breaches of contract, again there are both similarities and differences. The basic idea behind a contract is that it is a voluntary agreement between two parties, which creates duties from each to the other. If you make a contract to buy a car, for example, you voluntarily agree to accept a duty to pay the price agreed, and the seller voluntarily agrees to accept a duty to hand over the car. A breach of contract, therefore, is a failure to fulfil a duty that was voluntarily agreed to. Torts also involve failure to fulfil a duty, but in this case the duty is one that is applied by law, regardless of whether or not you agree to it. Going back to the example of James and Ted, tort law says that Ted, as a motorist, has a legal duty to take reasonable care for the safety of other road users, and breach of that duty will be a tort. Ted has that duty under the law whether he likes it or not; it is not something he has to agree to accept like a contractual duty.

Again, though, in practice some of these distinctions break down. In some cases, the fact that one party has agreed to something may change their duty in tort. For example, the tort of occupiers' liability provides that the occupier of a house has a duty to protect the safety of anyone who comes into it. But the extent of that duty will be different, depending on whether they have agreed that the person can come in, or whether the person enters without permission.

Another way in which the distinction between torts and breaches of contract blurs is that not all duties under a contract are accepted voluntarily. If we take the example of selling a car, the buyer voluntarily accepts the duty to pay the price, and the seller voluntarily accepts the duty to hand over the car. But in addition to these duties, the law states that their contract will contain other duties, including that the car must be of satisfactory quality, fit for its purpose and as described. Under the Sale of Goods Acts 1979 and 1994, these duties are implied into sales contracts regardless of whether the parties agree to them. That means that breach of these duties is not really breach of a duty voluntarily accepted by the parties but breach of a duty that is applied by law.

As with crime, the same act can make someone liable in both tort and contract. Let's say that Bob, a builder, builds a wall for Jane. Because of his poor workmanship, the wall falls down and injures Jane. Bob's contract contains a term requiring him to take reasonable care with regard to the standard of his work and he is in breach of that, but he is also likely to be liable to Jane in the tort of negligence because he failed to take reasonable care.

Practical issues in tort law

Before we go any further, there are some things about the way tort law operates in practice that will be useful for you to understand. These are:

- tort and lawyers;
- how cases work in practice;
- the role of insurance in tort law.

Tort and lawyers

As we have seen, there are lots of different torts, covering different types of activity and different types of harm. For the purposes of studying law, all these different types of claim fall under the general umbrella of tort. However, in practice, different torts and groups of torts tend to be treated as distinct and specialist branches of law, so there is no such thing as a 'tort lawyer' who would handle cases involving all the different types of tort. Instead, lawyers who are involved in tort cases tend to specialise. Some work mainly with one particular tort, such as defamation. Some might specialise in cases involving a particular type of harm, such as personal injury. Personal injury can happen as a result of a number of different torts, including negligence, occupiers' liability, employers' liability and product liability, so a personal injury specialist would deal with all these types of cases. Others will specialise in torts which are related by the kinds of situation they deal with; trespass to land and nuisance, for example, both deal with interests in land, and so a lawyer who deals with one will usually also deal with the other, and may also work on other areas of non-tort law that are related to land.

How cases work in practice

Something that you should bear in mind as you study the cases in this book is that they represent the tip of an iceberg, because the vast majority of tort claims never actually make it to court. If the defendant believes that the claimant has a chance of winning, there will usually be a process of negotiation, in which the defendant tries to persuade the claimant to accept a lower amount of money than they are claiming rather than take the risk of going to court and not only losing but having to pay the defendant's costs. Only if this process fails does a case go to court, but in most cases the parties agree and there is no need to go to court. This is called an **out-of-court settlement**. It may sound very harmonious and pleasant, but one thing to bear in mind is that in many tort cases the claimant is an individual and the defendant is a large company, and it is very easy for powerful defendants to put pressure on claimants to accept a settlement that may be much less than they could expect to win in court. We will look at this issue a bit more towards the end of this chapter, when we consider personal injury cases.

the vast majority of tort claims never actually make it to court

The role of insurance

Insurance is a very important issue in the tort system because, in the vast majority of cases, it is insurance companies who pay the damages if a case is lost. You have probably come across what is called first party insurance, which is designed to compensate the policyholder for any loss or injury that they personally suffer. An example would be home contents insurance, which pays out if your home contents are stolen, or damaged in a fire or other accident. There is also a second form of insurance, known as third party, which provides protection when the policyholder is liable for injury or loss caused to someone else. If you drive a car, for example, you are required by law to have third party insurance, which means that if you cause an accident anyone who is injured or has their car damaged can claim against your insurance.

Many, perhaps most, of the activities from which tort claims arise are covered by third party insurance. To give just a few examples, health trusts have insurance against claims by injured patients, employers have insurance against claims by injured employees, newspapers often have insurance against libel claims, and anyone running a building that is open to the public will have insurance protecting against someone suing for having an accident on the premises. Even normal household insurance usually includes a third party element, which protects the householder if anyone visiting the house should have an accident. Where a defendant has insurance, it is the insurance company who stands to pay damages if a claim is successful, and not the defendant themselves. In fact, if there was no insurance the vast majority of tort claims would never be brought at all, because there would be no money to pay them. For that reason, it is often argued that without insurance the tort system would no longer be able to function.

if there was no insurance the majority of tort claims would never be brought

Because of this, insurance companies have a great deal of power within the tort system. Faced with a claim, an insurance company can choose simply to pay it, or to contest it. If they contest it, they will usually negotiate with the claimant, to try to persuade them to take a lesser amount, and then **settle** the case out of court. If the claimant says no, they can then choose to pay what the claimant is asking, or go to court in the hope that the claimant will lose, or will be awarded lower damages than they have claimed. This means that, to a great extent, it is the insurance industry which decides which cases come before the courts, and which cases go to appeal. As a great deal of tort law is **common law**, coming out of the cases which come before the courts, you can see that the way in which the law develops very much depends on what cases go to trial. For example, if a case going to the higher courts is likely to lead to a development in the law which would be unfavourable to insurance companies, it is in the insurance industry's interests to settle that case, even at a high cost, and so prevent it going to court and creating a precedent that would end up costing insurers a lot of money. This happened quite recently, in the case of ***Fairchild* v. *Glenhaven*** (2002), discussed in the Law in Action box.

Case Navigator

Law in action The asbestos cases

An example of the power that insurance companies can have in shaping tort law can be seen in the case of *Fairchild* v. *Glenhaven* (2002). We will be looking at this case in more detail in Chapter 3 but, for now, the brief details are that the case concerned people who had suffered illness which would kill them, due to working with asbestos, and the question at stake was exactly what they had to prove to make their employers liable. In the Court of Appeal, the defendants, who were funded by their insurers, had won their case. When the claimants decided to appeal to the House of Lords the insurers offered them a full settlement, meaning that the claimants would get the entire sum of money that their lawyers believed the claim was worth. If the claimants had accepted the settlement, that would have meant that the appeal would not have been heard, preventing any chance of the Court of Appeal decision being reversed at that point. As a result, the claimants in the case would have been compensated, but thousands of other victims would have been unable to succeed in a claim unless someone else came along and took a case all the way to the House of Lords, which was not very likely to happen given that it is a long and expensive process.

Quite unusually, the claimants refused to accept the settlement and the Court of Appeal decision was reversed but, had they decided to accept it, it is quite possible that the law would still not allow a remedy for people in their situation, saving the insurance industry a great deal of money.

[*Reference*: 'Asbestos solicitors rap "cynical" insurers', *Law Gazette*, 29 April 2002]

Making tort law

A small number of torts take their rules from statutes, but the vast majority of tort law rules come from common law; that is, they were made by decisions of the higher courts in the cases that have come before them over the years. The most important tort of all, negligence, comes entirely from common law, and so do the key torts of nuisance, trespass to land and trespass against the person.

As well as the rules of individual torts, there are sets of general rules about how torts work, and many of these also come from common law. For example, as we have seen, most torts require that the defendant has done some sort of harm to the claimant, and therefore the claimant must prove that what the defendant did actually caused that harm. The rules about how this is done are known as the rules on **causation**, and they too have been created entirely by common law.

The role of policy in making tort law

Just like every other area of law, tort has a set of rules which judges use to decide whether a particular defendant is liable. However, in many cases these rules leave a certain amount of room for interpretation. For example, a very common concept within torts is that a defendant is required to take 'reasonable care', and this is clearly not a fixed and easily definable standard; what you might consider reasonable, I might consider unreasonable.

Because there is this room for interpretation in many areas, the way in which the courts apply the rules of tort, and make new ones when necessary, is often said to be shaped by policy. What do we mean by this? In general terms, when we say that judges make a decision on policy grounds, or are influenced by policy, we mean that they take into account what they see as the best interests of society as a whole. This can mean taking into account a wide range of issues, but there are three which commonly arise:

- insurance;
- the **'floodgates'** issue;
- the risk of deterring desirable activities.

Insurance

As we saw earlier, many of the activities from which tort claims arise are covered by insurance and, in a majority of tort cases, it is insurance companies who stand to pay damages and not the defendant themselves.

The way that insurance companies work is that the higher the risk of them having to pay out, the more they will charge for the insurance. This means that the more chance there is that a certain type of claim will be successful, the more expensive insurance against that type of claim will become. This can then have wider effects on society as a whole: for example, if health trusts have to pay more for insurance, that means more cost to the taxpayer and/or less money for the trusts to spend on healthcare. Similarly, if companies have to pay more for insurance, they will usually pass the cost on to consumers in higher prices, which hurts us all. In some cases, higher insurance costs can even put companies out of business, which means lost jobs and losses to businesses who supply that business.

Where does the law come into this? As you will know from having studied precedent on your English Legal System course, decisions by the higher courts do not just affect the parties in the case before them but also set new law for the cases that come afterwards. In tort, higher court decisions are often about the boundaries of tort: deciding whether, when a new factual situation arises, that situation should create liability. If a court decides that a certain type of situation does create liability, that means that the number of successful claims will increase. That will lead to increased costs for insurance companies and they will therefore put up their prices for that type of insurance, with all the effects mentioned above. For this reason, when the courts are deciding whether to extend liability in a particular area one of the issues they sometimes take into account is the effect on insurance costs.

You can read about an example of the effect a court decision can have on insurance premiums in the Law in Action box.

Law in action The *Mirvahedy* case

An example of a court case which had an effect on insurance costs is *Mirvahedy* v. *Henley* (2003), a case which was brought under the Animals Act 1971, which details when owners will be liable in tort for injury or damage caused by their animals. We will look at the case in more detail in Chapter 20, but the key point was that the House of Lords decided that the owners of some horses who caused an accident could be liable, even though the way the horses had behaved was quite normal in the circumstances. Up until the case was decided it had been thought that owners could only be liable for behaviour that was abnormal in their particular type of animal. The decision in the case meant that there would be more successful claims against animal owners, particularly owners of horses which, because of their size and the fact that they are often ridden on the road, are involved in a fairly high number of accidents. This in turn meant that companies providing insurance to riding schools and stables knew that they might have to make more payouts. Insurance costs went up by as much as 200 per cent, and many riding schools and stables said they might well be forced out of business by the increase.

Source: Pearson Education Ltd/Imagestate/John Foxx Collection

The 'floodgates' issue

A policy issue which the courts often refer to openly is what is known as the 'floodgates' issue. This refers to the fact that if the courts decide to extend liability in a particular case a huge number of similar claims may be brought. That has three possible implications. First, that the court system may be overwhelmed with claims. Secondly, as we have seen, that insurance costs may go up, and thirdly, that the change may place too much of a burden on those who would be sued and make it harder for them to predict whether they were likely to be sued. For example, if a decision made it very much easier for an employee injured at work to succeed in a claim against their employer, that would place greater costs on businesses, which would be passed on to consumers in higher prices and/or might make it difficult for smaller businesses to survive. In such a case, therefore, the courts have to decide between restricting protection for employees and leaving some claimants without a remedy, or putting that extra burden on businesses with all the wider effects that would bring.

This decision is even more difficult where the defendant is some kind of public body funded by the taxpayer. For example, take the situation where someone is seriously injured during an operation, and when they sue, the court has to decide whether the surgeon took reasonable care. Clearly, it is desirable that people injured by poor medical care should get compensation, and if the court sets the standard of reasonable care too high, fewer such victims will be able to claim. However, the more victims who can claim successfully, the more money hospitals will have to pay in insurance cover and/or damages, and that money comes from the taxpayer who expects it to be used for patient care. In all these cases, judges cannot realistically avoid taking policy into account, whether they refer to it in their decisions or not.

judges cannot realistically avoid taking policy into account

The risk of deterring desirable activities

The third common policy issue is one which has been very much in the news recently. This is the idea that if it becomes too easy to make a successful claim regarding a particular type of activity, potential defendants might avoid getting involved in that activity at all. For example, there have frequently been news reports that schools are reluctant to take pupils on trips because of the danger of being sued if something goes wrong, and that public events such as fêtes have been cancelled because the organisers are concerned about the danger of being sued. As we will see later, these fears are often based on a misunderstanding of the law, but in an attempt to address the issue the government introduced legislation which specifically permits the courts to take this aspect of policy into consideration when deciding cases. Section 1 of the Compensation Act 2006 states that when deciding whether a defendant should have taken particular steps to avoid harm, a court

> may . . . have regard to whether a requirement to take such steps might –
>
> (a) prevent a desirable activity from being undertaken at all, to a particular extent, or in a particular way, or
>
> (b) discourage persons from undertaking functions in connection with a desirable activity.

In other words, if the activity which has caused the harm is one which is considered to be good for society in some way, the courts can take this into account when deciding how wide liability for harm caused by that activity should be.

Law in action

A compensation culture?

The provisions of section 1 of the Compensation Act were put in place because of fears that Britain has developed a 'compensation culture', in which people are overly ready to sue, sometimes over quite trivial incidents, and it is said to have become common to try to blame someone for events which would once have been seen as nothing more than accidents. The media in particular give the impression that the number of cases is constantly rising and the courts are flooded with trivial claims; it is, for example, widely believed that the British courts allowed a claim against McDonald's by a woman who was scalded because her coffee was too hot.

Source: Pearson Education Ltd/Photos.com/Jupiterimages

In fact, when the government set up a taskforce to investigate the issue, its report, *Better Routes to Redress*, found that the overall number of people suing for personal injury has gone down in recent years, and there was no statistical evidence that the compensation culture actually exists (Better Regulation Taskforce 2004). As you will discover when you read the next chapter, it is not legally possible in England to claim for trivial accidents that are nobody's fault, and while it is true that McDonald's were sued in the USA for selling coffee that was too hot, an attempt to bring a similar claim in the English courts failed in *Bogle* v. *McDonald's* (2002) (see page 272).

On the other hand, the *Better Routes to Redress* report found that what does seem to be happening is that the belief that it is easy to be sued can make people and organisations reluctant to get involved in activities which involve any kind of risk. This could mean that the very idea of a compensation culture is causing problems all by itself, regardless of whether we actually have one.

[*Reference*: 'Judge rules against McDonalds scalding victims', *Daily Telegraph*, 27 March 2002]

Tort and the requirement of fault

As we saw earlier, most torts require the claimant to prove that the defendant was at fault in some way, meaning that they deliberately caused harm or failed to take reasonable precautions to prevent it. You might well think that this is just common sense, because it is obviously fairest to impose liability where the defendant is at fault. However, it can be argued that there are good reasons why fault should not be a requirement for tort liability, and there are some legal experts who argue that more areas of tort law, particularly those involving injury, should be subject to strict liability or should be taken out of the tort system altogether and compensated on a **no-fault** basis, where claimants would only have to prove that they had a particular injury rather than having to pin the blame on someone for it. Such a system exists in New Zealand and we will look at it a bit later. This issue often comes up on exam papers, so it is useful to look at some of the arguments for and against the requirement of fault.

Arguments in favour of a requirement to prove fault

There are three main arguments in favour of a fault requirement:

- The 'floodgates' issue: As we saw earlier, the courts are always concerned to avoid swamping the legal system with cases, or placing too heavy a burden on defendants. Requiring a claimant to prove fault clearly limits the number of cases quite considerably, because it rules out all those situations where a defendant has caused harm through no fault of their own, or where the claimant cannot prove fault.
- Deterrence: The requirement of fault is said to make people and companies more likely to take care to avoid harming others, because by taking care they can avoid being sued. If they were liable regardless of fault, it is argued, there would be no point in taking care.
- Fairness: The argument here is that it is only just to make someone pay for their wrongdoing if there was some way they could have avoided doing that wrong. If not, they are simply unlucky and should not have to pay for that.

Arguments against the requirement of fault

The fault requirement has a number of drawbacks. These are some of the arguments used against a requirement for fault, and in favour of strict liability in some areas of tort law:

- Expense: The need to prove fault increases the length and so the cost of tort cases. This increases the amount of money that is spent on lawyers and the court system, and if that money was saved it could be spent on compensating tort victims.
- The effect of insurance: The idea that the fault requirement helps deter wrongdoing is very much weakened when you consider that in the vast majority of cases damages are not paid by the wrongdoer but by their insurance company.
- Unpredictability: The fault principle makes it much more difficult to predict which party will win a case. This means that powerful and wealthy defendants can put pressure on claimants to accept an out-of-court settlement that might be much less than they could have won, because the claimant is afraid to take the risk of losing and getting nothing.
- Economic realities: Where a tort causes financial loss, that loss must either be borne by the defendant or by the claimant. In very many cases, the claimant in a case will be a private individual and the defendant will be a company. This would be the case where a patient sues a health trust, for example, where an employee sues their employer, and even where a pedestrian sues a motorist, since it will be the motorist's insurance company that stands to pay damages. In these cases, it can be argued that increasing the number of successful claims by removing the requirement of fault moves the financial loss to the party who can most easily bear it.
- Unjust distinctions: Requiring fault means that two people who have suffered exactly the same kind of harm may receive very different treatment. For example, let's say that Susan and Sophie are both seriously injured in separate car accidents. They both suffer the same amount of pain and suffering, and neither of them are ever able to work again. In Susan's case, she can prove the driver is at fault and is able to claim hundreds of thousands of pounds in damages that compensate for her pain and suffering, and for the financial loss caused by being unable to go back to work. In Sophie's case, however, the driver was not at fault, and so all she can expect to receive are the very low level of benefits provided by the social security system. To that we could add another imaginary case, Shirley, who has the same kind of medical problems as Sophie and Susan but was born with hers as a result of a hereditary disease. She too suffers in exactly the same way as they do, and will have done so for longer, but there is no compensation for her either. It could be argued that as tort damages are almost entirely paid for by insurance, and that cost is ultimately passed on to all of society, it might be simpler and fairer for society simply to compensate all victims of injury and illness through a no-fault system, with payouts that are smaller but more fairly distributed.

No-fault liability in practice

What would a system of no-fault liability look like? Such a system has actually existed in New Zealand since the 1970s, when the government abolished the tort system for all personal injuries caused by accidents. It was replaced with a state compensation scheme, paid for by taxpayers and extra charges on employers and motorists. Accident victims can simply apply for compensation, without having to prove that anyone was to blame for their injuries. The system has very low administrative costs compared with the tort system, and initially the payments made were just slightly less than people could have expected to receive in a tort case, though they have since been reduced. It was initially intended that the scheme should be extended to cover injuries resulting from other causes but this has never happened, so the system does not address the criticism that people who suffer illness or injury through, for example, hereditary disease are treated differently from accident victims.

In this country, the nearest we have to a no-fault system for injury victims is under the Consumer Protection Act 1987, which imposes strict liability for people injured by dangerous products. However, as we will see when we look at product liability in Chapter 10, there are a number of provisions in the Act which mean that liability is not quite as strict as it looks at first glance, and it can still be very difficult to win a case in this area.

Out and about

Have a look at **www.acc.co.nz**, which is the website of New Zealand's no-fault accident compensation scheme and gives a useful insight into exactly how such a scheme can work. Do you think the scheme sounds like a good idea? What advantages might it have over a system like ours, where people have to go to court for compensation? Can you see any drawbacks to it?

Tort and the Human Rights Act 1998

As you will probably know from studying the English legal system, the Human Rights Act 1998 brings into English law the provisions of the European Convention on Human Rights and allows people to bring cases regarding these provisions in the English courts. This has had a number of effects on tort law.

First, it means that the courts must interpret and apply statutes and case law in a way which is compatible with the rights protected under the Act, as far as it is possible to do so. In some cases, these rights may conflict with rights protected under tort law. The tort of defamation, for example, protects the right to reputation. Claims are most often brought against the media in an attempt to prevent them saying, or get compensation for the fact that they have already said, things which damage someone's reputation. However under the Human Rights Act, the media have a right to freedom of expression, and so the courts must balance this against a claimant's right to protect their reputation. We'll look at this issue in more detail in Chapter 16.

The second way in which the Human Rights Act is making an impact on tort law concerns the fact that the Act allows individuals to sue public bodies who may have breached their rights under the Act. In several areas, the rights protected under the Human Rights Act overlap with rights protected by tort. For example, Article 8 of the European Convention on Human Rights gives a right to respect for a person's private and family life, their home and correspondence, and there are some situations where this could overlap with the right, protected by the tort of nuisance, to peaceful enjoyment of your own land. If, for example, you live in a house which is near an airbase and low-flying aircraft cause noise and disturbance to you, that could potentially be a breach of Article 8, but could also be nuisance.

Because of these overlaps, there are an increasing number of cases where claimants sue both in tort and under the Human Rights Act 1998. Although it is possible for the same act or omission to be a breach of the Act and a tort, the claimant will not be compensated twice for the same injury. The advantage of bringing both claims is simply to increase the chances of winning; if one fails, the other might succeed. As we will see when we go on to look at specific torts, there are an increasing number of situations where tort law does not give someone a remedy, but the Human Rights Act does.

The tort system and personal injuries

As we have seen, torts protect against a wide range of different types of harm, from having your reputation damaged by a newspaper, to being unable to enjoy sitting in your garden because your neighbour's pigs are smelly. However, as you can see from the Key Stats box, the majority of tort claims involve personal injury, which essentially means anything which damages a person physically or mentally, whether permanently or not. That can also include fatal injuries; if a person dies as a result of a tort, the person who inherits their estate, meaning the money and property they leave behind, also inherits the same right to sue that the person would have had if they were still alive. In most cases, of course, it is the close relatives of the dead person who sue.

Key stats Tort cases begun in the High Court during 2010

This list gives you an idea of how tort cases divide up in terms of numbers. As you can see, the majority of cases involve personal injury, and these will mostly be cases involving the torts of negligence, occupiers' liability, employers' liability and product liability. **Clinical negligence** cases are those alleging poor treatment by medical staff, and so most of these are also likely to involve personal injury.

- Personal injury actions 1041
- Clinical negligence 752
- Other negligence 247
- Defamation 158
- Other torts 19

In case you were wondering about the other categories on the list, 'Other negligence' would cover other cases of negligence involving purely financial loss or damage to property, and defamation cases, as already explained, are those where the claimant is seeking to protect their reputation. 'Other torts' would include, for example, nuisance, the tort which protects against interference with your land, and trespass, which protects against people coming on to your land without permission.

[*Source*: Judicial and Court Statistics 2010]

Given that personal injury cases are such a big part of the tort system, it is worth looking at the way that system handles them, before we go on to look at the individual torts in detail over the following chapters. This background will help you understand some of the cases that we will look at later.

The personal injury 'obstacle race'

During the 1970s academics from Oxford University did an extensive survey of the experiences of injury victims in the tort system, which is usually referred to as 'the Oxford Survey'. One of the researchers, Donald Harris, likened the tort system to 'a compulsory long-distance obstacle race' (Harris 1984) because of all the hurdles that the system itself, and the law behind it, throws in the victims' way. Although the survey was completed over 30 years ago, none of those hurdles have disappeared (though we could say that some have been modified), and so the report's conclusions are still a useful guide to the way the tort system operates in personal injury cases. The hurdles it identified fall into three main groups:

- access to legal services;
- problems with settlements;
- difficulties of proof.

Access to legal services

The first hurdle, to continue Donald Harris's comparison, appears before the injured person even gets on to the race track. This is the hurdle of access to legal services. As you will know if you have studied an English Legal System course, there are a number of reasons why people who might have a legal claim never take any action to follow it up, including worries about how much legal action will cost, not knowing how to make a claim, being put off by the intimidating image of the legal profession, and not even realising that they have a claim. Since the Oxford Survey was done, two major changes to the legal system have happened, which you might expect to have had an impact on this problem. The first is that solicitors have been allowed to advertise, and many have chosen to incorporate in their advertising messages about the kind of injuries people can sue for – you will probably have seen adverts that begin 'Had an accident at work?' or 'Been injured in an accident that wasn't your fault?' On top of this has come the growth of claims management companies, who advertise for accident victims and then refer them on to law firms who pay them for the referral. You would imagine that this makes it much less likely that someone who might have a legal claim would not realise it. However, when the website **personalinjurylawyers.co.uk** did a survey in 2011, shown in the Key Stats box, they found that half of all accident victims still do not make a claim, and their reasons for not doing so were strikingly similar to the ones quoted in the Oxford Survey: not knowing how to claim, not realising they had a valid case, and unfamiliarity with the legal profession.

Key stats Attitudes to accident claims 2011

The research carried out by **personalinjurylawyers.co.uk** found that:

- 39% had suffered an accident for which they could have claimed compensation
- 36% had had an accident at work
- 25% had been hurt in a car accident
- 22% had been hurt by slipping or tripping over
- 64% had injuries severe enough for them to need time off work
- 48% did not claim compensation
- 52% said they did not know how to go about claiming
- 23% were worried about being able to find a reputable law firm to take their case
- 18% did not claim because they thought they would lose

[*Source*: **http://www.lawgazette.co.uk/news/half-accident-victims-do-not-claim**]

The second big change regarding access to legal services has been the arrival of **conditional fee agreements** (CFAs), often called 'no win, no fee', which were introduced during the 1990s. Under a CFA, a solicitor agrees not to charge a fee if they lose the case but, if they win, to take their usual fee plus an 'uplift', which can be anything up to twice the usual fee but no more. A claimant who wins will usually be able to claim these costs from the losing defendant, and will usually take out an insurance policy which will pay their opponent's costs if the claimant loses and has costs awarded against them. The existence of these arrangements has meant that ordinary individuals who would not be able to afford to pay for a court case themselves can still take legal action.

However, CFAs have their limits. Clearly lawyers will only take on cases on this basis if they are fairly certain of success, and most firms insist that there is at least a 60–70 per cent chance of success before they will consider a CFA. Given that some types of personal injury case can be very hard to prove, it is possible that there are many potential claimants who are not helped at all by the existence of CFAs. In addition, when the Oxford Survey was done legal aid was available for personal injury cases. During the period since CFAs were introduced, the availability of legal aid for personal injury cases has been drastically reduced and is now only available for medical negligence cases and cases of deliberate injury. This suggests that overall the financial barriers to legal action for personal injury victims are still a big problem.

some types of personal injury case can be very hard to prove

Problems with settlements

As mentioned earlier, most tort cases never come to court but are settled, with the parties agreeing compensation between them. Although this cuts costs, as the trial is the most expensive part of the process, it can have disadvantages for claimants. Hazel Genn's very important 1987 study, *Hard Bargaining*, looked at the experiences of personal injury claimants, and found that the two sides in a case were usually in very different positions. The defendants would be backed by insurance companies, and in the tort system insurance companies are what Genn called 'repeat players'. They are involved in a lot of cases, know the system very well and have no real emotional involvement with individual cases. By contrast, for most claimants that Genn studied their case would be the first time they had been involved with the tort system, it would have enormous personal importance to them and they were likely to find the whole process quite stressful. In many cases, they might also need to get their compensation quickly, in order to pay for care, or perhaps adaptations to their home to accommodate disabilities caused by the accident.

Given this imbalance of power between the two parties, Genn found, claimants often accepted much less in a settlement than they might have got if they had gone to court, and some even dropped their cases completely rather than continue with the process. Accepting a low settlement was most likely to happen in very serious cases, where the claimant's need for compensation was greatest and where damages ordered by a court were likely to be high, so that by achieving a settlement insurance companies stood to save themselves a lot of money.

This pressure on claimants to settle is increased by a provision in part 36 of the Civil Procedure Rules, which are the set of rules that govern the way tort and other civil cases are run. Under part 36, if one side makes a realistic offer and the other side turns it down and the case goes to trial, the existence of the offer can make a difference to the costs awarded. From a claimant's point of view, part 36 means that if they turn down an offer and then win their case but are awarded damages equal to or less than the offer, the court can decide that the claimant should pay their own costs and those of the defendant from the date at which the offer expired (instead of the defendant paying both sets of costs as they usually would). This can be a frightening prospect for claimants, and it is well known in the personal injury world that insurers use **part 36 offers** as a bullying tactic to put pressure on claimants to settle.

Difficulties with proof

Some types of personal injury case can be very difficult for a claimant to win, because of the need to prove fault and causation. One of the most difficult areas is clinical negligence, where what is alleged is that medical treatment has fallen below a reasonable standard, and by falling below that standard the medical professional has caused harm to the claimant. Given the complexity of modern medical care, it can often be very difficult to work out exactly what, or who, has caused the claimant's problems. For example, there are situations where the claimant might not have recovered fully from the condition or injury that took them to hospital in the first place, even if the treatment had been correct, but they claim that the medical treatment they got made their injury or illness worse, or their recovery less complete, than it would have been if the treatment had been correct. In such cases the claimant has to prove that it was the treatment that caused their problems, or at least some of them, and not the underlying condition. There may also be a variety of different problems and treatments which interact with each other, so that it is difficult to pinpoint exactly what has caused the harm, and a variety of different medical professionals involved in the treatment making it difficult to see who, if anyone, caused the damage. On top of that, the court has to decide what a reasonable standard of care for that particular condition would be, and that may be something that even medical professionals do not agree on.

All these complications mean that it may not be possible to know whether the case is worth pursuing without doing a substantial amount of research and consulting medical experts, and that preparatory work can easily cost £2,000–£5,000. It is perhaps not surprising then that the average chance of winning a clinical negligence case is only around 17 per cent, compared to 85 per cent for other personal injury cases. For this reason lawyers will often refuse to take these cases on a no win, no fee basis.

The People in the Law box gives you an insight into how the experience of making a claim can be for claimants, and the lawyers who work for them.

People in the law

Source: Marek Bednarczyk (*text and photo*)

Marek Bednarczyk is a Partner at Hart Brown solicitors in Guildford, Surrey, and specialises in personal injury claims. He came into the legal profession after working as a teacher for 10 years.

What kind of cases do you typically deal with? It's a huge variety – I do nearly all types of personal injury and clinical negligence, so I get road traffic accidents, occupiers' liability and accidents at work, as well as a lot of clinical negligence. I've been qualified for nearly 20 years, so I tend to get the more complex, high-value cases, from around £50,000 up to multi-million pound claims.

What attracts you to this area of law? I like the variety, and the fact that you're dealing with human beings. And it's not a dry and dusty area of law – you could call personal injury law many things, but it's definitely not dry.

Research shows that a proportion of accident victims never make a claim, because they don't realise they have a case, or don't know what to do about it. What do you think should be done to address that problem? Obviously it's not possible to teach everyone all about the law, but I'd like to see some basic legal education taught in all schools. I think that would go some way towards raising awareness. We often find, for example, that even if people do decide to make a claim, they don't realise that there are **limitation periods**, and they simply leave it too late.

How are most of your cases funded? The majority of our personal injury cases are funded by conditional fee agreements (CFAs). We do some legal aid work in clinical negligence, but it's a minority of cases. That's partly because this is a prosperous area of the country, so many clients don't fit the financial limits for legal aid, but also because the Legal Services Commission prefers to focus on the very highest value cases, so even getting funding for a case worth £50,000 can be a problem.

How do your cases typically progress? Quite often they'll start with a phone conversation, when I'll find out what's happened and what the injuries are. Then we ask the person to fill in a questionnaire, which we use to assess whether we can take on the claim. If not, we'll explain our thinking and the client won't be charged anything, so we're effectively giving free advice at that stage. If we are taking on the claim, we'll explore the funding options – they may have legal expenses insurance, for example as part of a home insurance policy, or we may want to look at a CFA.

Then we'll do a Letter of Claim, and the process of negotiation begins. In most cases, there'll be a series of offers, from both sides, and part of my job is to know when to settle and when to wait for a better offer. It's very rare for a first offer to be a reasonable one – insurance companies want to settle for as little as they can get away with, so the first offer will almost always be deliberately low. For example, in a case that eventually settles for half a million pounds, the first offer might only be £250,000. It's up to me to fight my client's case and get the best offer I can. You do need to be quite robust for that part of the job, but it's a part that I really enjoy. In the meantime, the other side will be doing all they can to minimise the claim, so they might use tactics like secret filming, or having people followed, to see if they're exaggerating their injuries.

Most cases take 1–2 years, but some settle within six months, some take much longer. Only a few will go to trial – most personal injury cases don't get anywhere near the door of a court, and I know personal injury lawyers who haven't had a court case in five years. That often surprises law students – reading court reports can give a misleading idea of how things really are, because the cases that end up in court are the minority.

How do claimants find the experience?

It can be quite stressful for them, especially in the higher value, more complex cases, where people might need 24-hour care for the rest of their lives, or might be unable to go back to their jobs, because for them the outcome is crucial. If an insurance company loses a million, it's not good news, but it doesn't change anyone's life – but if a client loses a million pound claim, that's devastating. It's part of my job to minimise the stress for them, but I can't completely eradicate it because the outcome is so important to them.

One client said to me recently that he felt as though he'd been accused of something and was having to prove his innocence, and that was spot on – the system is skewed in favour of the defendant, because it's the claimant who has to prove their case. People do find that difficult, because the way they see it, they're the victim, they haven't done anything wrong and yet they're the ones being secretly filmed or followed. Some – not all – insurance companies have the mindset that all claimants are malingerers and that incenses people. But having worked for defendants in the past, I've ordered that kind of surveillance myself, and although mostly you don't find anything, we did have one or two that were caught red-handed in fraudulent claims, so I do understand the need for it.

On the other hand, some people find that the process of **litigation** can be quite beneficial in itself, aside from the money. In clinical negligence cases, for example, people often have serious injuries, and they feel they've been very badly let down by a medical professional, and what they want, as much as anything, is to get vindication and acknowledgement that what happened to them was wrong.

What's your view on the idea that Britain has a compensation culture?

Lord Young's report [*Better Routes to Redress*] made a distinction between the reality of the situation and the perception, and I think that's accurate. There is a perception that we have a compensation culture, and I think lawyers have played a part in creating that perception, with all those 'If there's blame, there's a claim' adverts that you see. But the reality, looking at the statistics, is that over the past 10 years, there's actually been a drop in litigation. The underlying position is that most people are ignorant of their rights in pursuing claims – for example, if you look at the numbers of adverse incidents in the NHS every year, it's hundreds of thousands, and the number of people who actually pursue a claim against the NHS is a tiny fraction of that. And in my experience, even those that do claim are often quite reluctant about it – they'll say 'I don't really want to sue my doctor' or 'I don't really want to sue my employer'. So I don't think we're living in a society that's rife with litigation.

I also think the compensation culture debate has a slightly odd attitude to legal rights. No one would say 'Please take away some of my legal rights', yet criticising people for making a claim is effectively criticising them for pursuing their legal rights. And you have to remember that when people do sue, there can be very good reasons for that. If someone else's negligence means you've been so seriously injured that you need 24-hour care for the rest of your life, or you can't work anymore, you have a good reason to claim, and it's your legal right to do that. It's about holding people accountable for their mistakes, which as a principle I think is the right thing.

Alternative methods of compensating personal injury victims

We saw earlier that for victims of personal injury getting compensation through the tort system is not a straightforward activity at all. Fortunately, perhaps, there are a variety of other ways in which people may get financial support after being injured in an accident, and we can only really understand the role of the tort system if we look at how these run alongside it. Although these systems rarely provide as much money as a tort claim can, they have the benefit that the claimant does not have to prove anyone was at fault for their injury.

Employment benefits

All employees who earn £102 a week or more are entitled to Statutory Sick Pay (SSP), which pays a standard weekly rate for up to 28 weeks. At the time of publication the rate was £81.60. Some employers have their own sickness benefit schemes which pay more, for longer, and these may take over after the first 28 weeks, or be paid as well as SSP during that time. They rarely go on longer than six months, however.

The social security system

The vast majority of accident victims who need financial support get it not from a legal claim but through welfare benefits. As we saw in the survey by **personalinjurylawyers.co.uk**, around half of people who could have a legal claim do not take legal action, and to this we can add all the people who cannot claim because their injury was not (or could not be proved to be) anyone's fault. A proportion of these people will be unable to work, either for a temporary period or permanently, and once sick pay from their employer runs out their main source of support will be welfare benefits, unless they have insurance. The amount of money they can claim will vary, depending on the type of benefit they are eligible for, but in general benefits only pay enough to provide for the necessities of life. Tort compensation, by contrast, aims to put the claimant back in the position they would have been in if the accident had not happened, so someone who would have been earning a good salary can expect their tort damages to replace that money.

The advantages of welfare benefits over tort damages is that they can be obtained relatively quickly, and they offer certainty, in that if the claimant is entitled under the rules of a particular benefit they will get the money, unlike a tort case where a claimant may spend months and even years making their claim and then end up with nothing. The main disadvantage of welfare benefits is the very low amounts of money they offer. There is also a certain stigma attached to claiming benefits, with welfare payments referred to in the press as 'handouts' even though in most cases the people claiming them will have been supporting the social security system for years, through the tax and National Insurance that they have paid while they were in work. Welfare benefits also have an advantage over tort damages for society as a whole, in that they cost less to provide. During the 1990s, the judge Lord Woolf prepared a report into the civil legal system, called *Access to Justice*, which found that it costs 8–12p to provide every £1 of benefits, compared to as much as £1.35 to provide every £1 of tort damages (Woolf 1996).

Insurance

Some types of insurance policy offer cover for victims of accidents. The two most important are life insurance, which is designed to pay out when someone dies in order to take care of that person's family once their income is no longer available, and income protection insurance, which replaces part of a person's income if they are unable to work for a long time through illness and disability. It continues to pay out until the person can go back to work, or reaches retirement.

Life insurance is a very well-accepted product that most people buy if they have dependants, and, as the market is large, can usually be obtained at a reasonable price. Its main drawback is simply that it pays out only on death, so does not help accident victims who are only injured. Income protection insurance has more drawbacks, in that it is quite expensive and policies can be quite complex, which can mean that people do not always realise what they are buying. For example, many people assume their policy will pay out for as long as they are unable to do their old job, but then find that the policy will only pay out while they are unable to do any job at all.

Compensation schemes

There are also a number of schemes designed to offer compensation to victims of particular types of accident. One of the biggest is the Industrial Injuries Scheme, which provides benefits for people who have been injured at work, or who have developed certain illnesses, such as asthma or deafness, because of their work. Other schemes have been set up by the government to compensate children who suffer injury as a result of having vaccinations, and to compensate people who contracted HIV and/or hepatitis C through infected blood transfusions. These schemes offer levels of benefit that can compare with those in the tort system, and claimants who want to use them have to give up their right to sue in tort. The idea behind them is that, although the government does not accept legal liability for the injuries, they have been caused by activities run by the state and so the government accepts a responsibility to help those harmed.

There have for many years been plans for a compensation scheme for victims of poor medical treatment in the NHS. Since the mid-1990s, claims against the NHS for medical negligence have been increasing, and at the time of publication were costing the NHS around £500 million a year in compensation and legal fees. As a result, in 2001 the National Audit Commission looked into the issue of negligence claims against the NHS and concluded that money could be saved, and complaints dealt with more efficiently, if a new system specifically for NHS complaints was created.

The Commission pointed out that research showed that in many cases financial compensation was not the patient's main aim. Often, they were more interested in getting a genuine explanation of what had gone wrong, an apology, and some kind of reassurance that action would be taken to prevent other people being injured by the same sort of mistake. It was when the NHS failed to meet these needs that attitudes tended to harden, leading people to sue for compensation. The Commission concluded that if measures were put in place to address these issues, fewer legal cases might be brought.

A further report was produced in 2003 by the Chief Medical Officer, Liam Donaldson. In *Making Amends*, he too recommended the creation of a new scheme for NHS complaints, which would make it easier to get not just compensation but also acknowledgement of mistakes, and care and rehabilitation to deal with the results of the medical negligence. The emphasis in the report was on creating a system in which, instead of the patient having to prove fault and the NHS attempting to fight claims, NHS staff would be encouraged to admit mistakes and the organisation would take responsibility for improving practice by learning from such mistakes.

The government's response to *Making Amends* was the NHS Redress Act 2006. It allows the creation of an NHS Redress Scheme which, the explanatory notes to the Act state, will 'provide investigations when things go wrong, remedial treatment, rehabilitation and care where needed, explanations and apologies, and financial compensation in certain circumstances' without the need to make a legal claim. Only cases worth less than £20,000 will be handled by the scheme, and patients who accept redress offered under the scheme will have to waive their right to take legal action.

The Act is what is known as an Enabling Act, which sets out a broad framework for the scheme and then permits the detailed rules to be put in place by means of secondary legislation. It was passed in November 2006, and the government then began consulting with interested parties before deciding on the details of how the scheme will work. It was eventually decided that the scheme would be piloted in Wales.

The details of the scheme had not yet been approved when this book was published, but the proposals included provisions for claimants to receive compensation in the form of any care that they might need as a result of poor medical treatment; a duty for medical organisations to appoint a person responsible for ensuring lessons learned from complaints are put into practice; a more proactive approach to investigating negligence, with organisations required to review incidents where things have gone wrong, and investigate them, and the onus no longer on the patient to make a complaint. It was thought that the scheme would be restricted to complaints which, if brought as a tort case, would be worth less than £20,000, while more serious claims would still use the tort system.

All these systems runs alongside the tort system, and in some cases an individual claimant may use more than one. Someone whose accident means they are out of work for a long time, for example, may make a claim in tort and claim state benefits during the period while their case is in progress. However, remember that the aim of the tort system is to put the claimant back in the position they would have been in if the tort had not been committed. This means that the tort victim not only should not be worse off, but also should not be better off as a result of the accident. For this reason, when a tort claim includes a sum of money for loss of earnings any welfare benefits received will be 'set off' against that claim, so that the claimant is not compensated twice for the same loss. Insurance benefits, however, are not set off, as it is believed doing this would dissuade people from taking out insurance.

One other element that we should take into account when looking at the whole picture of support for accident victims is the NHS. Although not strictly speaking a source of compensation, the NHS does provide a major benefit for accident victims in the form of free care for their injuries. In any other system, they would have to pay for this care and then hope they could claim back the cost in a tort action. This may be one reason why tort damages here have never reached the incredible levels that they do in the USA, where many claimants may have to factor in tens of thousands of pounds worth of medical care.

Studying tort law: some advice

As we saw earlier, although a handful of torts have been created by statute, most of them have come from common law, meaning that their rules have been created by the decisions of judges in cases over the years. Sometimes students find that this makes the rules of tort harder to pin down than those of, for example, crime, where statute is much more heavily involved. Whereas a statute will usually state what the law is quite clearly and concisely, the rules on common law torts need to be picked out from the many thousands of words in a Court of Appeal or House of Lords/Supreme Court judgment, and this can lead to uncertainty about how a particular rule might apply in different cases, or for your current purposes, in problem questions. Try not to worry too much about this, though. When you are tackling problem questions, the main thing is not that you should know exactly what a court would decide, but that you can spot the issues the problem raises and what tests a court would use to decide those issues.

If we take, for example, a nuisance case where one neighbour's smelly pigs mean that the other cannot enjoy sitting out in his garden, an important issue the courts would look at is whether the pig owner's interference with her neighbour's enjoyment was reasonable. You do not need to know for certain whether they would find it was reasonable or not – remember that lawyers do not always know this either, because if they did there would never be any need to bring cases on the point to the courts. What you do need to be able to do is to spot that this is the issue the question raises, and then explain what factors the court would take into account in deciding this question. If you can refer to the decided cases that you will find in the relevant chapter, apply them to the situation described in the problem, and give a reasoned opinion on the question based on the law you have applied, you will be giving a good answer.

Summary

- Tort law aims to compensate the person who has suffered wrongdoing, and covers a wide range of different situations where one person (or organisation) has caused harm to another or infringed their legal rights.
- There are many different torts, covering different ways of doing wrong against someone else, and each one comprises a set of things that the claimant must prove in order to win their case.
- Not every kind of wrong will be a tort. The basis of tort law is that we all have interests which the law should protect, and only a wrong that infringes one of the interests that the law protects will be a tort.
- Most torts have four elements:
  - an act or omission by the defendant;
  - harm to the claimant, of a type that the law protects against;

- the harm must be caused by the act or omission;
- the defendant must be at fault.

A few torts do not require harm; these are called torts actionable per se.

Some torts do not require fault; these are called strict liability torts.

Torts differ from crimes in that crimes are committed against and prosecuted by the state, but torts are a matter between the wrongdoer and the person wronged. The aim is to compensate the claimant, not punish the wrongdoer. But there is some overlap between them, because criminal courts can order compensation for crime victims, and damages in a tort case are intended to be a deterrent to wrongdoing, just as punishments in a criminal case are.

Torts differ from breaches of contract in that torts are usually breaches of a duty owed by law, and breaches of contract are usually breaches of a duty voluntarily agreed to. But they overlap in that voluntary agreement can change the nature of a duty in tort, and some contractual duties are imposed by law, not agreement.

Most tort cases are funded by insurance and this means the insurance industry has a big say in which cases come before the courts. This is important because most tort law is case law.

Decisions in tort cases are often influenced by policy, which means the judges' view of what is best for society. Courts may consider the effects on the insurance market, the number of cases coming before the courts, the impact on business or publicly funded organisations, or whether widening liability might prevent desirable or useful activities.

An important question in tort is whether it is a good thing for the claimant to have to prove the defendant was at fault. Arguments in favour of this include:

- It limits the number of cases, preventing the system being swamped.
- It deters wrongdoing if people know they can avoid liability by taking care.
- It is fairer if people only have to pay for wrongdoing they could have avoided.

Arguments against the requirement of fault include:

- It makes cases longer and so more expensive.
- It cannot deter wrongdoing when damages are paid by insurers, not the wrongdoer.
- It makes cases unpredictable, which allows the more powerful party to put pressure on the weaker one.
- It makes sense for losses to be paid for by those who can best bear them, and the fault principle puts a barrier in the way of this.
- It means that similar injuries are treated in quite different ways, depending on whether fault can be proved.

The Human Rights Act 1998 is making an impact on tort law, in two ways:

- courts must interpret tort law in line with the provisions of the Act as far as possible;
- the Act gives rights which may overlap with rights protected by tort, or give remedies where tort does not.

Most tort cases deal with personal injuries and research shows that claimants in this area of law face a number of difficulties, including getting access to legal services, the imbalance of power between them and defendant insurance companies which can make settlements unfair, and problems proving their case.

Alternative methods of compensation for personal injury victims run alongside the tort system, including employment benefits, social security, insurance and special compensation schemes for particular types of injury.

Further reading and references

Better Regulation Taskforce (2004) *Better Routes to Redress*, London: Cabinet Office Publications.
This report looks at whether we really have a compensation culture, and gives suggestions for better ways to improve access to justice for those who have genuine claims. It has lots of useful background information on how the tort system works.

Cane, P. (2006) *Atiyah's Accidents, Compensation and the Law*, 7th edn, Cambridge: Cambridge University Press.
This book has been through many editions but still remains one of the best and most detailed explanations of the way the law treats personal injury claims. Easy to read and very interesting, it has lots of useful background information, and looks at current topical issues including funding and the 'compensation culture'.

Donaldson, Sir Liam (2003) *Making Amends*, London: Department of Health.
This report looks at the way claims against the NHS are handled and recommends the creation of a new scheme. Its recommendations led to the NHS Redress Act 2006.

Flood, Colleen (1999) 'New Zealand's No-Fault Accident Compensation Scheme: paradise or panacea?', 8 *Health Law Review*, 3.
A critical look at one of the world's best-known no-fault compensation schemes, which argues that recent reforms have brought back some of the disadvantages of the tort system. Useful material if you are writing about the advantages and disadvantages of the fault requirement.

Genn, Hazel (1987) *Hard Bargaining*, Oxford: Clarendon Press.
A fascinating study of the way the tort system works, particularly from a claimant's point of view.

Harris, D., et al. (1984) *Compensation and Support for Illness and Injury* (The Oxford Survey), Oxford: Clarendon Press.
Although it is now over 30 years old, this research still sheds useful light on the difficulties the tort system places in the way of claimants.

Morgan, J. (2004) 'Tort insurance and incoherence', 67(3) MLR 384.
An interesting article on the impact of insurance on decisions in tort cases. The author argues that decisions influenced by insurance issues have led to incoherent rules.

National Audit Commission (2001) *Handling Clinical Negligence Claims in England*, available online at http://www.nao.org.uk/publications/0001/handling-clinical-negligence.aspx
This is another report into the way clinical negligence claims against the NHS are handled, which reveals a number of weaknesses with the tort system as a way of dealing with this type of claim.

Taylor, S. (2008) 'Clinical negligence reform: lessons from France?' 52 ICLQ 737.
This very interesting article looks at a new system of compensating victims of medical accidents which has been set up in France, and considers what advantages it might have over our system of using the courts for these kinds of cases.

Woolf, Lord (1996) *Access to Justice: Final Report*, London: Department for Constitutional Affairs.
Lord Woolf's report led to a number of changes being made to civil justice procedure, and gives useful background to some of the problems with the system. Some have been remedied by his reforms, but some remain.

Visit **www.mylawchamber.co.uk/quinntort** to access tools to help you develop and test your knowledge of tort law, including practice exam questions with guidance, annotated weblinks, glossary and key case flashcards, legal newsfeed and legal updates and interactive 'You be the judge' questions.

Use Case Navigator to read in full some of the key cases referenced in this chapter with commentary and questions:

Fairchild* v. *Glenhaven Funeral Services Ltd and others
[2002] 3 All ER 305

Chapter 2
Negligence: general principles

Key points In this chapter, we will be looking at:

- ✦ How the tort of negligence began
- ✦ When a defendant will owe a duty of care
- ✦ When a duty of care is breached
- ✦ What amounts to damage for the purposes of negligence

Introduction

Negligence is the most important tort in modern law – and it all began with a snail. On 28 August 1928, Mrs May Donoghue left her house in Paisley, Scotland, and headed for the nearby Meadow Café, where she was meeting a friend for what she must have thought would be a quiet drink. When they arrived at the café, Mrs Donoghue ordered a ginger beer float, which was a scoop of vanilla ice cream with ginger beer poured on top. The café owner poured out a little of the ginger beer and left the rest in the bottle on the table. As was usual at the time the bottle was opaque, so it was impossible to see the contents, and when Mrs Donoghue poured out some more ginger beer, the remains of a very dead and decomposing snail slithered out of the bottle and onto her ice cream. In addition to ruining her evening, the drink made her ill, and Mrs Donoghue decided she wanted to take legal action. She had no idea that, thanks to that snail, she was about to play a part in creating a whole new branch of law, which today employs hundreds of lawyers and pays millions of pounds in **damages** every year.

How negligence began

Today, it seems perfectly normal that someone who is made ill by a product can sue the manufacturer, but at that time there was no such legal claim. If Mrs Donoghue's friend had been made ill by the drink, the friend could have sued the café owner in contract, because she had paid for the drink. But Mrs Donoghue had no contract with the café owner, so that kind of claim was not available to her. However, apparently by pure luck, she consulted a solicitor, Walter Leechman, who believed the law should recognise claims like hers and had tried to bring similar cases, though without success. With his help, she sued the manufacturer of the ginger beer, David Stevenson, and the case, *Donoghue* v. *Stevenson* (1932), went all the way to the House of Lords. There, Lord Atkin delivered one of the most famous judgments in legal history, and in doing so created the foundation for what we now know as the law of negligence.

Case Summary

Mrs Donoghue's claim sought only to establish that where a manufacturer supplies food or drink in a form that makes it impossible for the customer to inspect them, and through the manufacturer's carelessness the products are not fit to be eaten or drunk, the manufacturer should be liable to pay damages. The House of Lords not only accepted this argument, but went further, and created a general principle that, where someone causes loss or injury through lack of reasonable care, and they could have foreseen that their carelessness might cause loss or injury, they may be liable to pay compensation for the results.

Lord Atkin explained the principle as: 'You must take care to avoid acts or omissions which you can reasonably foresee would be likely to injure your neighbour.' This is sometimes known as the **neighbour principle**. By 'neighbour', Lord Atkin did not mean just the person who lives next door, but, as he put it, 'persons who are so closely and directly affected by my act that I ought to have them in contemplation as being so affected when I am directing my mind to the acts or omissions which are called into question'. In other words, anyone who you can foresee being harmed by something you do or don't do.

Building on that general principle, the law of negligence now covers a huge range of cases, from people injured in a car accident who sue the driver, to businesses which lose money because an accountant has failed to advise them properly, patients who sue doctors when medical treatment goes wrong and children wrongly taken into care by a local authority.

The basics of negligence

Although the law of negligence now covers many different types of situation, the basic rules are the same. Whether you want to claim against a doctor who has performed your operation badly, a driver who has crashed into your car, or a surveyor who told you your house was solidly built when in fact it is falling down, you must prove three things:

1. That the person (or organisation) you are suing had a duty of care towards you. A **duty of care** basically means a legal duty to pay compensation for the results of carelessness, but not every situation where someone carelessly harms someone else will create a duty of care. Whether a duty exists in a particular situation will depend on a number of different factors, including:
    - whether it was foreseeable that the defendant's actions might cause harm to the **claimant**;
    - the relationship (if any) between the claimant and the **defendant**;
    - the type of injury or loss caused;
    - whether it is in the public interest for there to be liability in particular situations.

    If there is no duty of care in a particular situation, there is no liability for negligence.
2. That there was a breach of their duty of care. If someone has a duty of care towards you, they are expected to carry out that duty to a reasonable standard. That means that, for example, a doctor operating on you is expected to perform the surgery as

well as any reasonable doctor at their level would do, and a driver is expected to take the same care to avoid injuring other road users as any reasonable driver would do. If someone who has a duty of care falls below the relevant standard of reasonableness, they are said to have breached the duty of care.

3. That the breach has resulted in damage. Damage in this case can be personal injury (which covers both physical and mental injury, usually referred to as **psychiatric injury**), damage to your property, or financial loss, or a combination of all three. If the courts consider that the type of damage you have suffered does not fit into one of these categories, there is no case in negligence. For example, a claim for psychiatric injury can only be brought if you have a recognised psychiatric condition, such as post-traumatic stress disorder or depression. The courts do not recognise shock or distress alone as a psychiatric injury, so there would be no claim for these.

These three elements are specific to negligence law, but there are also a number of rules which relate to all torts, which you need to know when applying the law of negligence. They concern:

- Causation: this is essentially a set of rules which dictate whether the defendant's carelessness has in fact caused the damage. This may seem obvious but, for example, there are cases where an injury has more than one possible cause and the courts have to decide whether, or how far, the defendant should be liable.
- Remoteness of damage: this is a legal test, which decides whether the defendant's carelessness is sufficiently closely related to the damage to make it fair for them to pay compensation. It is needed because there are cases where, for example, there is damage that would not have happened **but for** the defendant's negligence, but for which they cannot fairly be held responsible.
- Defences: these are a set of rules which mean that, in certain circumstances, a defendant who has breached a duty of care and caused damage as a result will not be liable for that damage, or will only be partly liable. For example, **contributory negligence** is a **defence** which applies where the claimant was partly responsible for the damage, and means that the defendant has to pay less compensation than they would otherwise have done.

In this chapter, we will be concentrating on the three basic elements: duty, breach and damage. We will go on to look at causation, remoteness and defences in the next chapter.

Duties of care

As we have seen, negligence is a branch of law that seeks to compensate people for the harm done to them by the carelessness of others. However, the law does not provide a remedy for every case of carelessness that causes damage, and the idea of the duty of care is the most important mechanism that the courts use to decide which types of situation should or should not give rise to a claim in negligence.

In many situations it will be well established whether a duty of care exists: for example, it is clear that doctors owe a duty of care to their patients, and that motorists owe a duty of care to other road users. However, where a new situation comes before the courts, the courts have to decide whether there should be a duty of care, not just

In many situations it will be well established whether a duty of care exists

in that case but in any future cases concerning the same situation. So when a court denies a new duty of care, or accepts one, they are effectively drawing and redrawing the boundaries of the tort of negligence, and deciding whether or not to allow more cases in.

But why would the courts want to restrict the situations in which a duty of care exists, and so limit the number of cases brought? Why not let everyone caused damage by negligence to make a claim? Their reasons fall into four main groups:

- the 'floodgates' argument;
- impact on activities and enterprise;
- impact on insurance;
- public policy.

The 'floodgates' argument

The **'floodgates'** argument assumes that without restrictions on the kinds of situation which can create a claim in negligence many more people would bring claims. Not only could this mean that the court system might become overloaded with claims, making it more difficult for people who have suffered harm to get justice, but more importantly it could also place too much of a burden on those who would be sued. For example, if a decision made it very much easier for someone injured by a faulty product to succeed in a claim against the manufacturer, that would place greater costs on businesses, which would be passed on to consumers in higher prices, and/or might make it difficult for smaller businesses to survive. In such a case, therefore, the courts have to decide between restricting protection for claimants and leaving some without a remedy, or putting that extra burden on businesses with all the wider effects that would bring.

In addition, by placing restrictions on claims, via the concept of a duty of care, the courts make it easier for individuals and organisations to know what they can and cannot do, and therefore to plan their affairs in order to avoid doing anything which could get them sued.

Impact on activities and enterprise

This argument suggests that creating too wide an opportunity to sue over lack of care can have a restrictive effect on business and other desirable activities. For example, it is often claimed that in the USA, where ordinary people are thought to be much more willing to sue doctors than here, medical professionals are more likely to avoid trying new techniques, or to cover themselves by ordering costly and often unnecessary tests, because of the danger of legal action. This means, it is suggested, that medical advances may be held back if it is made too easy to sue for medical negligence. Similarly, in cases involving injury at work, it is claimed that creating too wide a duty of care imposes unjustified costs on businesses.

Impact on insurance

As we saw in Chapter 1, in most negligence cases, one or both of the parties will in practice be insurance companies, even if the names on the cases are those of their policyholders.

If you are injured in a car accident, for example, you might sue the driver, but it is their insurance company who will fund their legal representation and pay the damages if you win. The same will usually apply if you sue your employer for an injury caused at work, or a manufacturer over a dangerous product, or a health authority for medical negligence.

The way the insurance industry works is by assessing risk

The way the insurance industry works is by assessing risk: if a policyholder wants to be covered for a particular risk, the insurance company looks at how likely it is that the risky event will happen, and how much it is likely to cost them if it does. The more likely and more expensive the risk is, the more it will cost to insure against it, and if the risk is very high and very expensive it may be impossible to get insurance at all.

This means that if, for example, a court decision allows a duty of care where none existed before, the chance of successful claims in that area becomes much higher, and so insurance for the relevant activity will cost more, or possibly become harder to get. In a situation involving car insurance, for example, this would mean all drivers paying higher premiums. In a situation involving companies it would mean they would put their prices up to cover their higher insurance premiums, and in a situation involving local authorities, hospitals or schools, it would ultimately mean higher costs for taxpayers.

Public policy

This is a catch-all category which covers cases in which the courts simply believe it is not in the public interest to allow a particular type of claim to succeed, for reasons of basic morality or public acceptability. An example would be a group of cases discussed on page 62, where claimants claimed for the cost of bringing up children born after they had undergone sterilisation operations, and those operations had failed due to negligence. The courts held that society in general considered the birth of a child to be a blessing, not a burden, and therefore not something to be compensated for. For that reason, it was not appropriate to impose a duty of care in that situation.

When will a duty of care exist?

Where it is not clear whether a duty of care is owed, the courts have developed a basic test, stated in the case of *Caparo* v. *Dickman* (1990), to decide whether a duty should be imposed. Before we look at the ***Caparo* test** though, you should be aware that there are situations where the courts use more complex rules to decide whether there is a duty of care. These are:

- where the damage is pure **economic loss**. This means a financial loss that does not result from a personal injury or damage to property;
- where the damage is psychiatric injury;
- where the defendant is a public authority (including the police and other emergency services, local authorities and healthcare trusts).

We will look at these situations in the following chapter, by which time you will already understand how negligence works, and so find them easier to follow.

However, before we move on to look at the rules surrounding when and where a duty of care will exist, there is one important point about the way cases may be brought that will help you make sense of some of the cases in this section. This is explained in the Law in Action box.

Law in action A practical point: striking-out applications

Where a case raises a question of law (such as 'Is there a duty of care in this situation?'), the defendant can make what is called a **striking-out application**. When this application is heard, the defendant is effectively arguing that even if the facts of what the claimant says are true this does not give them a legal claim against the defendant. So in duty of care cases, the defendant will be arguing that even if they caused the harm alleged to the claimant, there was no duty of care between them and so there can be no claim for negligence.

When a striking-out application is made, the court conducts a preliminary examination of the case, in which it assumes that the facts alleged by the claimants are true, and from there decides whether they give rise to an arguable case in law – so in a striking-out application for a duty of care case they are deciding whether, on the facts before them, the defendant may owe a duty of care to the claimant. If the court decides that there is no possibility that a duty of care could exist in that situation, the case can be dismissed (struck out) without a full trial. If the court finds that there is an arguable case for a duty of care, the striking-out application is dismissed and the case can proceed to a full trial.

Not all cases do proceed to a trial after a striking-out application is dismissed, because some are settled. So, rather annoyingly, there are some cases where a striking-out application decides that there might be a duty of care, but because the case does not go to trial we do not discover whether there actually is a duty in that situation.

If a case does proceed to a full trial, the claimant will then have to argue successfully that there is a duty of care, and prove that all the facts alleged are true, so it is possible to win a striking-out application and go on to lose the case (for an example, see *Swinney* v. *Chief Constable of Northumbria Police* (1996), on page 160).

The basic test for a duty of care – the *Caparo* test

In *Caparo* (we will look at the facts of this case below), the House of Lords held that the test for a duty of care involves three questions:

- Was the damage reasonably foreseeable?
- Was there a relationship of proximity between the claimants and the defendants?
- Is it just, fair and reasonable to impose a duty in this situation?

This is now the basic test for a duty of care in new situations. We will look at each question in turn, but note that they often overlap.

Was the damage reasonably foreseeable?

This element of the test has its foundations in the original neighbour principle established in *Donoghue* v. *Stevenson*, where, as we saw earlier, Lord Atkin said there was a duty to 'take care to avoid acts or omissions which you can reasonably foresee would be likely to injure your neighbour'. Essentially, the courts have to ask whether a reasonable person in the defendant's position would have foreseen the risk of damage.

Case Summary

A modern case which shows how this part of the test works is *Langley* v. *Dray* (1998), where the claimant was a policeman who was injured in a car crash when he was chasing the defendant, who was driving a stolen car. The Court of Appeal held that the defendant knew, or ought to have known, that he was being pursued by the claimant, and therefore he knew, or ought to have known, that if he increased his speed the defendant would do the same and therefore be at risk of a crash. The defendant had a duty not to create such a risk.

It is important to note that for the duty to apply, the defendant must not only foresee that they might cause damage, but foresee that they might cause damage to the claimant, either as an individual or as one of a group of people in a particular situation. In *Langley* v. *Dray*, this applied because the defendant knew, or could reasonably have been expected to know, that the police car was chasing him, so he knew that whoever was inside that car might be caused damage by his actions.

Case Summary

If, however, the defendant could have foreseen that their actions might cause damage, but could not have foreseen that that damage would affect someone in the claimant's situation, there is no duty of care to that claimant. This was the case in *Palsgraf* v. *Long Island Railroad* (1928). The case arose from an incident in which a man was boarding a train and a member of the railway staff negligently pushed him, which made him drop a package he was carrying. The box contained fireworks, which exploded, and the blast knocked over some weighing scales several feet away. The scales fell on the claimant and she was injured. She sued, but the Court held that it could not reasonably be foreseen that pushing the passenger would injure someone who was standing several feet away at the time, so there was no duty to her. There was a duty not to injure the man who was pushed, since it was obviously foreseeable that he might be injured, but that did not create a duty to the whole world.

Case Summary

In *Haley* v. *London Electricity Board* (1965), the Court of Appeal considered when a duty could be owed to a group or category of people, rather than specific individuals. The defendants had dug a trench in the street in order to repair some underground cables. They laid a shovel across the hole to draw pedestrians' attention to it, but that was not much help to the claimant, who was blind. He fell into the hole and was seriously injured. It was agreed in court that the precautions the workmen had taken were sufficient to protect a sighted person from injury, so the question was whether it was reasonably foreseeable that a blind person might walk by and be at risk of injury. The Court of Appeal said it was: the number of blind people living and working in London meant that it was foreseeable that one of them might be injured if better precautions were not taken, so there was a duty of care towards the claimant.

Proximity

In ordinary language, proximity means closeness in terms of physical position, but in law it has a wider meaning. For the purposes of negligence, proximity concerns the relationship, if any, between the defendant and the claimant. In some cases, this will mean that they know each other, but this is not essential. What the courts are looking for with the test is really something that links the two parties in such a way that makes it justified to impose liability in negligence. This is a bit of a slippery concept, however, and it has been used to mean different things in different cases.

Case Summary

Case Navigator

In some cases, proximity really means little more than foreseeability (and therefore overlaps with the first test). This was the case in ***Caparo* v. *Dickman*** (1990) itself (which is of course the case where the three-stage test was set down). The claimants, Caparo, were a company who had made a takeover bid for another firm, Fidelity, in which they already owned some shares. When they were deciding whether to make the bid, they had used figures prepared by Dickman, an accountancy firm, for Fidelity's annual audit (an independent examination which shows whether the financial figures a company publishes about itself are accurate). The audit showed that Fidelity was making a healthy profit, so they bought the shares. When the takeover was complete, however, Caparo discovered that Fidelity was in fact almost worthless. They sued Dickman, and the House of Lords had to decide whether Dickman owed Caparo a duty of care. Their Lordships pointed out that the preparation of an annual audit was required under the Companies Act 1985 for the purpose of helping existing shareholders to make sure that the company they had invested in was being run properly. An audit was not intended to be a source of information or guidance for potential new investors and therefore, they said, it could not be intended to help companies in Caparo's position to decide whether to buy more shares. It was not foreseeable that the audit would be used for this purpose, and therefore there was no relationship of proximity between Dickman and Caparo and no duty of care.

Case Summary

Case Navigator

In more recent cases though, the courts have looked for something more than foreseeability when they are deciding whether there is proximity between the parties. In ***Sutradhar* v. *Natural Environment Research Council*** (2006), Lord Brennan said that a key factor in deciding when there was proximity was whether the defendant has 'a measure of control over and responsibility for the potentially dangerous situation'. The claimant was a resident of Bangladesh, who had been made ill by drinking water contaminated by arsenic. The water came from wells near his home, and his reason for suing the defendants was that, some years earlier, they had carried out a survey of the local water system and had not tested the water for arsenic. He argued that they should either have tested for arsenic, or warned the public that they had not done such tests. By doing neither of those things, he claimed, they had led the local people to assume the water did not contain arsenic.

The House of Lords held that there was no proximity between the defendants and the claimant. Mr Sutradhar had never seen the defendants' report and so his claim had to be based on the idea that they owed a duty to the entire local population. Their Lordships said that this could not be the case. Proximity required some sort of control over the source of the injury, namely the water supply where Mr Sutradhar lived, and the defendants did not have any degree of control over that. They were simply doing general research into the performance of the type of wells that happened to be used in that area, they had no connection with the project that had provided the wells, and no one had asked them to test whether the water was safe to drink. The fact that someone might have expert knowledge of a subject did not impose a duty on them to use that knowledge to benefit anyone in the world who might require such help.

Case Summary

By contrast, in *Watson* v. *British Boxing Board of Control* (2000), the defendants were found to have sufficient control over the risk to create a relationship of proximity. The claimant was the professional boxer Michael Watson, who suffered severe brain damage after being injured during a match. He sued the Boxing Board on the basis that they were in charge of safety arrangements at professional boxing matches, and evidence showed that if they had made sure immediate medical attention was available at the ringside, his injuries would have been less severe. The Court of Appeal agreed that there was proximity between Mr Watson and the Board, because the Board was the only organisation in the UK which could license professional boxing matches, and so had complete control of and responsibility for a situation which could clearly result in serious harm to boxers if the Board did not exercise reasonable care.

Justice, fairness and reasonableness

The third test is that it must be just, fair and reasonable to impose a duty of care. Again, there are many cases where this requirement overlaps with the foreseeability and/or proximity requirements. In *Watson* v. *British Boxing Board of Control* and in *Sutradhar* v. *Natural Environment Research Council*, for example, the arguments we have just looked at, which were made under the heading of proximity, could equally well be seen as arguments relating to justice, fairness and reasonableness. It was obviously fairer to expect the Boxing Board in *Watson* to supervise a match properly, since that was their job, than it was to expect the researchers in *Sutradhar* to take responsibility for a task that was not their job, and which they had never claimed to have done.

However, the justice, fairness and reasonableness test can also be used as a kind of back-up, where the courts find that there may be foreseeability and proximity but conclude that it would be unfair in all the circumstances to allow a duty in that situation.

Case Summary

This was the case in *West Bromwich Albion Football Club* v. *Medhat El-Safty* (2006), which concerned a knee injury to a West Brom player, Michael Appleton. The club arranged for him to see the defendant, Mr El-Safty, who was a doctor who specialised in bone injuries, and he advised surgery. The operation was unsuccessful and Mr Appleton could no longer play. It was accepted by the defendant that the advice was negligent, as other treatment should have been tried first, and a claim by Mr Appleton was settled. However, as well as being a personal disaster for Mr Appleton, losing a player meant that the club lost money and so they sought to sue the defendant for their losses. The doctor clearly had a duty towards the player to take reasonable care to give competent medical advice, but the club could only claim if he also had a duty to take reasonable care not to damage their financial interest in the player. The Court of Appeal said that it was not just and reasonable to impose such a duty, because there was nothing to suggest that the defendant should have realised he would be taking on that responsibility, and to take on this additional duty could have conflicted with his duty towards the player who was his patient, if, for example, a certain form of treatment could have enabled him to play on but led to problems later in life. The defendant was therefore not liable to the club.

The justice, fairness and reasonableness test is also used to refuse a duty where there is foreseeability and proximity, but the court believes that allowing a duty would be against the public interest because of the wider impact it would have.

Case Summary

This was the situation in *Commissioners of Customs and Excise* v. *Barclays Bank plc* (2006). The government's Customs and Excise Department, which collects tax, was owed a lot of money in unpaid VAT by two companies who had accounts with Barclays. Customs and Excise got court orders called 'freezing injunctions', which should have meant that the companies could not withdraw their money from the bank. Although Barclays were told about the orders, through negligence they allowed the companies to withdraw over £2 million, which meant Customs and Excise were unable to get all the money they were owed. Did Barclays owe Customs and Excise a duty of care? The House of Lords said no. It was foreseeable that if the bank ignored the court orders Customs and Excise might be unable to get their money, and this also suggested there was some proximity. But it was unjust and unreasonable to make banks in this situation liable for what could be huge losses, when they would usually be caused by a minor mistake. If a bank breached a court order, the court which issued it had power to punish that breach, and that was enough to make sure that banks would usually comply with such orders.

Case Summary

Case Navigator

Public interest arguments were also used in ***Mitchell* v. *Glasgow City Council*** (2009), where the claimants were the wife and daughter of a man who had been killed by their neighbour. The neighbour rented a house from the defendant council, and had a history of aggression towards the claimants' family, including making threats to kill them. In an attempt to solve the problem, the council called the defendant to a meeting, and told him that if his behaviour did not improve they would consider evicting him. Within an hour he had gone back home and attacked his neighbour, inflicting injuries which proved fatal. The claimants argued that the council were aware that he had made death threats and had a duty of care to warn them about the meeting, because the council must have realised that he might attack anyone he suspected of complaining about him. The House of Lords said that it was not fair, just and reasonable to impose such a duty, because that would mean that a similar duty must apply to all other landlords, and to social workers, in similar situations. Imposing a duty to warn, and liability if warnings were not issued, would deter landlords from taking steps to deal with antisocial behaviour by tenants, which would not be desirable.

You be the judge

Q: Pat is a postman. One dark December morning, he is out doing his deliveries when he falls into a large hole in the garden of a house he is delivering to and hurts his leg badly. The hole was left there by Bob, a builder, who is building a shed for the householder. Some days earlier, the local milkman also fell into the hole, though he was not badly hurt. He complained to the householder, who asked Bob to leave a lantern by the hole. Bob usually does this now, but this time he forgot and the hole was hard to see in the dark.

Using the *Caparo* test, decide whether Bob owes a duty of care to Pat.

A: As you will remember, the *Caparo* test has three elements: foreseeability, proximity and fairness, justice and reasonableness. Regarding Pat, clearly it was foreseeable that someone could fall into the hole, as Bob knows someone already has. Is there proximity? The case of *Watson* would suggest there is, as Bob was the person who had control over the hazard. Is it just and reasonable to impose a duty? Without any policy reasons not to, the courts are likely to find that it is.

Source: Pearson Education Ltd/Imagestate/John Foxx Collection

Writing and drafting

Source: Pearson Education Ltd/81A Productions/ Photolibrary

Read the case of *Sutradhar* v. *Natural Environment Research Council* (2006). Now go through the case, and pick out the arguments in favour of Mr Sutradhar's claim – in other words, the reasons why he believed the Research Council should be liable. Note them down in your own words. Then go through again, picking out the arguments against his claim. The case before the House of Lords was to decide whether the defendants should succeed in having Mr Sutradhar's claim struck out without a trial (check the Law in Action box on page 33 if you can't remember what this means). They decided it should be struck out. Having looked at all the arguments, do you think that was the right decision? What factors do you think were most persuasive?

Handy tip: Judgments do not always take the arguments for and the arguments against in turn. A good way to organise your material is to use two sheets of paper (or open two documents if you're working on a computer), one for the argument for, and one for those against, and then jot them down as you work through the text.

Reflective practice

Did you find it easy to pick out the arguments made in the case? Were there some arguments that were easier to follow than others? You may find this kind of exercise difficult at first, but it will get easier as you get used to reading tort cases. Being able to identify and use the arguments made in previous cases is an essential skill for any lawyer who appears in court, so repeating this task again with other cases that you come across is very good practice.

Liability for omissions

You may remember that when Lord Atkin explained the neighbour principle in *Donoghue* v. *Stevenson*, he said that 'You must take care to avoid acts or omissions which you can reasonably foresee would be likely to injure your neighbour.' By including 'omissions' in the principle, Lord Atkin made it clear that a defendant could be liable not only for something they have done, but also for something they have failed to do. However, as the law has progressed over the years, the courts have decided that there will only be liability for things a defendant has failed to do in a limited range of cases.

The basic rule is now that, in negligence law, there is no general duty of care to help someone just because they might be in need of help. If you see someone drowning and you are a strong swimmer and could easily rescue them, you might have a moral duty to try to do that, but you do not have a legal duty to do it and you cannot be sued for negligence if you decide not to bother. However, there are a small number of situations where the law does impose a duty of care in negligence to prevent harm or loss to someone else, and they fall into three groups:

- where the defendant has some control over the claimant;
- where the defendant has assumed responsibility for the claimant;
- where the defendant has done something to make a danger worse.

Defendants with control over the claimant

This issue mostly arises in cases where the claimant is in police custody, and the courts have found that in this circumstance the police essentially have control of the claimant's situation and therefore have a duty of care to take reasonable steps to keep them safe. In *Reeves* v. *Commissioner of Police for the Metropolis* (1999), the claimant was the widow of a man who had committed suicide while he was in a police cell. Previous case law had established that the police had a duty to take reasonable steps to prevent mentally ill prisoners from trying to kill themselves, but Mr Reeves had no mental problems and so the police argued that they did not have the same duty of care towards him. The Court of Appeal disagreed. They said that although it was very unusual in negligence law to impose a duty of care to look after someone's safety, it was appropriate because the police would have a high level of control over a prisoner's situation, and it was well known that suicide was a risk among people held in custody.

Case Summary

Defendants assuming responsibility

Although there is no general duty of care to help someone in need, a duty of care can arise after a defendant does something which suggests that they are assuming responsibility for someone else's safety. An example of this is *Barrett* v. *Ministry of Defence* (1995), where the Ministry of Defence (MOD) was sued by the widow of a pilot who was in the Navy. He was posted to a remote base in Norway, and had died after getting very drunk there and choking on his own vomit. Evidence was given that heavy drinking was very common on the base, even though there were Royal Navy regulations against drunkenness. On the night he died, he had been found unconscious and an officer had organised for him to be put to bed, but nobody had been told to watch over him and make sure he didn't choke. The Court of Appeal said that the officer was not liable for failing to prevent the pilot from getting drunk, because adults could be expected to take responsibility for their own drinking and the consequences of it. However, once the officer ordered the pilot to be put to bed, he was at that point assuming some responsibility for his welfare and he owed a duty of care to take reasonable steps to carry out that responsibility, for example by getting medical help, or asking someone to make sure the pilot did not choke (which leads to the rather strange situation that the MOD, which had legal responsibility for the officer's actions, would have been better off if he had done nothing at all to help the pilot. No one ever said tort decisions were always entirely logical). The MOD was held liable because the officer had assumed responsibility for the claimant's welfare. However, because the situation was also partly a result of the pilot's own actions in getting so drunk, the Court held that the MOD had the defence of contributory negligence (see page 88), and reduced the damages payable to the claimant by two-thirds.

Case Summary

Defendants who create or worsen a danger

Case Summary

Where the defendant actually creates a danger, or a dangerous situation already exists but the defendant does something to make it worse, they may then have a duty to take reasonable steps to deal with that danger, and can be liable for negligence if they fail to do so. This was the case in *Capital and Counties plc* v. *Hampshire County Council* (1997), which concerned a fire at the claimant's property. When the fire brigade arrived, they ordered the claimant's sprinkler system to be turned off, and this enabled the fire to spread more rapidly than it would otherwise have done and so caused more damage. The Court said that the fire brigade did not have a general duty of care to individual building owners to turn up and fight a fire. However, if they did turn up and did something to make a fire worse or more dangerous, they then had a duty of care to take reasonable steps to deal with the situation. The same would apply where a defendant had actually caused the dangerous situation.

You may find it odd that the Court decided that a fire brigade had no duty of care to turn up and fight fires. But remember that the Court was not saying that they had no legal duty at all to do this, and clearly members of the fire services have obligations to fight fires under their employment contracts, for example. What the Court was asked to decide was whether the fire brigade had a duty to individual building owners, which would enable those building owners to sue if the duty was breached, and they concluded that they did not.

Figure 2.1 Liability for omissions

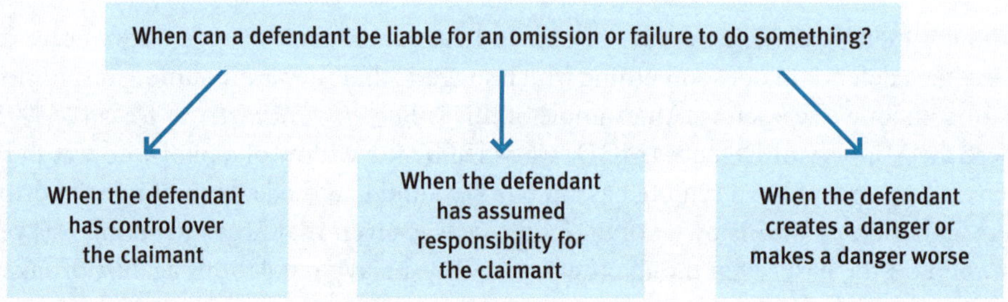

You be the judge

Q: **John is walking in the park when he sees a small girl, who he doesn't know, fall into the pond. It is obvious the child can't swim and there is no one else around. John can swim and could easily help her, but he doesn't and she drowns. Could John be liable in negligence?**

A: No. In general, negligence does not impose liability for a failure to act. John would only be liable if he had control over the child, had in some way assumed responsibility for her, or did something to make the situation worse.

Duties of care for other people's actions

We've now looked at situations where damage is alleged to have been caused by something that the defendant has done or failed to do. But what about situations where damage has been caused by someone else, because of something the defendant failed to do? Let's say, for example, that you have offered to feed your neighbour's cat while she is on holiday. You forget to lock the back door one evening and she is burgled. Should your neighbour be able to sue you for negligence? On the one hand, you could argue that it was the burglar who caused your neighbour's loss so you should not be liable, but on the other hand, your neighbour might argue that if you had not left the door unlocked the burglar would not have got into the house.

When it comes to cases like these, the basic rule is that there is no liability in negligence for damage caused by other people (usually called third parties).

However, there are a number of situations which the courts have said are exceptions to this rule, and in these situations a defendant can have a duty of care to prevent harm done by someone else. They fall into the following groups:

- where there is proximity between the defendant and the claimant;
- where there is proximity between the defendant and the third party who causes the damage;
- where the defendant has negligently created a source of danger;
- where the defendant knew or had reason to know that a third party was creating a risk on the defendant's property.

There is also a fifth situation, called **vicarious liability**, which applies where an employee commits a tort in the course of doing their job, and the law makes their employer liable for the damage. This is discussed in Chapter 8.

Proximity between defendant and claimant

As we saw earlier, in the case of the boxer who sued the British Boxing Board of Control, proximity basically means some kind of link between two parties that makes it reasonable for a duty of care to exist. Where there is such a link between two parties, that can mean there is a duty of care to prevent harm done by someone else. One example of this is where there is a contract between the two parties. This was the case in *Stansbie* v. *Troman* (1948), where the defendant was a decorator who was working on the claimant's house. The claimant went out and asked the decorator to make sure to lock the house properly when he left. He failed to do this and the house was burgled. He was held liable, because the fact that he was being paid to paint the claimant's house meant there was a contractual relationship between them. Case Summary

Proximity between the claimant and the defendant can also arise from things the parties have said and done. In *Swinney* v. *Chief Constable of Northumbria Police* (1996), the claimant was a woman who had supplied the police with information about a dangerous criminal. She had stressed that the information should remain confidential, because she was afraid of the criminal taking revenge, but thanks to negligence by the police the Case Summary criminal found out who had informed on him and subjected her to a terrifying campaign of violent threats. The Court of Appeal said that there was proximity here, since the claimant was someone who the police knew could be at risk from a particular criminal if they were negligent with the information she gave them. We can see how this works more clearly if we contrast this case with *Hill* v. *Chief Constable of West Yorkshire Police* (1986), which also involved police failure to protect someone from violent crime. In this case, the claim was brought by the mother of a woman who was murdered by the serial killer Peter Sutcliffe, known as the Yorkshire Ripper. Sutcliffe had already killed several women before he murdered Miss Hill, and her mother argued that the police had been negligent in failing to catch him earlier and so prevent her daughter's death. The House of Lords held that there was no duty of care here. There was no proximity between Miss Hill and the police, because she was not someone who they knew was in special danger. All the women in the area were potentially at risk while Sutcliffe was on the loose, but she was not at more risk than anyone else. (In both these cases, issues of public policy were important too, and this is discussed at page 157.)

Case Summary

Merely being able to foresee that the defendant is someone who might feasibly be caused harm is generally not enough to amount to proximity in this situation. In *P. Perl (Exporters)* v. *Camden London Borough Council* (1984), the defendant council owned two buildings next door to each other, numbers 142 and 144. The first was rented to the claimant and the second was empty. There was no lock on the door of number 144, which made it possible for thieves to get in and, by knocking a hole in the wall, get through to number 142 and burgle it. The Court of Appeal said that it was true that the council could have foreseen the risk of leaving number 144 without a lock, but by itself foreseeability was not enough to create a duty of care for the acts of a third party.

Case Summary

Proximity between defendant and third party

Another situation where there may be a duty of care to prevent harm by third parties is where a defendant is in a position of control over the third party who causes the damage. However, this will only create a duty of care towards a claimant who was at some kind of special risk, and not to the world in general.

Case Summary

This was the case in *Home Office* v. *Dorset Yacht Co.* (1970). Prison officers (employed by the Home Office) were in charge of a Borstal (a prison for young offenders) situated on an island. Due to their negligence, some boys escaped from the Borstal and took boats belonging to the claimants to try to get away from the island, damaging the boats in the process. The House of Lords found that the Home Office had a duty of care towards the boat owners, because the boys were under the Borstal officers' control (or at least they were supposed to be!), and it was clearly foreseeable that if boys from the Borstal escaped, they might try to get off the island by stealing boats. However, they stated that the officers' control over the boys did not create a duty of care to absolutely anyone who might suffer damage caused by the boys. The boat owners were at special risk and that was why there was a duty of care towards them.

Dangers created by the defendant

The third situation where there can be a duty of care to prevent harm done by a third party is where the defendant negligently creates a danger, and that danger is the source of the harm done by the third party. The case of *Haynes* v. *Harwood* (1935) explains how this can happen. The defendant left his horses unattended in a busy street. The third party here was a child, who threw stones at the horses, which made them run off down the road. A police officer saw the danger and ran to catch them, injuring himself in the process. The Court held that the defendant had a duty of care to him.

A duty of care will not, however, arise just because the defendant creates a situation which might make it possible for a third party to injure someone else. A case which illustrates this is *Topp* v. *London Country Bus (South West)* (1993), where a bus driver left his bus unattended outside a pub with the keys in the ignition. When the pub closed somebody got into the bus and drove it away, hitting and killing the claimant. The Court of Appeal held that there was no duty of care in this situation. The bus made it possible for someone to run over the claimant but, in itself, it was no more of a danger than any other vehicle parked on the road would have been. It only became a danger when the third party got in and drove off in it. The difference between this case and *Haynes* was that the horses in *Haynes* were a source of danger even without the actions of the child, because they could easily have got frightened and run off anyway.

Risks created on the defendant's property

Where a defendant knows, or has the means of knowing, that a third party has created a risk on the defendant's property, the defendant has a duty of care to take reasonable steps to prevent foreseeable danger to others, such as the occupants of adjoining buildings. Whether the danger is foreseeable will, in these cases, often depend very much on the facts. In *Smith* v. *Littlewoods Organisation* (1987), Littlewoods were the owners of a disused cinema, and while it stood empty vandals came and set fire to it. The fire spread to the building next door, owned by the defendant. The House of Lords held that in this situation there was no duty of care, because Littlewoods had no reason to foresee that anyone would set fire to the building: they had not been warned about any risk of arson by the police, and nothing especially flammable was stored in the building.

By contrast, in *Clark Fixing Ltd* v. *Dudley Metropolitan Borough Council* (2001), where the facts were similar, a duty of care was found to exist. Here again, vandals broke in and started a fire, which spread to the claimant's property, but in this case the damage was held to be foreseeable, because the defendants were aware that trespassers had entered the building and started fires on previous occasions, so they knew there was a risk of it happening again.

Figure 2.2 Liability for third parties

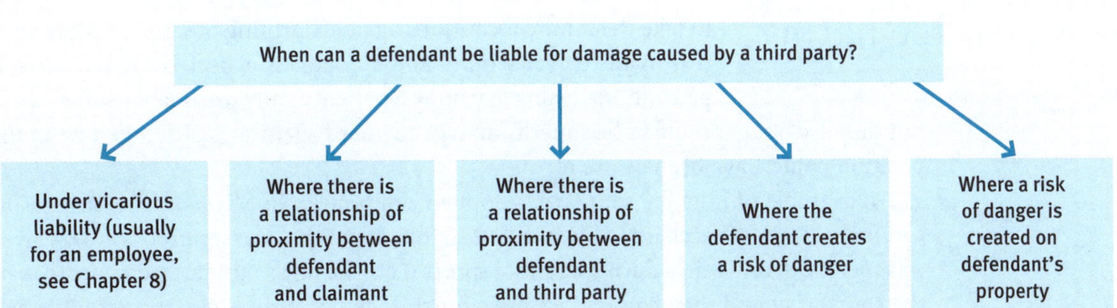

Case Summary

Similarly, in *Sandhu Menswear Co. Ltd* v. *Woolworths plc* (2006), a duty was found because the defendants had left piles of flammable material lying around outside, which clearly posed a risk that vandals might set light to it.

Out and about

Get a copy of your local newspaper, and go through it looking for any stories about people who have suffered physical injury in any way. For each story, use what you have learned in this chapter so far to try to work out whether someone had a duty of care towards that person and why. Remember that both organisations and individuals may have a duty of care, and that the person who causes the damage may not necessarily be the person who had the duty of care.

Duties of care: the problem situations

As mentioned earlier, there are a number of situations in which the courts have developed more complex rules about when a duty of care will exist: where the damage is psychiatric injury, or pure economic loss, or where the defendant is a public body. These are covered in Chapters 4, 5 and 6 and, if you want to cover the whole topic of duties of care in one go, you could move on to those chapters now and come back to this one afterwards. However, students often find it easier to understand the subject if they get a proper overview of how a negligence claim works before looking at the problem areas in duty of care. If you want to do that, carry on to the end of this chapter first.

Breach of a duty

Now we have looked at the issue of when a duty of care will exist, we can move on to consider when a defendant will be considered to have breached their duty. A duty of care essentially means a duty to reach a reasonable standard of behaviour in the situation concerned.

> a duty of care is not a duty to prevent every possible harm

It is important to realise that a duty of care is not a duty to prevent every possible harm or even to do everything possible to try to prevent harm. It is only a duty to do what a reasonable person would do to prevent harm occurring, and for this reason is often known as the standard of reasonableness. So, for example, a driver is expected to take the same precautions against harming other road users as any reasonable driver would, and a doctor is expected to take the same precautions against harming a patient as any reasonable doctor would, but they are not expected to be superhuman or to guard against risks that no one in their position could have been aware of.

Case Summary

An example of how the standard is applied can be seen in *Simmonds* v. *Isle of Wight Council* (2003). The claimant was a 5-year-old boy who was injured while playing, unsupervised, on swings during a school sports day. The boy's mother had come to watch the sports day and they had had a picnic lunch together near where the activities were taking place. Afterwards, she sent him back to join the activities but, unknown to her, he headed off to the nearby swings instead. While playing there alone he fell off and broke his arm. His mother claimed the school had a duty of care to prevent accidents on the swings, but the Court disagreed. It said that the sports day had been well supervised and the school had put in place measures to prevent accidents happening on the swings. It was not possible to make a playing field completely free of dangers, only to take reasonable precautions, and the school had done that.

An objective standard

The standard of reasonableness is an objective one, which means that it is tested against what the court finds that a reasonable person would do, and not what the defendant personally thinks is reasonable to do. Let's say, for example, that you are a talented skateboarder, and you skateboard through the local shopping centre at top speed, hitting and injuring someone in the process. A court would ask whether a reasonable person would have done what you did, not whether you personally believed you were entirely in control and not a risk to anyone. They might, for example, take expert evidence from someone who knows about skateboarding, and can say whether a skateboarder of your experience was likely to be able to skate through a crowded shopping centre without hitting anyone. From this, they will make up their own minds about whether a reasonable person would have foreseen that what you did was likely to lead to injury. If they conclude that it was not reasonable to expect you to foresee a risk of injuring someone, you will not be in breach of your duty of care. But if they decide, on the evidence, that a reasonable person would have realised that what you did was likely to cause someone injury, you will be in breach, regardless of whether or not you yourself were certain there was no risk.

Assessing the standard

When deciding what is a reasonable standard of behaviour in a particular situation, the courts consider a number of different factors, balancing them against each other. These include:

- how far it was practical to protect against the risk;
- the likelihood of harm;
- the seriousness of the harm;
- characteristics of the defendant;
- characteristics of the claimant;
- common practice in the relevant field;
- any benefits to society from the risky activity or situation;
- use of special skills.

Practicality of protection

As explained earlier, a duty of care is never an absolute duty to prevent all harm, but a duty to take reasonable steps to prevent harm. This means that the courts will take into account how difficult or expensive precautions against a risk would be (and therefore whether it would be reasonable for the defendant to take them). The more serious the risk, the more a defendant will be expected to do to protect against it, but defendants will not be expected to take expensive and difficult precautions against relatively minor risks.

Case Summary

In *Latimer* v. *AEC Ltd* (1952), the defendants ran a factory where the claimant worked. Heavy rain had caused some flooding in the factory, which left some very slippery patches on the floor, and although the defendants had covered some of them with sawdust they had not had enough sawdust to do them all. The claimant slipped on one of the uncovered patches and was injured. He argued that the claimants had not taken sufficient precautions to prevent his injury, and that the situation was so potentially dangerous that they should have temporarily closed the factory. The House of Lords agreed that closure would have been the only way to completely protect against the danger of people slipping over. However, they said that given the level of risk, and the fact that the slippery patches were clearly visible, it was unreasonable to expect the defendants to take such extreme precautions, and they were not liable.

Where a defendant is reacting to an emergency, they are judged according to what a reasonable person could be expected to do in their position, and with the same time available to decide what to do. This will often mean that behaviour that might not normally be considered reasonable will be accepted in an emergency situation.

The likelihood of harm

Case Summary

The courts will look at how likely it was that the harm would happen. If the risk is very small, fewer precautions may be required than for something which was very likely to happen, though this must be balanced against the seriousness of the harm that would be done. In *Bolton* v. *Stone* (1951), the claimant was standing outside her house when she was hit by a cricket ball from a nearby ground. Clearly, the cricketers could have foreseen that a ball might be hit out of the ground and this had happened before, but only six times in the previous 30 years. The pitch was some distance from the edge of the ground and there was a 17-foot fence around the ground. The House of Lords said that the chances of a ball being hit out of the ground and injuring someone were so small that there was no need to take more precautions than the defendants had done. The only way to make sure that an injury could not occur would be to build an extremely high fence, or possibly even a dome over the whole ground, and the trouble and expense of such precautions was completely out of proportion to the likelihood of the risk.

Seriousness of the harm

Case Summary

Where the potential harm is very serious, the standard of reasonableness may require extra precautions, even for a risk that is not very likely to happen. In *Paris* v. *Stepney BC* (1951), the claimant was employed by the defendants in a garage. As a result of a previous injury at work he was blind in one eye. One day, he was doing some welding when a piece of metal flew into his good eye and damaged it. Goggles would have protected him, but the defendant had not supplied any. The reasoning in the case is a good example of how the courts balance up the different factors involved in assessing the standard of care. The House of Lords accepted that for a worker with two uninjured eyes there was no duty of care to supply goggles, because the risk of this type of injury was quite small. However, they said that in this case, where the defendants knew that the claimant had already effectively lost one eye, there was a duty of care to provide goggles. The risk of an injury happening might be small, but if it did happen the risk to this employee was very serious and, in addition, it was not very difficult or expensive to supply goggles.

Characteristics of the defendant

Because the standard of reasonableness is objective, the courts will usually ignore any particular characteristics of the defendant. For example, if you drive on the road, the standard of care expected of you is that you will drive as any reasonable driver would, regardless of whether you are taking your first driving lesson or have been driving for years. In *Nettleship* v. *Weston* (1971), the claimant was a driving instructor and the defendant was having her third driving lesson with him. She drove into a lamp post, and the claimant was injured. The court held that she was required to come up to the standard of the average competent driver, and anything less amounted to a breach of the motorists' duty of care. It did not matter that she was doing the best she could after just three lessons (this may seem very unfair on the learner driver, but remember that in road accident cases, there will usually be insurance, so she would not have had to pay damages herself).

Case Summary

However, there are two characteristics which can mean that the courts will impose a lower standard, and these are when the defendant is a child, or is affected by illness. Children are not expected to reach the same standard of care as an adult would be, but they are expected to take the same precautions that an ordinarily careful and reasonable child of the same age would do. In *Mullin* v. *Richards* (1998), the defendant and claimant were two 15-year-old schoolgirls. They were pretending to sword fight with plastic rulers, when one of the rulers snapped and a piece of plastic flew into the claimant's eye, causing her to lose her sight in that eye. The Court of Appeal held that the correct test for breach of duty was whether an ordinarily careful and reasonable 15-year-old would have foreseen that the game carried a risk of injury. On the facts, what they were doing was something lots of children in the school did, and the girls had never been warned that it could be dangerous, so the injury was not foreseeable.

Case Summary

In *Orchard* v. *Lee* (2009), the Court of Appeal stressed that where the defendant was a child their behaviour would have to be 'careless to a very high degree' before they should be considered liable for negligence. The claimant in the case was a playground supervisor at a school, who was injured when a 13-year-old pupil ran into her while playing tag with a friend. The Court of Appeal confirmed that the test in *Mullin* was the correct approach, but said it was not the whole story. Courts did need to ask what a reasonable and prudent child of the defendant's age would have foreseen, but only as part of the wider question of whether the child had fallen below the standard of behaviour that could reasonably be expected from a child of that age. Only if there was a high degree of carelessness should a child be liable. In this case, that did not apply where a child of 13 was playing a game within a play area, was not breaking any rules or acting to any significant degree outside the rules of the game, so the claimant lost her case.

Case Summary

Where a defendant is suffering from some kind of illness which might affect their ability to reach the normal standard of reasonableness, the courts will look at whether the defendant knew this was the case. In *Roberts* v. *Ramsbottom* (1980), the defendant had suffered a stroke; he did not know that was what had happened, but he was aware of the symptoms he was suffering. He caused three accidents in his car, and the court held that he was negligent in continuing to drive when he knew that his driving was affected by his symptoms. A contrasting case is *Mansfield* v. *Weetabix* (1998), where a lorry driver had, unknown to him, an illness which lowered his blood sugar so far that his brain could not work properly. He did not know that his ability to drive was impaired, and there was evidence that he would have stopped if he had known. The Court of Appeal said the standard by which he should be measured was that of a reasonably competent

Case Summary

driver who was unaware that he suffered from a condition that affected his ability to drive. On this basis, he was found not to be negligent.

Characteristics of the claimant

If there is something about the claimant that increases the risk of harm to them, this may be relevant to the standard of care required. This was the case in *Paris* v. *Stepney BC*, the case of the welder who lost the sight in both eyes, discussed above.

Common practice

Case Summary

In deciding whether the precautions (if any) taken by the defendant were reasonable, the courts may look at what is normally done in similar situations in the relevant field. In *Wilson* v. *Governors of Sacred Heart Roman Catholic Primary School* (1997), the claimant, a 9-year-old boy, was hit in the eye with a coat by a fellow pupil as he crossed the playground to go home at the end of the day. It was argued that the school should have supervised the children at this time, but the Court of Appeal found that most primary schools did not supervise children when they were leaving at the end of the day. In addition, they pointed out that the incident could just as easily have happened outside the school gates, when the school would not have been expected to supervise the children. The school had therefore not fallen below the standard of reasonableness.

Case Summary

However, the courts have stated that a defendant who falls below the standard of reasonableness cannot avoid liability just because others in the same field would have done the same. In *Thompson* v. *Smith Shiprepairers (North Shields) Ltd* (1984), the claimant had gone deaf as a result of the noise levels in the defendants' shipyard where he worked. The defendants argued that the noise levels were common across the industry and so they did not fall below a reasonable standard of care. Mr Justice Mustill disagreed, stating that they could not avoid liability simply by proving that all the other employers were just as bad. He pointed out that the whole shipbuilding industry seemed to be indifferent to the problems caused by their working conditions, and said there were some circumstances in which an employer had a duty to take the initiative and seek out precautions which they could take to protect workers. However, he also said that it was still reasonable to take into account the cost and hassle of possible precautions, and employers were not expected to have safety standards that were way above those of other firms in the same industry.

Benefits of the risk

Case Summary

Some risks have potential benefits for society, and the courts will weigh up these benefits against the possible damage if the risk is taken. This was the case in *Watt* v. *Hertfordshire County Council* (1954). The claimant was a firefighter and was called, with his colleagues, to the scene of an accident, where a woman was trapped under a car. A heavy jack was needed to rescue her, and the vehicle in which the firefighters travelled to the incident was not designed to carry the jack. It slipped during the journey and injured the claimant. The court held that the risk taken in transporting the jack in the wrong vehicle was outweighed by the need to get it to the incident quickly, so there was no breach of duty. However, the court said that if the same kind of accident had occurred in a business situation, where the risk was taken in order to get a job done for profit, there would have been a breach of duty.

Case Summary

In *Cole* v. *Davis-Gilbert* (2007), the Court of Appeal specifically mentioned the danger of setting standards of care so high that they discourage socially useful activities. The case arose after Ms Cole was walking across a village green and stepped into a hole, breaking her leg. The hole had been used to hold a maypole for a village fête, and was dug by the local British Legion who organised the fête. After the pole had been removed they had filled in the hole, but by the time of Ms Cole's accident it had been left open again. It was not known how this had happened, but the Court assumed it was probably done by children playing on the green. The Court held that the British Legion was not in breach of their duty to people walking on the green, because they had taken reasonable steps to fill in the hole; equally the landowners, who were also sued, were reasonable in assuming the hole had been filled in and were not liable either. The Court commented that it was important not to set a higher standard of care than what was reasonable, because an unreasonable standard would eventually mean that events like village fêtes could not take place at all.

Use of special skills

Where the activity that causes harm to the claimant involves some kind of special or professional skill of the defendant, the courts will take this into account. In these cases, the standard of reasonableness is that the defendant must have acted as competently as an ordinarily skilled member of the relevant profession. A defendant who falls short of that standard, even if they might still be better at what they are doing than the average person in the street, will have breached their duty of care. In *Gates* v. *McKenna* (1998), for example, a woman who had been hypnotised during a stage show claimed that she had developed mental problems afterwards. The court said that the hypnotist was expected to take the precautions that a 'reasonably careful' stage hypnotist would have taken to protect people taking part in the show from psychiatric injury.

Case Summary

Special skills: levels of expertise

Obviously in many specialist areas there will be different levels of expertise: most of us would expect a consultant surgeon, for example, to be more skilled than a junior doctor. In *Bolam* v. *Friern Barnet Hospital Management Committee* (1957), the facts of which we will discuss a little later, the Court stated that where a defendant is using a specialist skill, he or she is expected to do so to the same standard as a reasonable person at the same level within that field. So, for example, a junior doctor is not expected to have the same level of skill as a consultant surgeon, but is expected to be as competent as a reasonably competent junior doctor, while a consultant is expected to show the competence to be expected of someone at their level in the profession.

This principle applies to all kinds of professionals and not just doctors, and we can see it in action in *Balamoan* v. *Holden & Co.* (1999). The defendant was a solicitor who ran a small high street practice, in which he was the only qualified lawyer. The claimant consulted him over a claim, and was advised that he could not hope to win damages of more than £3,000. He refused to accept the advice, and went on to conduct the case himself, winning a settlement of £25,000. He then sued the solicitor, arguing that if it had not been for the solicitor's negligence in, among other things, failing to gather all the evidence at an early stage, he could have won £1 million in damages. The Court of Appeal said the solicitor was only required to reach the standard of a solicitor with a general practice in a small country town, and was not expected to have the expertise of a big specialist firm. However, he had not even reached the standard of a solicitor in a

Case Summary

small country town, because he had delegated most of the work on the claimant's case to unqualified staff.

However, although the courts will adjust the standard of reasonableness to reflect the level a defendant has reached in their field, they will not take account of how long the defendant has been at that level. In *Djemal* v. *Bexley Health Authority* (1995), the defendant was a houseman (the most junior level of hospital doctor), and had only been at that level for four months. Even so, the court held that he was required to reach the standard of a reasonably competent houseman, whether he had been doing that job for a month or a year.

Case Summary

A defendant using specialist skills may be expected to do so as competently as someone who uses those skills as their trade, even if they are not in that trade. This was the case in *Wells* v. *Cooper* (1958). The defendant, who was a keen DIYer, had fixed a handle onto a door at his home but had used screws that were too short. The local fishmonger called to deliver some fish and was invited in for a cup of tea. When he was leaving, he pulled the door closed and the handle came away. Because the door was stiff and he had had to pull it hard, he was thrown backwards, and fell four feet from an unfenced platform outside the door, injuring himself. The Court of Appeal had to decide what the standard of reasonableness should be, and they decided that in doing a job like this, which could foreseeably cause injury if done badly, the defendant should be judged by the standards of a reasonably competent professional carpenter. On the facts, he had reached this standard, because a reasonably competent carpenter would not necessarily have realised the screws were too short, so he was not liable.

Case Summary

Special skills: differences of opinion

In assessing the standard of reasonableness when a defendant is using specialist skills, the courts have accepted that within any field of expertise there will be differences of opinion about the most appropriate techniques and procedures in any particular situation. The rule that applies in this situation was set down in *Bolam* v. *Friern Barnet Hospital Management Committee* (1957). The claimant had had electric shock therapy for psychiatric problems (this was a common treatment at the time), and because the treatment caused sudden, violent movements he had suffered a broken jaw. Usually, patients were either restrained or given muscle relaxing drugs to avoid the danger of fractures, but the defendant had done neither. However, there was evidence that not all doctors considered these precautions necessary. How was the Court to set the appropriate standard of reasonableness?

Case Summary

The answer was a formula which effectively let professionals set their own standard of reasonableness. According to Mr Justice McNair: 'A doctor is not guilty of negligence if he has acted in accordance with a practice accepted as proper by a responsible body of medical men skilled in that particular art.' Although it refers only to doctors, the judgment has since been used for other cases involving professional skills as well. It effectively meant that if a professional could find someone in the same field, who was prepared to state that what the defendant did (or failed to do) was in line with what some other professionals would do, they were not in breach of their duty of care. The fact that other professionals might not have acted as they did would not mean they were negligent.

The decision was much criticised as being unfair to claimants, and the test was modified by the House of Lords in *Bolitho* v. *City & Hackney Health Authority* (1997), though as we shall see, the practical difference this makes may not be much. The case involved a 2-year-old boy, Patrick Bolitho, who was taken into hospital because he was having trouble breathing. While in the hospital, Patrick had two very severe attacks of

Case Summary

breathing problems and the nurse looking after him called the senior doctor, but on both occasions she failed to come. About half an hour after the second incident, he had another attack during which his breathing failed completely. He suffered a heart attack and severe brain damage, and later died. His mother sued the health authority, arguing that he should have been seen by a doctor when she took him to the hospital, and that if he had been seen, and had had a tube inserted into his throat to help him breathe, he would not have suffered such serious brain damage. The doctor who was on duty at the time said that even if she had come to see Patrick she would not have inserted a tube anyway, which meant that the court had to decide whether she would have been negligent in not doing so. The claimant was able to call a number of expert witnesses who said that a reasonably competent doctor would have inserted a tube before the final incident happened, but the doctor also produced medical experts who said failing to insert a tube would not be out of line with accepted medical practice.

In this situation, the old *Bolam* approach would suggest that the doctor was not in breach of her duty because, even though other doctors might have disagreed with her actions, she could produce evidence that she had acted in line with a responsible body of medical opinion. But the House of Lords said that this was not necessarily the final word. Lord Browne-Wilkinson, who delivered the leading judgment with which the other judges agreed, said that although the ***Bolam* test** was still good law, it did not mean that a court was obliged to find that a doctor was not negligent just because some medical experts agreed that what they had done was in line with accepted medical practice. The court still had to satisfy itself that the medical experts' view was reasonable, in that they had weighed up all the risks and benefits, and had a logical basis for their conclusion. However, he then went on to water down this statement by saying that in most cases, the fact that medical experts held a particular view would in itself suggest that that view was a reasonable one, and that it would be only in rare situations that the court would want to reject such a view. The case itself was not one of those rare situations, and so the claimant lost.

Case Summary

Even so, there are signs that the *Bolitho* judgment is being used to ensure that medical professionals meet a more independent standard of reasonableness. In *Marriott* v. *West Midlands Regional Health Authority* (1999), the claimant had suffered a head injury after a fall at home, which left him unconscious for about half an hour. He spent a night in hospital but was sent home the next day. A week later he was still having headaches, so he saw his GP. The GP did some tests and found nothing wrong, but told the claimant's wife to ring again if her husband's condition got worse. A few days later the claimant became so ill that he was taken into hospital, where it was discovered that he had a fractured skull. This caused a blood clot in his brain, which left him partially paralysed. The claimant's medical expert claimed that a reasonably competent GP would have sent him back to the hospital for more tests, which might have uncovered the problem before so much harm was done. The GP's expert evidence was that although sending the claimant back to hospital would have been a reasonable course of action, it was equally reasonable to keep him at home with instructions to contact the GP again if his symptoms got worse. The old *Bolam* approach would have meant that the GP was not negligent, but the Court of Appeal held that the trial judge was correct to follow *Bolitho* and ask himself whether the defendant's argument was reasonable. The trial judge had concluded that, in the circumstances, the failure to refer the claimant back was unreasonable and a breach of duty, and the Court of Appeal upheld this decision.

For a real-life view on the operation of the *Bolam* test, and the effect of *Bolitho*, have a look at what solicitor Muiris Lyons has to say in the People in the Law box.

People in the law

Muiris Lyons is Head of Clinical Negligence at solicitors Stewarts Law in London.

Source: Muiris Lyons (*text and photo*)

What kind of cases do you typically do? My team specialises in cases involving very serious injuries to the brain and spine, caused by negligent medical treatment.

Can you tell us how a typical case might proceed? My cases will usually start with a telephone call, where the client explains what's happened, and from there you can get a very good idea of whether there is a good case. We're not doctors, we're lawyers, but because we specialise in brain and spine injuries, with experience you get to know how things are supposed to be done, and when things haven't been done the right way. I call it the eyebrow test – if they tell you something that makes you raise your eyebrows and think, that doesn't sound right, there's usually something worth looking in to.

Eight out of ten of the cases that come to us are turned away, either because they're not the kind of thing we do, or because we don't think there's a case that can be won. The other 20 per cent we then look at very carefully. The starting point is to go and see the client, and because of the nature of the injuries I'm dealing with, that usually means a hospital or home visit. It's quite time-consuming but you're possibly starting a relationship with a client that could last several years, so you need to make sure you're comfortable with them and they're comfortable with you.

Once we've established that we seem to have a case, and worked out how it's to be funded, the investigation process starts. We'll take a full statement from the client, get their medical records in, and instruct expert witnesses. Once we've done all our investigations, we'll review the case and decide whether to proceed. If we're going ahead, the health authority has four months to respond, and once they reply, you know whether they're going to put their hands up and admit liability or not – but it doesn't often happen at that stage.

Most of our cases are dealt with at the Royal Courts of Justice in the Strand, and they're run according to a set of case management guidelines specifically for clinical negligence cases. These days that means that from issuing proceedings a case will usually take no more than 12–18 months, which is considerably less than they used to take. A case can still go on for four or five years though, because the investigation stage alone might take two years, before you even know if there's a good claim.

What kind of issues are usually in question in your cases? Because we're dealing with cases of negligent medical treatment, duty of care is rarely in question, and the main issues tend to be breach of duty and/or **causation**.

How easy or difficult is it to prove breach of duty in this kind of case? It's extremely difficult for a claimant to prove breach of duty in a clinical negligence case, and one of the main reasons for that is the *Bolam* test. It effectively lets doctors set the standard of care, and you do get very good cases that are lost that way – I've had a couple myself.

If you look at the figures, very few clinical negligence cases that go to trial are won by the claimant – in 2005–2007, it was 29 per cent. The NHS won 67 per cent, and the rest were settled during the trial. Basically what's happening is that the NHS drags things out, because they know a high proportion of claims – about 40 per cent – are abandoned. If you know four in ten clients will give up, or lose their funding, or die, you're not going to settle early. Then they settle the ones that have a strong case, and only fight those where they have a very good chance of winning. So as a claimant's lawyer, you want to prevent the case going to court if you can, and if you do go to court you have to know you have an extremely strong case.

Has the decision in *Bolitho* changed anything? It has improved the situation a little. Before it, things really had got to the stage where the medics were deciding cases. *Bolitho* was the courts' way of clawing back the balance of power, and it means they can now examine and challenge the medical evidence. But it's still the case that the *Bolam* test makes it very hard to prove a doctor negligent. Even so, I think the test is overall a fair one, and it's hard to see another way of doing it. As a lawyer, you know that's the hurdle you face, and you just have to deal with it.

What qualities do you need to do your job? Obviously, you need to be fairly sensitive – you're dealing directly with clients, who have very serious injuries, or perhaps whose child has been brain-injured at birth, so you need to be easy to talk to. But you have to be commercially minded too. People who go into this area of law tend to be those who want to help people, and it can be hard when you have a very sad case in front of you, but you know they don't really have a claim. The temptation is to try to do something for them, but you're doing them no favours because you're giving them false hope, and you're also using time and effort that could be used on someone who does have a good case.

You have to be good at forensic investigation too – to be able to analyse a case, to grasp the issues and evaluate the evidence. And you need a strategic approach, so you can look at a case and think, what's the goal here and what's the best way to get to it? A lot of lawyers get very bound up in the process and just follow it step by step, but you really want to look for ways to short-circuit that process and get the result your client wants, as quickly as possible. You need to know when making the right phone call, or releasing the right piece of evidence at the right time, will get you there quicker, because that's what your client wants.

When looking at problem questions, remember that the *Bolam* test, as modified by *Bolitho*, is not just used in medical cases but can be used in any case involving specialist skills or expertise. In *Adams* v. *Rhymney Valley District Council* (2000), the claimants were parents whose children had died in a fire at the house they rented from the council. The house had double-glazed windows that could only be opened with a key, and the defendants had not been able to smash the glass quickly enough to get their children out. They argued that the council were negligent in supplying this type of window, and the question before the court was whether the *Bolam* test was the correct way to work out the standard of reasonableness. They decided that it was. In choosing the windows, the council had had to balance the risk of fire against the risk of children falling out of a window that was easier to open, and experts on fire safety would have different opinions as to whether they had got the right balance between these two factors. If a reasonable body of experts would consider that the council's choice struck the balance in a reasonable way, and the court found their reasoning logical, then there was no negligence, even though other experts might disagree.

Case Summary

Special skills: a duty to explain

In medical negligence cases, professionals have a duty not just to take reasonable steps to make sure their advice or action is right, but also to explain any potential risks to the patient. In ***Chester* v. *Afshar*** (2004), the claimant had had surgery for a back problem, and as a result of the surgery had ended up with severe nerve damage which paralysed one leg. This was a known risk of the type of surgery she had, though it happened very

Case Summary

Case Navigator

rarely, but the surgeon had not mentioned the risk at all beforehand. The House of Lords found that the surgeon was not negligent in the way he did the operation. The paralysis was something that could happen even when the surgery was carried out properly, as it had been here. But they said that he had been negligent in failing to warn the claimant of the risk, even though it was a small one. She had a right to choose what was or was not done to her, and she could only do that properly if she had full information. Providing such information was therefore part of the doctor's duty of care.

Case Summary

Attempts have been made to extend the duty to explain non-medical cases, but the courts have generally been against this idea. In *Moy* v. *Pettman Smith* (2005), the defendant was a barrister and the claimant a former client. The barrister was representing the claimant in a medical negligence case about an operation that went wrong, and a key part of the evidence was a report from a surgeon. The claimant's solicitors failed to get the report when they should have, and the barrister applied to have the case adjourned to allow more time to get the report. She was refused, but she planned to apply again. Just before the trial, the health authority offered to settle the case for £150,000 but the barrister advised the claimant not to accept it, and said she thought there would be no problem getting extra time to present the surgeon's report, which would help them win more than the settlement offer. In fact, she admitted later, what she really thought was that there was a fifty-fifty chance of getting more time, but that if they did not, and as a result the claimant won less than he should have, he could sue his solicitors for the difference. However, she did not explain any of this to the claimant.

The claimant took her advice and refused the offer, but her application for more time was refused and the court ruled that the hearing had to go ahead. Without the report, the claimant's case was much weaker, so she advised him to settle. But by this time the health authority had reduced their offer to £120,000. The claimant therefore sued the barrister and the court had to consider whether she was negligent in not explaining the full background to her advice. The House of Lords held that she was not. The advice she gave was within the range of advice that an ordinarily competent barrister might give in that situation, and as long as she had given the advice clearly, so that the client could understand it, there was no duty to spell out how she had come to that conclusion.

Special skills: changes in knowledge

Specialist knowledge in areas like medicine and technology never stands still, and procedures and techniques which are standard practice may become outdated as experts develop new, better and safer ways of solving problems. In some cases, practices once accepted as safe and normal may even be discovered to be dangerous. In *Roe* v. *Minister of Health* (1954), it was established that where this happens a defendant only has to reach the standard that was accepted at the time they acted.

Case Summary

The claimant in *Roe* was left paralysed after an operation, because the anaesthetic injected into his spine was contaminated with disinfectant. This happened because the glass tubes that the anaesthetic came in were kept in disinfectant, and there were microscopic cracks in the glass, invisible to the naked eye, through which the disinfectant leaked into the anaesthetic. At the time that the claimant was injured, in 1947, it was not known that this could happen. By the time the case came to court the risk was known about, and it was standard practice to add dye to the disinfectant so that any contamination became visible. The court held that the defendant could only be judged on the knowledge that a doctor would have had, or should have had, at the time of the accident, and so he was not liable.

Setting the standard

The importance of each factor will vary from case to case

The factors we have just looked at are the kinds of issues that the courts will consider when deciding where to set the standard of reasonableness in a particular case. However, they are not used as a checklist, and not every factor will be considered in every case. Nor do they come in any order of priority. The importance of each factor will vary from case to case, and they must be balanced against each other. So, for example, if a type of damage is not very likely to occur, and protecting against it would be very difficult, the courts will expect less of the defendant than they would if the damage was not very likely to occur, but it would have been easy to protect against it. Similarly, if a type of damage is very serious but not very likely to occur, the courts will usually allow fewer precautions to be taken than if the damage was potentially serious and quite likely to occur.

Writing and drafting

You are a solicitor in a firm specialising in personal injury claims. You have a client who has a claim for negligence against a doctor. He wants to know how the court will decide whether the doctor was negligent or not. In your own words, write a short explanation of the factors a court will take into account when deciding whether the doctor has breached his duty, and how they will balance them against each other. Use case examples where you think they will make the rules clearer.

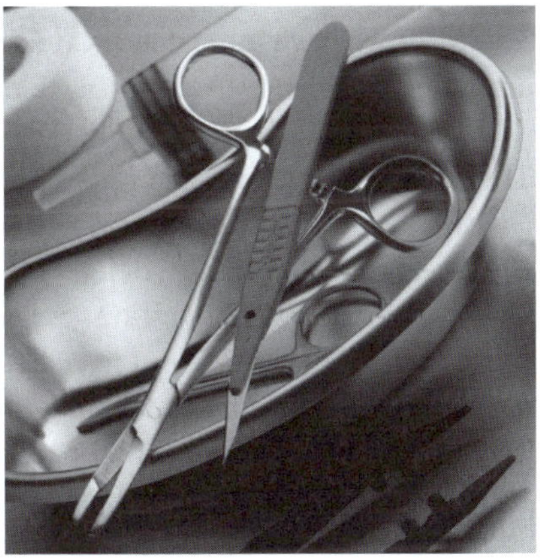

Source: Pearson Education Ltd/Photodisc/Don Farrall

Handy tip: Remember your client is not a lawyer, so use clear, simple language, and assume that he does not have any prior knowledge about the law.

Reflective practice

Did you find this task easy or was it difficult? Explaining legal concepts in your own words is a good way to check whether you have really understood them, so if it was tricky, you might want to go back over the text and make sure you really get to grips with this part of the law and how it works.

Table 2.1 Assessing whether there is a breach of duty

Factors in favour of the defendant	Factors in favour of the claimant
The damage was not very likely to happen	The damage was very likely to happen
The damage was not very likely to be serious	The damage was very likely to be serious
It would have been difficult and/or expensive to take precautions against the risk	Taking precautions against the risk would have been simple and inexpensive
The precautions taken were in line with common practice, or it was not common practice to take precautions against this risk	It was common practice to take precautions against this risk, or better precautions than the defendant took
The risky activity had social benefits	There were no social benefits associated with the risky activity

Proving negligence

The cases we have looked at in this section show how the courts decide what the standard of reasonableness is in any particular set of circumstances. The courts set this standard, and then it is for the claimant to prove that the defendant's behaviour fell below it. This means that a case can raise two separate sets of questions: the legal issues, such as whether there is a duty of care, and what the standard of care should be; and the factual issues, covering what the defendant actually did, and when. Because most legal textbooks only discuss the questions of law it is easy to get the impression that every case raises some of these questions, but in real life there are a great many cases where the law is not in question, because it is clear that, if the claimant's version of what happened is true, the defendant had a duty of care, breached it and caused damage that was not too remote. In those situations, the court case will be about whether the claimant can prove that the defendant did what the claimant says they did. This can be very difficult, and often expert evidence will be needed (for example, from doctors in medical negligence cases), which is one of the things that can make negligence cases so expensive. The Law in Action box looks at a real-life example of how difficult it can be to prove negligence.

often expert evidence will be needed

Law in action Claims for MRSA

Over the past few years, there has been widespread media coverage of the 'superbug' MRSA, a potentially life-threatening bacterial infection which has affected increasing numbers of hospital patients and is associated with a lack of cleanliness in hospitals. Many of the patients who have contracted MRSA have ended up seriously ill, or in some cases have died, and not unnaturally many of them have wanted to sue the hospitals. Given that they went into a place that was supposed to make them better, and instead came out more seriously ill (or didn't come out at all), you might imagine that their cases were relatively simple, but in fact they are a good example of how difficult it can be to prove the facts of a negligence case.

Imagine that you are a solicitor with a client who has contracted MRSA after a very minor operation and wants to sue. You would want to show that the infection was caused by the hospital's negligence, in the form of poor cleaning standards, and that means that you would have to prove that the hospital was unreasonably dirty, at the time she was in there, and that she caught MRSA as a result of that negligence.

Your first hurdle is that the MRSA bacteria is very common, and is carried harmlessly on the skin by around 30 per cent of people (it becomes dangerous only when it enters an open wound, which is one reason why infections so often happen in hospital). You therefore have to prove that your patient wasn't already carrying MRSA when she went into hospital. If the hospital tested her for MRSA when she was admitted, a negative result is good evidence that the bug was caught in hospital, but until recently not all hospitals did these tests routinely, so if your client went into hospital some time ago there may be no evidence of whether she was carrying her own MRSA when she went into the hospital (people do not always decide to make a legal claim straightaway, so there can be a time lag between the injury and going to a solicitor).

Then there is the problem of proving that the hospital was negligently dirty. Your patient tells you that the ward was filthy, and relatives who visited her in hospital are willing to give evidence that backs up this claim. But the hospital will deny that the ward was dirty, and say that the relatives' evidence cannot be relied on because they are obviously biased towards the claimant's interests. There will often be very little evidence in the claimant's medical records of what the staff were (or were not) doing with regard to hygiene, so you would therefore have to find independent evidence to prove that the hospital was dirty, for example by combing through the hospital's own records of their infection control procedures to see if there was a recorded lapse in the procedures at the time, and getting expert evidence from a clinical microbiologist.

To add to your problems, MRSA infection can happen even where standards of cleanliness are adequate, so even if you can prove that what your client says about the lack of cleanliness is true, you would have to prove, on a **balance of probabilities**, that she caught the bug through that lack of cleanliness and not just through sheer bad luck.

The issue becomes even more complicated if, as in many cases, your client was already seriously ill when she went into hospital, and as a result of the MRSA her illness worsened. In these cases, you would need to get medical evidence to show that but for the MRSA the original illness would not have become so serious. Clearly that can be very difficult as doctors cannot always accurately predict how a disease will progress. It is perhaps not surprising then that relatively few attempts to sue in negligence for MRSA infection have succeeded.

Reversing the burden of proof

There are two situations where the **burden of proof** is effectively reversed. The first is where the defendant has already been convicted of a criminal offence based on the same facts as are alleged in the negligence action, such as, for example, where the defendant has been convicted of dangerous driving and the claimant is suing for injuries caused as a result of that dangerous driving. Under section 11 of the Civil Evidence Act 1968, the conviction counts as substantial evidence of negligence, and it is for the defendant to disprove it if they can. The second situation is where a legal principle called **res ipsa loquitur** applies.

Res ipsa loquitur

Res ipsa loquitur is Latin for 'the thing speaks for itself', and it can be used in cases where the accident is one that could not normally happen without some kind of negligence.

Examples might be one train crashing into another, or a surgeon cutting off a patient's right leg when they should have amputated the left one. If a claimant can successfully argue res ipsa loquitur, they need not put forward detailed evidence about what the defendant did or did not do.

In order to use res ipsa loquitur, the case must be one where:

- the type of accident is one that would not normally happen without negligence; and
- the cause of the accident was under the defendant's control; and
- there is no explanation for the accident.

The type of accident

Case Summary
Case Summary

An example of a case where the courts found that an accident would not normally happen without negligence is *Scott* v. *London and St Katherine's Docks* (1865), where the claimant was injured by some bags of sugar, which fell out of the open door of the claimant's warehouse above. There was no evidence of negligence, but the Court of Appeal held that negligence could be assumed from the facts of what happened, because sacks of sugar do not normally fall out of the sky unless someone has been negligent. Similarly, in *Mahon* v. *Osbourne* (1939), the claimant was left with a swab inside him after a stomach operation, and the court held that this could not have happened unless someone had been negligent.

Case Summary

In *George* v. *Eagle Air Services* (2009), the claimant's partner and the father of her children was killed when a plane operated by the defendants crashed as it was about to land. She claimed that the pilot must have been negligent in his handling of the plane. The defendants responded that the plane had been checked and found safe, and they had not authorised the pilot to carry out any activities that would be outside the safe operation of the plane. They offered no other evidence to show that they were not negligent. The **Privy Council** found that modern air travel had a reasonable safety record, and plane crashes would not normally occur without some kind of failure on the part of someone involved in flying, maintaining or designing the aircraft. Therefore, in the absence of any evidence to rebut the presumption, res ipsa loquitur could apply.

Under the defendant's control

Case Summary
Case Summary

This requirement is illustrated by two contrasting cases. In *Gee* v. *Metropolitan Railway* (1873), the claimant fell out of a train, just after it had left a station, because the door was not properly shut. It was the railway staff's job to shut the doors, and because the train had only just pulled out of the station it could be inferred that they had not shut the doors properly. However, in *Easson* v. *LNE Railway* (1944) the facts were similar but the train was seven miles past its previous station when the door flew open. In this case the situation was not under the control of the defendant's staff, because anyone could have interfered with the door during the time since they had closed it. They might have been negligent, but it was not possible to assume that from the facts and so res ipsa loquitur could not be used.

No explanation for the accident

Case Summary

Res ipsa loquitur can only be used where there is no evidence to show what happened, as was the situation in the two cases we looked at earlier. If there is evidence, the court will examine that in the normal way rather than assuming negligence under res ipsa loquitur. This was the case in *Barkway* v. *South Wales Transport Co. Ltd* (1950). The claimant was injured when a bus he was travelling in mounted the pavement and crashed down an embankment. He tried to use res ipsa loquitur, but there was evidence that the crash was caused by a defect in one of the tyres on the bus, and that the defendants had not instructed their drivers to report any heavy blow to a tyre even though it was known this could cause it to burst later. The court held that the proper approach was to examine this evidence to see if there was negligence (and on this basis, the defendants were found liable).

The effect of res ipsa loquitur

If a claimant successfully puts forward a claim of res ipsa loquitur, the court will assume that there was negligence, unless the defendant can provide a plausible explanation that shows the accident could have happened without negligence.

Case Summary

In *Ward* v. *Tesco Stores* (1976), the claimant slipped on some yogurt in a branch of Tesco. She had no evidence of how it came to be there, or how long it had been there, though she did have evidence that a few weeks earlier spilt orange juice had been left on the floor for 15 minutes. Tesco claimed that the floor was swept several times a day and that staff who spotted a slippage were told to stand by it and call for someone to clear it up, but they could not explain how, if that had happened, the claimant had come to slip on the juice. The Court of Appeal said that res ipsa loquitur could apply. The claimant had shown that something had happened which was more likely to be a result of negligence than not to be. The defendants could still escape liability if they could provide an explanation of how the accident might have happened, and that explanation would show that the accident was at least equally likely to happen if there was a proper system in place to protect customers. They had not shown this and so they were liable.

Damage

The third element of a claim for negligence, outlined earlier under 'The basics of negligence', is that the defendant's breach of duty must have caused damage to the claimant. If you have a duty of care towards someone, and you breach that duty but (perhaps just by luck) no damage is caused, they cannot successfully sue you in negligence. Take, for example, a situation where you are driving far too fast along a road and a pedestrian steps out in front of you. You are going too fast to stop, but at the last moment someone grabs the pedestrian and pulls them out of the way, so they are not injured at all. In that case, you have clearly breached a duty of care, and most people would agree that you were doing something wrong, but if you have not caused injury or loss to anyone there is no one who can sue you for it in negligence (though you may of course be prosecuted for speeding by the police).

Types of damage

There are three basic types of damage that negligence will compensate for:

- personal injury;
- damage to property;
- economic loss.

Personal injury

This can be physical injury, or psychiatric injury such as depression or post-traumatic stress disorder. There are restrictions on the situations in which claims can be brought for psychiatric injury, and we will look at these in Chapter 4.

Case Summary

In *Rothwell* v. *Chemical and Insulating Co. Ltd* (2006), the Court of Appeal looked at what could and could not amount to physical injury for the purposes of a claim in negligence. The claimants in the case were a group of workers who had been negligently exposed to asbestos while working for the defendants. If asbestos gets into the lungs, it can cause one of a range of fatal diseases. At the time the case was brought none of the defendants had any of these diseases, but they did have what are known as pleural plaques. These are a form of scarring on the lungs, which show that asbestos has been inhaled. The plaques do not cause any symptoms, or make it more likely that the person will get one of the asbestos-related illnesses, but because they are evidence that asbestos has entered the person's lungs having them is a sign that that person may be at risk of asbestos-related illness. This naturally caused great anxiety among the claimants. The Court of Appeal held that the plaques could not be considered a physical injury, because they did not actually affect the claimants' physical health. They were evidence that the claimants' had an increased chance of suffering illness in the future, but there was no claim in negligence for an increased chance of illness. They would only be able to claim if the illness actually happened. Nor could they claim for the distress and anxiety caused.

Damage to property

This covers anything which makes a claimant's property less useful or less valuable, which would of course include completely destroying it. So if another driver crashes into your car, damaging it and injuring you, you can claim for both your injury and the damage to the car.

Case Navigator

Case Summary

In ***Hunter* v. *Canary Wharf*** (1995), the Court of Appeal said that compensation in negligence could only be given for damage that amounts to a physical change in property. The claimants in the case lived near a large building site, and sought to claim for the huge amount of dust that was constantly blown into their homes from the site. The Court said this could not be considered damage. (This kind of thing might, however, allow a claim in nuisance; see Chapter 14.)

For the purposes of a negligence claim, all kinds of physical objects can be classified as property, from a car to a coat, but the Law in Action box looks at a case that raised a rather unusual question about what can and cannot be considered property.

Law in action Is sperm property?

Advances in medical knowledge can result in new and unusual questions coming before the courts, and this was the case in *Yearworth and Others* v. *North Bristol NHS Trust* (2009). The claimants in the case were all men who had undergone chemotherapy treatment for cancer. This kind of treatment can leave men sterile, and so it has become common for hospitals to offer patients the chance to have a sperm sample frozen under medical conditions so that they still have at least a chance of having children if they later want to. The storage and use of the sperm samples is regulated by the Human Fertilisation and

Embryology Act 1990, which lays down rules about who can store the samples and how they can be used.

The claimants' sperm samples had been stored by one of the defendants' hospitals but, owing to negligence, they had been allowed to thaw, making them useless, and the claimants sued the NHS Trust for negligence. The Trust admitted that it had a duty of care to take reasonable care of the samples, and that it had breached this duty. However, it denied liability because, it argued, the loss of the samples was not damage of a kind that was recognised in the law of negligence.

There were two possible ways in which the sperm could be classified as damage: either its destruction was a personal injury to the men who provided it, or alternatively, the sperm could be considered to be the men's property. Trying first to argue that the damage was personal injury, the claimants' lawyers said that the sperm had been inside the men's bodies, and if it had been damaged there that would clearly have counted as a personal injury. Why, they argued, should the situation be any different because the sperm had been ejaculated? They went on to argue that the sperm was different from body parts which were intended to be discarded, such as nail clippings or amputated limbs, because it was always intended to be kept. The purpose of keeping it was exactly the same as the purpose it had while still in the men's bodies, namely to create a baby, and it was still biologically active and therefore had a 'living nexus' or connection with the men. The Court of Appeal dismissed these arguments, stating that 'it would be a fiction to hold that damage to a substance generated by a person's body, inflicted after the removal of that substance, constituted a bodily or personal injury to him'. Unfortunately they didn't provide much in the way of reasoned explanation for this conclusion, beyond saying that to accept destruction of the sperm as personal injury would 'generate paradoxes, and yield ramifications, productive of substantial uncertainty, expensive debate and nice distinctions in an area of law which should be simple, and the principles clear'.

The Court of Appeal therefore considered the alternative argument, that the sperm was the men's property. The Trust's lawyers had argued that the sperm could not be considered property, because the Human Fertilisation and Embryology Act had restricted the rights that would normally go with ownership. For example, the Act states that only organisations licensed under the Act can store the samples and use them to bring about a pregnancy, so it would not have been possible for the men to ask for the samples back and store them themselves. That being the case, the Trust argued that the men could no longer be said to own the sperm. The Court of Appeal disagreed. They said that the men's bodies had produced the sperm, and the reason for giving the sperm samples was that the sperm could later be used for their benefit. They agreed that the Act restricted the men's use of the samples, but pointed out that many statutes imposed restrictions on the use of property, without suggesting that this means the owner does not own it – for example, planning laws restrict a landowner's choice of how to use their land, but that does not mean that the land is not property or not owned. The Court further pointed out that as well as placing restrictions on what they could do with the sperm, the Act also gave the men rights over it, such as that the men could at any time withdraw their consent to having the sperm stored. They also pointed out that the men's recognised rights over the sperm, namely to decide its future use, exactly coincided with the result of the Trust's breach of duty, which was to prevent its future use. They therefore agreed that the sperm samples could be regarded as property, and so the Trust could be liable for negligently destroying it.

Economic loss

This means financial loss which is not part of a claim for personal injury or property damage. It is sometimes known as 'pure' economic loss, to distinguish it from financial losses that arise out of a personal injury, such as loss of earnings if an injury means a claimant cannot work. An example of pure economic loss would be where a surveyor negligently valued a house you were planning to buy and, as a result, you got a house worth much less than you paid for it. Claims for 'pure' economic loss are subject to special rules and we will look at these in Chapter 5.

Other types of loss

There are types of loss for which negligence does not offer a remedy. For example, if you have studied contract law you will know that it can, in certain cases, offer compensation for disappointment, distress and loss of enjoyment. If, for example, you buy a package holiday, and the hotel turns out to be a building site, infested with cockroaches and five miles from a beach when you were told it was across the road, you can sue the holiday company for breach of contract, and as well as claiming your money back you can claim for loss of enjoyment and disappointment. This is not the case in negligence. If, while on holiday, you injure yourself due to the hotel's negligence, and spend the rest of the stay in hospital, you will be able to claim for your injury, and for financial losses that result from it, but not for disappointment and loss of enjoyment of your holiday. Similarly, there is no claim in negligence for the shock or distress caused by an accident, unless it causes a recognisable psychiatric illness.

You be the judge

Q: Ben runs a business hiring out DIY equipment and tools. One of his ladders comes back from a customer with a rung near the top damaged. Ben plans to fix it but doesn't get round to it. The next morning, Kate comes into his shop wanting to hire a ladder that day. The broken one is the only one in stock and, forgetting about the damage, Ben lets her hire it. When Kate is at the top of the ladder, the broken rung gives way and she falls, but luckily she lands on a bush and isn't hurt at all, although she was frightened by the fall and is very cross with Ben. Does Kate have a claim against Ben?

A: No. Although Ben owed Kate a duty of care and breached that duty, there was no damage that is recognised by the law of negligence, so she has no claim.

The 'wrongful birth' cases

In most situations, it will be clear whether a type of damage can be compensated for in negligence or not, but in a series of cases brought over the past few years the courts considered a difficult ethical issue: could the birth of a child be considered damage? The cases all involved situations where one of the parents had been sterilised but, unknown to them, the operation had not worked and so an unwanted pregnancy had happened.

Case Summary

In *MacFarlane* v. *Tayside Health Board* (1999), the claimants had four children and had decided they did not want any more, so Mr McFarlane had a vasectomy. When Mrs MacFarlane became pregnant again, they sued for the pain and discomfort of pregnancy and birth, and for the costs of bringing up their fifth child. The House of Lords allowed the claim for pain and discomfort, since this, they said, was no different from any claim for personal injury. However, they would not allow a claim for the costs of bringing up the child, because, they said, the birth of a baby was generally considered to be a blessing, not a burden, and could not therefore be viewed as damage.

Case Summary

A similar claim was brought in *Parkinson* v. *St James and Seacroft University Hospital* (2001), but in this case the claimants' child was born with severe disabilities. The Court of Appeal repeated the argument that the birth of a child was something to be welcomed. They said that having children meant both advantages and disadvantages for parents, with one of the disadvantages being the cost of bringing them up. As it was impossible to calculate the advantages of having children, the fairest approach was to assume that the advantages were sufficient to cancel out the costs, and so the courts should not give compensation for the basic costs of bringing up any child. Where a child was disabled, however, they would bring just as many advantages to their families as any other child, but they would usually cost more to bring up. Therefore the advantages did not cancel out the costs, and so the Court awarded damages designed to represent the extra amount that the child would cost to bring up as a result of his disabilities (but not the basic costs that his parents would have faced even if he was not disabled).

Case Summary

The issue took a slightly different twist in *Rees* v. *Darlington Memorial Hospital* (2002). Here the claimant had a hereditary condition which made her almost blind and, because of this, she did not want to have children. When she became pregnant after a negligently-performed sterilisation, she claimed for the basic costs of bringing up her son (who was not disabled), and for the extra costs that arose from her disability. The House of Lords once again refused to give compensation for the costs of bringing up a healthy child, on the grounds that this would offend most people, especially as the money would have to come from the NHS. However, they said that where a defendant's negligence had resulted in a birth that the mother did not want and had asked them to prevent, a legal wrong had been done that went beyond the pain and suffering involved in pregnancy and birth. Lord Bingham gave examples of the results of this legal wrong, such as the situation of a single mother who might already be struggling to make ends meet and would now have to wait longer before she could go back to work, or a mother who might have been longing to start or resume a much-wanted career and was now prevented from doing so. The Lords held that there should be recognition of this wrong, and awarded £15,000 on top of the damages for pain and suffering, stating that this award should be made in all cases where a child is born as a result of negligence concerning sterilisation.

Summary

- Negligence has three basic elements:
  - a duty of care;
  - breach of that duty;
  - damage caused by the breach.

- A duty of care is a legal concept which dictates which types of situation should give rise to a claim in negligence. When the courts decide whether or not to allow a duty of care in a new situation, they are redrawing the boundaries of the tort of negligence.

- The basic test for a new duty of care comes from *Caparo* v. *Dickman*. It asks:
  - Was the damage reasonably foreseeable?
  - Was there a relationship of proximity between the claimants and the defendants?
  - Is it just, fair and reasonable to impose a duty in this situation?

- Negligence liability is usually imposed for things the defendant has done, not things they fail to do, but there are three situations where liability can be imposed for things the defendant has failed to do:
  - where the defendant has some control over the claimant;
  - where the defendant has assumed responsibility for the claimant;

- where the defendant has done something to make a danger worse.

Negligence usually only imposes liability on the person who has caused damage, but there are five circumstances where a defendant can be liable for damage caused by someone else:

- where there is proximity between the defendant and the claimant;
- where there is proximity between the defendant and the third party who causes the damage;
- where the defendant has negligently created a source of danger;
- where the defendant knew or had reason to know that a third party was creating a risk on the defendant's property;
- where there is vicarious liability.

A defendant will be in breach of their duty of care if their behaviour falls below the standard to be expected of a reasonable person doing what they are doing. The test is objective, and requires the defendant to take reasonable precautions, not to eliminate every possible risk. In deciding on the standard to be expected, the courts weigh up several factors:

- characteristics of the defendant;
- characteristics of the claimant;
- the likelihood of harm;
- the seriousness of the harm;
- how far it was practical to protect against the risk;
- common practice in the relevant field;
- any benefits to society from the risky activity or situation;
- use of special skills.

These areas are balanced against each other; there is no set order of priority.

The burden of proof is reversed where the defendant has been convicted of a criminal offence arising from the same facts; or res ipsa loquitur applies.

There are three types of damage which can be compensated in negligence:

- personal injury;
- damage to property;
- economic loss.

Other types of loss cannot be compensated.

Question and answer*

Problem: Josie is a young chef and has just opened her own café. One day, she puts chicken curry and rice on the menu, but makes a mistake and cooks twice as much rice as she needs. She decides to save some for the following day. Most chefs would know that cooked rice which is not refrigerated quickly can cause food poisoning and Josie vaguely remembers being told something about this during her training, but she decides that as it is a cold day there should be no problem with leaving the rice out of the fridge. She leaves the rice out in the kitchen overnight and the next day Tom, a customer, orders some and later suffers food poisoning.

Because her business is only just getting going, Josie also does cat-sitting to make some extra money and is currently looking after two cats for Cherie, who is away on holiday. On the day that she hears about Tom having food poisoning, she is so upset and worried that she forgets to lock the front door when she leaves Cherie's house. While Josie is at the café that day, burglars break into Cherie's house. They are furious when they discover that she has no flat screen TV, no stereo and nothing else that they consider worth stealing, so they smash her collection of antique china.

Advise Tom and Cherie on any claims they may have against Josie.

You should allow yourself no more than 40 minutes to complete this task.

Essay: One of the main reasons why the law of negligence exists is to encourage people and organisations to take care in what they do, and avoid carelessness that might cause damage or loss to others. How well do the rules about how the standard of care is defined meet this aim?

This question should be answered in 40 minutes.

* Answer guidance is provided at the end of the chapter.

Further reading

Brazier, M. and Miola, J. (2000) 'Bye-bye *Bolam*: a medical litigation revolution?', 8 Med LR 85.
A very clear and interesting article looking at how the *Bolam* test is used in practice and arguing that the policy of letting professionals set their own standard has crept into other areas of medical law, such as consent to treatment. The authors argue that the decision in *Bolitho* v. *City and Hackney Health Authority* can and should make a difference. If you're interested in medical law this is a good read.

Conaghan, J. and Mansell, W. (1993) *The Wrongs of Tort*, Ch. 2, London: Pluto Press.
This very interesting book looks at tort law from a critical perspective, which means that it challenges many of the assumptions that are contained within the rules of tort. This chapter examines duties of care, and how they really work.

McBride, N. (2004) 'Duties of care – do they really exist?', 24 OJLS 417.
This thought-provoking article looks at the issue of whether a duty of care means you have a duty to be careful, or a duty to pay compensation if someone suffers as a result of you not being careful.

Teff, H. (1998) 'The standard of care in medical negligence – moving on from *Bolam*?', 18 OJLS 473.
This is another article looking at the impact of *Bolitho*, with reference to concerns about the use of expert witnesses in negligence cases. It gives lots of good background information on how medical negligence cases work in practice.

Witting, C. (2005) 'Duty of care – an analytical approach', 25(1) OJLS 33.
This article looks at the *Caparo* test, and argues that although they may appear to overlap the three elements of the test all have a distinct job to do. The second part of the article is about **negligent misstatement**, which is covered in Chapter 5, so you may want to read that part later.

Question and answer guidance

Problem: When dealing with problem questions, it is always best to take a systematic approach, taking each possible claim in turn and working through the elements of the tort that are relevant to them. So, taking Tom first, you need to look at the three elements of negligence: duty of care, breach of duty, and damage. Starting with duty of care, you can apply the *Caparo* test: was the injury foreseeable, was there proximity, and is it just and reasonable to impose a duty? Use the cases on these issues to help make your argument. Then move on to the issue of whether Josie has breached her duty. She is someone who is acting in a professional capacity, so use the rules that apply to defendants using special skills. The fact that most cooks would know that unrefrigerated rice carries a risk of food poisoning is relevant here, and you should explain that the standard is an objective one, so the fact that Josie thought it would be OK to leave the rice out does not help. Finally, deal briefly with damage; food poisoning is a form of personal injury and we know that negligence compensates this kind of damage.

Turning to Cherie, the main issue here is whether Josie can have a duty to take steps to prevent harm done by a third party (the burglar). You will remember that in most cases there is no liability for harm done by someone else, but there are exceptions to this rule and one of them is where there is proximity between the parties. The case of *Stansbie* v. *Troman* is relevant here because, like the defendant in that case, Josie has a contractual relationship with Cherie because she is being paid to look after the cats. Then look at whether Josie has breached her duty, pointing out which factors the courts are likely to weigh up – an important one will be practicality, since it would have been very easy for Josie to lock the door. Finally, there is clearly damage in the form of Cherie's smashed china, and again, we know that damage to property is compensated in negligence.

Essay: The first thing to note with this question is that you are being asked to talk about the rules concerning the standard of care, so you need to stick to that area of law. You will probably have a lot of material on duties of care that relates to the issue of whether the law encourages people to take care, but that is not relevant here.

A good way to start would be to outline the basis of the rules on breach of duty: the standard of reasonableness; the objective approach; and the factors which the courts will weigh up in order to assess reasonableness. You can then go on to discuss specific areas in more detail, picking out those which raise issues about how well the rules work to discourage dangerous behaviour. Regarding the objective standard, you might point to the fact that it can be vague, and in some cases unachievable. The cases of *Nettleship* v. *Weston*, *Mansfield* v. *Weetabix* and *Roberts* v. *Ramsbottom* are all useful ones to discuss here. Given the impact of insurance in these cases, is the standard more about shifting the loss than discouraging dangerous behaviour?

Another useful area to discuss is that of defendants using special skills, and the criticism that the *Bolam* test allows professionals to set their own standards: how far can that be said to discourage negligent behaviour? The material in the articles by Brazier and Miola and Teff may be useful here. You could also look at the fact that the standard of reasonableness can only go so far to discourage dangerous behaviour, because it only requires defendants to take reasonable steps and not to eliminate all risks; the cases of *Latimer* v. *AEC* and *Bolton* v. *Stone* are relevant here. You might want to consider briefly whether strict liability might be a better way to discourage dangerous activities, and you will find useful material for this at page 12.

Visit **www.mylawchamber.co.uk/quinntort** to access tools to help you develop and test your knowledge of tort law, including practice exam questions with guidance, annotated weblinks, glossary and key case flashcards, legal newsfeed and legal updates and interactive 'You be the judge' questions.

Use Case Navigator to read in full some of the key cases referenced in this chapter with commentary and questions:

Caparo Industries plc* v. *Dickman and others [1990] 1 All ER 568
Chester* v. *Afshar [2004] 4 All ER 587
Hunter* v. *Canary Wharf Ltd [1997] 2 All ER 426
Mitchell* v. *Glasgow City Council [2009] 3 All ER 205
Sutradhar* v. *Natural Environment Council [2006] 4 All ER 490

Chapter 3
Negligence: causation, defences and time limits

Key points In this chapter, we will be looking at:

- The rules covering how a claimant must prove that the defendant caused their injury, damage or loss
- Defences to negligence
- Time limits within which negligence actions must be brought

Introduction

To illustrate what this chapter is about, let's take two similar imaginary cases. In the first, Johnny is walking along the street when a car comes round the corner. The driver, Susie, is sending a text message on her phone, is not looking at the road ahead and is going too fast. She loses control of the car and swerves onto the pavement, running Johnny over. He suffers a broken leg. From what you have learned so far, you can see that Susie is clearly liable in negligence for Johnny's injury. As a motorist, she had a duty of care to other road users. She was in breach of that duty because her driving was obviously below the standard of a reasonable driver, and it is obvious that her breach of duty caused damage to Johnny.

Now take a situation that is slightly different. Susie comes round the corner as before, going too fast and not watching the road because she is sending a text message. But this time Johnny walks out into the road without looking to see if any traffic is coming, and Susie hits him in the middle of the road, breaking his leg. Is it still clear that Susie is liable? An ambulance is called for Johnny, but on the way to hospital it crashes and he breaks his ribs in the accident. Is Susie liable for that injury as well as the broken leg? Johnny gets to the hospital and is treated for his injuries, but he falls out of bed and hits his head, suffering a brain injury. Is Susie liable for that? Finally, a doctor accidentally gives him the wrong drugs, which kill him. Is Susie liable for his death?

As you can see, it is not always enough to know that there is a duty, breach and damage. The courts often have to look at whether the defendant's negligence actually caused the damage: here, Johnny would not have broken his ribs, hit his head or died from the drugs if Susie had not run him over, but does that mean she caused those things? Courts also have to consider whether the **defendant** might have a **defendce**, which is a reason why they should not be held liable for damage they have caused, or should only be partly liable. In our example, the fact that Johnny walked into the road may mean a court will find that he is partly responsible for what happened, which would give Susie the defence of **contributory negligence**, and mean that the **damages** she pays would be lower than if Johnny had not been partly to blame.

In this chapter then, we will look at the rules that decide whether a defendant can be said to have caused an accident or the resulting injury, where that is not obvious from the facts. These are known as the rules on **causation** and **remoteness of damage**. We will then consider what defences are available in negligence, and how they work. Finally, we will look at a third issue, which is the time limits within which negligence cases have to be brought.

The rules on causation and remoteness also apply to other torts where the claimant has to prove damage. They are discussed here because is it useful to get a complete overview of how one tort works before you move on to the others (and because most of the cases have arisen in negligence), but remember when you go on to look at the other torts that these rules apply there too.

Causation

As you know, there will only be a claim in negligence if the defendant's breach of duty caused the **claimant** damage. This means that the claimant not only has to prove that there was damage, but that something the defendant did or did not do caused that damage. As we saw in the example of Susie and Johnny above, this is not always as simple as it might seem at first. To deal with these problems the courts have developed two sets of tests, which answer two different questions:

- Tests for factual causation: these look at whether the defendant's negligence was a factual cause of the damage. The essential question here is whether the damage would have happened if the negligence had not happened.
- Tests for remoteness of damage: these are used where the defendant's negligence is a factual cause of the damage, but the law states that the negligence and the damage are too distantly related for the defendant to be liable to pay compensation. For example, in our imaginary case of Susie and Johnny, Susie's negligence could be said to be a factual cause of Johnny's death from the wrong drugs, because he would never have been in the hospital if she had not been driving negligently. However, the law would almost certainly find that his death was too remote from Susie's negligence for her to be liable for it (we will look at why later in this chapter). Tests for remoteness are therefore legal tests, rather than factual ones.

Causation: the 'but for' test

The basic test for causation is known as the '**but for**' **test** and, as the name suggests, it simply asks whether the damage would have happened but for the breach of duty. A good example of the way the test works is *Barnett* v. *Chelsea and Kensington Hospital* (1968). The claimant's husband arrived at the hospital in the early hours of the morning, after doing a night shift, and said he had been feeling sick since drinking a cup of tea at work. The nurse on duty called a doctor, who refused to examine the man and advised him to go home and consult his GP if he still felt unwell later. Five hours later the man died of arsenic poisoning. His wife sued on his behalf, and the Court accepted that the hospital had been negligent. However, there was evidence that even if he had been examined at the hospital, by that stage the poison had already taken effect, so it was too

Case Summary

late for any treatment to save his life. Therefore it could not be said that but for their negligence he would not have died, and the hospital was not liable.

Case Summary

A similar result was reached in *McWilliams* v. *Sir William Arrol* (1962), where a man was killed in a fall at work. It was claimed that the defendant, his employer, was negligent in not providing him with a safety harness, but there was clear evidence that if a harness had been provided he would not have worn it anyway. It could not therefore be proved that but for the defendant's negligence he would not have fallen, and so the defendant was not liable.

We looked earlier at the case of *Bolitho*, where the little boy died after having breathing difficulties. You may remember that the doctor in the case did not come to examine him and so did not insert a breathing tube which, it was argued, could have saved his life. When the Court addressed the question of whether she was negligent in not coming to see him, she argued that even if she had she would not have inserted a tube, so it could not be argued that but for her failure to turn up he would not have died. The House of Lords refused to accept this argument. They said that causation could clearly be proved if she *would* have inserted the tube if she had seen the patient. But it could also be proved if she *should* have inserted a tube if she had seen the patient, because it would have been negligent not to do so.

You be the judge

Q: Stacey is out riding her horse when she falls and hurts her arm. She is taken to hospital, and is told that she has just sprained it and to go home and take some paracetamol. When the pain is still getting worse the next day she goes back, and this time the doctor realises she has broken her arm. As a result of the break, she is left with permanent damage to her arm. Medical evidence shows that this was an inevitable result of the kind of fracture that she suffered, and that no treatment could have prevented it. Does she have a claim against the hospital for the permanent damage to her arm?

A: No. The hospital's misdiagnosis may have been negligent, but the permanent damage would have been caused anyway, even if she was diagnosed on her first visit, so the hospital has not caused it and is not liable.

Writing and drafting

You are a solicitor, and a potential client came to see you after her husband died of a lung condition. The illness was misdiagnosed on his first visit to the local hospital and only correctly recognised two weeks later. The medical evidence suggests that the illness was one which a competent doctor should have spotted, but it also shows that the illness was incurable even before the first visit to the hospital, so an earlier diagnosis would not have prevented his death; in other words, the 'but for' test means that the hospital is not liable. Your client is very angry with the hospital and believes they should be made to pay for the fact that they misdiagnosed her husband. You have explained that she could not possibly win a case against them, but she was upset and angry and you don't think she took in everything you said. You want to make sure she understands the position. Write her a letter, explaining the legal principle that prevents her case from succeeding.

Handy tip: Make sure you know how to set out a business letter, and how to start and finish it correctly (if you haven't done this before, you'll find a useful guide at **http://www.excellencegateway.org.uk/media/KSSP/c11_businessletter_child.pdf**). Use complete sentences – do not write in note form – but keep your language clear and simple. Remember that your client is not a lawyer and wants an explanation she can understand.

Reflective practice

How easy or difficult did you find this task? Being able to explain legal concepts in plain, simple language that anyone can understand is a very useful skill for a lawyer, and while you are studying, it is also a good way of checking that you have understood the concept yourself.

Other tests for causation

There are a number of situations in which the 'but for' test does not work particularly well, and in these cases the courts will sometimes (though not always) modify the test. The problem areas can be classified as:

- damage with more than one possible cause;
- damage caused by a chain of events;
- loss of a chance.

More than one cause

In some cases damage or injury will have more than one cause, and in these cases the 'but for' test does not work well. Let's say, for example, that there is an imaginary illness called X Fever. People can get it from being exposed to a substance called Xon gas, but it is also possible for the illness to happen without exposure to the gas in people who have a certain genetic weakness. Nick gets X Fever, and it turns out that his employer has negligently exposed him to Xon gas at his workplace. But Nick also has the genetic weakness that can cause X Fever to happen without exposure to the gas, and doctors are unable to say whether he got the disease because of his genetic weakness, or because he was exposed to the gas. In this situation, it is not possible to say that but for the negligent exposure to the gas he would not have got X Fever. But equally, his employer has negligently exposed him to a dangerous substance, and that negligence may have caused his illness. Should the employer bear any liability?

In cases like this, the courts have modified the 'but for' test, and tried to find tests for causation that will operate more fairly where there is more than one possible cause of damage. But because it can be very difficult in this type of case to find a solution which is fair to both sides, the courts have actually taken two different approaches, and have themselves had trouble explaining the difference between them and how to tell which will be applied in any particular case in the future.

Case Summary ↓

The first approach was developed in *McGhee* v. *National Coal Board* (1972). The claimant worked for the defendants, and in his job he came into contact with brick dust, which caked his skin and caused a skin condition called dermatitis. Exposing workers to the dust was not in itself negligent, because it was an unavoidable part of the work they did, so the defendants could not have avoided it by taking reasonable steps. However, the claimant argued that they were negligent in not providing showers where workers could wash off the dust at the end of the day. This would have shortened the time the dust was on his skin and, he claimed, reduced the risk of getting dermatitis. Since he might have got the dermatitis anyway, from being in contact with the dust during working hours, it was not possible to show that it would not have happened but for the defendant's negligence. There were two possible causes, one 'innocent' (being exposed to the brick dust in the first place), and one 'guilty' (not being given the showers and so prolonging exposure to the dust).

The House of Lords said that in cases where there was more than one possible cause, the 'but for' test could be modified and causation could be proved if the defendant's negligence materially increased the risk of the injury occurring. It was not necessary to show that the negligence was the only possible cause. The lack of showers had materially increased the risk of dermatitis and so the defendants were liable.

Case Summary

The 'material increase' approach was used by the Court of Appeal in the more recent case of *Bailey* v. *Ministry of Defence* (2008). The claimant, Miss Bailey, suffered brain damage while she was in a hospital run by the defendants. The defendants admitted that they had been negligent at an earlier stage of her care, but the brain damage was caused after this when Miss Bailey suffered a heart attack due to inhaling her own vomit. This was something which could have happened without any negligence, and the defendants argued that their breach of duty did not cause it to happen. But Miss Bailey's lawyers claimed that it had happened because she was in a weakened state, and that weakened state had been caused by the defendants' earlier negligence. The Court of Appeal found in favour of Miss Bailey, on the basis that but for their negligence she would not have been in a weakened state and so their negligence made a material contribution to what happened.

Case Summary

Although, as *Bailey* shows, the *McGhee* approach continues to be good law, the courts also use a different test, often in cases which would appear to be very similar to *McGhee*, and this test can lead to a quite different result. This test was explained in *Wilsher* v. *Essex Health Authority* (1988). The claimant, Martin Wilsher, had been born three months too early. He was put on an oxygen supply, and as a result of a doctor's admitted negligence was given too much oxygen. He was found to have a condition called retrolental fibroplasia, which eventually made him go blind, and it was admitted in court that this condition could be caused by an overdose of oxygen. However, there was medical evidence that retrolental fibroplasia could also be the result of as many as five different, non-negligent causes. The trial judge found for Martin, but the case was appealed all the way to the House of Lords. They said that the claimant had to prove, on a balance of probabilities, that the defendant's negligence was a material cause of the blindness. 'On a **balance of probabilities**' means that there is more than a 50 per cent chance, or in other words that it was more likely than not, that the negligence was a material cause of the blindness. It was not enough to prove that the defendant's negligence had increased the risk of blindness occurring. The House of Lords held that the case should be retried.

In fact, as you can read in the Law in Action box, the *Wilsher* case itself never went to a retrial, but the importance of the House of Lords decision in it is that it established another test for causation in cases where there are multiple causes: on a balance of probabilities, was the defendant's negligence a material cause of the damage?

Law in action The *Wilsher* case

Reading the official reports of the cases which make legal history sometimes tells you only half the story. In Martin Wilsher's case, it is often assumed that he lost his claim after the House of Lords case. In fact, the dispute still had some years left to run. The House of Lords ordered that the case should be retried, using the test for causation that they had outlined. They were not saying that he could not prove his case, only that the wrong test had been used in the original trial, so Martin's win there could not stand and the case needed to be looked at again using a different test of causation. However, this must have come as a huge blow for Martin's parents. By the time the case came to the House of Lords, Martin was 9, so their legal battle had already been going on for some years, and after the House of Lords decision they were back to square one.

Negotiations between the parties began again, and eventually the Health Authority agreed to settle the case, so a retrial never occurred and we will never know what the result would have been. The Health Authority paid Martin the sum in damages that had been awarded in the original trial, but without interest, which by that time should have doubled the amount. The loss of interest meant that in practice the settlement worked out to be considerably less than Martin was originally awarded, because

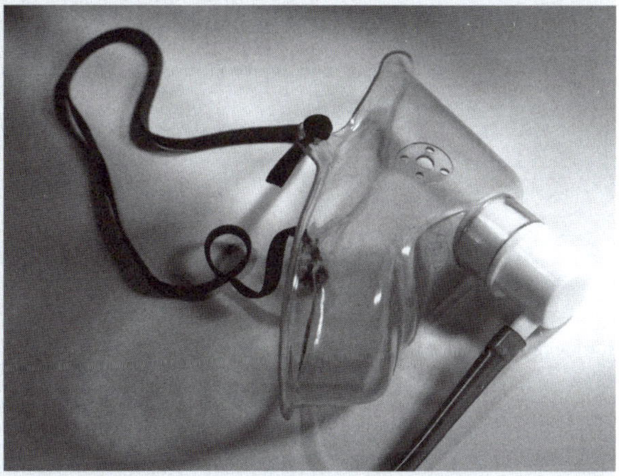

Source: Pearson Education Ltd/Jupiter Images/Brand X/Alamy

lump sums are usually invested so that they offer an income and Martin had already missed out on several years of investment.

Ironically, in later years medical research into conditions like Martin's progressed, and it became known that an overdose of oxygen was the only likely cause of the condition which caused Martin's blindness. If this had been known at the time of his original trial, he would almost certainly have won his case.

[*References*: 'Brushes with *Bolam*' by James Badenoch (2004) 72 *Medico-Legal Journal* 127; http://www.ncbi.nlm.nih.gov/pmc/articles/PMC2545124/pdf/bmj00277-0053.pdf]

Multiple causes: which test?

McGhee and *Wilsher* left the courts with two quite different tests for cases involving multiple causes of injury and damage and, clearly, the choice of test can have a big impact on the chances of a claimant winning their case. Unfortunately, there is still no certain way to predict which approach a court will take in a particular case, so when you are faced with a problem question raising this kind of issue, it is usually safest to explain that there are two possible ways in which a court might approach causation, and then to apply both tests in turn.

There is one area of causation where the House of Lords have set down special rules on causation. This is in cases where claimants have suffered a disease called mesothelioma, a type of cancer which is almost always caused by exposure to asbestos and which is always fatal.

The mesothelioma cases

The issue of causation in mesothelioma cases was first addressed by the House of Lords in ***Fairchild* v. *Glenhaven Funeral Services*** (2002), a case where the claimants all had mesothelioma. It is not clear quite how exposure to asbestos causes mesothelioma, but it is

Case Summary

Case Navigator

thought possible that it could be caused by as little as one fibre penetrating a cell in the lining of the lungs and causing a tumour. The important thing about this for the issue of causation is that it means that once the 'guilty fibre' has penetrated the lung the disease will happen, but any later exposure to asbestos will not make it worse. This suggests that under the 'but for' test only the employer that the defendant was working for at the time when the fibre entered their lung should be liable. As it can take anything from 10 to more than 30 years for the symptoms to show and, over the years, the defendants in *Fairchild* had worked for many different employers who had exposed them to asbestos, you can see that it would have been quite impossible for them to prove causation using the 'but for' test. Yet all the defendants, their employers, had negligently exposed them to a substance which was known to put them at risk of dying early and painfully. Could it be fair that they should escape liability?

Recognising this, the House of Lords held that, as in *McGhee*, the 'but for' test could be modified, and the claimants could prove causation against any defendant if they could prove that that defendant negligently exposed them to asbestos, and therefore materially increased their risk of suffering the illness. Applying that approach, the claimants could prove causation and the defendants were held liable.

The *Fairchild* decision was very unpopular with insurance companies, who would be paying the damages in mesothelioma cases. They attempted to fight back, and minimise their liabilities, in *Barker* v. *Corus* (2006), which again involved a group of mesothelioma victims. They had all worked for different employers over their careers, and many of those employers, and their insurers, had gone out of business by the time the case was brought (this is a common problem with asbestos **litigation**; see Law in Action, page 75). The claimants therefore sought to sue those who were still in business, on the grounds that, following *Fairchild*, it was enough to prove that each of those employers had negligently exposed them to asbestos. The defendant employers appealed the case all the way to the House of Lords, arguing that where an employee was exposed to asbestos by more than one employer, each employer's liability should be calculated according to the length of time the employee spent with them. The House of Lords accepted this argument, and said that each employer should pay damages in proportion to the amount of exposure they caused.

Case Summary

This verdict was potentially devastating for mesothelioma claimants, because it meant that unless they could find every employer they had worked for, and all those employers and their insurers were still in business, they could not hope to claim the full amount of damages that was appropriate to their illness. For example, where a claimant had worked for a roughly equal amount of time for three different employers and two of those employers were now out of business (which in practice is quite likely), the claimant would get only one-third of the damages that would normally be awarded for such a serious illness. It also meant that cases would take longer because of the need to trace as many employers as possible, which was particularly important as by the time a claimant realises they might have a case they usually do not have very long to live.

The decision was, not surprisingly, welcomed by the insurance industry, which was set to save millions of pounds as a result, but was widely criticised by the media, victims' groups and personal injury lawyers. The government agreed that it was unfair, and in response took the unusual step of inserting a clause into the Compensation Bill, which was going through Parliament at the time, which reverses the decision in *Corus*. Section 3 of the Compensation Act 2006 now provides that when a person (or company) is responsible for negligently exposing another to asbestos, and that person gets mesothelioma as a result of exposure to asbestos, the party responsible for the negligent exposure can be fully liable, even if it cannot be proved that it was that episode of exposure and not another that caused the illness. Where several parties have all negligently exposed the claimant to asbestos, the one who is sued can claim a contribution towards the damages from the other(s), but there is no need for the claimant to sue more than one of them.

Case Summary

Case Navigator

In ***Sienkiewicz* v. *Greif (UK) Ltd*** (2011), the claimant had been exposed to asbestos by only one employer. There was evidence that he might have got mesothelioma from this exposure, but it was also possible that he got it from low-level exposure to asbestos in normal daily life. The evidence suggested that the exposure to asbestos at work only increased his risk of getting mesothelioma by 18 per cent. Nevertheless, the Supreme Court said that the rule set in *Fairchild* applied here too, because the employer had materially increased the risk. The Court said that the only situation in which this would not be the case was where the negligent exposure was too insignificant to take into account.

These rules were developed because of the special nature of mesothelioma cases, in that medical science does not yet really understand how the disease develops, making it impossible to decide causation using standard tests. They do not apply in other types of case.

Law in action The asbestos litigation

The mesothelioma litigation results from what has been called an epidemic of illness caused by asbestos, a mineral that for many years was widely used in building materials because it is very resistant to heat and fire. As well as mesothelioma, it causes abestosis, a serious and disabling lung illness, and lung cancer. The Health and Safety Executive estimates that there are now over 3500 deaths a year from asbestos-related disease and, because the illness takes so long to show, these rates are predicted to double over the next 20 years. Currently, five people a day are diagnosed with mesothelioma, and there are thought to be two cases of asbestos-related lung cancer for every case of mesothelioma.

Although it was suspected that asbestos was a risk to health by the 1930s, workers in Britain continued to be widely exposed to it until 1980, and insurers like those who stood to pay the claims in *Fairchild* and *Corus* would have been taking premiums for decades during which the risks of asbestos exposure were known to them, as well as to the employers responsible for the exposure.

The way in which the insurance industry can, in practice, manipulate the tort system can be seen in their behaviour regarding the *Fairchild* litigation. In the Court of Appeal, the defendants (who were funded by the insurers) had won their case. When the claimants decided to appeal to the House of Lords, the insurers offered them a full settlement, which, if the claimants had accepted it, would have meant that the appeal would not be heard, preventing any chance of the Court of Appeal decision being reversed. As a result, the claimants in the case would have been compensated, but thousands of other victims would have been unable to succeed in a claim unless someone else came along and took a case all the way to the House of Lords (which was not very likely to happen, since it is a difficult, time-consuming and expensive process and any potential future claimants would, like the *Fairchild* ones, be very ill with only a short time to live).

The then President of the Association of Personal Injury Lawyers, Frances McCarthy, called the offer to settle 'a cynical and underhanded attempt to prevent the cases being heard'. In the event, the claimants very bravely decided to continue with their fight (which, remember, they could have lost, leaving them with nothing) and, as a result, thousands of very ill people can now get the compensation they deserve.

[*References*: 'Asbestos solicitors rap "cynical" insurers', *Law Gazette*, 29 April 2002; **http://www.thelawyer.com/playing-with-lives/77223.article**]

People in the law

Ann-Marie Christie works for Thompsons, a large firm of personal injury solicitors. She specialises in cases of people negligently exposed to asbestos.

Source: Ann-Marie Christie (*text and photo*)

What made you want to specialise in this area? I was drawn to the asbestos cases because I feel very passionately about their situation. Many of them are dying, through no fault of their own, and they should be compensated. They often come to me straight after getting a diagnosis, but by then they often haven't got long to live, and they want to make sure their families will be taken care of when they die.

How do you get started on a case? I'll start by talking to the claimant, to find out all the facts of the case. They might have worked for 20 or 30 different employers, and the exposure may have been many years ago, so it can take a while to get everything clear. Quite often people are nervous about meeting me, because they might not have talked to a lawyer before, and the case is very important to them. You have to be able to put them at their ease, but still control the interview – often my clients are quite elderly, and they're talking about what they were doing 30 or 40 years ago, so it can be quite difficult to get them to stick to the bits you need to know. But at the same time, you have to let them tell their story.

In these cases there's a fair bit of detective work to do, because you have to track down the employers and their insurers, and possibly people the claimant worked with as witnesses. Many of the employers and insurers will have gone out of business, but as long as you have at least one who's insured, you can then make the claim. Often though, I'll be suing as many as 15 different defendants, which does make things more complicated compared to other personal injury cases, where you only usually have one defendant.

How long does a typical case take? The courts are very strict about timetables these days, especially the High Court, which is where most of my cases would go. In the old days, a case could trundle on for ages, but the majority of mine take around six months now, which is much better for the claimants. With asbestos cases it's the sooner the better, because the claimant has so little time left.

Do most cases settle? Yes, very few of my cases go to a full trial, though you can never predict at what stage a settlement will happen. It can be quite late.

What's at issue in the cases that do go to court? Often the issue of liability is already clear, because it's accepted that the claimant was exposed to asbestos while working for the defendant, so what's in question is how much the damages should be. Each case is different, and the court has to take into account things like the dependants left behind, and whether the claimant is still working, so that can be quite complex.

Cases that go to trial will be presented by a barrister, but I'll still be there, because you have a relationship with the client by then. I never mind handing over the case to the barrister – that's not a part of the job I ever wanted to do. I think the two roles are quite different, but each contribute a lot. And by that stage the client knows that you've already put a lot of work in, so you don't feel that you've done all the work just to hand it over to someone else.

What's the most difficult part of working on these cases? Having to tell someone who's been exposed to asbestos, and who's dying as a result, that I can't help them because there is no one they can sue. Because the disease takes so long to show up, we're mostly talking about exposure that happened 30 or 40 years ago, so it can be that none of the companies they worked for exist any more. That's very, very difficult, and it happens a lot. We're not talking about a cut finger – these are people who are dying. To their mind, someone has caused that and someone should pay, so it's very hard to tell them there is no viable case.

You do get involved with the clients, and it can be very difficult when you've formed a relationship with them and their family, and then one day the wife rings up and tells you that her husband has passed away. But I don't think you could do this job properly if you didn't get involved. And when you do get damages for someone, that's very satisfying. No amount of money can really compensate my clients for what's happened to them, but when you get them compensation, within their lifetime, and they know that their family will be taken care of, they're very grateful.

Chains of events

The 'but for' test also causes problems where injury or damage is caused by a chain of events, rather than just one, or where later events make an injury worse. This was the imaginary situation we looked at earlier, where Susie drove negligently and hit Johnny, breaking his leg, and then the ambulance that took him to hospital crashed, breaking his ribs, he fell out of his hospital bed, getting a head injury, and the doctor gave him the wrong drugs and he died. If we use the 'but for' test alone, Susie could potentially be liable for all these things, since, but for her negligence, Johnny would never have been in the ambulance, nor the hospital. But is it fair to make her liable for all of it?

In cases where two different events cause the same damage, the 'but for' test can still work. This was the case in *Performance Cars* v. *Abraham* (1962), where the claimant's Rolls Royce was involved in two separate collisions (it's not always fun being rich). Both the crashes were caused by the other drivers' negligence, and both damaged the same area of the car. The High Court held that the driver in the second crash was not liable to pay for a respray. At the time of the second accident the car already needed a respray as a result of the first crash, so it could not be said that but for his negligence the car would not have needed the respray.

Case Summary

However, where later events in a chain cause new injuries or damage, the position is more difficult, and so the courts have again modified the 'but for' test. However, as with *McGhee* and *Wilsher*, there are two different approaches and it is not always clear which one will be used.

The first approach was used in *Baker* v. *Willoughby* (1970). The claimant injured his leg in a road accident caused by the defendant's negligence. Some time after the accident, he was shot in the same leg by an armed robber, and ended up having to have his leg amputated. The armed robber was never caught and so could not be sued. Clearly the car driver was not responsible for the fact that the claimant had had his leg amputated, but where did his liability end? Normally, the claimant would have claimed for the effects of the defendant's injury to his leg (such as pain and suffering or inability to work), for as long as those effects lasted. But the defendant claimed that he should only be liable for the effects up until the time of the robbery, because once the robbery happened it was not possible to say that but for his negligence the leg would have been uninjured. The House of Lords rejected this view. They said that compensation was not just for the injury itself, but for the inability to lead a full life which that injury had caused, and that inability continued after the robbery. In addition, even if the robbers

Case Summary

had stayed around to be sued they would only have been liable for the damage to an already injured leg, so the claimant could not have got full compensation using the 'but for' test.

Case Summary

The second approach was taken in the apparently similar case of *Jobling* v. *Associated Dairies* (1982). The claimant was employed by the defendant and, through their negligence, he hurt his back at work in 1973. This meant he could only do work that paid around half the salary he was earning previously. In 1976, he discovered that he had a back disease, which was not related to the injury at work, and by the end of that year the back disease had got so bad that he could not work at all. His employers argued that they should only be liable for the effects of the back injury up to the point where the back disease began. Applying *Baker* v. *Willoughby*, they would have been liable for his 50 per cent reduction in earning capacity for the rest of his life, because that reduction would have continued even if he had not got the back disease. But the House of Lords rejected this approach, and applied the 'but for' test. They pointed out that when a court calculated damages for a tort, they usually took into account what are called 'the vicissitudes of life', or in plain language, the chance that something bad may happen during a claimant's life. So, for example, when calculating a claim for loss of future earnings, the courts do not assume that the claimant would definitely have done the same job for the whole of their life, because that might not happen: they might get ill and only be able to do a less well-paid job, or no job at all, or they might be sacked and never be able to get another job. The courts therefore allow for these possibilities when deciding how much damages a claimant should get. The claimant's illness was just the kind of event that would fit into this category, and the House of Lords argued that if it was normal to allow for bad things that might or might not happen, they could not ignore the fact that one already had. Therefore the defendants were only liable for the effects of the injury up until the back disease began.

In *Jobling*, the House of Lords criticised the decision in *Baker*, but they did not say it was wrong and should not be applied in future cases. So again, there are two possible tests, each leading to quite different results in most cases. This means that in a problem question involving a chain of events, you will usually need to explain that there are two tests, apply both and explain how the results would differ.

Out and about

Read the cases of *Baker* v. *Willoughby* and *Jobling* v. *Associated Dairies*. Now try to write down, in your own words, the court's main arguments for not imposing the test used in *Baker* to the facts of *Jobling*. Do you think they were right?

Handy tip: Some tort cases are easier to read than others and these two are quite tricky to follow – but take your time, make notes as you go, and you should be able to get to grips with them. As a lawyer, you'll need to develop the skill of reading and understanding cases, so the earlier you start the better!

Loss of a chance cases

There is a third type of case where the 'but for' test causes problems, and this is where the claimant alleges that the defendant's negligence caused them to lose a chance. This might be the chance to get money (or more money), for example, or the chance to recover from an injury. An example would be where the claimant has cancer, and their cancer would normally have, say, a 50 per cent chance of being cured if found early, but because their doctor negligently fails to diagnose it early enough, the chances are reduced to 20 per cent by the time it is found. In loss of a chance cases involving personal injury, the courts have to decide whether the delay can be said to have caused the patient not to be cured, or whether they would not, on a balance of probabilities, have been cured anyway (remember that 'on a balance of probabilities' means that something was more likely to have happened than not to have happened). In two key decisions, the House of Lords have decided that damages for loss of a chance are not available for personal injury cases. However, they have allowed loss of a chance claims to succeed in cases where the loss is purely financial.

Loss of a chance: personal injury

Case Summary

The first key case on loss of a chance in personal injury is *Hotson* v. *East Berkshire Health Authority* (1987). The claimant, a young boy, had gone to hospital after falling from a rope he was swinging on. The hospital X-rayed his knee, but found nothing seriously wrong and sent him home. Five days later, he was still in pain, and when he went back to the hospital they discovered that he had in fact injured his hip in the accident. By this time, the hip injury had caused a condition called avascular necrosis, which can happen when the blood supply to an injury is restricted, and which eventually left him with a deformed hip. Avascular necrosis can occur even if an injury is treated properly and quickly, but medical evidence showed that if the injury had been spotted and treated when he first went to the hospital, there was a 25 per cent chance that the injury would have healed and the avascular necrosis would not have happened. The Court of Appeal found the defendants liable but reduced the damages to 25 per cent to reflect the fact that there was only a 25 per cent chance. However, the defendants appealed, and the House of Lords held that the Court of Appeal had taken the wrong approach. They said that the issue here was not how much the damages should be, but whether the defendants' negligence had actually caused the avascular necrosis. The claimant had to prove that, on a balance of probabilities, the defendants' delay in treating the injury had caused the avascular necrosis, or in other words, that there was a 51 per cent chance of not developing the condition if the condition had been treated from the start. The medical evidence only showed that there was a 25 per cent chance, so causation was not proved.

Case Summary

Case Navigator

This approach was challenged in ***Gregg* v. *Scott*** (2005), but without success. The claimant had visited his GP, complaining of a lump under his arm, but the doctor said it was nothing to worry about. Nine months later, the lump was still there, so he consulted another GP who referred him to a specialist. The lump was then diagnosed as cancer, and it was shown to have grown during the time between visiting the first and second GP. The claimant was treated, and the cancer went into remission (this means that the cancer has responded to treatment and symptoms can no longer be seen, but it can be a temporary stage, and does not mean the cancer is cured). There was no way to tell whether he was actually cured, or whether the cancer might come back again.

The claimant sued the first GP, claiming that the delay in finding his cancer had made it less likely that he would be cured. However, it was not possible to prove this. Medical evidence showed that out of every 100 people who developed the same kind of cancer, 17 would be cured if they had early treatment, but not if their treatment was delayed by more than a year; 25 would be cured even if their treatment was delayed by a year; and 58 would not be cured, regardless of when they were treated. The claimant added together the figures for those who would be cured even if treatment was delayed, and those who would only be cured if treatment was given early, and said this meant he had originally had a 42 per cent chance of being cured. By delaying his treatment, the doctor had reduced his chances to 25 per cent, and that he should be able to claim for loss of the original, better chance. The House of Lords rejected the argument, confirming that there was no claim for loss of a chance. The claimant could only succeed if he could prove that it was more likely than not that his cancer could have been cured but for the GP's negligence. The medical evidence showed that there was a 58 per cent chance he would not have been cured anyway, so causation was not proved.

Loss of a chance: economic loss

Case Summary

By contrast, the courts will allow a loss of a chance claim in cases of pure financial loss. In *Allied Maples Group* v. *Simmons* (1995), the claimants were buying a business and some properties. The defendants were advising them on how best to do this, and the contract that was drawn up included a clause that made the claimants liable for certain losses associated with the properties. There should have been another clause which would mean the sellers would repay such losses, but due to the defendant's negligence it was left out, and the claimants ended up having to cover the losses. It was possible that the seller might not have agreed to the repayment clause even if it had been put in. The Court of Appeal held that where the alleged damage depends on the possible actions of a third party (in this case the sellers deciding whether or not to accept the clause if it had been put in), the claimant had to prove that they had lost a substantial chance. It was not enough just to show that something might have happened. If they could prove that they had lost a substantial chance through the defendant's negligence, causation was proved, and the size of the lost chance could simply be taken into account in calculating the damages.

Remoteness of damage

As we saw earlier, the law has a second category of test related to causation, which is called remoteness of damage. Once the claimant has proved that the defendant's negligence is the factual cause of their damage, using the 'but for' test or one of its modifications, they may then have to prove that the damage is not too remote from the defendant's negligence. Like the tests for duty of care, the tests for remoteness are legal tests, which form one of the ways in which the law draws the line between situations in which damage will be compensated for and situations in which it will not. This means that there are some circumstances where a defendant has a duty to the claimant, and has breached that duty and caused damage, but in law they are not held liable for it because the damage is considered to be too remote.

> the tests for remoteness are legal tests

There are two tests for remoteness of damage in tort:

- the **direct consequence test**;
- the **reasonable foreseeability test**.

The test for remoteness in negligence is now reasonable foreseeability, but the direct consequence test still applies in some other torts. For convenience both tests are explained here, and in the chapters on other torts you will find details of which test applies there.

The direct consequence test

Case Summary

The original test for remoteness of damage was laid down in *Re Polemis* (1921), and essentially imposed liability for all direct physical consequences of a defendant's negligence. The claimants were the owners of a large cargo ship, which the defendants had hired. The defendants loaded it with cans of petrol, and during the voyage some of them leaked, filling the hold with petrol vapour. The ship docked at Casablanca, where it was unloaded by employees of the claimants. They positioned some heavy planks as a platform over the hold, and due to their negligence one of the planks fell into the hold. It caused a spark, which set the petrol vapour on fire, and the ship was completely burnt. The claimants sued for the value of the ship, which was around £200,000. The trial judge found that the defendants could reasonably have foreseen that some damage to the ship might be caused by the falling plank, but there was no way they could reasonably have foreseen that it would cause a fire and destroy the ship completely. The Court of Appeal said this was irrelevant. They held that a defendant was liable for any damage which was a direct result of their breach of duty, even if it might be a different type of damage or much more serious than any damage they could reasonably have foreseen. Damage would only be considered too remote if it was 'due to the operation of independent causes having no connection with the negligent act, except that [the defendant] could not avoid its results'.

The reasonable foreseeability test

As time went on, and the tort of negligence grew, the direct consequence test came to be seen as unfair to defendants and it was replaced by the reasonable foreseeability test. This was laid down in *Overseas Tankship (UK)* v. *Morts Dock & Engineering Co. (The Wagon Mound)* (1961), which is more often referred to as *Wagon Mound No. 1* (a second case, *Wagon Mound No. 2*, arose from the same incident, but raised different issues; it is discussed later). The incident that gave rise to the litigation was an accident that happened in Sydney Harbour, Australia. The defendants in *Wagon Mound No. 1* were the owners of a ship which was loading oil there, and owing to the negligence of their employees some of it leaked into the sea and spread, forming a thin film on the surface of the water. Within hours, it had spread to a neighbouring wharf, owned by the claimants, where another ship was being repaired by welders. The oil initially just caused some relatively minor damage to the slipway, but a few days later much more serious damage was caused when sparks from the welding operations set the oil on fire. The evidence showed that the damage to the slipway was reasonably foreseeable, but that the fire was not reasonably foreseeable, because the oil had to be raised to a very high temperature before it would catch fire from a spark and there was no reason to believe this would happen. Under the *Re Polemis* direct consequence test, the defendants would still have been liable for both types of damage, because both were a direct result of their negligence. However, the **Privy Council** took a different view, and stated the direct consequence test should no longer be the test of remoteness in negligence. They introduced the reasonable foreseeability test instead, which states that a defendant will only be liable for damage that was reasonably foreseeable at the time of the breach of duty. Using this test, the defendants were only liable for the damage to the slipway, and not for the fire damage. This is now the standard test for remoteness of damage in negligence.

Case Summary

Defining the type of damage

In *Wagon Mound No. 1*, it was very clear that there were two different types of damage, one of which was much more likely to happen than the other, and so it was quite straightforward to say that one was reasonably foreseeable and the other was not. However, things are not always quite so clear-cut, as the two contrasting cases of *Hughes* v. *Lord Advocate* (1963) and *Doughty* v. *Turner* (1964) show.

Case Summary

In *Hughes* v. *Lord Advocate*, the defendant's employees had opened a manhole in the street. They left it open when they finished work for the day, fixing a canvas shelter over the top and arranging paraffin lamps around it so it could be seen. The claimant, an 8-year-old boy, picked up one of the lamps and took it into the shelter, and while he was playing there he knocked the lamp over, causing an explosion in which he was badly burnt. The defendants argued that although they could have foreseen a risk that someone might be burnt by one of the lamps, they could not reasonably have foreseen an explosion, and so the damage was too remote. The House of Lords rejected this view: it was foreseeable that someone might be burnt, and that was what had happened. It did not matter that the burns were caused in an unforeseeable way.

Case Summary

This all seems very straightforward, which is what makes the decision in *Doughty* v. *Turner* rather surprising. In *Doughty*, the claimant was employed by the defendants, and was injured at work when an asbestos cover was knocked into a vat of hot liquid. A chemical reaction between the asbestos and the liquid made the liquid bubble up and erupt over the edge of the vat, burning him. The chemical reaction was not foreseeable, but the claimant argued that it was foreseeable that if the lid was knocked into the vat, liquid could splash out and burn him, so the foreseeable damage would have been precisely the same damage as actually happened. The Court disagreed, stating that an eruption was different from a splash and so the damage was not foreseeable.

Case Summary

Although *Doughty* has never been overruled, it does appear that the courts today favour the less strict approach as seen in *Hughes*. One of the most recent House of Lords cases on the subject is *Jolley* v. *Sutton London Borough Council* (1998), a case involving a claim under the Occupiers' Liability Act 1957 (which is discussed in Chapter 9). The claimant, a 14-year-old boy, came across an old boat that had been abandoned on the council estate where he lived. He and a friend decided to try to repair it, and propped it up with a car jack. The jack collapsed and the boat fell on the claimant, injuring him so badly that he was left paralysed. The council admitted that they should have removed the boat, because it was reasonably foreseeable that children might play on it and possibly fall through the rotten floor. However, they claimed that what the claimant and his friend had done was not a foreseeable use of the boat, and so the accident itself was not foreseeable either.

The House of Lords disagreed. They said it was foreseeable that children would muck around with the boat, and might be injured as a result, and that was enough to make the claimant's injury foreseeable. It did not matter that the council could not foresee exactly how that injury might happen. Their Lordships made the point that children quite often find surprising ways to put themselves in danger, and that the council should have taken this into account when deciding what precautions needed to be taken regarding the boats. They also commented that the council had admitted the risk of children playing on the boat was foreseeable, and that they should have removed the boat to avoid this risk. They could have avoided the risk of what actually happened in exactly the same way, so it would not have involved any more effort or expense.

Predicting the extent of the damage

As long as the type of damage is foreseeable, it does not matter if it turns out to be more serious than could reasonably have been foreseen. This is known, rather gruesomely, as the '**eggshell skull rule**' (the name comes from the idea that if you negligently cause someone a head injury that would normally just cause a headache, but they have a very thin skull and their skull fractures, you are liable for the fracture, even though you did not know you would cause such serious damage).

The way the rule works can be seen in *Smith* v. *Leech Brain* (1962). The claimant worked for the defendants, and was burnt on the lip at work as a result of the defendants' negligence. Unknown to them, he had a pre-cancerous condition, which meant that the cells in his lip could become cancerous as a result of injury, and this is what happened. When he died, his widow sued and the court held the defendants liable for the cancer.

Case Summary

In *Lagden* v. *O'Connor* (2003), the House of Lords confirmed that a version of the eggshell skull rule could also apply in cases of **economic loss**. The claimant was involved in a car accident, caused by the defendant's negligence, and needed a replacement car while his own was being repaired. Normally, there would be no problem with making a defendant liable for the cost of hiring a replacement car, but the complication here was that the claimant was unemployed and had very little money, so he could not afford to hire a car. The only way he could afford to get a replacement car was through what is called credit hire, which meant he did not have to pay anything and the hire company would instead get their money from the defendant's insurers. This, however, was more expensive than normal car hire, and the defendant claimed that they should not be liable for the extra cost, only the amount it would have cost to hire a car in the normal way. The House of Lords disagreed. They said that defendants had to take claimants as they found them, and that included their financial situation. If a claimant was hard up and as a result of that the defendant's negligence caused them extra costs, the defendant was liable for those costs, as long as they were reasonable. An extra cost would be considered reasonable if the claimant could not have avoided it without making unreasonable sacrifices.

Case Summary

You be the judge

Q: Terry has a back problem which causes him a lot of pain. He has been warned that he should avoid certain activities involving sudden movements, as these could cause permanent damage to his back. One day he is driving along in his car when he is hit from behind by Janet, who was sending a text and not looking where she was going. Although she is driving slowly, the jolt causes the permanent damage to Terry's back that he had been warned about. Medical evidence shows that if Terry had not had the back condition beforehand, he would not have been seriously injured in the accident. Is Janet liable?

A: Yes. The 'eggshell skull rule' applies here. It was clearly foreseeable that Terry could have sustained some injury in the accident, so Janet is liable even if it was not foreseeable that it would be so serious.

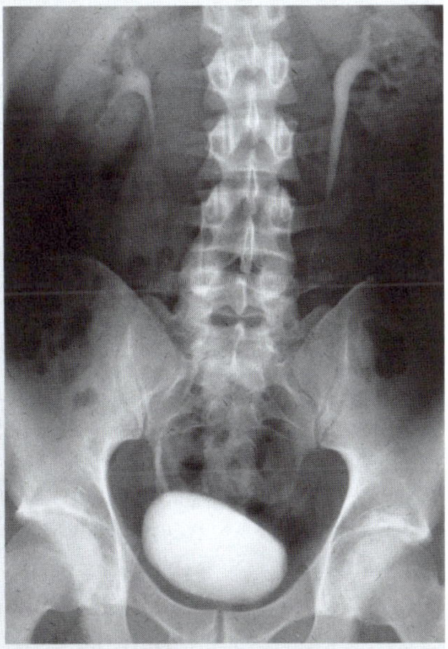

Source: Pearson Education Ltd/Jupiter Images/Brand X/Alamy

How likely does the damage have to be?

Case Summary

As long as the type of damage that happens is reasonably foreseeable, it will not be too remote, even if the chances of it happening were low. This rule was established in *Overseas Tankship* (UK) v. *Miller Steamship Co. (The Wagon Mound No. 2)* (1967), which, as explained earlier, arose out of the oil spill incident in Sydney Harbour that gave rise to *Wagon Mound No. 1*. In this case, the defendants were again the owners of the ship that spilt the oil, but the claimants were the owners of some other ships which were also damaged in the fire. The trial judge had found that although there was a foreseeable possibility of the oil catching fire, it was so unlikely to happen that it was reasonable for the defendants not to have taken precautions against it. The Privy Council reversed the decision. They said it did not matter that the damage was very unlikely to happen, if the type of damage was reasonably foreseeable, the defendants should have taken reasonable precautions against it. At this stage you may be wondering why the court found that the fire was not foreseeable in *Wagon Mound No. 1*, but was foreseeable in *Wagon Mound No. 2*; the answer is simply that the cases were heard six years apart, and the trial judges drew different conclusions from the expert evidence.

Intervening events

In some cases, the defendant may breach their duty, but damage is actually caused by something that happens after the breach. This is known as an **intervening act** or event (or sometimes by the Latin phrase for the same thing, ***novus actus interveniens***). As an example, let's say that you are in a public toilet and you find that the door will not open. You shout for help, but there is no one around, so eventually you decide to climb out over the door, but you fall and hurt yourself. The local council owns the toilets and was negligent about maintaining the locks, which is why you got locked in. But your injury was caused by you climbing over the door. Are they liable for your injuries?

In situations like this, the question the courts ask is whether the intervening event has broken the chain of causation. If it has, the defendant will only be liable for any damage that happened before the intervening event. But if the intervening event is judged not to have broken the chain of causation, the defendant will be liable for all the damage. The way the courts will decide this question varies slightly according to the cause of the second event, and the cases fall broadly into three groups:

- things done by the claimant;
- natural events;
- things done by a third party.

Things done by the claimant

If the claimant does something which causes them injury or damage, the courts will consider whether what they did was reasonable in all the circumstances. If it was reasonable, the chain of causation is not broken and the defendant is liable for all the damage. But if the claimant acts unreasonably, the chain of causation is broken and the defendant is only liable for any damage that happened before the claimant acted. Essentially this is just an aspect of the reasonable foreseeability test, since it should be possible to foresee what a reasonable person would do.

Two contrasting cases, *Wieland* v. *Cyril Lord Carpets* (1969) and *McKew* v. *Holland* (1969), illustrate this principle. In *Wieland* v. *Cyril Lord Carpets*, the claimant had been injured as a result of the defendant's negligence. Because of her injuries, she could not wear her glasses and, as a result of not having her glasses on, she missed her footing when going down some stairs and hurt herself. The court said that it was not unreasonable for her to walk down the stairs, and so the chain of causation was not broken, and the defendant was liable for the second set of injuries as well. In *McKew*, the claimant had hurt his leg in an accident at work, caused by the defendant's negligence, and his leg was still very weak. When he walked down a very steep staircase with no handrail, his leg gave way and he fell down the stairs, causing new injuries. The court held that he had chosen to put himself in a dangerous situation, knowing that his leg was weak, and that this was unreasonable behaviour which broke the chain of causation.

Case Summary

However, in a more recent case, *Spencer* v. *Wincanton Holdings* (2009), the Court of Appeal made it clear that unwise behaviour by the claimant will only break the chain of causation if that is a fair result. The claimant was injured at work and because of the continuing pain of the injury eventually decided to have part of his leg amputated. His car needed to be adapted to allow him to use it wearing his false leg, but until this could be done, he was able to drive around without the leg on because the car was an automatic so had only one foot pedal. Because putting the leg on was a cumbersome and time-consuming procedure, if he was only briefly getting out of the car, he would usually use sticks to help him walk instead. One day he stopped at a petrol station and although he would usually have sounded the horn to get help from an attendant, he got out, without his sticks or his false leg, and by steadying himself against a pump was able to fill the car himself. His intention was to get back into the car and call an attendant to take his payment, but as he was doing so he caught his foot and fell, causing serious damage to his good leg. His employers accepted that their negligence had caused his original injury, and the amputation which clearly happened as a result of it. But were they liable for the fall at the petrol station as well? (It was established that the petrol station had not been negligent in any way.)

Case Summary

The Court of Appeal said that the basis of the doctrine of intervening acts was fairness: it was unfair to hold a defendant liable for something which was actually not a result of their negligence. Therefore, the fact that Mr Spencer had chosen to get out of the car without his leg or his crutches could only break this foreseeable chain of events if it would be unfair to hold the defendants responsible for the damage done by it. The Court held that what happened to Mr Spencer was a foreseeable result of the defendants' negligence. They may not have been able to foresee the exact circumstances of the accident in the petrol station, but it was possible to foresee that if their negligence caused a man to lose his leg, that man would be more likely to hurt himself in an ordinary fall than someone who had two legs and would more easily be able to regain their balance. Therefore it was not unfair for the defendants to be held responsible for the injury caused by the fall. However, the Court of Appeal upheld the trial judge's decision to cut the damages by one-third for contributory negligence, in recognition of the fact that Mr Spencer had chosen not to use his leg or sticks and so increased the risk of falling.

Incidentally, in case you were wondering whether next time you get locked in a toilet you should climb out and then sue if you get hurt, or if it would be safer to stay put, the situation described above actually happened, in *Sayers* v. *Harlow Urban District Council* (1958). The court held that it was not unreasonable of the claimant to try to climb out, and so the chain of causation was not broken (though damages were reduced

Case Summary

as the court held that she had been contributorily negligent – see page 88 for details of this defence).

Case Summary

There are, however, some kinds of case where considering the reasonableness of the claimant's action is not very useful. In *Reeves* v. *Commissioner of Police for the Metropolis*, the case discussed earlier where the claimant's husband committed suicide in police custody, the police argued that his decision to kill himself broke the chain of causation. Clearly it was not appropriate to consider whether, in committing suicide, Mr Reeves behaved reasonably or not, so the House of Lords analysed the situation in a different way. They said that in this situation, where Mr Reeves was known to be a suicide risk, the police's duty towards him was to take reasonable steps to prevent him from harming himself. They could not therefore argue that the very act which was a breach of that duty broke the chain of causation.

Natural events

Natural events can include anything from storms, floods and fire, to a tree falling down or even a chemical reaction. The key issue here is that if a natural event is held to break the chain of causation, the claimant will have no one to sue for the damage that was caused by it, and this may mean that a defendant would evade liability, even if the damage would never have happened but for their breach.

Case Summary

If the natural event is a natural consequence of the situation the defendant has caused, the chain of causation is not broken, and the defendant will be liable for the full damage. This was the case in *Vacwell Engineering* v. *BDH Chemicals* (1971). The defendants supplied the claimants with industrial chemicals, and failed to warn them that the chemicals could cause an explosion if they came into contact with water. The claimants washed the tubes that held the chemicals with water and, when one smashed in the sink, there was a huge explosion that killed a scientist and severely damaged the claimants' factory. The chemical reaction was a natural consequence of the failure to warn the claimants, and so the defendants were liable.

Case Summary

An example of a natural occurrence that was considered to be an intervening event can be seen in *Carslogie Steamship Co.* v. *Royal Norwegian Government* (1952). The claimants' ship was damaged in an accident caused by the defendants, and needed repairs which would take 10 days, but these could not be done in England. The ship set sail for America where the repairs were to be done, but an unusually violent storm blew up during the voyage and the ship was damaged more seriously, so that by the time it reached America it needed an extra 30 days' repair. The ship would not have made the journey had it not been for the accident but, even so, the court held that the storm was an intervening event, because it was something that could happen on any voyage. The defendants should only be liable for the original damage done in the accident. This seems to suggest that a defendant will not be liable where their negligence does no more than put the claimant in the place where the natural event happens.

Things done by a third party

Where a third party does something, after the defendant's breach, that causes damage to the claimant, the courts will look at whether the third party's act was a natural consequence of the original breach, or whether it was a new cause that breaks the chain of causation. They also take account of whether the third party acted negligently or even just unreasonably; negligent or unreasonable behaviour is more likely to break the chain of causation.

Case Summary

In *Knightley* v. *Johns* (1982), the defendant caused a road accident in a tunnel. A police officer at the scene told a police motorcyclist to ride through the tunnel, in the opposite direction to the traffic, even though this was against normal police practice. The motorcyclist caused a second accident, which injured the claimant. Was the defendant liable for that as well? The Court of Appeal said no. The second accident was not a 'natural and probable consequence' of the defendant's earlier negligence, but a new cause that broke the original chain of causation.

Case Summary

A contrasting case is *The Oropesa* (1943). Two ships, *The Oropesa* and *The Manchester Regiment*, collided in rough seas, due to the negligence of *The Oropesa*'s crew. *The Manchester Regiment* was badly damaged and the captain sent most of his crew over to *The Oropesa*. The weather got worse and a few hours later the captain decided to go over to *The Oropesa* with the rest of his crew, to discuss what to do next. However, the seas were by now so rough that the lifeboat they were in sank, and nine of the 16 sailors died. The owners of *The Oropesa* said they were not liable for the deaths, because the captain's decision to leave the ship broke the chain of causation. The Court disagreed, saying that his decision was the natural consequence of the emergency in which the defendants had placed him and so they were liable for the deaths. To act as an intervening event, the Court said, an event would have to be 'a new cause which disturbs the sequence of events, something which can be described as either unreasonable or extraneous or extrinsic'.

Case Summary

Where a third party deliberately acts in a wrongful way, the courts are more likely to find that their act breaks the chain of causation. In *Lamb* v. *Camden LBC* (1981), the defendants had done some work on the claimant's house, which caused a flood. The claimant had to move out temporarily, but while he was gone squatters moved in, and when they were eventually evicted they trashed the house. The Court of Appeal held that their deliberate vandalism broke the chain of causation, even though it was foreseeable, and the defendant was not liable for the damage they caused.

Writing and drafting

You are a solicitor, about to meet a new client for the first time. She contracted the superbug MRSA during a stay in hospital, and she wants to sue the health authority for negligence. Using what you now know about what a claimant needs to show in a negligence case, draw up a list of questions you would want to ask her in order to start preparing the case.

Handy tip: Have a look back at the Law in Action box on page 5, which deals with MRSA cases.

Reflective practice

Take a few minutes to think about how this exercise went. What did you find difficult? What did you find worked well for you? Is there anything you would do differently if you did a similar exercise?

Figure 3.1 The effect of intervening events

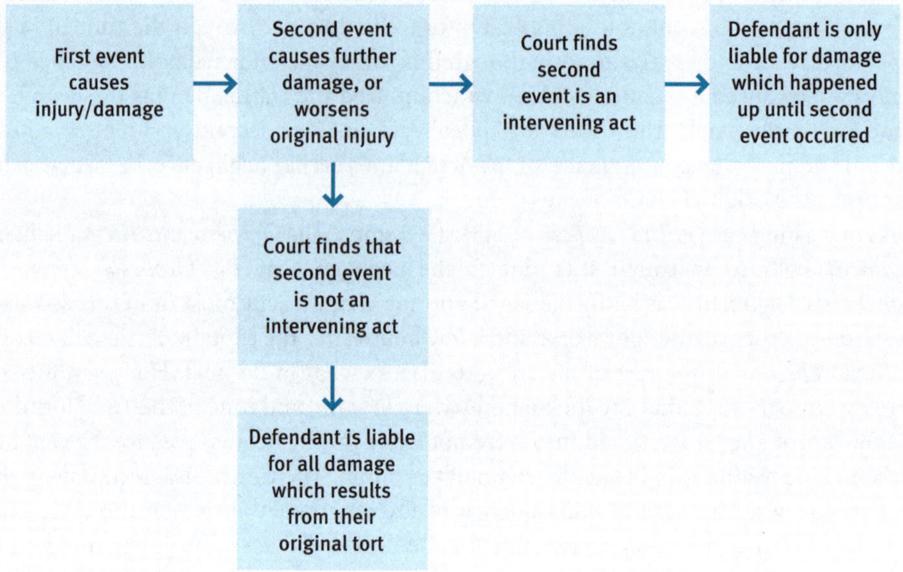

Defences

In some circumstances, a defendant will have breached a duty of care and caused damage that is not too remote, but there are reasons why the law believes they should not be held liable for that damage, or should be only partly liable. This is called having a **defence**. There are three defences to negligence:

- contributory negligence, where the claimant is partly at fault;
- *volenti non fit injuria*, where the claimant voluntarily accepts the risk;
- illegality, where the claimant was injured or caused loss as a result of doing something illegal.

Contributory negligence

Contributory negligence covers situations where the defendant causes the claimant damage but the claimant also contributes to the damage in some way, either by partly causing the damage or by doing or not doing something which makes the damage worse. For example, if you are hurt in a car crash caused by another driver's negligence, but your injuries are worse than they would otherwise have been because you were not wearing a seatbelt, the other driver can use the defence of contributory negligence and the damages you get will be reduced to reflect the fact that they were not entirely to blame.

The defence was introduced in the Law Reform (Contributory Negligence) Act 1945. Before that, **common law** provided that anyone who was partly responsible for damage done to them could not sue at all, which could be very unfair on claimants and allowed defendants to avoid liability even in cases where they had caused serious injury. Section 1(1) of the 1945 Act provides that where a claimant is partly responsible for the damage they suffer, a court can reduce the damages that would normally be awarded for that injury 'to such extent as the court thinks just and equitable having regard to the claimant's share in the responsibility for the damage'. The court will usually express the claimant's share of the responsibility as a percentage, and reduce the damages accordingly. So, for example, if a claimant would have received £100,000 in damages if they had not been contributorily negligent, and the court decides they were 25 per cent to blame for their damage, they will receive £75,000.

Note that contributory negligence can only apply where both the defendant and the claimant have caused the damage (though there may be other, non-negligent causes as well). It is not possible for a court to find that a claimant was 100 per cent contributorily negligent.

Where a defendant raises contributory negligence, the court will ask two questions:

- Did the claimant fail to take reasonable care for their own safety?
- Was that failure a cause of the damage they suffered?

Did the claimant take reasonable care?

In deciding whether the claimant has taken reasonable care for their own safety, the courts essentially use the same standard of reasonableness as they use to decide whether a defendant has breached a duty of care (though claimants do not need to have a duty of care towards the defendant). So they will look, for example, at issues such as how likely the damage was to occur, how serious it was likely to be, and any special characteristics of the defendant or the claimant which affect the risk of damage. The basic question to be asked is, did the claimant act as a reasonable person would when involved in the activity which caused the damage?

Case Summary

The way that this works can be seen in *Baker* v. *Willoughby* (1970), the case discussed earlier, where the claimant was run over by the defendant and then shot by a robber. In the first incident, he was crossing the road and, although the defendant was driving negligently, the claimant had a clear view of the road for the last 200 yards travelled by the car, yet made no attempt to get out of the way. The Court of Appeal found that he was 50 per cent contributorily negligent (in other words, that both parties were equally to blame) and his damages were reduced by half.

Case Summary

Not all cases are as straightforward as *Baker*. In *Badger* v. *Ministry of Defence* (2005), the claimant's husband had died of lung cancer, which had been caused partly by being exposed to asbestos while working for the defendants, and partly by smoking for most of his life. Did the smoking make him contributorily negligent? The High Court found that he was not contributorily negligent for starting to smoke, because he had started in 1955, when it was not widely known that smoking could cause cancer or any other health problems. However, the connection between smoking and lung cancer was widely known by the mid-1970s, and before that, in 1968, Mr Badger had been told by his doctor that he should give up smoking for the sake of his health. The court held that a reasonable person in his position would have given up smoking by the mid-1970s, and so he was contributorily negligent from that point onwards, but not before.

Reasonable care and child claimants

A claimant who is a child is not expected to take the same amount of care for their own safety as an adult. They will only be found contributorily negligent if they have failed to take the amount of care for their own safety that is to be expected from a child of their age.

Case Summary

In *Yachuk* v. *Oliver Blais* (1949), a 9-year-old boy bought some petrol from the defendants, saying that his mother needed it for her car. He used it to make a flaming torch for a game, and was seriously burnt. The company was found negligent for selling petrol to such a young child, but the claimant was not contributorily negligent because he was considered too young to know the dangers of playing with petrol. By contrast, in *Evans* v. *Souls Garage* (2001), the claimant was a 13-year-old who bought petrol from the defendants and ended up being burned. In this case the court found that he should have known that what he was doing was dangerous, and found him to be one-third responsible for his injuries.

Note, however, that these cases do not establish that a 9-year-old can never be contributorily negligent, or that a 13-year-old can always be. They are a useful guideline to the way courts approach cases involving children, but in each new case the courts will look at whether a child of the claimant's age could be expected to recognise the particular risk which caused the damage.

Reasonable care in emergency situations

Where the defendant's negligence has created an emergency situation, and the claimant takes action which ends up causing or increasing the damage, the courts will take the emergency into account when deciding whether the claimant took reasonable care for their own safety. In *Jones* v. *Boyce* (1816), the claimant was riding on top of the defendant's horse-drawn coach, when one of the horses' reins broke and it looked as though the coach might topple over. The claimant jumped down off the coach, breaking his leg. As it turned out, the driver was able to keep the coach on the road, so if the claimant had stayed in his seat he would not have been injured. Clearly he had contributed to his own injury, but the court held that he had no liability as he had acted reasonably in what seemed to be a dangerous situation.

Case Summary

Did the claimant's lack of care help cause the damage?

Contributory negligence will only provide a defence it if helped to cause the accident, or the damage, or made the damage worse. If a claimant does not take a reasonable standard of care for their own safety, but the accident would have happened anyway and the damage would have been just the same, there is no defence. If, for example, you are involved in a car accident and you are not wearing a seat belt, then in order to establish contributory negligence the defendant has to show that your failure to wear a seat belt was a cause of your injuries. If you are thrown forward and hit your head on the windscreen, then failing to wear a seat belt has clearly contributed to your injuries and you will usually be held contributorily negligent. However, if your injuries were caused by something crashing through the windscreen and crushing you against the seat, it would have made no difference whether you were wearing a seat belt or not, and so the failure to wear one will not make you contributorily negligent.

Case Summary

In *Smith* v. *Finch* (2009), the claimant was a cyclist injured when he was hit by the defendant's motorbike. The claimant was not wearing a helmet and the defence alleged that this made him contributorily negligent. However, evidence showed that helmets do not protect the head if an accident happens at the speed at which the defendant was travelling, and that helmets did not protect against blows to the back of the head, which was what had happened here. The court found that it was not proved that wearing a cycle helmet would have reduced the claimant's injuries, and so there was no reduction in the damages.

Nature of the risk

In order for the claimant's lack of care to be a cause of the damage, the damage that happened must be related to the risk they were taking. This can be seen in *Jones* v. *Livox Quarries* (1952). The claimant was riding on the back of a vehicle at the defendants' quarry where he worked. That particular type of vehicle was not designed to have passengers on the back, and the staff had been warned not to travel this way. The claimant was injured when another of the defendants' vehicles was driven negligently into the back of the vehicle. He said that he was not contributorily negligent, because the risk he was taking was that he might fall off the vehicle, and it was not a fall that caused his injuries. The court disagreed, and said that being hit from behind was within the range of risks arising from his behaviour, so he was contributorily negligent. The situation would have been different if his injury had been caused by something he could not be said to have taken the risk of, such as being shot in the eye while riding on the vehicle, by a negligent sportsman out shooting near the quarry.

Case Summary

Out and about

Read the case of *Jones* v. *Livox Quarries* carefully. Now imagine you are a barrister representing Mr Jones. What arguments would you make to persuade the court that they should not find him contributorily negligent? You can use arguments that are referred to in the judgment but put them in your own words.

The type of damage

Most of the key cases on contributory negligence involve accidents which cause personal injury, but the defence can also apply in cases where the damage is economic loss and the claimant has failed to take reasonable care of their own financial interests. In *Cavendish Funding Ltd* v. *Henry Spencer and Sons Ltd* (1998), the claimants, Cavendish, had lent money for the purchase of a building which had been negligently valued by the defendants. The defendants had valued it at over £1.5 million, and the claimants had also had a valuation from another company, for around £1 million, so there was a half a million pounds difference between the two. The property was actually worth only around £250,000. Cavendish gave a loan based on the defendants' valuation, lost money, and sued the defendants for their loss. The Court of Appeal held that they had been contributorily negligent, because the difference between the two valuations should have made it clear that something might be wrong, and they should have checked this out before lending the money.

Case Summary

Calculating the damages

As explained above, where a claimant is contributorily negligent, the Law Reform (Contributory Negligence) Act directs courts to reduce damages by a proportion that they consider 'just and equitable'. This means that they must decide what reduction is fair in each case. An example of the kind of calculations that may be made can be seen in *Badger* v. *Ministry of Defence*, the case we discussed earlier about

the court must decide what reduction is fair in each case

the man whose lung cancer was caused both by his smoking and the defendants exposing him to asbestos. The defendants accepted that they were more to blame than Mr Badger, because they had exposed him to asbestos at a time when the safety risks of doing so were already known. The court found, therefore, that the claimant's liability should be no more than 50 per cent. However, there was a further factor to take into consideration, in that for the first 20 years that Mr Badger smoked the health risks of smoking were not widely known, so he did not know he was taking a risk and could not be said to have behaved unreasonably. Therefore, the court concluded, the appropriate reduction was 20 per cent.

Case Summary

In one of the most common examples of contributory negligence, failure to wear a seat belt, the courts have laid down a standard set of reductions. In *Froom* v. *Butcher* (1976), it was stated that in cases where using a seat belt would have prevented the claimant's injuries from happening at all, the appropriate reduction is 25 per cent. If wearing a seat belt would not have prevented the injuries, but would have made them less serious, the reduction should be 15 per cent.

Volenti non fit injuria

Case Summary

The name of this defence is Latin for 'no injury can be done to a willing person' and it applies where the claimant has voluntarily taken a risk of harm. If a defendant successfully pleads ***volenti non fit injuria*** (usually known as *volenti*), the claimant gets no damages at all. For example, in *Morris* v. *Murray* (1991), the claimant accepted the defendant's offer to take him for a ride in his private plane, even though he knew that the defendant was very drunk. Not altogether surprisingly, the plane crashed and the claimant was seriously injured. The Court of Appeal found that the defendant's drunken state was so obvious that the claimant had voluntarily taken the risk of an accident and so he received no damages.

For the defence of *volenti* to apply, the courts look at two questions:

- Did the claimant accept the risk?
- Was the acceptance really voluntary?

Did the claimant accept the risk?

Case Summary

Clearly there will be very few cases where there is evidence that the claimant actually said that they would accept the risk, and the courts are not able to look inside the head of a claimant and discover what they were thinking. Therefore, the courts have to decide whether, on the basis of what the claimant did, they can infer that the claimant accepted the risk. This was the case in *ICI* v. *Shatwell* (1965). The claimant and his brother, James, were employed in the defendants' quarry. They needed to test some detonators, and had been told by their employers to follow a set of safety precautions when they did it. They decided to do the test without taking these precautions, and there was an explosion which injured the claimant. Because James was employed by the defendants, the claimant was able to sue them for negligence (this is an example of the principle of **vicarious liability**, which we will look at in Chapter 8). However, the Court held that the claimant was fully aware of the risk he was taking, because he had been warned to take precautions, and in going ahead anyway he had clearly consented to it. *Volenti* applied and he got no damages.

Knowledge of the risk is not enough

Case Summary

The fact that a claimant clearly knew that there was a risk may be evidence that they consented to take that risk, but it is not conclusive proof on its own. In *Smith* v. *Baker* (1891), the claimant worked in the defendant's quarry, and while he was working a crane was being operated above his head, swinging huge rocks. The claimant knew this was happening and had complained to the defendant several times that there was a risk of one of the stones falling on him. Sure enough, one did fall, and he was seriously injured. His employers pleaded *volenti*, arguing that in continuing to work when he knew of the risk he was accepting it. The House of Lords said no. If a person took on work that would have been dangerous even if their employers took proper precautions, they might be said to be accepting the risks involved in that work. But in this case, the work itself was not dangerous, but was made so by the defendant's negligence (and the claimant had tried to get the danger removed). Therefore merely continuing to do the work when he knew of the risk did not mean he consented to it.

Was acceptance voluntary?

The defence of *volenti* can only be successfully used against someone who had genuine freedom of choice. There will be no *volenti* where a claimant only accepted a risk because they were under some kind of pressure to do so. This issue has arisen most often in cases of accidents at work, and since the late nineteenth century the courts have generally accepted that an employee who does something dangerous because they are told to by their employer cannot really be said to be voluntarily accepting the risk, because unless they want to lose their job they may feel they have little choice. This was part of the reason why the courts found there was no *volenti* in *Smith* v. *Baker*, above, whereas in *ICI* v. *Shatwell*, it was clear that the claimant was not acting under pressure from his employer, because they had told him to take precautions. Where a person is incapable of giving genuine consent, *volenti* will not apply. This rule was applied in *Kirkham* v. *Chief Constable of Greater Manchester* (1990), where the claimant's husband committed suicide while in police custody. The police pleaded *volenti*, but the Court of Appeal held that as the claimant was clinically depressed at the time he could not be said to have made a voluntary decision. (In fact it appears that *volenti* cannot be used in any suicide case, as the defence was denied in the similar case of *Reeves* v. *Commissioner of Police for the Metropolis* (1999), even though in that case the man who committed suicide was not mentally ill.)

Case Summary

Volenti and exclusion clauses

In some cases, harm may arise from an activity that was the subject of a contract between the claimant and the defendant. Many contracts contain what are called exclusion clauses or disclaimers, which state that the seller of the goods or services does not accept liability for certain forms of harm to the buyer or user.

Exclusion clauses are often inserted into written contracts, but they can also become part of a contract in other ways, whether the contract itself is a written one or not. For example, you may have noticed that public car parks often display signs saying that the owner of the car park accepts no responsibility for damage to cars or things left in cars parked there. These are intended to be exclusion clauses, and they will become part of the contractual agreement if the buyer was given sufficient notice of them. In the car park example, this would mean a sign can become a term of the contract between the car park and people using it so long as it is clearly visible to someone entering the car park, before they have to commit themselves to parking there and therefore enter a contract by doing so.

the use of exclusion clauses to avoid liability for negligence is restricted

If someone supplying something under a contract is sued for negligence, and an exclusion clause was part of the contract (whether written into the contract or elsewhere, such as a sign), they can claim that *volenti* applies, because the claimant voluntarily took a risk knowing that the defendant was disclaiming liability. However, the use of exclusion clauses to avoid liability for negligence is restricted by the Unfair Contract Terms Act 1977, which applies to any contract made in the course of a business or from business premises. Section 2 of the Act sets out two provisions:

- Section 2(1) provides that it is not possible to use an exclusion clause to avoid or restrict liability for death or personal injury caused by negligence.
- Section 2(2) states that liability for other types of damage can only be avoided or restricted where it is reasonable to do so. The test for reasonableness is whether the clause is 'a fair and reasonable one . . . having regard to the circumstances which were, or ought reasonably to have been, known to or in the contemplation of the parties when the contract was made.'

In addition, section 2(3) provides that 'where a contract term or notice purports to exclude or restrict liability for negligence, a person's agreement to or awareness of it is not of itself to be taken as indicating his voluntary agreement of the risk'. This means that the existence of an exclusion clause is not in itself enough to prove that *volenti* applies; there must be additional proof that the claimant voluntarily took a risk.

Volenti in road accident cases

Volenti cannot be used as a defence when the claimant is a passenger in a road vehicle that the defendant is driving. This is because of a provision in section 149 of the Road Traffic Act 1988, which states that, where a person uses a vehicle which is required by law to be insured (which effectively means any vehicle used on the road), any attempt to

You be the judge

Q: Bill and Ben have been out drinking, after driving to the pub. Both of them are very drunk, but they decide that as Bill is slightly less drunk he should drive. Bill tells Ben to put on his seat belt but Ben refuses, saying seat belts are for wimps. The car hits a wall, and Ben is thrown against the windscreen, fracturing his skull. He sues Bill for negligence. Does Bill have any defence(s)?

A: You might assume that in this case Bill would have the defence of *volenti*, as Ben clearly consented to being driven even though he knew that Bill was drunk. But the decision in *Pitts* v. *Hunt* makes it clear that *volenti* cannot apply in cases involving road traffic accidents, because of the provisions of the Road Traffic Act 1988. However, Bill may have the defence of contributory negligence, because Ben refused to wear a seat belt. If it can be shown (as looks likely) that this made his injuries worse than they would otherwise have been, he is partly to blame and the damages ordered against Bill will be lower.

evade liability to a passenger will be ineffective. In *Pitts* v. *Hunt* (1991), the claimant was a pillion passenger on a motorbike being driven by the defendant. The claimant knew the defendant had been drinking, but not only still got on the bike with him but also encouraged him to drive dangerously. The Court of Appeal held that this would have been a case of *volenti*, but the defence could not apply because of the Road Traffic Act.

Case Summary

Volenti and sports

Where a person voluntarily plays a game or a sport, they are assumed to have accepted the normal risks associated with that sport when it is played according to the rules. In *Simms* v. *Leigh Rugby Football Club* (1969), the claimant broke his leg when he was thrown against a wall during a tackle. The tackle was within the rules of the game, and so the court held that he had accepted the risks involved, and *volenti* applied. This contrasts with the decision in *Condon* v. *Basi* (1985). Here the claimant also broke his leg as a result of a tackle, but it was a foul and not within the rules. The court held that *volenti* could not apply.

Case Summary

Case Summary

Similar rules apply to spectators at sporting events. In *Wooldridge* v. *Sumner* (1963), where the claimant was injured by an out-of-control horse at a showjumping event, the court held that a spectator voluntarily assumes the risk of any damage 'done in the course of and for the purposes of the game or sport', unless the participant's conduct shows 'a reckless disregard for the spectator's safety'. On the facts, the rider who lost control of his horse had just made an error of judgement and not been negligent, so there was no liability anyway.

Case Summary

Volenti and rescuers

Where a defendant's negligence causes an emergency and, as a result, the claimant deliberately takes a risk to themselves in order to prevent harm to others or to rescue someone in danger, *volenti* will not apply. This is partly on the grounds of social policy, in that it would be bad for society if people were discouraged from acting as rescuers, and unfair to penalise the rescuers. It also reflects the fact that a person who performs a rescue is acting in response to someone else's need, and so the rescuer's choice could be seen as not genuinely voluntary. Deciding to rescue someone from a burning building is not the same kind of decision as, for example, the choice to go up in a plane with a drunken pilot. In addition, in rescue cases the defendant's negligence has usually happened before the rescue, so it is hard to see that the rescuer has consented to it, and they may not even know about it.

In *Haynes* v. *Harwood* (1935), the defendant's employee left his horses unattended in a busy street, and the horses ran off when a child threw a stone at them. The claimant, a police officer, ran after them and managed to catch them, but was injured in the process. The defendant pleaded *volenti*, but the Court of Appeal said it could not apply because the police officer was not acting voluntarily but doing his duty of protecting the public.

Case Summary

The same rule applies even if the rescuer is not under a professional duty. In *Chadwick* v. *British Railways Board* (1967), the claimant suffered **psychiatric injury** as a result of spending many hours helping victims in the wreckage of a terrible train crash near his home. The defendants said that as he was not related to any of the victims, or involved in the crash himself, he had made a voluntary choice to help, and *volenti* should apply. The court rejected the defence.

Case Summary

However, *volenti* may apply even in rescuer situations if the claimant took a risk that was not actually necessary. This was the case in *Cutler* v. *United Dairies* (1933), which,

Case Summary

like *Haynes*, involved runaway horses. This time the horses ran off into a field, and the claimant went after them to try to recapture them and was injured. However, the evidence showed that the horses were not creating any risk of harm to people or property where they were. The court said that in this case *volenti* could apply.

Illegality

Case Summary

Case Summary

The defence of **illegality** can apply where the damage or injury to the claimant is connected with the fact that they have committed an illegal act (it is sometimes known as ***ex turpi causa non oritur actio***, which is Latin for 'no action may be based on an illegal cause'). The basic reason for the defence is public policy: many people would find it offensive if, for example, someone who steals your car could sue you for negligence because the brakes were not working and they crashed and hurt themselves. An example of the defence in action is *Ashton* v. *Turner* (1981), where both claimant and defendant had taken part in a burglary. The defendant had the job of driving the getaway car, but did it so badly that the claimant was injured. He attempted to sue his co-burglar for the injury, but the court held that the claim was prevented by the defence of illegality.

In *Clunis* v. *Camden and Islington Health Authority* (1998), the claimant was mentally ill and had murdered a young man, Jonathan Zito. The claimant should have had psychiatric care from the defendants and claimed that, but for their negligence in not providing this care, he would never have committed the murder. The Court of Appeal said that he could not use his own illegal act to create the basis of a claim.

In *Gray* v. *Thames Trains Ltd* (2009), the claimant had been involved in a serious train crash caused by the defendants' admitted negligence, and had suffered post-traumatic stress disorder as a result. As a result of this condition, he killed someone, and when he was found guilty of the killing the Criminal Court imposed a hospital order, which meant he was detained in a mental hospital for treatment. It was accepted that up until the train accident the claimant had been, in Lord Brown's words, 'a decent and law-abiding citizen', and that had it not been for the post-traumatic stress disorder it was impossible to believe he would ever have killed anyone.

Mr Gray sued the train authority in negligence for causing the post-traumatic stress disorder, and part of his claim included a sum for loss of earnings while he was detained in hospital, and for damages for the remorse and shame he felt over the killing. Despite expressing sympathy for the claimant's situation, the Court of Appeal refused to allow either of these parts of the claim. They said that *ex turpi causa* applied, because even though the claimant's responsibility for the killing was reduced by the mental problems that he was suffering from, it was still clear that he knew what he was doing and was responsible for what he did. It would be offensive to public opinion about the fair distribution of resources to compensate him for the consequences of killing someone. In addition, in imposing the hospital order on him the Criminal Court had removed his earning capacity for as long as the order was in force. It would be contrary to public policy for a civil court to undermine the order by allowing him to claim back the lost earnings from the defendants.

The limits of illegality

Case Summary

Illegality will only apply where there is a clear link between the illegal act and the damage. In *National Coal Board* v. *England* (1954) (the facts of which are not important on this point), the court gave two examples to illustrate this principle. They said that if two burglars, A and B, agreed to blast open a safe, and A handled the explosives negligently and injured B, the defence of illegality would prevent B from claiming against A. But if A and B are going to a house that they intend to burgle, and on the way, B picks A's pocket and steals his watch, the defence of illegality would not prevent A suing B in tort. In the first situation, A's injury arises directly out of the illegal activity he is involved in but in the second one there is no real link between the burglary and the theft of the watch: B could just as well have stolen the watch when they were on their way to a football match.

Inapplicable defences

There are a couple of circumstances which students often imagine might provide a defence in negligence, but which in fact do not. They are:

- mistake;
- inevitable accident.

Mistake

Negligence claims often arise because someone has simply made a mistake, but this does not act as a defence. If the defendant made a mistake that any reasonable person could make, then they have not breached their duty, and so there is no negligence and no defence is needed. An example of this situation would be *Roe* v. *Minister of Health* (1954), the case where disinfectant leaked into tubes of anaesthetic, and the claimant was paralysed. Storing the tubes in disinfectant was a mistake, but because of the state of scientific knowledge at the time it was not one that any reasonable person could have been expected to know about and avoid, so there was no negligence.

If, on the other hand, the defendant made a mistake that no reasonable person would make, they will have fallen below the standard of reasonable care, and the mistake, far from offering a defence, is the thing which makes them negligent. In *Roe*, for example, if medical staff had known that there was a serious risk attached to putting the ampoules in disinfectant but someone had perhaps got distracted and put one back in the wrong place, a court would be likely to find that that was a mistake that no reasonable member of the medical staff would make, and so there would be negligence.

Inevitable accident

An inevitable accident is one which the defendant could not have avoided, no matter how much care they took. Like mistake, it has no application as a defence in negligence, because if the claimant cannot prove that the defendant could have avoided the accident by taking reasonable care, there is no negligence anyway, so no defence is needed.

Use the flowchart in Figure 3.2 to work your way through problem questions about negligence.

Figure 3.2 Is there a claim in negligence?

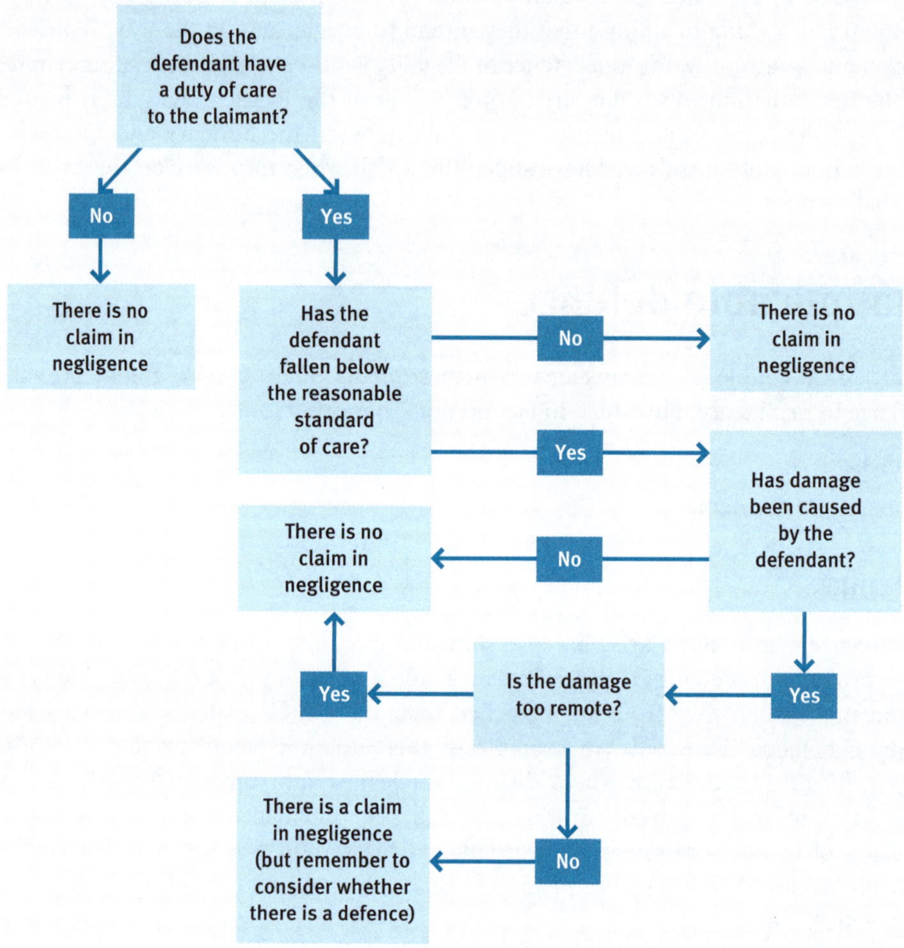

Law in action Negligence in the news

Now that you know the basics of negligence, you will begin to notice that negligence cases often hit the news, so it is worth knowing that they are often misrepresented.

This certainly happened with much of the coverage of *Harris* v. *Perry* (2008), a case you may have read about, in which a young boy was injured while playing in a bouncy castle that had been hired for a friend's birthday party. When, at first instance, the claimants won their case, it was widely reported in the press that the parents who had hired the castle would have to pay damages of over £1 million, and that the case was an example of the 'compensation culture', in which people seek to blame someone and get compensation for even the most minor injury. The facts of the case did not, however, fit this picture. First, the Perrys, like most householders, had home insurance, and it was their insurers who would have to pay the damages (in practice, it is extremely unlikely that an ordinary person without such insurance would be sued for negligence). In taking premiums from the Perrys, the insurance company was accepting the risk that they might, one day, have to pay out on the policy, which they would have assessed as a risk worth taking, in the knowledge that they might equally well have been able to take the premiums for years and years and never have to pay out a penny. Secondly, the boy injured in the castle suffered severe brain damage, and will need 24-hour care for the rest of his life. His parents were not seeking to get rich at the expense of someone else, but to be able to pay for that care.

The Perrys appealed, and the Court of Appeal overturned the decision. However, very few newspapers bothered to report that decision prominently, so the general public is largely left with the impression that if a child is injured at your house in this way you will be liable, even though the Court of Appeal held that that was not the case. The Harrises sought to appeal to the House of Lords but were refused permission.

[*Reference*: 'Bouncy castle couple win appeal over liability for brain damage', *The Telegraph*, 31 July 2008]

Time limits

The right to bring a claim in negligence (or any other tort) does not last for ever. It is considered to be unfair to defendants for claimants to be allowed the unlimited right to sue them many years after causing damage or injury, and there would be practical problems too: memories fade, witnesses may die, and evidence can be lost. In addition, as we have seen, the majority of tort claims are actually paid by insurance companies, and it would be very difficult for them to plan their business affairs if there was absolutely no time limit on claims, and so they had no idea of their potential liabilities.

For these reasons, the Limitation Act 1980 lays down specific time limits for different types of court case. In tort, the basic **limitation period** is six years, but different rules apply for defamation, discussed in Chapter 16; product liability, discussed in Chapter 10; and personal injury cases, discussed below. In cases of negligence not involving personal injury, the six-year time limit means that a claimant must bring their case within six years of the date when the damage was caused. However, there are some situations where a claimant may not realise that damage has occurred until some time later. This is called **latent damage**, and special rules apply to cases where it occurs.

the Limitation Act 1980 lays down specific time limits for different types of court case

Latent damage

Imagine that a lorry drives into your house. Your front window is smashed and there is some minor damage to the brickwork, and the lorry driver's employer pays for this to be repaired without argument. Seven years after the accident, you notice cracks appearing in your walls. You consult a building expert, who says that the crash must have made the walls unstable. He tells you that over the years this instability has made the walls move, and that is why they are cracking now. This is what is known as latent damage, meaning damage that does not appear until some time after the event which caused it. The lorry firm deny liability, and the standard six-year time limit to sue them has already passed.

In recognition of this problem, the Latent Damage Act 1986 was passed. It amends the Limitation Act 1980 by adding a new section 14A and 14B, which applies to all negligence claims, except those for personal injury. Section 14A provides that where damage is not apparent when it is first caused, the time limit is either six years from the time when the damage occurred, or three years from the time when the claimant knew, or ought to have known, of the damage, whichever is later. The stage at which it is considered that a claimant ought to have known of the damage is when they are aware of such facts as would enable a reasonable person to realise that there might be damage. This is called having constructive knowledge.

Section 14B imposes a final time limit of 15 years from the time that damage occurs. This means that if damage does not show until more than 15 years after it is caused, the claimant has lost their right to sue.

Personal injury cases

As we saw when we looked at the asbestos cases earlier in this chapter, there are situations where personal injury may not become obvious until very many years after the negligence has happened. With the asbestos-related diseases, for example, many claimants are not diagnosed until 30 years or more after being negligently exposed to asbestos, and there are other diseases that can take a similarly long time to show symptoms.

In recognition of this problem, the Limitation Act 1980 lays down separate rules for personal injury cases. Here, the time limit is three years, but it begins to run only from the later of these two points:

- when the damage was done; or
- when the claimant first had knowledge of the following facts:
  - that the injury was significant;
  - that it was wholly or partly caused by the defendant's negligence;
  - the identity of the defendant;
  - if the allegation is that someone other than the defendant committed the negligence, the identity of that person, and why the defendant should be liable.

it can be difficult to prove exactly what someone knew and when

If the defendant can prove that the claimant had the relevant knowledge more than three years before bringing the claim, they can avoid liability, so often in these cases there will be argument about when the client had knowledge of the above issues. Clearly, it can be difficult to prove exactly what someone knew and when, since a court cannot look inside their head. For this reason, where there is a dispute, a claimant will be considered to have the relevant knowledge from the time when they might reasonably have been expected to acquire it, from facts which could be seen, or could have been found out, with or without the help of medical or other experts.

Case Summary

An example of the way this rule is applied can be seen in *Forbes* v. *Wandsworth Health Authority* (1996). The claimant had had an operation on his leg, which went wrong. He was operated on a second time, but this surgery failed too, and he ended up having to have his leg amputated. Ten years later, he was told by a doctor that the amputation had only been necessary because the first operation was not done properly. He argued that the limitation period should run from the time he got this information from the doctor. The Court of Appeal disagreed. It said that it was reasonable to allow a claimant a period to get over the shock of the operation not working. But the damage in this case was very serious, and it was reasonable to expect that within 12–18 months someone who had had an operation go this badly wrong would start asking questions. Therefore they held that Mr Forbes had constructive knowledge 18 months after the first operation, and so his claim was too late.

Extending the limitation period in personal injury claims

There is also a second way in which the law recognises and allows for the problems caused by time limits in personal injury cases. Section 33 of the Limitation Act gives the courts a wide discretion to extend the limitation period for personal injury claims that are outside the normal time limit, where they think it is fair to do so. In deciding this, the Act says a court should look at all the circumstances of the case, and in particular the following issues:

- the length of the delay and the reason for it;
- the effect of the delay on the evidence;
- the conduct of the defendant after the cause of action arose;
- how long the claimant's disability lasted;
- whether the claimant acted reasonably once they knew they might have a claim;
- the steps taken by the claimant to get expert advice, and the nature of that advice.

Case Summary

In *McGhie* v. *British Telecommunications plc* (2005) the Court of Appeal explained that in applying section 33 the courts should consider the 'balance of prejudice' between claimant and defendant; in other words, whether it would be more unfair to the defendant if the limitation period was extended, or more unfair to the claimant if it was not. Mr McGhie worked for the defendants, who most of us know better as BT. He hurt his back in an accident at work, which might have been caused by BT's negligence, but he did not realise at the time that he might have a case against them. Later he had an operation, which made his back problem much better, and at that time he learnt that he should have been given special training and equipment for his job, and that in not providing this BT might have been negligent. By that time, he was outside the normal time limit. The Court of Appeal applied the 'balance of prejudice' test, taking into account the fact that there had been a two-year delay, Mr McGhie did not have particularly strong evidence for negligence, and as his problem was now better, his claim would have been for a relatively small amount of money. On balance, it was more unfair to BT to allow the claim to proceed than it was to Mr McGhie to refuse it.

Case Summary

An example of a case where the limitation period was extended is *Das* v. *Ganju* (1999). The claimant had a child who, it was claimed, was injured by medical negligence. She had consulted a solicitor, who told her that if she waited until her daughter was over 18, the daughter could sue on her own behalf and would be able to get legal aid for this. This was incorrect, but the claimant did not discover that until two years outside the limitation period. The court held that it should exercise its discretion under section 33 and extend the limit, because the delay was not the claimant's fault and she should not be disadvantaged by her solicitor's negligence.

Summary

- The claimant must prove that the defendant's negligence caused the damage.
- The main test for causation is the 'but for' test, which asks whether the damage would have happened but for the negligence.
- The 'but for' test can be modified in cases where there is:
  - damage with more than one possible cause;
  - damage caused by a chain of events;
  - loss of a chance.
- The claimant must also prove that the damage is not too remote from the defendant's negligence. This is a legal test, not a factual one.
- There are two tests for remoteness:
  - the direct consequence test;
  - the reasonable foreseeability test.
- The remoteness test in negligence is reasonable foreseeability: was the type of damage reasonably foreseeable? The extent of the damage need not be foreseeable.
- Damage may be too remote if an intervening event breaks the chain of causation.
- Three defences may apply in negligence:
  - contributory negligence;
  - *volenti non fit injuria;*
  - illegality.
- The following defences do not apply:
  - mistake;
  - inevitable accident.
- Negligence claims not involving personal injury must be brought:
  - within six years of the damage occurring; or
  - within three years from when the claimant knew/ought to have known about the damage.

  Claims cannot be brought more than 15 years after the damage occurred.
- Personal injury claims must be brought:
  - within three years of the damage; or
  - within three years of the time the claimant knew of the damage.

  The courts have discretion to extend this limit where it is fair to do so.

Question and answer*

Problem: Mr Steady is driving his 18-year-old son Keith to football practice when a red Ferrari, driven by Nigel Speedy, comes round a bend towards them. Nigel is going much too fast and talking on his phone to his girlfriend. He loses control of his car and hits Mr Steady's car head-on. Mr Steady hurts his back in the crash and Keith hits his head on the windscreen. They are taken to hospital. The police contact Mrs Steady, who rushes to the hospital to see them. She is so worried about them that she cannot concentrate properly on her driving, and crashes her car. She is unhurt, but the car is a write-off.

At the hospital, Mr Steady is left in the A&E department for six hours before he sees a doctor. When he is eventually seen he is told that, as a result of the accident, he will be paralysed from the waist down. Medical evidence shows that the injury he got in the crash leads to paralysis in 100 per cent of cases.

Keith has a small injury to his head, which is treated quickly. He tells the doctor his leg hurts as well, but the doctor says it is only bruised. Some days later, his leg is still painful and he returns to the hospital. An X-ray shows that his knee was fractured in the accident. Six months later, his knee is still weak, and he is told it is unlikely to get better. Medical evidence shows that of patients with the same original injury as Keith, 35 per cent will get this kind of weakness if their injury is not treated promptly, 25 per cent will get the weakness even if they are treated promptly, and 40 per cent will recover completely from the injury, with no weakness.

Advise Mr and Mrs Steady and Keith as to any potential claims they may have. You can assume that Nigel was driving negligently.

You should allow yourself no more than 40 minutes to complete this task.

Essay: How far do the rules relating to causation and remoteness of damage in negligence achieve the aim of compensating claimants for harm done to them?

This question should be answered in 40 minutes.

* Answer guidance is provided at the end of the chapter.

Further reading

Conaghan, J. and Mansell, W. (1993) *The Wrongs of Tort*, Ch. 3 (pp. 45–9), London: Pluto Press.
This chapter takes a critical look at the ideas behind the rules on causation and remoteness, pointing out problems with the key cases that have shaped the law. Very useful material for essays.

Hill, M. (1991) 'A lost chance for compensation in the tort of negligence by the House of Lords', 54 MLR 511.
This article looks at the concept of loss of a chance after *Hotson*. Clear and easy to understand, it is a good guide to this quite tricky area.

Law Commission Report 160 (2001) *The Illegality Defence in Tort*, London: The Stationery Office.
This report from the Law Commission looks at problems with the defence of illegality, and makes some recommendations for reform. Useful for essays.

Morgan, J. (2003) 'Lost causes in the House of Lords: *Fairchild* v. *Glenhaven Funeral Services*', 66 MLR 277.
This is a clear and critical account of the decision in *Fairchild*, and a useful look at the principles of causation.

Stapleton, J. (1985) 'Compensating victims of disease', 5 OJLS 248.
Most of the case law on causation deals with cases involving accidents, but personal injury cases involving disease can raise different issues. This is a good, clear and interesting look at the problems of proving causation in these kinds of case.

Question and answer guidance

Problem: As you are told that Nigel was driving negligently, you can ignore issues of duty, breach and damage here, and instead turn straight to the questions of causation and remoteness. As always in a problem question, take each person's claim in turn.

Starting with Mr Steady, it is clear that he has a claim against Nigel because the medical evidence shows that the accident caused his paralysis. Although he may have been treated negligently by the hospital in being left so long without seeing a doctor, he has no claim against them because his injury would have happened in just the same way whether he was seen promptly or not. The case of *Barnett* v. *Chelsea and Kensington* is relevant here.

Turning to Keith, he also has a claim against Nigel, because the accident caused his original injury, but the question here is whether the misdiagnosis of his leg injury breaks the chain of causation, so that Nigel would only be liable for the initial injury, and not for the fact that Keith is unable to walk again. This is a loss of a chance case, so you need to apply *Hotson*, and *Gregg* v. *Scott*, and work out whether, on a balance of probabilities, the misdiagnosis and the resulting delay in treatment caused the permanent injury, and what the answer means for the liability of Nigel and the hospital.

Finally, turning to Mrs Steady, clearly but for Nigel's negligence her husband and son would not have been in hospital, so she would not have gone there and crashed her car on the way. However, her decision to get in the car and drive to the hospital is an intervening event, so what we have here is a question of remoteness. You need to explain how the courts treat intervening events when the event is something that the claimant has done, so look at the cases of *Wieland* v. *Cyril Lord*, *McKew* v. *Holland* and *Spencer* v. *Wincanton*, and apply the tests explained there to Mrs Steady's situation.

Essay: A good way to start this essay would be to explain briefly the role of the rules on causation and remoteness, that one is a factual test designed to show whether the injury did in fact happen as a result of the negligence, and the other is a legal test designed to decide whether it is fair to hold the defendant liable for the harm. You need to point out that compensating claimants is only one aim of the rules; they are also there to make sure that defendants are not held liable for damage where it would be unfair to do so because, for example, a later event is a more important cause of the damage.

Then work through the rules, highlighting the way in which they strike this balance. The 'but for' test, for example, is very clearly aimed at making sure defendants are not held liable when there was nothing they could have done to prevent the damage, and in this sense it protects defendants more than claimants. On the other hand, some of the modifications of the 'but for' tests, such as the test in *McGhee*, mean that claimants can be compensated even when it cannot be proved that but for the negligence the injury would not have happened, and so can be seen as leaning more towards achieving the aim of compensation for harm. Then work through the rules on remoteness, highlighting the same issues; do the tests work most to ensure compensation for claimants, or to protect defendants from unfair liability? As you work through each test, make sure to mention the cases that illustrate the points you are making. Then finish with a conclusion that sums up the points you have made about the way in which the law strikes the balance between compensating claimants and protecting defendants.

Visit **www.mylawchamber.co.uk/quinntort** to access tools to help you develop and test your knowledge of tort law, including practice exam questions with guidance, annotated weblinks, glossary and key case flashcards, legal newsfeed and legal updates and interactive 'You be the judge' questions.

Use Case Navigator to read in full some of the key cases referenced in this chapter with commentary and questions:

Fairchild* v. *Glenhaven Funeral Services Ltd and others [2002] 3 All ER 305
Gregg* v. *Scott [2005] 4 All ER 812
Sienkiewicz* v. *Greif (UK) Ltd [2011] 2 All ER 857

Chapter 4
Negligence: psychiatric injury

Key points In this chapter, we will be looking at:

- What psychiatric injury means in negligence law
- When there is a duty of care regarding psychiatric injury
- Problems with the law on psychiatric injury

Introduction

Imagine that you are walking along the street one day, when a car comes speeding round the corner, the driver loses control and mounts the pavement towards you. At the very last moment, he swerves and you are not hit, but you are badly frightened and shocked. Assuming the driver was negligent, should you be able to sue him for the fear and panic he has caused you? Now imagine the same incident happens, but you are more seriously affected: you cannot sleep, you have nightmares, and you have flashbacks to what happened. Your doctor says you have a recognised mental illness called post-traumatic stress disorder. Should you be able to sue the driver for that? Finally, imagine that the incident was slightly different; you were standing well out of the way, but as the car sped round the corner, it went out of control and ploughed into the front of a sweet shop, killing 13 small children who were queuing up to buy lollipops. You saw the whole thing, and it affects you so badly that you become depressed and cannot carry on with your law degree. Should you be able to sue the driver for this?

The question these scenarios raise is this: how far should the law allow compensation when negligence causes injury to a claimant's mind, rather than (or as well as) to their body? It is a question which the courts have wrestled with as the tort of negligence developed, not always with entirely logical or consistent results. In this chapter, we look at the answers they have come up with.

What is psychiatric injury?

In legal terms, when we talk about **psychiatric injury** we mean an injury that affects the mind rather than the body, or an injury which affects the body but is triggered by a shock to the mind or emotions. Examples would be clinical depression, or post-traumatic stress disorder. Traditionally, the courts have referred to such injuries as '**nervous**

shock', and sometimes they still do, but in fact this is a very misleading term. It suggests that **claimants** can get **damages** because they are shocked by the result of a **defendant**'s negligence, or perhaps upset, frightened, worried or grief-stricken, but this is definitely not the case. In order to have a chance of claiming in negligence for a psychiatric injury, a claimant has to prove that they have a genuine illness or injury. This illness or injury must fall into one of the following categories:

- a physical illness or injury, caused by a mental shock; or
- a recognised mental illness.

Physical illness or injury caused by mental shock

In some cases, the defendant's negligence may cause an event so shocking that it leads to a physical injury or illness. An old example of this is *Dulieu* v. *White* (1901), where the claimant was working in a pub when the defendant's horse-drawn van came crashing through the window. She was pregnant, and the shock caused her to suffer a miscarriage. She was able to claim damages.

Case Summary

A recognised mental illness

Most cases which fall under the category of psychiatric injury are those where the claimant suffers some kind of mental illness, such as clinical depression or post-traumatic stress disorder (see Law in Action box for more information on the types of psychiatric injury). The claimant will need to bring medical evidence to prove both that they have the illness, and that the illness was caused by the shocking event that the defendant was liable for.

Law in action Types of psychiatric injury

As we saw above, negligence law does not provide compensation for simple distress, worry, shock or anxiety. A claimant will only be able to claim for psychiatric injury if they can prove, with medical evidence, that they have a recognised psychiatric illness. The following are some of the most common psychiatric illnesses that arise in this type of case:

Depression

Symptoms vary but the person may experience withdrawal from their usual activities, or loss of interest or pleasure in activities that were once enjoyed; a dramatic change in appetite, often with weight gain or loss; trouble sleeping or excessive sleeping; agitation, restlessness, and irritability; fatigue and lack of energy; feelings of worthlessness, self-hate, and inappropriate guilt; extreme difficulty concentrating; thoughts of death or suicide.

Generalised anxiety disorder

The person persistently feels anxious and nervous, and there may also be trembling, muscular tensions, sweating, light-headedness, palpitations, dizziness and stomach pain. Victims sometimes worry obsessively that they or a relative will become ill or have an accident.

Panic disorder

The victim suffers recurrent and unpredictable panic attacks, with palpitations, chest pain, choking sensations and dizziness. There is often also a secondary fear of dying, losing control, or going mad.

Post-traumatic stress disorder

This illness is only diagnosed where the victim has experienced an extremely traumatic event. This could be an incident in which they were seriously injured, or at risk of death or serious injury, or it could involve witnessing serious harm to or the death of someone else. The victim will usually suffer nightmares and flashbacks about the traumatic event, accompanied by symptoms similar to those of generalised anxiety disorder.

Chronic pain syndrome

The victim suffers persistent, severe pain that severely affects their day-to-day life or ability to work but no physical cause for it can be found. There is evidence that this type of pain may be triggered by psychological factors such as depression.

Where a claimant's case is based on the fact that they have one of these or another psychiatric condition, they will always need to produce evidence from a psychiatrist or other specialist to confirm that they have been diagnosed as having the relevant illness.

Liability for psychiatric injury

Given that psychiatric injury can be every bit as serious and life-destroying as physical injury, you might expect that it would be treated in the same way by the courts, but this has never been the case. At one time it was not possible to sue for psychiatric injury at all, and although it is now possible to do so, the circumstances are restricted.

You might remember that in Chapter 2 we looked at the fact that the courts have traditionally used the concept of a duty of care to draw the boundaries of negligence. If the higher courts, when examining a new factual situation, decide that there is a duty of care in that situation, the number of potential negligence cases will grow, but if they decide there is no duty of care in that situation, it will not. Psychiatric injury cases are one area of the law where the courts have used the duty of care concept in this way. By making the duty of care for psychiatric injury more restrictive than that for physical injury, the courts have limited the number of cases that can be brought.

Why is liability restricted?

There are three main reasons why the courts have been so reluctant to allow compensation for psychiatric injury. The first is simply historical: at the time when negligence law was first expanding, doctors understood very little about mental illness and how it was caused. There was a general belief that mental illness was the result of a weak character, and something that people should try to overcome. For example, during the First World War many soldiers became unable to go on fighting because of the terrible psychiatric trauma their horrific experiences had caused. Today, we would recognise them as suffering from post-traumatic stress disorder, but in those days they were widely regarded as cowards. Against this background, judges seem to have felt it was undesirable to encourage such 'weakness' by allowing compensation for it.

> when negligence law was first expanding, doctors understood very little about mental illness

The second reason, related to the first, is that judges used to believe that psychiatric injury was easy to fake. In a case today, a claimant can bring evidence from a medical expert, but in the past, the main evidence might be the claimant's own statement about their condition. Unlike a broken leg, or a head injury, mental illness was not visible, and the courts were not too keen on taking a claimant's word for it.

Today, though, the main reason for restrictions on liability for psychiatric injury is the much repeated **'floodgates'** argument. As you may remember from Chapter 1, this is the argument which suggests that unless negligence liability is restricted in certain ways, too heavy a burden could be placed on those who have to pay damages, leading to increased insurance costs, which are ultimately passed on to us all. There is also a problem of unpredictability: when someone does something negligent, there is usually a relatively small number of people who can be physically injured by that negligence, but there may be a much higher and less predictable number of people who could suffer psychiatric injury, for example by seeing an accident. This makes it difficult for insurers to calculate risks, and can expose them to liabilities for which they have not planned.

Although this argument clearly has some force, it should be pointed out that there are situations where negligence may cause very widespread physical injury (such as where a medicine causes dangerous side effects), and there is no suggestion that these should be subject to restrictions to avoid the floodgates problem. Even so, it is still the case that the courts will only allow compensation for psychiatric injury in limited circumstances.

The duty of care

In Chapter 2 we saw that a defendant will only be liable for physical injury caused by their negligence if they owe the claimant a **duty of care**, and the test for a duty of care regarding physical injury is the three-part ***Caparo* test** (foreseeability; proximity; justice, fairness and reasonableness).

However, when it comes to psychiatric injury, the courts apply a different test, which was established in *White and others* v. *Chief Constable of South Yorkshire* (1998), the leading modern case on psychiatric injury in negligence. It arose from the 1989 Hillsborough disaster, where 96 football fans died as a result of negligent police decisions that caused horrific overcrowding during an FA Cup semi-final (we will look at the facts in more detail later in this chapter).

The test set down in *White* divides claimants into three categories:

- Those who are physically injured by the defendant's negligence, as well as psychiatrically injured.
- Those who are put at risk of physical harm, but actually suffer only psychiatric injury.
- Those who are not put in danger of physical injury to themselves, but who suffer psychiatric injury as a result of witnessing, or hearing about, such injury to someone else.

The first two categories of claimant are called **primary victims** and the third **secondary victims**. There is one duty of care for primary victims and a different, much more restrictive, one for secondary victims.

You be the judge

Q: John and Maureen are driving to the supermarket. As they approach a bend, Jeremy comes round the corner in his new sports car, going far too fast, and hits John and Maureen's car. Peter, who lives on the street where the accident happens, sees the whole thing. John is left paralysed in both legs, but Maureen is not physically injured. Later on, John is told he will never be able to go back to his old job and he becomes clinically depressed. Both Maureen and Peter suffer nightmares and flashbacks, and their GP diagnoses them as having post-traumatic stress disorder.

All three want to sue Jeremy for psychiatric injury. Would the courts classify them as primary or secondary victims?

A: John is a primary victim, because he was physically injured as well as suffering psychiatric harm. Maureen is also a primary victim, because she was at risk of physical harm, even though she was not actually physically hurt. Peter is a secondary victim, because he witnessed the event but was not physically injured or at risk of physical injury.

Figure 4.1 Primary and secondary victims in psychiatric injury cases

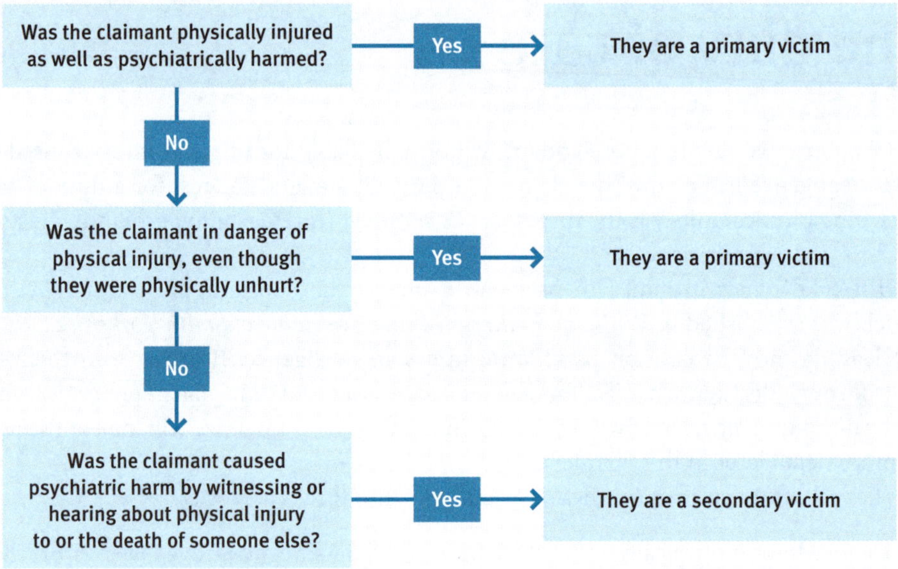

Primary victims

In *White*, it was stated that if a person negligently exposes another to a risk of physical injury they will be liable for any psychiatric injury that results, whether or not the physical injury actually happens. This means that if a claimant suffers both physical and psychiatric injury, or is put at risk of physical injury and suffers psychiatric injury, they can claim under the normal rules of negligence that apply to physical injury. If there is a question about whether a duty of care applies, the test is the standard *Caparo* test, though in practice these will often be cases where the duty of care is already established, such as medical negligence or car accidents.

Case Summary

The leading modern case in this category is *Page* v. *Smith* (1996). The claimant was involved in a car accident caused by the defendant. The accident could have injured him but in fact he was unhurt. Some years earlier, he had suffered an illness called myalgic encephalomyelitis (ME), but had believed he had recovered from it. However, shortly after the accident, the symptoms began coming back, and he claimed that the shock of the accident had caused the illness to recur. ME is a disease that doctors still do not really understand, and there is some debate about whether it has a physical or a psychiatric cause, but in *Page* the courts seem to have assumed it was psychiatric. The House of Lords held that where it was reasonably foreseeable that the defendant's negligence would expose the claimant to a risk of physical injury, the defendant has a duty of care with regard to any injury that the claimant suffers, whether physical or psychiatric.

Case Summary

A case where the claimant suffered both physical and psychiatric injury is *Simmons* v. *British Steel* (2004). The claimant was employed by British Steel, and was physically injured in an accident at work. As a result of his shock and anger at what had happened to him, he developed a severe skin condition, which meant he had to take a lot of time off work. This in turn led to him developing a severe depressive illness. The House of Lords held that his employers were liable for the skin condition and the depressive illness, as well as the original injury. They had exposed him to a foreseeable risk of physical injury, and they were therefore liable for all the injuries that resulted from that risk. It did not matter that they could not have foreseen a psychiatric injury.

Primary victims: how serious must the risk be?

Case Summary

As we have seen, a primary victim put at risk of physical injury can claim for psychiatric injury even if the physical injury did not happen. What about cases where the defendant's negligence makes the claimant fear they will be physically injured, and their fear causes psychiatric injury, but it is later discovered that they were not in physical danger after all? This was the situation in *McFarlane* v. *Wilkinson* (1997), which arose out of a terrible explosion on the Piper Alpha oil rig in 1988 in which 167 people died. The claimant was a painter on the rig and at night lived on a support boat about 55 metres from the rig. He saw the fire from the boat and afterwards suffered psychiatric illness as a result. The Court of Appeal rejected his claim, because the boat he was on was clearly never in any danger and so his fears for his own safety were not reasonable.

What remains unclear, however, is what happens when a claimant was not in physical danger, but had reasonable grounds for thinking they were. Will they still be classed as a primary victim? The two leading judgments in *White* differ slightly in this area. Lord Steyn says that the claimant must have 'objectively exposed himself to danger or *reasonably believed* that he was doing so', but Lord Hoffmann refers only to primary victims being those who are 'within the range of reasonably foreseeable physical injury'. Of course, in the majority of cases, if a claimant reasonably believes they are in danger, that will be because they are. However, in the middle of an emergency situation, it may be quite easy to become terrified even if in fact there is no risk to you at all, and it would have been useful if the House of Lords had been clearer on this point.

Secondary victims

As we saw earlier, claimants who suffer psychiatric injury but were not at risk of physical injury are classified in *White* as secondary victims. These claimants tend to fall into five groups:

- People who have suffered psychiatric injury as a result of witnessing the death of, or injury to, relatives, friends or work colleagues.
- People who have suffered psychiatric injury as a result of helping out at the scene of an accident. These people are usually referred to as 'rescuers' but the category includes people who give any kind of help, not just dramatic actions such as running into burning buildings and carrying people out. It includes both ordinary members of the public who voluntarily give help at the scene of an accident, and people such as police officers who do so as part of their job.
- Employees who suffer psychiatric injury as a result of witnessing an accident at work.
- Bystanders, who are people with no connection to the accident or the people involved in it, who just happen to be on the scene when it happens.
- People whose psychiatric injury has been caused because they did the thing that brought about the death of or injury to someone else, or feared they might have done so, even though the the ultimate cause was someone else's negligence. This group is usually called 'unwitting agents'.

Until *White*, each of these groups had been treated differently by the law, but *White* establishes that they are all secondary victims and subject to the same rules. These rules were set down in two earlier cases, *McLoughlin* v. *O'Brian* (1982) and *Alcock* v. *Chief Constable of South Yorkshire* (1992). Together, these three cases make it clear that secondary victims can only claim for psychiatric injury in very limited circumstances.

Secondary victims: how the law developed

Case Summary

In *McLoughlin* v. *O'Brian*, the claimant's husband and children were involved in a serious car accident, caused by the defendant's negligence. One of her daughters was killed, and her husband and two other children were badly injured. The claimant was not with her family when the accident happened, but was told about it immediately afterwards and rushed to the hospital. There she saw her husband and the two surviving children covered in dirt and oil, and her badly injured son screaming in fear and pain. As a result, she suffered clinical depression and changes to her personality, and claimed against the negligent driver for psychiatric injury.

Until Mrs McLoughlin's case was brought, the courts had only allowed claimants who were actually present at an accident to claim compensation for psychiatric injury, but the House of Lords allowed her claim. The judgment itself was rather confused, however. Lord Bridge said that Mrs McLoughlin could claim because her psychiatric injury was reasonably foreseeable, and that was enough to create liability. Lords Wilberforce and Edmund-Davies favoured a different, more complex approach. They said that while psychiatric injury in secondary victims did have to be reasonably foreseeable, that alone was not enough to create a duty of care. Secondary victims would also have to satisfy a series of other requirements, concerning the cause of their psychiatric injury, their relationship to the primary victims of the accident, and their position with regard to the accident.

This second approach is the one that now forms the modern law on secondary victims, and it was explained in detail in *Alcock* v. *Chief Constable of South Yorkshire.* Like the case of *White*, *Alcock* arose from the Hillsborough disaster which, as mentioned earlier, took place during the 1989 FA Cup semi-final, between Liverpool and Nottingham Forest. As a result of poor decisions by the police, a section of the ground became grossly overcrowded, and people inside it were crushed to death. The police admitted negligence, and settled out of court with the families of those who were killed, and with those who were injured in the stadium. However, there were two further groups who wished to claim against the police, in both cases for psychiatric injury caused by witnessing the events. The first group were relatives and friends of those who were killed and injured, whose claims were examined in *Alcock*; and the second group were police officers who were on duty at the ground, and were the claimants in *White* (the fate of their claim is discussed later, see page 121).

Case Summary

The claimants in *Alcock* included grandparents, parents, brothers, brothers-in-law, fiancées and friends of the dead and injured. Between them they had either been at the match when the disaster occurred and witnessed it first-hand; or had seen it on the television; or heard about it and then gone to the stadium to look for someone close to them; or been told that a loved one was injured or dead in the crush; or had to identify someone in the temporary mortuary at the ground. The police argued that they did not owe any of these people a duty of care with regard to their psychiatric injury.

The claimants argued, following Lord Bridge's judgment in *McLoughlin*, that a duty of care was owed because it was foreseeable that people in their situation would suffer psychiatric injury. However, the House of Lords took a different view, following the approach that Lords Wilberforce and Edmund-Davies had set out in *McLoughlin*. They said that while it was clear that deaths and injuries in traumatic accidents commonly caused suffering that went well beyond the immediate victims, it was generally not the policy of negligence law to compensate everyone who suffered in this way. Where someone was not the primary victim of an accident, their claim for psychiatric injury had to be subject to much stricter requirements than someone who was actually involved in the accident. As a result, none of the claimants in *Alcock* succeeded.

We will see why as we go through the tests the court used, but before we do that, the Law in Action box explains a bit more about the disaster which gave rise to the claims. Students reading this case sometimes wonder why the police were blamed for what sounds like a tragic accident, but a detailed look at the facts (which you may find upsetting to read) will help you understand why the police were sued, and why so many people suffered serious psychiatric injury as a result of the disaster.

Law in action The Hillsborough disaster

The key cases in this area, *Alcock* and *White*, both arise from the tragic events which took place at Hillsborough football stadium in Sheffield on 15 April 1989, where the FA Cup semi-final was due to be played between Liverpool and Nottingham Forest.

All tickets for the match had been sold, and it was being shown live on television. Kick-off was scheduled for 3.00 pm and, because many fans had been delayed by unexpected roadworks, by around 2.30 pm there was a large build-up of people outside the turnstiles at one end of the ground. A bottleneck developed, made worse by the fact that fans with no tickets were being turned away but could not move for the crush behind them. The normal policy in this kind of situation would be to delay the kick-off, but the senior police officer refused to do this.

Source: Pearson Education Ltd/Photodisc/Don Tremain

The crush outside became worse once fans heard the game inside begin, so the police decided to open some exit gates, without realising that this would cause a rush of fans into the ground and through a narrow tunnel into the centre of the stand. At this time football grounds were not all-seater stadiums, and the stand was just a series of steps where fans found a place and stood. It was divided into three 'pens'. By this stage the centre pens were already overcrowded and the crowd coming in should have been directed towards the side pens, but because the police failed to do this, people continued to surge into the centre pens. Those at the back of the surge could not see how crowded the pens were, and those at the front of it could not turn back because of the weight of people behind them.

Fans at the front of the stand were crushed against the fence around the pitch, and the pressure was so great that people began to suffocate. Eventually the gates in the fence which led to the pitch sprang open under the weight of the crowd, but they were twice closed by police officers who assumed fans were trying to invade the pitch and cause trouble. It was six minutes before senior officers realised what was going on and stopped the match. The inquiry into the accident found that many of the people who were being crushed would have suffered irreversible brain damage within four minutes, and death shortly after. Ambulances were called, but communication problems led to delays in paramedics reaching the victims. Families of the victims still believe that some of them could have been saved if they had received medical attention. In all, 96 people died and over 700 were injured.

A public inquiry found that poor policing was the main cause of the disaster. The Director of Public Prosecutions decided there was not enough evidence to prosecute anyone from the police force, so families of the victims brought a private prosecution against the two most senior officers. One was acquitted, and the jury failed to reach a verdict on the other. The judge ruled out a re-trial.

[*References*: 'How the Hillsborough disaster happened', **http://news.bbc.co.uk/1/hi/uk/7992845.stm**; Lord Justice Taylor (1989) 'The Hillsborough Stadium Disaster – Interim Report', HMSO Cmnd 765]

Secondary victims: the test for a duty of care

Taken together, *McLoughlin*, *Alcock* and *White* created a new test for secondary victims of psychiatric injury. A secondary victim can only claim where:

- psychiatric injury was a reasonably foreseeable result of the defendant's negligence; and
- they have a recognised psychiatric injury which was caused by a sudden shock; and
- they have a close relationship with the primary victim; and
- they were at the scene of the shocking event, or witnessed its 'immediate aftermath'.

Was psychiatric injury reasonably foreseeable?

In *White*, the House of Lords said that psychiatric injury in a secondary victim could only be considered reasonably foreseeable if a person of 'reasonable fortitude' would have suffered psychiatric injury in the same circumstances. A person of 'reasonable fortitude' simply means someone who has a normal degree of emotional strength; the opposite of someone with reasonable fortitude would be someone who, for some reason, was more likely to suffer psychiatric injury through witnessing a shocking incident than most other people would be. So if the claimant only suffers psychiatric injury because something about them makes them more prone to this kind of illness, reasonable foreseeability will not be proved and there will be no need to look at the other parts of the test for a duty of care.

This confirms an old rule which was stated in *Bourhill* v. *Young* (1943). The claimant in the case, Mrs Bourhill, was a pregnant woman, who was getting off a tram when the defendant's motorbike hit a car, about 40 metres away from her. She did not see the crash, but she heard it and later saw blood on the road. She claimed that the shock of this caused her baby to be stillborn. The House of Lords said that she could not claim, because it was not reasonably foreseeable that a person of reasonable fortitude, in her position, would suffer psychiatric injury. Drivers were entitled to assume that ordinary members of the public had 'sufficient fortitude to endure such incidents as may from time to time be expected to occur [on the roads], including the noise of a collision and the sight of injury to others'.

Case Summary

Was the psychiatric injury caused by a sudden shock?

Like primary victims, secondary victims must prove that their psychiatric injury amounts to a recognised psychiatric illness. Unlike primary victims, they also have to show that their psychiatric illness was caused by them suffering a sudden shock, resulting from what Lord Ackner in *Alcock* described as a 'horrifying event'.

This means that secondary victims will not be able to claim if they suffer psychiatric injury as a result of someone else's negligence but that psychiatric injury results from anything other than witnessing a sudden shocking event. There would be no claim if, for example, they are caused psychiatric injury through the grief of watching a loved one slowly dying of an illness caused by someone else's negligence, or where psychiatric injury is brought on by the stress of having to look after a relative who has been disabled through someone else's negligence. In *Sion* v. *Hampstead Health Authority* (1994), the claimant had developed a stress-related psychiatric illness as a result of watching his son slowly die in intensive care as a result of negligent medical treatment. It was held that the health authority had no duty of care regarding his psychiatric injury because it was not caused by a sudden shock.

Case Summary

In most cases where the psychiatric injury is triggered by a 'horrifying event', this event will involve injury to, or the death of, someone else. However, the courts have allowed a claim for psychiatric injury triggered by a sudden shock caused by witnessing damage to property, rather than injury to a person. In *Attia* v. *British Gas* (1988), British Gas were installing central heating in the claimant's house. She had spent many years improving and decorating her home, and was very emotionally attached to it. She went out, leaving the heating fitters at work, and came back to find her house on fire as a result of their negligence. It took the fire brigade four hours to get the blaze under control, by which time the house was very seriously damaged. British Gas accepted liability for the damage to the house, but the claimant also sought to claim for psychiatric injury brought on by the shock of seeing her home on fire. The Court of Appeal accepted that there could be a duty of care regarding psychiatric injury in this situation.

Case Summary

In many cases, causation will be difficult to prove, because in addition to the required 'sudden shock', the claimant will also have suffered the grief of bereavement, which

Case Summary

could equally well have caused their psychiatric injury. This was the case in *Vernon* v. *Bosley (No. 1)* (1996), where the claimant had witnessed his children drowning in a car that was negligently driven by their nanny. The medical evidence suggested that his psychiatric injury was partly caused by the shock of witnessing the accident, and partly by the sheer grief of losing his children. The Court of Appeal said that so long as it was clear that the sudden shock was part of the cause, that was sufficient for this part of the test. However, in these cases, it is still open to the defence to argue that the claimant's psychiatric injury is entirely caused by the grief of bereavement and would have happened even without the sudden shock; it will often be very difficult for the claimant to prove otherwise.

In *Alcock*, there was clearly no problem with establishing that the claimants had suffered their psychiatric injury as a result of a horrific event. However, once a claimant has proved this, they have two more tests to face, and, for the claimants in *Alcock*, these were to prove more difficult.

Was there a close relationship?

A secondary victim can only claim for psychiatric injury if they can prove that they have a close personal relationship with the primary victim(s). In establishing this rule in *McLoughlin* and *Alcock*, the courts could have introduced some clarity to the law, by making a rule that, for example, only those with the closest relationship to the primary victim could claim. They could, for example, have specifically limited claims to children, parents and spouses of the primary victim, or to all blood relatives plus spouses. Or they could have said that anyone who could prove a close emotional relationship could claim. However, they chose to do neither, and the result is a test that is difficult to apply and hard to justify.

In explaining the test in *McLoughlin*, Lord Wilberforce said that, in terms of closeness to the primary victim, potential claimants stretched all the way from the closest, which were parents, children and spouses of the victim, to the least close, which would be someone who just happened to see the accident. The law was already clear that parents and children and spouses were sufficiently close to be able to claim, assuming they passed the other tests, and mere bystanders were not. Where a secondary victim fell in between these two extremes, their Lordships refused to rule anyone in or out, and instead said each case would have to be judged 'in the light of other factors, such as proximity to the scene in time and place, and the nature of the accident'. In other words, less close relatives, partners outside marriage or friends might be sufficiently close, but might not.

Just to make things a little more complicated, in *McLoughlin* Lord Wilberforce stated that for a secondary victim to be considered sufficiently close to the primary victim, the tie between them had to be close 'not merely in relationship, but in care', and this was confirmed in *Alcock*. This means that a claimant not only has to prove that the type of relationship was one which would usually be assumed to be close, such as brother and sister, but also has to prove that the relationship was in fact a close and loving one. This test knocked out a number of the *Alcock* claimants, including one who was present at the stadium when his brother was killed, but could not prove that they had an emotionally close relationship.

The result is now that a secondary victim must either be a spouse, parent or child of a primary victim, or be able to prove that there was a close emotional bond between them.

You be the judge

Q: Brian's brother Eric is killed in a car accident caused by Tina's negligence. Brian is a witness to the accident, and later suffers post-traumatic stress disorder as a result. Is he considered to have a 'close relationship' to Eric under the *McLoughlin/Alcock* rules?

A: Not necessarily. Anyone who is not the spouse or child of the primary victim has to prove that their relationship with the victim was a close one 'in care' as well as in fact. So Brian will have to prove that he and his brother had an emotionally close relationship; the mere fact that they are brothers is not enough.

Did the claimant witness the accident or its immediate aftermath?

In *Alcock*, some of the claimants had seen the disaster from other areas of the stadium, others had heard about it on the radio or seen it on television, and one had seen it begin on a TV near the stadium and had immediately gone to the stadium to find his son (who turned out to have been killed). The House of Lords said that to make a claim for psychiatric injury, a secondary victim would usually have to have been present at the scene of the accident, or its immediate aftermath.

The House of Lords would not specify exactly what they meant by 'immediate aftermath', and each of the judges gave a slightly different interpretation. Lord Keith said that the aftermath continues for as long as the victim remains in the state caused by the accident, but Lord Ackner thought that the situation in *McLoughlin* (where the claimant saw her family in hospital immediately after an accident, still covered in dirt and blood and obviously in pain) was on the borderline. Identifying the body of a loved one in the temporary mortuary, eight hours after the accident, was stated to be outside the immediate aftermath. The House of Lords also made it clear that merely being informed of the accident by someone else was not sufficient.

An unusual element of the Hillsborough situation was that the match was being shown live on television, and so the disaster was seen by millions of people sitting at home, as well as those inside the stadium. It was not possible to see individuals, as broadcasting guidelines ban television companies from showing the death or suffering of recognisable individuals, and the broadcasters stuck to this rule. However, many of the viewers would have known that their loved ones were in the crowd, and even knew exactly where in the ground they were likely to be. Was there a duty of care to people who suffered psychiatric injury from watching the events on television, assuming they could pass the other two tests?

The House of Lords said no. They stated that watching a recorded broadcast would never be sufficiently proximate to create a duty of care for psychiatric injury, and even watching a live broadcast was very unlikely to create a duty. This was because the broadcasting guidelines meant individuals would not usually be shown, and so seeing the events on television was not the same as actually being on the scene. If the broadcasting guidelines were broken, so that individuals were shown, this would be an intervening act, which would break the chain of causation (see page 84), and so the party which caused the shocking event (in this case the police) would not be liable.

Their Lordships did say that there might be very rare occasions where a shocking incident was shown live and broadcasting regulations were breached without breaking the chain of causation. The example they gave was of a publicity-seeking organisation arranging an event where a party of children were taken up in a hot air balloon, and shown live on television. If the balloon suddenly burst into flames, the suddenness of the explosion might mean that it was impossible for the broadcasters to prevent viewers from seeing it. This would be reasonably foreseeable to the party whose negligence caused the accident, and so they could be liable to anyone who was psychiatrically injured through watching the broadcast, and passed the other three tests for secondary victims.

People in the law

Source: Wendy Wright (*text and photo*)

Wendy Wright is a partner at London law firm Osbornes, and works on personal injury cases arising from accidents, including those involving psychiatric injury.

What kinds of psychiatric injury do your clients have? Most of the psychiatric injury cases we work on are ones where people have also been physically injured. A common problem is chronic pain syndrome. I have had clients who are in so much pain that they can't use one of their arms, for example. If no physical cause can be found for the symptoms, we have to get a psychiatrist's report to see if we can establish whether there's a psychiatric cause.

How difficult are these cases to prove? The main issues we face are having to prove that the claimant's psychiatric injury amounts to a diagnosable psychiatric condition, and also that the client's symptoms have been caused by the accident. If their medical records show that they've had any kind of mental trauma before, the defence will try to prove that their ongoing symptoms are not accident-related. The question of prognosis [how likely the illness is going to last] is also a big issue with psychiatric injury, because it's much harder to predict than for physical injuries.

There is also still a feeling among some judges that clients might be malingering, because you can't see a psychiatric injury like you can a broken leg. And of course the other side will be seeking to show that there isn't a psychiatric injury at all. It's quite common for claimants to be secretly followed or filmed to try to prove this – I had one case where the defendants said that my client couldn't be depressed because they'd seen him going to a café and laughing and talking with friends.

Have you dealt with secondary victims as well? Yes, I've handled two cases where parents have suffered psychiatric injury after their children were killed in car accidents. Both of their children were sadly killed by drivers going through red lights. The parents were very badly affected – the mother in both of the cases was unable to work again – and it completely changed their lives.

What do you think of the law on secondary victims? I feel very strongly that the law relating to these cases is wrong. The requirement for secondary victims to have witnessed the accident or its immediate aftermath is completely unfair and arbitrary, and because the concept of the immediate aftermath is so vague, every judge will put their own interpretation on it.

In the first of my two cases, the parents saw their son's body two hours after the accident, and the barrister who advised us said that they were unlikely to win in court because that wouldn't be accepted as the immediate aftermath. In the second, they saw the body after about an hour, and liability was admitted by the defendants. That distinction really makes no sense. It's completely outside the parents' control when they see the body and what state it's in, and it really doesn't make any difference to the effect on them. Yet the law makes a distinction between the two cases and only one wins.

The other big problem in these cases is that you have to prove that the psychiatric injury is caused by the shock of seeing the body, and not just from the general effect of losing your child in an accident. But how can you realistically distinguish between the two? I've got a case at the moment where the other side's expert is adamant that what my client is experiencing is nothing more than the normal reaction to grief, and it's very difficult to prove otherwise.

How do you think the law should be reformed? I'd like to see the immediate aftermath requirement removed, and for it to be accepted that parents, children and spouses can claim without any extra hurdles in fatal cases. But I do understand that this would open the floodgates to many claims. It's a difficult issue because it means that, for example, in cases involving a child you're going to pretty much double the number of claimants, because there aren't many cases where someone isn't seriously affected by losing a child. They'd still have to prove they have a psychiatric injury of course. I can see the problem, but at the moment, the law is really a minefield that draws very arbitrary distinctions between when secondary victims can claim and when they can't.

Secondary victims: the position of rescuers

Imagine that you are watching television one evening, when you hear a terrible crash outside. You run out and see that two cars have been involved in a head-on collision; two passengers are trapped in one of the cars and are screaming with pain and fear, while the driver of the other has been thrown right through the windscreen and is lying on the ground, unconscious and covered in blood. You are experienced in first aid, so you give what help you can until the ambulance service arrives, but the unconscious driver dies in front of you. You later suffer post-traumatic stress disorder caused by everything you saw and experienced. Should you be able to claim against whoever caused the accident?

Until *White and others* v. *Chief Constable of South Yorkshire Police* (1998), it had always been assumed that the law made special allowances for people who suffered psychiatric injury as a result of helping at the scene of an accident. This was on the grounds of public policy, working on the principle that someone who made the effort to help others in an emergency was performing a service to society, and should therefore be compensated if they suffered any kind of injury as a result.

Case Summary

The leading case which supported this approach was *Chadwick* v. *British Railways Board* (1967), where the claimant spent 12 hours helping victims of a terrible train crash that happened near his home, and in which over 90 people were killed. After the incident he became severely depressed and anxious and ended up unable to work, and the courts allowed his claim for psychiatric injury.

Case Summary

Case Navigator

However, in ***White and others* v. *Chief Constable of South Yorkshire Police*** (1998), the House of Lords stated that rescuers were not to be considered a special category, and should be subject to the same rules as every other kind of secondary victim. As explained earlier, *White* (like *Alcock*) arose from the Hillsborough disaster, but the claimants here were police officers who were on duty at the ground. Three of the four claimants had been at the scene of the crushing incident, and had been involved in getting dead and injured people out of the fenced-in areas and trying to resuscitate the victims. The fourth had moved bodies into the temporary mortuary set up at the opposite end of the ground, and had obtained first aid for some of the injured.

The claimants argued that, as rescuers, they were not secondary victims at all and so should not be subject to the restrictions laid down in *Alcock*. The House of Lords rejected both arguments. It stated that only those who were in danger of physical injury (and possibly those who were not but reasonably believed they were: see Lord Steyn's view on page 111) could be viewed as primary victims. Everyone else was a secondary victim. This meant that, even if a claimant was a rescuer, they could not make a claim for psychiatric injury unless they had a close relationship with at least one primary victim. As none of the police officers had such a relationship with any of the victims, none of them could claim as rescuers (we will look at their claim as employees in the next section).

The claimants in *White* were not, of course, in exactly the same position as the claimant in *Chadwick*. He was an ordinary member of the public who helped out voluntarily, whereas the claimants in *White* were helping as part of their job. The House of Lords could, therefore, have kept the special treatment of voluntary rescuers like Mr Chadwick but ruled that professional rescuers should be treated like any other secondary victims. This approach could have been justified by the argument that there should be no need to encourage professional rescuers to act in ways that were already expected of them in their jobs, and so the public policy reasons do not apply to them in the same way. However, in *White* the House of Lords chose to go further than this, and state that voluntary rescuers were not a special category and must be treated in the same way as professional rescuers. Where a rescuer, whether voluntary or professional, was themselves in physical danger, they could claim as a primary victim, but where they were not at risk of physical harm they would be secondary victims and must pass the tests set down in *Alcock*.

Two main reasons for the ruling were given by Lord Hoffmann. First, that allowing rescuers to be a special case would sooner or later lead to difficult distinctions. If you abandon the line between those who are in physical danger and those who are not, how much help would someone have to give in order to be considered a rescuer and not merely an onlooker? Secondly, said Lord Hoffmann, it would be seen as unjust to allow the police officers to claim, given that their conditions of employment provided for them to be compensated in other ways (such as sick pay), when the families of the dead had been given nothing. While this may be true (and the public was already angry about the denial of the families' claims), it does not explain why the House of Lords felt it necessary to use the case to make rules about voluntary rescuers.

Another strange element of the decision is that Lord Hoffmann claimed his judgment was not a change in the law. He said that existing rescuer cases were merely examples of the standard rules on cases of psychiatric injury, because those claimants who had been compensated were all at risk of physical injury, and so were treated as primary victims. In the leading case of *Chadwick*, at least, this is questionable. There was a theoretical risk that the railway carriage the claimant was in could collapse, but it is very clear that the court did not treat that as a main reason for allowing his claim. Lord Hoffmann's reasoning on this point makes the impact of the judgment less clear than it seems at first. If Mr Chadwick could be considered a primary victim, it may be that what the *White* decision actually does is to allow the courts to take a wide view of whether a claimant was in physical danger. They can then use that reasoning to allow or refuse a claim. This would mean that some rescuers would still be able to make a claim, because if the court decided they were at physical risk they would be considered primary victims.

Out and about

Read the case of *White* v. *Chief Constable of South Yorkshire Police* (1998), concentrating particularly on the sections relating to the police officers' claim as rescuers. Now go through the text again, and note down, in your own words, the main arguments made in favour of allowing rescuers to be treated as a special case, and the main arguments made against this. Which seem strongest to you? Do you think the decision was right? Can you think of any other arguments you would have made if you were the barrister representing the police officers?

Writing and drafting

You are a trainee solicitor. Your firm likes to encourage the staff to think critically about the law, and your boss has asked you to do a presentation on the position of rescuers who suffer psychiatric injury so that a group of colleagues can debate the subject. Prepare a PowerPoint presentation explaining what the current position is, and what criticisms can be made of the current law. If you can, try to think of how the law could be defined in a way that you think would be fair to both rescuers and those they would be seeking to sue. You might also want to suggest some questions for your colleagues to debate.

Secondary victims: employees

At the time of *White and others* v. *Chief Constable of South Yorkshire Police* (1998), it was, and still is, established law that employers owe a duty to take reasonable care that employees are not physically injured at work. So, as an alternative to their claim as rescuers, the police officers in *White* also tried to claim that they were owed a duty of care as employees of the party whose negligence caused the shocking event that triggered their psychiatric injury. This, they said, meant they should not be considered as secondary victims. Case Summary

The House of Lords rejected their claim. They said that the employers' duty to employees was not a separate tort with its own rules, but an aspect of the law of negligence, and therefore subject to the normal rules of negligence. This meant that, where a claimant suffered a type of injury that was subject to special restrictions on when a duty of care would exist, these rules applied in just the same way as they usually would, regardless of the fact that the claimant was the defendant's employee. There was no special duty of care regarding psychiatric injury caused by employers to their employees, just the normal rules. Those rules meant that unless an employee was in physical danger, they would be treated as a secondary victim, and as none of the police officers had a close relationship with any of the dead, they could not claim as secondary victims.

An example of a case where an employee was treated as a primary victim is *Cullin* v. *London Fire and Civil Defence Authority* (1999), where the claimant was a firefighter. He suffered psychiatric injury after an incident in which two colleagues were trapped inside a burning building. The claimant was among those who tried to rescue his colleagues, but it proved impossible and he was there when their bodies were carried out. His employers tried to have the claim struck out, on the grounds that his situation was similar to that of the police officers in *White*, but the Court disagreed. It was at least arguable that he was, or reasonably believed himself to be, in physical danger during the rescue attempt, and so the case should not be struck out. Case Summary

Secondary victims: bystanders

White, *Alcock* and *McLoughlin* make it clear than bystanders who have no relationship with the victims of an accident, and are not themselves in any physical danger, are very unlikely to be able to sue successfully for psychiatric injury. This upholds the traditional position spelt out in *Bourhill* v. *Young*, the case we looked at earlier, where the claimant suffered psychiatric injury as a result of seeing the aftermath of a motorbike accident, but the court ruled that an ordinary bystander could be expected to withstand the shock of such a sight.

However, in *Alcock* the point was made that there might be very rare occasions when an incident was so horrific that psychiatric damage even to uninvolved bystanders might be foreseeable, and there a duty of care would arise. The House of Lords gave the rather lurid example of a petrol tanker crashing into a school playground full of children and bursting into flames. If something as terrible as this were to happen, they suggested, even a passer-by who had no connection with anyone in the school might have a claim for psychiatric injury.

Secondary victims: unwitting agents

There is one category of claimant whose position was left unclear by the decision in *White*, and to some extent is still unclear. This is the group known as 'unwitting agents', who suffer psychiatric injury because something they have (or fear they have) done caused the death of another, but the ultimate cause is someone else's negligence. An example of this situation is *Dooley* v. *Cammell Laird* (1951). The claimant was operating a crane at the docks where he worked. Through no fault of his, the crane dropped a heavy load into the hold of the ship that was being unloaded. His colleagues were working in the hold and Mr Dooley was terrified that they might have been hurt or killed. In fact no one was injured, but Mr Dooley suffered psychiatric injury as a result of the incident. He was able to claim successfully against the defendants, whose negligence caused the load to fall.

Case Summary

Until *White*, *Dooley* and a couple of similar cases were regarded as establishing that unwitting agents had a right to sue for psychiatric injury, even if they were not themselves at risk of physical injury. But in *White*, Lord Hoffmann stated that there was no such right. He pointed out that all the unwitting agent cases were first instance cases that did not reach the higher courts, and were decided before the *Alcock* restrictions were put in place. However, he said that there might be grounds for treating unwitting agents as a special case, and not subjecting them to the *Alcock* control restrictions. Rather unhelpfully though, as the question was not actually at issue in *White*, their Lordships did not decide it either way.

The issue was examined again in *Hunter* v. *British Coal* (1998). Here Mr Hunter was a driver in a coal mine who accidentally hit a water hydrant while manoeuvring his vehicle. Water immediately began spurting out of the hydrant, so he went to find a hose, to channel it away safely, leaving behind a colleague, Tommy Carter. When Mr Hunter was about 30 metres away he heard the hydrant explode, and rushed to find the valve to turn it off, which took about 10 minutes. During that time, he heard a message over the public address system saying that a man had been injured, and on his way back to the accident scene he was told by another worker that it looked as though Mr Carter had been killed. This turned out to be correct, and Mr Hunter's belief that he had caused his colleague's death caused him to suffer clinical depression.

Case Summary

When it became clear that in fact the accident had happened because his employer had failed to put certain safety procedures in place, he sued. The Court of Appeal rejected his case. They regarded him as a secondary victim, and said his claim failed because he was not present at the accident or its immediate aftermath. His depression had been caused by hearing about the death, and that was not sufficient.

However, it is not clear that *Hunter* definitely means an unwitting agent is a secondary victim. The latest House of Lords word on the subject comes in *W* v. *Essex County Council* (2000). The claimants were foster parents who had four young children of their own. The council assigned them a foster child who had a history of sexually abusing other children, but did not tell the foster parents this. He abused their children and the foster parents suffered psychiatric injury as a result. There was no risk of physical injury which would make the parents primary victims, and it appeared that they could not claim as secondary victims either because they did not actually witness the abuse. The council therefore applied to have the case struck out, but the House of Lords refused and said it was at least arguable that there was a duty of care in this situation.

Case Summary

Lord Slynn confirmed that the category of primary victims was not closed after *Alcock*, and might still include, for example, people who suffer psychiatric injury because they believe they have contributed to causing harm to another. Lord Slynn said that if this category did count as primary victims, the foster parents might fall within it, as their psychiatric injury was partly triggered by their feelings of guilt, because it was their decision to allow the foster child into their home (even though they did not know his history) and/or because they did not spot what was happening earlier.

Lord Slynn emphasised that he was not saying that there was definitely a duty of care in the claimants' situation, only that it was arguable that there might be. Unfortunately the question remains unanswered because the case never came to trial. It was settled out of court in January 2002, with the council paying compensation of £190,000.

Out and about

Working in pairs, take turns at playing a claimant and their solicitor. The claimant is seeing the solicitor because they have suffered post-traumatic stress disorder as a result of an accident which was caused negligently. The student playing the role of the claimant should prepare a (fictional) story to form the facts of the case. The accident can be as dramatic or unusual as you like, and you can be a witness to the accident, a rescuer, an unwitting agent, or a relative of someone killed in the accident, or a combination of these. Decide whether you were at the scene, and if so, how you were involved; or whether you found out about it afterwards, and if so, when and how. Add as much detail as you can, whether or not you think it is relevant to the legal case.

The solicitor should then interview the client, with the aim of working out whether they may have a claim, and then explain their conclusion to the client.

Handy tip: The solicitor needs to find out whether the claimant passes the tests set down in *White*, but remember, your client is not legally trained. That means that there is no point in asking, for example, 'Did you witness the immediate aftermath?' because the client will not know what this means. Instead, to find out whether they witnessed the immediate aftermath, you need to establish when and how they found out about the accident, and then look at the cases of *McLoughlin*, *Alcock* and *White* for guidance on whether it counts as the immediate aftermath. You will need to follow a similar process with the other tests for secondary victims.

To make the exercise realistic, the student playing the victim should remember that something terrible and shocking has happened to them – feel free to get upset, to ramble on endlessly about irrelevant details, or find it difficult to 'remember' certain details!

Reflective practice

Take a few minutes to think about how this exercise went. What did you find difficult? When you played the solicitor, was it easy to decide what questions to ask, or more difficult than you expected? What did you find worked well for you? Is there anything you would do differently if you did a similar exercise?

Psychiatric injury not caused by shocking events

The cases so far in this chapter have all concerned psychiatric injury caused by witnessing or being involved in a shocking event such as a serious accident, but there are other ways that psychiatric injury can be caused. The courts have tended to apply different rules for these, declining to use the primary/secondary victim approach detailed in *Alcock* and *White*.

Case Summary

In *CJD Group B Claimants* v. *The Medical Research Council* (1998), the claimants had all had medical problems as children, which stopped them growing properly. They were treated with a growth hormone which, it was later discovered, might have been contaminated with the virus which causes Creutzfeldt-Jakob Disease (CJD), a fatal brain condition. It was known that anyone who had received the contaminated injections was at risk of developing the illness, but it was not possible to find out which batches of the growth hormone had been contaminated, nor to test the claimants to find which of them had received the contaminated hormone. As a result, the claimants were having to live with the knowledge that they might develop the disease, and this had caused them to suffer psychiatric injury.

It was established that the defendants had been negligent, because they had carried on giving the hormone injections even after the risk of transmitting CJD was suspected. The claimants argued that, with regard to psychiatric injury, they were owed a duty as primary victims, because the injections they were given made them more than mere bystanders. Their situation, they said, was more like that of the claimant in *Page* v. *Smith*, who you may remember was involved in a car accident which could have physically injured him but instead reactivated a previous psychiatric injury (see page 111).

Mr Justice Morland disagreed with this approach. He said they were not primary victims in the usual sense, because it was not the injections that triggered their psychiatric injury but the knowledge, which came later, that they might be at risk of developing CJD. Even so, he allowed their claim, but neither as primary nor as secondary victims. Instead, he used a straightforward application of the *Caparo* test: there was a relationship of proximity between the parties, the psychiatric injuries were reasonably foreseeable, and it was fair, just and reasonable to allow the claim.

Similarly, there have been a number of cases involving psychiatric injury caused by stress at work, and the courts have not used the *Alcock*/*White* approach in these either. Instead, they treat these cases as part of the law covering an employer's duty to take reasonable steps to protect their employees' safety. This is covered in Chapter 7.

Figure 4.2 Liability for psychiatric injury

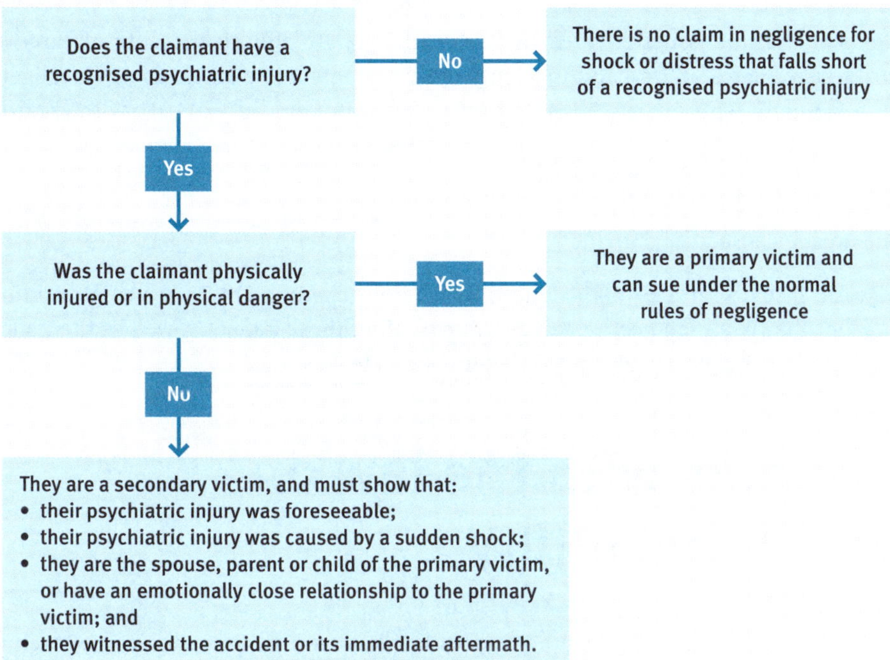

Key stats Compensation for psychiatric injury

How much compensation a claimant can be awarded for psychiatric injury will depend on how far the injury affects their day-to-day life. Claims generally fall into one of four bands:

- *Minor*: the psychiatric injury was temporary and the claimant has recovered. Damages in this kind of case are usually between £800 and £3,250, depending on how far the injury affected the claimant's daily activities, their work or their sleep.
- *Moderate*: the claimant is unable to cope with ordinary life and work, and their future is unclear, but by the time of the trial their condition is improving and the chances of recovery are good. These cases typically result in damages of £3,250 to £10,500.
- *Moderately severe*: the claimant is unable to cope with ordinary life and work, and their future is unclear, but the medical evidence suggests their illness may get better. In these cases damages are typically between £10,500 and £30,000, with the majority of cases around the middle of this range.
- *Severe*: the claimant is unable to cope with ordinary life and work, and the situation is not expected to get much better. These cases typically attract damages of £30,000 to £63,000.

Tackling psychiatric injury questions

Remember that the issues covered in this chapter relate only to the duty of care with regard to psychiatric injury, and that duty of care is only one element of any negligence case. A claimant who can establish that the defendant has a duty of care with regard to their psychiatric injury also has to prove the other elements of negligence:

- the defendant breached the duty of care;
- the breach caused the damage.

If you are faced with a problem question where a claimant has a psychiatric injury, remember that you may need to cover some or all of these issues, as well as the issue of duty of care, and you may also need to consider defences.

Problems with the law on psychiatric injury

McLoughlin, Alcock and *White* have muddled rather than clarified the law

Usually, when an area of law has seen a number of cases reach the House of Lords in recent years, the result is that the law becomes clearer. But if anything, the cases of *McLoughlin, Alcock* and *White* have muddled rather than clarified the law, and it is very hard to find a logical justification for large parts of the decisions. The following issues are some of the problems that now arise.

The requirement for 'reasonable fortitude'

In *White*, the House of Lords confirmed that someone who witnesses an accident but is not at personal risk can only be compensated for psychiatric injury if a person of 'reasonable fortitude' would have suffered psychiatric injury in the same circumstances. There is no comparable rule for physical injury, and creating one for psychiatric injury seems to hark back to the old belief that psychiatric injury is linked to emotional weakness, and that people can somehow choose whether or not to give in to it.

The position of rescuers

As we saw earlier, rescuers were formerly thought to be a special case with regard to psychiatric injury. Because it was considered a good thing for society that people volunteered to help those involved in accidents, a rescuer who suffered psychiatric shock would not be subject to the same restrictions as a mere bystander. *White*, as we saw, changes this, but this aspect of the decision was criticised by Lords Goff and Griffiths, who gave dissenting judgments in the case. A key element criticised by Lord Goff was Lord Hoffmann's claim that rescuers had in fact never been a special case. The previous leading case on rescuers had been *Chadwick* (where the claimant helped train crash victims), and Lord Hoffmann said this fitted in with his analysis because there was a danger of the train carriage collapsing, which put the claimant at physical risk and therefore made him a primary victim. Lord Goff disputed this argument. He pointed out that the trial judge in *Chadwick* treated the potential danger to the claimant as irrelevant, and was right to do so because it was not the physical risk to himself that caused Mr Chadwick's psychiatric injury, but the horror of spending hours surrounded by the terrible sights and sounds of the accident scene.

Lord Goff also pointed out that making rescuers' claims dependent on whether they were at risk of physical injury could lead to unjust distinctions. He gave the example of two men going to help in the aftermath of a train crash, one at the front of the train and one at the back, where the situation happened to be that helping victims in the front half of the train involved some threat of physical danger, and working in the back half did not. Each of the two men might perform the same service, suffer the same trauma and end up living with the same degree of psychiatric injury, yet one would be able to claim compensation and the other would not. This distinction, said Lord Goff, was 'surely unacceptable'.

The 'immediate aftermath' requirement

It was established in *Alcock* that secondary victims must also have been present at the accident, or to have witnessed its 'immediate aftermath'. It is not enough to be told about the accident by a third party, or to see it on television. Again, it is very difficult to see a rational justification for this distinction. In *McLoughlin*, the deciding factor seemed to be that the sight of the claimant's relatives, still covered in blood and clearly in pain, was particularly distressing and shocking. But is it necessarily more shocking than, for example, sitting down to watch a football match on television, and then witnessing fans being crushed to death, when you know your own son is at the match and could be one of them? Is it any more distressing than hearing about the accident at Hillsborough and then spending all night at the ground, searching for your brother, as one of the *Alcock* claimants did?

In practical terms, the proximity requirements clearly work as a way of setting limits on the numbers of people who can sue, because there will only ever be a limited number of people who witness an accident or its aftermath, while there may be many more who hear about it afterwards in some way. Whether they achieve justice for victims is another question.

The 'sudden shock' requirement

As with the proximity and closeness of relationship requirements, it is hard to find a rational basis for the line drawn between psychiatric injury caused by a sudden shock, and the same injury caused by, for example, the long-term stress of caring for a relative seriously injured by another's negligence. So long as the psychiatric injury is a foreseeable result of the claimant's negligence, why should it matter whether it was caused by a shock or not?

Take, for example, the case of *Sion* v. *Hampstead Health Authority* (1994). Here a father suffered psychiatric injury after watching his son slowly die as a result of negligent medical treatment. Had the son died suddenly as a result of a fatal heart attack caused by his poor medical treatment, and his father been there to witness it, the father might well have been able to get compensation for psychiatric injury suffered as a result. Why should the fact that he watched his son die slowly, with all the stress and grief that must cause, change his situation? The defendant's treatment of his son was no less negligent because it did not cause a sudden shock. Nor is the father's psychiatric injury less real, or less foreseeable.

why have two completely different sets of rules for the same type of injury?

The sudden shock requirement makes even less sense when you consider that the courts allow claims for psychiatric injury caused by prolonged stress at work, using a different set of rules to those for accident cases. Why should stress in the workplace be considered more harmful than the stress of seeing a loved one in pain and distress over a long period of time, or of having to look after someone who has been seriously injured and will never recover? And why have two completely different sets of rules for the same type of injury?

Reform of the law

The law on psychiatric injury with regard to secondary victims has been widely criticised, and as far back as 1998 the Law Commission's report, *Liability for Psychiatric Illness* found that the current law was too restrictive. The Commission argued that the requirement for a close tie between primary and secondary victims was justified and should remain, but said this should be enough. The requirements of proximity and sudden shock should be abandoned. To date there appear to have been no moves towards this, either by the courts or Parliament.

Writing and drafting

You work at the Law Commission, which oversees reform of the law. The Commission decides to prepare a new report on liability for psychiatric injury. You are asked to look at the question of whether it should be made easier for the parents, children or spouses of accident victims to claim for psychiatric injury. Draw up a list of the problems you see with the law as it stands (if any), and suggest how you think the law could be improved, or whether it should stay the same. If you suggest changes, remember to consider any problems that your changes could cause, and how you would address those.

Handy tip: As well as the material in this chapter, you may find it useful to look at the material on pages 6–8, which assesses how the tort system works in practice.

Summary

- To claim for psychiatric injury, a claimant has to prove that they have a medically recognised illness or injury which is either:
  - a physical illness or injury, caused by a mental shock; or
  - a recognised mental illness.
- Psychiatric injury victims are categorised as:
  - primary victims, who are themselves physically injured or at risk of physical injury;
  - secondary victims who suffer psychiatric injury from witnessing physical injury to others.
- Secondary victims fall into four groups:
  - relatives and friends;
  - rescuers;
  - employees;
  - bystanders.
- The position of unwitting agents is still unclear, but they may be primary victims.
- Primary victim cases use the *Caparo* test for duty of care.
- The duty of care test in secondary victim cases is that the claimant must:
  - suffer psychiatric injury that is foreseeable;
  - suffer psychiatric injury caused by a sudden shock;
  - have a close relationship with the primary victim; and
  - witness the shocking event or its immediate aftermath.
- Problems with the law include:
  - the requirement for 'reasonable fortitude';
  - the position of rescuers;
  - the 'immediate aftermath' requirement;
  - the 'sudden shock' requirement.

Question and answer*

Problem:

Stinkychem Ltd is a company which makes industrial cleaning products. The manufacturing process uses some dangerous chemicals. Owing to Stinkychem's negligence, some of the chemicals have been wrongly labelled, and when one of their employees, Nigel, mixes the wrong two chemicals together there is a big explosion. Nigel is not physically hurt but Kenton, a colleague, is killed in the explosion. Nigel is later diagnosed with post-traumatic stress disorder.

Lizzie is walking past Stinkychem's factory when the explosion happens. She doesn't know anyone who works there, but the incident shocks and frightens her and she later develops an anxiety disorder.

Kenton's brother, Phil, works for another company whose offices are across the road. Kenton and Phil had a huge row a year ago and have not spoken since. Phil hears the explosion and rushes outside, and half an hour later he is present when Kenton's body is brought out of the building. He is later diagnosed with depression.

Advise Nigel, Lizzie and Phil as to whether they can sue Stinkychem in negligence.

You should allow yourself no more than 40 minutes to complete this task.

Essay:

The law on secondary victims of psychiatric shock has been widely criticised as over-complex, vague and lacking in rational principles. Do you agree?

This question should be answered in 40 minutes.

* Answer guidance is provided at the end of the chapter.

Further reading and references

Law Commission Report 249 (1998) *Liability for Psychiatric Illness*, London: The Stationery Office.
This Law Commission report criticises the law on secondary victims, and recommends that wider liability should be allowed.

Mullender, R. and Speirs, A. (2000) 'Negligence, psychiatric injury and the altruism principle', 20 OJLS 645.
This very interesting article looks at the position of rescuers. It argues that not allowing their claims goes against a principle of law, that of encouraging altruistic behaviour, but that even so, refusing such claims is defensible in the interests of society as a whole.

Stapleton, J. (1994) 'In Restraint of Tort', in P. Birks, *The Frontiers of Liability*, Vol. 2, Oxford: Oxford University Press, p. 95.
Jane Stapleton is a very well-known and respected expert on tort law, who always has an interesting argument to make. In this article she argues that there is no reasonable basis for allowing claims for nervous shock, and they should not exist.

Teff, H. (1992) 'Liability for psychiatric illness after Hillsborough', 12 OJLS 440.
This is a detailed look at the key cases on psychiatric injury, in which the author argues that the current law is too restrictive. It is a good, clear read with lots of useful arguments you can quote in essays.

Teff, H. (1998) 'Liability for negligently inflicted psychiatric harm: justifications and boundaries', 57(1) CLJ 91.
In this article, the author argues against some of the views put forward by Jane Stapleton (see above), and discusses where the boundaries for psychiatric injury claims could and should be drawn. Taken together, these two sets of views will give you lots of useful material for essays.

Question and answer guidance

Problem: In any problem question involving psychiatric injury, your starting point should be to decide whether each person you need to look at is a primary or a secondary victim. Starting with Nigel, it would appear that he is a primary victim, because he was in the explosion which killed Kenton, and so we can assume that he too was at physical risk, even though he was not in fact physically hurt. As a primary victim, he can sue for his psychiatric injury using the standard *Caparo* test for personal injury, and you should explain what this is and apply it to his situation.

Turning to Lizzie, she is clearly a secondary victim, because she was not physically injured herself, nor at risk of physical injury. You therefore need to apply the four tests set down in *McLoughlin* and *Alcock*. Of particular importance in Lizzie's case is the fact that she is a mere bystander with no connection to the accident or anyone at risk in it.

Phil is also a secondary victim, so again, apply the *McLoughlin*/*Alcock* tests. Here, the important elements will be Phil's relationship to Kenton – given the fact that they have not spoken for a year, is it close in care and fact? – and whether he was there at the 'immediate aftermath' of the explosion. You will need to use material from the key cases to back up your arguments.

Essay: A good way to begin this essay would be to explain what secondary victims are, and why they are subject to special rules. Then, to give your essay a clear structure, you could take each criticism in turn, and give some examples of areas of the law to which it applies – which parts of the law do you find vague, which over-complex, and which lacking in rational principles? You will find useful material for making these arguments in the section on pages 126–128, and in the articles suggested in the Further reading section. As a conclusion, you could say whether you think the law could be improved, perhaps mentioning the proposals for reform put forward by the Law Commission.

Visit **www.mylawchamber.co.uk/quinntort** to access tools to help you develop and test your knowledge of tort law, including practice exam questions with guidance, annotated weblinks, glossary and key case flashcards, legal newsfeed and legal updates and interactive 'You be the judge' questions.

premium mylawchamber
unrivalled support for legal education

Use Case Navigator to read in full some of the key cases referenced in this chapter with commentary and questions:

White and others* v. *Chief Constable of the South Yorkshire Police and others [1999] 1 All ER 1

CASE NAVIGATOR
POWERED BY LexisNexis

Chapter 5
Negligence: economic loss

Key points In this chapter we will be looking at:

- What economic loss is
- The circumstances in which negligence law allows a claim for economic loss
- Reasons why claims for economic loss are restricted

Introduction

There is probably no one in Britain who likes roadworks. They delay our journeys, divert our buses, and just when one lot are finished someone else always seems to come along and start all over again. But next time you are stuck in a traffic jam because someone is digging up ahead, spare a thought for the owners of a company called Spartan Steel, who, back in 1969, had more reason than most of us to get annoyed about holes in the road – and as a result, gave us a case which very neatly explains the subject of this chapter.

The case is called *Spartan Steel* v. *Martin* (1972), and it arose because in June 1969 workers digging up a road near Spartan Steel's factory damaged an electricity cable, which meant the factory had no power for nearly 15 hours. The factory usually made steel 24 hours day but it could not work without electricity, and the power cut cost the firm £2,535 (which would be the equivalent of around £25,000 today). Yet when they sued the contractors who had negligently damaged the power cable, the court said they were only entitled to compensation of £768 (about £7,550 in today's money). This was because part of the claim was for what is known as pure economic loss, and, as we will see in this chapter, the courts have traditionally been reluctant to compensate this form of loss. To some extent this is still the case, though we will also see in this chapter that there are now some important exceptions to this rule.

What is pure economic loss?

Of course, many losses arising from negligence can be described as economic, in the sense that they involve money. If your house burns down because of someone's negligence, or if someone crashes into your car, the loss is economic in the sense that it will cost money to rebuild the house or fix the car. Even personal injury often involves some economic loss, if it means the victim cannot work. But there is no problem with compensating these losses, because there is a **duty of care** regarding both property damage and personal injury, and these losses arise from breach of one of those duties.

Pure economic loss (which we will refer to from now on simply as **economic loss**) is loss that does not result from property damage or personal injury, though it does result from the **defendant**'s negligence.

We can see how this works if we look at the claim in *Spartan Steel*. At the time the electricity went off, the factory was melting metal in a furnace so that it could be made into steel bars. With no power to keep the furnace hot, there was a risk that the metal might solidify and damage the inside of the furnace. To get it out, the workers at Spartan Steel had to add oxygen to the liquid metal, and this reduced the quality of the metal. That made it worth £368 (about £3,620) less than it had been before, so they claimed this amount from the defendants. The damaged metal was Spartan Steel's property and, as we have already seen, property damage is a standard form of damage in negligence, so there was no problem with allowing this part of the claim. If they had been able to make the metal into bars as planned, Spartan Steel would have made a profit of £400 (£3,930) on it. The court also allowed this second part of the claim, because the loss of profit was a foreseeable consequence of the damage to the metal.

However, the third element of their claim was a different story. During the 14.5 hours that the power was off, Spartan Steel would have worked on a further four batches of steel in the furnace, which would have been sold at a profit of £1,767 (£17,400). They claimed this amount too, but this part of the claim was refused. This was because the court found that it was pure economic loss, which did not result from any damage to Spartan's Steel's property. The defendants had a duty to take reasonable steps not to damage Spartan Steel's property, but they did not have a duty to protect their profits, and so there was no liability for this part of the claim.

Before we go on to look at liability for economic loss, it is important to know that there are two basic ways in which economic loss can be caused: by actions and by words. The loss in *Spartan Steel* is an example of economic loss caused by action: the digging up of the road and the resulting damage to the cable. But how can this kind of loss be caused by words alone? As an example, let's say you are thinking of buying a business and you want to know how much money you could make from it. You do not want to take the word of the person selling it, because they may exaggerate its potential profits, so you check with their accountant, who says the company is making a good profit. You buy the business but, as it turns out, the accountant has been negligent and the business is in fact making a loss. If you then fail to make the profit that the accountant led you to expect, you could argue that the accountant's advice caused your loss. Similarly, if you are offered a job, but the offer is withdrawn because your previous boss negligently mixes you up with another employee and gives you a bad reference, their words have clearly caused you economic loss. As we will see later, the distinction between economic loss caused by acts and that caused by words is an important one.

You be the judge

Q: **Grant owns a small car repair business. Owing to his negligence there is an explosion in his workshop, which causes a fire. The fire causes smoke damage to the café next door owned by Ian, and as a result he is unable to open the café for a week. It costs him £1,000 to get the damage cleaned up, and he loses £5,000 in profit through not being able to open. Peggy owns a pub a few doors down from Grant's workshop. Although her pub is not damaged in the fire, the street was closed off for a whole evening while the fire brigade fought the fire, and she lost £300 in profit because no customers were able to get to the pub.**

Is Ian's claim pure economic loss? Is Peggy's?

A: Ian's claim is not pure economic loss, because it results from the damage to his café. Therefore he can claim for both the damage itself and the loss of profit caused by that damage. Peggy's claim, however, is pure economic loss, because there was no damage to her property, nor injury to her. She will not be able to claim for her loss of profit.

Liability for economic loss

So now we know what economic loss is, we can look at when a defendant will be liable for it. The traditional position in tort law was that there was no duty of care for economic loss. This has been modified to an extent over the past 50 years, but before we look at the current position it is worth understanding why the court sought to limit claims for economic loss in the first place. One of the reasons for this is one which you should by now be familiar with: the '**floodgates**' argument. While in most situations an act or omission can only cause personal injury or property damage to a limited number of people, the same act or omission could cause economic loss to many more. In *Spartan Steel*, for example, the damaged electricity cable might have been supplying electricity to a large number of different businesses, all of whom might potentially have lost profits if their power was cut off for nearly 15 hours. The courts have decided that, even though such losses would clearly be caused by the defendant's negligence, such wide and potentially unpredictable liability is not desirable.

A second reason for limiting claims for economic loss is that traditionally these claims belonged in the law of contract. A contract is typically an agreement between two parties, in which each party gives something for what they get. Both of them know and agree what they are expected to give, and what they expect to get, and if one party fails to deliver the agreed benefit, contract law allows a claim for it. This provides certainty, especially in business, because defendants can only be liable for losses caused by their own failure to fulfil an agreement. Allowing such claims in negligence, by contrast, could create uncertainty, because defendants might find themselves liable to a wide number of claimants with whom they have not made any agreement. As part of the law's job is to provide people and companies with a framework within which they can plan their activities, this kind of uncertainty is seen as a bad thing.

> The position of claims for economic loss in negligence has varied over the years

The position of claims for economic loss in negligence has varied over the years, with the law swinging backwards and forwards between allowing such claims and restricting them. The result is that today there is generally a duty of care regarding economic loss caused by negligent statements and advice, though only in very specific circumstances, but there is no duty of care for economic loss which is caused by a negligent act. To understand how this quite strange situation came about, we need to look at a bit of legal history, which will help you understand the current law when we come to look at it.

The traditional rule

The traditional position was that there was no duty in law not to cause economic loss unless there was a contractual relationship. This can be seen in the case of *Cattle* v. *Stockton Waterworks Co.* (1875). The **claimant** was involved in building a tunnel for a landowner called Mr Knight, and the price for the work had been agreed under the contract between them. The defendants negligently damaged a water pipe, which flooded the tunnel, and the delays this caused meant Mr Cattle's profit on the job was reduced. He sued the defendants for his loss, but the Court held that he could not claim back the money because it was pure economic loss. *Cattle* v. *Stockton* was decided before the modern law of negligence really began but, as we will see, the principle continued into modern law.

Case Summary

Cattle v. *Stockton* concerned economic loss caused by a negligent act, but traditionally the same rule applied where economic loss was caused by a negligent statement, as we can see from the case of *Candler* v. *Crane Christmas and Co.* (1951). Here Crane Christmas, who were a firm of accountants, had prepared some accounts for a company, knowing that the figures would also be shown to Mr Candler who was thinking of investing in that company. On the basis of the figures they supplied, Mr Candler did invest, but the accounts had been prepared negligently and were inaccurate. As a result, he lost money and sued Crane Christmas. The Court of Appeal held that his claim failed, because there was no duty of care to prevent economic loss where there was no contractual relationship.

Case Summary

The swing towards wider liability

As we saw in Chapter 2, the modern law of negligence really began in 1932 with the case of *Donoghue* v. *Stevenson*, which established the **neighbour principle** – the principle that you are liable for damage caused to anyone who you can foresee being damaged by something you do or fail to do. In the years following that case the courts began to expand the situations in which the neighbour principle applied, but they did so quite cautiously. When a new factual situation came before them, they would look to see whether there was already a precedent for applying the **neighbour test** in a similar situation. For example, it was already established that motorists owed a duty to other road users, and employers to employees, so the neighbour test was applied to these situations. If the situation before them was not one where a duty already existed, the courts might create a new one, but they would first ask if there were good policy reasons for doing so. This means that they would consider not just the legal framework, but whether society would benefit from such a duty. Only if the answer was yes would they create a new duty. One result of this cautiousness was that the traditional rule against liability for economic loss was kept.

In the early 1960s, the House of Lords made a major change to the law, in the case of *Hedley Byrne* v. *Heller* (1963). They said that claims for economic loss caused by misstatements should now be allowed, but only where there was a 'special relationship between the parties', and the defendants had supplied advice or information knowing that the claimants would rely on it for a particular purpose. This type of claim is known as **negligent misstatement**, and it is now an important part of the law of negligence. We will look at the facts of this case and the changes it made later in this chapter, but for now let's carry on with an overview of the history.

So, after *Hedley Byrne*, the position was that claims for economic loss caused by negligent misstatements were allowed in certain circumstances, but claims for economic loss caused by acts or omissions were not. By the 1970s, however, the original cautious approach to negligence was being widely criticised by some judges, who believed that the law should be used to create wider liability for damage negligently caused to others. Their view began to gather support, and in *Anns* v. *Merton London Borough* (1978), the House of Lords decided it was time to move the law on.

Case Summary

The claimants in *Anns* were living in flats in a block which was negligently built and sued the builders, and the council who had approved the building works, for the cost of repairs. The case against the builders was settled, but the council argued that it had no duty of care. At first glance the damage in this case might look like property damage, but the courts had always held that a defect in property is not the same thing as damage. Where a defect caused personal injury or property damage, the victim could claim for those types of damage, but the defect itself was always considered economic loss because it arises from the reduced value of the defective thing. So, following the traditional principle, the claimants would not have been able to claim.

However, the House of Lords decided that it was time to change this, and in the process widen the scope of the law of negligence generally. Lord Wilberforce, giving the leading judgment, said that the approach to new duties of care should change. In order to decide whether a duty of care existed in a new factual situation, the courts should use a two-stage test. First, they should ask whether the parties satisfied the neighbour test: was the claimant someone to whom the defendant could reasonably be expected to foresee a risk of harm? If they were, the second test was to ask whether there were any reasons of policy which suggested that a duty should not exist. If not, a duty of care should be imposed. This meant that new duties of care could be created wherever the neighbour test was satisfied, unless there were good policy reasons not to. It was no longer necessary to find a good policy reason in favour of creating a new duty, only to make sure that there was no good reason not to. This made it likely that many more claims would be allowed.

In *Anns* itself, the claimants clearly passed the neighbour test and the House of Lords decided that there were no good policy reasons for denying a duty. But Lord Wilberforce neatly skipped over the issue of whether this new approach meant that economic loss for negligent acts should now be compensated, by simply deciding that the defect in the building was property damage for which there had always been a duty of care.

Case Summary

However, the House of Lords faced the issue head-on in the case of *Junior Books* v. *Veitchi* (1983). The claimants had had a factory built for them under a contract with a building firm. The factory needed a special type of floor in order to support the weight of the machinery they planned to use, and they asked the builders to use Veitchi, a specialist flooring firm, to provide the floor. After Veitchi laid the floor it was found to be defective. If the factory owners had contracted directly with Veitchi they could have sued in contract, but their only contract was with the building company and it was

Veitchi, not the builders, who had been negligent. The floor was not dangerous, and nor did it cause damage to the building, which meant that Junior Books' claim for the cost of replacing the flooring was pure economic loss.

Applying the *Anns* two-stage test, the House of Lords said the claimants passed the neighbour test, because it was clearly foreseeable that if Veitchi carried out the work negligently Junior Books would suffer a loss. Regarding the second stage of the test, the only reason which had been put forward for not imposing a duty was that the claim was for economic loss, and such claims had not been allowed before. Lord Roskill, giving the leading judgment, said this was not a good enough reason to deny a duty of care. The House of Lords therefore found that there was a duty of care from the flooring company to the factory owners. This meant that it was now possible to claim for economic loss by acts, using the new two-stage *Anns* test, as well as for economic loss caused by statements, under the rules in *Hedley Byrne*.

The judicial retreat

The decision in *Junior Books* was controversial, for two reasons: first, it seemed to sweep away the distinction between contract and tort; and secondly, it substantially increased the number of claims which could now be brought, and therefore increased the need for, and cost of, insurance against such claims. It was widely criticised, and the courts seemed to agree that they had gone too far because, in a number of cases over the following few years, they began tightening the law up again.

Case Summary

This process came to a head in *Murphy* v. *Brentwood District Council* (1990), where the House of Lords decided not just to call a halt to the expansion, but to wind things back a little. As you will know if you have studied the English legal system, in 1966 the House of Lords created a power for themselves to overrule their own previous decisions. In *Murphy* they decided to use this power to overrule *Anns*. They stated that the two-stage test for a duty of care no longer applied, and that the courts should go back to a more gradual approach. They could still find new duties of care, but the way to do this was by building the law step by step, using comparisons with established duty of care situations, although policy would still be a relevant consideration.

The facts of *Murphy* were quite similar to those of *Anns*, involving defects in a building. The House of Lords reverted to the pre-*Anns* position, where such defects were classified as economic loss, and stated that there was no liability for them. This meant that after *Murphy* it was no longer possible to claim for economic loss caused by acts.

Liability for economic loss: the law today

After this series of swings backwards and forwards, the current position is that the law on economic loss in negligence essentially has two separate categories, which are treated differently:

- loss caused by negligent acts;
- loss caused by negligent statements, advice and in some cases, services.

Loss caused by negligent acts

There are three main types of situation in which pure economic loss can be caused by a negligent act:

- Negligent manufacture or building may create a product or building with a defect that makes it less valuable, as in *Anns* and in *Murphy*.
- A three-way business arrangement like that in *Junior Books* may mean that one of the parties is caused loss by the second, but only has a contract with the third.
- A claimant may be caused pure economic loss because of damage to property that belongs to a third party, such as an electricity cable as in *Spartan Steel*.

It is now clear that there is no duty of care for economic loss in any of these situations.

Defects in products and buildings

Case Summary

In the first of the above categories, *Murphy* v. *Brentwood* established that there was no duty of care regarding economic loss caused by defective buildings. The issue of other defective products was examined in *Muirhead* v. *Industrial Tank Specialities* (1986). Here the claimant planned to run a business which involved buying lobsters at times when they were inexpensive, and keeping them in tanks in order to sell at a profit when prices were higher. Unfortunately the pumps he bought for the tanks were made in France, and the voltage they used was not the same as in the UK. As a result, many of his lobsters died. Although he had a contract with the seller, that firm had gone bankrupt, so he sued the manufacturer in negligence instead. The Court of Appeal said he was able to claim for the cost of the dead lobsters, but not for the profit he expected to make on them because this was pure economic loss.

Three-party agreements

Case Summary

Regarding the second of the categories above, three-party business agreements like those in *Junior Books*, the same applies: there is no duty of care. *Junior Books* itself has never been specifically overruled, but in a series of cases on three-party agreements the courts have declined to follow it, and it is no longer thought to be good law. In *Simaan General Contracting Co.* v. *Pilkington Glass* (1988), Simaan were a company who were constructing a building in Abu Dhabi. The building was to have a glass wall panel, and the claimant's clients had specified that the glass had to be a particular shade of green. Simaan were using another firm to do some of the work (this is called sub-contracting), and that firm ordered the glass from Pilkington. Pilkington supplied the wrong colour, and Simaan's client refused to pay. Usually Simaan could have sued the sub-contractors, but they had gone out of business, so they sued Pilkington in negligence. The Court of Appeal said that Pilkington could not have a duty of care towards Simaan to supply the right kind of glass, because the only loss caused by their failure to do so was economic.

Damage to property owned by a third party

Finally, there is no duty of care in the third category, of economic loss caused by damage to property belonging to a third party. As we saw, this was the case in *Spartan Steel*, and although it was decided before the temporary expansion of negligence, it still applies. In

Case Summary

Londonwaste v. *AMEC Civil Engineering* (1997), Londonwaste's business was burning rubbish to generate electricity, which they sold to companies that supply electricity to homes and businesses. AMEC's employees negligently severed a cable, which carried electricity from the Londonwaste site and was owned by another company, Eastern Electricity. The power cut caused some damage to Londonwaste's machinery, and also meant that they had to pay to get rid of the rubbish that arrived during the power cut and could not be burnt. They also lost the profit they would have made on the electricity they would have generated if the power had not been cut off. The court allowed them to claim the cost of the damage to their machinery, but not the cost of disposing of the rubbish, nor the loss of profit. These did not result from damage to Londonwaste's property, and were pure economic losses.

You be the judge

Source: Pearson Education Ltd/Shenval/Alamy

Q: Superfun Parks Ltd is the owner of a theme park, which decides to expand. They ask a firm called BigFun Builders to build a new area of the park. As part of this project, BigFun Builders agrees to buy a roller coaster from Rollicking Rollercoasters. There is a contract between Superfun Parks and BigFun Builders, and one between BigFun Builders and Rollicking Rollercoasters. The roller coaster is negligently built, and as a result an hour after the new area of the park is opened there is an accident in which 12 visitors are seriously injured. Superfun Parks is forced to close the park for the rest of the day, and give back every visitor the cost of their ticket. A week later, BigFun Builders goes bust.

Do Rollicking Rollercoasters owe a duty of care to Superfun Parks? Do they owe a duty of care to the visitors who are injured?

A: Rollicking Rollercoasters do not owe a duty of care to Superfun Parks, because the loss they caused to the park company results from a defect in a product and so is considered pure economic loss. They do owe a duty to the people on the ride because their loss is personal injury.

Loss caused by negligent statements (negligent misstatement)

When it comes to economic loss caused by statements, the situation is different. In the case of *Hedley Byrne* v. *Heller* (1963), the House of Lords decided that it should be possible to claim for economic loss caused by statements, providing certain requirements are met. This came to be known as a claim for negligent misstatement.

The *Hedley Byrne* principles

Case Summary

Case Navigator

The claimants in ***Hedley Byrne* v. *Heller*** (1963) were an advertising agency, who had been asked by a firm called Easipower to buy substantial amounts of advertising space on their behalf. Hedley Byrne wanted to make sure Easipower would be able to pay, so they asked their own bank, National Provincial, to check on them. National Provincial contacted Heller, who were Easipower's bank, and Heller confirmed in a letter that Easipower were creditworthy. The letter contained a disclaimer, which said the information was provided 'without responsibility on the part of this bank or its officials'. Relying on that information, Hedley Byrne went ahead with the arrangement with Easipower and bought £17,000 worth of advertising space for them. Easipower later went bust, leaving Hedley Byrne to pay the bill for the space. They then sought to claim this amount from Heller, on the grounds that the advice had been provided negligently.

The House of Lords held that the fact that Heller had issued the information with a disclaimer meant there could be no duty of care, and so the claim failed (as we will see later in the chapter, the effect of the disclaimer might be different if the case was decided today). However, their Lordships decided to consider what the position would have been if there had been no disclaimer, and this is where the importance of the case lies. They stated that, in appropriate circumstances, there could be a duty to be careful when giving advice or information, and that breach of that duty could give rise to liability for negligence, even though the only loss was economic.

However, the decision does not establish that there will always be a duty of care for loss caused by negligent advice or statements. In order to establish a duty of care under *Hedley Byrne*, their Lordships said, four requirements must be met:

- there must be a 'special relationship' between the parties;
- there must be a voluntary assumption of responsibility by the party giving the advice;
- the party receiving the advice must rely on it; and
- it must be reasonable for that party to have relied on that advice.

The requirements are to some extent interlinked, but some specific principles can be drawn out from cases in which *Hedley Byrne* has been applied. Since the 1990s, there has been a tendency to apply the *Hedley Byrne* principles in combination with the three-part ***Caparo* test** of foreseeability, proximity, and justice, fairness and reasonableness.

Negligent misstatement: the 'special relationship'

In *Hedley Byrne*, Lord Reid said a special relationship would arise where 'it is plain that the party seeking advice was trusting the other to exercise such a degree of care as the circumstances required, where it was reasonable for [the party seeking advice] to do that, and where the other gave the information or advice when he knew or ought to have known that the enquirer was relying on him'. In other words, there will be a 'special relationship' if the person asking advice was putting their trust in the person they asked, it was reasonable for them to do that, and the person giving the advice realised that or should have realised that the other person would trust their advice.

Case Summary

An example of this kind of special relationship can be seen in *Esso Petroleum Co. Ltd* v. *Mardon* (1976). The claimant had leased a petrol station after Esso advised him that he could expect to sell at least 200,000 gallons of petrol a year. In fact he managed to sell only 78,000 gallons in 15 months, and so made much less money than he had expected. The Court of Appeal held that Esso had special knowledge of the petrol market, which the claimant did not have, and as a result they knew that he was relying on their advice; in fact they intended him to rely on it in order to convince him to take on the petrol station.

The party giving advice need not be a specialist in the relevant area, nor someone whose job or business is giving advice, as long as it is reasonable for the claimant to have trusted their advice, and they knew or should have known that. In *Lennon* v. *Commissioner of Police of the Metropolis* (2004), Mr Lennon was an officer in the Metropolitan Police, who was changing jobs to go to work in the police force in Northern Ireland. He had been entitled to a housing allowance, and wanted to make sure this would continue, so he asked a personnel officer at the Metropolitan Police whether taking time off between finishing his old job and starting his new one would affect his entitlement to the allowance. She advised him that it would not be a problem. In fact, under the rules about the allowance, taking time off between the two jobs was counted as a break in employment, and by taking this break he lost the allowance for ever. He sued the Metropolitan Police, and the Court of Appeal upheld his claim. They said that even though the personnel officer was not a professional adviser, she had a managerial job in the police service and had, or had access to, special knowledge about the effect of job changes on the type of allowances Mr Lennon had asked about. In addition, she had allowed the claimant to believe that he could rely on her advice, when she could have simply told him that the question was outside her area of expertise and suggested he took advice from elsewhere.

Case Summary

Advice given outside business settings

In *Hedley Byrne*, Lord Reid made it plain that the special relationship will only arise when advice is given within a business context. He said:

> Quite careful people often express their opinions on social or informal occasions, even when they see that others are likely to be influenced by them; and they often do that without taking the care which they would take if asked for their opinion professionally, or in a business connection . . . there can be no duty of care on such occasions.

This means that where someone gives advice in a purely social setting, no duty of care will arise, even if they have expertise in the area which the advice covers. For example, both doctors and lawyers frequently complain that as soon as they disclose their profession at parties, there will always be a fellow guest who wants free advice on their back problem or their dispute with their neighbour. Lord Reid's words make it clear that, even if they cannot escape those boring conversations, they can at least be sure that they cannot be sued for negligence if the advice they give is wrong.

Curiously, there is one case in which a claimant successfully sued under the *Hedley Byrne* principles, even though the advice was given in a purely friendly setting. In *Chaudry* v. *Prabhakar* (1988), the defendant and the claimant were friends. The claimant was planning to buy a used car and the defendant, who claimed to know about cars, advised on the choice. However, he failed to notice that the car he recommended had been in an accident and was in fact unfit to be driven. The claimant sued him and succeeded, despite Lord Reid's words in *Hedley Byrne*. However, it appears this may have been because, for some reason, the defendant's lawyer did not attempt to deny that there was a duty of care and so the judges were not required to decide this point. One of them said that if they had been asked to decide this point, no duty of care would have been found. *Chaudry* does not, therefore, change the basic rule that only advice given in a business setting will lead to liability for economic loss.

Case Summary

Negligent misstatement: voluntary assumption of responsibility

In *Hedley Byrne*, Lord Reid pointed out that someone who is asked for advice in a business context has three choices: they can refuse to give any advice; they can give advice but warn the other person that it should not be relied on (they might for example suggest that the person does further research elsewhere); or they can give the advice without any such warning. In general, someone who chooses the third option will be considered to have voluntarily assumed responsibility for the consequences of giving that advice.

Case Summary

An example of voluntary assumption of responsibility can be seen in *Dean* v. *Allin & Watts* (2001). Mr Dean was a mechanic, and not widely experienced in business. He was approached to lend money to a firm called Citizen Homes, which bought rundown houses, did them up and sold them on for a profit. He agreed to lend them £50,000, on the understanding that one of the flats they owned would be put up as security. This meant that if the loan was not paid back, Mr Dean would get the flat instead. The borrowers suggested that their solicitor could draw up all the necessary paperwork, which they paid for. Mr Dean made it clear that he would not be using a solicitor of his own, and the borrowers' solicitor did not suggest that he ought to take independent legal advice.

The solicitor advised that in order for the flat to stand as security, it was sufficient for Mr Dean to hold the title deeds (the document which proves who owns a property). This was incorrect, because the arrangement should have been put in writing; merely holding the deeds did not give Mr Dean any rights over the property. Eventually the borrowers failed to pay back the money and the mistake was discovered. Mr Dean now had neither his £50,000, nor the flat. He sued the solicitor's firm. The Court of Appeal held that, as the solicitor knew that Mr Dean was inexperienced in business and was not taking legal advice from anywhere else, he knew that Mr Dean was relying on him to ensure that there was security for the loan. By going ahead when he knew this, and without advising Mr Dean to get independent legal advice, he was voluntarily accepting responsibility to him. Had he advised Mr Dean to consult a solicitor of his own, there would have been no duty of care because that would have meant that the solicitor was declining responsibility towards Mr Dean.

Responsibility assumed to someone unknown?

In Mr Dean's case, the solicitor had met him and knew his circumstances, but this need not necessarily be the case. In *Hedley Byrne*, Lord Bridge said that a defendant could be judged to have assumed responsibility where they knew the information they gave would be passed on to the claimant personally and relied on by them, but also where the claimant was 'a member of an identifiable class' that would receive the information and rely on it. That means that the defendant need not know the claimant personally, or even have met them, for liability to arise.

Case Summary

An example of a claimant who was not personally known to the defendant but was a member of an identifiable class can be seen in *Smith* v. *Eric Bush* (1990). Mrs Smith had bought a house, which had been surveyed by the defendants, a firm of surveyors. A survey is an examination of a house, designed to tell if it has any serious faults and how much it is worth. Where a homebuyer wants a mortgage, as Mrs Smith did, the mortgage lender commissions a survey to make sure the property is worth the amount they are being asked to lend. The contract for the survey is between the lender and the surveyors, but the lender usually charges the cost of the survey to the would-be homebuyer. The homebuyer may or may not meet the surveyor, and does not get to choose the firm or the individual who does the work. Clearly the information the survey provides is useful to the homebuyer as well as the lender, because without it they could not get a mortgage. In addition, although some buyers commission their own surveys, it is very common for buyers to rely on the survey undertaken for the lender when deciding whether the property is worth buying. This is what Mrs Smith did. The survey was done negligently, and the house turned out to have serious faults which made it worth much less than Mrs Smith had paid for it. Could she sue the surveyors for negligence?

The House of Lords held that she could. They said that even though surveys commissioned by lenders were not done for the purpose of advising homebuyers, surveyors were well aware that the buyer would rely on them. Therefore there was a duty of care from surveyors to buyers. An important factor in the decision was that it did not impose particularly wide liability: the extent of a surveyor's liability would never be more than the value of the house concerned, and would not be owed to anyone but the buyer.

Writing and drafting

Read the case of *Smith* v. *Eric Bush*. Now go through it again and, in your own words, note down the main arguments in favour of the claimant's case and the main arguments against it. Do you think the decision was the right one?

The effect of disclaimers

As we saw in *Hedley Byrne* itself, sometimes people or companies give advice but accompany it with a disclaimer, stating that they do not accept responsibility or liability for the advice. You might expect that where a disclaimer exists, a defendant cannot be said to be voluntarily assuming responsibility, since they are clearly warning that their advice should not be relied on. However, this is not necessarily the case.

As you will remember from Chapter 3, the Unfair Contract Terms Act 1977 (UCTA) provides that in some cases disclaimers in consumer contracts will be ineffective. In *Smith* v. *Eric Bush*, the surveyor's report contained a disclaimer, and the surveyors argued that this protected them against liability to Mrs Smith. The House of Lords found that the provisions of UCTA applied not just to contracts but also to the giving of information or advice where there was no contract. Mrs Bush's situation was therefore covered by section 2(2) of UCTA, which provides that someone acting in the course of a business can only restrict their liability for loss or damage other than personal injury where it is reasonable to do so. When would such a restriction be reasonable? Lord Griffiths said there were four factors to consider:

- Were the parties of equal bargaining power?
- How far was it practical, in terms of cost and time, for the claimant to have obtained independent advice?
- How difficult was the task that was the subject of the disclaimer? The harder the task, the more likely it would be that a disclaimer was reasonable.
- What were the practical consequences of allowing or not allowing the disclaimer, in terms of costs to each party, and their ability to bear those costs?

On all four factors, the House of Lords held that the disclaimer in *Smith* v *Eric Bush* was not reasonable, and should not be allowed to prevent liability.

First, the parties were not of equal bargaining power, because the disclaimer was imposed on Mrs Smith and she had no opportunity to object to it. This is often the case where an individual deals with a company, because disclaimers are frequently part of a firm's standard terms and conditions, which an individual may be unaware of and has no chance to alter even if they are aware. Secondly, it was not very practical for Mrs Smith to have commissioned an independent survey, because this would have meant paying twice for the same information. The court accepted that at the cheaper end of the property market most buyers could not easily afford to do this. Thirdly, the valuation was not an especially difficult task, and was one of the more routine parts of a surveyor's job. Finally, the consequences of liability for surveyors were not disastrous, as the cost would never be more than the value of the house, and surveying firms would carry insurance against such claims. By contrast, if the disclaimer was allowed to prevent liability, the result would be a financial catastrophe for the homebuyer.

disclaimers are frequently part of a firm's standard terms and conditions

Lord Griffiths pointed out one of the key factors that made the disclaimer unreasonable in this case was that the property was 'a dwelling house of modest value'. In similar cases where the purchases are of higher value, or involve commercial property such as factories or shops, the courts expect buyers to be more knowledgeable, to understand the effect of disclaimers and take their own precautions if necessary. In *Omega Trust Co. Ltd* v. *Wright, Son & Pepper* (1997), it was decided that a surveyor's disclaimer was reasonable in a purchase of commercial property, and the same applied in *McCullagh* v. *Lane Fox* (1996) to the purchase of a house at the upper end of the market.

Negligent misstatement: reliance by the claimant

In order for the principle in *Hedley Byrne* to apply, the claimant must rely on the statement or advice. In most cases, reliance will be shown by the fact that the claimant used the information or advice to help them decide whether or not to do something. In *Hedley Byrne* itself, for example, the advertising agency used the bank's credit reference to help them decide whether to spend money on behalf of Easipower, while in *Smith* v. *Eric Bush*, Mrs Smith used the surveyor's report to help her decide whether to go ahead and buy the house at the agreed price.

Case Summary

As a general rule, the claimant must therefore be able to show that the defendant's advice or information had an effect on their own actions. If they would have done what they did anyway, there is no reliance. This was the situation in *Commissioners of Customs and Excise* v. *Barclays Bank* (2006), the case we looked at in Chapter 2, where the bank failed to follow a court order preventing two of their customers from withdrawing money which was owed to Customs and Excise. The House of Lords said it was not possible to make out a case under the *Hedley Byrne* principles because Customs and Excise were not in a position to do anything differently as a result of Barclays' failure to follow the court order. The only thing they could do to protect their own financial position was to get the freezing injunction. They had done that, but not as a result of anything the bank did or did not do. As we saw in Chapter 2, the House of Lords also applied the *Caparo* test in this case, which confirmed there was no duty of care.

You be the judge

Q: Sharon is thinking of buying a hairdressing business. She has never run her own business before, so her friend John, who has run his own salon for years, offers to have a look at the business she is planning to buy and give her some advice. She agrees, and John tells her she can expect to make about £100,000 a year. Sharon thinks this sounds ridiculous, and suspects John has just plucked a figure out of the air because he doesn't really know what he is talking about. She buys the business anyway, thinking it will probably make her about £30,000 a year, but in fact it only makes £15,000 a year. Does she have a claim against John?

A: No, for two reasons. First, John's advice was not given in a business context. He was merely acting as a friend, so there is no 'special relationship'. Secondly, Sharon clearly did not rely on John's advice; she did not believe what he said and it did not influence her decision to buy the business. Therefore she has no claim against him.

Negligent misstatement: reliance must be reasonable

The fourth part of the *Hedley Byrne* principle is that the claimant must show that not only did they rely on the defendant's negligent misstatement, but that it was reasonable for them to do so. The courts have held that reliance will not usually be reasonable where advice given for one purpose is relied on for a different purpose. This was the case in ***Caparo* v. *Dickman***, the case we looked at in Chapter 2, which introduced the three-stage test for a duty of care. As you may remember, Caparo had used figures prepared by Dickman, a firm of auditors, when deciding whether to buy shares in another company. The figures had been produced negligently and gave a misleading picture of the company's financial position. The House of Lords said Caparo could not make a case under the *Hedley Byrne* principles, because auditors' reports were produced to show existing investors whether a company was being run properly. It was not reasonable for Caparo to rely on the report for the different purpose of deciding whether to buy shares.

Case Navigator

A similar result was reached in *Reeman* v. *Department of Transport* (1997). Mr Reeman was the owner of a fishing boat, which required an annual examination by the Department of Transport (DoT) to certify that it was seaworthy. Without a DoT certificate, it could not be used at sea and would be worthless. The boat had a certificate when Mr Reeman bought it, but it was later discovered the inspector who issued it had been negligent. The certificate should not have been issued and would not be renewed. Mr Reeman would not have bought the boat if he had known this. His claim against the DoT failed, because the certification scheme was designed to promote safety, and not for the purpose of establishing a boat's commercial value. It was therefore not reasonable for Mr Reeman to rely on the DoT report for that purpose.

Case Summary

However, since reasonableness is by nature a flexible concept, the courts are willing to look quite closely at the circumstances of the case, and there are situations where they have found reasonable reliance even though advice or information was given for a different purpose. In *Law Society* v. *KPMG Peat Marwick* (2000), they found that the fact that advice was given primarily for one purpose did not mean it could never be reasonable to rely on it for another purpose at the same time. The defendants were accountants to a firm of solicitors, and were asked by the firm to prepare their annual

Case Summary

accounts. These accounts had to be submitted to the Law Society, which oversees the solicitors' profession. A senior partner in the solicitors' firm had been defrauding hundreds of clients, but the accountants failed to see the evidence of this. The Law Society runs a scheme to compensate clients who have suffered fraud by solicitors, and when the frauds eventually came to light over 300 clients claimed under the Law Society scheme. The Society sued the accountants, claiming there was a duty under *Hedley Byrne* because they had relied on the information in the accounts. They said that if the accountants had spotted problems earlier, the Society could have stopped the frauds and would have had to pay less compensation as a result.

The Court of Appeal analysed the situation using the three-part *Caparo* test of foreseeability, proximity and fairness and reasonableness, in conjunction with the *Hedley Byrne* rules. They said that it was clearly foreseeable that, if the accountants failed to highlight the fact that a fraud might be happening, there could be claims on the Law Society's compensation fund, and there was clearly sufficient proximity between the two parties because the accountants would have known that that was the situation. The main issue in question was fairness and reasonableness, and here the Court used reasoning similar to that in *Smith* v. *Eric Bush* (the case of the negligent surveyor's report that we looked at above). They said that it was fair and reasonable to impose a duty, because doing so would only expose the accountants to limited liability. The amount of compensation claimed would never be more than the amount of clients' money lost in the frauds, and because reports were delivered annually, negligence in one year could be uncovered by a non-negligent report the following year.

References and wills: the expansion of *Hedley Byrne*

Since the mid-1990s, there has been a small crop of cases where the courts have found a duty of care for economic loss caused by negligent advice, information and even services, even though the circumstances did not really fit perfectly into the *Hedley Byrne* criteria. The two areas where this expansion has occurred concern employment references, and wills.

Hedley Byrne and employment references

Case Summary

In *Spring* v. *Guardian Assurance* (1995), Mr Spring had been employed by the defendant company but was sacked. He was offered a new job and asked Guardian for a reference. They supplied one, which said that he was incompetent and dishonest. Not surprisingly, his job offer was withdrawn. He sued Guardian for the economic loss caused by not getting the job. The trial judge found that Mr Spring was not dishonest, and that while the manager who had written the reference had honestly believed it was true, he had been negligent in the way he reached that conclusion. The House of Lords agreed that a duty of care existed in this situation, and Guardian had breached it.

Two factors make *Spring* v. *Guardian Assurance* different from the usual *Hedley Byrne* case. First, the information which caused the loss was not given *to* the person who was caused economic loss by it, but was *about* him. Secondly, it is hard to see how it can fairly be said that there is a voluntary assumption of responsibility in this situation. You may remember that in *Hedley Byrne*, Lord Reid said that someone asked for advice or information had three options: to say nothing; to give advice with a warning not to rely on it; or to give the advice without any such warning. Given that there was such a choice, someone who chose the third option could fairly be judged to have assumed responsibility for their words. But this analysis cannot be applied to the situation where someone is asked for a job reference. Someone who refuses to give a reference at all is effectively giving a bad reference, because the new employer will assume there must be something to hide. Equally, giving a reference but saying it is not to be relied on is likely to sound very suspicious. An ex-employer asked for a reference is therefore forced to take responsibility, whichever option they choose.

A third issue is that claims involving untrue statements that affect a person's reputation would more usually fall under the tort of defamation. Mr Spring had chosen not to pursue a claim in defamation because it was clear that, under the rules on defamation, Guardian would have had a **defence**, whereas they did not have one in negligence. In allowing the claimant to get round that defence by suing in negligence instead, it could be argued that the rules on defamation were undermined.

The wills cases

The other area where liability for economic loss has been expanded, despite not fitting the *Hedley Byrne* criteria, is in the area of wills. In *White* v. *Jones* (1995), two daughters had had an argument with their father, and he cut them out of his will. After a while they made up their quarrel, and the father instructed his solicitor to amend his will again, leaving £9,000 to his daughters. A month later, he discovered that this change had not been made, and reminded the solicitors to do it. When he died, it was found that the solicitors had still not changed the will, and this meant that the daughters could not legally receive the £9,000 their father had wanted them to have. They sued the solicitors and the House of Lords allowed the claim.

Case Summary

Like *Spring* v. *Guardian Assurance*, the decision in *White* v. *Jones* is quite difficult to fit into the *Hedley Byrne* principles. Wills are drawn up to put into practice the wishes of the person making the will (called the testator). Although in this case the daughters knew their father had wanted to leave them money, it is often the case that people who stand to inherit from a will (called the beneficiaries) are not aware that money has been left to them. How then can they be said to have relied on a solicitor drawing up the will properly? Clearly the solicitor assumes a responsibility to the testator to put their wishes into practice, but do they also assume a responsibility towards the beneficiaries? The House of Lords admitted that it was hard to argue that they did, but even so they were prepared to find a duty of care.

What seemed to have swayed them here (and perhaps in *Spring* too) was the practical justice of the claimant's case. The solicitor had been negligent and someone had suffered loss as a result. But the only party who would have had a claim under traditional *Hedley Byrne* principles was the testator, and he had suffered no financial loss. As Lord Goff pointed out, there was a 'lacuna', or loophole, in the law which, he said, needed to be filled.

The exact legal basis for the decision is, however, quite difficult to discover, because their Lordships disagreed about quite how the facts of the case were to be fitted into the *Hedley Byrne* principles. Lords Browne-Wilkinson and Nolan argued that in taking on the job of writing the will, the solicitor had voluntarily accepted responsibility for doing the job properly, and that that responsibility included a duty to the claimants. Lord Goff, on the other hand, held that the solicitor had only assumed responsibility to the testator, but that the law could and should fill the loophole by extending that responsibility to the beneficiaries.

Limits to the expansion of *Hedley Byrne*

Case Summary

The apparent mood of expansion seen in *Spring* and *White* is not, however, a consistent one. In *Goodwill* v. *British Pregnancy Advisory Services* (1996), the Court of Appeal resisted an attempt to expand the *Hedley Byrne* principles into a new factual area, even though in some ways the circumstances of the case were a more comfortable fit with *Hedley Byrne* than either *Spring* or *White*. The claimant, Ms Goodwill, had become pregnant by her boyfriend. Three years before their relationship began he had had a vasectomy, performed by a clinic run by the defendants. They had advised him that it had been successful, and he would not need to use contraception in the future. He told Ms Goodwill this, and she stopped using contraceptives. In fact the vasectomy had reversed itself. She sued the defendants for the cost of bringing up her daughter, claiming that if she had known about the chances of this happening she would have taken contraceptive precautions.

The Court of Appeal said that in order to claim for economic loss arising from reliance on the defendants' advice, a claimant had to show that the defendants knew, either because they were told or because it was obvious, that their advice was likely to be relied on by the claimant, either as an individual or as one of a specified group. It was also necessary to show that, at the time they gave the advice, the defendants knew the purpose for which the claimant was relying on the advice, and that the claimant had suffered a disadvantage through relying on the advice. In this case, they said, these requirements were not fulfilled. When the advice was given, the claimant was not known to the defendants, and was simply one of a potentially large class of women who might at some stage have a sexual relationship with their patient. They could not be expected to foresee that, years later, their advice to the patient might be passed on to and relied on by her for the purpose of deciding whether or not to use contraception. The Court suggested that the situation might be different where a man and his partner were advised at the same time, or possibly even where the man was in a relationship at the time and the clinic knew this.

In common-sense terms, this distinction is a difficult one. Clearly, as Ms Goodwill pointed out, in this day and age it was not unlikely that a man of her boyfriend's age would have a sexual relationship with future partners. While the class of potential partners might be large, the number of them who would end up pregnant was not, given that once that happened it would be known that the vasectomy had reversed itself. In addition, the purpose for which she had relied on the advice was exactly the same as the purpose for which the patient would rely on it: in order to decide whether they needed contraceptive precautions or not.

Out and about

Working in teams of three, read the full facts of *Goodwill* v. *British Pregnancy Advice Service* and the full judgment in *Hedley Byrne* v. *Heller*. Now assign one of your group as barrister for Ms Goodwill, one as barrister for the British Pregnancy Advice Service and the third as the judge. Each of the barristers should prepare their case, referring to the principles of *Hedley Byrne*, and to any of the other cases detailed in this chapter, plus any policy considerations that you feel are relevant. You then have ten minutes each to put your case to the judge. The judge then has ten minutes to prepare a judgment, detailing which side they find for, and why. Remember that as a judge you should try to put aside your own personal views, and make up your mind after you have heard both sides, not before.

Reflective practice

If you can, take a few minutes to think about how this exercise went. What did you find difficult? Was it easy for the barristers to work out which points to make, or more difficult than you expected? Was the judge's decision easier or more difficult to make than you expected? What did you find worked well for you? Is there anything you would do differently if you did a similar exercise?

Hedley Byrne and contract

As we saw earlier, part of the reason for the courts' resistance to allowing economic loss claims in negligence was that contract was traditionally seen as the correct method for dealing with economic loss. For this reason, it was generally considered that where there was a contract between two parties, and one was caused loss but for some reason contract law did not allow a remedy, it was not possible to sue under *Hedley Byrne* instead, because this would undermine the certainty of contract law. However, this changed during the apparent expansion of *Hedley Byrne* that we discussed above.

Case Summary

In *Henderson* v. *Merrett Syndicates Ltd* (1995), the claimants were all investors in Lloyd's, which is a very big insurance provider. For many years, Lloyd's had run a scheme under which wealthy individuals, called Lloyd's Names, put up their own money as backing for insurance policies offered by companies who were members of Lloyd's. When the Names suffered large losses through this scheme (see the Law in Action box on the Lloyd's **litigation**), many of them alleged that they had been misled about the nature of the investment, and sought to sue the agents through whom they had invested. Some of them had contracts with these agents but a claim in contract has to be brought within three years, and for some of the Names this three-year period had already expired. Negligence actions can usually be brought for up to six years, and one of the issues in *Henderson* was whether the Names could take advantage of this fact, and sue in negligence instead.

The prospect of contract law's rules being undermined in this way was one of the main reasons why the courts had traditionally disliked the idea of allowing a tort action between parties to a contract. Even so, the House of Lords found that there could be a duty of care. Lord Goff said that the basic question was whether the *Hedley Byrne* principles of assumption of responsibility and reliance were fulfilled. If they were, a duty of care could arise, and the fact that there was a contractual relationship did not prevent this. A claimant who had potential remedies in either contract or tort could choose whichever was most advantageous, unless the terms of their contract specifically prevented them from doing so.

Negligent misstatements often take place during the negotiation period when one party is trying to persuade the other to make a contract – an example would be *Esso* v. *Mardon*, the case where the would-be buyer of a petrol station was misled about the amount of money he could expect to make. As *Esso* v. *Mardon* shows, the *Hedley Byrne* principles can apply in those situations but in practice this type of case is now more often brought under the Misrepresentation Act 1967, which imposes liability for false statements made during contractual negotiations, because it is generally easier to make out a case using the provisions of the Act.

Law in action The Lloyd's litigation

Henderson v. *Merrett* was just one of a huge number of cases in what became known as the Lloyd's litigation, stretching from the early 1990s right up to 2009. The cases arose from the Lloyd's Names system, which invited rich individuals, known as Names, to use their personal wealth as backing for insurance policies offered by companies who were members of Lloyd's. The deal was that the Names got a share of the profits from the policies, but if a loss was made they had unlimited liability for covering those losses. That meant that if there was a loss, a Name could be called upon to pay everything they had, up to and including losing their home. Explained that way, you might imagine most sane people would run a mile from this kind of investment, but during the 1970s and 1980s, the insurance market was doing well and many people made a huge amount of money from being a Name. As a result, it came to be seen as a way to get easy money if you were rich enough to be allowed in on it. Because individuals had to prove they had a certain level of wealth in order to join the scheme, there was also social status attached to being a Name, and it became the fashionable thing to do in wealthy circles.

Source: Pearson Education Ltd/Photodisc/Neil Beer

In the early 1990s, however, the easy profits came to an end when the insurance industry was hit by a number of unusually big claims. These were partly the result of major accidents and disasters, including a fire on the Piper Alpha oil rig, a particularly bad hurricane in the USA, and a major oil spillage at sea, and also the fact that claims for asbestos-related illness, which we looked at in Chapter 3, were beginning to pile up. As a result, the Names were called upon to pay, and because their liability was unlimited many of them faced financial ruin.

As explained above, the Names then sought to sue Lloyd's and/or the agents who had brought them into the scheme, claiming that they had been negligent in the way they had explained and run the scheme. Although the unlimited liability of the Names was well known, most of them knew nothing about the insurance market, and said they did not understand how big a risk they were taking or how the system really worked, and simply trusted the agents to look after their interests. The litigation in the early 1990s hit the headlines, and was the subject of much debate: while some newspapers ran sympathetic stories about Names who stood to lose everything, others criticised them for being happy to sit back and take the profits during the good years, and then complaining about the system when things went wrong.

Because there were so many cases about to come before the courts, the parties agreed that it was sensible for the court to determine the key legal issues in advance, and this was what was done in *Henderson* v. *Merrett*. As we saw, *Henderson* v. *Merrett* established that there was a duty of care towards the Names, and so they then proceeded to sue in negligence. In 1996, a settlement was reached with 94 per cent of the Names, under which they could pay to transfer their liabilities to a new company, but others chose to fight on. In the most recent cases they have accused Lloyd's of deliberately misleading them about what they were taking on, but these cases have not succeeded, and the High Court has issued restraint orders which mean that the Names cannot bring any further cases without the Court's permission.

[*References*: 'Lloyd's names face bankruptcy as court battle ends', *The Telegraph*, 4 June 2009; 'Court of Appeal ends names litigation', Lloyds News, **http://www.lloyds.com/News_and_Insight/News_and_features/Lloyds_News/Lloyds-News_2009/02/Court_of_Appeal_ends_Names_litigation**]

Liability for economic loss today

This area of negligence is quite a complex one, so now that we have looked in detail at it, you might find it useful to have a summary of the law as it currently stands.

There is no claim for economic loss caused by:

- defects in buildings or products;
- three-party agreements like those in *Junior Books* v. *Veitchi*;
- damage to property belonging to someone other than the claimant, as in *Spartan Steel*.

There is a claim for economic loss caused by statements or advice, under the principles set down in *Hedley Byrne* v. *Heller*. These are that:

- there must be a 'special relationship' between the parties;
- there must be a voluntary assumption of responsibility by the defendant;
- the party receiving the advice must rely on it, to the extent that it affects their behaviour; and
- it must be reasonable for that party to have relied on the advice.

There is also a claim for economic loss caused by:

- employment references made negligently;
- negligent preparation of wills, where the economic loss is suffered by an intended beneficiary and they have no other way to claim.

Problems with the law on economic loss

As we have seen in this chapter, the courts have frequently struggled with the issue of liability for economic loss in negligence, and the result is that the law is fractured, inconsistent and, in many ways, still has an unsettled air. These are some of the problems that now arise.

Too many restrictions?

The powercut cases of *Spartan Steel* and *Londonwaste* illustrate that the distinction between pure economic loss and other kinds of loss can be a very fine one – and one that in common-sense terms is hard to justify. In both cases, it was very clear that the defendants' negligence caused all of the claimants' losses and all of their losses were foreseeable. So why should the defendants have been liable to compensate some of those losses and not others? To the non-legal eye, distinguishing between them seems completely illogical – as indeed it must do to a claimant who is left with a loss caused by someone else and who has no redress. In many cases this can be seen as allowing a defendant to get away with seriously careless behaviour, regardless of the loss caused to others.

Too few restrictions?

On the other hand, it can be argued that rather than not allowing sufficient redress for pure economic loss, the tort system in fact allows too much. In most cases of pure economic loss, what we are really talking about is not loss but failure to make a gain. This is obvious in the will case, *White* v. *Jones*, for example, but also in the housebuying case of *Smith* v. *Eric Bush*. A homebuyer is entering into a market transaction, and these always run the risk of creating a loss as well as the possibility of making a gain. Mrs Smith did not actually have money taken from her, she simply bought a house that was worth less than she thought.

Traditionally, the role of tort law is to compensate those who have actually suffered loss. It can be argued that those who want to protect their expectation of gain should do so through contract, and those who have given nothing in return for a service should not be compensated when that service lets them down financially. One answer to the latter view is that in many of the cases where claimants have not contracted, and therefore not paid, for a service, the defendants nevertheless gain a commercial benefit from the situation. This was clear in *Smith* v. *Eric Bush*, where the surveyors only had the work because homebuyers were willing to pay for it, even if indirectly, and in *White* v. *Jones*, where the solicitor had been paid to draw up the will, albeit not by the claimants. However, a commercial benefit can also be seen in less obvious situations. In *Hedley Byrne*, for example, Lord Goff pointed out that in establishing whether the special relationship existed in a particular case,

> it may be a material fact to consider whether the adviser is acting purely out of good nature, or whether he is getting his reward in some indirect form. The service a bank performs in giving a reference is not done simply out of a desire to assist commerce. It would discourage the customers of the bank if their deals fell through because the bank had refused to testify to their credit when it was good, and so it is in the bank's interest to be able to give references.

Overlap with contract law

The issue of the relationship between contract and tort causes particular problems, and especially the assertion in *Henderson* that a claimant who has a contractual claim as well as a possible action in negligence can choose between them. As well as making the limitation period for contract essentially meaningless, it allows the claimant to pick and choose in other ways. For example, in contract a loss will only be compensated if there was a very high degree of probability that it would arise from the breach of contract, whereas in tort liability can be allowed for quite unlikely losses, so long as they are reasonably foreseeable. On the other hand, if the existence of a contract ruled out liability in negligence, this would mean that someone who had paid for advice would be in a worse position than someone who had not.

in tort liability can be allowed for quite unlikely losses

Summary

- Pure economic loss is loss that does not result from personal injury or property damage.
- Liability for economic loss falls into two categories:
  - economic loss caused by acts;
  - economic loss caused by statements or advice.
- Economic loss caused by acts occurs in three main ways:
  - defective products or property;
  - three-way agreements;
  - loss caused by damage to another's property.

  None of these situations create a duty of care for economic loss.
- There is a duty of care for economic loss caused by statements under the principles set out in *Hedley Byrne* v. *Heller* (1963), where there is:
  - a 'special relationship'; and
  - voluntary assumption of responsibility; and
  - reliance; and
  - reliance is reasonable.
- A claimant who may have a case in contract or tort can choose which to bring.

Question and answer*

Problem: Erica and Ernie Fryer decide to open a fish and chip shop, The Happy Plaice. It is the first time they have ever attempted to run a business. Using a mortgage, they buy a shop with a flat above it, where they intend to live. Their mortgage lender commissioned a survey on the building, which the Fryers paid the mortgage company for. The survey said the building was worth £125,000, and they paid this amount. The survey also included a statement that 'This report is provided without liability on the part of the surveyors'. Erica and Ernie also invest £30,000 in equipment for the shop, including a fish fryer, from Fishy Wishy Shop Supplies. Unknown to them, the fish fryer has been negligently manufactured and on the day they open, it explodes, injuring Erica and causing a small fire which destroys their new counter. They have to close the shop for two weeks, during which time they lose £1,000 in profit.

Just before they reopen, they notice that the back wall of the building has a long crack in it. They later discover that the wall is falling down, and the building is worth only £40,000 as a result.

Advise Erica and Ernie as to any claims they may have in negligence.

You should allow yourself no more than 40 minutes to complete this task.

Essay: How satisfactory is the current law on liability in tort for pure economic loss?

This question should be answered in 40 minutes.

* Answer guidance is provided at the end of the chapter.

Further reading

Barker, K. (1993) 'Unreliable assumptions in the modern law of negligence', 109 LQR 461.
This article looks at the different ways of approaching economic loss, and how the *Hedley Byrne* test relates to the *Caparo* test. The author argues that the courts pick and choose their approaches according to moral or policy concerns arising from the facts of a particular case, and that this has produced incoherence. It is quite a complicated read, but worth the effort – take notes as you go and you will find it easier to keep track of the arguments.

Markesinis, B.A. and Deakin, S. (1992) 'The random element of their Lordships' infallible judgment: an economic and comparative analysis of the tort of negligence from *Anns* to *Murphy*', 55 MLR 619.
A very useful look at the way the law has developed on economic loss. The authors point out inconsistencies in the rules, and compare our treatment of economic loss with that of other legal systems.

Smith, J.C. and Burns, P. (1983) '*Donoghue* v. *Stevenson*: the not so golden anniversary', 46 MLR 147.
This article looks at the state of the law pre-*Murphy*, and gives a good indication of the concerns that led to that decision.

Witting, C. (2000) 'Justifying liability to third parties for negligent misstatements', 20 OJLS 615.
This article looks at the basis of liability for negligent misstatement, and argues that it is not really about responsibility and reliance, but about the link between what the defendant does and the harm caused. It contains a detailed look at key cases.

Question and answer guidance

Problem: There are three potential claims here: against the manufacturers of the fish fryer, against the surveyor, and against the builder. To give your answer a clear structure, take each one in turn. Starting with the manufacturer of the fish fryer, Erica will want to claim for her injuries, and this is straightforward because we know from *Donoghue* v. *Stevenson* that a manufacturer has a duty of care towards anyone who might foreseeably be harmed by their products. The Fryers will also want to claim for the damage to their counter, and again this is straightforward because it is property damage. But can they claim for the loss of profit? This may look like pure economic loss, but it is not: because the closure of the shop results from the damage to the fryer, it is loss arising from property damage, so it is part of the same claim.

Turning to the surveyor, the Fryers will want to claim the difference between what they paid for the building and what it was worth, on the basis that his advice was negligent. You need to apply the principles of *Hedley Byrne* v. *Heller* and *Smith* v. *Eric Bush*, and in particular consider whether the Fryers fit the criteria laid down in *Smith*.

Finally, turning to the claim against the builder, this is a case of defective property, and so you need to apply *Murphy* v. *Brentwood*.

Essay: A good start to this essay would be to summarise the current law on economic loss, stating when liability will exist and when it will not. You can then go on to work through some of the problems with the law which are highlighted in this chapter, including the fact that the law is complex, that some of the distinctions made can seem unjust, and that some cases – such as *Spring* v. *Guardian Assurance* and *White* v. *Jones* – do not seem to fit very well into previous case law. As you work through each criticism, refer to cases which illustrate your point. As a conclusion, you might want to say why you think the law in this area has become so problematic.

Visit **www.mylawchamber.co.uk/quinntort** to access tools to help you develop and test your knowledge of tort law, including practice exam questions with guidance, annotated weblinks, glossary and key case flashcards, legal newsfeed and legal updates and interactive 'You be the judge' questions.

Use Case Navigator to read in full some of the key cases referenced in this chapter with commentary and questions:

Caparo Industries plc* v. *Dickman and others [1990] 1 All ER 568
Hedley Byrne & Co. Ltd* v. *Heller & Partners Ltd [1963] 2 All ER 575

Chapter 6
Negligence: public bodies

Key points In this chapter we will be looking at:

- When a public body such as the police or local authority will owe a duty of care in negligence
- Why public bodies are sometimes treated differently from other types of defendant
- The influence of the Human Rights Act 1998 on this area of law

Introduction

Between 1979 and 1981 the city of Leeds was terrorised by a series of savage murders, committed by a killer who soon became known as the Yorkshire Ripper. By the time the police discovered that the Ripper was a Bradford lorry driver called Peter Sutcliffe, he had killed 13 women, including a 20-year-old student called Jacqueline Hill, who was his last victim. After Sutcliffe was charged, details began to emerge of how the police had handled – or mishandled – the investigation. Among other things, they had interviewed Sutcliffe nine times, but had failed to put together the different pieces of evidence which could have revealed that he was likely to be the killer.

As you may remember from Chapter 2, Jacqueline Hill's mother sued the police, in *Hill* v. *Chief Constable of West Yorkshire Police* (1986). She claimed that if they had not conducted the investigation negligently, Sutcliffe would have been caught earlier, and her daughter would not have been killed by him. We saw in Chapter 2 that the House of Lords found that the police had no **duty of care** to Miss Hill because there was no proximity between them, but that was not the only issue in the case. The other, equally important, part of the question was whether it should even be possible to sue the police for doing their job negligently. Should taxpayers' money, which would otherwise pay for services that benefit the whole community, be used to compensate individuals? When the police had lots of different calls on their budget, should the courts be able to decide that they should spend more money and manpower on one case than another? Might the threat of legal action make the police spend time and effort covering their backs, instead of getting on with the job? But on the other hand, should not the police, who do one of the most important jobs in society, be called to account if they fail to do that job properly?

Similar questions can also be asked about claims against other publicly-funded bodies, such as local councils. In this chapter, we look at how the courts have tried to resolve these very difficult issues.

Police liability for negligence

As a general rule, police officers can be sued just like anyone else for damage or loss that they negligently cause while going about their work. So, for example, if a police car crashes into yours, you can sue the police for any damage to the car or injury to you and your passengers, just as you would any other driver. In practice in these cases, a **claimant** sues the Chief Constable of the relevant force, who is held liable for the actions of his or her officers. This is called **vicarious liability** and is covered in Chapter 8.

However, there are some situations in which the courts have held that special rules should apply. They make a distinction between:

- operational matters, which essentially means the way in which the police carry out their work; and
- policy matters, which means decisions made about issues such as where money and manpower should be allocated, and which types of work should have priority.

The traditional view was that there could be a duty of care towards members of the public for negligently performed operational matters, but not for policy matters. The practical difference between the two types of issue can be seen in *Rigby* v. *Chief Constable of Northamptonshire* (1985). The police were pursuing an armed man, who took refuge in a shop owned by the claimant. The police used CS gas, which is highly flammable, to get the gunman out, but the gas exploded and the fire damaged the claimant's shop. The shop owner argued that the police's decision to equip themselves with CS gas was negligent, because the gas was known to be flammable and there was a non-flammable alternative that they could have used instead. The House of Lords said that the choice of which gas to use was a policy decision, and it was not up to the courts to say whether or not it was the right one. However, they held that the police had been negligent in failing to bring firefighting equipment to the scene, because that was an operational matter, in that it concerned how effectively and safely they carried out their duties. It was their choice whether or not to use CS gas, but having decided to use it they had a duty to take reasonable precautions when it was used.

Case Summary

Police immunity

Until relatively recently, the distinction made between policy and operational matters meant the police were effectively immune from negligence actions brought by members of the public, concerning the way they deal with crime. The reasons for this were explained in *Hill*, the case brought by the mother of the Yorkshire Ripper's last victim. The House of Lords said that if the police could be sued for failing to prevent a particular crime, the courts would need to look into the decisions the police had made on things like which areas of inquiry to pursue and where to prioritise the resources available to them. These were policy areas that it was not appropriate for the courts to decide on. To defend themselves against such claims, the police would effectively have to reopen old cases and show that they acted reasonably, and that would take up police time which could otherwise be used for fighting crime. Lord

To defend themselves against such claims, the police would effectively have to reopen old cases

Templeman said the real questions in the case were issues like whether the Yorkshire police selection and training procedures were good enough, whether rates of pay were high enough to attract good people, and whether financial restrictions prevented the use of sufficiently modern equipment. A negligence claim against a particular police force or police officer could not answer any of these questions.

Case Summary

For these reasons, it was held in *Alexandrou* v. *Oxford* (1993) that the police were not liable to a member of the public who was burgled after they ignored a message that his burglar alarm had gone off. The police had assumed that the message was a false alarm, and so had not bothered to go and investigate. The court held that this was not negligent because there was no duty of care even to go and check. Similarly, in *Vicario* v. *Commissioner of Police of the Metropolis* (2007), the Court of Appeal held that, when making the decision on whether to prosecute a suspected offender, the police have no duty of care towards the alleged victim of that offender.

Case Summary

Cases like this can seem quite strange at first glance, but remember that the courts are not saying that the police do not have a duty to do their job properly. What they are doing is using the concept of a duty of care to draw the boundaries of negligence and say when an individual will have a right to sue for **damages**. So although society clearly expects the police to do a good job, and there are ways that individual police forces and police officers can be held to account through **public law**, the courts do not believe it is in the interests of society to allow individuals to claim damages for harm caused by negligent police work.

Osman: a challenge to police immunity

Hill was traditionally considered to create a blanket immunity for the police in cases involving the investigation of crime, because these would always involve policy issues. However, in 1998 this approach was challenged in the European Court of Human Rights and, since then, the House of Lords has stated that the immunity is not absolute, and that it is still necessary to judge whether there is a duty of care in each case.

Case Summary

The challenge came in the case of *Osman* v. *UK* (1998), brought by the wife of a man who was murdered by someone who had an obsession with their son. The police had for a long time been aware of both the obsession and of the threatening behaviour of the eventual killer. He had, for example, attacked a friend of the Osmans' son and threatened to 'do a Hungerford', referring to a gunman who went on a shooting spree in the Berkshire town of Hungerford in 1987, killing 14 people. However, although the police interviewed the man twice, they took no other steps and eventually the man stole a gun, attacked their son and shot and killed Mr Osman. Mrs Osman sought to sue the police for negligence in failing to protect them, despite the clear evidence that they were at risk, but the case was struck out on the grounds of the *Hill* immunity, as it was understood then.

Mrs Osman went to the European Court of Human Rights (ECHR) and sued the UK government for breach of the Human Rights Act 1998. Article 6(1) of the ECHR gives the right to a fair trial, which includes the right to a hearing. Mrs Osman argued that she had not had a hearing, because of the way the *Hill* immunity was used at the time. Where a claimant brought a case which seemed to involve policy issues, the police would apply to have it struck out on the grounds that *Hill* established there was no duty of care in such cases, and this had happened to Mrs Osman's claim. As we saw in Chapter 2, in a **striking-out application** the courts do not assess the facts of the case but simply look at whether, if the facts were true, there could be a viable legal claim. Only if they find that there may be a legal claim does the case go on to be tried fully on the facts. This meant that cases like Mrs Osman's were being filtered out without a full hearing of the facts, and her lawyers claimed that this contravened the Article 6 right to a fair trial.

The ECHR agreed that the *Hill* immunity could act to prevent a fair trial, and had done so in Mrs Osman's case. The judgment pointed out that the Court of Appeal had not looked at the facts on which her case was based, or considered whether there were any policy reasons why it should succeed. They had simply assumed that because it was a case that challenged police policy decisions in a particular criminal investigation, as the original *Hill* case had done, the police could not be liable.

The ECHR said that there were clear public interest reasons for the *Hill* rule, but because Mrs Osman's case had been struck out the Court of Appeal had not considered whether there might also be public interest reasons in favour of her claim. They pointed out that her case did involve important issues of public interest: the allegations involved a catalogue of failures that amounted to grave negligence, rather than minor acts of incompetence, and the harm done as a result was of the most serious kind. In order not to breach Article 6, the ECHR said the Court of Appeal should have looked at these issues, and they had not done so.

The implications of *Osman*

The ECHR's decision in *Osman* came as something of a surprise to the English courts, and the lawyers who work in them. It seemed to suggest that, where cases might raise issues of public policy, it would rarely be possible to use the striking-out procedure to decide whether a duty of care existed. This would apply not just to cases against the police, but also to those against other public bodies where, as we will see later, a similar approach had been taken. So there was a sigh of judicial relief when the ECHR took another look at the issue, in *Z* v. *UK* (2001), which involved the liability of local councils. The facts of the case will be discussed later in this chapter, but the key point here is that *Z* v. *UK* involved a claim which had been struck out because the **defendant** was a public authority. Would the ECHR say that the striking-out procedure should not be used for this type of claim either? This time, however, the ECHR admitted that their decision in *Osman* had been based on a misunderstanding of English law. Article 6 was designed mainly to deal with procedural barriers to a fair trial such as, for example, rules preventing certain types of case being heard in public. But the apparent immunity of the police and some other public bodies to certain types of claim was not a procedural issue; it was part of the English law of negligence. When a court says that there is no duty of care on the police in a particular type of situation, they are not saying that the police are immune from liability, but that there is no liability for them to be immune from. The ECHR said they had failed to understand and take this into account.

Case Summary

However, although the ECHR admitted to this misunderstanding, they did not say that the decision in *Osman* was wrong. Their decision in *Z* v. *UK* was not unanimous either, and it was clear that some of those who dissented still felt that the view taken in *Osman* was right. As a result, the ECHR's view on the position of public bodies in negligence is still not entirely clear or predictable and, as we will see, this has had an effect on the way the English courts now approach the issue.

Police immunity after *Osman*

Since *Osman*, the courts have been noticeably more reluctant to dismiss duty of care cases in a striking-out action, and the *Hill* principles no longer operate as a blanket immunity for the police. In *Swinney* v. *Chief Constable of Northumbria Police (No. 2)* (1999), Mrs Swinney was a pub landlady, who had told the police the identity of a hit-and-run driver who had killed a police officer. The person she identified was known to the police as a violent and ruthless criminal. Not surprisingly, Mrs Swinney made it very clear to the police that she was giving them the information confidentially and did not want to be identified as their informant. However, the police recorded her name in a document containing the details she had supplied. A police officer left the document in an unattended police car, from where it was stolen. It eventually reached the man Mrs Swinney had identified, who then began a series of terrifying threats against Mrs Swinney and her husband. She was so badly affected that she suffered **psychiatric injury** and had to give up running the pub.

Case Summary

When Mrs Swinney sued the police, they argued that, as in *Hill*, there was no proximity between them and her, and there were good policy reasons why there should be no duty of care. The Court of Appeal disagreed. On the proximity question, they said that Mrs Swinney's position was different from Miss Hill's. Miss Hill had been at exactly the same risk of attack from the Ripper as any other woman in the area, and the police had no more reason to think that she would be attacked than anyone else. In Mrs Swinney's case, however, the police knew that if they let the information she had given fall into the wrong hands, there was a clear risk that a very violent criminal would want to take revenge on her for informing on him. In addition, in agreeing to keep the information confidential, they had undertaken a responsibility to her personally. The Court of Appeal said that informers were not in the same position as any ordinary member of the public: in giving the police important information, they created a special relationship, which gave rise to a duty of care.

On the policy issue, the police claimed that the arguments made in *Hill* also applied here: allowing liability would take money and manpower away from normal police work and so make it harder for the police to fight crime. The Court agreed that these arguments were relevant. However, they said that in this case, there were also policy arguments in favour of allowing a duty of care towards informants, because it would encourage people to come forward to help the police, and so help rather than hinder the fight against crime. In line with the ECHR's approach in *Osman*, they said that these arguments had to be balanced against each other in a full hearing, and so it was not appropriate to strike out the claim.

When the case went to trial, the judge found that there was a duty of care towards Mrs Swinney, but she lost her case because, on the facts, the police were not in breach of their duty of care. As you'll remember from Chapter 2, this simply means that they did not fall below the standard of behaviour to be expected in the relevant situation, but simply made a mistake that any reasonable person could make.

Case Summary

In *Waters* v. *Commissioner of Police for the Metropolis* (2000), the claimant was a police officer who had been bullied and shunned by her colleagues after she alleged that another officer had raped her. She suffered psychiatric injury, and claimed that the police had been negligent in failing to stop the bullying. Again, the police argued that, as in *Hill*, allowing a duty of care would distract resources from real police work. But the

House of Lords said there were also policy reasons in favour of liability, in that if the claimant's allegations were true there was a serious problem within the police, which should be brought to public attention so it could be dealt with. They refused to strike out the claim, and said the issue of duty of care should be assessed on a full hearing of the facts.

In both these cases, the claimants were in some kind of special relationship with the police, Swinney as an informant and Waters as an employee. What is the situation where the claimant is simply an ordinary member of the public? This was the case in *Brooks* v. *Commissioner of Police for the Metropolis* (2005), which arose out of the murder of Stephen Lawrence, a young black student who was stabbed to death in a horrific gang attack in 1993. The claimant, Duwayne Brooks, was Stephen's friend. He was with him at the time of the murder and was also attacked by the gang. The police investigation into the attack was so badly mishandled that an official inquiry into it was ordered. The inquiry found that when the police arrived after the gang had left and saw a young black man agitated and, in their words, 'aggressive', they automatically assumed he had been involved in a fight. This mistake, the inquiry said, was due to racial stereotyping, and because of it the police did not treat Mr Brooks as a victim of crime and, at first, did not take his evidence seriously.

Case Summary

Mr Brooks suffered post-traumatic stress disorder after the incident. Although he accepted that this was initially caused by witnessing the murder, he claimed that his treatment by the police had made it worse, and sued for negligence. The basis of his case was that the police owed him a duty of care to find out if he was a victim, and treat him as one, and to take reasonable notice of his evidence and act accordingly.

The House of Lords was unanimous in holding that there was no such duty of care to someone in Mr Brooks's position. They repeated the arguments used in *Hill*, saying that the police's main duty was to prevent and investigate crime, and allowing a duty of care in this case would divert resources from that task. The House accepted that the police should treat victims and witnesses with respect, but said that creating liability in damages for not doing this was going too far. However, they confirmed that it was no longer appropriate to think of the *Hill* arguments in terms of an absolute immunity. It would, they said, be rare for a duty of care to be found in cases involving investigation of crime, but there might be exceptional cases or, as Lord Keith put it, 'cases of outrageous negligence by the police' that could fall outside the general position in *Hill*.

However, the case of *Smith* v. *Chief Constable of Sussex* (2008) suggests that as far as ordinary members of the public are concerned, cases will have to be very exceptional indeed before the police can be held liable for failing to protect an individual. Mr Smith had had a succession of death threats from his former partner, Gareth Jeffrey. He reported these to the police but they took no action, and even refused to look at the threatening emails and texts. Eventually, Mr Jeffrey attacked Mr Smith with a hammer so violently that he was arrested for attempted murder. Mr Smith survived, and sued the police for negligence.

Case Summary

Despite the fact that the police had had clear information that Mr Smith was under threat from a particular individual (as opposed to the situation in *Hill*, where there was no way of knowing who the killer's next victim would be), the House of Lords held that they were not liable. Although they admitted that it was a difficult balance to strike, they accepted the arguments in *Hill* and *Brooks* that creating a specific duty to an individual would be against the public interest, because it would skew the way in which police resources were used. They also pointed out that there would be many cases, especially in the area of relationship breakdown, where one person claimed to be under threat from another. Imposing a duty to protect the accuser could mean taking unjustified action against the person accused, who might well be innocent. As in *Brooks*, the House did not rule out the idea that there might be situations where the police would have a duty to protect a specific individual, but said this was not such a case.

The current position then seems to be that the courts are no longer allowing the *Hill* arguments to operate as a blanket immunity, and are willing to look at policy arguments for and against liability. But it will still be very difficult for an ordinary member of the public to argue successfully that the police owe a duty of care to prevent a crime against them.

Figure 6.1 Timeline: police liability

1996: *Hill* v. *Chief Constable of Northumbria Police* establishes that the police do not have a duty of care to individual victims of crime

↓

1998: *Osman* v. *UK* challenges the *Hill* immunity in the European Court of Human Rights, and it appears that striking out actions can no longer be used in police cases. Although the ECHR later admits it misunderstood the way the duty of care concept works, the courts become more careful about using *Hill* as a blanket immunity for the police

↓

1999: In *Swinney* v. *Chief Constable of Northumbria Police*, the Court of Appeal allows a claim by a police informer for negligence in not protecting her from attack

↓

2000: In *Waters* v. *Commissioner of Police for the Metropolis*, the House of Lords allows a claim by a police officer for failure to stop her being bullied by fellow officers, even though the police argue that the *Hill* principles apply

↓

2001: In *Z* v. *UK*, the ECHR says it misunderstood the law on duty of care, but the English courts continue to be more cautious about striking out applications in police cases

↓

2005: In *Brooks* v. *Commissioner of Police for the Metropolis*, the House of Lords says the *Hill* principles are no longer to be viewed as a blanket immunity, and in exceptional cases, there may be liability to an ordinary member of the public, though the claimant loses his case

↓

2008: In *Smith* v. *Chief Constable of Sussex*, the House of Lords hold that the police are not liable to a claimant who was attacked almost fatally after reporting a series of death threats to them.

Out and about

Working in groups of three, read the facts of *Smith* v. *Chief Constable of Sussex*. Now assign one of your group as barrister for Mr Smith, one as barrister for the police, and the third as the judge. Each of the barristers should prepare their case, referring to the cases in this chapter on police liability and any policy considerations that you feel are relevant. You then have ten minutes each to put your case to the judge. The judge then has ten minutes to prepare a judgment, detailing which side they find for, and why.

Source: Pearson Education Ltd/Photodisc/Photolink/R. Morley

Handy tip: Remember that as a judge you should try to put aside your own personal views, and make up your mind after you have heard both sides, not before.

Reflective practice

Take a few minutes to think about how this exercise went. What did you find difficult? Was it easy for the barristers to work out which points to make, or more difficult than you expected? Was the judge's decision easier or more difficult to make than you expected? What did you find worked well for you? Is there anything you would do differently if you did a similar exercise?

The Human Rights Act 1998: an alternative to negligence?

Because the *Hill* rules have made it so difficult for crime victims to sue the police for negligence, attempts have been made to sidestep the issue, by basing a claim on the Human Rights Act rather than negligence. As we saw earlier, in *Osman* v. *UK*, the wife of a murdered man went to the ECHR to claim that the *Hill* rules breached the right to a fair trial. Mrs Osman's case also had a second strand, in which she claimed that in failing to protect her husband the police had breached his right to life, under Article 2 of the ECHR. The ECHR said that, on the facts, the right to life under Article 2 was not breached, largely because the police could not have been expected to know that the Osman family would be a target. However, it did say that there were circumstances where national authorities such as the police could have an obligation to take preventive action to protect an individual whose life was at risk from the criminal activities of another. This obligation would arise, they said, where the authorities knew or ought to have known of a real and immediate risk to the life of an indentified individual from the criminal activities of someone else, and they failed to take measures which were within the scope of their powers, and might reasonably have been expected to protect the person concerned.

Case Summary

The issue was considered again in *Van Colle* v. *Chief Constable of Hertfordshire* (2008). Mr and Mrs Van Colle were the parents of a man who was shot dead just before he was due to give evidence in a criminal trial. Their son, Giles, had been called as a witness in the trial of a man called Daniel Brougham on charges of dishonesty. During the run-up to the trial there was a series of threats and incidents of interference with witnesses. Mr and Mrs Van Colle had evidence that showed the police officer in charge of the case knew, or should have known, about this. Nevertheless, no protection was provided for Giles, and days before the trial he was shot by Daniel Brougham, who was later convicted of his murder. Mr and Mrs Van Colle argued that the police had put Giles at risk by requiring him to give evidence, and there were reasonable precautions that they could and should have taken to protect him. They said their failure to take these precautions put the police in breach of Article 2.

Mr and Mrs Van Colle won their case at first instance and in the Court of Appeal, but the House of Lords reversed the Court of Appeal decision. They said that the key question, based on the *Osman* decision, was whether the officer in charge of the case, making a reasonable and informed judgement in the circumstances known to him at the time, should have realised that there was a real and immediate risk to Giles's life. If he should have realised this, there would have been a breach of Article 2, because appropriate steps to protect Giles were not taken. However, on the facts, the House held that there had been no breach.

Law in action 'Osman warnings'

In June 2008, *The Times* reported that the *Osman* case has led to a change in the way that the police carry out their work. As we have seen, where the police know of a serious threat to a particular individual and do nothing about it, they could be liable under Article 2 if that person is killed or seriously injured. *The Times* found that where police forces receive information that a particular individual may be the subject of a murder plot, but do not have enough evidence to make an arrest, it has become standard procedure to warn that person about the threat to their safety, a practice known as issuing an '*Osman* warning', after the case of *Osman* v. *UK*. In some cases the people concerned will be potential witnesses to crime (and may enter the witness protection programme as a result of the warning), in others they are themselves known criminals, particularly drug dealers and gang members, who are under threat from rivals or former associates. Over 1,000 *Osman* warnings were issued across the country during 2007, but by 2010 a Freedom of Information request made by the BBC found that the Metropolitan Police alone had issued over 350 warnings that year, three times the number they had issued in 2007. It is thought that the increase was due to a rise in gang violence.

[*Reference*: 'Metropolitan Police "Osman" murder warnings treble', http://www.bbc.co.uk/news/uk_england_london_13753554]

Liability of local councils and public authorities

Many of the arguments against police liability in negligence can also be used against liability for local councils and other public authorities. As with the police, damages will often ultimately be paid by the taxpayer, resources may be diverted from public services to defending legal cases, and staff may become more concerned with covering themselves than doing their job well. However, there is a further problem with cases involving public bodies, and in particular democratically elected ones. That is the issue of 'justiciability', which simply means suitability for examination by a court.

'justiciability' simply means suitability for examination by a court

The justiciability issue arises because, in many cases, the actions and decisions of public bodies can only be properly examined by reference to factors which the court process is not equipped to assess. Public bodies are often given legal powers to act, but allowed a choice as to how, when and even whether they use those powers. For example, imagine that a statute says that local councils 'may establish patrols to round up stray dogs'. This means that a local council that wants to set up patrols can do so. But it does not mean that they have to. It is up to the council to decide whether there is a need for this service in their area, and if there is, whether money would be well spent on meeting that need, or whether there might be some other need that is more important. Similarly, if a council did decide to set up dog patrols under the statute with this wording, it could decide how often and where they should be used.

Although our statute here is an imaginary one, there are many Acts of Parliament which allow public bodies to make these sorts of choices: this is usually referred to as allowing them a discretion. How a public body exercises this discretion will depend on lots of different factors, including:

- what the local needs are;
- how much money and manpower they have available;
- whether there are other demands on those resources;
- whether there are different ways of solving a problem or meeting a need.

As an example, take the facts of *Stovin* v. *Wise* (1996). Mr Stovin was injured when his motorbike was hit by a car driven by Ms Wise. Her insurance company paid Mr Stovin, but they claimed that the accident was partly caused by the negligence of the local council and so claimed a contribution from them. The basis for the claim was that Ms Wise had been unable to see Mr Stovin approaching because an overhanging bank of earth was obstructing her view. The council had a statutory power to order a landowner to remove this kind of obstruction, but they had not done so.

Case Summary

We will discuss the court's decision later in this section, but for the time being the facts of the case illustrate very well the problem of justiciability. The council did know about the obstruction, and had previously asked the landowner to remove it, but had not followed up when this was not done. They also knew that other accidents had happened in the same spot. But there were even worse accident blackspots in other areas of the county, and there were also other problems that demanded the council's money and attention. The council's budget was limited, as every council's is. How should a court decide whether the council, which had been democratically elected by local people, should have spent its money and manpower on removing this particular obstruction rather than on something else?

The traditional position

Until fairly recently, these problems meant that the courts generally took the view that it was not desirable to impose duties of care on councils and other public bodies. The case which established this approach was *X* v. *Bedfordshire County Council* (1995), in which the House of Lords heard five cases, which were grouped together because they all raised the issue of local authority liability in negligence. Three of the cases were brought by claimants who, as children, had had special needs. They claimed that their local councils had been negligent in failing to provide adequate education for them. The other two concerned allegations of negligence in local councils' use of their powers to take children into care. In one case, four siblings had suffered terrible neglect and abuse at the hands of their mother, who locked them in filthy bedrooms, which they were forced to use as toilets, and failed to feed them so they got so hungry that they scavenged food from dustbins. They said the council was negligent in not taking them into care. In the other case, a local council had wrongly taken a child into care, and both the child and its mother had suffered psychiatric injury as a result.

Using the ***Caparo* test**, the House of Lords held that it was not just and reasonable to impose a duty with regard to protection from child abuse. They said this was an area where councils had to exercise their discretion, and in any individual situation there might be different views as to the best course of action. If the courts were to impose a duty of care to individuals, council staff might begin making decisions with one eye on whether they might be sued, and the need to defend claims in negligence would take money and manpower from the important work of protecting children at risk. In addition, there were other ways that an individual who was unhappy with a council's actions could challenge them, including appeals procedures contained in child protection statutes, and the right to bring a complaint to the local authority ombudsman, who oversees their work.

In the education cases, however, the House of Lords found that it was arguable that a duty of care might arise, where advice was being given directly to, and relied on, by parents. However, the House did not decide that there definitely was a duty of care, just that arguably there might be.

Case Summary

A similarly restrictive approach was taken in *Stovin* v. *Wise*, the road accident case we looked at above. The claimant argued that the existence of a statutory power for councils to order the removal of obstructions created a relationship of proximity between the council and users of their roads. The House of Lords disagreed. They said that the fact that Parliament had given local councils a power to act, rather than a duty, suggested the statute was not meant to create any liability to individuals.

A change of approach

These cases seemed to suggest that the courts intended to keep strict limits on the liability of public authorities and councils for negligence. However, just as with the police cases, the influence of the Human Rights Act has led to a shift in approach in recent years. In the previous section, we looked at the case of *Osman* v. *UK*, which suggested that allowing immunities to liability for certain categories of defendant might be a breach of the Article 6 right to a fair trial. *Osman* itself made the courts more reluctant to strike out duty of care cases generally, and it was followed by *Z* v. *UK* (2001), which specifically dealt with the liabilities of local councils. The claimants in the case were the same four siblings whose claim had been part of *X* v. *Bedfordshire*, where they alleged the council had been negligent in failing to take them into care. In *Z* v. *UK*, they claimed that the UK had breached their Article 3 right to protection from 'inhuman and degrading treatment'. The ECHR agreed, and ordered damages to be paid.

Case Summary

The ECHR decision meant that people in the position of the claimants would have a claim under the Human Rights Act. The English courts could, therefore, have kept the restrictive rules on public authorities' liability in negligence, because claimants would have an alternative remedy in human rights law. But in logical terms, this made no sense. Essentially, the reason why the claimants' rights under the Human Rights Act were breached was because a public authority failed to take reasonable care for their safety. How then, was it possible to say that the same authority could not be liable in negligence, when negligence in this case would mean failure to take reasonable care for their safety?

claimants would have an alternative remedy in human rights law

Recognising this problem, the courts have now moved away from their former strict approach to public authority liability, and in a series of cases duties of care have been found in situations involving public authorities. One of these cases was *W* v. *Essex County Council* (2000), the case we looked at briefly in Chapter 4, where the claimants were foster parents and the local council placed with them a boy who had a record of sexually abusing other children. He then abused the couple's children. The Court of Appeal said that the council had a duty of care towards the foster parents and their children.

Case Summary

In *Barrett* v. *Enfield London Borough Council* (1999), the claimant had been taken into care as a child. He was moved from home to home, had a thoroughly unpleasant and difficult childhood, and was never given treatment for the psychiatric problems he suffered from. The Court of Appeal said that councils could have a duty to the children in their care.

Case Summary

In *T* v. *Surrey CC* (1994), the council recommended a childminder to a local mother, even though the minder was being investigated for abuse. She later injured the claimant's child, and it was found that councils could have a duty of care in this situation. In ***Phelps* v. *Hillingdon LBC*** (2001), the House of Lords found that councils could owe children a duty of care to provide an education appropriate to their needs, and in *Bradford Smart* v. *West Sussex CC* (2001), that schools could owe pupils a duty to take reasonable steps to prevent bullying.

Case Summary

Case Navigator

Finally, in ***D* v. *East Berkshire NHS Trust*** (2005), the House of Lords overruled the decision in *X* v. *Bedfordshire* on the duty of care owed in child protection cases. Again, this was three cases heard together. The claimant in the first case was a mother who had been wrongly suspected of harming her daughter; in the second, a father whose daughter had been taken into care on the incorrect suspicion that she was being sexually abused by him; and in the third, a mother and father whose daughter was taken into care for a year after they were wrongly suspected of injuring her. In each case, the claimants had suffered psychiatric harm as a result of the events, and sought to sue their local NHS Trust and/or local council, who had been responsible for the decisions made.

Case Navigator

Case Summary

The defendants sought to rely on *X* v. *Bedfordshire*, where it had been said that it was not fair, just or reasonable to impose a duty on public authorities with regard to child protection. They said that the reasons given there still applied: council staff might begin making decisions with one eye on whether they might be sued, and the need to defend claims in negligence would take money and manpower from the important work of protecting children at risk. But the House of Lords said that, since the Human Rights Act was passed, things had changed. A local authority could no longer avoid the adverse effects of a risk of being sued in negligence, because claimants could sue anyway under the Human Rights Act. Therefore, there were no longer any policy reasons for refusing to impose a duty of care in negligence between public authorities and the children they were supposed to protect. This did not mean that there would be such a duty in every case; there could still be situations where it was not fair, just or reasonable to impose a duty of care. But each case would have to be determined on its individual facts, rather than covered by a blanket rule of no liability for public authorities.

However, the House made it clear that where there was a duty it could only be owed to children, and not to parents. This was because where child abuse was suspected the interests of the child might be in conflict with the interests of the parents. It would be difficult for social workers or doctors to do their duty to a child who they suspected was being abused if, when deciding whether to take the child into care for its own protection, they had also to think about whether they might be sued for causing psychiatric injury to the parents. The child's interests had to take priority, so there were still good policy reasons for refusing a duty to parents in this situation, but not to children.

Interestingly, the House also specifically stated that the decision should apply equally to cases concerning negligence which happened before the Human Rights Act was passed. This was important in practical terms, as in many of the cases the events concerned will have happened many years ago, when the claimants were children. Had the House not done this, claimants in that situation would not have been able to sue in negligence.

Writing and drafting

Imagine that it is 2005 and you are a lawyer. The case of *D* v. *East Berkshire* has just been decided, and your boss thinks it may lead to some new avenues of work. She wants to know the full details of the decision. Read the case, then write a brief memo, detailing the law before the case was decided, and the changes it makes.

Handy tip: You may find it useful to read the case through fully, making notes, and then put the key points in order of priority before you start drafting your memo.

Source: Pearson Education Ltd/Photodisc/C Squared Studios

Law in action Child protection cases

As we saw above, the case of *D* v. *Berkshire* established that local authorities owed a duty of care to children at risk of abuse, and opened the way for children who had been abused at home to sue for a local authority's failure to take them into care. In 2008, newspapers reported on one of the first cases of this kind to reach the higher courts, *Pierce* v. *Doncaster Metropolitan Borough Council* (2008). The claimant had been beaten by his parents almost daily since he was a baby, left naked outside for hours at a time, and warned that if he told anyone he would be killed. When he was six months old he was briefly taken into care but then returned to his parents. His aunt later contacted social services when she saw burns on his body, but her warnings were ignored. He was not taken into care until he was 14, and had run away from home after his father threatened him with a knife. By that time he had a severe personality disorder. He argued that the local council had failed in their duty to him, by returning him to his parents after his initial stay in foster care. The council argued that they were not in breach of their duty of care, but the Court of Appeal disagreed, and Mr Pierce won his case. He was awarded £25,000 in damages. After the case, *The Times* reported that between 200 and 300 similar cases were being prepared by lawyers. Most of them were expected to be settled, with damages of between £15,000 and £100,000.

The issue hit the headlines again in 2009, with the story of Baby P, later identified as Peter. The 17-month-old died after months of vicious abuse, with eight broken ribs and a broken back, despite the fact that social services had regularly visited his home. They were criticised for failing to take him into care, and Baby P's father, who did not live with his mother, threatened to sue the local council on his son's behalf. At the time of publication it was not known whether that claim is to go ahead.

[*Reference*: 'Hundreds of abused children to sue', *The Times*, 24 Dec 2008]

People in the law

Rawdon Crozier is a barrister at King's Bench Chambers, in Plymouth, who has dealt with negligence litigation against local authorities by claimants who have spent time in care.

How did you get involved in this area of work? I've always done professional negligence work, and my first encounter with a negligent care proceedings case came as a result of having two relatively recent care leavers walk in off the street. Their first concern had simply been to have sight of their care records, but the local authority in question had run them from pillar to post and so they'd felt the need to engage a solicitor.

Essentially, the truth was that their mother had split from their father, moved away and become an alcoholic and started to form unsuitable attachments. There were suggestions that she'd engaged in prostitution and formed a relationship with another prostitute and that they had allowed unsuitable people into the home, while at the same time they had been very successful at keeping social services out. There was physical abuse and a strong suspicion of sexual abuse, and apart from that the children had been left to run wild. There had been a number of referrals to social services over a period of years, and numerous visits at which social services had failed in trying to see the children. Before the children were finally taken into care, they had not been seen by a social worker for about 14 months.

Source: Rawdon Crozier (*text and photo*)

The children were only taken into care when their mother finally succeeded in drinking herself to death. However, the only information they had from the council had simply said more or less 'Your mother was an alcoholic, no one really knew anything until she died'. At the time I became involved in that case, *X* v. *Bedfordshire* was still notionally good law, and the impact of *Z* v. *UK* had not been assessed domestically, so it was something of a flyer to advise granting them legal aid.

What are the main practical problems you face with this kind of case? First, the quantity of documentation, and assessing it coherently, and secondly, finding the right expert. Thirdly, the clients. This is not being pejorative – they are often damaged individuals who need careful handling; simply wading in and asking direct questions about childhood trauma could itself be psychologically damaging. Fourthly, avoiding being rushed into bad decisions because the limitation period is about to run out – often these cases involve incidents which happened a long time ago, and generally the limitation period runs out three years after the client becomes 18. But recognising the problems is the first step to overcoming them.

Do you think *D* v. *East Berks* was a good decision? An immensely good decision, and a brave and intelligent one too. It would have been very easy for the Court of Appeal to have decided the issue on narrow grounds and avoided examining the impact of *Z* v. *UK* almost completely. Equally, they could just have considered the effect of *Z* after the introduction of the Human Rights Act, and left pre-2000 cases in the limbo of having to fail to obtain a domestic remedy and then go off to Europe for compensation. Instead they effectively 'reverse-engineered' the **common law** to found a duty of care retrospectively. It's the legal equivalent of inventing a time machine and I can't think of another instance of anything similar.

There were concerns that allowing local authorities to be sued for negligence in child protection would 'open the floodgates'. Do you think this will happen? How common do you think it is for people to want to sue for negligence in child protection? I know that there will be more claims than there were previously (self-evidently when one is starting from a base-line of zero) but I do not think there will be a flood. For a start, it will be rare that a case which has involved a delay while the local authority has given itself reasonable time to reflect upon the right course of action, or has left a child in the home while, say, attempting rehabilitation will give rise to a viable claim. I think that the margin of appreciation given to local authorities will be wide enough to keep the numbers of claims that are brought to a low level.

I would expect quite a number of care leavers to seek advice as to whether they might have a claim, however. I know the solicitors who instructed me in the case to which I have referred have had enquiries from other potential claimants and that has happened simply from word of mouth within a small provincial town. But I do not see that as being likely to open the **'floodgates'**.

Does the standard of care as explained in *Pierce* [see Law in Action box] give sufficient protection to children, or could it amount to the social work profession setting their own standard? I think it's a mistake to see *Pierce* as something concerned with protecting children per se. *Pierce* is about the remedy afforded to a child when protection measures have failed in circumstances in which they should not have done. If I may be allowed to butcher analogy, *Pierce*, in common with all other professional negligence litigation, is not concerned with seeing that the stable door is shut but in deciding how much the owner should be paid for the horse that has bolted.

Having said that, the existence of *Pierce*-type claims may help to focus the minds of social workers and thereby have an incidental benefit to child protection. However, generally best practice social work is adequate to ensure child protection; it is the lack of resources that is usually responsible for standards falling below that level. The interesting question as the field develops will be to see to what extent underfunding is going to be allowed to be used as a **defence**. There is a world of difference between judging child care decisions by the standard of 'the reasonable local authority' and 'the reasonable but near-bankrupt local authority'. Unfortunately I see there being quite a lot of litigation on this topic.

As to the standards: very largely the social work profession is setting, or strictly, has set, its own standards, because the proof of negligence involves expert evidence from a social work professional. But the courts always have the fallback of being able to say that a particular practice was so unreasonable as to be negligent, however widely it was followed within the profession.

Do you think there are any problems with the law in this area? Limitation and the striking of a fair balance between giving the deserving a remedy and allowing local authorities a fair opportunity to defend their actions will be, I anticipate, an ongoing area of controversy.

Summary

- Negligence cases against public bodies raise difficult issues because damages may be funded by the taxpayer, fighting cases diverts resources from services, and fear of being sued may affect the way services are run and delivered.
- For police liability, a distinction is made between operational issues, where a standard duty of care applies, and policy issues, where a duty of care traditionally did not apply.
- This distinction traditionally meant police had no duty of care to protect an individual member of the public from crime, but this approach was successfully challenged in the ECHR case of *Osman* v. *UK*.
- There is no longer a blanket immunity for negligence claims concerning police handling of criminal cases, but so far case law has only found a duty of care towards people in a special relationship with the police, such as informers or employees. There can only be a duty to ordinary members of the public in exceptional circumstances.
- Public authority cases raise the extra problem of justiciability, in that some questions involve decisions about allocation of resources and choice of policy, which are not appropriate for a court to decide.
- The courts were traditionally reluctant to allow a duty of care in public authority cases, but the position has changed since *Osman* v. *UK* and *Z* v. *UK*. A duty of care can now exist to children given inadequate education and children at risk from abuse at home, among others.

Question and answer*

Problem:

Susie Seeker is a reporter on a newspaper. She has been working undercover on an investigative report into criminal gangs, and she learns that one gang plan to kidnap Johnny Rich, the son of a wealthy local business owner. She decides to give the information to the police, but she makes it clear that she is giving it to them confidentially, and that she does not want the gang members to find out it came from her in case they try to take revenge.

The police do not take her information seriously, and a week later Johnny is kidnapped. He escapes, but was badly beaten up during his captivity. During the investigation into the kidnapping, an officer leaves a report detailing Susie's evidence in a local café, and it eventually reaches the hands of the gang leader. He sends two men to track down Susie and beat her up.

Advise Johnny and Susie whether either of them has a claim against the police in negligence.

You should allow yourself no more than 40 minutes to complete this task.

Essay:

'Cases involving negligence by the police or public authorities present the courts with a difficult balancing act.'

Do you think the current law strikes the right balance?

This question should be answered in 40 minutes.

* Answer guidance is provided at the end of the chapter.

Further reading

Bailey, S. (2006) 'Public authority liability in negligence: the continued search for coherence', 26 LS 155.
This interesting article argues that treating public authorities as a special case in negligence has led to the creation of unnecessary and unworkable tests, and that it would be better to use other ways of holding them to account.

Gearty, C. (2001) 'Unravelling *Osman*', 64(2) MLR 159, and

Gearty, C. (2002) '*Osman* Unravels', 67 MLR 87.
In the first of these articles, the author takes a detailed look at the reasoning in *Osman* and how it impacted on English law, and in the second, he looks at the case of *Z* v. *UK*, and how far this repairs the damage. Clear and easy to read, these are a good guide to these two very important cases.

McIvor, C. (2010) 'Getting defensive about police negligence: the *Hill* principle, the Human Rights Act 1998 and the House of Lords', 69(1) CLJ 133.
An interesting and up-to-date look at the key cases on police liability.

Wright, J. (1998) 'Local Authorities, the Duty of Care and the European Convention on Human Rights', 16 OJLS 1.
A very clear and detailed look at the key case of *X* v. *Bedfordshire*.

Question and answer guidance

Problem: Taking Johnny first, the starting point in cases involving police negligence is *Hill*, so you should apply the rules there to Johnny's situation. You can then go on to point out that in *Brooks* v. *Commissioner of Police for the Metropolis*, it was held that there might be exceptional situations where there is a duty of care towards an individual and then consider the case of *Smith* v. *Chief Constable of Sussex*, and how that applies to Johnny's position.

Turning to Susie, the situation is a bit different, in that she is an informer. You therefore need to apply the case of *Swinney*, and consider why this might make a difference.

Essay: A good way to begin this essay is to explain why these cases present the courts with a difficult balancing act, and talk about issues like who pays the damages, how the threat of liability might affect day-to-day work, and why the questions raised in these cases may not be suitable for courts to decide. Then work through some of the cases in this chapter, explaining how the courts have sought to strike the right balance, and highlighting some of the problems that have arisen. You might mention, for example, the difficulties in deciding liability in *Stovin* v. *Wise*, and the problems with being fair to both adults and children in the child protection cases. You should also mention the impact of the Human Rights Act, and you might conclude by considering whether this has improved the courts' ability to perform their balancing act or not.

Visit **www.mylawchamber.co.uk/quinntort** to access tools to help you develop and test your knowledge of tort law, including practice exam questions with guidance, annotated weblinks, glossary and key case flashcards, legal newsfeed and legal updates and interactive 'You be the judge' questions.

Use Case Navigator to read in full some of the key cases referenced in this chapter with commentary and questions:

D* v. *East Berkshire Community Health NHS Trust and others [2005] 2 All ER 443

Phelps* v. *London Borough of Hillingdon*, *Anderton* v. *Clwyd County Council*, *Jarvis* v. *Hampshire County Council*, *Re G (a minor) [2000] 4 All ER 504

Chapter 7 Employers' liability

Key points In this chapter we will be looking at:

- The duty of care owed by employers to their employees
- Types of harm for which an employer can be liable
- Breach of the employer's duty
- Defences to a claim

Introduction

If someone were to ask to you to list activities that were dangerous, you might suggest things like skydiving or hang-gliding, perhaps rock-climbing or motor racing. You probably would not have on your list 'going to work' and yet the workplace is one of the most common situations for accidents and injuries to occur. These can range from horrific deaths caused by workers being trapped in machinery, or fatal industrial illnesses such as asbestosis, to conditions such as repetitive strain injury or depression, which are typically caused in the apparently safe environment of an office but can be sufficiently serious to mean that an employee may never be able to work again.

Up until the early nineteenth century the law provided little help for anyone injured at work, but as increasing industrialisation made accidents more common, the courts began to develop rules to protect employees, and eventually created a **common law** duty on employers to take steps to protect employees' health and safety. That duty is the subject of this chapter. As you will see, it is really a specialised branch of the general law on negligence and, as such, many of the rules and concepts are the same.

Key stats Accidents and injuries at work

During 2009–10:

- 1.3 million people were suffering from an illness that they believed was caused or made worse by their work.
- 550,000 people developed an illness which they believed was caused by their work.
- 152 employees were killed at work, which works out at 1 in every 200,000 workers.
- 233,000 employees reported being injured at work, which works out at 840 injuries per 100,000 employees.
- 28.5 million working days were lost to work-related illness or injury.

[*Source*: Health and Safety Executive, **www.hse.gov.uk**]

Liability for harm to employees

For most of this chapter, we will be looking at an employer's common law duty for the safety of their employees. Before we start though, it is worth knowing that there are several other ways that an employer can be liable under civil law for harm done to an employee:

- Vicarious liability: this arises when one employee injures another, in circumstances where the law regards the employer as being legally responsible for the employee's acts, and is discussed in the next chapter.
- Breach of statutory duty: this arises where statute imposes a duty on the employer with regard to the safety of the employee, this duty is breached and the statute allows for a claim. It is discussed in Chapter 11.
- Breach of contract: all employment contracts contain an **implied term** (meaning one which the law assumes is there, regardless of whether it is written down) that the employer will take reasonable care to protect the health and safety of their employees.

In certain cases an employer who breaks health and safety laws can also be liable for a criminal offence, up to and including manslaughter.

Employers' liability: the traditional position

Before we look at the law on employers' liability as it is today, it is worth having a brief look at the history of the law in this area, as that will help you put the current law in its practical context. As we saw in the introduction, special legal protection for employees has really only existed since the nineteenth century. Before that, three legal principles existed which made it practically impossible for injured employees to make a claim against their employers, even where it was clear that the injury was caused by the employer failing to take even basic safety precautions. These principles have become known as the 'unholy trinity', and consist of the following:

special legal protection for employees has really only existed since the nineteenth century

- the doctrine of 'common employment';
- the **defence** of **contributory negligence**;
- the defence of ***volenti non fit injuria***.

The doctrine of common employment, established in *Priestley* v. *Fowler* (1837), meant that if an employee suffered harm caused by another employee, the employer was not liable for this, even if the ultimate cause was the employer's failure to take adequate safety precautions. The only exception was if the employer had failed to make sure that the employee who did the harm was competent (and it was very difficult to prove that). The theory behind the doctrine was that every contract of employment had in it an implied term stating that the employee accepted the risk of negligence by a fellow employee. In practice this was nonsense, as most workers in those days were not in a position to accept or reject any terms or conditions, but had to take what the employer offered or find another job. There were no trade unions to fight for fair terms, and individual workers had little, if any, say in their working conditions. The second element of the 'unholy trinity', the defence of contributory

most workers were not in a position to accept or reject any terms or conditions

negligence, is one we looked at in Chapter 3. You will remember that, in modern law, it applies where the claimant was partly to blame for the accident or injury and reduces the **damages** to reflect that. However, this position was only introduced in the Law Reform (Contributory Negligence) Act 1945. Before that, common law provided that anyone who was partly responsible for damage done to them could not sue at all, and this meant that if it could be argued that the employee was in any way at fault they had no claim.

We have also come across the third element of the trinity, the defence of *volenti*, before, and you will remember that this applies where the claimant has voluntarily taken the risk of being harmed. As we will see later, the modern courts are aware that accepting a job which carries risks may not be a genuinely voluntary choice, given that many people have to take whatever work they can find in order to earn a living. Back in the nineteenth century, however, the courts did not take this view, and it was easy for an employer to claim that if an employee had chosen to do a job that was dangerous the defence of *volenti* applied.

employers could impose extremely dangerous conditions and practices on their employees

Taken together, these three doctrines meant that employers could impose extremely dangerous conditions and practices on their employees, with practically no risk of being sued. This was a time when Britain was industrialising and many employees worked in factories, mills and mines where the machinery was highly dangerous, safety precautions were scarce, and hours were long, so accidents were common, and if someone was seriously injured there was no NHS to look after them and no welfare benefits to support them if they were unable to work again. But industry was making Britain prosperous, and the courts were reluctant to disturb this by exposing employers to the costs of either taking safety precautions, or paying compensation for the harm done by not taking safety precautions. The approach of the law was therefore that it was up to employees to look after their own safety, and if they failed to do so they could not expect to make the employer liable.

How the law developed

Towards the end of the nineteenth century things began to change, for three main reasons. First, the increase in industry, and in particular, the huge amount of work being done to build railways, led to greater awareness of the numbers of serious accidents being caused to workers and the harshness of the law regarding them. Secondly, workers were beginning to organise into trade unions and, together, they were able to fight for better treatment in a way that individual workers could not do for themselves. Thirdly, a market in insurance cover for business owners was developing, and this meant that if an employer was sued they would not have to pay the costs themselves.

both the courts and Parliament began to offer more protection to injured employees

As a result of these developments, both the courts and Parliament began to offer more protection to injured employees, though it took some time. The first major development came in *Smith* v. *Charles Baker* (1891), the case we looked at in Chapter 3, where a worker was injured when a large stone fell on him.

Case Summary

As you may remember, the **claimant** worked in the defendant's quarry, and while he was working, a crane was being operated above his head, swinging huge rocks. The claimant had complained to the **defendant** several times that there was a risk of one of the stones falling on him, but when that happened, and he sued, his employer pleaded *volenti*, arguing that in continuing to work when he knew of the risk he was accepting it. The

House of Lords disagreed. They said that if a person took on work that would have been dangerous even if their employers took proper precautions, they might be said to be accepting the risks involved in that work. But in this case, the work itself was not dangerous, but was made so by the defendant's negligence. Therefore merely continuing to do the work when he knew of the risk did not mean he consented to it, and *volenti* did not apply. This made it much more difficult for employers to use the *volenti* defence in cases where the only acceptance of the risk was taking the job, or carrying on doing it.

The other major developments took a little longer, but by the 1930s the key case of *Wilsons and Clyde Coal* v. *English* (1938) had established that employers had a duty towards the safety of their employees. The claimant was a miner at the defendants' coal mine. As he was leaving the mine at the end of his shift, some machinery that should have been switched off was turned on, and he was crushed. The defendants said that they had employed a competent manager, whose job it was to look after the technical operations of the mine, and since they had done that they should not be liable. The House of Lords disagreed. They stated that employers had a duty to provide a competent staff, adequate materials and a proper system of work, and that this duty was '**non-delegable**'. That meant that although an employer could delegate the task of doing those things to someone such as a manager, they could not delegate the legal liability for them.

Case Summary

Finally, during the 1940s, the remains of the 'unholy trinity' were dismantled. As we saw earlier, the 1945 Law Reform (Contributory Negligence) Act altered the contributory negligence defence so that it could only reduce damages and not prevent a claim completely. Three years later, the Law Reform (Personal Injuries) Act 1948 abolished the doctrine of common employment, making it possible to sue employers for torts committed by their employees (we will look at why this is so important in the next chapter, when we look at vicarious liability).

Further protection for employees came in 1969, when the Employers' Liability (Compulsory Insurance) Act provided that employers must take out insurance against workplace accidents. In practical terms this was very important, as it made it much more likely that employers would be able to pay damages if they were sued.

The employer's duty

As we saw above, *Wilsons and Clyde Coal* v. *English* established that employers have a duty to take reasonable care to ensure the safety of their employees. This duty works in the same way as duties of care in negligence, such as the motorist's duty to take reasonable care not to injure other road users, in that it is not an absolute duty to prevent any harm occurring but a duty to take reasonable care to prevent reasonably foreseeable harm.

The duty is owed only by employers to employees, and not to anyone who happens to visit the workplace, or to what are called 'independent contractors', meaning people who come to the workplace to do a job but are not, in law, employed there (an example would be a plumber who comes to fix a leak in a factory, but is not employed by the owners of the factory).

In *Wilsons*, the House of Lords said that the duty had the first three elements listed below, and over the years the fourth has also come to be accepted as part of the duty:

- a competent staff;
- adequate materials;
- a safe system of work;
- a safe workplace.

A competent staff

An employer who takes on someone without sufficient experience and/or training for a particular job, or fails to take action when a worker is incompetent in some way, will be liable if this results in another employee being injured. In practice, this part of the duty has become much less important since the creation of the doctrine of **vicarious liability**, which means that an employee injured by a colleague can usually sue the employer for what the colleague did (we will look at how this works in the next chapter). It will usually be easier to prove a case on vicarious liability, which looks at what the colleague actually did, than to prove that the harm they caused was the result of the employer recruiting someone insufficiently experienced, or failing to train or supervise them properly.

Case Summary

However, there are still some situations in which the employer's duty will provide a claim when vicarious liability will not. An example can be seen in *Hudson* v. *Ridge Manufacturing Co. Ltd* (1957). The claimant was injured by a colleague, Harold, who had a habit of playing around at work, including tripping people up and play-fighting or, as the court put it, 'engaging in horseplay'. Vicarious liability did not apply, because it is only available when harm is caused by an employee acting 'within the course of employment'. This is a concept we will look at more fully when we examine vicarious liability in Chapter 8, but for now a simple explanation is that what the colleague was doing must be part of their work or closely connected to it. Harold's mucking around could not be considered to be something he was doing 'in the course of his employment', so it was not possible for the claimant to make the employer vicariously liable for what had happened. However, it was clear that the employers knew about Harold's tendency to boisterous behaviour, and had known for some time, and the court found that it was obvious that this kind of thing was likely to lead to injury at some point. Therefore the employers were in breach of their duty to the claimant, because they had not taken reasonable steps to stop Harold's behaviour.

Adequate material

Case Summary

Employers have a duty to take reasonable care that the tools, equipment and materials employees use are reasonably safe, and to maintain them in a safe condition. In *Bradford* v. *Robinson Rentals* (1967), for example, an employer was found liable when the claimant suffered frostbite after making a long journey in a van which had cracked windows and no heating.

The duty also requires employers to provide safety equipment where it is reasonable to do so, but it is possible for an employer to escape liability if they can show that the employee would not have used the equipment even if they had provided it. This is simply an application of the **'but for'** test of **causation** that we looked at in Chapter 3. As you will remember, a claimant has to show that but for the defendant's negligence, their accident or injury would not have happened. Even if an employer is clearly negligent in not supplying safety equipment, if it can be shown that the claimant would not have worn it anyway the 'but for' test is not satisfied, because the accident or injury would have happened even if the equipment had been provided. This was the situation in

Case Summary

McWilliam v. *Sir William Arrol & Co. Ltd* (1962), where the claimant was a steel erector who fell to his death because he was not wearing a safety harness. His employers had not actually provided a harness, but there was strong evidence that the claimant had never used safety harnesses even when they were available, and so the House of Lords held that it was reasonable to infer that he would not have worn one on the day of the accident either. He would therefore have suffered the same injury even if the employers had not been negligent and so they were not liable.

In the past there was a serious loophole in this area of the law, which concerned defective equipment (both safety equipment and the ordinary equipment used to do a job, such as tools or machinery). If an employee was injured because of a defect in equipment that could not be discovered using reasonable care, the employer would not be liable under common law, and the employee's only option was to sue the manufacturer of the equipment in negligence (which, as we will see in Chapter 10, can be extremely difficult). This gap was closed by the Employers' Liability (Defective Equipment) Act 1969. Section 1(1) provides that

> Where . . . an employee suffers personal injury in the course of his employment in consequence of a defect in equipment provided by his employer for the purposes of the employer's business and the defect is attributable wholly or partly to the fault of a third party (whether identified or not) the injury shall be deemed to be also attributable to negligence on the part of the employer.

This means that if the employee can show that, on a balance of probabilities, the defect resulted from negligence or other fault during manufacture, and the defect caused their injury, they can sue the employer. The employer will usually have a claim against the manufacturer, either in negligence or for breach of contract. Since the Act was passed the courts have given a wide definition to the term 'equipment', and in *Knowles* v. *Liverpool City Council* (1992), where the claimant was injured by a flagstone he was laying, the House of Lords said that 'equipment' included any article of any kind provided by the employer for the employee to do their job.

Case Summary

You be the judge

Q: Giles is a builder, working on a site run by Dodgy Developments Ltd. He is working in a building that was partly destroyed by an explosion. Large areas of the roof were damaged, and every so often, huge chunks of wood fall into the building. Usual practice in the industry is to wear hard hats on site but the foreman, who is in charge of the safety equipment, has gone off to another job, and no one knows where to find the key to the Portakabin where the hats are kept. Giles doesn't care; he finds hard hats uncomfortable and never wears them, and the foreman never insists. Giles sets to work, but a roof timber falls on him, causing a serious head injury. Does he have a claim against Dodgy Developments?

Source: Pearson Education Ltd/David Sanderson

A: No. It does look likely that not supplying the hard hats was negligent, and as we have seen, the duty to provide safety equipment is non-delegable, so Dodgy Developments could be liable even though it was the foreman's job to supply the hats. But in this case, it appears that Giles would not have worn a hard hat even if one had been available. That means the 'but for' test is not satisfied, because his injury would have happened even if there was no negligence, so his employers are not liable.

A safe system of working

This part of the duty covers things like the way jobs are organised and carried out, the number of employees involved in particular tasks, safety precautions other than equipment, and safety instructions and warnings, especially to new or inexperienced employees. The employer must take reasonable care to ensure that employees are not caused injury as a result of any of these factors, or anything else relating to the system of working. In *Johnstone* v. *Bloomsbury Health Authority* (1991), the claimant was a junior doctor who was contracted to work for 40 hours a week, and to be on call for an additional 48 hours. This meant he often went without adequate sleep, and he claimed that the hours he was forced to work had caused stress and depression, which, as we saw in Chapter 4, are recognised as forms of personal injury. The court agreed that a breach of the duty to provide a safe system of work could occur if an employee was made to work such long hours that it affected their health.

Case Summary

This duty may go further than simply providing a safe system of work; depending on the circumstances, it may be considered reasonable to expect the employer to make sure that employees work according to the safe system. In *Pape* v. *Cumbria County Council* (1992), the claimant developed a painful skin condition as a result of contact with cleaning products. Although the employer had provided protective gloves, which might have prevented the problem, they were held liable for breach of duty because they had not given employees sufficient warnings about the risks of the chemicals they were working with, nor instructed them to wear the gloves at all times.

Case Summary

In some cases, employers will argue that an employee should have been aware of the risk and realised the need to take precautions. The courts tend to reject this argument, even where the employee is experienced. In *General Cleaning Contractors* v. *Christmas* (1953), the claimant was a window cleaner with 20 years' experience, who was working on second floor windows. His employer had told him to clean as much as he could from the inside, and then to stand on the windowsill outside, holding on to the window frame, to clean the rest. The building concerned had sash windows, which have a top and bottom pane that each open independently, and the method of working was to open one of the panes, which allowed the claimant to hold on to the frame of the other one. While he was doing this the open pane closed, trapping his fingers and making him lose his balance and fall. It was clear that this was a potentially dangerous way of working, but it could have been made safe if Mr Christmas had wedged one of the panes open. The employer argued that because he was experienced he should have known to take this precaution. The House of Lords disagreed; it was the employer's duty to devise a safe system of work, and give employees such safety instructions as a reasonable employer who has considered the risks would be expected to give. The employer could not shunt that duty on to the employee, even if he was experienced. In fact, a reasonable employer should realise that employees are often careless about the risks involved in their work, and should bear this in mind when issuing safety warnings.

Case Summary

Where an employee is inexperienced, the courts may require employers to take even greater care. In *Fraser* v. *Winchester Health Authority* (1999), the claimant was a 21-year-old support worker who was employed by the health authority to work in a centre for handicapped young people. She was sent on a camping trip with some of the residents, and was burnt when she attempted to change a gas cylinder near a lit candle. She had not been given any training or instructions for using the camping equipment. The Health Authority argued that the risk of changing a gas cylinder near a naked flame was so obvious that she could be expected to see it, and that it was not therefore

Case Summary

reasonable to expect them to have warned her about it. The Court of Appeal disagreed: given the seriousness of her responsibilities, and the fact that she was very inexperienced, she should have been given more training. However, they accepted that she really should have had some awareness that what she was doing was dangerous, and so reduced the damages by one-third for contributory negligence.

A safe place of work

the employer is not expected to eliminate all possible risks

Employers must take care to ensure that the workplace is safe for employees. However, as with the other aspects of the duty, this is a standard of reasonableness; the employer is not expected to eliminate all possible risks (which in some types of workplace would be impossible), but is expected to take such steps as are reasonable and practical. In *Latimer* v. *AEC Ltd* (1952), the claimant worked for the defendants in their factory. Heavy rain had caused some flooding in the factory, and the water had mixed with an oily substance used in the manufacturing process, which left some very slippery patches on the floor. Although the defendants had covered most of them with sawdust, they had not had enough sawdust to do them all. The claimant slipped on one of the uncovered patches and was injured. He argued that the claimants had not taken sufficient precautions to prevent his injury, and that the situation was so potentially dangerous that they should have temporarily closed the factory. The House of Lords agreed that closure would have been the only way to completely protect against the danger of people slipping over. However, they said that given the level of risk, and the fact that the slippery patches were clearly visible, it was unreasonable to expect the defendants to take such extreme precautions. The precautions they had taken were reasonable in all the circumstances, and so they were not liable.

Case Summary

Offsite workers

Of course, not all employees work at their employer's premises. If you are employed as a window cleaner, a decorator or a plumber, for example, you will do your work in a variety of business premises or homes. Similarly, if you work for a company with clients overseas, you may from time to time have to work in the premises of those overseas clients. Even in these situations, your employer still has a duty to take reasonable steps to ensure that the workplace is safe but, here again, the courts will use a standard of reasonableness to judge what those precautions should be. In *Wilson* v. *Tyneside Window Cleaning Co.* (1958), the claimant was a window cleaner who was employed by the defendants to clean windows at the premises of different customers. He was injured when he was cleaning the outside of a kitchen window, standing on the sill, and the handle he was holding on to gave way. Evidence was given that the window was very obviously in poor repair, and that one handle was already missing. The employers did not inspect the premises that they sent employees to, nor had they warned about the specific danger of a handle giving way. However, they had told employees that if ever they had doubts about whether a particular window could be cleaned safely, they should not attempt to do so. The Court of Appeal held that they had done enough to fulfil their duty to the employee, and said it was not reasonable to expect an employer sending employees to a series of private houses to go and inspect all the premises beforehand.

Case Summary

Case Summary

A similar approach is taken where the employee is sent abroad. In *Cook* v. *Square D Ltd* (1992), the claimant was an electronics engineer who was sent to work on the installation of a computer system at a client's premises in Saudi Arabia. He tripped on a loose tile there and injured his leg. The Court of Appeal found that the employers had checked that the client in whose premises the accident happened were reliable and aware of their safety responsibilities. Considering the distance involved, they said this was all that the employers could reasonably be expected to do, and therefore they had fulfilled their duty. The Court pointed out that if several employees were being sent to a particular premises abroad, or if one or two were being sent there for a considerable period of time, it might be reasonable to expect the UK employer to take more steps to ensure the workplace abroad was safe, possibly including visiting to inspect the site.

You be the judge

Q: Ben is an electrician. He and nine other colleagues were sent by their firm to work on a new building in Dubai. While they are there, Ben falls from a ladder and is seriously injured. The ladder is found to be faulty. Ben's employer claims they cannot possibly be liable because the accident did not happen on their premises. Are they right?

A: No. An employer may still be liable even if an accident happens away from their premises, if they did not take reasonable precautions to check that the other premises were safe. Whether they are liable will depend on whether a court finds that the precautions they took, if any, were reasonable, and in this situation a court would look at whether it was practical for Ben's employer to check the site in Dubai. The fact that several employees were sent there may suggest they should have made a greater effort than if there had been only one employee sent out.

Source: Pearson Education/Image Source

Now you know what the employer's duty consists of, and we have looked at some cases which show how the courts apply it in different circumstances. Before we go on to the next section, try the practical exercise in the Writing and Drafting box to see how well you can apply the law.

Writing and drafting

You are a trainee solicitor, and your firm has recently taken on a client who has come up with an idea for a new product and is about to set up a small factory to make it. This is the first time she has run a factory, and she wants to make sure she takes reasonable precautions to protect her employees, and protect herself against common law liability for any injuries. She has asked your firm for advice and your boss asks you to write her a letter, explaining the basics of an employer's duty to their employees. Describe the elements of the duty in simple terms that a non-lawyer can understand, and explain what practical precautions she may need to take.

Handy tip: Remember that you are giving advice, not writing an essay, so you need to use practical instructions and address the client directly – for example, you might say 'Telling your employees about safety precautions may not be enough; it is safer to ensure that they follow them' rather than 'The case of *Pape* v. *Cumbria* provides that employers must make sure safety precautions are taken'.

Reflective practice

How easy did you find this exercise? If you found it difficult to give advice based on the summaries of the cases here, you may want to read some of the cases in more detail. It can be quite tricky to switch from essay writing mode to giving practical advice, but it is a good way to reinforce your understanding of the law, as well as excellent practice for the skills you will need as a lawyer.

Types of harm

Most employers' liability cases arise from accidents at work, or unsafe practices which cause illness over time, and so the majority of claims are for physical injury. However, in recent years the courts have seen a number of claims from people who have been caused mental health problems because of stress at work, and it is now clear that employers have a duty to take precautions against psychiatric injury, though the rules are quite restrictive. The courts have also found that employers' liability can include a duty to take steps to protect employees against economic loss, though this is very much more limited.

employers have a duty to take precautions against psychiatric injury

Psychiatric injury

The rule that employers must take reasonable steps to protect employees against **psychiatric injury** was established relatively recently, in the case of *Walker* v. *Northumberland County Council* (1995). Mr Walker was employed by the council to manage a team of four social workers, in an area where there were a lot of children at risk of harm. This created a huge caseload for Mr Walker's department, and eventually the stress and pressure led him to have a nervous breakdown, which kept him off work for three months. When he went back to work, the council promised to provide help to cut down his workload, but although some assistance was provided, it was not enough to make a real difference. Six months later, Mr Walker had another breakdown, and was not able to go back to his job again. He sued the council and the court held that the council was liable for the second nervous breakdown, because once the first one had happened it was reasonably foreseeable that Mr Walker would suffer further mental problems if the cause of the stress was not tackled. The council had failed to take reasonable steps to do this.

Case Summary

The decision in *Walker* led to a number of similar cases being brought against employers and, as so often happens when a new area of tort law is opened up, there was concern (particularly among employers) that the case might open the **'floodgates'** to a vast number of claims. In *Hatton* v. *Sutherland* (2002), the first of these reached the Court of Appeal, and the Court took the opportunity to lay down guidelines for dealing with workplace stress claims. The case involved four separate claims, which were heard together because they raised similar issues. Three of the claimants – Ms Hatton and Mr Barber, who were teachers, and Ms Jones, an administrative assistant – were arguing that overwork and lack of help had caused them to suffer clinical depression. The fourth, Mr Bishop, who was a factory worker, had had a nervous breakdown after his employer changed his job and required him to take on work that he was unable to cope with.

Case Summary

The Court of Appeal said that the duty on employers to take steps to protect against psychiatric injury was a part of the standard employers' duty, and subject to the same rules. Under the normal rules on employers' duty, an employer will only be liable where injury was reasonably foreseeable, and this is the same where the injury is psychiatric. However, the court pointed out, psychiatric injury may be much more difficult to foresee than physical injury. For this reason, they held, employers were entitled to assume that an employee was mentally able to cope with the demands of their job unless the employer was aware of some particular problem or vulnerability. Some of the defendants had argued that certain occupations (such as teaching) were stressful by nature, and that in these areas it was always foreseeable that employees might suffer from psychiatric injury, but the court rejected this view; the issue was whether in the claimant's particular situation, it was reasonable to foresee that they personally might suffer from stress problems.

As we will see, this reasoning has made it more difficult for employees to make a successful claim.

In deciding whether psychiatric injury was reasonably foreseeable, the Court of Appeal in *Hatton* said courts should look at:

- whether the workload was much heavier than normal for that kind of job;
- whether the demands on the employee were unreasonable compared with the demands made on other employees in similar jobs;
- whether there were signs that others doing the same job suffered from stress, such as an abnormal number of people off sick;
- whether the claimant was especially vulnerable to stress, or had previously suffered from illness due to stress at work;
- whether the claimant had taken an unusual amount of time off sick;
- whether the claimant or anyone else had warned the employer of a potential problem with stress.

There would usually, the court said, need to be 'signs of impending harm to health' which would make it plain to a reasonable employer that the employee was likely to 'go over the edge' unless steps were taken to alleviate the stress. The court also stated that if an employee said they were coping, the employer was entitled to take this as the truth, unless there was good reason not to. They did not have a duty to check whether it was true.

In line with the standard rules on employers' duty, the court stressed that there was no absolute duty to prevent psychiatric injury, only a duty to take reasonable precautions. In deciding what precautions were reasonable, the courts could take into account the size and financial resources of the firm, and the need to treat other employees fairly, for example when redistributing the claimant's workload. A company which provided a confidential advice service for employees, which could refer them to appropriate counselling services, would, the court said, usually be considered to have taken reasonable steps to prevent psychiatric injury.

Although the Court of Appeal stressed that their guidelines were simply an application of the normal rules on employers' liability, we can see how they made it much more difficult for employees to claim for mental than physical injury if we look at the fate of the four claimants in *Hatton* v. *Sutherland*. In Mr Bishop's case, the main issue was what steps his employer could have taken to prevent the problem. The court said they could not be under a duty to give him his old job back because it no longer existed. The only other possible action was to sack him for his own good, but Mr Bishop had said that he did not want to leave and would prefer to try to carry on. The court therefore found that there was nothing the company could reasonably have done to prevent his nervous breakdown, and so they were not liable.

With regard to the other three claimants, the court focused on whether the employers could reasonably have foreseen their psychiatric injury. In Ms Hatton's case, she had not told her bosses that she felt she was in danger of a breakdown if her workload was not reduced, but she had suffered periods of illness during her time in the job. However, the court held that it would have been easy to assume these were due to causes other than stress at work, so her employers could not reasonably have been expected to realise that she was at risk of psychiatric injury. The same reasoning applied to Mr Barber. He had taken three weeks off work, his sick note from his GP said that he had been suffering from stress, and he had complained about his workload. But as the complaint was made at the end of a term, the court held that it was reasonable for his employers to think that he would be rested and able to cope by the time he came back to work after the summer holidays. Therefore they could not reasonably be expected to realise that he was at risk of psychiatric injury if his workload was not reduced.

The only one of the four claims that was accepted – and even then rather reluctantly – was that of Ms Jones. The difference in her case was that she had complained about her workload and the stress it caused from an early stage, and the court accepted 'with some hesitation' that she had done enough to make it reasonably foreseeable that, if her employer did not take steps to help, she might suffer psychiatric damage.

A shift in approach?

Hatton laid down quite a strict approach to workplace stress cases, which made it very difficult for claimants to succeed, as you will see when you come to read the People in the Law box a little later in the chapter. Since then, however, there have been a handful of cases in which the courts have clarified the tests set down in *Hatton*, and these appear to show a slight shift in favour of a more flexible approach.

Case Summary

Case Navigator

In **Barber v. Somerset County Council** (2004), the case was an appeal by the Mr Barber who had been one of the claimants in *Hatton* v. *Sutherland*, and this time round he won. The House of Lords looked again at the question of whether the school should have realised that there was a problem. The Court of Appeal's view, as we saw above, was that employers were entitled to assume an employee was coping unless there was something to suggest an increased risk of stress, and were not obliged to make 'searching or intrusive enquiries'. The House of Lords confirmed that this was 'useful practical guidance' but said it should not be an inflexible rule. The real test was whether an employer had acted reasonably in the light of everything they knew or ought have known, and had weighed up the risk of injury and the likely effectiveness, cost and inconvenience of any precautions that they could have taken. In this case, the evidence had been that Mr Barber was an experienced and hardworking teacher, and the fact that someone like this had taken time off for stress, and made an official complaint about his workload, meant that the school could reasonably be expected to have realised there might be a problem and taken steps to help Mr Barber cope. The decision does not depart from the general approach taken in *Hatton*, which the House of Lords specifically said it approved, but it makes clear that there will be some situations where it is reasonable to expect an employer to see a risk, even if the employee has not made the problem absolutely plain to them.

Case Summary

In *Daw* v. *Intel Corporation* (2007), the claimant had worked for the defendants for many years, was highly thought of and considered to be a hard worker. Over the years, her workload had become heavier and heavier, and she had told her employers at least 14 times that she was struggling to deal with it. She was eventually promised help but it was not provided, and in the end she had a nervous breakdown, leading to severe depression, and was unable to work again. In *Hatton*, the Court of Appeal had said that an employer who provided a confidential advice service for employees would usually be considered to have taken reasonable steps to prevent psychiatric injury, and as they had such a service, which Ms Daw had not wished to use, Intel argued that they could not be liable. The Court of Appeal rejected their argument, saying that in this case, a counselling service would not have been able to help, because the problem arose from Ms Daw's workload. They held that Intel should have taken steps to deal with the problem as soon as they were in a position to realise that the increase in workload was having an effect on the claimant's mental health.

Case Summary

In *Dickins* v. *O2* (2008), the claimant had started working for the defendant telecommunications company as a secretary, had a good work record, and had progressed to become a manager. While doing that job, she had told her bosses on several occasions that she needed help with her workload, but none was provided. By March 2002, after a particularly busy period, she was exhausted and asked to be moved to a less stressful job. Her employer told her to hang on for three months, but the following month she felt she could not go on any longer and asked for a sabbatical (a period of time off without pay). Nothing was done. A month later she asked again, telling her boss that she felt she was at the end of her tether. Her employer suggested she see the company's occupation health department, but she was not given an urgent appointment, and within a few days she was diagnosed as being completely unfit for work due to anxiety and depression. Her employment was eventually terminated in November 2003.

O2 argued that they were not liable, on the basis of *Hatton*, because it was not reasonably foreseeable that Ms Dickins would suffer psychiatric harm because of her workload; there were no 'signs of impending harm to health', as required by *Hatton*. The Court of Appeal rejected this argument, saying that the fact that Ms Dickins had complained about her workload and had said she did not think she could keep going was enough to fulfil this requirement.

O2 also argued, again on the basis of *Hatton*, that they should not be liable because they had offered Ms Dickins access to a confidential counselling service in the form of the occupational health department. The Court of Appeal said that this would only strengthen an employer's case where the employee was unwilling to admit the problem to their manager. Where, as in this case, the employee had made their manager aware of the problem and made the severity of it clear, referring them to a counselling service was not enough to avoid liability. The Court of Appeal upheld the judge's finding that, on the evidence, O2 could only have fulfilled their duty by sending the claimant home on full pay while the occupational health department investigated the issue. The decision suggests that the courts now expect employers to be more aware of potential risks, and where they are aware, to take steps to alleviate stress at an early stage.

Key stats Stress at work

- Stress is the second most common type of work-related illness.
- Over 400,000 people a year are thought to suffer from stress caused or made worse by their job.
- Almost 10 million working days a year are lost to work-related stress.

[*Source*: Health and Safety Executive, **www.hse.gov.uk**]

People in the law

David Marshall is a Managing Partner at Anthony Gold Solicitors in London, and an expert on workplace stress claims.

Source: David Marshall (*text and photo*)

What attracted you to this area of work?
I've always done some employment law as well as personal injury, and in stress cases there is a certain amount of crossover between the two, which I find intellectually interesting. They're legally complex, and you have to analyse a work environment in great detail – a lot of personal injury work, particularly accidents, is about single incidents, but with stress claims, whether it's bullying or overwork, it's usually gone on over a period of time, so you get to look into how they've been managing the situation, and what's led up to the problem. For me that makes it interesting.

Have you seen an increase in claims for workplace stress in recent years? There's certainly been an increase in enquiries, in people thinking they might be able to bring a claim. That's partly because of growing awareness that there are potential remedies, because of coverage in the media, but also, I think, because with the economic recession, workplaces are far more stressful than they were a few years ago – staff cuts mean people are put under pressure and that can lead to more stress in the workplace.

How are your cases funded? We do almost all our stress work on **conditional fee agreements**. A lot of stress cases are funded by trade unions as well, though we don't do very many of those cases.

How severely affected would a typical claimant be? All claimants for workplace stress have to have a recognised psychiatric injury, of course, but even if they do, if it's just a mild depression, for example, and hasn't really impacted on their ability to work, the damages are going to be so low that it's not worth bringing the case. So almost by definition, the cases we take involve quite significant psychiatric injury. Usually, that will present itself in the form of clinical depression, which may go on for years, but some will have had serious psychiatric breakdowns. What's very common is that people can become quite obsessed about what's happened to them, and that can lead to quite a paranoid approach to the world – I had one case where a client couldn't physically bring herself to go anywhere near the part of central London where her old employer's offices were. So they are quite serious cases.

How easy or difficult is it to prove stress cases? They're hard cases to prove, for either side – we only work for employees, but I think people working for employers would say the same. One reason for that is the interpretation of the law in *Hatton* – with sixteen different principles that you have to get over, it's not at all easy to establish that there's a case in law. But they're also evidentially quite difficult, because it's not very easy to get witness evidence when most of the people who are involved are still working for the employer, and may be fairly reluctant to come forward and give evidence. On the employer's side, you'll usually find that there's not just one person involved – if the situation has gone on for a long time, other managers will have got involved, and you could have three or four people all saying no, we didn't realise it was as serious as that and backing each other up. So you really do need some extra evidence, because unless there are obvious inconsistencies in the witness evidence, the judge is going to find it very difficult to find for the claimant.

What other evidence can you use? There's often quite a lot of written evidence nowadays, a lot of documents and particularly emails. Large numbers of emails are kept, and people are surprisingly open in them, compared to what they would say in a letter, so that can be very useful. There are also responses to grievances – even if later the employer might claim they didn't realise there was a problem, you'll sometimes find that if you look at the early investigations of an employee's complaint, you can see that there was something dodgy going on.

You also need a good psychiatrist, because it's not just a question of diagnosing the psychiatric injury and the prognosis – you also have to be able to link that to the employer's breach of duty, so you need an expert witness who understands the legal principles as well as the medical issues.

Did *Hatton* make it much more difficult to prove a claim? Yes, it did. *Hatton* established that the key point about stress cases is foreseeability of the likelihood of psychiatric injury. If you've got a physical injury in the workplace, if there's an unguarded machine or something, and someone chops their arm off, foreseeability is pretty much taken as obvious. But with levels of work or bullying, it's much harder to foresee that that would cause psychiatric injury if the employer's not on actual notice because the employee has already complained, or because they're aware of a vulnerability there. That makes it very difficult.

I have a case at the moment, where the guy was suspended on false grounds, and seven years on, he's still very badly affected, but it's going to be very difficult to make a case. Employers aren't generally going around trying to suspend people on false grounds, even if it turns out afterwards that that's what happened, and as the employee had no background of any problems, the employer didn't really have any way of knowing that he was going to react that way.

The foreseeability requirement means employers have to be aware that what they were doing was likely to cause psychiatric injury, and often they're not. So you get this position where 'second breakdown cases', as they're known in the trade, are rather more easy to establish than first breakdown cases – but then the damages might be a bit lower because the person was already vulnerable to psychiatric injury first time round.

So *Hatton*, by making foreseeabilty of psychiatric injury the key element, makes it particularly difficult to win. To be fair to the court though, there were some rather bizarre decisions, going both ways, beforehand, where judges seemed to have forgotten about issues like causation, so there's lots of good in *Hatton*. But it's clear that the court was very conscious of the floodgates issue and wanted to put a real check on that.

There's a perception, especially in the tabloid press, that a lot of the people bringing claims for workplace stress are just 'trying it on'. What's your view on that? There are obviously a few people, but I don't think there are a lot. We get two or three enquiries a month, and we probably turn down 90 per cent of them, but that's not because people are trying it on, it's because in most of them, there isn't a strong enough case. That's not because people are making things up, or what's happened isn't very serious for them, but because there simply isn't a legal remedy. That might be because, although the person is very angry and distressed about what's happened to them, they haven't actually suffered a recognised psychiatric injury, or it might be because we can't prove foreseeability, for the reasons I've already mentioned. Or perhaps we can't prove causation because there may have been other things going on in their life that contributed to the psychiatric illness – they may believe that the situation at work was the straw that broke the camel's back, but proving that is very difficult.

There's also the issue that these cases are usually pretty complicated, so they're fairly costly, and that means it's only where people are likely to be able to show a significant loss that it's really worth bringing a claim – if damages are going to be less than £10,000, that's out of proportion to what it would cost to bring the claim. So no, I don't think there are large numbers of people trying it on. In fact I think most people are quite surprised at how hard it is to prove a case.

Does the law as explained in *Hatton* strike the right balance between the interests of employers and employees?
No, it's weighted too much in favour of employers. I can see why the Court of Appeal felt that the foreseeability issue had to be used to avoid the floodgates problem. Stress is the second most common reason for absence from work, and I think at the back of their minds, the court thought that hundreds of thousands of people might start suing. But the fact that a claimant has to have suffered a recognised psychiatric injury restricts the number of possible cases in itself, so I'm not sure the law has to be weighted quite so far in favour of employers.

When *Hatton* was decided in 2003, most of the cases under appeal were from the late 1990s, early 2000s, where the claimant's last day at work would usually have been in the early 1990s. I think the understanding of stress at work has moved on since then – the Health and Safety Executive has produced a lot of guidance about work-related stress and what employers should be doing, so to some extent it has become more difficult for employers to say we didn't realise that people might need help managing their workloads, or that you shouldn't shout at people. There are some signs that the Court of Appeal is recognising that – we saw in *Daw* v. *Intel* and *Dickins* v. *O2* that they were a bit more sympathetic to claimants working for big organisations who really ought to know what they're doing. It's still difficult but the world has moved on a bit and hopefully that's the way it'll continue to go.

Psychiatric injury by fellow employees

The cases we have looked at so far mainly involve stress caused by heavy workloads and/or the demands of a job. The courts have also held that employers have a duty to protect employees against psychiatric injury which is caused by the actions of other employees. In *Waters* v. *Commissioner of Police for the Metropolis* (2000), the claimant had accused another officer of sexually assaulting her. Her complaint was not pursued because of lack of evidence, but her colleagues knew the complaint had been made and began a campaign of victimisation against her, which caused her to suffer a psychiatric injury. She sued the police for failing to protect her against the victimisation and they attempted to have the claim struck out. The House of Lords refused, saying that employers had a duty to take reasonable care to prevent foreseeable harm to employees, and in this case it had been foreseeable that she would suffer victimisation from her colleagues after making a complaint against one of them, and that this could cause mental harm.

Case Summary

Employees who suffer stress at work through bullying also have another way to claim against their employers, at least in some circumstances. In *Majrowski* v. *Guy's and St Thomas' NHS Trust* (2006), the claimant said he had been bullied by his department manager, and that the bullying amounted to harassment under the Protection from Harassment Act 1997 (we'll look at this Act in detail in Chapter 12, but for now all you need to know is that most cases of workplace bullying, which happen on more than one occasion, are likely to be covered by it). He sued his employer on the basis that they were vicariously liable for the manager's behaviour. The House of Lords confirmed that there was nothing in the legislation to prevent vicarious liability, and it was therefore possible for an employer to be liable when one employee harassed another. This has important

Case Summary

implications for workplace stress cases where the stress is caused by actions that could be said to amount to harassment. In this situation there would be no need for the claimant to prove that their psychiatric injury was foreseeable, or even that the stress amounts to an actual psychiatric injury. It does not apply, however, where the stress is caused by a heavy workload or general workplace stress.

Law in Action Workplace bullying on the rise

The Guardian reported in 2010 that cases of bullying in the workplace were increasing, apparently due to the pressures caused by the economic downturn. The conciliation service ACAS told the paper that one in ten employees had experienced bullying or harassment, while a survey by the union Unison found that one-third of their members said they had been bullied within the previous six months. The Andrea Adams Trust, a charity set up to help victims of workplace bullying, said it had been so overwhelmed with calls that it had had to close down its helpline. Lyn Wetheridge, who ran the helpline, said that the numbers of calls had doubled since the economic downturn, and suggested some managers were bullying people as a way of getting them to leave without having to make them redundant.

Victims of workplace bullying have included a *News of the World* reporter, who was awarded almost £800,000 by an employment tribunal, and the first female Beefeater at the Tower of London, who was subjected to a bullying campaign by two colleagues who were eventually sacked.

[*References*: 'Bullying in the workplace on the rise', *The Guardian*, 4 Jan 2010; 'Bullying at Work Day – Union outs bullies', **http://www.unison.org.uk/asppresspack/pressrelease_view.asp?id=1639**]

We have looked at the main cases on workplace stress now, so try the practical exercise in the Writing and Drafting box to test how well you understand the principles contained in them. Don't forget about the issue of stress caused by other employees.

Writing and drafting

You are a trainee solicitor and your boss has asked you to produce a simple presentation for employers, explaining what they need to know about liability for workplace stress. After reading through the section above, pull out the key points which emerge from the cases and prepare them as a PowerPoint presentation, remembering that your audience are not lawyers so you need to use clear, accessible language and no jargon.

Handy tip: think about how you organise your material. Employers don't need to know what happened in each case, and they don't want a chronological account of how the law has developed. What they want is a simple list of what they should and should not be doing, so a good way to approach this task is to go through the cases, pick out the relevant points and then put them in a logical order.

Source: Pearson Education Ltd/Photodisc/ Michael Matisse

Economic loss

It is clearly established that employers have a duty to take reasonable steps to protect employees against foreseeable physical or mental injury. But what about **economic loss**? Clearly, there are many situations where an employer can foresee that an employee is at risk of losing money as a result of something the employer does or fails to do: where a firm decides to close one of their premises, for example, so that employees there lose their jobs, or where it invests in machinery which means fewer workers are needed. You could even argue that an employer who makes a poor business decision which cuts its profits, and then has to cut costs by making redundancies, can foresee that the poor decision may lead to economic loss for employees. However, it would clearly make life impossible for businesses if they had to compensate employees for money lost in this way and, as you might expect, the employer's duty to employees does not include a general duty to prevent them suffering economic loss.

However, the courts have found that there may be a duty to prevent economic loss in very limited circumstances. In *Spring* v. *Guardian Assurance* (1995), the claimant had worked for the defendant, and when he applied for another job the defendant gave a reference which said he was dishonest; this ruined his chances of getting the other job. What was said in the reference was not true, and the employer had been negligent in not checking the facts. The case was brought in negligence and, applying the ***Caparo* test** for a duty of care, the House of Lords held that it was fair, just and reasonable that an employer who, through negligence, deprives an employee of their chance of earning a living, should be liable. This was, they said, comparable to the duty to take reasonable steps to protect an employee's physical safety. Similarly, in *Scally* v. *Southern Health and Social Services Board* (1992), the defendant was found liable for negligently failing to advise the claimant, who they employed, that he was entitled to certain pension rights.

Case Summary

Case Summary

The courts have made clear, however, that these are very specific situations, and there is no general duty on employers to prevent economic loss to employees. In *Crossley* v. *Faithfull and Gould Holdings* (2004), the claimant had lost out on certain benefits available under his employer's insurance scheme because he had resigned from his job. He had not known this would happen if he resigned, and although his employer did know they had still advised him to resign. He argued that employers had a general duty to take reasonable care to protect an employee's financial well-being, but the Court of Appeal disagreed. They said that where an employer had taken on the responsibility for giving financial advice to an employee, they had a duty to take reasonable care to give correct advice, but they did not have a duty to give advice in the first place, nor a general duty to protect an employee's financial situation.

Case Summary

Breach of the employer's duty

As we have seen in some of the cases discussed above, the employer's duty is not an absolute duty to protect the employee against harm; it is a duty to take reasonable steps to prevent harm. This means that the fact that an employee has suffered harm due to factors that fall within the employers' duty (such as unsafe working conditions or incompetent colleagues) does not necessarily mean the employer is liable. We can see

Case Summary

this in the case of *Withers* v. *Perry Chain* (1961). The claimant had suffered from a painful skin condition caused by contact with grease at work, so her employers switched her to new duties, where the risk of coming into contact with grease was not eradicated but was the lowest of any work they had. The problem reoccurred and she sued, claiming they had a duty not to allow her to do any work which caused a risk of causing skin problems. The Court of Appeal rejected her claim, because the employers had done all they could reasonably be expected to do.

Case Summary

The duty is owed to each employee individually, so where there is something about a particular employee that increases the risk of harm to them, that may mean it is reasonable to expect the employer to take stronger precautions than normal. In *Paris* v. *Stepney BC* (1951), the claimant, who worked in the defendant's garage, had only one eye and the defendant knew this. The work the claimant did involved a risk of eye injury, and he ended up losing his remaining eye in an accident at work. He argued that the defendants should have given him safety goggles, but there was evidence that the work was not of a kind where safety goggles would usually be required. The court upheld the claim; although it might be reasonable not to supply goggles to other workers, the fact that the risk to the claimant was potentially more severe, in that he could be completely blinded, meant the employers should have taken greater precautions.

Law in action Slips, trips and dangerous horses

Accidents and injuries at work can happen in all sorts of ways – these are some of the most recent cases reported by the magazine *Hazards*:

- A train driver was paid £6,000 after injuring his back in a fall. He stepped onto rubbish that had been left on a train, which caused him to fall back onto the platform.
- An civil servant received £16,500 after injuring a knee when the lift she was travelling in went into freefall.
- A lorry driver won £3,500 after his finger was crushed by a 50 kilo beer keg that he was trying to unload. His delivery vehicle was so overloaded that it was impossible to move the kegs safely.
- A factory worker was awarded £3,500 after slipping on a wet floor and breaking her elbow. The slip was caused by a coolant unit which had been leaking for five years; management had ignored a series of complaints about the risk.
- A jockey received £85,000 after he was kicked by a horse, which broke his leg and ended his career.
- A worker in a food factory won £3,800 after burning his arm, which left a large scar, because he was given inadequate safety gloves.
- An employee of a firm which sorts change collected by banks was awarded £13,500 after he injured his back lifting bags of coins weighing up to 7 kilos.
- An office worker won £10,000 after suffering a back problem caused by an unsuitable office chair. Her injury meant she was no longer able to work and was forced to take early retirement.
- An employee at a shipbuilders received £5,750 after being exposed to excessive noise at work, which permanently damaged his hearing.
- A nurse won £17,500 after slipping on a wet floor and injuring her spine and ankle.

[*Source*: **hazards.org**]

Delegating the duty

As we saw earlier, the case of *Wilsons and Clyde Coal* v. *English* established that the employer's duty is non-delegable, which means that an employer can delegate the performance of the duty to someone else, such as a manager, but cannot delegate the legal liability for it. The reason for this is that, even by the 1930s when the case was decided, industrialisation meant it had become less and less common for workplaces to be managed by the person who owned them, and more and more common for it to be the job of managers or supervisors to look after workplace safety. If employers could argue that, therefore, any accidents were the responsibility of the manager, this would be very likely to leave an injured employee without compensation, as managers would simply not have the money to pay. This principle is even more important these days when there are very few situations where an employer takes day-to-day responsibility for safety precautions, and in big firms they may not even be in the same building as all of their workers.

The fact that the duty is non-delegable means that regardless of whose job it is to look after employee safety on a day-to-day basis, it is still the employer who is liable for any breach of the employer's duty. In *McDermid* v. *Nash Dredging* (1987), the claimant was employed by the defendants as a ship's deckhand, but on the ship he was supervised on a day-to-day basis by the captain, who was employed by a different company. He was injured due to the captain's negligence. On the facts, it was found that the employer had devised a safe system of work, but the captain had not been operating that system. The defendants argued that they should not be liable for the captain's failure to operate a safe system of work, but the Court of Appeal disagreed, stating that

Case Summary

> The essential character of the [employer's] duty is that, if it is not performed, it is no defence for the employer to show that he delegated its performance to a person, whether his servant or not his servant, whom he reasonably believed to be competent to perform it. Despite such delegation the employer is liable for the non-performance of the duty.

Defences

The defences of contributory negligence and *volenti* are available in actions for breach of the employer's duty (if you need a reminder of how these defences work, you can find a full explanation in Chapter 3). However, the courts are aware that in a workplace situation, employees do not always have a free choice about what they do and the risks they take, and this is taken into account in deciding cases involving injury at work. An example can be seen in *Smith* v. *Baker* (1891), discussed at page 93.

Summary

- Under common law, employers have a duty to take reasonable care to ensure the safety of their employees.
- The duty is owed only by employers to employees, and not to anyone who happens to visit the workplace, or to 'independent contractors'.
- The employer must take reasonable care to provide:
  - a competent staff;
  - adequate materials;
  - a safe system of work;
  - a safe workplace.
- The duty covers physical injury, psychiatric injury and, to a more limited extent, economic loss.
- The employer is not required to eliminate every risk, only to take reasonable precautions.
- The employer can delegate performance of their duty, but they remain liable for any breach of the duty.
- The defences of contributory negligence and *volenti* apply, but the courts take into account that employees do not always have a free choice about what they do at work.

Question and answer*

Problem: Carol and John are chefs who work at a restaurant owned by Jackie. Thanks to their cooking, the restaurant has become very busy over the past two years, and Carol and John's workload has increased. Carol has also had to take on a lot of paperwork for the business. Over the past year she has been feeling increasingly stressed and having problems sleeping, and this has got worse since her husband left her six months ago. At around that time, she told Jackie how she was feeling, and asked if they could take on an extra chef for the busiest nights, and/or someone to help with the paperwork. Jackie said the business was not making enough money to justify doing that. Last week, Carol phoned in sick and her doctor has diagnosed a nervous breakdown.

With Carol away, John is forced to cope on his own. On the Saturday night, they have a party of 15 booked in. Jackie informs him that they are very important clients, and she insists that he must make sure they are served quickly. All 15 people order fish and chips. The kitchen has two deep fat fryers, one of which is large but has a fault which occasionally causes it to overheat, and a smaller one which takes only half as much food. Jackie knows about the fault and has told John and Carol only to use the smaller one until she can get the bigger one fixed. However, John knows that if he uses the smaller fryer he can only fry half the order at once, so he uses the large fryer instead. While the chips are cooking, John gets on with the desserts, which are usually Carol's job, and does not notice that the fryer is overheating. Hot oil bubbles up out of it, causing John serious burns.

Advise Carol and John as to any claim they may have against Jackie.

You should allow yourself no more than 40 minutes to complete this task.

Essay: 'The law on liability for accidents at work needs to strike a balance, so that employees are protected but employers are not subject to unfair burdens.'

How well does the common law on employers' liability strike this balance?

This question should be answered in 40 minutes.

* Answer guidance is provided at the end of the chapter.

Further reading

Barrett, B. (2001) 'Policy issues concerning compensation for psychiatric injury', 30(1) *ILJ* 110.
This article looks at the subject of workplace stress and the way the courts have approached the problem.

Conaghan, J. and Mansell, W. (1993) *The Wrongs of Tort*, London: Pluto Press, pp 70–8.
This book takes a critical look at tort law, and in this section looks at the development of tort law against the background of increasing industrialisation during the nineteenth century. Not an especially easy read, but very interesting.

***Hatton* v. *Sutherland* [2002] 1 WLR 1089.**
This case is definitely worth reading in detail if you are doing an essay on workplace stress claims.

Mullany, N.J. (2002) 'Containing claims for workplace mental illness', 118 LQR 373.
A useful look at the Court of Appeal decision on claims for workplace stress in *Hatton* v *Sutherland*.

Question and answer guidance

Problem: Beginning with Carol, the claim here would be for psychiatric injury, and we know from *Walker* that the employer's duty includes a duty to take reasonable precautions against this type of harm. You should consider the principles laid down in *Hatton* v. *Sutherland* and later clarified in *Barber* and *Daw*, and apply them to the facts here: relevant issues include the fact that Carol has told Jackie about the problems and asked for help, but Jackie has refused it. You also need to consider the fact that Carol's marriage breakdown may have contributed to her nervous breakdown.

With regard to John, the issue is physical injury, which the employers' duty clearly covers. What you need to look at here is whether Jackie did or failed to do something which she could reasonably have been expected to do to prevent John's injury. You should explain that the courts will apply a standard of reasonableness, which will entail balancing relevant factors against each other. We know that the duty requires an employer to provide a sufficient staff to do the job, so the courts will want to look at whether it was reasonable to expect John to cope alone, given that Jackie already had reason to know that the workload was excessive for two people, let alone one. On the other hand, they will also look at the fact that John decided to use the larger fryer even though he had been warned not to. This will mean that Jackie may put forward the defence of *volenti*, and you should explain how this works in employers' liability cases and consider whether John can really be said to have been acting voluntarily.

Essay: A good way to start this essay might be by briefly explaining exactly why it is important for the law to strike this balance – why is it good for society? You should then go on to look at the ways in which the law strikes the balance. Perhaps the most important is the fact that it applies a standard of reasonableness, rather than giving employers an absolute duty to prevent all risks, and you should look at some of the cases on this issue, explaining how they strike a balance between the differing interests of employers and employees, and whether you think the cases have always struck the right balance or whether the law in some cases might be unfair to one side or the other.

Another good issue to mention is the operation of the defences, where the courts have addressed the fact that within an employment relationship the parties do not have equal power. Again, use the cases to show how the law has struck a balance between competing interests.

One area that can be considered problematic is that of psychiatric injury, where the courts have subjected claims to more restrictions than apply to claims for physical injury. Look at the cases, and explain whether you think employees are being given adequate protection and/or whether there are unfair burdens on employers.

You should finish with a conclusion which sums up the points you have made, and explains whether you feel the current balance is a good one, or whether changes should be made.

Visit **www.mylawchamber.co.uk/quinntort** to access tools to help you develop and test your knowledge of tort law, including practice exam questions with guidance, annotated weblinks, glossary and key case flashcards, legal newsfeed and legal updates and interactive 'You be the judge' questions.

Use Case Navigator to read in full some of the key cases referenced in this chapter with commentary and questions:

Barber* v. *Somerset County Council [2004] 2 All ER 385

Chapter 8 Vicarious liability

Key points In this chapter we will be looking at:

- When an employer will be liable for torts committed by their employees
- Reasons why this liability is imposed
- Other types of liability for torts involving multiple tortfeasors

Introduction

Imagine that you are walking past a building site, and a bricklayer working above negligently drops a brick on your head. It causes you serious injury, and you are unable to work again. **Damages** for this kind of injury would normally run into tens of thousands of pounds, perhaps more, but the bricklayer does not have the money to pay such a claim, nor any insurance cover, so there is no point in suing him or her. However, that does not necessarily mean you will be unable to claim compensation for your injury.

Instead of leaving victims without a claim in this kind of situation, the law imposes what is called **vicarious liability** on the employer. This means that the employer becomes jointly liable for the whole of the damage, and you can sue them instead of the employee. This is obviously useful to **claimants**, as the employer is likely to have more money and/or insurance. Vicarious liability is not a tort in itself, but a form of liability that can apply to most torts. So just as our builder's employer could be vicariously liable for negligence in the example above, a hospital can be vicariously liable for trespass against the person if a doctor operates without the patient's consent, and a factory owner could be vicariously liable for nuisance if their staff cause a problem which intereferes with neighbouring properties.

Technically speaking, vicarious liability means that the claimant can sue either the employee, the employer, or both. In practice, however, most claimants simply sue the employer, because they will be able to pay. This is why you will have seen many cases in which the name of the **defendant** is a company or organisation, even though the damage was done by an individual.

If you think back over the cases we have looked at so far, you can see that there are very many in which torts happen at, or are associated with, work: doctors who negligently injure patients, police officers who fail to protect an informant, surveyors who make mistakes in their reports and accountants who give inaccurate advice, to name just a few. This means that, in practical terms, vicarious liability is a very important principle and arises in a high number of cases. However, it does not automatically apply in every single case where the tort is committed by an employee, and in this chapter we will look at the rules on when it does and does not apply. At the end of this chapter, we will also look at some other types of liability that apply when there is more than one **tortfeasor**.

Why does vicarious liability exist?

Before we take a detailed look at how vicarious liability works, you might at this stage be wondering why it exists at all. As you will have realised by now, a basic principle of tort law is that people who cause injury or damage to others should be held responsible for their actions, and where possible, compensate for the damage. Vicarious liability can be seen as being in direct conflict with this principle, because it seeks to hold someone other than the wrongdoer responsible, and means the person who commits the tort is not usually required to pay any compensation. Why then does it exist? The following are some of the reasons which have been put forward to justify it.

Control

A traditional argument for vicarious liability was that an employer is in overall control of what their employees do, and so it is fair for them to take responsibility for their employees' acts. While this may have been true in the past, where the tasks most employees did were relatively simple and easy to supervise, it does not fit so well with the modern world of work. In today's workplaces, employees will often have expertise and skills that their employers do not share; to say, for example, that a local health authority controls the work of a surgeon in one of their hospitals is simply not accurate.

However, the idea does make sense if we look at it in a wider context. In the modern world, employers set profit and performance targets, staffing levels and budgets, either formally or informally. If these mean that there is insufficient time or staff to do a job properly, and that results in, for example, someone being injured through negligence, it would be true to say that that situation was within the employer's control. They could have taken steps which would have prevented it happening, and if they chose not to it seems fair that they should take responsibility.

Benefits to employers

It can also be argued that employers benefit from the work done by their employees and so ought to be liable for any damage which arises from that work. This is linked to the point about profit targets above: if an employer benefits from, for example, cost-cutting practices, they should be liable for any risks arising from that cost-cutting.

Availability of resources

In practical terms, the strongest argument for vicarious liability is simply that an employer is usually better placed to insure against potential claims than an employee. Companies routinely take out this kind of insurance and for them it is merely one of their standard costs. By contrast, requiring employees to take out insurance would be very expensive for individuals.

Spreading risk

Making employers responsible for the torts of their employees is a way of spreading risk so that it is paid for by many people instead of just the person committing the damage. In his book, *Vicarious Liability in the Law of Torts* (1967), the renowned tort academic P.S. Atiyah suggests that this is the main, and most sensible, justification for vicarious liability today:

> In the great majority of cases an employer who has to pay damages for the torts of his servants does not in fact have to meet those liabilities out of his own pocket. The cost of the liabilities is distributed over a large section of the community, and spread over some period of time. This occurs partly because of the practice of insurance, and partly because most employers are anyhow not individuals but corporations. Where the employer insures against his legal liabilities he will charge the cost of insurance to the goods or service which he produces. In general this cost will be passed on by the employer in the form of higher prices to the consumer.

In this way, the cost of paying compensation is effectively spread thinly among many people. It can be argued that most modern industry carries some degree of risk, and yet society as a whole benefits from its existence, so it makes sense for society to pay for that risk through the higher prices charged to cover the cost of insurance.

Promotion of care

It can be argued that imposing liability for the acts of their employees makes employers more likely to take care to prevent those employees causing damage, by careful recruitment, training and supervision. If employers were not liable for torts committed in the course of employment, there might be a temptation to 'turn a blind eye' to unsafe practices, especially if those practices resulted in a benefit to the employer through lower costs and/or higher profits. On the other hand, it might also be argued that vicarious liability could make employees more likely to be careless, if they know that if they cause damage the employer will be sued and not them.

Elements of vicarious liability

In most cases involving torts committed by an employee, it will be clear that vicarious liability applies. If a doctor negligently injures a patient during an operation, for example, it is standard practice for vicarious liability to be imposed on the health authority that employs the doctor. However, there are situations where it is not clear whether vicarious liability applies, and here the courts have to ask two questions:

- Was the tortfeasor an employee?
- Was the tort committed in the course of their employment?

Vicarious liability will only apply if the answer to both questions is yes. The issue usually arises because a claimant seeks to sue the employer of someone who has caused damage, and the employer wants to avoid this liability. If they can establish that the answer to one of the above questions is no, they or their insurance companies can save themselves a lot of money.

Was the tortfeasor an employee?

At first glance, this might seem like a funny question: surely it is obvious whether you work for a particular company or not? However, modern working practices mean this is not always as clear as you might imagine. The law makes a distinction between employees, who are actually on the staff of a company or organisation, and independent contractors, who might be doing work for the company but in law are actually self-employed or employed by an agency. There can be vicarious liability for the torts of an employee, but not for those of an independent contractor. But in recent years changes to the labour market have blurred the distinctions between these two groups. Many companies now prefer to take on workers on a casual or temporary basis, or to use self-employed people to do work as and when it is needed, rather than taking staff on permanently. Yet in many workplaces, those casual, temporary or freelance workers will work alongside permanent staff, doing the same work. Similarly, in industries such as media and computing, many people prefer to be self-employed, but nevertheless may spend months at a time working for one firm, at their offices, and under the same supervision as an employee would be. In those situations, when the courts ask whether they are an employee, what they are really asking is whether the person's working circumstances are so similar to the traditional view of an employee that it would be fair to impose vicarious liability on the company for that person's actions.

In approaching this question, the courts have developed a number of different tests. Some of the tests they use were not originally developed in tort cases but come from tax or employment law. This is because the question of whether someone is an employee or an independent contractor can also be relevant to their rights at work, or the way they are taxed. However as the question is the same, the same tests are often carried across to tort cases.

Tests for employee status

Traditionally, the way the courts decided whether someone was an employee or not was by looking at the amount of control that the supposed employer had over them. If the employer decided what work the person should do, and how and when they did it, the person was likely to be considered an employee. If, however, a person was paid to do a particular task, but could decide for themselves how, when and perhaps where to do it, they were not usually classified as an employee. This worked well back in the times when companies were small, and the person who owned a factory, for example, would often be an engineer who understood how everything and everyone in the factory worked.

However, as many types of work became increasingly skilled and specialised, this test came to be less useful. Take, for example, a large company which employs, among others, a team of IT technicians to look after the computers that all the other staff use. The managing director of that company would probably not have the technical expertise to tell the computer technicians how to do their job, but in common-sense terms it is obvious that that fact alone does not mean the technicians are not employees. Similarly, the head of a health authority is unlikely to issue day-to-day instructions to a surgeon but the surgeon is clearly still an employee of the health authority. So, these days, the control test is still used but it is no longer the single, or even the main, decisive factor. Instead, the courts apply a variety of different tests, depending on the type of work involved, and look at all the circumstances of the case.

Case Summary

One test that is frequently used is whether the person can be said to be 'in business on their own account'. This was applied by the Court of Appeal in *Hall* v. *Lorimer* (1992), a tax case in which Mr Lorimer, a freelance TV technician, wanted to establish that he was an independent contractor because it gave him certain tax advantages. Mr Hall, the tax inspector, sought to claim that Mr Lorimer was an employee, because the TV companies he worked for would hire him for set periods of time during which they could tell him where, when and how long to work. The Court of Appeal said the key test was whether Mr Lorimer was 'in business on his own account'. Factors which would suggest that he was in business on his own account included providing his own equipment, taking financial risks (such as doing work on credit), hiring helpers, charging varying amounts for different jobs, and having a number of different clients. Mr Lorimer was not, on this test, in business on his own account, and so he was judged to be an employee. However, the Court pointed out that although this test was relevant to Mr Lorimer's situation, it would not work in every case:

> The question whether the individual is in business on his own account, though often helpful, may be of little assistance in the case of one carrying on a profession or vocation. A self-employed author working from home or an actor or a singer may earn his living without any of the normal trappings of a business.

Case Summary

Another test was suggested in *Ready Mixed Concrete* v. *Minister of Pensions* (1968). Here, the Court said that three factors would point towards a person being an employee rather than an independent contractor. First, that they agree to provide work and skill in return for payment. Secondly, that they agree to be subject to the employer's control. They might give this consent explicitly, for example by signing a contract with terms about control, or the consent might be given by implication, where it is obvious that the arrangement between them makes them subject to control. Thirdly, that all the other terms of the contract between them are consistent with them being an employee. If, for example, the person's contract stated that they should have to buy all their own tools, or that they are allowed to employ others to help do the job, that would suggest that they are not an employee. The Court also said that, for there to be an employer–employee relationship, there had to be some form of mutual obligation between the parties, in which the company was obliged to give the worker work, and the worker was obliged to do that work.

Often, there will be a written contract between the parties that says whether they are to be considered an employee or not. However, the courts are well aware that companies sometimes seek to classify someone as an independent contractor because this means they can evade certain responsibilities under employment law, as well as vicarious liability for tort. Therefore, although the courts will look at the wording of any contract, it will not be decisive if the actual working arrangement seems to suggest something different. This was the case in *Ferguson* v. *Dawson* (1976). The claimant was a building labourer who had a contract that said he was self-employed. The company argued that this meant he was not covered by certain safety legislation that only applied to employees. However, the Court of Appeal looked at the work he was doing and the way it was managed, and concluded that, despite the wording of the contract, he was an employee.

Case Summary

You be the judge

Q: Susie works as a chef at a small restaurant owned by Malcolm. Due to her negligence a customer got serious food poisoning and now wants to sue the restaurant. However, Susie's contract describes her as self-employed. Malcolm believes this means he cannot be vicariously liable for her negligence, because she is not an employee. Is he right?

A: No. Malcolm is correct in thinking that if Susie is not an employee, he cannot be vicariously liable for her negligence. But a court which is asked to decide whether someone is an employee or not will not take the words of the contract as the final say on the matter; as the case of *Ferguson* v. *Dawson* shows, they will also look at the reality of the working arrangements, which may tell a different story.

Try the practical exercise in the Writing and Drafting box to test your knowledge of what you have read so far.

Writing and drafting

You are a solicitor and one of your clients is a large building firm. They are being sued by a woman who was injured when a plank of wood fell on her as she was passing a building that the company was working on. The person who dropped the plank is a temporary worker that the building firm call in now and then when they are short-staffed. They have always considered him to be self-employed, and they hope to avoid vicarious liability by proving that he is not their employee. Based on the cases discussed above, draw up a list of questions that you would ask the building firm in order to decide whether they may be able to avoid vicarious liability.

Agency workers

In many industries, it is common for employers to get staff through agencies rather than hiring them directly. The advantage of this situation is that the agency does all the work of finding suitable staff, and the company can keep them for as long as they need them and then simply end the arrangement without having either to sack them or to make them redundant, both of which can legally be done only under certain conditions. What happens then if an agency worker commits a tort? Can the company which is hiring their services from the agency be vicariously liable? In most cases, the answer is no, because it is usually very clear that the employee is actually employed by the agency: they recruit the worker and have the power to end their employment, and the payment arrangement is usually that the agency pays the worker and charges a fee to the company using the worker, rather than the company paying the worker directly.

However, the courts have found instances where a company using agency staff can be deemed to be their employer, and therefore vicariously liable for torts committed by them in the course of their employment. This was the case in *Hawley* v. *Luminar Leisure* (2006). The case arose when a nightclub bouncer, Mr Warren, assaulted the claimant, Mr Hawley, causing him permanent brain damage. The assault was found to be within

Case Summary

the course of Mr Warren's employment but there was a question as to who was his employer. Luminar were the owners of the nightclub, but they had not employed the bouncer themselves but got staff from a security company, ASE Security Services. However, he worked at Luminar's premises on a day-to-day basis and had done so for two years. ASE had gone bust, so the claimant sued Luminar.

The Court of Appeal said that the question was 'who was entitled and therefore obliged to control Mr Warren's act so as to prevent it?' They found that it was Luminar. ASE's only role in the situation was to employ Mr Warren in the first place, send him to Luminar at their request, and pay his wages for as long as Luminar wanted to use his services. It was Mr Warren's line manager at the nightclub who had the power to control his behaviour. The court also highlighted two further factors which in their view, made it right to impose vicariously liability on Luminar. The first was that Mr Warren would have been recognised as working for Luminar by members of the public, as he had been standing on their door, wearing their uniform, for two years. The second was that Luminar did not have to use an agency to supply door staff; they could have employed their own bouncers. The fact that they chose not to was clearly because they wanted to avoid certain aspects of employment law, which would have restricted the way they could manage the club. The Court was not willing to allow this to prevent liability. Therefore Luminar were vicariously liable for the assault.

Casual workers

Increasingly, companies now use workers on a casual basis, which means they are asked to work when the company needs them but cannot demand to work and be paid when the company chooses not to use them. In *Carmichael* v. *National Power* (2000), the House of Lords looked at whether someone working in this way could be considered an employee. The claimants in the case worked as tour guides, showing visitors round a power station owned by the defendants. National Power would call them and ask them to work when they needed them, and usually the claimants did so. However, it was clear that if on any occasion the claimants were asked to work and chose not to, National Power did not take any disciplinary action against them; in other words, they could choose whether or not to work. The House of Lords held that they could not be employees, because there was no mutual obligation between them: the company was not obliged to give them work, and they were not obliged to take it if it was offered.

Case Summary

Employees on loan

In some industries it is common for one employer to 'lend' an employee to another, for example where one company hires equipment and the services of someone to operate the equipment come as part of the deal (although the court have tended to refer to this as a loan, it is in practice more like temporarily hiring the employee). If an employee commits a tort while they are 'on loan', which of the two companies has vicarious liability for their actions?

Case Summary

The traditional approach to this question was laid down in *Mersey Docks and Harbour Board* v. *Coggins & Griffiths* (1947). The Harbour Board had hired out one of their cranes, with a driver, to Coggins, whose business was loading and unloading ships. As a result of the crane driver's negligence someone was injured, and to work out which company was vicariously liable, the court had to work out of which company the crane driver was an employee. The case went to the House of Lords, and they laid down a number of principles to be used in deciding similar cases.

- The worker's permanent employer (in this case the Harbour Board) would usually be vicariously liable, unless they can show good reason why liability should be placed on the company 'borrowing' the worker.
- If the permanent employer alleges that there is good reason for the other company to bear liability, a key question will be who had the immediate right to control the employee's method of working. If the company which borrowed the worker has this right, that may point to them being liable.
- Courts should identify the act which caused the negligence, and ask who had responsibility for preventing that act.
- Other important questions to consider were who paid the worker and who had the right to dismiss them. The company which paid them and had the right of dismissal would be more likely to be the employer.
- The terms of the contract between the two companies were not to be considered as deciding the matter.

In the case before them, the contract of hire between the Harbour Board and Coggins said that the driver was employed by Coggins, but during the period of the loan the Harbour Board paid his wages and had the power to sack him. The House of Lords therefore decided that the Harbour Board had not shown that there was good reason for liability to be imposed on Coggins, so the Harbour Board was liable.

The approach taken in *Mersey Docks* required the courts to choose one employer or the other to bear vicarious liability, but more recently the courts have suggested that in some circumstances it might be more appropriate for the employers to share responsibility. This approach was developed in *Viasystems (Tyneside) Ltd* v. *Thermal Transfer* (2005), a case which was even more complicated than Mersey Docks because it involved three companies. The claimants in the case owned a factory, where they were having air conditioning installed. While this was happening a worker involved in the job, Mr Strang, negligently caused a flood, which damaged the property. The claimants had hired the defendants, a company called Thermal Transfer, to do the work. Thermal Transfer had subcontracted some of the work to another company, Darwell, and Darwell had hired Mr Strang from a third company, CAT Metalwork. The Court therefore had to decide whether Mr Strang was employed by Thermal Transfer, Darwell or CAT Metalwork. Mr Strang worked alongside, and under the instructions of, a fitter from CAT Metalwork but both of them were supervised by a foreman employed by Darwell. The Court of Appeal found that both the fitter and the foreman, and therefore the companies they worked for, had the right and the responsibility to control Mr Strang's work. Therefore, they said, it was fair that both companies should be vicariously liable for his negligence, and both should contribute equally to the damages.

Case Summary

The *Viasystems* approach suggests that joint vicarious liability may now apply in many 'borrowed employee' cases, since there will often be shared control of the employee's work. However, there will still be cases where the approach used in *Mersey Docks* will be more appropriate. In his article 'Vicarious liability and joint employees' (2005), Andrew Tettenborn suggests that shared vicarious liability would not apply where, for example, company A hires a digger and driver from company B to do some work on company A's premises, since company A would not be in the position of telling the digger driver how to do the job and so would not have effective control over the work. Similarly, when an employment agency supplies a secretary to a company, the employment agency is unlikely to share vicarious liability, because they would not have day-to-day control over the secretary's work. The *Viasystems* case therefore seems to offer a new approach to the problem, but the principles in *Merseyside Docks* will still apply in some cases.

Writing and drafting

You are a solicitor at a firm whose clients include Dodgy Dinners, a catering company, which provides cooks for parties and events. An advertising agency, Clever Pics, hired one of Dodgy Dinners' cooks for a party they were holding for special clients. Due to her negligence, there was a serious fire in the kitchen, and one of the guests who was standing nearby was hurt. The guest is suing Dodgy Dinners, but Dodgy Dinners say that Clever Pics were vicariously liable for what the cook did because it happened on their premises and they were in charge. Draw up a list of questions you would ask Dodgy Dinners in order to establish whether they may be vicariously liable.

Source: Pearson Education Ltd/Photodisc/Cole Publishing Group/Michael Lamotte

In the course of their employment

We saw at the beginning of this chapter that there are two elements that must be proved if a claimant wants to establish that an employer is vicariously liable for a tort. Once it is established that the person who has committed a tort is an employee, the court then needs to ask whether the tort was committed in the course of employment. If it was committed in the course of their employment, the employer will be liable, but if not, the employer is not liable. When reading the cases on this issue, you may come across the phrase 'on a frolic of their own'. This is simply a term the courts sometimes use to mean 'not in the course of employment'.

You might imagine that a tort would be considered to have happened in the course of employment if it happened while the employee was at work and/or within working hours. These are factors, but they are not the only ones, and over the years the courts have developed some rather more complex tests. This is partly because there are many cases where, if vicarious liability cannot be found, a victim who may have suffered very serious injury will not be compensated. Faced with this prospect, the courts have often applied the law in quite unexpected ways in order to do justice in the case before them. Because of this, as you will see, there are some cases in this area where the facts look very similar, and yet in one case the courts will find vicarious liability, and in the other

the courts have often applied the law in quite unexpected ways

not. This can be confusing but remember that, as a student, you are not expected to know which way a court would decide if that is not something a lawyer would be able to predict either. What you need to do is get a good grasp of the case law, so that when you are faced with a problem question you can say what the relevant case law is, and how the courts might apply it, even if it is not possible to be certain what the result would be.

Tests for 'in the course of employment'

The traditional test for whether a tort was committed in the course of employment was taken from a classic tort textbook, *Salmond on Torts*, first published in 1907. Salmond stated that a tort would be classified as done in the course of employment

> if it is either (a) a wrongful act authorised by the master [an old-fashioned legal term for the employer] or (b) a wrongful and unauthorised mode of doing some act authorised by the master.

The first part of this principle is obvious: if an employer has given permission for the tort to be committed, and therefore actually paid for it to be done, it is clear that they should bear liability for the results. However, the second part of Salmond's analysis suggests that employers should be liable even where an employee acts without permission, if their harmful act can be seen as one of the tasks involved in their job but done in a way that the employer would not have permitted. In *Century Insurance* v. *Northern Ireland Road Transport* (1942), the defendants' employee, Mr Davison, was the driver of a petrol tanker. He was unloading petrol from his tanker to underground storage in the claimant's garage when he struck a match to light his cigarette and then threw the match on the ground. Not surprisingly (though presumably it surprised Mr Davison), this caused an explosion, and although no one was hurt the fire damaged the defendant's property. It was agreed that he lit the match for his own purposes, and not those of his employers, but even so the Court held that the defendants were vicariously liable, because what Mr Davison was doing at the time (unloading the tanker) was part of his job, even though doing it while smoking was negligent and not something his employers permitted.

Case Summary

A similar result was reached in *Bayler* v. *Manchester Railway Co.* (1873). A member of the railway staff thought the claimant was on the wrong train and, meaning to be helpful, dragged him off it so forcefully that he was injured and, just to make things worse, missed his train. The railway company was held to be vicariously liable, because helping passengers to get to their destination was part of the employee's job, even if he had done it so badly as to have completely the opposite effect.

Case Summary

In contrast to the cases above, there are situations where an employee commits a tort during work time, at the workplace and/or using work equipment, but the courts will not find the employer vicariously liable because there is not sufficient connection between the job itself and the act committed. This situation is often referred to as the employee being 'on a frolic of their own'. An example is *Heasmans* v. *Clarity Cleaning Co.* (1987), where the employee of a cleaning firm was employed to go to different offices. She used the opportunity to make long-distance phone calls while she was there, and one of the firms wanted to sue the cleaning company for her actions. The Court of Appeal refused to apply vicarious liability, because the job only provided the opportunity for misusing the phones. Making the calls was not actually connected with what she was employed to do and could not be regarded as doing her job in an unauthorised way.

Case Summary

Journeys and detours

Case Summary

One area that has caused problems for the courts is where a tort (usually negligence which causes an accident) happens on a journey that may or may not be taken in the course of employment. In *Hilton* v. *Thomas Burton* (1961), four workmen were out in their employer's van, which they were allowed to use for travelling to a demolition site out in the countryside. After half a day's work, they decided to stop and go to a café seven miles away for tea. On the return journey, there was an accident caused by the van driver's negligence, and one of the passengers was killed. His widow sought to make the employer vicariously liable for the negligence, but the Court held that there was no vicarious liability. Although the driver was using the van with the employer's permission, he was doing something he was not employed to do when the accident happened.

Case Summary

However, in *Williams* v. *Hemphill* (1966), a lorry driver who took a long detour was held to be acting within the course of his employment. It was his job to carry passengers to Glasgow, and while they were on board he took a detour, during which part of the journey there was an accident. Were his employers liable for the accident? The House of Lords said they were, because it was his job to transport the passengers, and they were on the lorry at the time, so it could not be said that he was taking the detour merely for his own purposes. Lord Pearson said:

> Had the driver in the present case been driving a lorry which was empty or contained nothing of real importance, I think that so substantial a deviation might well have constituted a frolic of his own. The presence of passengers, however, whom the servant is charged . . . to drive to their ultimate destination makes it impossible . . . to say that the deviation is entirely for the servant's purposes. Their presence and transport is a dominant purpose of the authorised journey, and, although they are transported deviously, continues to play an essential part . . . [T]heir transport and safety does not cease at a certain stage of the journey to be the master's business, or part of his enterprise, merely because the servant has for his own purposes chosen some route which is contrary to his instructions.

Case Summary

In *Smith* v. *Stages* (1989), the House of Lords took the opportunity to clarify the issue. The case involved a road accident involving two of the defendant's employees. They were usually based in the Midlands, but their employer had asked them to do a job at a power station in Wales. It was agreed that they would be able to claim travel expenses, and would be paid for the time it took to get to and from the job, as well as the time they spent working. Negligent driving by one of them caused an accident on the way home, and the other one was injured. Was the employer vicariously liable? The House of Lords said that in most cases, travelling to and from work would not be considered within the course of employment, but in this case, because of the arrangements about being paid for the travelling time, the men were 'on duty' at the time of the accident, and what happened was within the course of their employment.

Lord Lowry then went on to clarify the whole issue of vicarious liability arising from journeys:

- An employee travelling from home to their regular place of work is not acting within the course of their employment, even if the vehicle is provided by the employer, unless the contract of employment states that he or she must use transport provided by the employer. If the contract does say he or she must use transport provided by the employer to get from home to work and back, the employee will be in the course of employment during such journeys, unless the contract says otherwise.

- An employee will be acting in the course of employment when they are travelling between two workplaces. This would cover both an employee who usually works at one place but occasionally has to go to another, and employees such as meter readers or salespeople whose job may take them to lots of different workplaces.
- If an employee is paid for time spent travelling, then the travelling will be within the course of their employment, even if the employee is able to choose when and how to travel. However, being able to claim travel expenses does not mean that a journey is within the course of employment.
- An employee travelling during the employer's time (meaning time the employer is paying them for) will be within the course of their employment if they are travelling from home to a workplace other than their regular one, or if they are travelling between different workplaces due to the nature of their job (such as a travelling salesperson), or if they are travelling to the scene of an emergency related to their work.
- If an employee is on a journey that is within the course of their employment, and they take a detour or interrupt the journey, they will no longer be within the course of their employment, unless the detour or interruption is 'merely incidental'.
- If an outward journey is within the course of employment, the return journey will be too.
- Any of the above principles can be displaced by express agreements between employer and employee.
- Where an employee is salaried, the issue of whether they were travelling on the employer's time may not be significant. The distinction here seems to be between jobs where the employee can claim overtime for extra hours worked, and those (usually in professional and managerial occupations) where the salary remains the same even if extra hours are worked, so it is harder to say whether the journey is on the employer's time.

You be the judge

Q: Jack is employed by Wishy Washy Ltd as a plumber and his work takes him to customers' houses. He starts work at 8.30 am and finishes at 5.30 pm. At 2.30 one afternoon he has just finished installing a bathroom at one house when he gets a call from his boss, asking him to go to unblock a toilet in another house about 10 miles away. He sets off, but halfway there remembers that it is his wife's birthday. As he has to drive right past a flower shop, he pops in and buys her some flowers. As he pulls away from his parking space outside the flower shop, at 4.30, he negligently hits another vehicle. Are Wishy Washy liable for the accident?

Source: Pearson Education Ltd/Imagestale/John Foxx Collection

A: It seems likely that they are. Taking the principles explained by the House of Lords in *Smith* v. *Stages*, factors which appear to make Wishy Washy liable are that Jack is travelling between two workplaces, during time he is paid for. The only question is whether going into the flower shop can be considered a diversion or detour (which seems unlikely as it was directly on his route), and whether it was more than 'incidental'.

Acts forbidden by the employer

As we saw earlier, an employer can be liable for an act even if they have not given the employee permission to do it. What about acts which the employer has actually banned the employee from doing? You might imagine that an employer could never be liable for these, but this is not the case. The rule is that if the actual act the employee does is banned, the employer will not be liable, but if the ban is not on a specific act but on a way of doing their job, the employer can be liable.

Case Summary

This is a very slippery concept and, as we will see, has led to some very odd distinctions between different cases. It was applied in *Limpus* v. *London General Omnibus Co.* (1862), where a bus driver caused a collision while racing a bus from another company to be the first to a bus stop. His employers had issued written rules banning their drivers from racing against other drivers, but the court held that the accident happened in the course of his employment because it took place when he was driving a bus in a way calculated to help his employer's business and that was an act he was authorised to do. His employers had not banned him from driving, only from driving in a particular way, and this level of ban was not enough to prevent vicarious liability.

Case Summary

The difficult distinctions this approach can cause can be seen in two very similar cases, which had different results. In *Twine* v. *Bean's Express Ltd* (1946), the defendant's employee was a van driver and gave the claimant's husband a lift in the van. As a result of the employee's negligence the husband was killed. The driver had been told by his employers not to give lifts in the van to anyone except a list of authorised passengers, and there was a notice on the side of the van repeating this. The Court held that in giving the lift, the driver was doing something that the employer had expressly banned and so the employer was not vicariously liable. By contrast, in *Rose* v. *Plenty* (1976), an employer was found liable for injury to someone riding in one of their vehicles, even though their employer had been told not to take passengers. In this case, the employee was a milkman who had been told by his employer not to allow passengers on his float, nor to let children help him deliver the milk. He ignored those orders and paid the claimant, who was 13, to help him on his rounds. As a result of his negligent driving, the claimant was injured while riding on the milk float. The Court of Appeal held that his employer was vicariously liable, because the injury happened when he was doing the job that he was authorised to do, even though he was doing it in a way that had been banned by his employers.

Case Summary

One distinction between the two cases, put forward by Lord Denning in *Rose* v. *Plenty*, was that in *Rose* the injured boy was helping with deliveries and therefore the milkman's decision to take him benefited his employer, whereas in *Twine* there was no benefit to the employer from giving the lift. This may be the case, but clearly this was a benefit the employer in *Rose* did not want, especially as it ended up involving them in liability. In practice what seems to be happening in these cases is, again, that the courts are trying to do justice for a claimant who would otherwise have no way of getting compensation in situations where the employer is in some way benefiting from the banned practice.

Criminal acts

What is the position where the employee's act is not only a tort but also a criminal act? For example, if a nightclub bouncer gets annoyed with a customer and punches them on the nose, can the owner of the nightclub be liable? The answer, you might be surprised to know, can be yes. If a criminal act is so closely related to the employee's job that it can be considered part of that job, then the employer can be vicariously liable for it.

Before we look at the cases, it is important to understand that when we talk about vicarious liability for criminal acts committed by employees, we do not mean that the employer is prosecuted for the act instead of the employee. Where an employee does something, in connection with their job, which is a crime, he or she is prosecuted for the crime by the state in the normal way. So in the example above, the nightclub bouncer could be prosecuted for assault, and the case would be heard in the criminal courts. But if the crime also amounts to a tort, the victim can also sue for damages. As few individuals are wealthy enough to be worth suing, the victim will try to impose vicarious liability so that they can sue the employer instead.

if the crime also amounts to a tort the victim can also sue for damages

Vicarious liability for criminal acts: the traditional approach

In some cases, the courts have found vicarious liability for criminal acts simply by applying the Salmond test: was the tort an unauthorised way of doing the job that the employee was paid to do? As with the cases we have already looked at, the result will largely depend on how the court defines the employee's job. In *Morris* v. *Martin* (1966), the claimant sent a fur coat to be cleaned and one of the defendants' employees, a Mr Morrissey, stole it. The claimant sued for conversion, which is a tort that can be committed by taking someone else's property. It would, quite clearly, have been possible to argue that Mr Morrissey's job was to clean the fur and stealing it was not part of that job. But the Court of Appeal defined his job more widely, stating that the conversion was within the course of employment, because he was trusted with looking after the fur and it was in the process of doing so that he stole it. Lord Diplock explained:

Case Summary

> [The defendants] put Morrissey as their agent in their place to clean the fur and to take charge of it while doing so. The manner in which he conducted himself in doing that work was to convert it. What he was doing, albeit dishonestly, he was doing in the scope or course of his employment.

The key point here is that Mr Morrissey's job was not just something that gave him the chance to steal the fur. If, for example, he had worked in a restaurant and stolen the fur when a customer left it on the back of a chair, there would not have been liability because looking after the fur would not have been part of his job.

The same principle was applied in *Warren* v. *Henley's Ltd* (1948). Here the defendants were the managers of a petrol station. Their employee mistakenly accused the claimant of trying to leave without paying and, after he had paid, the customer threatened to complain about the employee to his managers. The employee replied by punching the customer on the nose. The Court held that the assault was not committed in the course of employment. Although it was part of the employee's job to stop customers leaving without paying, the assault occurred after the customer had paid and was no longer anything to do with the job but the result of the employee's annoyance at the customer threatening to complain about him. There would only have been vicarious liability if the assault was committed as part of the process of stopping the customer leaving without paying.

Case Summary

Widening liability: the 'close connection' test

Case Summary

There remain some types of criminal act where the courts have found problems with applying the Salmond test. In *Trotman* v. *North Yorkshire County Council* (1999), the claimant was a pupil at a school for children with learning disabilities, and was sexually abused by the deputy headmaster during a school trip to Spain. Applying the Salmond test, the Court of Appeal held that there was no vicarious liability, because it was not possible to say that sexually abusing a child was an unauthorised way of the teacher doing his job. In fact, it might be said to be the opposite of the job a teacher was expected to do.

Case Navigator

Case Summary

However, in ***Lister* v. *Hesley Hall*** (2001), the House of Lords took another look at the issue, and introduced a new, wider test. The facts of the case were very similar to those of *Trotman*, in that the claimants in the case were boys at a school for children with emotional problems, who had been sexually abused by the school warden, an employee of the defendants. At first instance, there was no possibility of arguing vicarious liability for the abuse itself, because the court at first instance would have had to follow the *Trotman* decision. So the claimants instead argued that, as part of the warden's job, he had a duty to report to his employers anything that could harm the welfare of children in his care. He would, for example, have a duty to report if some other member of staff had abused them. Therefore, it was argued, he had a duty to report his own abuse, and the defendants were vicariously liable for his failure to do that.

It was an unusual argument to say the least and, as you can see in the People in the Law box a little later in the chapter, even the barrister in the case was surprised when it succeeded at first instance. But because it did succeed at first instance, the case was then appealed all the way to the House of Lords. Because the Lords did not have to follow the Court of Appeal's decision in *Trotman*, it became possible to take a broader look at the issue, and a new test was introduced (the story of this case gives you some idea of how far important changes in the law can be a matter of chance, depending entirely on when or whether a particular point of law makes it up the appeals ladder).

In *Lister*, the Lords looked back at the traditional Salmond test for vicarious liability, which, as we saw earlier, says that an employer will be liable for acts that, though not authorised by the employer, amounted to doing the job the employee was paid to do, only in an unauthorised way. Clearly, the case did not appear to fit into the traditional definition of vicarious liability, because what the defendant did could not be seen as merely doing his job in an unauthorised way. His job was to look after the boys and what he did was the opposite of that. However, the House of Lords referred to a phrase which Salmond used to explain the test, in which he said that 'a master . . . is liable for acts which he has not authorised, provided they are so connected with acts which he has authorised, that they may rightly be regarded as modes – albeit improper modes – of doing them'. The House of Lords said that the key words were 'so connected'. The question to ask was whether the connection between what the employee had done and what he was supposed to do in his job was so close that it would be 'fair and just' to impose vicarious liability on his employers.

To answer this, it was necessary to ask what was the task that the employer had delegated to the employee. In this case, the school had responsibility for looking after the boys on a day-to-day basis, and they had delegated this task to the warden. The sexual abuse had been carried out during the day-to-day routine of looking after the children, and the nature of the job was part of the reason why the employee was able to commit the abuse. Therefore, the House of Lords held that the sexual abuse was 'inextricably linked' with the job that the employee had been employed to do, and so it was fair to make the school vicariously liable. They explained that this would not have been the case if, for example, the employee had been a gardener and his job had merely given him access to the boys. The essential factor was the close link between the nature of his job and the tort he committed. This is essentially the same reasoning as was used in *Morris* v. *Martin*, where the employee's job was to take care of the fur.

Case Summary

The *Lister* test was applied in *Bernard* v. *Attorney-General of Jamaica* (2004), a case heard by the **Privy Council**. Here a police officer, who was not in uniform, approached a man using a public phone, said he was a police officer and told the man to get off the phone so that he could use it. The man refused, and the police officer pulled a gun and shot him. The police officer appeared not to have been on duty at the time (he had since fled the country so it was impossible to find out for sure). But the court held that the police force still had vicarious liability for his actions. They pointed out that the shooting happened immediately after he identified himself as a police officer, the gun was supplied by the police, and these factors made the criminal act so closely connected with the man's job that it was fair to impose vicarious liability. The court also said that employers should expect to be liable for risks which are reasonably incidental to their business. In this case, the police had created the risk by supplying guns and allowing officers to keep them while off duty.

Case Summary

In *Mattis* v. *Pollock* (2003), the Court of Appeal said that where an employee's criminal act involves violence, the employer is more likely to be found vicariously liable if the job also involved using violence. The case concerned a bouncer at a club, who stabbed a customer, leaving him paralysed. The stabbing came after a series of incidents in which the bouncer had behaved in an intimidating way to a particular group of customers. On the night in question, this had led to a fight at the club, in which the bouncer came off worse and ended up running away. He later went back to the club, armed with a knife and apparently looking for revenge. The customers he had fallen out with had left the club, but he met them in the street and stabbed the claimant. The claimant sued the owner of the nightclub, Mr Pollock, who claimed he was not vicariously liable, because the stabbing did not happen in the club, although it did happen in the bouncer's normal working hours. However, the Court of Appeal found that the stabbing was not an isolated incident, but part of a pattern of violent behaviour by the bouncer. There was evidence that Mr Pollock had encouraged the bouncer to be intimidating and use violence, and had ignored warnings from other bouncers that the man's behaviour had gone beyond acceptable levels. Therefore they found that it was fair and reasonable to impose vicarious liability for the stabbing.

In *Maga* v. *Trustees of the Birmingham Archdiocese of the Roman Catholic Church* (2010), the Court of Appeal examined a case that was in some ways similar to *Lister*, but with some important differences. The claimant alleged that when he was a teenager he had been sexually abused by a Catholic priest, Father Clonan, and sought to sue the Church as being vicariously liable for the priest's actions. What made the claim significantly different from that in *Lister* was that the boy was not a Catholic, and the occasions on which he was abused were not directly to do with the Church. He and Father Clonan had met when he was admiring the priest's sports car one day, and Father Clonan had invited him to a church disco that he ran, which was open to all local young people and not just Catholics. The claimant later began doing small jobs for Father Clonan, such as washing his car or cleaning the house where he lived, which was owned by the Church. It was on these occasions that much of the abuse happened. The claimant did not attend the Church and Father Clonan apparently did not attempt to persuade him to do so. The Church therefore argued that the abuse could not be said to be so closely connected with

Father Clonan's work that it would be fair and just to hold them liable. They pointed out that although his position as a priest gave him the opportunity to abuse the claimant, it was made clear in *Lister* that there had to be a closer connection than mere opportunity.

The Court of Appeal took a different view. Lord Neuberger pointed out that whenever Father Clonan met the claimant he was dressed in his priest's robes, and that symbolised the fact that he had a role involving trust, responsibility and moral authority. In addition, part of his job was to spread the Catholic faith, and an element of this involved getting to know and befriend non-Catholics and to spend time alone with them, which was what he had done with the claimant. It did not matter that his reason for doing so was not to spread the faith but to commit abuse; the relationship with the claimant was still brought about under the guise of his duties as a priest. It was also relevant that Father Clonan had been given special responsibility by the Church for working with young people, and that the event which drew the claimant in (the disco) was held on church premises and organised on behalf of the Church. The work abuse itself had also frequently happened on church premises, when the claimant was cleaning the priest's house. Taken together, these factors meant that the abuse passed the *Lister* test, and the Church was vicariously liable.

Case Summary

A contrasting case, where the *Lister* test led to vicarious liability being refused, is *N* v. *Merseyside Police* (2006). The claimant came out of a club in the early hours of the morning and was very drunk. An off-duty police officer was sitting in his own car nearby, and offered to take her to the nearest police station for safety. She agreed, but instead he drove her to his own home where he raped her. He was charged and pleaded guilty. The claimant then sued the Chief Constable, arguing that he was vicariously liable for the officer's actions. The claim was rejected. The court held that the case differed from *Lister*, in that the employee there had been given the job of looking after the boys whereas the police officer had not been given the responsibility for looking after his victim. He had not actually been carrying out any police duties at the time, and the only connection with his job was that he had used his uniform and warrant card to persuade the woman to get into his car. This was not a sufficiently close connection between the job and the rape to make it fair for vicarious liability to be imposed.

The principle that seems to emerge from these cases is that the courts will look closely at all the circumstances when deciding whether the connection is sufficiently close to make vicarious liability fair. One key issue, which is clearly linked to fairness, appears to be whether the employer was in some way at fault. In *Lister*, the school failed to detect the abuse: in *Bernard*, the police helped create the risk by allowing off-duty officers to keep their guns; and in *Mattis* v. *Pollock*, it was clear that the club owner had ignored warnings that the bouncer's behaviour was beginning to get out of hand. By contrast, in *N* v. *Merseyside* the police officer merely took advantage of his job, and it is hard to see what the police could have done to prevent him doing what he did.

These cases show that the principle in *Lister* makes it possible for the courts to take into account all the circumstances and deliver practical justice, as we saw in the case itself. The defendants in the case were in a vulnerable position, and by failing to detect or prevent the abuse the school had let them down. Without vicarious liability they had no real chance of compensation, and for both these reasons there is a clear degree of practical fairness in the decision.

the principle set down in *Lister* has been criticised as being too vague

However, the principle set down in *Lister* has been criticised as being too vague. The *Lister* decision extends the Salmond test with the question of whether the tort and the job are so closely linked that it is 'fair and just' to impose vicarious liability. But we are not told exactly what makes it fair and just in one case and not in another, beyond the fact that the job must do more than merely make it possible for the tort to be committed. As we saw in the chapter on the duty of care in negligence, 'fair and just' can amount to nothing more than a value judgement on the part of whichever judges happen to hear a case. This can make the law unpredictable and uncertain. On the other hand, it could equally well be argued that in making the test wider, the Lords created sufficient flexibility for vicarious liability to be imposed where the circumstances of the case made it fair to do so, and for it to be denied where that would be fair. In this approach, they were merely following a wider trend in tort law, for preferring general principles over very detailed rules: the ***Caparo* test** in negligence and the rules on foreseeability are just two more examples of this. It can be argued that such flexibility is necessary, given the wide variety of different situations that tort law can cover, and that it is better to sacrifice predictability for fairness.

An interesting alternative view has been taken by the Canadian courts, in *Bazley* v. *Curry* (1999), a case where the facts were similar to those in *Lister*. As we saw earlier, in *Lister*, the House of Lords focused closely on existing law and drew out their new test from the basis of the Salmond test, so that the key question was still what the employee was employed to do. By contrast, in *Bazley* the Canadian court focused openly on the policy issues around vicarious liability. Mr Justice MacLachlin said:

> the question in each case is whether there is a connection . . . between the employment enterprise and [the tort] that justifies imposition of vicarious liability on the employer . . . in terms of fair allocation of the consequences of the risk and/or deterrence.

Like the House of Lords in *Lister*, the Canadian court is using the 'close connection' test, but instead of focusing on what the job was, they look specifically at who is best placed to pay damages and/or be deterred by vicarious liability. In practice, of course, the *Lister* test is wide enough to allow the courts to look at exactly those issues as well, but it could be argued that, in bringing the policy issues out into the open, the Canadian approach allows their courts to strike a better balance between flexibility and predictability, since it makes the question of which factors will make vicarious liability fair much clearer in advance.

People in the law

Rosalind Coe was a barrister, who appeared for the claimants in *Lister* v. *Hesley Hall* and has now been appointed as a Circuit Judge. The interview below was conducted while she was still a barrister.

Can you describe the kind of work you do? I specialise in clinical negligence cases, and over the past few years, I've done a lot of cases which, like *Lister*, deal with child abuse that happened in children's homes some years ago. Usually I'm involved in big group litigation cases, where you're bringing the case on behalf of perhaps hundreds of claimants.

Is most of your work done in court? No, I only spend about a third of my time in court, because most of my cases get settled, but that can be at a very late stage – around 50 per cent are settled at the last minute, sometimes on the morning of the hearing. About once or twice a week, I might have a meeting to try to negotiate a settlement, and the rest of the time is spent on advisory work. At the moment, for example, I'm preparing skeleton arguments for a hearing, and I've got 20 files in front of me, full of witness statements, expert reports, claimant's medical and education records and case reports, which I'll need to work through to make my arguments.

How much contact do you have with the clients you represent? Not very much. I'll usually meet them once, but it's quite possible, if a case is settled, that I won't meet them at all. The disadvantage of that is you're very reliant on the solicitors who instruct you. I work from the witness statements they give me, and that can mean they miss a piece of information you might have got and used. But the advantage is you can be objective – when a solicitor works on a case over a long period, they can get quite involved with the client's perspective, whereas I can stand back and look at what's there, without preconceptions.

Is there a typical working day for you? There's no routine to my work at all. One day I might have to get up at 5.30 to get to court somewhere, another I'll work at home. For a big group action, a solicitor might get an enquiry, and once they've looked into it, they'll come to me and ask if I think it's got good prospects. If I think it does, they'll go away and do more work, and it might be another year before I get more closely involved, and then five or six years before it goes to court or settles.

In other cases, I only get involved at the last minute – a solicitor might expect a case to settle, for example, and then when it doesn't, I might get instructed a week before, and have to very quickly get to grips with all the evidence. I might even get a call at lunchtime to do a hearing tomorrow morning, so in this job, you have to be able to master a lot of information quite quickly, and to be able to deal with unpredictability – if you get instructions at the last minute, you can't say, well it's five o'clock and I'm going home to watch the TV. You have to be know how to think on your feet as well. If you're examining a witness in court, and they say something you weren't expecting, you've got to come up with a way to deal with that, there and then.

Did you have any way of knowing that *Lister* was going to be a groundbreaking case? No, I had no idea. It was returned to me at the last minute – I got the instructions on the Friday for a hearing on the Monday and as I read the papers over the weekend, I could see it was a very problematic case.

How did you go about deciding on your arguments? Because of the decision in *Trotman*, we couldn't argue vicarious liability, so we initially went for negligence on the part of the employers. But I knew that was going to be difficult, because we had to show that the employers knew or should have known about the abuse, and as it had all taken place away from the school and behind closed doors, it was quite difficult to prove that they should have known it was happening.

That approach wasn't working, so I came up with the idea of arguing that the warden had a duty to report to his employers anything that might harm the boys in his care, that his abuse was something that he therefore should have reported, and that they were vicariously liable for his failure to report it. It was quite an academic argument, and I was pretty surprised when the judge accepted it and we won at first instance. The case was appealed on that point, and the Court of Appeal rejected it, saying it was ridiculous to claim that someone could have a duty to report their own abuse. But then once it was appealed to the House of Lords, they were able to move on from that argument and take a wider look at the issues. So although my argument didn't win, it was the reason the case got as far as the Lords, and we got the law changed.

How did you prepare for the House of Lords? In that kind of case, which affects a general point of law, you know that they're going to want to take a very broad look at things, so you have to do a lot of research. Their Lordships looked at the whole history of the issue – I think the earliest case cited was from the 1700s – and at cases from other jurisdictions as well.

It was my first time in the Lords, and though I wouldn't say I was nervous exactly, you do feel a certain amount of anticipation when you're doing something like that for the first time. Their Lordships have already read all the relevant evidence and the cases you want to cite, so they get down to details quite quickly. It's very quick fire and you have to be on the ball, but I loved it. And to win was a very good feeling. The law had become too restrictive, in my view, and we knew straightaway that the case would have a big impact. When you look at the cases that came after it, you can see how much it changed the law – in my opinion, in the right direction.

Source: Rosalind Coe

The employee's liability

Vicarious liability can only arise if the employee was liable for a tort in the first place. If what the employee did does not amount to the relevant tort, the employer cannot be vicariously liable for that tort either. Similarly, if the employee has a **defence**, the employer will also be covered by the defence.

Case Summary

This was the situation in *ICI* v. *Shatwell* (1965), where two brothers, George and James, were employed by ICI. Their job was to test electrical circuits and the company regulations required them to take safety precautions while they were doing it. This made the job take longer, so the brothers agreed between them not to bother with the safety rules. There was an explosion and George was injured. He sued ICI, claiming they were vicariously liable for James's failure to take the proper safety precautions. However, if George had sued James, James would have had the defence of consent, because George agreed not to use the safety precautions. Therefore, ICI were also covered by the defence and there was no vicarious liability.

Suing both employer and employee

a victim can sue both the employee and the employer if they choose to

The fact that vicarious liability can be established against an employer does not mean that the employee who committed the tort is no longer legally liable. Vicarious liability is a form of **joint liability**, which means that a victim can sue both the employee and the employer if they choose to. In practice however, it is usually only the employer who is sued, because they are most likely to be able to pay damages. Can the employer then sue the employee to get back the damages they have paid out? The answer, perhaps surprisingly, is yes, though in practice this does not happen often. This right was first established in *Lister* v. *Romford Ice and Cold Storage* (1957). In that case, a lorry driver drove negligently in the course of his employment and ran over his father, who was also employed by the same company. The father recovered damages on the basis of the employer's vicarious liability for his son's negligence, and those damages were paid by the employer's insurance company. The employer then sued the son, arguing that his careless driving was not just a tort against his father, but was also a breach of his employment contract because he had not exercised reasonable care in doing his job. The House of Lords agreed, saying that the employee who committed the tort should not be able to avoid paying damages for it. They ruled that the son should pay his employer damages equivalent to the amount paid to his father. In practice, of course, the claim was brought by the employer's insurance company, even though it was in the employer's name, and the result was that they got back the damages they had paid out under the insurance policy.

Case Summary

The case was widely criticised as undermining the whole principle of vicarious liability. It was pointed out that the decision effectively allowed the company's insurers to reclaim money from the employee, which meant that the employers had been paying the insurers to cover a risk which ended up costing the insurers nothing. Although the case has never been overruled, in practice it now has little real effect, because after it was decided, insurance companies made an informal agreement that they would not attempt to sue under the principle in *Lister* v. *Romford Ice*, unless there was evidence that the employee and employer had, between them, misrepresented the situation in order to make the insurers pay, or committed some other misconduct regarding the insurance cover.

An employer who is sued for an employee's tort also has a right to get their money back from the employee under the Civil Liability (Contribution) Act 1978. This provides that where two or more parties are jointly liable for a tort, and only one of them is sued and pays damages, that tortfeasor can then make a claim against the other(s) for a proportion of the money paid in damages. This claim is a matter between the tortfeasors, and does not affect the claimant who already has his or her money. In practice, however, this provision is not often used in employer–employee cases, because the employee will not usually have the money to pay substantial damages. It is more often used in cases involving two or more tortfeasors who are not in an employment relationship but are liable for the same tort, a situation which we will look at later in this chapter.

Liability for independent contractors

As we saw earlier, a company will not have vicarious liability for torts committed by independent contractors, only for those committed by employees. However, there are situations in which a company can be directly liable for the acts of contractors that they use, because the company has a **non-delegable duty** to the claimant and something the independent contractor has done has breached that duty. As we saw in the previous chapter, a non-delegable duty is one where the company can delegate the work of performing the duty to someone else (the independent contractor), but they still have the legal responsibility for making sure the work is done properly.

> Whether a duty is non-delegable or not is a question of law in each case.

Whether a duty is non-delegable or not is a question of law in each case. Many non-delegable duties arise from statute, and here the wording of the Act will often indicate whether the duty is delegable or non-delegable. For example, the Occupiers' Liability Act 1957, which we will look at in the next chapter, states that an occupier has a duty to make premises reasonably safe but this duty can be delegated, provided that they use a competent independent contractor to deal with a potential risk, such as maintaining electrical wiring. Where the wording of the statute does not make it clear whether the duty is delegable or non-delegable, it is up to the courts to interpret the statute in order to decide whether the duty is delegable.

Even where a duty is delegable, and a company delegates it to an independent contractor, they can still be liable if they have failed to take reasonable steps to find a competent person or firm to do the work, or to make sure it was done properly. Just as with non-delegable duties, the liability in this situation arises from the company's own duty to the claimant and not to any kind of vicarious liability.

You be the judge

Q: Counties Water are a water supply company who have a non-delegable duty to repair a water pipe. They pay Perfect Pipes to do the work, but Perfect Pipes do not fix the pipe properly and there is a huge leak, which causes damage to the home of Mary, a local resident. Mary now wants to sue Counties Water. Could they be liable?

A: Yes. Because their duty is non-delegable, Counties Water cannot delegate legal liability for it, even though they delegated performance of the duty to Perfect Pipes.

Source: Pearson Education Ltd/Pearson Education Asia Ltd/Coleman Yuen

Limits of liability

In both the situations described above (where a duty is non-delegable, or a duty is delegable but the company which has the duty fails to take reasonable steps to make sure the independent contractor they use is competent), the company using the independent contractor will be liable only if the tort was part of the work the independent contractor was hired to do. Acts which fall outside the work they are hired to do are called collateral negligence, and the company which uses them will not be liable for this. An example of this principle is *Padbury* v. *Holliday and Greenwood* (1912). Independent contractors were hired to work on the windows of a house the defendants were building. While working on the windows, the contractor negligently placed a heavy iron tool on the window sill and it fell off and injured the claimant. Putting the tool on the windowsill was not a normal part of the work the contractor was doing, and so it was held that the claimant's injuries were caused by collateral negligence, for which the defendants were not liable. The Court said that for the defendants to be liable, the negligence had to be central to the work the contractors were asked to do, and not just casually connected to it.

Case Summary

Should vicarious liability be widened?

As we saw at the beginning of this chapter, one of the reasons why vicarious liability is imposed is that it moves the loss to the party most able to pay compensation, because employers have insurance, whereas individual workers generally do not and cannot afford to pay damages out of their own pockets. In his article 'Vicarious liability and independent contractors – a re-examination' (1990), Ewan McKendrick argues that restricting vicarious liability to cases where the tortfeasor is an employee is undermining the ability to spread losses fairly and practically. Increasing numbers of companies now use freelance or temporary staff to do work that would previously have been done by employees, often in an attempt to avoid employment protection legislation or gain tax advantages. As McKendrick points out, many of these self-employed workers could no more afford tort damages than an ordinary employee could, and are unlikely to have taken out insurance cover. Yet the law defines them as independent contractors, which means the person making use of their services bears no liability for any torts they may commit. McKendrick argues that even where there is not technically an employment relationship, vicarious liability should still apply in many of these cases because the person using their services will be best placed to bear the cost of damages, and spread their effect through insurance and prices. There is some evidence, in cases such as *Hawley* v. *Luminar Leisure* and the *Viasystems* decision, that the courts are beginning to take this approach as well, and are looking very carefully at the reality of employment relationships to determine where it is just to impose liability.

Other types of multiple liability

Vicarious liability applies when one party (the employer) is sued for a tort committed by another (the employee). What about situations where a tort is actually committed by more than one party? Here, liability will be divided between the tortfeasors in one of three ways:

- independent liability;
- several liability;
- joint liability.

Which form of liability applies will depend on how the damage was done, and whether or not the parties were acting together.

Independent liability

Independent liability applies where the claimant suffers damage which is caused in two completely separate incidents by different tortfeasors. Imagine, for example, that you are driving along the road one day, and a van drives into you, damaging the right-hand side of your car. You exchange details with the van driver and go on your way, but then, as if your day was not bad enough, another car comes out of a side road and hits you, damaging the left-hand side of your car. In this situation, the van driver and the car driver would each be independently liable, which means each is liable for the damage that they caused and, if the claim(s) had to go to court, you would sue each of them separately for that damage and only that damage.

Several liability

Several liability arises where two or more tortfeasors act independently of each other, but the result of their acts is damage to the claimant. Take, for example, a situation where two motorists are both driving negligently: Annie is talking on her phone and not looking at the road, and Billy is going much too fast. They are coming in opposite directions and, because of their negligent driving, they crash into each other. The two cars spin across the road, and into a third car driven by Carrie, who is not driving negligently. Carrie is injured. In this situation, Annie and Billy would both be liable for all of the damage caused to Carrie. She can sue either Annie or Billy for the full amount of her claim or she can sue both of them at once for the full amount of her claim. Once a claimant has received the total amount that is relevant to the damage, whether from one or more of the defendants, they cannot receive any more (so a claimant could not, for example, recover damages twice by suing two different defendants for the full amount).

Joint liability

Joint liability can arise in two ways. Vicarious liability is one, and the other is known as common design, and applies where the same wrongful act is committed by two or more people together, with a joint purpose. In either type of joint liability, a claimant can sue one, some or all of the defendants. If the claimant chooses to sue only one or some of the defendants (usually because the other(s) cannot afford to pay damages), they can claim the total amount from those they do sue; there is no reduction for the fact that others are involved. Let's say, for example, that Alan and Billy commit a tort against Charles in circumstances which make them jointly liable. Alan is very wealthy, but Billy is not. Charles can choose to sue one or both of them, but there is little point in suing Billy because he will not have any money to pay damages. So in practice he will probably choose to sue just Alan, and because there is joint liability he can claim the full amount from him. However, it is not possible to get full damages more than once. In our example above, if Billy was later to become wealthy, but Charles had already sued Alan for the full amount, he could not then go on to sue Billy as well.

An example of joint liability by common design can be seen in *Brooke* v. *Bool* (1928). Mr Brooke was renting a shop from Mr Bool, and there was also a lodger in the same building. The lodger smelled gas one day and told Mr Bool, so they went together to see if there was a leak. The defendant told the lodger to light a match, which he did and, not surprisingly, there was an explosion which damaged the claimant's property. Presumably because the lodger would not have been able to afford to pay damages, the claimant sought to sue Mr Bool, as being jointly liable for the damage. The Court agreed that Mr Bool was jointly liable because although the lodger lit the match they were acting together for the same purpose. This meant that the claimant could get the full amount of damages from Mr Bool.

Case Summary

Contributions between tortfeasors

As you can imagine, if two tortfeasors are responsible for damage to the claimant, but the claimant sues only one of them for the whole amount, the party who is sued might well see this as an unjust result. To address this situation, the Civil Liability (Contribution) Act 1978 provides that where this is joint or several liability, and only one of the tortfeasors is sued and pays damages, that tortfeasor can then make a claim against the other(s) for a proportion of the money paid in damages. This claim only involves the tortfeasors, and not the claimant, who already has his or her money.

We can see how this works if we apply it to the car crash example we looked at above, under several liability. There, Annie and Billy's negligence caused injury to Carrie, and Carrie can choose to sue one or both of them. Let's say she chooses to sue only Annie, and is awarded damages of £30,000. Carrie then has her damages, and her role in the dispute is over. But Annie can then sue Billy, to make him pay her a portion of the damages that she has paid to Carrie. The court will decide how much it is fair for Billy to contribute, by examining how far each of the parties was responsible for the damage.

Summary

- Vicarious liability is a legal concept which makes employers liable for torts committed by their employees.
- Vicarious liability applies where:
  - the tortfeasor was an employee;
  - the tort was committed within the course of their employment.
- Tests for employee status include:
  - Does the employer control the employee's work?
  - Is the tortfeasor 'in business on their own account'?
  - Did the tortfeasor agree to provide work and skill in return for payment, and be subject to the employer's control?
  - Are the terms of the contract consistent with employee status?
  - Is there a mutual obligation between the parties?
- Liability can also be shared between two or more employers.
- A tort is committed in the course of employment if it was:
  - a wrongful act authorised by the employer; or
  - a wrongful and unauthorised way of doing some act authorised by the employer.
- An employer can be liable for behaviour they have forbidden, if it can be seen as banning a way of doing the job rather than a specific act.
- Employers can be liable in tort for criminal acts, if they are so closely connected with the job that it is fair to impose vicarious liability.
- Vicarious liability can only arise if the employee was liable for a tort in the first place.
- Companies can be liable for torts committed by independent contractors if:
  - there is a non-delegable duty; or
  - the duty is delegable but the company fails to take reasonable steps to find a competent person or firm to do the work, or to make sure it was done properly.
- Liability for independent contractors only applies where the tort was part of the work the independent contractor was hired to do.
- There are three types of liability for torts committed by more than one party:
  - Independent liability, where the damage was caused by separate incidents;
  - Several liability, where two or more tortfeasors caused damage in the same incident;
  - Joint liability, where the tortfeasors were acting together.
- The Civil Liability (Contribution) Act 1978 provides that where there is joint or several liability any tortfeasors sued can claim against the others.

Question and answer*

Problem:

Ronnie Razzle is the owner of a club called Total Tracks. Security for the club is provided by a firm called Heavies 4 Hire, which supplies Ronnie with two bouncers who work on the door of the club each night. One of the bouncers, Trevor, gets into an argument with a customer, Jeremy, one night and refuses to allow him into the club. Jeremy is furious, and insults Trevor, but walks away. On his way home that night, Trevor sees Jeremy again, goes up to him and punches him on the nose. Ronnie has been warned by the other bouncer that Trevor can be violent, and a week before the incident he told Trevor that if he 'went too far' he would not be able to work at the club any more.

Tina also works at the club, though she is part of the permanent staff there. One of her jobs is to drive a minibus which takes the other employees home when the club closes in the early hours of the morning. She has just dropped off the last employee when she sees a friend, Bob, walking home after missing the last bus. Although she has been told by Ronnie that she may not give anyone except employees of Total Tracks lifts in the bus, she takes Bob home, and on the way the bus crashes, due to her negligent driving, and Bob is injured.

Advise Jeremy and Bob about any claims they may have in tort.

You should allow yourself no more than 40 minutes to complete this task.

Essay:

'The doctrine of vicarious liability has not grown from any clear logical or legal principle, but from social convenience and rough justice' Lord Pearce, in *ICI* v. *Shatwell* (1965).

How far do you think Lord Pearce's description is true? In the light of your answer, do you think the current law on vicarious liability is satisfactory?

This question should be answered in 40 minutes.

* Answer guidance is provided at the end of the chapter.

Further reading

Atiyah, P. (1967) *Vicarious Liability in the Law of Tort*, London: Butterworths.
Patrick Atiyah is probably the most renowned expert on tort, and although this book was written over 40 years ago his explanation of the background to vicarious liability is still worth reading, especially if you are writing an essay on the subject.

Giliker, P. (2009), 'Making the right connection: vicarious liability and institutional responsibility', 17 Torts Law Journal 35.
A very interesting look at the decision in *Lister*, and the way it has been applied in later cases. *Lister* is the most important modern case on vicarious liability so this is well worth reading.

McKendrick, E. (1990) 'Vicarious liability and independent contractors – a re-examination', 53 MLR 770.
McKendrick looks at modern employment practices, such as the use of agency and temporary workers, and argues that the courts should be more ready to find that companies using these arrangements are employers, or the aims of vicarious liability will be undermined.

Stevens, R. (2007) *Torts and Rights*, Oxford: Oxford University Press, pp. 257–74.
The point made by Lord Pearce in *ICI* v. *Shatwell*, and used in the essay question above, is one which academics have long puzzled over: how does vicarious liability fit in with the wider principles of tort law? Stevens attempts to answer this question

with the theory that the law is not imposing liability on employers for the torts of their employees, but reflecting the fact that the employing companies are acting through their employees. A very interesting read.

Tettenborn, A. (2005) 'Vicarious liability and joint employees', 155 NLJ 1750.
In this commentary on the *Viasystems* case, the author suggests how far the principles set down in the case can be applied.

Question and answer guidance

Problem: Taking Jeremy's claim, the first question here is whether Trevor is actually an employee of the club, so you need to look at the tests the courts have used for this; the case of *Hawley* v. *Luminar* is clearly particularly relevant here. Then move on to consider whether the assault can be considered to have been committed in the course of Trevor's employment; as it is a criminal act, you will need to look at the 'close connection' test explained in *Lister*, and the case of *Mattis* v. *Pollock*.

Regarding Bob's claim, we know Tina is part of the permanent staff, so the first part of the test for vicarious liability has been passed. The main issue here is whether Tina was acting in the course of her employment, so you will need to look at the 'lifts' cases, *Twine* v. *Bean* and *Rose* v. *Plenty*, and the principles set down in *Smith* v. *Stages*.

Essay: A good way to start this essay would be to define what vicarious liability is and when it applies. You could then go on to explain Lord Pearce's comment by referring to the reasons why vicarious liability is imposed – spreading losses to those most able to bear them can be seen as something done for social convenience, while making employers liable because ultimately they may benefit most from the activities of their businesses is a form of rough justice (rough justice in this context really means doing what seems to be morally right, even if it might not fit strict legal principles).

You can then go on to look at some of the cases on vicarious liability, explaining whether you think they are based on social convenience and/or rough justice, and highlighting where there might be any lack of logic or legal principle – *Lister* is an obvious example of this, as are the 'lifts' cases where very similar factual situations led to different results.

In the light of the cases you have looked at, say how satisfactory you find this area of law. Do you think the aims of vicarious liability are valid ones? Is it worth sacrificing logic and legal principles if the results seem just? Or has this approach made the law too muddled and inconsistent? There is no right or wrong answer to this part of the question, as long as you can make sure your arguments are backed up by reference to the law, rather than just stating what you think is fair or unfair.

Visit **www.mylawchamber.co.uk/quinntort** to access tools to help you develop and test your knowledge of tort law, including practice exam questions with guidance, annotated weblinks, glossary and key case flashcards, legal newsfeed and legal updates and interactive 'You be the judge' questions.

premium mylawchamber
unrivalled support for legal education

CASE NAVIGATOR
POWERED BY LexisNexis

Use Case Navigator to read in full some of the key cases referenced in this chapter with commentary and questions:

Lister* v. *Hesley Hall Ltd [2001] 2 All ER 769

Chapter 9
Occupiers' liability

Key points In this chapter we will be looking at:

- How an occupier of premises can be liable for accidents that happen to people who have permission to be there, under the Occupiers' Liability Act 1957
- How an occupier of premises can be liable for accidents that happen to people without permission to be there, under the Occupiers' Liability Act 1984
- How far it is possible to exclude either type of liability
- Defences applicable under each Act

Introduction

Let's suppose that you live in a house with a long front garden. On the path leading up to the front door there is a loose flagstone, and one day the postman trips on the flagstone and breaks his leg. Would you be liable to pay him compensation for that injury? What about if it was not the postman who trips on the path but a burglar, creeping up to look through the window to see if anyone is in – would you be liable then? These kinds of issues are the subject of this chapter, which looks at liability for harm that is caused by dangerous places or buildings. The occupier of a building, or land, can be liable for this harm, whether the person harmed is there with permission or not.

Occupiers' liability

The rules of tort that we have looked at so far come mostly from **common law**, having been built up over the years by the decisions of judges in cases that come before the higher courts. Occupiers' liability also started out this way, but its rules have since been clarified and set down in two statutes, which, taken together, state the current law on liability for dangerous premises:

- The Occupiers' Liability Act 1957, which sets out the duty towards people who enter premises with the occupier's permission (usually known as visitors);

- The Occupiers' Liability Act 1984, which explains the duty towards people who enter premises without permission (usually known as non-visitors or trespassers; for the purposes of this chapter both words mean the same).

Before these Acts were passed, liability for harm caused by dangerous premises was covered by the ordinary law of negligence. However, case law had developed different levels of protection for different categories of people. Someone who entered the premises as part of a contract (such as a plumber coming to fix a pipe, or a guest at a hotel) was covered by a higher standard of care than someone who was invited in for business purposes (such as a customer browsing in a shop), while a third standard, lower still, covered anyone who was just a guest on the premises (such as a friend coming round for dinner). Someone who did not have permission to be on the premises had very little protection at all; if they were injured, the occupier could only be liable for deliberately or recklessly causing them harm and not for negligence. Bear in mind that this category would not just include people who deliberately entered premises knowing they should not be there, but also someone who got lost, or a child who was too young to understand that they needed permission to enter, and you can see that there was potential for injustice in the law, as well as over-complexity and confusion, which gave rise to a huge amount of litigation.

there was potential for injustice in the law, as well as over-complexity and confusion

The situation was widely criticised, and in 1954 a report by the Law Reform Committee recommended legislation to clarify the law. The result was the Occupiers' Liability Act 1957, which established one standard of care to cover all the different categories of people who enter premises with permission. This made the law much less complex and more consistent. However, it still left one problem unsolved, in that people who did not have permission to enter premises were not covered by the Act, and so had very little protection. Over the years, this was increasingly seen as unjust; there were, for example, a number of cases where children had strayed on to land without permission and been injured, as well as adults hurt in situations where, although they did not have permission to be there, they would not generally be seen as having done anything wrong, yet it was difficult for them to make a claim. In response to this problem, the Occupiers' Liability Act 1984 was passed, which establishes that occupiers do have a **duty of care** for the safety of people who enter the land without permission, although it is more limited than the duty under the 1957 Act that they owe to people who do have permission to enter.

For convenience, the two Acts are sometimes referred to in the following text simply as 'the 1957 Act' and 'the 1984 Act'. The key point to remember is that *the 1957 Act deals with people who enter with permission,* and *the 1984 Act deals with people who enter without permission.*

You will notice as you read through the chapter that some of the cases we look at were decided before the two Occupiers' Liability Acts were passed. This is because the Acts are partly based on the common law that existed before, so these earlier cases are still good law. You will probably also notice that a lot of the principles contained in the Acts are similar to those in negligence. This is because cases involving dangerous premises would usually have been brought in negligence before the Acts were passed, and so the common law principles that formed the basis of the Acts mostly come from negligence.

Occupiers and premises

Before we look at the provisions of the two Acts, we need to establish two preliminary questions, which apply to both of them:

- Who is the occupier of land?
- What counts as 'premises'?

Who is the occupier?

the occupier is the person (or organisation) who has control of the premises

In ordinary language, the occupier of premises would be the person who is physically occupying it – the person living in a house, for example, or the firm carrying on business in a factory. Under common law, however, the term has a wider meaning than this, and means the person (or organisation) that is in control of the premises. The Occupiers' Liability Acts also use this common law definition. The 1957 Act says that 'the persons who are to be treated as an occupier . . . are the same . . . as the persons who would at common law be treated as an occupier', and the 1984 Act says that anyone who is an occupier under the 1957 Act is also an occupier under the 1984 Act. In both cases, therefore, the occupier is the person (or organisation) who has control of the premises.

What does it mean to say someone is 'in control' of land or premises? This will be a matter of fact in each case, but the essential principle is that they are in a position to allow or prevent people entering. This would obviously cover someone who owns premises, or who is renting and living or working in them, but it is also possible, in legal terms, to be in control of premises without being physically present. In *Harris* v. *Birkenhead* (1976), the case concerned a house which the local council had bought from the owner as part of a slum clearance programme. The owner had been renting the house out, and it was agreed that, although the house had been sold and was now owned by the council, the tenant could stay there until a specified date. After the tenant moved out, a child got into the house and was seriously injured after she fell from a window. The council knew that children commonly entered empty premises to play, and they usually boarded houses up to prevent this, but in this case they had not done so. They were sued for negligence (at this time there was no Act to cover liability to trespassers) and argued that they were not the occupier because they had not taken over possession of the house. The Court of Appeal disagreed, saying that the sale of the house meant the council had the legal right to control the house (including the right to take precautions against trespassers entering), and this meant they could be considered the occupiers.

Case Summary

More than one occupier

The fact that the occupier does not have to be physically on the land means it is possible for there to be two or more occupiers at the same time, both of whom can be liable. A common example is where a property is owned by a landlord, but lived in by a tenant. This was the case in *Wheat* v. *Lacon* (1966), where the **defendants** owned a pub, which was managed by a Mr Richardson. Mr Richardson and his wife lived on the top floor of the pub, and had permission from the owners to take in lodgers. The **claimant** was one of these lodgers, and one night he fell down the stairs and was

Case Summary

killed. The defendants argued that they were not the occupiers because the Richardsons were living in the relevant part of the building, but the House of Lords rejected this argument. They said that a person was an occupier if he or she has 'a sufficient degree of control over the premises that he ought to realise that any failure on his part to use care may result in injury to a person coming lawfully there'. Therefore both the Richardsons and the defendants were occupiers, though in fact neither of them was held liable because the evidence was that the accident was not caused by anything they had done or not done.

What counts as 'premises'?

The Acts impose liability on the 'occupiers of premises'. In the majority of cases, 'premises' will be a building or an area of land. However, both the Acts give 'premises' a wider definition than just buildings or land. Section 1(3) of the 1957 Act defines premises as including land, buildings and 'any fixed or movable structure, including any vessel, vehicle or aircraft'. The definition is therefore quite broad, and the courts have been happy to give it a wide interpretation: in *Bunker* v. *Charles Brand* (1969), for example, 'premises' was held to include a digging machine used to construct a tunnel.

Case Summary

What about the 1984 Act? Section 1(2) of the 1984 Act states that 'premises' includes 'any fixed or movable structure'. It does not specifically mention vessels, vehicles and aircraft, but it could certainly be argued that these are included within the term 'movable structure', so in effect both Acts have very similar, and similarly broad, definitions of 'premises'.

Although in practice most cases will involve buildings or land, keep the above provisions in mind when you are tackling problem questions, as examiners will sometimes set occupiers' liability problems on boats, trains or other odd places to test your knowledge of the wording of the legislation.

You be the judge

Q: **Jeremy, unluckily, has accidents in all the following places. Which of them could lead to a claim under one of the Occupiers' Liability Acts?**

(a) a supermarket;
(b) a park;
(c) a train;
(d) a friend's house;
(e) a roller coaster.

A: As far as the Occupiers' Liability Act 1957 is concerned, any of these could give rise to a claim, as the Act specifically states that it covers land, buildings or 'any fixed or movable structure, including any vessel, vehicle or aircraft'. Under the 1984 Act, (a), (b) and (d) would definitely give rise to a claim, as these are clearly premises. It is not entirely clear whether (c) and (e) would be covered but it could certainly be argued that they are 'movable structures'.

Liability to visitors: the Occupiers' Liability Act 1957

As we saw above, the 1957 Act defines an occupier's liability to people who enter the premises with permission, normally referred to as visitors. One important thing to note here is that section 1(3)(b) of the Act states that the occupier's duty of care to visitors covers both personal injury and damage to property. For convenience, in this section we talk about keeping visitors safe, but everything said here also applies to keeping a visitor's property safe and undamaged.

Who is a visitor?

In ordinary language, a visitor is someone who you invite in, such as a friend coming round for coffee. For the purposes of the Act, however, 'visitor' has a wider meaning, which covers anyone who is lawfully on the premises. This covers three main groups:

- people with express permission to enter;
- people with implied permission to enter;
- people with a legal right of entry.

People with express permission to enter

This covers anyone who the occupier has actually invited on to the premises, or given permission to enter. Examples would be a friend invited round for dinner, a plumber called in to fix a leak, or a pet-sitter who holds a key and comes round to look after the cat while the occupier is on holiday. The permission might be given in advance, as in the case of friends invited round for dinner, or on the spot, as when a neighbour calls and you invite them in.

People with implied permission to enter

This covers anyone who can show that the circumstances were such that they could assume they had permission to enter. It is generally recognised that anyone has implied permission to enter premises and 'state their business' to the occupier, though what this means in practice depends on the situation. For a domestic house, it would mean that anyone has implied permission to walk up the garden path and knock on the door, but not to walk into the house uninvited; with a shop, on the other hand, there would usually be implied permission just to walk in and look around or go up to the counter to ask for what you want, but not to walk through a door marked 'Staff only'; in a hospital, there would be implied permission to walk into the accident and emergency department, or into a ward during visiting hours if you are visiting someone, but not to start wandering around looking into consulting rooms and operating theatres.

There will not be implied permission if the occupier makes it clear that they are not giving permission to enter. For example, a door-to-door salesperson would normally be regarded as having implied permission to go and knock on anyone's door in order to sell their goods, but many people put signs on their doors or gates saying 'No salesmen', and this would mean that there was no implied permission even to enter the front garden and go up to the door.

In some cases, permission can be implied by the occupier's own behaviour. In *Lowery* v. *Walker* (1911), the defendant, a farmer, occupied land which was regularly used as a short cut by local people. The defendant knew this and had never taken steps to prevent it, largely because most of the people who used the short cut were customers who bought his milk. Mr Lowery was injured when he took a short cut across the field and a wild horse that the farmer had put there attacked him. The Court held that Mr Lowery had implied permission to be on the land because Mr Walker had never done anything to prevent or discourage people from walking across it. This case and others like it have been seen as the courts finding a way to offer a claim to deserving cases who, if they were found to be trespassers, would not have been able to get compensation. This type of decision is less likely to arise now that the 1984 Act provides a duty towards trespassers.

Case Summary

People with a legal right of entry

The 1957 Act includes in the definition of a visitor anyone who enters premises under a right conferred by law, with or without the occupier's permission. Examples would be police officers who have a warrant, or who are covered by statutory powers of entry, such as the power to search premises for drugs under the Misuse of Drugs Act 1971.

All of the above categories are covered by the term 'visitor' under the 1957 Act, so remember when you see this term that it covers more than just the friend you have invited round.

People not classified as visitors

There are two groups of people who you might expect to be classified as visitors but who are not:

- *People using rights of way*: In *Greenhalgh* v. *British Railways Board* (1969), it was stated that people using a public right of way are not to be treated as visitors under the 1957 Act. This would include someone walking down an ordinary street, for example.
- *Walkers and ramblers*: The Countryside and Rights of Way Act 2000 gives a general right to walk over land which falls within the description of 'mountain, moor, heath or down'. This has become known as the 'right to roam'. The 2000 Act provides that people exercising this right are not visitors, so are not covered by the 1957 Act. They are covered by a restricted duty of care under the 1984 Act.

Limitations on permission

Both express and implied permission may be subject to restrictions, and that can affect which Act applies if someone is harmed. As you will remember, the key difference between the Acts is that the 1957 Act covers people who have permission to enter, and the 1984 Act covers people who enter without permission. If, for example, you invite someone to your house, but specifically ask them not to go into your bedroom, they would have express permission to be in the house, but no permission to be in the bedroom. Therefore if they tripped on a loose carpet in the bedroom and hurt themselves, any claim would be decided under the 1984 Act because they do not have permission to be there. But if the accident took place anywhere else in the house, the 1957 Act would apply because they do have permission to be there. This is important because, as we will see later, it is easier to make a claim under the 1957 Act than it is under the 1984 Act.

Restrictions can also be – and often are – implied from the circumstances. For example, if you get a plumber in to fix the sink in your kitchen, they would have implied permission to go into the kitchen, and perhaps to the room where your stopcock was to turn off the water. But that permission would not allow them to go wandering round the bedrooms, and if an accident happened there they would be covered by the 1984 Act and not the 1957 one.

If a person is given permission to enter premises at a particular time, they will be considered a visitor when they enter at that time, but as a trespasser if they enter at another time. Similarly, if a visitor is permitted to enter the premises for a particular purpose, they will be a visitor then, but a trespasser if they enter for a different purpose. So, for example, if you give a builder the key to come into your house and do some work, they would be considered a visitor while they are there doing that work, and any accident which happened during that time would be covered by the 1957 Act. But if they were to come back later, let themselves in and sit down to watch a DVD, they would not have permission to be there for that purpose – so if they were injured then, they would be covered by the 1984 Act and not the 1957 one.

You be the judge

Q: Carrie and her young son Tom go into the local bakers to buy some bread. While Carrie is choosing what she wants at the counter, Tom wanders off and sees a door marked 'Staff only'. He goes through it and falls down some stairs. Might Tom have a claim under the Occupiers' Liability Act 1957?

A: No. Although Carrie and Tom have implied permission to go into the shop, the fact that the door was marked 'Staff only' means there is no implied permission to go through it. In law Tom is therefore a trespasser and if he has a claim, it would be under the Occupiers' Liability Act 1984 and not the 1957 Act.

Source: Pearson Education Ltd/Image Source

The issue of which Act applies when permission contains restrictions comes up a lot in problem questions, so it is worth taking time to make sure you are clear about this. The exercise in the Out and About box will help.

Out and about

Make a list of at least 10 types of place that you have implied permission to enter. If you are stuck, take a walk through your nearest town centre – you should get plenty of ideas from the buildings you see there. In each case, work out what that permission allows you to do. Are there areas you do not have permission to enter, or things you might do which would put an end to the right to be there? Pick three buildings where there are restrictions on your permission, and work out where/when you would be covered by the 1957 Act if you had an accident in those buildings, and where/when you would be covered by the 1984 Act.

The duty of care to visitors

So, now we know who will be considered a 'visitor' under the 1957 Act, we can look at the duty of care which an occupier will owe to them. The duty of care owed to visitors under the 1957 Act is described as 'the common duty of care' and is based on the duty which was previously owed under the common law of negligence. Section 2(2) of the Act states that:

> The common duty of care is a duty to take such care as in all the circumstances of the case is reasonable to see that the visitor will be reasonably safe in using the premises for the purposes for which he is invited or permitted to be there.

The important thing to note here is that the Act does not impose a duty to make sure that visitors are not at any risk of harm whatsoever. It only requires the occupier to take reasonable steps to make sure the visitor is reasonably safe. This is essentially a question of balance, and the courts will look at the same kind of factors as they do with breach of duty in negligence, weighing the seriousness of the risk against the practicality of taking precautions against it (if you want to remind yourself of what these factors are and how this balancing act works, have a look back at pages 45–55).

Case Summary

An example can be seen in *Horton* v. *Jackson* (1996), where the claimant lost the sight in one eye after being hit by a ball when playing at a golf club. He sued the golfer who hit the ball, and the golfer brought the golf club in on the action, claiming that the accident was partly their fault. He argued that it was known that there was a risk of such accidents at that particular part of the course, and there was in fact a sign asking players at the tee concerned to wait until those behind had moved on, but this policy was not enforced. The club could have put up screens between the two tees to prevent balls hit at the first from hitting people at the second, and he claimed that in not doing so they were in breach of their duty under the 1957 Act. The Court of Appeal disagreed: there was expert evidence suggesting that a screen would not have prevented the accident, and the fact that in 800,000 rounds of golf at the club only one other accident had ever occurred at the spot meant the trial judge was entitled to conclude that the existing precautions were reasonable in the circumstances.

The Law in Action box gives a real-life example of how difficult this balancing act can be.

Law in action The graveyard dilemma

As we have seen, the Occupiers' Liability Act 1957 requires occupiers to take reasonable precautions regarding the safety of visitors (and we will see later that the 1984 Act contains a similar duty to non-visitors). But how easy is it for occupiers to assess what the law will consider 'reasonable'? And can efforts to make premises safe sometimes cause other problems? An example of this dilemma is outlined by academics Bennett and Gibbeson in their study of precautions taken by local councils to make cemeteries safe, after a young boy was killed when a gravestone toppled over and fell on him. His family sued the council, which ran the cemetery, and were paid £33,000 **damages** in an **out-of-court settlement**.

The accident, which happened in 1980, set alarm bells ringing among local councils, and after the Health and Safety Executive issued a warning about the risks posed by old and unstable headstones, councils across the country began checking their cemeteries. Tens of thousands of headstones deemed to be a risk were laid flat or even destroyed, sometimes without the knowledge of relatives of the people buried there. The action led to a huge backlash from the public and the media, as relatives spoke of arriving at cemeteries to find what looked like mass vandalism, and then discovering it had been done deliberately by the council. The councils were criticised as going too far: a columnist for *The Times* pointed out that there had been just six fatal accidents in graveyards in 12 years, and compared that to the number of people killed on Britain's roads, which was six every 14 hours. He also pointed out that in one area the council's own safety experts had pointed out that laying down the stones actually caused a further safety issue, because people could trip over them, so the council had to pay to have the stone embedded into the surrounding grass.

The situation was a perfect example of how difficult it can be to weigh up competing factors and decide what is reasonable. The number of previous accidents was small, which suggests the risk of one happening again was also small. However, if a tombstone did fall on someone, it was potentially very dangerous, so although an accident was not very likely to happen, the risk if it did was a serious one. This in turn had to be balanced against the distress caused to bereaved relatives by what they saw as official vandalism.

Just to make things even more difficult, Bennett and Gibbeson's study points out that there was not even agreement among experts on precisely when a gravestone should be considered safe. The device used to measure whether a stone was likely to fall over was called a Topple Tester, and it showed how much force a stone could withstand before it would fall. However, there was disagreement about exactly what degree of force a stone should be able to withstand in order to be classified as safe; the manufacturers of the Topple Tester suggested 35 kg, but other safety experts preferred a lower figure. In addition, the makers only recommended the device for use on stones that were at least a metre high, and many of the stones tested were smaller than this and so may have been less likely to fall than the Topple Tester suggested. Not surprisingly, cemetery managers told Bennett and Gibbeson that they felt they were in a no-win situation, where they were 'damned if they do and damned if they don't'.

[*Reference*: L. Bennett and C. Gibbeson (2010) 'Perceptions of occupiers' liability risk by estate managers – A case study of memorial safety in English cemeteries', *International Journal of Law and the Built Environment*, 1(1), 76–93]

Child visitors

Where the visitor is a child, the law recognises that it may be necessary to take extra precautions. Section 2(3) of the 1957 Act makes special provision for visitors who are children, stating that:

An occupier must be prepared for children to be less careful than adults. If the occupier allows a child to enter the premises then the premises must be reasonably safe for a child of that age.

This means that safety precautions that might be reasonable for adult visitors may not be sufficient for children: an obvious example would be a warning notice, which would be useless if a child was too young to be able to read or understand it. Similarly, something which would not be a hazard to adults may be considered a risk to a child. This was the case in *Glasgow Corporation* v. *Taylor* (1922), where a 7-year-old child died from eating poisonous berries that he had picked in a park that was under the control of Glasgow Corporation (the name then given to the local council). The Corporation knew the berries were poisonous but had taken no steps to keep children away from them. The House of Lords held that they were liable because they knew that the berries, which looked like cherries, might be attractive to children, and that small children are 'inquisitive and easily tempted' and would not understand the risk of eating the berries. As they knew that, they should have taken precautions such as fencing off the bush, and they had not done so. This case was decided before the 1957 Act was passed, but as the common duty of care is based on the common law rules of negligence that existed before the Act, it still represents the law regarding children.

Case Summary

In *Jolley* v. *Sutton London Borough Council* (2000) the claimant was a 14-year-old boy. He and a friend found a broken old boat abandoned on the council estate where they lived, and decided to try to repair it. They propped it up with a car jack, but it collapsed, pinning the claimant under it and injuring him so badly that he was paralysed. He won his case, but on appeal the Court of Appeal said the council was not liable. They agreed that the boat was both an allurement to children and a risk because it was broken, but they said these factors were not the causes of the accident. The accident, they said, had happened because the boys had jacked the boat up, and this was not the kind of normal playing in the boat that the council could have foreseen. The House of Lords, however, reinstated the claimant's victory, saying that it was foreseeable that children would meddle with the boat in some way, and that this could cause injury. That was enough to have required the council to take some precautions, such as removing the boat.

Case Summary

Where a child is very young, an occupier may be entitled to expect that their parents will take responsibility for them, and not let them go where there may be danger. In *Phipps* v. *Rochester Corporation* (1955) the claimant was a 5-year old boy who was injured when he fell into a trench on a piece of open land owned by the Rochester Corporation (the local council). The Corporation knew that children played on the land, but had done nothing either to keep them out or make the area safe. Even so, the Court held that the occupiers were not liable, because it was the duty of a parent to make sure that very young children did not wander about by themselves, or if they did allow their children out alone, to make sure that the places they went to were safe. However, the Court said the position might be different where the land concerned was a public park or playground, which parents were entitled to expect would be safe.

Case Summary

A similar approach was applied in the tragic case of *Bourne Leisure* v. *Marsden* (2009), which involved the death of a 2-year-old boy. The Marsden family were staying at a caravan park operated by Bourne Leisure, and while Mrs Marsden was talking to another camper, her son Matthew wandered away without her noticing. After a frantic search, he was found drowned in a pond on the site. The Marsdens sued Bourne Leisure, claiming that the pond should have been fenced off to prevent danger to children, but the Court of Appeal disagreed. It found that the park owners did not have a duty to fence

Case Summary

off the site, because guests at the park were made aware of the existence of this and two other ponds, and it would have been clear to any parent that these ponds would have presented a danger to any small child who wandered off on their own. The Court of Appeal pointed out that this decision did not mean that the Marsdens, who were described as 'responsible, attentive and caring' parents, were at fault, because it was well known that children could 'disappear in an instant'. But the fact that they were not at fault in losing sight of Matthew did not mean that the park was liable for his death.

Writing and drafting

You are a trainee solicitor, and you and your boss have just had a meeting with a client, Jerry Jolly, who is about to open a local restaurant. He wants to encourage families to eat there, but is worried about liability if a child were to have an accident on the premises, which also has outside tables in a pretty garden with a fishpond and children's play area. Your boss asks you to draft a letter to Mr Jolly, summarising the law on occupiers' liability to child visitors, and pointing out anything that Mr Jolly needs to be aware of and any precautions he should take. Go through what you have read so far, and draft the letter.

Handy tip: Remember that Mr Jolly is not a lawyer, so you need to use simple, practical language, and explain the legal rules that come out of cases, rather than referring to the cases themselves. Tell him what he needs to do, rather than giving him a detailed explanation of the legal principles.

Visitors doing a job

Sometimes a visitor who is on the premises for work purposes will be at risk of harm from dangers that are to do with the job they are doing. A fireman who attends a house fire, for example, is always at risk of being injured fighting the blaze, while a window cleaner is always at risk of falling off a ladder. The 1957 Act makes special provision for these types of danger. Section 2(3)(b) of the 1957 Act provides that

> An occupier may expect that a person, in the exercise of his calling, will appreciate and guard against any special risks ordinarily incident to it, so far as the occupier leaves him free to do so.

The term 'in the exercise of his calling' simply describes the situation where someone enters premises in order to do a particular job. The effect of section 2(3)(b) is that where a risk normally arises in the course of someone's work, the occupier does not need to take special precautions to guard the visitor against that risk, as long as they allow the visitor to take their own precautions.

Case Summary

In *Roles* v. *Nathan* (1963), two chimney sweeps were poisoned by carbon monoxide gas when they were working on the chimney of a boiler that was alight at the time. The occupier was held not liable, because the risk of carbon monoxide poisoning in that situation was well known to sweeps, and they had actually been warned about it. Lord Denning pointed out that the situation would have been different if, for example, the stairs in the house had given way, injuring the sweeps, because that was not a risk that arose out of their job. In that case an occupier could be liable.

However, if someone 'exercising a calling' takes all the normal precautions of their trade but, despite that, is injured by a hazard that is associated with their job, the occupier may still be liable. In *Salmon* v. *Seafarers Restaurant* (1983), a fireman was injured while fighting a fire in a fish and chip shop. The fire happened because the occupier had left the fryers on, and the blaze was so serious that there was clearly a risk of firefighters being injured even if they took normal safety precautions.The shop owner argued that the risk of being injured in a fire was a normal part of the claimant's job and something an occupier could expect him to guard against for himself. However, the Court held that although an occupier was entitled to expect a fireman to take precautions against the normal risks involved in their job, the occupier could not escape liability if the fireman had taken the normal precautions but these were not sufficient to prevent injury. This approach was approved by the House of Lords in the similar case of *Ogwo* v. *Taylor* (1988), also involving a fire, where the situation was such that no amount of care by the fireman could have prevented his injury.

Case Summary

Case Summary

Independent contractors

What is the situation where a hazard on premises is the result of work done by someone other than the occupier? For example, faulty maintenance or construction are the cause of many injuries that could give rise to a claim, and in many cases this maintenance or construction will not have been done by the occupier but by a tradesperson or company. If, for example, you ask a builder to build a wall in your house, and because of their poor workmanship, the wall collapses and kills a visitor, should you be liable, or the builder? This issue is covered by section 2(4) of the 1957 Act, which states that:

> In determining whether the occupier of premises has discharged the common duty of care to a visitor, regard is to be had to all the circumstances, so that (for example) –
>
> . . .
>
> (b) Where damage is caused to a visitor by a danger due to the faulty execution of any work of construction, maintenance or repair by an independent contractor employed by the occupier, the occupier is not to be treated without more as answerable for the danger if in all the circumstances he had acted reasonably in entrusting the work to an independent contractor and had taken such steps (if any) as he reasonably ought to in order to satisfy himself that the contractor was competent and that the work had been properly done.

This essentially means that an occupier who employs an independent contractor to maintain, repair or build something on their premises can avoid liability for harm caused by that contractor's work, if it was reasonable for them to trust the work to a contractor, and they have taken reasonable steps to make sure the contractor is competent and the work is done properly.

What amounts to 'reasonable steps' will depend on the nature of the occupier, the premises and the work done: on a large-scale, complex project such as a council building a school, a court might find that reasonable steps would include employing an architect or other professional to supervise the work, whereas for a small job such as installing a central heating system in a private house, the occupier would probably not need to do more than choose a contractor they had good reason to believe was reliable and competent. On the other hand, even on a small household job, an occupier who knowingly employs a 'cowboy' builder because they were cheap might not be considered to have taken reasonable steps.

Case Summary

The more technical the work is, the more likely it is to be reasonable for the occupier to rely on the contractor, and not have to take their own steps to make sure the work is done properly. In *Haseldine* v. *Daw* (1941), the claimant was killed when a lift failed and plunged to the bottom of its shaft. The Court held that the building's occupiers were not liable for the death, because they had used an apparently competent firm to maintain the lift, and as the work involved was highly technical they could not be expected to check themselves whether it had been done correctly.

Case Summary

However, where the work done is of a kind that can easily be checked, the occupier may be liable, even if the hazard was caused by the independent contractor. In *Woodward* v. *Mayor of Hastings* (1945), the claimant, a cleaner, slipped on a step that was covered in snow and was injured. There was some question as to whether she was an independent contractor, but on the assumption that she was, the Court held that the occupiers could be liable, because no special technical knowledge was required to see that a step had not been properly cleaned of snow. The occupier was required to take the same degree of care as an ordinarily prudent person would, no more or less.

Where a claimant cannot sue the occupier because they have taken reasonable steps with regard to employing an independent contractor, it will often be possible to sue the contractor under the usual principles of negligence.

A duty to check insurance cover?

Case Summary

In a recent case, the Court of Appeal has held that in some situations an occupier may reasonably be expected to check that independent contractors have adequate insurance against accidents. In *Gwilliam* v. *West Hertfordshire Hospital NHS Trust* (2002), the hospital was holding a fund-raising fair in their grounds, and hired a contractor to supply and operate a 'splat wall': a fairground attraction comprising a trampoline, a Velcro-covered wall and a Velcro suit, where the idea was for people to wear the suit, bounce on the trampoline and throw themselves at the wall. The wall was set up wrongly, and Mrs Gwilliam was injured while using it. Unknown to the hospital, the contractor's insurance had run out four days before the fair. The Court of Appeal held that the occupier's duty to make sure that a contractor was competent included taking reasonable care to check that an independent contractor who was supplying potentially hazardous equipment had adequate insurance. On the facts, however, the hospital was not in breach of the duty because they had asked whether the contractor had insurance and were told that they did, which was true at the time of the booking. The Court held that asking the question was sufficient to count as taking reasonable steps; it was not reasonable to have expected them to ask to check the insurance certificate, which would have shown that the policy was to run out before the fair took place.

Case Summary

The suggestion in *Gwilliam* that there might be a duty to check whether independent contractors have insurance was controversial, and in later cases it seems the Court of Appeal has drawn back from this approach. In *Naylor* v. *Payling* (2004), the claimant was injured by a nightclub bouncer (yes, another one), who was employed by an independent contractor which provided security services to the nightclub. The contractor was not insured so the claimant could not sue them, and the facts were such that it was not possible to claim that the bouncer was actually employed by the club, and so make them vicariously liable. So, on the basis of *Gwilliam*, the claimant tried to sue the nightclub for their failure to check whether the contractor had insurance. The Court of Appeal rejected the idea that an occupier would always have a duty to check whether a contractor had insurance. They said that such a duty could only arise in 'special circumstances', such as where there was a statutory requirement to make such a check. The Court said that the decision in *Gwilliam* could be explained by the fact that the hospital trust was using the contractor for a one-off occasion, were not especially experienced in choosing this type of service, and had simply obtained the name of the contractor from the *Yellow Pages*. In that situation, checking whether the contractor had insurance cover was something that they might well be expected to do as part of assessing whether the contractor was competent. The situation in *Naylor* was different, because the bouncers supplied by the contractors were licensed by a scheme run by the local council and the local police, which checked that they were of good character and had been properly trained.

Warnings

As we saw above, the 1957 Act says that the visitor should be made 'reasonably safe', not that the premises have to be safe. This means that an occupier can fulfil their duty of care, even if there are hazards on their premises, by warning visitors about those hazards. However, not all warnings will have this effect, only those that are sufficient to enable the visitor to be reasonably safe. As Lord Denning explained in *Roles* v. *Nathan* (1963), if a house has a dangerous bridge in front of it, and that bridge is the only means of getting to the house, the occupier will not fulfil their duty by posting a notice warning visitors of the risk. The sign would not make visitors reasonably safe, since they would have to use the bridge anyway. However, if there are two bridges, one dangerous and one safe, an occupier could fulfil their duty by displaying a notice warning visitors not to use the unsafe bridge. If the visitor used the dangerous bridge anyway and was injured, the occupier would not be liable.

Case Summary

To take a more common example, let's look at two contrasting situations, concerning a leisure centre. In the first situation, the floor has just been cleaned. It is still wet and a little bit slippery, but anyone who knew this could walk safely across it if they took care. The leisure centre puts up a warning notice saying 'Take care – slippery floor'. In this case, the notice would be enough to make visitors 'reasonably safe', because the warning is enough to enable people to stay safe. Now take a second situation, where one of the staff made a mistake and used the wrong liquid to clean the floor. The liquid they used is very oily, and has made the floor so slippery that it would be impossible to walk across it without slipping over. In that case, putting up a notice saying 'Take care – slippery floor' would not be enough to make the visitor 'reasonably safe', because even knowing of the risk they are likely to slip if they try to walk across the floor.

You be the judge

Q: Ned runs a pub. One lunchtime, as he is opening up, he notices that the step in front of the door is loose. There is no time to fix it before opening time, so he puts a notice on the door saying 'Be careful, loose step'. A few minutes later, his first customer of the day, Sharon, arrives. She sees the sign and treads carefully, but as she steps on to the step, it gives way and she falls and breaks her ankle. Ned claims that he cannot be in breach of the 1957 Act because he posted a clear warning of the risk. Is he right?

A: No. A warning sign can only help an occupier avoid liability if it is sufficient to make a visitor 'reasonably safe'. In this case, Sharon had no alternative but to use the step, and on the facts we have here it seems that Ned's warning was not enough to make her reasonably safe.

Excluding the common duty of care

In many situations, occupiers will try to avoid liability to visitors by using warning notices, or exclusion clauses in contracts. You will probably have seen signs in places like car parks, hotels and gyms, saying things like 'The management accept no liability for loss of or damage to guest's property', or 'Patrons enter at their own risk'. These are attempts to avoid liability under the Occupiers' Liability Act 1957 – but are they legally valid? The answer is, only sometimes.

The 1957 Act does allow an occupier to 'restrict, modify or exclude' the duty owed to visitors, for example by using warning signs, or terms in a contract. However, another Act, the Unfair Contract Terms Act 1977, sets down some circumstances where this kind of exclusion of liability will be invalid. The Act, commonly known as UCTA, was put in place to try to give ordinary consumers better rights against companies and traders, and applies where the premises are used for business or the occupier is acting in the course of their business. It has two important provisions regarding occupiers' liability:

- Section 2(1) prevents an occupier from excluding liability for death or personal injury. This means that if, for example, a hotel put up a sign saying 'Guests enter at their own risk', this would be completely ineffective against claims for death or personal injury; regardless of the notice, someone injured on the premises could successfully sue.
- Section 2(2) prevents an occupier from excluding liability for other forms of damage (such as damage to property), unless it is reasonable to do so. This means that if, for example, a gym you go to puts up a notice saying 'We take no responsibility for loss or damage to members' property', and owing to the gym's failure to take reasonable safety precautions there was a fire which damaged your property, you may still be able to sue, regardless of the notice, if a court considers it was unreasonable for them to exclude liability. If, on the other hand, the court considers it was reasonable for them to exclude liability, you will not have a claim.

Note that the Act applies wherever premises are used in the course of a business, whether or not the visitor was there for a purpose related to the business. Business premises would include premises used by government organisations and local authorities. However, UCTA does not apply where the visitor comes on to the premises for recreational or educational purposes, unless those purposes are within the business purposes of the occupier. So a church which allowed the local badminton club to practise in its hall could exclude occupiers' liability to them, but a leisure centre hiring out badminton courts to the club could not.

Out and about

Over the course of a week, look out for signs which exclude occupiers' liability. Each time you see one, remember the terms of UCTA, and work out whether the sign could actually protect the occupier against a legal claim. You may well come across signs which have no legal effect at all because of UCTA, or have less effect than they claim to. Why do you think these signs might be used even though UCTA makes them meaningless?

Handy tip: Places where you might see this kind of sign include car parks, leisure centres, pubs and business premises of all kinds. Remember that they may not necessarily use the words 'exclude' or 'liability'; a common phrase in car parks for example is 'Cars are parked at the owner's own risk', which effectively implies 'So you can't sue us for any damage'.

Before we move on to look at defences under the 1957 Act, try the exercise in the Writing and Drafting box to check your understanding of what you've read so far.

Writing and drafting

You are a trainee solicitor, and your firm has a client, Sue Shapely, who has just set up a local gym. She has consulted you because a friend has told her that if she puts up a sign saying 'The Lovely Bodies Gym accepts no liability for injuries, however caused', she cannot be sued if a gym member should hurt themselves while exercising. Write a letter to Sue, advising on whether she should put up the sign, and explaining, in simple terms, what her legal duty under the Occupiers' Liability Act 1957 is.

Source: Pearson Education Ltd/Imagestate/John Foxx Collection

Defences under the 1957 Act

As we have seen, an occupier can, in some circumstances, use warnings and exclusions to avoid liability to visitors under the Occupiers' Liability Act 1957. In addition, there are two general defences which an occupier sued under the Act can use:

- contributory negligence; and
- *volenti*.

Contributory negligence

As we saw in Chapter 3, **contributory negligence** in a negligence case applies where the accident or injury is partly the fault of the claimant. If the defendant successfully pleads contributory negligence, the damages payable will be reduced to take into account how much of the blame should fall on the claimant. The **defence** works in just the same way under the 1957 Act. As we saw earlier, an occupier's duty under the Act is to 'take such care as in all the circumstances is reasonable'. This means that, when deciding whether an occupier has breached their duty under the Act, a court will look at all the circumstances of the case, and section 2(3) provides for a defence of contributory negligence by stating that the circumstances to be taken into account include 'the degree of care, and want of care, which would ordinarily be looked for in such a visitor'. Where an accident and/or the harm caused is partly the fault of the claimant, their damages can be reduced to reflect this.

Let's say, for example, that you regularly go to a gym, where the showers often flood because the management have not maintained them properly. You know this, but you leave your gym bag on the floor and while you are in the shower there is a flood and your expensive watch is damaged. You can sue the gym under the Occupiers' Liability Act 1957, but there is a good chance that they will successfully plead contributory negligence, because your own carelessness made you partly to blame for the damage to your watch. This would mean that your damages would be reduced.

Volenti

The second available defence, ***volenti non fit injuria***, is also one that we came across in Chapter 3, and you will remember that it applies where the claimant has voluntarily accepted a risk of harm. It applies in just the same way under the 1957 Act. Section 2(4) states that 'The common duty of care does not impose on an occupier an obligation to a visitor in respect of risks willingly accepted as his by the visitor'.

As an example of *volenti* in an occupiers' liability situation, let's say that a theme park has a ride in which passengers loop the loop and are held upside down at the top of the loop. A notice in front of the ride says 'People with back or neck problems are advised not to travel on this ride'. Susie has a back problem, but she really wants to go on the ride so she ignores the notice, but sure enough the ride makes her back problems worse and she sues the theme park. They will be able to use the defence of *volenti*, because Susie knew the risk and voluntarily took it.

The Act goes on to say that whether a risk had been willingly accepted is to be judged on the same principles as in other cases where a duty of care is owed by one person to another. This means that the rules we looked at in Chapter 3, with regard to *volenti* in negligence, apply in just the same way here. If you want to remind yourself about these, you'll find them on page 93.

Liability to non-visitors: the Occupiers' Liability Act 1984

As we have seen, if you are on someone's land with permission, whether express or implied, the occupier owes a duty with regard to your safety under the Occupiers' Liability Act 1957. But what if you are on land or premises without permission? In legal terms this makes you a trespasser, and until 1984, your situation would have been covered by the common law of negligence, which traditionally treated trespassers as having done something wrong and so imposed only very limited duties on occupiers to take safety precautions to protect them.

Lord Moulton summed up the reasoning behind this approach in *Addie & Sons Ltd* v. *Dumbreck* (1929): Case Summary

> Towards the trespasser, the occupier has no duty to take reasonable care for his protection or even to protect him from concealed danger. The trespasser comes on to the premises at his own risk. An occupier is, in such a case, liable only where the injury is due to some wilful act involving something more than the absence of reasonable care. There must be some act done with the wilful intention of doing harm to the trespasser, or at least some act done with reckless disregard of the presence of the trespasser.

This meant that an occupier could only be liable to a trespasser if the occupier had deliberately harmed them, or had done something that harmed them without bothering to think whether they might be harmed. Many people would think this was fair enough: why should an occupier have a duty to protect the safety of a burglar, or someone who enters their premises when they should not be there? However, there are many cases where someone might be on premises without permission, but in circumstances where we would generally not consider them to have done anything wrong: they might have got lost and wandered on to the land accidentally, for example, or in the case of children, they might not understand that they should not be there without permission. The approach described by Lord Moulton could operate very harshly in these kinds of cases, and so the courts began to find ways round it. An example of this can be seen in *Glasgow Corporation* v. *Taylor*, the case we looked at earlier where the council was liable for leaving poisonous berries on land accessible to children, where the court decided that since it was clear the berries were an 'allurement' to children, they should have taken safety precautions. Similarly, *Lowery* v. *Walker*, the case we looked at earlier where the claimant was injured by a milkman's horse, was an example of the courts finding implied permission to enter, so that the claimant was not considered a trespasser and could claim under the 1957 Act. Case Summary

Gradually, this less harsh, more balanced approach began to find favour, at least in cases involving 'innocent' trespassers such as children. In *British Railways Board* v. *Herrington* (1972), the case involved a 6-year-old child who suffered severe burns from an electrified railway line when he was trespassing on the defendant's land. He had got on to the land through a gap in their fence, which was routinely used as a short cut by other local people; the Railways Board knew this, and also knew that children had got on to the land that way, but had not mended the fence. The House of Lords found them liable, and stated that although occupiers owe a lower standard of care to trespassers than to visitors, they still have a duty to act humanely. Lord Wilberforce explained: Case Summary

> It must be remembered that we are concerned with trespassers and a compromise must be reached between the demands of humanity and the necessity to avoid placing undue burdens on occupiers. What is reasonable depends on the nature and degree of the danger. It also depends on the difficulty and expense of guarding against it. The law, in this context, takes account of the means and resources of the occupier – what is reasonable for a railway company may be very unreasonable for a farmer.

This approach – which essentially requires the occupier to take reasonable precautions regarding the safety of trespassers or 'non-visitors' – is known as the 'duty of common humanity' and eventually became the basis for the Occupiers' Liability Act 1984, which now contains the law on occupiers' liability to people who enter without permission.

Who is a non-visitor?

The old law of negligence in this area tended to use the term 'trespasser' to cover anyone who was on an occupier's premises without permission. The 1984 Act does not use this term, and instead talks about people who are 'not [the occupier's] visitors', but the meaning is the same. Both 'trespassers' and 'non-visitors' mean anyone who goes on to land without permission, whether deliberately or accidentally, where the occupier does not know they are there or objects to them being there. This means that both terms include not only burglars and squatters, but also anyone who, for example, wanders on to land because the boundaries are not marked or because they are lost.

> it is possible to become a trespasser or non-visitor in certain parts of a building

As we saw in the first part of this chapter, it is possible to become a trespasser or non-visitor in certain parts of a building or piece of land, even though you count as a visitor to the place as a whole, or to become a trespasser because of something you do, even though you had permission to enter.

Case Summary

Case Summary

An example of this situation was given in *The Calgarth* (1927), by Lord Justice Scrutton, who pointed out that: 'When you invite a person into your house to use the staircase, you do not invite him to slide down the banisters'. Similarly in *Hillen* v. *ICI (Alkali) Ltd* (1936), the Court of Appeal found that dock workers who were lawfully on a barge for the purpose of unloading it became trespassers when they went on to an inadequately supported hatch cover in order to unload some of the cargo, because they knew that they were not supposed to use the covered hatch for this purpose.

Case Navigator

Case Summary

A more recent case on this point is ***Tomlinson* v. *Congleton Borough Council*** (2003). Mr Tomlinson visited a public park, where there was a lake with a beach where people often sunbathed, paddled or rowed boats. Swimming was forbidden, however, and there were signs warning 'Dangerous water; no swimming'. Deciding to swim anyway, Mr Tomlinson dived into a shallow area and was very seriously injured. The House of Lords held that his claim should be judged under the 1984 Act, because although he was a lawful visitor to the park, he became a non-visitor when he ignored the signs and dived into the water.

As we saw earlier, the Countryside and Rights of Way Act 2000 introduces a 'right to roam' on open countryside. The 2000 Act provides that occupiers owe a duty under the 1984 Act to people exercising the right to roam, but it is a more limited duty than that owed to other non-visitors. An occupier cannot be liable for injuries caused by natural features of the landscape, or caused while crossing fences or walls, except by means of gates or stiles, unless the occupier has intentionally or recklessly caused a danger. When judging cases relating to the right to roam, the courts should not use the right to put an undue burden on occupiers, and should take account of the importance of preserving the essential character of the countryside.

You be the judge

Q: Pat owns a farm, which once a year holds an open day for visitors to come and see how the farm works. Tina is one of the visitors, and particularly wants to see inside the dairy where Pat makes their cows' milk into yogurt. Pat explains that they cannot allow visitors inside the building because they have to keep the area scrupulously clean to avoid contaminating the yogurt. While Pat is talking to another visitor, Tina takes her chance and sneaks into the dairy. She trips on a loose flagstone and seriously injures her knee. Which of the Occupiers' Liability Acts would Tina's claim be judged under?

Source: Pearson Education Ltd/Imagestate/John Foxx Collection

A: The 1984 Act. Although Tina has permission to be on the farm, she clearly does not have permission to go into the dairy, so she is a non-visitor.

The duty of care to non-visitors

How much does an occupier have to do to fulfil his or her duty to non-visitors under the 1984 Act? As with the duty under the 1957 Act, it is essentially a duty to take reasonable care, rather than a duty to eradicate all possible risks. Section 2(4) states that occupiers have a duty 'to take such care as is reasonable in all the circumstances of the case to see that the non-visitor does not suffer injury on the premises by reason of the danger concerned'. This is essentially the same standard of reasonableness as applies in negligence, and requires the courts to weigh up factors such as the seriousness of the risk, the social usefulness of the activity and the practicality of taking precautions (if you want to remind yourself how this balancing act works, have a look back at pages 45–55).

Case Summary

An example of the way in which the courts juggle the factors relating to reasonableness is *Tomlinson* v. *Congleton*, the case we looked at above where the claimant was injured diving into a lake where swimming was banned. The court heard that it was quite common for people to swim in the lake, despite the signs, and the claimant's lawyers therefore argued that the occupiers, who were the local council, should have taken steps to prevent this, such as planting over the beach so it could no longer be used. The House of Lords rejected this view. The duty was to do what was reasonable, and the council had fulfilled that by putting up the signs. There was a social value in allowing access to the beach and lake to those who wanted to use them in a responsible way, and there would be a cost involved in making the beach unusable. The council should not be expected to take away this amenity, and incur considerable costs, in order to protect a minority of people who choose to take irresponsible risks when the dangers were obvious.

As we saw earlier, the 1957 Act provides that an occupier may be expected to take greater precautions for child visitors than for adult ones. The courts have ruled that exactly the same principle applies to child non-visitors under the 1984 Act. In *Keown* v. *Coventry Healthcare NHS Trust* (2006), where a young boy was injured falling from a fire escape, the Court of Appeal said that precautions considered reasonable for the safety of adult non-visitors might not be sufficient for children.

Case Summary

Out and about

Look up the case of *Tomlinson* v. *Congleton*, and have a close look at the way the courts balanced the issue of whether the council had acted reasonably. What factors did they take into account? Do you think they struck the right balance? Are there any other arguments you would have made if you were representing either side?

As we have seen, the duty owed by occupiers under the 1957 and 1984 Acts are very similar, in that they both require occupiers to take reasonable precautions rather than to eradicate all risks. However, there are two major differences between the two Acts:

- when the duty applies;
- the type of harm covered.

These two differences mean that it can be more difficult for non-visitors to make a claim under the 1984 Act than it is for visitors to make a claim under the 1957 Act.

When does the duty apply?

One very important distinction between the two Acts is that under the 1957 Act an occupier will *always* owe a duty of care to a visitor, but under the 1984 Act a non-visitor must prove three extra elements before a duty will apply to them. These are contained in section 1(3) of the 1984 Act, which says that an occupier only owes a duty of care to non-visitors where:

- the occupier is aware of a danger on their premises, or has reasonable grounds to believe that a danger exists; and
- the occupier knows or has reasonable grounds to believe that the non-visitor is in the vicinity of the danger, or might come into the vicinity of the danger; and
- the risk is one against which, in all the circumstances of the case, the occupier may reasonably be expected to offer the non-visitor some protection.

Where a defendant actually knows about a danger, and actually knows that non-visitors are or might go near it, these conditions are straightforward. As we will see in the next three sections, where we look at each of these requirements in turn, more tricky judgements arise where the courts have to consider whether a defendant 'had reasonable grounds to believe' that a danger existed and/or that a non-visitor was or might go near it. To have reasonable grounds to believe something basically means that you have some information which makes it reasonable to expect you to have realised or worked out something else. So, for example, if I live next to a family with children, and I know that, when they accidentally kick a ball into my garden, they have sometimes climbed over my fence to fetch it, I can obviously work out that this is something they might do again and so I have reasonable grounds to suspect that they might do that. But if I don't know that they climbed the fence before, and the fence is a high one, I do not have reasonable grounds to suspect that they would climb over it. When a court is considering what a defendant had reasonable grounds to think, they cannot look inside the defendant's mind, so they have to look at what the known facts were, and decide what a reasonable occupier would have concluded from those facts.

Awareness of or reasonable grounds to suspect a danger

If an occupier knows there is a danger on their premises, this requirement is obviously fulfilled. But what if the danger is one that was hidden? How do the courts decide whether the occupier 'had reasonable grounds to believe' that it existed? This was the question in *Rhind* v. *Astbury Water Park* (2004). The claimant was playing football in the park, and his ball went into a lake. He dived in to get it, and hit his head on a fibreglass container that was in the lake, suffering serious injuries. There were signs all round the lake saying 'Private property: no swimming', which meant that the claimant was considered to be a non-visitor, and the case was judged under the 1984 Act. The container had been lying on the bed of the lake, covered in silt, and was invisible from the surface of the lake, so there was nothing to make the defendants suspect it was there. The Court of Appeal ruled that the defendants did not know about it nor have reasonable grounds to think it was there, so they were not liable. Case Summary

Presence of the non-visitor in the vicinity of the danger

The second element the claimant must show is that the defendant knew, or had reasonable grounds to believe, that a non-visitor was or might be in the vicinity of the danger. Again, if it is not clear that the defendant knew non-visitors might be near the danger, the court will look at what they did know, to determine whether they had reasonable grounds to suspect the presence of a non-visitor. In *Swain* v. *Natui Ram Puri* (1996), the claimant was a 9-year-old boy who was injured when he fell from the defendants' factory roof. There was no evidence that the defendants knew children could or would climb onto the roof, but the claimant's lawyers argued that the defendants ought to have known that children might do so, and the defendants were therefore in breach for not taking precautions against this. The Court of Appeal disagreed, stating that 'reasonable grounds to believe' meant that the defendants had to know about actual facts which provided grounds for the belief, not that in the circumstances they ought to have known. As there was no evidence of previous trespass, and the fences around the factory were quite high, even if not completely intruder-proof, there were no reasonable grounds for the defendants to suspect that children might get in. Case Summary

In *Higgs* v. *Foster* (2004), the claimant was a police officer who was investigating a sighting of a stolen trailer parked in the delivery yard of a supermarket. The defendant's premises were next door, and the claimant went in there to try to get a good look into the supermarket delivery yard. He fell into an uncovered inspection pit and was injured. The case was judged under the 1984 Act, and the judge found that although the defendant knew the pit would be a danger to trespassers, they did not have reason to believe that trespassers would come anywhere near it. The only reason they had to believe that anyone would enter the premises at all was that the area was only partially fenced in, but even if someone got in that way the pit was at the back of the premises and as there was nothing there to attract anyone there was no reason to think that anyone would go near the pit. Case Summary

Case Summary

An example of a case where the defendant was held to have reasonable grounds to believe that non-visitors might go near a danger is *Scott* v. *Associated British Ports* (2000). The defendant owned land on which there was a railway line. There were two separate accidents on the land, four years apart, both involving young boys who were seriously injured when they played on the line and attempted to get on to moving trains. The Court held that the defendant did not owe a duty to the victim of the first accident, because at the time when it happened, they were unaware that children were getting on to the land and playing about on the railway line. After the first accident, however, they clearly did know about this problem and therefore, the court held, they had reasonable grounds to suspect that non-visitors might be at risk and so owed a duty under the Act to the second victim. They were, however, not liable for breaching the duty because the evidence was that reasonable precautions (such as fencing off the area) would not have stopped the boys from getting in.

Reasonable expectation of protection against the risk

The third question a court will look at when deciding whether the claimant was owed a duty under the 1984 Act is whether the risk was one which, in all the circumstances of the case, the defendant could reasonably be expected to provide protection against. This is essentially a balancing act, and the courts will take into account factors such as the cost and practicality of taking precautions, and the effect on activities taking place on the premises.

Case Summary

This was one of the questions the House of Lords examined in *Tomlinson* v. *Congleton*, the case we looked at earlier where the claimant was injured diving into a lake where swimming was banned. The House of Lords held that this was not a risk which the occupier should be expected to provide protection against, because there were warning notices all round the lake which meant the risk was obvious, and taking any further measures to protect against it would have meant destroying the beaches completely, and therefore preventing other people from enjoying them. Lord Hoffmann said:

> It is unjust that the harmless recreation of responsible parents and children with buckets and spades on the beaches should be prohibited in order to comply with what is thought to be a legal duty to safeguard irresponsible visitors against dangers which are perfectly obvious. The fact that such people take no notice of warnings cannot create a duty to take other steps to protect them.

You be the judge

Q: Amina inherited a large piece of land from her aunt. The land is some distance away from her house and she has not yet visited it. On the land is a deep hole. Local children often play on the land, and one of them, Peter, falls into the hole and is seriously injured. Amina did not know about the hole, but a neighbouring landowner had written to warn her that children were playing on the land. Could Peter have a claim under the Occupiers' Liability Act 1984?

A: On the facts we have here, no. To be liable, Amina must know about the danger or have reasonable grounds to believe it exists, and we know from *Swain* v. *Natui Ram Puri* that 'reasonable grounds to believe' means there must be facts on which the belief could be based. This does not appear to be the case here, so Amina will not be liable. The fact that she was told about the children playing there would only be relevant if she knew about the hole in the first place.

Warnings

Can giving a warning about a risk be enough to amount to taking reasonable care?

As we saw earlier, an occupier's duty to non-visitors under the 1984 Act is to take reasonable care to see that the non-visitor does not suffer injury. Can giving a warning about a risk be enough to amount to taking reasonable care? The Act provides that it can: section 1(5) states that an occupier can fulfil their duty towards non-visitors 'by taking such steps as are reasonable in all the circumstances of the case to give warning of the danger concerned or to discourage persons from incurring the risk'. Note that this is another difference between the two Acts. Under the 1957 Act, a warning has to be enough to make the visitor reasonably safe (remember the examples of the dangerous and non-dangerous bridges, and the slippery floors?). Under the 1984 Act, however, all the occupier has to do is to take reasonable steps to warn the claimant of the danger or discourage them from taking the risk.

Excluding liability

We saw when we looked at the 1957 Act that occupiers may try to exclude liability under the Act by, for example, displaying notices or including clauses in a contract saying things like 'Guests enter at their own risk' or 'The management accept no liability for loss of or damage to property'. The 1957 Act allows occupiers to limit or exclude their liability in this way, subject to the provisions of the Unfair Contract Terms Act 1977. Can liability under the 1984 Act be excluded in the same way? The answer, unfortunately and perhaps surprisingly, is not clear from the wording of the Act, which says nothing about whether the duty under it can be excluded by the occupier. It has been argued that it should not be possible to exclude the duty, because it is based on the 'duty of common humanity' developed in earlier case law, which was designed to be a minimum standard of lawful behaviour. However, if the duty under the 1957 Act cannot be excluded, but the duty under the 1984 Act can, this potentially leaves trespassers better off than legal visitors, which seems inconsistent with the rest of the Acts, which in several respects give more protection to visitors.

Unfortunately the point has never been decided by the courts, so we do not know whether the duty is excluded or not. If it should arise in a problem question, you would need to explain this, and examine what the situation would be if the duty is excludable, and what it would be if it were not.

Defences under the 1984 Act

We saw earlier that the 1957 Act provides two defences, contributory negligence and *volenti*. The 1984 Act, however, only provides one: *volenti*.

Section 1(5) states that 'No duty is owed by virtue of this section to any person in respect of risks willingly accepted as his by that person'. This provision was applied in

Case Summary

Ratcliff v. *McConnell* (1999), where the claimant was a 19-year-old student who had been out drinking with a couple of friends. In the early hours of the morning, they decided to go swimming and climbed over the gate of an open-air pool. A sign at the shallow end of the pool warned that it was dangerous to dive in there and the claimant was aware of the sign. He dived in at a point close to where the shallow end began and suffered such serious injuries that he was paralysed. The Court of Appeal held that the occupiers owed him no duty under the 1984 Act, because he knew that it was dangerous to dive into shallow water and had chosen to take the risk anyway.

As with the 1957 Act, the section goes on to say that whether a risk had been willingly accepted is to be judged on the same principles as in other cases where a duty of care is owed by one person to another, so the rules applicable to *volenti* in negligence also apply here. If you want to refresh your memory about them you can find them on page 92.

People in the law

Kevin Walker is Head of the Personal Injury department at solicitors Myers Lister Price in Manchester, and has wide experience of occupiers' liability cases.

Source: Kevin Walker (*text and photo*)

What kinds of occupiers' liability cases do you deal with? There's a wide variety of this type of claim where an accident occurs on property or land owned by someone else. I deal with a lot of slip and trip claims – particularly those occurring in supermarkets, playground and play centre accidents, swimming pools, and have dealt with cases of people being injured by falling branches when they've been out walking.

In the majority of cases, injuries are relatively minor and the compensation tends to average somewhere between £5,000 and £10,000. I do have considerable experience of dealing with catastrophic injuries though and one such case I'm dealing with at the moment involves my client who has been left tetraplegic following a tragic diving incident in a hotel swimming pool. Dependent on liability, this claim is expected to settle for several million pounds.

Do you mainly work for claimants, or both claimants and defendants? Just claimants for approaching 20 years.

How difficult or easy are these cases to prove? They can be particularly difficult. You usually have to put in a lot of legwork with Occupier's Liability cases compared to a minor road traffic accident, for instance. By way of example, I dealt with a case where the defendant had fabricated inspection and maintenance records once the claim was put to them, to show that they 'took all reasonable precautions to ensure their premises were safe for their visitors'. When a defendant has documentation it's very difficult to disprove it and it may uphold a complete defence to your client's claim. As in my case where the defendant occupier had been fraudulent, that is where witness evidence is so important – it pays to obtain evidence as soon as possible following the accident because memories of witnesses do fade in time and in that particular instance a promptly obtained witness statement proved my client's case.

What kind of evidence would you normally need to produce? Evidence can be in the form of witness statements from your client, other people who were close by when the incident happened, or those who can verify information about the state of the premises/land at the time of the incident. CCTV footage and photographic evidence should also be obtained at the earliest opportunity.

As a solicitor, you should always make prompt and thorough enquiries as to the availability of evidence to support your client's claim. Workplaces and other areas open to the public should have an accident book, where any accident is recorded, and the accident book entry is evidence of when the incident occurred and that it occurred in the way your client states. If your client has sought prompt medical attention, the relevant medical authorities will have recorded the accident circumstances, details of any injuries, treatment and investigations and the mechanics of how the injuries were sustained.

I recently settled a claim where my client had slipped on a wet floor at his local sailing club. The club denied liability and claimed they had clear warning signs around the premises and a good system of cleaning in place. They also evidenced this. The claimant was banned from the club and it was difficult to obtain witness evidence in support because other members were unwilling to speak out against the club for fear of losing their membership too. I instructed an engineer whose report showed that the warning signs (and indeed the screws used to affix the signs to the wall) were new, old photographs at the club did not show the signs being present and a slip resistance test of the club floor showed it to be well below the required standard.

Evidence to support your client's claim should be considered paramount when taking initial instructions from your client and it should be noted that most CCTV footage will be erased after just 28 days. There are so many CCTV cameras around, which could show the incident itself, or you might see evidence of the conditions that caused the incident in question.

In my swimming pool case, a key issue is that the pool should have had warning signs and depth notices around the pool area and it should have been supervised. Our alleged lack of supervision at the hotel meant my client was left alone in the swimming pool under water for almost four minutes. I have obtained medical evidence which supports this, but if there is also CCTV evidence, we will have a stronger case to prove negligence.

Have cases like *Tomlinson* v. *Congleton* and *Ratcliff* v. *McConnell* made it more difficult for people to sue successfully in this area? Yes. We are finding that judges are being influenced by this notion that we have a compensation culture in the UK, and that's coming out in decisions. Unfortunately judges are listening to insurers who argue that the UK is health and safety mad with people making claims today where they would not have done say 20 years ago. I concur that common sense needs to play a part, but there also has to be a place for health and safety and occupiers need to uphold their duty of care to visitors. People are much more aware of their right to claim today and occupiers are expected to conduct risk assessments and warn people about any possible dangers or hazards on their premises/land.

Do people in general, and potential clients, underestimate how difficult it is to sue successfully? Yes they do. It's not enough to show that you've been injured. You need to show someone else was negligent and that this negligence caused the injuries. For the most part people also don't realise how long a case can take. You have to manage client expectations. I will always explain how the personal injury claims process works, but timeframes can change because every case is different, depending on a number of variants particular to the individual client's case and their injuries.

To ease the obvious stresses following an injury, it is important to obtain an admission of liability as early as possible and to arrange any appropriate rehabilitation to help clients get back to living their life as quickly as possible.

Is there anything about your job that you think would surprise a law student? *The hours*: I know very few personal injury lawyers who work 9–5. I certainly don't. I'm often in the office early and stay working through till late in the evening, which allows accessibility to clients who work normal office hours. It's very important to give a good quality service, so all my clients have my direct dial number and email address. I'll also take calls over the weekend when necessary.

Salaries: contrary to what most people believe, we don't all earn a fortune like bankers in the City.

Go into the law because you love it and want to help make a difference – whatever field of expertise you choose. As head of the personal injury department at MLP, as well as dealing with my own caseload and supervising/training others in my team, I am also heavily involved in budgets and marketing.

What's the most difficult part of your job? Probably time management. You have to be a bit of a juggler and wear lots of different hats. Often with a full case-load and other responsibilities within the firm, you will never be completely up-to-date. There is always something on the to-do list.

What's the most rewarding part? Exceeding the client's expectations, both in the amount of the settlement and in the service I am able to give.

What kind of skills and qualities do you think are important in your job? You need to have a good rapport with your client, but you can't be too 'matey' and you should always keep the relationship on a professional footing. Patience and the virtue of being a good listener are also essential.

In order to achieve the best results for your client, you need to understand your client's individual needs, to be able to think out of the box in order to achieve what your client needs and know when to be an aggressive litigator.

You also require a high level of business acumen with one eye constantly on the forever changing personal injury landscape.

Cases not covered by the Occupiers' Liability Acts

> The occupancy duty applied where harm was caused by the state of the premises themselves

The fact that a claimant is injured on the occupant's land does not necessarily mean that their claim will be covered by either of the Occupiers' Liability Acts. Before the 1957 Act was passed, the common law made a distinction between what were called the 'occupancy duty' and the 'activity duty'. The occupancy duty applied where harm was caused by the state of the premises themselves, and was covered by special rules on occupiers' liability (such as the difference between the duty owed to different types of visitor that we looked at on page 246). The activity duty applied where harm was caused by something the occupier was doing on the premises, and was covered by the ordinary rules of negligence. So, for example, if a restaurant had a loose carpet and a customer tripped and injured themselves, the occupancy duty would apply because the accident was caused by the state of the premises. But if a customer got food poisoning because the chef had not taken hygiene precautions, the activity duty would apply, because the harm was caused by something done on the premises, rather than any danger arising from the premises themselves.

Does this distinction continue under the Occupiers' Liability Acts? If it does, this would mean the provisions of the Acts apply only to cases involving the occupancy duty (such as the loose carpet), and not those involving the activity duty (such as the food poisoning). You might well wonder why this is important; as long as the claimant can sue in either negligence or under one of the Occupiers' Liability Acts, why does it matter which? Well, for your purposes, of course, it matters because you need to know which area of the law applies when you are tackling problem questions. But in some cases the distinction is important for claimants too. If a case falls under the Occupiers' Liability Act 1957, the claimant only needs to show that the defendant is the occupier and the claimant is a visitor, and the duty will arise automatically under the Act. However, if the situation is covered only by the normal rules of negligence, the claimant has to show that they are owed a duty of care in negligence, which in some cases will be more difficult. In cases where the claimant is a non-visitor, on the other hand, it will sometimes be more advantageous to show that the Occupiers' Liability Act 1984 does not apply, because if the claimant can sue in negligence they can claim for damage to property, which is not covered by the 1984 Act.

So, do the Occupiers' Liability Acts apply only to cases involving the occupancy duty, or are cases involving the activity duty covered as well? Taking the 1957 Act first, the wording of the Act is unclear on this issue, with two sections apparently contradicting each other. Section 1(1) of the Act says that the duty under the Act is owed 'in respect of dangers due to the state of the premises or to things done or omitted to be done on them', which seems to cover both dangerous conditions and dangerous activities. However, section 1(2) refers to harm suffered 'in consequence of a person's occupation or control of premises', which suggests that only dangerous conditions are covered.

However, it now seems that the courts have decided that the distinction between occupancy and activity duties does still apply, and that the 1957 Act only covers cases involving the occupancy duty. You may remember the case of ***Fairchild* v. *Glenhaven Funeral Services*** (2002), which we looked at in negligence, where the claimants had been made ill by exposure to asbestos by a number of different employers. As well as their claim in negligence, it was suggested that the claimants might have a case under the Occupiers' Liability Act 1957, as their employers had been the occupiers of the premises where the exposure to asbestos had taken place. The Court of Appeal held that the Act related solely to 'the static condition of the premises' and claims relating to activities which took place on the premises were not covered by the legislation.

Case Summary

Case Navigator

What about the 1984 Act, covering liability to visitors? Similar words to those in the 1957 Act are contained in section 1(1)(a) of the 1984 Act, which provides that the duty is owed to non-visitors 'in respect of any risk of their suffering injury on the premises by reason of any danger due to the state of the premises or to things done or omitted to be done on them'. This suggests that the Act covers both occupancy and activity duties. Again, however, the courts have decided that only the occupancy duty is covered. In *Keown* v. *Coventry Healthcare NHS Trust* (2006), the claimant was 11 years old at the time of the accident which gave rise to the case. He was climbing on a fire escape attached to a building at one of the Trust's hospitals, and fell, hitting his head and suffering severe brain damage. The Court of Appeal held that the Trust was not liable because the accident was not caused by the state of the fire escape; there was nothing wrong with it and it was not dangerous if used for its proper purpose. The danger was caused by the claimant deciding to climb on it, and that was not a danger due to the state of the premises or to anything the defendant had done or not done.

Case Summary

The same approach was taken in the case of *Revill* v. *Newbery* (1996). The defendant had an allotment, on which there was a shed containing all his tools. The allotments had recently suffered a lot of vandalism and burglary from sheds, and so Mr Newbery took to sleeping in his shed, with his shotgun beside him, in order to protect his property. The claimant, who had already broken into two other buildings that night, attempted to break into Mr Newbery's shed, and Mr Newbery poked his shotgun through a small hole in the door and fired, injuring the claimaint. The claimant tried to make a case of

Case Summary

liability under the Occupiers' Liability Act 1984, but the Court of Appeal rejected this claim. They said that the legislation did not apply because the defendant's liability did not come from the fact that he was the occupier of the land where the shooting happened. What happened to the claimant could have happened just as easily if the defendant had been, for example, a friend of the occupier who was staying in the shed. (The claim for negligence, however, did succeed, though damages were reduced for the claimant's contributory negligence.)

Table 9.1 The Occupiers' Liability Acts 1957 and 1984 at a glance

	The Occupiers' Liability Act 1957	**The Occupiers' Liability Act 1984**
What type of claimant is covered?	Visitors – people who have permission to enter	Non-visitors/trespassers – people who do not have permission to enter
What type of damage is covered?	Personal injury and damage to property	Only personal injury
What is the duty?	The occupier must take 'such care that the visitor is reasonably safe'	The occupier must take 'such care as is reasonable in all the circumstances of the case'
When does the duty apply?	It applies automatically to anyone who is a visitor	It only applies if the occupier • knew or had reasonable grounds to suspect the danger existed; and • knew or had reasonable grounds to suspect a non-visitor was near or might go near the danger; and • the risk was one that it was reasonable to expect them to provide protection from
Can the duty be satisfied by using warnings?	Yes, if the warning enables the visitor to be 'reasonably safe'	Yes, if reasonable steps are taken to warn the non-visitor of the danger (so no need for warning to make non-visitor 'reasonably safe')
What defences apply?	Contributory negligence and *volenti*	*Volenti*
Can the duty be restricted or excluded?	Yes, but subject to the provisions of the Unfair Contract Terms Act 1977	Not clear from the words of the legislation

So, from the cases we have looked at, it appears that the distinction between the occupancy duty and the activity duty remains good law, despite the lack of clarity in the wording of the Acts. This means that a case will only be covered by the Occupiers' Liability Acts where the harm arose from a danger or risk related to conditions on the premises, rather than to something which was being done on the premises. If you try to remember the loose carpet/food poisoning examples we looked at above, and apply that distinction when you are tackling problem questions, you should find it is easy to tell whether or not the Acts will apply.

Writing and drafting

Look up the case of *Keown* v. *Coventry Healthcare NHS Trust* and read it. Now summarise, in your own words, the arguments that the judges used to rule out liability under the Occupiers' Liability Act 1984. Do you agree with them? Are there any arguments you could make in the claimant's favour?

Summary

- Occupiers' liability arises under the Occupiers' Liability Acts of 1957 and 1984. The 1957 Act applies to people who enter premises with permission; the 1984 Act applies to people who enter without permission.
- An occupier of land or premises is the person in control of them. They need not be the owner, and there may be more than one occupier at the same time.
- The Occupiers' Liability Act 1957 states that an occupier must take reasonable care to see that the visitor is reasonably safe. In deciding what is reasonable, the courts will look at the same kind of factors as for breach of duty in negligence.
- The 1984 Act creates a duty to take such care as is reasonable in all the circumstances of the case to see that the non-visitor does not suffer injury.
- The duty under the 1984 Act is only owed where:
  - the occupier is aware of or has reasonable grounds to suspect a danger on their premises;
  - the occupier knows or has reasonable grounds to believe that the non-visitor is or might be in the vicinity of the danger; and
  - the risk is one against which, in all the circumstances, the occupier may reasonably be expected to offer the non-visitor protection from.
- The duties under both Acts can be fulfilled by the use of warnings.
- Contributory negligence and *volenti* are defences under the 1957 Act; *volenti* is a defence under the 1984 Act.
- Liability under the 1957 Act can be excluded, subject to the provisions of the Unfair Contract Terms Act 1977. It is not clear whether liability under the 1984 Act can be excluded.
- Both Acts only cover harm caused by conditions on the land, and not activities undertaken there.

Question and answer*

Problem: John takes his son Kevin, aged 6, to the local park, which is owned by the council. A sign at the entrance to the park says 'Anytown Borough Council accepts no liability for injury or damage to property'. A little while after they arrive John needs to use the toilet, but the park's toilets are locked. He decides to find a convenient tree, but there are none nearby. He spots a fenced-off area and decides that looks private enough. The gate to the area is bolted and there is a sign saying 'Danger: Do Not Enter', but John is desperate by now and goes in anyway. Just inside the gate is a deep hole concealed by a sheet of wood. John falls into the hole, breaks his leg and smashes his expensive watch.

By now Kevin has fed all the bread they brought to the ducks, and he is wondering where his father is. He goes to look for him and comes across a bush with bright red berries. There is a sign saying that the berries on it are poisonous and should not be eaten and a low fence around the bush. Despite the fence, the bush is quite easy to reach and, as Kevin is feeling quite hungry by now, he picks a handful of the berries and eats them. He becomes seriously ill.

Advise John about any claims he or Kevin may have against the council under the Occupiers' Liability Acts 1957 and 1984.

You should allow yourself no more than 40 minutes to complete this task.

Essay: Critically examine the differences between the duty owed to visitors under the Occupiers' Liability Act 1957, and the duty owed to non-visitors under the Occupiers' Liability Act 1984.

This question should be answered in 40 minutes.

* Answer guidance is provided at the end of the chapter.

Further reading and references

***Bourne Leisure* v. *Marsden* [2009] EWCA Civ 671.**
This very sad case is very clearly explained, and worth reading as an example of the factors which the courts have to balance when deciding whether an occupier has breached their duty.

Buckley, R. (2006) 'Occupiers' liability in England and Canada', 35 Common Law World Review 197.
A good overview of the English law in this area, with an interesting comparison to the law in Canada.

Jones, M.A. (1984) 'The Occupiers Liability Act – the wheels of law reform turn slowly', 47 MLR 713.
A detailed look at the 1984 Act, which highlights its strengths and weaknesses. It includes a discussion of the difficulties involved in shaping a law that would protect 'innocent' trespassers yet exclude people such as burglars – difficulties which meant it proved impossible to include such a distinction in the 1984 Act.

Law Commission (1976) *Liability for Damage or Injury to Trespassers and Related Questions of Occupiers' Liability*, No. 75, Cmnd 6428.
This is the Law Commission report whose recommendation eventually led to the passing of the Occupiers' Liability Act 1984, and it gives a very clear view of the problems that the law was designed to solve.

Law Reform Committee Third Report (1954) *Occupiers' Liability to Invitees, Licensees and Trespassers*, Cmnd 9305.
This report, from the forerunner to the Law Commission, led to the creation of the Occupiers'

Liability Act 1957, and is a useful overview of the problems that existed in the common law.

McMahon, B.M.E. (1975) 'Conclusions on judicial behaviour from a comparative study of occupiers' liability', 38 MLR 39.
This very interesting article looks at the historical background to the law on occupiers' liability, and how the courts dealt with problems such as 'innocent' trespassers, and also compares our law to that in other countries. It is not an easy read, but contains some very useful material for essays on the two Acts.

Payne, D. (1958) 'The Occupiers' Liability Act', 21 MLR 359.
Written shortly after the 1957 Act, this article looks at the state of the law before the Act and highlights the problems it was designed to solve.

Question and answer guidance

Problem: Taking John's potential claim first, you need to look at whether he is a visitor or a trespasser. Clearly he has permission to be in the park, but does he have permission to go into the fenced-off area? The case of *Tomlinson* will be relevant here. If – as it appears – he is a trespasser, the relevant legislation is the 1984 Act, so you need to explain what the council's duty is under this Act and apply it to the facts. Clearly the council knows about the danger, since there is a warning on the gate, but do they know or have reasonable grounds to suspect that someone might go near it? We do not have much information to tell us the answer to this, but you can use decided cases to indicate what kinds of factors a court might looking at when deciding this. You should point out the explanation of what 'reasonable grounds' means from *Swain*. You will also need to consider the importance of the warning sign on the gate: look back at what the 1984 Act says about warnings. You should also look at the issue of *volenti*; can John be said to have accepted the risk?

Note that John has two claims, for his personal injury and the damage to his watch. You should point out that although both types of damage are covered under the 1957 Act, the 1984 Act covers only personal injury, so if John is a trespasser he cannot claim for the damage to his watch.

Finally, you need to consider whether the council can avoid liability because of the sign at the entrance to the park. We know that it is possible to exclude liability under the 1984 Act, but does UCTA make the notice unenforceable?

Regarding Kevin, he is a clearly a lawful visitor, so you should point out that the relevant legislation is the 1957 Act. Outline the council's duty under the Act, explaining the relevance of the fact that Kevin is a child. You should explain that the courts will seek to work out what it was reasonable to expect the council to do to protect children from the risk of eating the berries: were the warning and the fence enough? You should discuss the cases of *Glasgow Corporation* v. *Taylor*, regarding 'allurements' to children, and *Phipps* v. *Rochester*, which points out that occupiers are entitled to expect the parents of young children to look out for their safety and not let them wander alone – but note that the court in the latter case specifically said that in a public park or playground it might be reasonable to expect a child to be safe.

Again, you also need to consider the effect of the exclusion notice at the park gate. Explain that we do not know whether the duty under the 1984 Act can be excluded, but also consider whether, if it can be excluded, UCTA would make the sign unenforceable.

Essay: The key word here is 'critically'. This means that to get a good mark it is not enough simply to list the differences between the two Acts, you also need to look at the implications of them; the underlying question is really whether one Act gives much more protection than the other, or whether the levels of protection are roughly equal. A good way to start would be by briefly explaining where each Act applies, i.e. the 1957 Act to visitors and the 1984 Act to non-visitors/trespassers, and stating what these categories of person mean. It would also be useful to explain why it was considered necessary to provide statutory protection for trespassers, with reference to the pre-1984 cases such as *Glasgow Corporation* v. *Taylor*.

You should then work through the differences between the Acts, looking first at what each Act requires the occupier to do and in what circumstances. You can use decided cases to show how – or whether – the duty differs in practice. Does one require much more of the occupier than the other? Does one give more protection than the other? In the same way, look at the defences available, and at the possibility of exclusion.

You could finish with a conclusion that, based on the arguments you have made and the cases you have referred to, says whether you think the differences – or lack of them – between the two Acts strike the right balance regarding the levels of protection that are appropriate to lawful visitors and trespassers.

Visit **www.mylawchamber.co.uk/quinntort** to access tools to help you develop and test your knowledge of tort law, including practice exam questions with guidance, annotated weblinks, glossary and key case flashcards, legal newsfeed and legal updates and interactive 'You be the judge' questions.

premium mylawchamber *unrivalled support for legal education*

Use Case Navigator to read in full some of the key cases referenced in this chapter with commentary and questions:

Fairchild* v. *Glenhaven Funeral Services Ltd and others [2002] 3 All ER 305
Tomlinson* v. *Congleton Borough Council and another [2003] 3 All ER 1122

CASE NAVIGATOR POWERED BY LexisNexis

Chapter 10
Product liability

Key points In this chapter we will be looking at:

- Liability for dangerous products in negligence
- Liability for dangerous products under the Consumer Protection Act 1987

Introduction

Imagine that you have just bought a nice, juicy burger, or a big slice of chocolate cake. You take a bite and break a tooth on a stone. Or you buy a bike, and while you are riding it the front wheel comes off, throwing you into the road. Or your doctor prescribes a drug for your hayfever, and when you take it your legs swell up and you can not walk for a week. Do you think you could sue anyone for your injuries? The answer is that you can, and the rules on these kinds of claims are the subject of this chapter.

In Chapter 2, you will have read the story of the unfortunate Mrs Donoghue. As you will remember, her encounter with a decomposing snail not only ruined her evening out, but went on to form the basis of the case that gave birth to the modern law of negligence, *Donoghue* v. *Stevenson*. One of the reasons why the case was such a landmark decision was that, before it, a consumer who was injured by a product only had a remedy if they had a contract with the seller of the product. Today, injured consumers can sue in negligence, or under the Consumer Protection Act 1987. They can also, of course, still sue in contract, if they are the person who bought the product.

Product liability in negligence

As we saw in Chapter 2, *Donoghue* v. *Stevenson* established the basic **neighbour test** for deciding whether a duty of care arises in a new factual situation, which states that a **defendant** will be liable for acts that they could reasonably foresee would be likely to injure their neighbour. But the case also established the specific **duty of care** for cases involving dangerous products, which is often referred to as the 'narrow rule' from the case (as opposed to the wider neighbour test). Lord Atkin defined the duty as follows:

> a manufacturer of products, which he sells in such a form as to show he intends them to reach the ultimate consumer in the form in which they left him, with no possibility of intermediate examination . . . owes a duty to the consumer to take reasonable care.

This basically means that if a manufacturer makes something which is intended to be used directly by a consumer, and which would not be checked by someone else between leaving the manufacturer and reaching the consumer, the manufacturer has a duty of care to that consumer.

Who can sue?

The 'ultimate consumer' referred to by Lord Atkin has been defined quite widely in the years since *Donoghue*. As well as people who are actually eating, drinking, wearing or using a product, it can apply to someone who was not doing any of these things, but was still injured as a result of coming into contact with a defective product. Some examples include *Brown* v. *Cotterill* (1934), where a child was injured when a gravestone fell on him; *Stennett* v. *Hancock* (1939), where a pedestrian was hit by a wheel that fell off a passing lorry; and *Barnett* v. *H and J Packer* (1940), where the owner of a sweet shop was injured by a piece of metal sticking out from a sweet.

Who can be sued?

In *Donoghue*, Lord Atkin spoke only of the duty being owed by manufacturers, but the courts quite quickly widened its scope. It is now established that the same duty is owed to consumers by anyone who:

- repairs a product;
- puts it together;
- distributes it or hires it out; or
- makes component parts that go into a product.

In some circumstances, even someone who only sells a product can owe a duty of care. This applies where the circumstances are such that it is reasonable to expect the seller to have inspected the product for dangerous defects. This was the case in *Andrews* v. *Hopkinson* (1957). The defendant was a second-hand car dealer, who sold an 18-year-old car to the **claimant**, without checking whether it was in a roadworthy condition. In fact the car had a dangerous problem with the steering, which failed a week after the claimant bought it, causing an accident in which he was injured. Expert evidence suggested that it was common for very old cars to develop problems with the steering mechanism, and that the defect could very easily have been spotted by a competent mechanic. The Court held that, given the seriousness of the risk involved, and the fact that finding the defect would have been easy, the supplier owed a duty to have the car examined by a mechanic before selling it, or at least to warn a potential buyer if it had not been examined.

Case Summary

Types of product covered

Lord Atkin's words made it clear that the duty extended beyond food and drink to all other categories of product, and since *Donoghue*, decided cases have covered everything from tombstones to underpants. The duty also covers any packaging that a product comes in.

As we saw above, in *Donoghue* Lord Atkin specified that the duty would only apply where products were intended to reach the consumer in the same form in which they left the defendant, 'with no possibility of intermediate examination'. The idea behind this requirement is that a defendant should only be liable for defects that were present when the product left their hands, and not for anything that may have happened since then. In *Evans* v. *Triplex Safety Glass Co. Ltd* (1936), Mr Evans bought a car with a windscreen made of what was described as 'toughened safety glass', manufactured by Triplex. A year later, he was driving along in the car when the windscreen suddenly shattered, for no apparent reason, injuring Mr Evans and his wife and son. He sued Triplex, but the company successfully argued that they should not be liable because the accident happened a long time after the sale of the windscreen, and it was known that the glass could be put under strain during the installation process, which Triplex were not involved in. This meant the defect could have been caused after the glass left their factory, and it would have been possible for the windscreen to be inspected for defects before the car was sold to Mr Evans.

Case Summary

However, the possibility of intermediate examination will only prevent liability if it gives the defendant reason to expect that any defects would be revealed, so that the product could either be made safe or be prevented from reaching a consumer. In *Griffiths* v. *Arch Engineering Co.* (1968), the claimant was involved in some repair work at a dock. He was working alongside employees of some other firms, and he asked one of them if he could borrow a grinding machine from him. The machine in question had been borrowed by the man's employers from another firm. That firm had fitted an incorrect part to it, and as a result Mr Griffiths was injured. He sued both firms: the company that borrowed the machine was the first defendant, and the one that owned it was the second defendant. The second defendant argued that they should not be liable, because it was possible for the first defendant to examine the machine before anyone used it. However, the Court said that although it was possible that the machine might be checked, the second defendant had no reason to believe that a check would definitely happen. Therefore both firms were equally liable.

Case Summary

In *Grant* v. *Australian Knitting Mills* (1936), the claimant bought a pair of long woollen underpants, which gave him a painful skin condition. The manufacturer claimed they should not be liable, because the pants were not sold in a sealed package but in a paper bag, which meant they could have been opened and inspected. The Court held that the duty of care established in *Donoghue* did not only apply to products in sealed packages.

What counts as a defect?

The law of negligence only covers defects in products which make the product dangerous. A defect which simply makes a product work less well or look less attractive, or which makes it less valuable, is not enough on its own. These types of defect can, however, create a claim in contract, if the claimant has a contract.

Types of damage covered

As you will remember from Chapter 2, a negligence claim requires proof of damage, so the product has to have caused the claimant harm. A claimant cannot sue in negligence on the basis that a product is clearly dangerous and could cause harm, if no harm has actually occurred. The types of harm covered in product liability cases are personal injury and damage to property other than the defective item itself. As we saw in Chapter 4, damage to the product itself, even if it results from a dangerous defect, is classified as pure **economic loss** and is not recoverable in negligence. So, for example, if you buy a defective TV and it blows up, setting fire to your living room, you can claim in negligence for the value of the damage to the room and everything else in it, but not for the cost of the TV itself, because a defect in a product is considered economic loss.

The problem of component parts

The rule that a claimant can get compensation for damage to other property but not to the defective item itself raises interesting questions about exactly what counts as 'other property'. Take the situation where a car tyre is faulty, and it explodes causing the car to crash. On one view, a defect in one item, the tyre, has caused damage to another, the car. But it might equally be argued that a tyre is part of the car, so a faulty tyre is a defect in the car, in which case there would be no damage to 'other property' and so no claim in negligence.

The way the courts have resolved this issue is that, as a general rule, where the defective component is a replacement for an earlier part, any damage it does to the bigger product can be compensated. Imagine, for example, that you buy a car, and three years later you replace two of the tyres because the original ones have worn out. If one of the replacement tyres is faulty, and causes an accident, you can claim for any damage done to the car, as well as any injuries, though not for the cost of the tyre itself because that is economic loss. If, on the other hand, a component is made and assembled by the same firm that makes the rest of the product, and added at the time the whole product is assembled, the component will not be treated as a separate product. So if you buy a car and the engine blows up, causing a fire that destroys the car, you would not be able to claim for the car or the engine, because they are considered one product and the defect in that one product is economic loss. But you would be able to claim for any damage the car causes to other property (such as anything you had left in the car).

Defects in packaging

Similar issues arise when a defect in packaging causes damage to the contents of the pack. In *M/S Aswan Engineering Establishment Co.* v. *Lupdine Ltd* (1987), Aswan were a building company who had bought a waterproofing product, called Lupguard, for use on a project in Kuwait. The Lupguard was packaged in plastic buckets, and when the order was delivered by ship to Kuwait the buckets were stacked on the quayside. The very high temperatures melted the buckets and the Lupguard spilled away. Aswan sued Lupguard's manufacturers, and the manufacturers of the packaging. The action failed because the Court of Appeal said it was not foreseeable that the plastic might melt, but the court also considered whether the buckets should be considered a separate product from the Lupguard. If they could, then the loss of the Lupguard would be damage to

Case Summary

property; if not, it was pure economic loss. The majority of the Court held that the Lupguard was a separate product. However as the issue was not really in question once the Court found that the damage was not foreseeable, the question is still unclear.

Breach of the duty of care

Product liability cases are subject to the same basic rules as any other negligence case: the claimant must prove that their damage was caused by the defendant's failure to take reasonable care. In product liability cases, this translates as proving that the failure to take care caused the defect which made the product dangerous. As in other negligence cases, the courts may balance a number of different factors, with the most important in practice being the seriousness of the risk, and how practical it would have been for the defendant to prevent it.

Manufacturing defects and design defects

Claims in product liability generally involve one of two different kinds of defect. The first are defects that arise because something has gone wrong in the manufacturing process. These will often affect only a limited number of batches of the product, or sometimes even just one single item. The second kind of defect is one which arises from the product's actual design, recipe or formula. This kind of defect will affect every example of that particular product. To illustrate the difference, take the situation where you buy a chair which breaks when you sit on it. If it broke because one of the legs was not screwed on properly, that is a manufacturing defect. But if it broke because the material used to make the legs was not strong enough to take the weight of a person sitting on it, that is a design defect.

With both types of defect, proving a breach of duty is potentially quite difficult, since it will usually involve examining the technicalities of how the product was designed or made. In cases of manufacturing defects, the courts have recognised this problem, and made it clear that claimants do not have to identify what exactly went wrong, only that the defendant must have fallen below a reasonable standard of care for the defect to arise.

Case Summary

This was the approach taken in *Grant* v. *Australian Knitting Mills*, the case we looked at above where the claimant was caused a nasty skin disease by a new pair of underpants. Tests showed that the rash was caused by high residues of sulphites, which were chemicals used in the manufacturing process. The defendants said that they had not been negligent because they had special procedures in place to prevent such residues being left in the fabric. However, the Court said that this in itself showed that someone in the factory must have been at fault, because the procedures clearly had not been put into practice. That being the case, the claimant did not have to show who exactly had failed to follow the procedures, or what they had done wrong. This looks very like the doctrine of **res ipsa loquitur**, which we looked at in Chapter 2, but the courts have tended not to label it as this and instead treat it as part of the rules on breach in product liability cases.

Proving breach in cases of an alleged design defect is more difficult. A claimant in this kind of case will need to bring evidence about the way the company went about designing or creating the product, to show whether they took reasonable care or not.

Once a claim is started, they can make the company disclose documentation about the design process, but to get to that stage they either have to pay legal costs themselves, or find a lawyer who will take the case on a no win, no fee basis, without knowing yet what the documentation will show. Not surprisingly the majority of decided cases in negligence are about manufacturing defects.

Instructions and warnings

Defects in the product itself are not the only way in which negligence can occur. A defendant can be in breach of duty if their product is made unsafe not by a defect in it but by instructions which are not reasonably adequate. For example, a manufacturer who supplied paracetamol without stating on the pack how many tablets equal a safe dose would clearly fall below a reasonable standard of care.

If a product has a known danger, a defendant can fulfil the duty of care by taking reasonable steps to warn about the risk. This was the case in *Kubach* v. *Hollands* (1937). The claimant was a schoolgirl who was injured when chemicals used in a science lesson exploded. The manufacturers knew that the chemicals could become unstable over time, and so they sold them to retailers with a warning that they should be tested before resale. The retailer who sold the chemicals to the claimant's school ignored the warning, and sold the chemicals without retesting them or warning that the school should test them. The Court held that the retailers were liable, but the manufacturers were not.

Case Summary

However, there is a difference between a warning that essentially says 'This product is unsafe if you do/do not do this with it' and one which says 'We do not accept liability for harm caused by this product'. The second type of warning is an attempt to avoid legal liability and is likely to be invalid, or subject to a requirement of reasonableness, under the Unfair Contract Terms Act 1977 (for a reminder of how the Act works, have a look back at page 240).

Defences

The usual **defences** to negligence apply – if you want to remind yourself of what they are, have look back at pages 88–95. In practice, the most important **defence** in product liability cases is **contributory negligence**, which you will remember applies where the accident or damage is partly the claimant's own fault. In product liability cases, this is often because the product has a dangerous defect but the claimant has contributed to the problem by using the product in an unexpected or unusual way.

Evaluating product liability in negligence

The development of negligence law since *Donoghue* v. *Stevenson* was a major benefit to people injured by dangerous products who, as we saw earlier, could previously only sue if they had a contract with the retailer. However, as a solution to product liability problems it still had one major drawback for claimants: the need to prove fault. As we have seen, the claimant must prove fault, by showing that the defendant did not take reasonable care to prevent foreseeable injury. You might think that sounds perfectly reasonable: why should a manufacturer be liable for something that was not their fault and which they could not have prevented? Accidents happen, after all.

> Detailed technical knowledge may be needed to spot the problem that caused the defect

The first point to bear in mind in response to this argument is that a negligence claim does not just require that the defendant was at fault; it requires that the claimant can prove the defendant was at fault. In product liability cases, this can be very difficult. Detailed technical knowledge may be needed to spot the problem that caused the defect, which adds to the cost of cases, and the most convincing evidence of faults in a manufacturing, design or quality control process may come from someone involved in that process, who may be unwilling to testify against their employer. Similar difficulties may be involved in proving that the lack of care actually caused the injury, especially in cases involving drugs and medications.

Over and above these difficulties, there is an argument that liability for dangerous products should not rest on fault anyway, and that manufacturers should bear responsibility for injuries caused by their products, whether or not they were to blame. The reasoning behind this argument is well expressed by the judge in the American case of *Escola* v. *Coca-Cola Bottling of Fresno* (1944). The judge, Mr Justice Traynor, argued that the manufacturer of a dangerous product should be held liable, regardless of whether they were negligent or not, because:

> Public policy demands that responsibility be fixed wherever it will most effectively reduce the hazards to life and health inherent in defective products that reach the market. It is evident that the manufacturer can anticipate some hazards and guard against the recurrence of others, as the public cannot. Those who suffer injury from defective products are unprepared to meet its consequences. The cost of injury and the loss of time and health may be an overwhelming misfortune to the person injured, and a needless one, for the risk of injury can be insured by the manufacturer and distributed among the public as the cost of doing business. It is to the public interest to discourage the marketing of products having defects that are a menace to the public. If such products nevertheless reach the market, it is to the public interest to place the responsibility for whatever injury they may cause upon the manufacturer, who, even if he is not negligent in the manufacture of the product, is responsible for its reaching the market.

In other words, this is an argument about practicality rather than fairness; manufacturers can easily insure against liability and add any costs to their prices, whereas consumers can do very little to protect themselves, and may find their lives ruined by an injury caused by a defective product.

The Law in Action box looks at a case which highlighted the problems with the law, and contributed to pressure for legislation to protect consumers, eventually resulting in the Consumer Protection Act 1987.

Law in action The Thalidomide scandal

One of the main driving forces behind the passing of the Consumer Protection Act 1987 was an outcry over a drug called Thalidomide, which caused serious birth defects in thousands of babies born during the 1950s and 1960s. The drug was considered to be safe, and one of the things it was prescribed for was morning sickness. It was taken by pregnant women in over 40 countries, and when there was a sudden rise in the number of babies being born with particular deformities, scientists began investigating and found the link to the drug.

The most typical defect was drastically shortened limbs, so that many victims had hands and feet but no, or very short, arms and legs. Many also had heart, kidney and digestive system problems. Over 10,000 babies were thought to have been affected worldwide, and about 40 per cent died before their first birthday. Of those born in the UK, 456 survived to adulthood.

Sixty-two of the British Thalidomide victims sought to sue Distillers, the company that made and marketed the drug in this country, and their struggle to get compensation highlighted the shortcomings of negligence law. They had to prove that the company had not taken reasonable care to make sure that the drug was safe. But Distillers pointed to the fact that, at the time the drug was put on sale, nobody knew that it could cause birth defects. This is the same argument that was successfully used in *Roe* v. *Minister of Health*, the case we looked at in Chapter 2, where the claimant was paralysed because a disinfectant leaked through tiny cracks in an ampoule of anaesthetic. As you may remember, the court there said that a defendant was entitled to be judged by the standards, and state of knowledge, that were accepted at the time they acted. Distillers brought evidence suggesting that the drug testing procedures that were accepted as standard at the time would not have revealed the risk of birth defects.

At first glance this may sound fair, if very unfortunate for the Thalidomide victims. But the picture looks a little different when you know that the drug was refused approval for sale in the USA because their Food and Drug Administration (FDA) had doubts about its safety. Clearly then, it was possible to realise the drug was risky, because the FDA did just that. But as we saw in Chapter 2, English negligence law does not require a defendant to recognise and eliminate all risks. It only requires them to take reasonable steps, and using the standard testing procedures of the time could amount to reasonable steps.

A further problem for the victims was proving that the drug caused their birth defects. Although many scientists were sure that the drug caused the problems, no one knew exactly how it caused them (in fact this was only worked out by scientists in 2009), and similar defects could also arise from genetic abnormalities. This meant that the only evidence they had to suggest that the drug caused their medical conditions was that these problems were much more common in babies whose mothers had taken the drug.

These and other problems made it increasingly obvious that the Thalidomide victims had little chance of succeeding in a claim for negligence and, in 1968, they were advised by their lawyers to accept an **out-of-court settlement**. This paid each child around 40 per cent of the amount that they were likely to have got if they had won in court. In return, they had to withdraw their allegations of negligence. The low amount of money offered caused a public outcry, and *The Sunday Times* began a campaign to make Distillers pay more. After going to court to try to gag the newspaper, and failing, the company did later increase the settlement. They have, however, never admitted negligence.

[*Reference*: 'Thalidomide victims still fighting for justice 35 years on', *The Independent*, 9 Oct 2009]

The Consumer Protection Act 1987

The Consumer Protection Act 1987 was designed to strengthen consumer rights against companies who make or sell dangerous products. Although there had been concern about this issue in the UK for some time, because of the Thalidomide scandal, the actual trigger for the new law came from the EEC, which was the forerunner of what we now call the European Union, or EU. Part of the reason for the EEC coming into being was to boost trade by establishing a 'single market' across all the member countries, making it easy for any firm based in the EEC to sell goods in any EEC country. One of the requirements for a single market is that all the member countries need to have similar laws affecting trade, so that firms from one country do not have an advantage over those in another. Imagine, for example, if in France, the law was that a manufacturer of a dangerous product was only liable if the injured consumer could prove negligence, but in Sweden, the law was that consumers only had to prove that the product caused their injury. This would mean that French manufacturers were much less likely to be found liable. As liability costs money, this would give them a competitive advantage over Swedish manufacturers, which defeats the purpose of a single market. It might also encourage them to have lower safety standards.

The EEC therefore decided that product liability laws across the member countries should be harmonised. They issued a Directive, which is an order to the member states to pass legislation which achieves the aim set out in the Directive. In this case the aim was harmonisation of product liability laws, and the Consumer Protection Act 1987 was the legislation passed to put it into practice in the UK.

the Directive and the Act were said to impose strict liability

The big difference between negligence law and the new legislation was that the Directive and the Act were said to impose strict liability. This, as we saw in Chapter 1, means that a claimant does not have to prove that the defendant was at fault. In negligence, as we have seen, a claimant has to prove fault in the sense that the defendant fell below a reasonable standard of behaviour. With **strict liability**, they only have to prove that the defendant caused their injury or damage, so a defendant can be liable even in situations where there was nothing they could have done to avoid the damage or injury. In theory, this approach gives a much higher level of protection to consumers. However, as we shall see, there has been considerable debate about whether the Directive and the Act actually do impose strict liability in practice.

Who can sue?

Anyone who suffers personal injury and/or property damage from a dangerous product can sue under the Act. As with a negligence claim, the claimant need not be the person who bought the item, and can be anyone who comes into contact with it and not just someone who eats, drinks, uses or wears it.

Who can be sued?

The Act imposes liability on the 'producer' of the defective product, and gives this term a wide definition. It includes manufacturers, and anyone who 'wins or abstracts' the product, a term which would apply, for example, where products are mined or excavated. It also applies to someone who is responsible for a process that adds 'essential characteristics' to a product. Exactly what this covers is still not entirely clear. It would probably include, for example, processing food by putting it into tins or jars, but probably not simply freezing fresh vegetables, as this would not seem to add an 'essential characteristic'.

Retailers' liability

There are two circumstances in which retailers can be liable under the Act. The first is where the product is made by another company but the retailer sells it under their own brand. Most of the major supermarkets, for example, sell a wide range of food and other goods labelled with their own brand, e.g. 'Waitrose' or 'Tesco', but which are made for them by other companies. Similarly, large chain stores like Marks & Spencer, Top Shop and Next sell most things under their own labels, but do not make any of the goods themselves. The idea of this provision is that if a product is sold with a particular store's label, the consumer should not have to find out who actually made it but can simply sue the retailer.

However, a retailer will only be liable for dangerous defects in own brand goods if they can be said to 'hold themselves out' as being the producer. Exactly what this means has not yet been tested by the courts. It is arguable, for example, that a store which used labels with phrases like 'Made for Tesco' or 'Selected for Morrisons' could be said to be making it clear that they were not the manufacturers, and might be able to avoid liability that way, but as the point has not been tested we do not know if that would carry any weight in court.

The second way in which retailers, and anyone else involved in the supply chain, can be liable is under section 2(3) of the Act. This provides that, where a claimant does not know who the producer of their item is, they can ask the place they bought it from to tell them. If the seller does not identify either the producer, or their own supplier, within a reasonable time, they will be liable as if they were the producer. The idea of this provision is to enable a claimant to trace goods back along the supply chain to the actual producer. Making firms liable if they do not assist in this process is designed to encourage them to keep good records of their own suppliers, and ensure that consumers are not left without a claim if the actual producer cannot be identified.

Out and about

Get together some examples of own brand goods you can find at home. Have a look at the wording on the packaging. Do you think a court would, or should, find that the retailer is 'holding themselves out' to be the manufacturer? Are there any words on any of the packs that you think would make a court more or less likely to find this? What other factors do you think a lawyer might put forward to show that an own brand retailer should, or should not, be considered to be holding themselves out to be the manufacturer?

Handy tip: There are no right or wrong answers because this issue has not been tested in the courts, so don't be afraid to come up with original ideas and arguments – the idea is to get you thinking like a lawyer.

Imported goods

The Act covers both goods made in the EU and those imported into it from elsewhere. Where a product is made outside the EU, the person or firm who first imported it into an EU member country can be liable under the Act, just as a producer would be. Again, this measure is designed to make it easier for consumers to get redress for dangerous products. It will be much easier to trace and sue the importer, who will be based in the EU, than to try to sue a manufacturer elsewhere in the world.

Liability does not, however, apply to anyone who imports goods into one EU country from another (unless they are liable for some other reason under the Act, such as selling the goods under an own brand, or being responsible for a process that adds essential characteristics to them). It only applies to whoever first imported the product from outside the EU into an EU country.

Suing more than one defendant

Liability under the Act is **joint** and **several**, which means that where two or more people or firms have caused the problem, a claimant can sue either or both of them. So a consumer who is injured by a product imported into the EU by one firm and sold by another could sue either or both.

You be the judge

Q: Mary buys a kettle, which blows up the first time she uses it, scalding her. The kettle was made in China and imported into Sweden by a firm called Hettvatten AB. Hettvatten sold a consignment of the kettles, including Mary's, to a firm called Makeacuppa, which imported them into the UK. Mary bought hers from a small retailer called Little Electricals, who sold the kettle under their own brand name Who can she salue under the Consumer Protection Act?

Source: Pearson Education Ltd/Comstock Images

A: Mary can sue Hettvatten, because they imported the kettle into the EU, and/or Little Electricals, because they sold the kettle under their own brand. As liability is joint and several, she can choose to sue either or both of them. She cannot sue Makeacuppa, because they only imported the kettle from one EU country into another.

What types of product are covered?

blood is a product and covered under the Act

A product is defined in section 2(1) 'any goods or electricity', so the Act covers all the usual kinds of consumer products, including food. The Act further explains that 'goods' includes 'substances, growing crops, and things comprised in land by virtue of being attached to it, and any ship, aircraft or vehicle'. In *A and Others* v. *National Blood Authority* (2001), it was accepted that blood is a product and covered under the Act (see below for more on this case).

The Act also states that 'product' includes 'a product which is comprised in other products, whether by virtue of being a component part, raw material or otherwise'. Where injury or damage is caused by a component part, or the raw material the product was made from, the consumer can sue the producer of the part/raw material, and/or the producer of the final product.

Buildings are not covered, but their component parts are. This means that a house which was dangerous because of defects in its design or the way it was built would not be covered, but one which was dangerous because of the material used to build it would be. So a company could be liable if, for example, they made defective roof timbers which led to a roof collapsing and injuring someone.

Liability for information

Information is not 'a product' for the purposes of the Act. This means, for example, that if you buy a book on DIY which gives you incorrect instructions on how to put up shelves, and as a result your shelves fall down on your head, you could not sue the publisher under the Act. But if the paper the book was made from was contaminated with a chemical that gave you a rash, you could.

However, a producer can be liable under the Act if they provide inadequate or misleading information in the form of things like instructions or warning leaflets for a product, and the instructions or warnings contribute to making the product dangerous.

What kinds of defect are covered?

Like negligence law, the Act only covers defects which make a product dangerous, and not those which only make it work less well or look less good, or reduce its value. Section 3 states that a product will be defective under the Act if 'the safety of the product is not such as persons generally are entitled to expect'. It is important to take notice of the word 'entitled'. This essentially means that the courts can set the standard according to what it is reasonable to expect. The fact that the claimant might personally have expected a higher standard of safety is irrelevant.

In assessing the standard expected, the Act directs the courts to take into account 'all the circumstances'. It mentions three factors which are relevant to this, though they need not necessarily be the only things the court takes into account. The three factors are:

- the way the product is marketed;
- what might reasonably be expected to be done with or in relation to the product;
- the time when the product was supplied.

The way the product is marketed

This may include any advertising claims, instructions or warnings that come with the product. Clearly, the way a product is advertised can affect the standard of safety that consumers are entitled to expect: a skin cream marketed as hypo-allergenic, for example, might reasonably be expected to be less likely to cause a rash than other brands. Similarly, products which are dangerous if used in the wrong way can be brought within the standard of safety by warnings and instructions. An obvious example would be a medicine like paracetamol, which is dangerous if taken in large amounts. As long as its packaging makes the recommended dose clear, and warns about the dangers of taking more than the recommended dose, the product can be considered safe under the Act.

Case Summary

In *Worsley* v. *Tambrands* (2000), Mrs Worsley suffered a condition called toxic shock syndrome (TSS), which is known to be associated with the use of tampons. She had used tampons made by Tambrands, which were supplied with a leaflet warning about how to avoid TSS and advising customers to seek immediate medical attention if TSS symptoms appeared. However, Mrs Worsley's husband had thrown away the leaflet from the box she was using at the time. She argued that given the seriousness of the disease, which can be fatal, Tambrands should have printed the warnings on the box, or presented them more strongly in the leaflet so that she would have remembered them from reading it earlier. The Court held that her claim failed: the leaflet was mentioned on the box, the leaflet itself was clear and easy to read, and manufacturers could not be expected to take precautions against people losing it or throwing it away.

What might reasonably be expected to be done with the product

This point of this provision is to encourage the courts to look at whether the product was dangerous in itself, or because it was used in an unexpected or unusual way. For example, a bed should obviously be safe to sleep on, and a court would probably find that it should also be safe for children to jump up and down on, because that is something that is quite likely to happen, even if it is not the use a bed is made for. However, a bed would not be considered unsafe because it failed to protect a consumer who chose to shelter under it during a hurricane, because that is not something anyone would reasonably expect a bed to be used for.

As well as the way the product is used, the courts may also look at issues such as whether a product is likely to fall into the hands of children; it would be considered reasonable to expect a higher standard of safety in products that children might be likely to get hold of.

When the product was supplied

As manufacturers develop their products, they may add new safety features that were not there on earlier models. The Act makes it clear that claimants cannot argue that a product is defective purely because similar products which were supplied later are safer. The idea behind this provision is to make sure producers are not deterred from adding new safety features to their products for fear of being sued over earlier, less safe versions.

The safety standard in practice

Although the Act has been in force for over 20 years, relatively few cases have been brought under it, probably because companies faced with a good claim will usually settle the case rather than attract bad publicity. However, the handful of cases that have been heard shed some useful light on how the courts define the safety standard detailed in the Act.

Case Summary

In *Bogle and Others* v. *McDonald's* (2002), the Court heard a number of cases together, all brought by claimants who had been scalded by hot drinks at McDonald's. Most of those who were injured had been children at the time, but in all cases the drinks were bought by an adult. The claimants argued that the drinks were served at a dangerously high temperature, and that the cups they were sold in were unsafe because the lids could come off if they were tipped over. The Court disagreed. It said that it was to be expected that tea and coffee would be hot, because that was the way most people preferred to drink them. Staff were trained to put the caps on securely and the caps did not necessarily come off if a cup was tipped up. They did come off if a cup was knocked over violently, or fell onto a table or the floor, but any precautions which would prevent this would also have made it difficult or impossible for customers to remove the lid for drinking, which many preferred to do. The Court pointed out that no one would have expected McDonald's to sell lukewarm coffee, in cups without removable lids, in order to prevent scalding accidents. In addition, tea and coffee would almost always be bought by adults, who would be aware that the drinks were likely to be hot and could cause scalding, and would know that they needed to take care especially if they were with children. Therefore McDonald's had not fallen below the level of safety detailed in the Act.

Case Summary

In *Richardson* v. *LRC Products Ltd* (2000), the product concerned was a condom. The tip of it broke at a rather crucial moment, with the result that Mrs Richardson became pregnant. She sued for the costs of bringing up the baby, but failed. The main reason for this was that, as we saw in Chapter 2, the English courts have ruled that there is no claim for the costs of bringing up a healthy child, because a child is considered to be a benefit and not to count as damage. However, the Court also looked at whether the standard of safety under the Act had been breached and decided that it had not. They said that it was in the nature of condoms that they would occasionally fail, and so people were not entitled to expect that this would never happen. The fact that this one had broken did not therefore mean it was defective under the Act.

Case Summary

In *A and Others* v. *National Blood Authority* (2001), the claimants had all been infected with the Hepatitis C virus through having transfusions of contaminated blood. The blood was thought to have been taken from donors who did not know they had the hepatitis C virus. At the time of the claimants' transfusions, the medical profession knew there was a danger of blood being contaminated in this way, but the general public did not. There was no way to test the blood for the virus. The claimants held that they were entitled to expect that donated blood was safe. The National Blood Authority said that the Act required the courts to take into account 'all the circumstances', and that this included the question of whether there was any way they could have prevented the use of contaminated blood. Since there was no way they could have done this, they held that the public was not entitled to expect a standard that was impossible to achieve.

The Court disagreed. The general public did not know about the risk, so they were entitled to expect that donated blood was safe unless they were warned otherwise. Whether or not the risk was avoidable was not something that a court should take into account, because it was clear that the Directive had intended that consumers should not have to prove fault. The contaminated blood was therefore defective within the meaning of the Act.

Case Summary

In *Pollard* v. *Tesco Stores Ltd* (2006), the case involved a boy who was a year old, who became seriously ill after swallowing some dishwasher powder. The claim was that the product was defective, because the little boy had opened the cap himself despite the fact that it was supposed to be child-resistant. There was a British Standard for childproof caps of the type used, which set out how much force the caps should be able to resist, and evidence was brought to show that the Tesco cap could be opened with much less force than that required for the British Standard. However, British Standards are not a legal requirement but a voluntary scheme which allows manufacturers to show that their products meet certain criteria. Manufacturers of dishwasher powder are not legally obliged to meet the standard for childproof caps, nor even to fit childproof caps at all.

In considering the standard of safety which consumers were entitled to expect, the Court of Appeal found that members of the public would have no idea what the British

Standard for childproof caps would be, so they were not entitled to expect that the cap would meet that standard. They were only entitled to expect that a childproof cap would be more difficult to open than a normal one, and the cap in this case had met that standard. This is in some ways a strange decision, since it suggests that manufacturers should be able to take advantage of public ignorance about safety standards, which hardly seems to be within the spirit of the legislation. Although it is undoubtedly true that few if any ordinary consumers would know what the British Standard for childproof caps was, it seems quite likely that consumers would expect that, if there was such a standard, major companies like Tesco would meet it.

The type of damage

The Act only covers personal injury and damage to property worth £275 or more. Property damage worth less than £275 is not covered, and nor is economic loss, including damage to the defective product itself.

There is also another important restriction, in that the Act does not cover damage to business property. This is defined as property which is not ordinarily intended for private use, occupation or consumption, and which was not intended by the person who suffers the injury or damage for their own private use, occupation or consumption. This means that, for example, if a computer which was used purely for private purposes, in a private house, blew up and burnt the house down, the house owner could claim under the Act. But the Act would not apply if the same thing happened but the computer was sitting in and used by a commercial office. There are, however, grey areas. Someone who works from home, for example, might use their computer for their job, but also for shopping online, downloading music and social networking. The Act does not make it clear whether this kind of mixed use means the user would be covered by the Act or not.

You be the judge

Q: Lucy buys a new flatscreen TV for her flat. She is watching *America's Next Top Model* one evening, when the TV blows up. Lucy puts out the fire very quickly and is unhurt, but a pile of books and CDs that was beside the TV is destroyed. The books and CDs together are worth around £200, and the TV cost £350. Assuming the TV is defective, does Lucy have a claim under the Consumer Protection Act?

A: No. She cannot claim for the TV, because that is classified as economic loss. The damage to her books and CDs counts as property damage, which is covered under the Act, but because their value is less than £275, Lucy has no claim under the Act. She may however have a claim for the books and CDs in negligence.

What must be proved?

The main difference between a claim under the Act and a product liability claim in negligence is that the Act is said to impose strict liability. A claimant has to prove that the product is defective within the meaning of the Act, and that this defect has caused them personal injury, or property damage worth £275 or more. They do not have to prove that any of this was the defendant's fault, or that there was anything they could or should have done to prevent it.

However, as explained earlier, there is some debate about whether liability really is strict. We will look at this issue later in the chapter.

Defences

The defence of contributory negligence applies under the Act. As we saw in Chapter 2, this defence applies when the damage caused to the claimant is partly their own fault and partly the defendant's. Under the Act, it can be used where the claimant has been caused damage partly as a result of a defect in a product, and partly because of something they have done, such as using the product in an unsafe way.

There are also six defences which are specific to the Act and which are set out in section 4:

- compliance with the law;
- product not supplied;
- non-commercial supply;
- defects arising later;
- component products not defective;
- the 'development risks' defence.

Compliance with the law

A defendant can avoid liability by proving that the defect is 'attributable to compliance with any requirement imposed by law'. Take, for example, a situation where the law required that bread had to contain a certain type of preservative, and this preservative was later found to be harmful, either to people generally or the claimant in particular. In this case, the producer of the bread would have a defence, because the law required them to put the preservative in the bread.

The defence applies only where the law requires the thing that causes the defect and not merely where the law allows it. So in the bread example above, there would be no defence if the law permitted manufacturers to add the preservative but did not insist on it.

You be the judge

Source: Pearson Education Ltd/Photodisc/Cole Publishing Group/Kevin Sanchez

Q: Yummy Dinners Ltd make ready meals. Several of their customers become ill after eating their lasagne, and expert evidence shows their symptoms were caused by the fact that the lasagne contained higher levels than usual of a chemical used to give the food an attractive colour. Food safety laws allow this chemical to be added to food, but also allow manufacturers to use other colourants instead of this one. Do the food safety laws mean Yummy Dinners have a defence under the Consumer Protection Act?

A: No. They would only have a defence if the food safety laws required them to use the chemical. Here, they have a choice, so there is no defence.

Product not supplied

This applies where the defendant can prove that they did not supply the product. However, supplying is widely defined and includes selling, hiring out or lending a product. The defence means that a supplier would not be liable if, for example, the product was stolen and sold on. A seller of branded products would also use this defence if they could show that the product in question was not theirs but was a fake.

Non-commercial supply

The Consumer Protection Act was designed to impose liability on businesses, rather than ordinary individuals. It does not, therefore, apply to goods which have not been supplied in the course of a business, or not with a view to making a profit. So if you make a cake for a charity fair and it poisons the person who buys it, you would not be liable under the Act.

Defects arising later

Producers will not be liable for defects that arise after a product leaves them. This defence applies to cases where a product has been interfered with or misused after it leaves the producer, or where a defect arises from normal wear and tear. It can also be of use where goods are perishable (such as food which goes off), or need regular servicing. Where a consumer is trying to trace back through the supply chain to find the producer, anyone in the chain can avoid liability if they can show that the defect did not exist when the product left them.

The defence can only be used if the product had actually left the hands of the defendant before the defect arose. This means there is no defence where, for example, a product is deliberately sabotaged before it leaves the defendant's factory or warehouse, either by a member of their staff or by someone else. In that situation strict liability still applies, so the fact that the sabotage was not the company's fault is irrelevant. If a defendant wants to use this defence, it is up to them to prove that the defect was not there when the product left them. The claimant does not have to prove that the defect was already there at that time.

Case Summary

The defence was successfully raised in *Piper* v. *JRI (Manufacturing) Ltd* (2006). Mr Piper had had a hip replacement operation, using an artificial hip joint made by JRI. The operation seemed to have been successful, but a while later the artificial hip broke into two. Mr Piper argued that the hip must have been defective. However, JRI were able to show that they had an inspection system which would have picked up any such defect, if the defect had existed at the time when the product was supplied, and so they were not liable.

Component products not defective

The Act allows a defence where the defendant has supplied a component which is incorporated into a product (referred to in the Act as the 'subsequent product'), and they can prove that the defect is in the subsequent product, not the component. For the defence to apply, the defect must be entirely due to the design of the subsequent product, or to the producer of the component complying with instructions from the producer of the subsequent product.

The 'development risks' defence

This is the most controversial provision in the Act. It provides that a producer has a defence where

> the state of scientific and technical knowledge at the relevant time was not such that a producer of products of the same description as the product in question might be expected to have discovered the defect if it had existed in his products while they were under his control.

An example of a situation in which the defence could apply is where a drug company launches a drug which later turns out to have side effects. If the company can prove that at the time the drug was launched no one knew about the possible side effects, they will be covered by the defence.

Applying the development risks defence

As we saw earlier, the Consumer Protection Act was passed to put into effect the requirements of an EEC Directive. When the Act was passed, there was controversy over the fact that the wording of the development risks defence in the Act differs from that in the Directive. The Directive states that the defence will only allow a producer to avoid liability where 'the state of scientific and technical knowledge at the time when he put the product into circulation was not such as to enable the existence of the defect to be discovered'. The Consumer Protection Act defence, however, says a producer can avoid liability where 'the state of scientific and technical knowledge at the relevant time was not such that a producer of products of the same description as the product in question might be expected to have discovered the defect if it had existed in his products while they were under his control'. The difference here is that the Directive refers to the general state of scientific and technical knowledge, whereas the Act appears to narrow the standard to what members of a particular industry could be expected to know. Take, for example, a situation where at the time a product was launched the possibility of a risk had been suggested in a handful of scientific journals, but had not filtered down to become known in the relevant industry. The wording of the defence in the Act seems to suggest that the producer could avoid liability, whereas the wording of the Directive seems to suggest that the development risks defence should not apply, because the state of scientific knowledge was such that the defect could have been discovered, even if it might have been quite difficult. So had the Act really applied the Directive correctly?

had the Act really applied the Directive correctly?

As you will know if you have studied EU law, the European Commission can bring a case before the European Court of Justice (ECJ) against any EU country which the Commission believes has failed to apply EU law properly. In *European Commission* v. *UK* (1997), the Commission brought a case against the UK, arguing that the difference in wording between the Directive and the Act meant the Directive had not been properly

Case Summary

applied. In its judgment, the ECJ clarified how the development risks defence was supposed to apply. It acknowledged that the 'state of scientific and technical knowledge' was not a rigid position. When scientists first recognised that a particular risk might exist, the idea might be criticised and rejected by other experts, but then over time, if the evidence built up, it would come to be accepted more widely and eventually be recognised as correct. The question was, at what point in that process could it be said that the state of knowledge was such that the risk could be discovered?

The Court said that once even one expert had raised the issue of a risk, it was clearly possible in theory for producers to find out about it. But they accepted that at that stage it would be very difficult for producers to be aware of the risk. On the other hand, it would be unacceptable if producers could argue that they could not be expected to know of a risk because it was not yet absolutely accepted as true by all the experts. The stage at which producers could be expected to be aware of a risk had to lie somewhere between the two points.

In deciding what the state of knowledge was at the time a product was launched, the ECJ said, the courts should 'include all data in the information circuit of the scientific community as a whole, bearing in mind, however, on the basis of a reasonableness test, the actual opportunities of the information to circulate'. They gave the example of two pieces of research, one undertaken by a researcher an American university and published in an English language journal, and the other carried out by an academic in a remote part of China and published in Chinese in a local scientific journal (remember they were talking at a time when the internet was not as widely used as it is today). They said that it was clearly more reasonable to expect an EU producer to know about the first piece of research than the second, and a producer should not be held liable purely because someone, somewhere knew about a particular risk.

Did this mean that the development risks defence in the Act was in line with the Directive? The ECJ said that it did. It was true that the words of the Act could be interpreted as meaning that a producer only needed to know what anyone else in the same industry would know, but they need not be interpreted this way. It was equally possible to interpret them as describing the defence intended in the Directive, where a producer would only escape liability if the general state of scientific and technical knowledge did not make it possible to identify the risk. As there had been no UK case law on this issue, the ECJ had no reason to think that the courts would choose an interpretation of the Act that did not comply with the Directive.

Cases involving the development risks defence

The ECJ had therefore made it clear how the Act should be interpreted in order to conform with EU law, and the English courts have followed this approach in the two cases where the defence has arisen.

Case Summary

In *Abouzaid* v. *Mothercare* (2000), the claimant was 12 at the time he was injured. He had been helping his mother to get a baby's sleeping bag known as a 'Cosytoes' attached to his little brother's buggy. The sleeping bag was designed to be attached by two elastic straps, which went round the back of the pushchair and clipped together with a metal buckle attached to the end of one of the straps. As the claimant tried to clip the straps together, the buckle flew off and hit him in the eye. It damaged his retina, leaving him with severely reduced vision in that eye.

Mothercare argued that, in 1990 when the sleeping bag was bought, they did not know that there was a danger of injury from the straps. They said that no similar accidents had been reported to them, nor recorded in a database of product-related accidents reported to hospital accident and emergency departments. This, they argued, meant that the state of scientific knowledge in 1990 was such that they could not have been expected to know about the risk. The Court of Appeal rejected this argument. It said that the defence was concerned with whether a producer should be aware of advances in technical knowledge, not to the issue of whether or not anyone had given any thought to a possible risk. There was evidence that simple tests could have revealed the risk, and it would have been easy to use another, safer type of fastening.

Case Summary

The defence was also put forward in *A and Others* v. *National Blood Authority*, the case we looked at earlier where the claimants got hepatitis C through contaminated blood transfusions. The Blood Authority argued that they were covered by the defence because at the time the transfusions were given it was not possible to find out whether a particular batch of blood was contaminated. The Court disagreed. The Blood Authority had known there was a risk of passing on hepatitis C through contaminated blood, and the defence could not apply where a risk was known. They said that if a producer chooses to supply a product knowing of a risk to its consumers, they must take the consequences if people are injured as a result.

Exclusion clauses

As we have seen in previous chapters, companies sometimes try to limit or even exclude their liability for injury or damage by using exclusion clauses, but these kinds of clauses are invalid under the Consumer Protection Act. Section 7 of the Act provides that claims 'shall not be limited or excluded by any contract term, by any notice or any other provisions'. Producers cannot therefore avoid liability by using disclaimers or any other kind of exclusion clause. This provision gives consumers wider protection from exclusion clauses than the Unfair Contract Terms Act 1977, which makes some types of exclusion clause invalid but allows others to stand if they pass a test of reasonableness.

Limitation periods

Claims under the Consumer Protection Act fall into the standard **limitation periods** for personal injury or property damage, set down under the Limitation Act 1980. This means that claimants must start their legal proceedings within three years of the time when the damage was caused, or when it was reasonable to expect the claimant to discover it. As we saw in Chapter 3, this Act gives the courts discretion to extend the time limit. However, the Consumer Protection Act also contains an additional provision on time limits, which states that the right to claim is lost once 10 years have elapsed since the product was supplied.

People in the law

Source: Gordon Hayward, Consumer Safety Expert Network (*text and photo*)

Dr Gordon Hayward is an engineer who has acted as an expert witness in many product liability cases, including *Abouzaid* v. *Mothercare* (2000) which we looked at earlier. He works through the Consumer Safety Expert Network, a database of experts in different fields.

As an expert witness, what's your role in a case? My main job is accident reconstruction: trying to work out how the accident happened, either because it's not clear, or because there's a major disagreement between the two sides about it. I'll examine the product – there's a steady stream of strangely-shaped parcels arriving here every day – and try to work out what would have needed to be wrong with it in order for the accident to have happened as the claimant said it did. Then I'll see if that fault is there. I also test products – I might get a new sample of the product, for example, and do a strength test on it.

The other thing I do is advise on safety standards. The Consumer Protection Act requires that the safety of a product is 'such as persons generally are entitled to expect', so I'll look at what official safety standards there are for that type of product. In most cases, there'll be a standard set down by the British Standards Institute, but if there isn't, I might look at codes of practice in the industry, or general good engineering practice, to work out what the normal safety standard would be. I'll put my conclusions in a report, which the court can use to help them decide whether the alleged defect means that the safety is or isn't 'such as persons generally are entitled to expect'.

Sometimes I'm asked just to provide a preliminary opinion, a sort of gut feeling about whether there might be something wrong with the product. If I can't see that there is, then I'll tell the solicitor that, and they'll use that opinion to help them decide whether to press on with the case.

What products most often give rise to claims? One of the most common products is ladders – I've dealt with more of them than any other type of product. Ladder manufacturers tend to fight quite hard, presumably because if they admitted that a certain design was defective, they would get huge numbers of claims. And the thing is, a ladder is a product that you can just fall off, even if there isn't anything wrong with it.

I also see a lot of cases involving baby products, because people do expect them to be very safe, and stairlifts, because they tend to be used by quite vulnerable people. Cases involving power tools are very common too, especially hire tools. Often in those cases it's not about a defect in the product, but instead it comes down to whether the instructions and warnings were adequate, because we're talking about tools that were really designed to be used by tradesmen but are hired by ordinary members of the public. And then a lot of cases involve products that no one would think could be dangerous – people hurting themselves on tin cans, for example.

How serious do the claimants' injuries tend to be? They vary widely. At one extreme, you get people who have been so badly injured that they almost have no choice but to try and sue, because they can no longer work, or they may even have to pay for care. And then at the other extreme, there are people whose injury isn't really serious, but who've perhaps complained to the company and to their local Trading Standards department and not got anywhere, and who really feel they want to make a point. Often it's because, although they haven't been seriously injured, they believe that someone else could be if the product isn't made safe. I've been quite impressed by how public-spirited people are about that kind of thing.

Ironically though, it often doesn't work that way anyway – if you've got a case, the company will usually just pay to settle the claim, and there'll be no publicity. People who just want to draw attention to a danger and stop other people getting hurt would usually have been better off going to a newspaper, but they don't realise that.

There's a perception that people make trivial claims against companies because they think it's an easy way to get money – have you seen any evidence of that? I've come across very few people who I've thought were trying it on. People do sometimes think big companies might be a soft touch because they want to protect their reputations, but solicitors seem to do a good job of weeding those people out. And you need a fair amount of persistence to carry on with a product liability case – they're not easy to prove, so I don't think many people do it lightly.

What impact do you think the Consumer Protection Act has had on this area of the law? It's made it much easier for consumers to sue, because they no longer need to prove fault. The Consumer Protection Act is a piece of legislation that's deliberately tipped in the consumer's favour, because the EU decided, when it harmonised safety standards across the member states, that it would adopt the highest standards found. I sometimes have to explain to defendants that that's the purpose of the law, and that, yes, it is tipped against them – they're not just reading it wrong!

Although it's still harder with some types of company than others, it is now possible for an ordinary consumer to take on a big company and win. The Woolf reforms to civil procedure have helped as well – before companies would drag things out, and make the whole process as expensive as possible, but with case management, they can't really get away with that now.

Even with a fairly high degree of contributory negligence, a consumer can get **damages** under the Consumer Protection Act. I had one case where a man was injured by a drill. He hadn't read the instructions or worn goggles, even though he knew he should have, but the instructions were in very small print and the drill bit didn't conform to the required standard, and he won quite a high settlement.

Do you think the Consumer Protection Act has a deterrent value, making manufacturers less likely to put dangerous products on the market? I'm not sure the product liability law in the UK provides that much of a deterrent. We don't see the huge damages that juries award in the US, so the thought of being sued isn't such a huge threat, except in areas like drugs, where you get big class actions.

Evaluating the Consumer Protection Act 1987

The Consumer Protection Act was designed to tighten up the law on dangerous products, making it much easier for consumers to get compensation and, in the process, encouraging manufacturers to take more care to make their products safe. However, there is some debate as to how much it has really improved protection for consumers. These are some of the problems identified.

Is liability really strict?

The main benefit of the Act for consumers was said to be that it imposed strict liability, so that consumers no longer had to prove a manufacturer was at fault as they did with a negligence claim. But how far does the Act really impose strict liability?

Take, for example, the standard of safety under the Act: a product will be considered defective if its safety 'is not such as persons generally are entitled to expect'. When they assess this question, it has been argued that the courts could take into account many of the same factors they would look at when setting a standard of care in negligence, such as how likely the product was to cause injury, how serious the injury would be, and how practical it was to take precautions against such an injury. This would essentially turn it into a test of reasonableness that was very difficult to distinguish from the test in negligence. However, the approach of the courts in recent cases suggests they are holding a firmer line, which upholds the principle of strict liability. The clearest example of this is *A* v. *National Blood Authority*, where the court ruled that the defendants could be liable even though there was nothing they could do to check whether the blood was contaminated. This contrasts with the approach in negligence, where the practicality of precautions is a key part of assessing the standard of care.

the claimant must show that the defect caused their damage

A more difficult problem is the issue of **causation**. As we saw with the Thalidomide case, it can be very hard for claimants in negligence to prove that damage was caused by a product, and the Act does nothing to change this. It provides that the claimant must show that the defect caused their damage, and as no special rules are provided for how this is to be done, the usual rules of causation from negligence apply.

The most criticised area, however, is the development risks defence, which some critics have argued has the potential to weaken severely the concept of strict liability. By allowing a producer to argue that they are not liable because they could not have been expected to know about a risk, the defence is essentially asking whether the damage was foreseeable, and whether it is reasonable to impose liability, which looks very like negligence. In fact, as we saw in the negligence case of *Roe* v. *Minister of Health*, the state of knowledge at the time of the injury is a relevant factor in assessing breach of duty. You may remember that this is the case we looked at in Chapter 2, where the claimant was paralysed because a disinfectant leaked through tiny cracks in an ampoule of anaesthetic; the Court said that a defendant was entitled to be judged by the standards, and state of knowledge, that was accepted at the time they acted. The development risks defence looks very similar to this approach.

As we saw in *Abouzaid* v. *Mothercare* and *A* v. *National Blood Authority*, the courts have so far been quite strict in keeping use of the defence in line with the Directive's aims, but it remains to be seen whether it could compromise strict liability in other situations.

The limitation period

The 10-year limit on cases brought under the Act was designed to protect producers from claims arising many years after they have supplied a product. However, it has the potential to weaken protection for consumers, because there are situations where damage caused by a defective product may take a very long time to become apparent. For example, during the early 1980s British beef cows were infected with a disease called bovine spongiform encephalopathy (BSE, also known as mad cow disease). At the time, experts said that eating the infected beef could not pass the disease to humans, but from the early 1990s doctors began to see cases of a fatal condition called variant Creutzfeldt-Jakob Disease (vCJD), which experts recognised as the human form of BSE. Since then, strong evidence has been produced suggesting that vCJD is caused by eating infected beef. However, it is thought that the period between getting the disease from eating beef and showing symptoms can be as long as 20 years, so many of the victims would be prevented from trying to sue under the Consumer Protection Act.

Use of settlements

As we have seen, very few cases under the Act have been brought before the English courts, and the situation is similar in the other EU member states. This is likely to be because if a claim is strong enough for the claimant to be willing to go to court, a company will usually prefer to settle it in order to avoid bad publicity. Allegations that a product is unsafe and has hurt customers will almost always damage the reputation of a product and the company which makes it, even if in fact the company wins its case.

However, this can limit the usefulness of the Act in deterring companies from selling unsafe products, and/or making customers aware of risks. This is because settlements are often offered on condition that the claimant accepts a confidentiality clause, preventing them from talking about the case, or the settlement itself. This means that companies can effectively cover up unsafe products, and also makes it very difficult to assess how far the Act has improved consumer protection.

companies can effectively cover up unsafe products

By contrast, in the USA, the Consumer Product Safety Act requires companies to notify the Consumer Product Safety Commission if a product is the subject of three or more settlements or judgments in a two-year period and the claims involve serious injury or death. Though this can only catch the most serious cases, it does allow for more transparency than the UK system, which potentially allows companies to bury even highly dangerous products for as long as they can persuade injured consumers to take the money instead of going to the press. The Royal Society for the Protection of Accidents has called for a Europe-wide database of all product liability cases to be set up, so that it would be possible for both consumers and the media to find out about dangerous products.

Should liability be strict?

Most of the criticisms of the Act relate to problems with its protection of consumers, but it has also been criticised from the opposite point of view, that strict liability puts too heavy a burden on businesses. Imposing strict liability is said to stifle innovation and enterprise, making companies reluctant to bring out ground-breaking new products because they can be sued if the products prove defective, even if the company is not at fault. Alternatively, it is argued, strict liability can make companies take excessive safety precautions, pushing up the costs of products to the consumer.

Are decisions suitable for the courts?

This criticism is one that applies to both negligence claims and claims under the Consumer Protection Act. We saw at the start of the chapter that in a negligence claim the courts have to decide whether a defendant has taken reasonable care, and that involves weighing up factors such as the likelihood of injury, the seriousness of the injury and the practicality of taking precautions against it. And in a claim under the Consumer Protection Act, a court has to judge whether the safety of the product was such as people were entitled to expect, which also involves value judgements about what defendants should and should not be expected to do, and what kinds of risk should be considered acceptable.

These are often difficult choices, and in product liability cases they can be choices that the courts are not well equipped to make. Take, for example, the situation where a company discovers a cure for heart disease, but later the drug is found to cause side effects which can kill some patients although it cures many others who would otherwise have died of their illness. Is a tort action really the place to decide whether that drug should have been put on the market? Are judges qualified to decide whether the risk to one group outweighs the benefit to the other? Or should this kind of decision be made somewhere else, where it is not linked to an individual's claims for compensation, and where the whole social context can be examined?

Law in action Fake claims in the USA

In America, claims for product liability can lead to huge damages – sometimes running into millions of dollars – and because big companies are known to be both wealthy and keen to avoid bad publicity about their products there are some consumers who believe fake product liability claims are an easy way to make money. The prizes for the three most outrageous claims surely have to go to these three US consumers:

- In 2005 a woman from California sued a fast-food chain, claiming that she had found a human finger in a bowl of chilli. Suspecting fraud, the chain asked police to investigate. Their scientific experts discovered that the finger had not come from any employee of the restaurant, or its suppliers, and pointed out that its condition 'was not consistent with an object that had been cooked in chilli at 170 degrees for three hours'. The finger was later traced to a work colleague of the woman's husband. It had been severed in a work accident a year earlier. The woman was sentenced to 9 years in prison for fraud, with a 12-year sentence for her husband who supplied the finger.
- In 2001 a man from Colorado attempted to sue the manufacturers of his car after he drove it into a lake. He said the manufacturers should be liable because it did not say anywhere in the car manual that it was not suitable for use in water.
- In 2004 a woman from Virginia claimed to have found a mouse in her soup at a restaurant. She offered not to sue if the restaurant paid her $500,000 dollars, but was arrested when tests showed the mouse had no soup in its lungs, showed no signs of being cooked and had died of a fractured skull.

[*References*: 'Chilli finger pair plead guilty', **http://bbc.co.uk/1/hi/world/Americas/4232018.skm**; 'Mouse soup extortion plot', **abcnews.go.com/us/crimeblotter/story?id=90044&page+1**]

Dangerous products and criminal law

As well as civil law claims in contract, negligence or under the Consumer Protection Act 1987, companies which make or sell unsafe products can be prosecuted under the General Product Safety Regulations 2005. These Regulations are enforced by the Trading Standards Departments of local councils. Usually acting on complaints from members of the public, they can test products to see whether or not they are unsafe. However, although they have powers to prosecute companies this is treated as a last resort, and Trading Standards Officers will usually try to persuade companies to remove unsafe products from the market instead.

Writing and drafting

You work for the law reform body, the Law Commission. The Commission is looking into how it can be made easier for consumers to get compensation if they are injured by dangerous products. Prepare a short report detailing what you believe are the problems with the current law, and suggest any ways in which you think it could be improved.

Summary

- A person caused injury or damage by a defective product can sue in negligence or under the Consumer Protection Act.
- In negligence, a claimant can sue the manufacturer, or anyone who hires out, repairs or produces parts for a product. All types of product are covered, as long as they are supplied to the consumer without intermediate checks.
- For a negligence claim, the claimant has to prove that the defendant did not take reasonable care to ensure the safety of the product. Only defects which make a product dangerous are covered, and the product must have caused personal injury or property damage.
- The usual defences in negligence apply.
- Claimants under the Consumer Protection Act 1987 must prove that the safety standard is not such as persons generally are entitled to expect. The Act imposes strict liability, so a claimant does not have to prove fault. Only defects which make a product dangerous are covered.
- The product must have caused injury or property damage worth £275 or more. A claimant can sue the manufacturer, anyone who 'wins or abstracts' the product; anyone responsible for a process that adds essential characteristics; retailers selling under their own brand; other suppliers, where the producer is unknown and they do not identify their supplier; or importers into the EU.
- All kinds of product are covered but products must be intended for personal and not business use.
- Seven defences apply:
  - contributory negligence;
  - compliance with the law;
  - product not supplied;
  - non-commercial supply;
  - defects arising later;
  - component products not defective;
  - development risks.
- Claims fall into the standard three-year limitation period for personal injury or property damage under the Limitation Act 1980, and can be extended under the rules of that Act, but the Consumer Protection Act adds a final 10-year limit after which claims cannot be made.

Question and answer*

Problem: David is out shopping for a birthday present for his wife, Victoria. She wants a new hairdryer, and he finds one at what seems to be a bargain price. He also spots a deep fat fryer, and knowing that Victoria loves chips, he buys that as well. On the way home, he sees that their local church is running a summer fair to raise money for charity, so he pops in and buys Victoria a birthday cake from the cake stall.

Victoria is delighted with her presents, but when she switches the hairdryer on she finds that it does not work. David decides to cheer her up by making some chips but the deep fat fryer overheats, causing a small fire in their kitchen that burns a section of the wall. They decide to have a cup of tea and a piece of the cake instead, but when Victoria takes a bite of her slice, she cracks a tooth on a piece of metal.

The following week they read a newspaper report which says that the manufacturers of the deep fat fryer are recalling the model that David bought, because of a scientific report suggesting that a fault in its casing material could lead to overheating. The story quotes a spokesperson for the manufacturers, who says: 'We had no idea that there was a problem with this product, but we take customer safety very seriously, so we are not taking any chances.'

Advise David and Victoria as to any claims they may have in negligence, or under the Consumer Protection Act 1987.

You should allow yourself no more than 40 minutes to complete this task.

Essay: How far has the Consumer Protection Act 1987 improved the law on defective products?

This question should be answered in 40 minutes.

* Answer guidance is provided at the end of the chapter.

Further reading

Albanese, F. and Del Duca, L. (1987) 'Developments in European product liability', 5 *Dickinson Journal of International Law* 193.
This article looks at the Directive which formed the basis for the Consumer Protection Act, and examines why reform was thought to be needed, by looking at product liability law prior to the Directive in several different countries including the UK.

Griffiths, Lord, De Val, P. and Dormer, R.J. (1988) 'Developments in English product liability law: a comparison with the American system', 62 *Tulane Law Review* 353.
An interesting article that compares the approach of the Directive with product liability law in the USA.

Hodges, C. (1998) 'Development risks: unanswered questions', 61 MLR 560.
This article looks at the development risks defence as set down in the Directive, and offers a detailed criticism of it.

Law Commission (1977) *Liability for Defective Products*, No. 82, Cmnd 6831.
This report looks at the law on product liability before the Consumer Protection Act, and many of its proposals were adopted in the Act.

Mildred, M. and Howells, G. (1998) 'Comment on "Development risks: unanswered questions"', 61 MLR 558.
This article is a response to the one by Hodges, above, and challenges some of his comments. Taken together, they will give you lots of useful material for essays.

Stapleton, J. (1986) 'Products liability reform: real or illusory?', 6 OJLS 392.
Jane Stapleton's articles are always well written and thought-provoking, and this one is no exception. It looks at the theoretical basis for product liability, and is very good on the arguments for and against strict(er) liability.

Question and answer guidance

Problem: Starting with the hairdryer, the key issue here is that the product is defective but not dangerous, so there is no claim either in negligence or under the Consumer Protection Act. You could mention that David will have a claim in contract as he bought the hairdryer.

Moving on to the deep fat fryer, this product has caused property damage, so there is the possibility of a claim in negligence or under the Consumer Protection Act for the damage to the wall. Go through each possible claim in turn, explaining who could be sued, and what David would have to prove. Note that the fault is in the casing material so you need to consider whether this counts as a separate component. You will also need to take into account the information in the newspaper article: do you think there might be a defence?

Finally, consider Victoria's claim with regard to the cake. Again, this is personal injury, so there may be a claim in negligence and/or under the Consumer Protection Act. A key issue here is where David bought the cake: could this provide a defence?

Essay: For this essay, you need to briefly explain what the Consumer Protection Act is, and then go on to look at the state of law before it was passed. Highlight the problems that exist with product liability in negligence, including the difficulties with causation and the need to prove fault, referring to cases that illustrate your points. You may also want to mention the Thalidomide **litigation** as an example of the difficulties, but keep this brief. Then explain what improvements the Consumer Protection Act brought to the law, again referring to cases which show how it gave added protection to consumers. Finally, you can talk about any issues which remain problematic, such as the need to prove causation and the doubts about the development risks defence.

Visit **www.mylawchamber.co.uk/quinntort** to access tools to help you develop and test your knowledge of tort law, including practice exam questions with guidance, annotated weblinks, glossary and key case flashcards, legal newsfeed and legal updates and interactive 'You be the judge' questions.

premium mylawchamber
unrivalled support for legal education

Chapter 11
Breach of statutory duty

Key points In this chapter we will be looking at:

- ✦ When a statute will create a right to sue in tort
- ✦ How the courts decide whether a statutory duty has been breached

Introduction

Among the hundreds of statutes enacted by Parliament, many will impose legal duties on individuals or organisations. A statute may, for example, require a local authority to provide certain services for its residents, or require companies to take particular safety precautions to protect workers, or require motorists to obey specified rules when driving. The issue discussed in this chapter concerns what happens when someone (whether an individual or an organisation) fails to perform the duty laid down in a statute, or to perform it properly, and someone else is caused injury or loss by that failure. Can the person harmed then sue for breach of the duty, in the same way as they could for any other tort, and win damages? As we will see, the answer is sometimes yes, and sometimes no, depending on how the courts interpret the words of the statute.

Claims for breach of statutory duty

Claims for breach of statutory duty arise when the **claimant** believes that they were owed a duty under a particular statute, and that duty has either not been performed, or not been performed properly. In the majority of cases, the **defendant** will be an organisation, such as a local authority, or a company. For example, if a statute provides that local authorities should provide 'adequate and suitable education' for local children, someone who feels they have not been given an adequate and suitable education might try to sue the local authority for **damages**, perhaps on the basis that if they had got a better or more suitable education they could have got a better job, or not been unemployed. Similarly, if someone is injured at work because their employer has breached safety legislation, they might wish to claim for personal injury.

However, the fact that a statutory duty has been breached and this breach has caused harm is not enough to make a claim possible. This is because the law does not automatically assume that a statute gives individuals a right to compensation if a duty under it is breached; in fact, the general assumption is that statute law is there to impose general rules which benefit everyone, and not to create individual rights to damages if duties imposed under a statute are not carried out. Therefore, a statute will only be found to create an individual right to sue if the courts find that Parliament intended to create such a right when creating the statute. This means that in statutory duty cases, a large part of the court's job is to look very closely at the relevant statute and decide whether a right to sue exists, and if it does, what the duty is and who it applies to. So, in making a claim for breach of statutory duty, the claimant must prove three things:

the law does not automatically assume that a statute gives individuals a right to compensation

- that the statute creates a right to sue;
- that the statutory duty was breached;
- that the breach caused damage or loss that is of a kind the statute is designed to prevent.

Is there a right to sue?

In some cases, a statute will specifically state whether breach of a duty contained in it will create a right for anyone caused harm or loss to sue. For example, the Sex Discrimination Act 1975 creates a duty not to discriminate against women by denying them access to a school or to other goods, facilities and services, and section 66 provides that someone who has committed an act of discrimination as defined by the Act 'may be made the subject of civil proceedings in like manner as any other claim in tort'. In other words, someone caused loss by a breach of the duty under the Act can sue the person or organisation responsible, just as they could if that person had been negligent or committed nuisance or trespass.

In very many cases, however, a statute says nothing about whether it creates a right to sue or not, and in this situation, the courts have the job of deciding whether a claim can be brought. As you will know if you have studied the English legal system, statutes are considered the highest form of English law because they are produced by Parliament, which is democratically elected. This means that when deciding whether a statute should create a right to sue, the traditional view is that judges attempt to use the words of the statute to work out what Parliament would have intended the answer to be, rather than simply deciding whether they think a right to sue ought to exist. How far this is actually realistic, however, is questionable. With older statutes, it may not have been obvious that a situation could arise in which someone would seek to sue, so Parliament may simply not have considered the issue. With more modern ones, legislators do know that the issue is likely to arise, so if they still choose not to state whether a provision should give rise to a right to sue, this must be assumed to be deliberate. In *M v. Newham Borough Council* (1994) Lord Staughton suggested that where a statute imposes a duty on a public authority, the question of whether there is a

statutes are considered the highest form of English law because they are produced by Parliament

private right to sue may be ignored because it is politically embarrassing for the legislators to admit that they do not intend to provide a remedy for someone injured by a public authority's failure to fulfil its legal duty.

Even so, the courts generally still express the view that what they are trying to do is find out what Parliament intended. Their starting point is that breach of a statutory duty does not create a right to sue, unless the words of the statute suggest that Parliament intended to create such a right. In assessing this, they take into account a number of factors, including the following:

- Who the statute was intended to benefit.
- How specific the duty is.
- Whether any other remedies for breach of the statutory duty are available.
- The background to the legislation.

No single one of these factors is decisive; the courts look at all of them, and may include other factors as well. This approach has been approved by the House of Lords in a number of cases, including *X* v. *Bedfordshire County Council* (1995) and *Lonrho* v. *Shell Petroleum (No. 2)* (1982) (see below).

Who the statute was intended to benefit

The question here is whether the statute was designed to benefit society as a whole, or a specific group of people; the courts are more likely to find a right to sue where the Act is intended to benefit a particular group. An example was *Ex Parte Island Records* (1978), where the statute in question provided that it was an offence to record a live music performance without the performers' consent. The Court of Appeal found that the statute was clearly intended to benefit a specific class of people, namely professional musicians, and they agreed that professional musicians should therefore be able to sue for loss caused by breach of this duty. Similarly, legislation on safety at work has generally been interpreted as being for the benefit of employees, and so employees have been given a right to sue under it.

Case Summary

However, the fact that a specific class of people stands to benefit from the existence of a statutory duty will not necessarily be taken to mean that the statute was *intended* to benefit them; the courts may decide that it was intended for another purpose completely. This was the case in *Lonrho* v. *Shell Petroleum (No. 2)* (1982). Shell had made a contract with Lonrho, which allowed Shell to use a pipeline owned by Lonrho to transport their petroleum products to Rhodesia. Rhodesia was a British colony, but in 1965 it declared itself independent (it is now the country we know as Zimbabwe). The declaration of independence was made because Britain wanted the country to make democratic reforms that would give more representation to the black majority, but the Rhodesian government, which was made up from the white minority, wanted to prevent this. The new independent state was not recognised by the British government, and as part of a programme of sanctions designed to undermine the Rhodesian government, it became illegal to supply oil to Rhodesia, under the Southern Rhodesia (Petroleum) Order 1965. Shell continued to supply oil, using different means, which was a breach of the order. Lonrho sought to sue them for that breach, arguing that by continuing to supply oil they were helping the illegal government to stay in place, and this had caused loss to Lonrho because while the illegal government was still there they could not use their pipeline. The House of Lords said that although companies in

Case Summary

Lonrho's position would ultimately benefit from the legislation, that was not its purpose. Its purpose was to undermine the illegal regime, and so Lonrho had no right to sue under the order.

Case Summary

The same approach was taken in *X* v *Bedfordshire County Council* (1995), the case we looked at in Chapter 6 regarding negligence by local authorities. The legislation here required local authorities to put in place protection for children at risk of abuse, and to provide educational services for children with special needs. The claimants were people who had been abused as children and claimed the council should have protected them and others who claimed they had not been given the educational services they were entitled to under the legislation. The House of Lords found that neither group could make a claim under the Act, because its purpose was to provide a general benefit to society, rather than a right to sue for individuals. Lord Browne-Wilkinson said:

> Although regulatory or welfare legislation affecting a particular area of activity does in fact provide protection to those individuals particularly affected by that activity, the legislation is not to be treated as being passed for the benefit of those individuals, but for the benefit of society in general.

Out and about

Look up the case of *X* v *Bedfordshire*, and read the parts of the judgment that deal with breach of statutory duty. In your own words, explain the reasons why the court held that there was no claim for breach of statutory duty. Do you find their reasons convincing? Can you find any problems or inconsistencies with their reasoning?

Reflective practice

How did you get on with the exercise above? Did you find it easy to locate the relevant parts of the judgment, and pick out the arguments? This is a key skill for a lawyer, so it's well worth practising, and the more you do it the easier you'll begin to find it.

How specific is the duty?

Some statutes set down in detail what they require to be done, but many simply state a looser duty, and allow those who are required to act a certain amount of choice in exactly how they put the duty into practice. For example, legislation regarding local authorities' duties to provide education tend to include broad duties such as to 'provide an adequate and suitable education' rather than, for example, stating that they should employ one teacher for every 20 children, or spend a particular amount on books. This means that local authorities can choose for themselves how they go about providing 'an adequate and suitable education'. This is important for cases involving breach of statutory duty, because the courts are more likely to find a right to sue where the statute makes it absolutely clear what there is a duty to do (such as 'Employ one teacher for every 20 children'), and simply requires that thing to be done, than where a statute contains a wide duty that allows discretion about exactly how it is to be performed.

Case Summary

This was one of the issues in *X* v. *Bedfordshire*, the case mentioned above, because the legislation imposed very wide duties such as 'to safeguard and protect the welfare of children within [the area] who are in need', which allowed the authorities a broad discretion as to how they went about doing this, as opposed to setting out, for example, that they had to employ a certain number of social workers, or visit every family with children so many times a year. The House of Lords concluded that Parliament was unlikely to have intended to provide a right to sue for breach of a duty that was so widely drawn and allowed for so much discretion. Cases where a right to sue was allowed were usually those where the duty was 'very limited and specific', said Lord Browne-Wilkinson, 'as opposed to a general administrative function . . . involving the exercise of administrative discretion'.

Case Summary

A similar approach was taken in *Danns* v. *Minister of Health* (1998). The claimant had had a vasectomy, but it had reversed itself and his wife became pregnant. Under the Ministry of Health Act 1919, the Minister of Health had a duty to give out such information as was desirable for the health of people in the country. A medical research paper published before Mr Danns's wife became pregnant had suggested that there was a 1 in 2,000 chance that vasectomies could reverse themselves, and the claimant argued that the Minister of Health had breached the duty under the 1919 Act because he had not warned the public about the risk of vasectomies reversing themselves. The Court of Appeal rejected this argument, saying that the statute gave the Minister a wide discretion over how the duty was performed, and warning the public about the research was not the only reasonable way to perform the duty.

This is one reason why a right to sue for breach of a statutory duty has mostly been found in cases involving workplace safety legislation, which tends to impose clear and very specific duties such as fitting specified protective equipment to machinery.

Are other adequate remedies available?

statutes which impose duties on public authorities may provide a complaints procedure

Most statutes which impose duties also provide a mechanism to enforce those duties. For example, some statutes on workplace safety make it a criminal offence to breach duties set down under the Act, so someone who does so can be prosecuted and fined or even sent to prison. Similarly, statutes which impose duties on public authorities may provide a complaints procedure which can be used by anyone affected by a breach of the statutory duties (but which may not necessarily involve compensation). The courts will look at the remedies offered under the Act, and decide whether they can be considered an adequate way of dealing with problems; if they can, this is usually taken to indicate that Parliament did not intend any other remedies to be available and a right to sue should be refused.

Case Summary

This was the situation in *Todd* v. *Adam* (2001). Four fishermen were killed when their boat sank, and their families sought to sue the owner of the vessel, who they said had breached his duty to take safety precautions under the Fishing Vessel (Safety Provisions) Rules 1975. The Court refused to allow them to sue, because the rules provided for boat owners who breached the rules to be prosecuted and this was considered an adequate remedy.

The courts will also look at whether other remedies are available outside the statute. If the **common law** already provides what it considers to be adequate remedies, this is seen as a reason not to grant a right to sue. This was the case in *McCall* v. *Abelesz* (1976), where the claimant tried to sue their landlord for breach of the statutory duty not to harass tenants. The Court pointed out that Mr McCall could sue in trespass or for breach of his rental contract, and so there was no need to allow a right to sue for breach of the statutory duty.

Case Summary

You be the judge

Q: Section 1 of the (imaginary) Dangerous Factories Act 1925 provides that factory owners must ensure that all cutting machinery is equipped with safety guards. Section 2(1) of the Act states that failure to equip cutting machinery with safety guards is a criminal offence, punishable by a fine of up to £10,000. If an employee is injured by a machine that is not equipped with a safety guard, does the provision in section 2(1) make it more or less likely that it will be possible for them to make a claim for breach of statutory duty?

A: Less likely. The existence of alternative remedies is one factor that the courts use in deciding that Parliament did not intend to create an individual right to sue.

Source: Pearson Education Ltd/Photodisc/Malcolm Fife

The background to the legislation

As the courts take the approach that they are trying to work out the intention of Parliament, they will sometimes look at the background to the legislation to see if it provides a clue. In *Ziemniak* v. *ETPM Deep Sea Ltd* (2003), the claimant was a seaman who had been seriously injured when he was testing a lifeboat on the defendant's ship and the chain holding it gave way. Safety legislation required that such chains were 'of adequate strength' to hold lifeboats in place, and the defendant admitted breaching this duty, but argued that the legislation did not give a right to sue. The Court of Appeal looked at the background to the relevant statute, which was secondary legislation, made under the Merchant Shipping Act 1979. This had built on earlier legislation, the Merchant Shipping Act 1970. The 1970 Act was the first real attempt to address the issue of workplace safety for seamen, and the notes to that Act explained that its purpose was to bring workplace safety at sea in line with the law in workplaces on land. The Court said that this purpose had also been carried over into the 1979 Act, and pointed out that most legislation concerning safety at work on land includes a right to sue for breach of the duties contained in it. They therefore allowed the claimant a right to sue.

Case Summary

Breach of the duty

If it can be established that a statute gives a right to sue, the next question to be asked is whether the defendant has actually breached the duty imposed under the statute. In order to answer this question, the court will look at the words of the statute, in order to work out exactly what the duty is. This may involve looking at two different aspects of the duty:

- ✦ What the duty requires the defendant to do.
- ✦ What degree of fault amounts to breach of the duty.

What the duty requires the defendant to do

In some cases, it will be very clear what the statute requires: for example, if a statute says that 'Safety guards must be fitted to every machine', it is obvious that a defendant can comply with the statute by fitting safety guards, and will breach the duty if they do not. In many cases, however, the duty set down in the statute is less precise, and the courts need to work out exactly what it requires.

Case Summary

In *R* v. *East Sussex County Council, ex parte Tandy* (1998), the council had been supplying five hours a week of home teaching to a child who was unable to go to school because of illness. It then reduced those hours in order to save money, and was sued for breach of statutory duty. The relevant statute was the Education Act 1993, which stated that councils had a duty to provide suitable education to local children who could not attend school because of illness. This clearly makes the duty much more vague than a statute saying 'All machines must be fenced'. If the statute had said 'Children unable to attend school through illness shall be given five hours of home tuition a week', the case would have been clear-cut, but a statute that imposes a duty to supply a suitable education does not state whether, in the claimant's case, a suitable education was five hours of home tuition, or three, or ten. It leaves the decision on what is a suitable education in each case to be made by the council. How, then, could the courts decide whether the duty had been breached? They did this by looking at how the legislation suggested the council should make their decision. In other sections of the statute, it was provided that councils could take into account financial considerations when making a decision on which service to provide. In the section stating the duty to supply a suitable education, however, there was no mention of taking financial considerations into account. The House of Lords therefore concluded that if Parliament had intended councils to be able to take costs into account when deciding what was a suitable education, they would have said so in this section as well. As they had not done so, cutting back the child's tuition hours to save money was a breach of the duty.

Case Summary

In *Gorringe* v. *Calderdale Metropolitan Borough Council* (2004), the claimant was injured when she crashed her car into a bus, which had been hidden from view over the crest of a hill. The Highways Act 1980 gives local councils a duty to 'maintain the highway', and Mrs Gorringe argued that they were in breach of this duty, because they had not painted warning signs on the road to encourage drivers to slow down. The House of Lords disagreed: the words 'maintain the highway' meant to keep the roads in good repair. Providing information and warnings was not part of this duty, and so there was no breach.

The degree of fault

In some cases, a statute may create absolute liability with regard to a duty, which means that if the defendant fails to do what the statute requires them to do, they are liable. For example, if a statute says that 'All grinding machines shall be fitted with a safety guard', a defendant who had failed to fit a guard would be liable, regardless of why the guard was not fitted. In this situation, an accidental failure to put the guard back on after cleaning would create liability just as much as a deliberate decision not to fit a guard because the machine could be operated more quickly without it.

Case Summary

An example of absolute liability is *Galashiels Gas Co.* v. *Millar* (1949), which involved the death of a man when the lift at his workplace failed. The Factories Act 1937 stated that 'every hoist or lift shall be properly maintained', and the House of Lords held that this meant there was an absolute duty to keep lifts in working order. Although there was no evidence that the factory owners had done anything wrong, or could have done anything to prevent the accident, they were in breach of the duty. This type of liability is most often found in legislation about safety at work.

Case Summary

More often, statutes impose qualified liability, which allows for a standard of reasonableness similar to that in negligence. This means that the courts have to perform the same sort of balancing act between factors as they would in a negligence case. This was the case in *McCarthy* v. *Coldair Ltd* (1951), where the relevant statute stated that 'there shall, as far as is reasonably practicable, be provided and maintained safe means of access to every place at which any person has at any time to work'. The claimant in the case had been injured when he fell from a short ladder, which slipped on a shiny floor that had been splashed with paint. He claimed that his employer was in breach of the statutory duty, because it would have been 'reasonably practical' to have another employee holding the ladder steady and the employer had not taken this precaution. The Court recognised that, as the employer had pointed out, the risk of harm from falling off such a short ladder was not great, and, usually, placing another employee at the foot of the ladder would have been more than an employer could reasonably be expected to do in view of the size of the risk. However, because the floor was slippery, the risk increased, and this meant it was reasonably practical to take that extra precaution, and the employer was in breach.

Did the breach cause the kind of damage the statute seeks to prevent?

Case Summary

In a claim for breach of statutory duty, the claimant must not only show that the defendant's breach caused damage, but also that the damage was of a kind that the statute was designed to prevent. Again, in deciding this, the courts will look closely at the words of the statute. In *Gorris* v. *Scott* (1874), the claimant was the owner of some sheep, who were being transported by sea by the defendant. The Contagious Disease (Animals) Act 1869 required that animals on board should be held in pens, to prevent the spread of disease. The defendant did not do this, and as a result the claimant's sheep were washed overboard. The court rejected the claim, because the statute was designed to prevent the spread of contagious diseases between different groups of animals on board, not to prevent financial loss to the owners of livestock.

Case Summary

A more difficult question arises where the damage caused is the kind that the statute is designed to prevent, but the damage happens in a different way from that referred to in the legislation. In these cases, the courts have sometimes made conflicting decisions. In *Donaghey* v. *Bolton and Paul* (1968), regulations made under a statute required that special safety equipment should be used when employees had to climb onto 'roofs . . . covered with fragile materials through which a person is likely to fall a distance of more than ten feet'. The claimant was injured by falling through a roof, rather than through fragile materials covering a roof, but the House of Lords held that he could claim damages for breach of statutory duty because the harm caused to him was exactly that which the statute sought to prevent. It did not matter that it was caused in a different way from that which the makers of the regulations had in mind.

Case Summary

In other cases, however, the House of Lords have taken a more restrictive approach. In *Close* v. *Steel Co. of Wales* (1962), the relevant legislation imposed a duty to fence off the moving parts of dangerous machinery. The purpose of this was to prevent workers from being injured by getting caught in the machines. The machine Mr Close was using was not properly fenced off, and a piece of metal flew out of it, hitting him in the eye. The House of Lords held that there was no claim, because the legislation was there to keep employees' hands out of the machines and not to prevent anything from flying out.

Out and about

You are a solicitor in a small high street practice. A client has come to you after being bitten by her neighbour's dog, which is a breed called a Japanese Tosa. She has read in the newspapers that under the Dangerous Dogs Act 1991 this breed of dog must be muzzled and kept on a lead in public places. The dog which bit her was running off the lead in a public park, and not wearing a muzzle. She would like to know if she can sue the dog owner under the Dangerous Dogs Act, and claim compensation. Look up the Act (you'll find it at **http://www.legislation.gov.uk/ukpga/1991/65/contents**) and, using the principles explained above, work out whether your client may have a valid claim for breach of statutory duty.

Source: Pearson Education Ltd/Lord and Leverett

Defences

The main **defence** to a claim for breach of statutory duty is **contributory negligence**, which as we saw in Chapter 3 applies where the claimant was partly to blame for the accident and/or the harm done. In theory, the defence of ***volenti*** can also apply, where the claimant voluntarily takes the risk of harm. However, in cases involving safety at work, which is the main area where breach of statutory duty arises, the courts recognise that in a workplace situation what looks like a voluntary act may in fact be something that the employee had little real choice about. If you want to remind yourself about how the defences of contributory negligence and *volenti* work, you will find all the details on pages 89–99.

Figure 11.1 Liability for breach of statutory duty

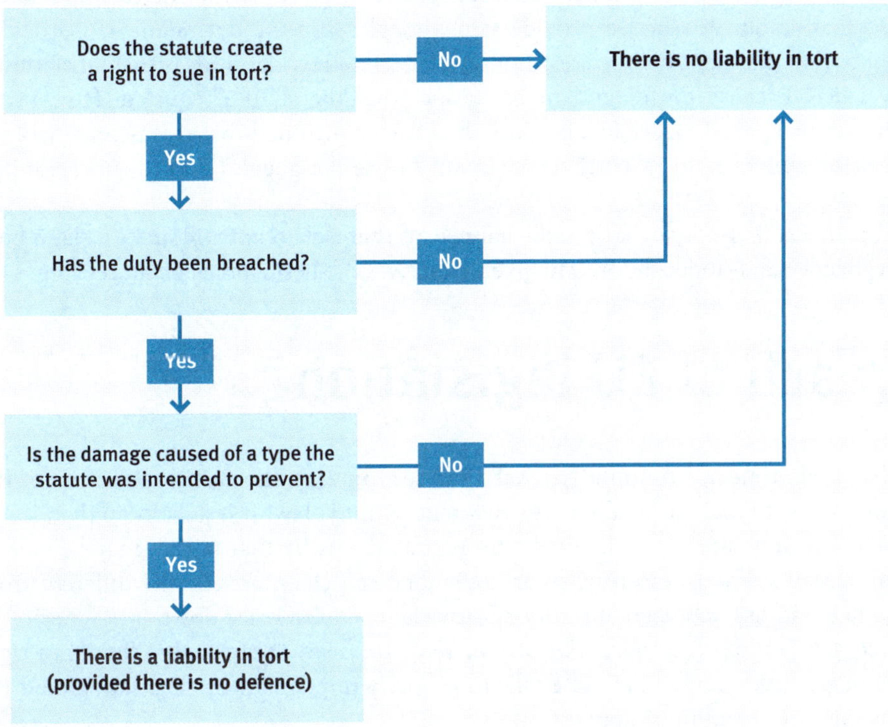

Breach of statutory duty v. common law employers' liability

Cases involving breach of statutory duty most often arise in the area of legislation on safety at work, where someone has been injured because the employer has not taken safety precautions set down in legislation (though they can arise from other types of legislation as well). As we saw in Chapter 7, there are also common law rules on employers' liability for workplace safety, so how does a claimant choose which type of claim to make? The answer will often depend on the facts of the case.

Sometimes making a claim under the relevant Act, rather than under the common law rules on employers' liability, can be easier, because statutory duties in this area are often clear-cut. For example, let's say that Jane works in a factory, and statute says that the kind of machine she uses should only be operated with a protective guard fitted. Jane's employer has fitted a guard, but after being removed for cleaning it was accidentally not replaced. Jane's hand gets trapped in the machine, and she is injured. To make a claim under common law, Jane would have to prove that her employer fell below the standards of a reasonable employer in not making sure the guard was replaced, and if it can be shown that the accidental non-replacement was a mistake even a reasonable employer could make, she will not succeed. But if she can make a claim under the safety legislation, she only needs to show that her employer did not replace the guard, which is much more straightforward.

Case Summary

On the other hand, there may be situations where a negligence claim will succeed where a claim for breach of statutory duty does not. This was the case in *Bux* v. *Slough Metals* (1974), where the claimant suffered an eye injury at work. The relevant statute stated that employers should provide safety goggles and the defendant had provided them, but the claimant had decided not to wear them. His claim for breach of statutory duty failed, because the defendant had done what the statute required. However, a claim for negligence succeeded, because the Court concluded that it was reasonable to expect the employer to instruct the claimant to use the goggles and to supervise him in doing so.

In practice, therefore, what usually happens is that a claimant will make a claim both in negligence and under the Act, to give themselves the best chance of succeeding.

Breach of EU legislation

Case Summary

Under the European Communities Act 1972 section 2(1), the British government has a duty to ensure that national law is consistent with EU law. If it fails to do that, it will breach that duty, and an individual who is caused loss by that failure may be able to claim damages. The rules on when an individual can claim are slightly different from those in a traditional breach of statutory duty claim, and were set down in *R* v. *Secretary of State for Transport, ex parte Factortame (No. 4)* (1996). It states that there is a right to damages where a member state fails to properly implement EU legislation, and the following three conditions apply:

- the EU law which is breached was intended to give rights to individuals;
- the breach was 'sufficiently serious'; and
- there is a direct causal link between the breach and the damage suffered.

The first and third conditions are the same kind of issues we have looked at in the claim for breach of statutory duty. The difference is in the second requirement, that the breach must be 'sufficiently serious'. In deciding this, the courts must look at whether the state has shown an obvious and serious disregard for its obligations under EU law.

Summary

- Claims for breach of statutory duty arise where a statute creates a duty, the duty is breached, and the claimant suffers harm as a result. But not all statutes which create a duty also create an individual right to sue.
- The courts generally assume there is no individual right to sue unless Parliament intended to create one. If the statute does not state a right to sue, the courts try to work out what Parliament intended by looking at factors including:
  - how precise the duty is;
  - who it is intended to benefit;
  - whether other remedies are available;
  - the background to the legislation.
- To decide whether a duty has been breached, the courts look at what the duty requires the defendant to do, and what the required degree of fault is.
- There will only be a claim for damage which is of a kind the statute was designed to prevent.
- The defences of *volenti* and contributory negligence apply.

Question and answer*

Problem: John works at a factory owned by Mega Machines Ltd as a maintenance engineer. One morning, a part in one of the machines at the factory has got jammed and John is asked to have a look at it. Safety legislation covering this type of machinery states that 'All machinery must be completely switched off before and during maintenance or repair', and states that failure to follow this rule is a criminal offence. However, the machine that John has to look at needs 10 minutes to warm up after it is completely switched off and, because they have a lot of work on, John's employer does not want to lose any more time than necessary, so he asks John to work on the machine without switching it off fully. John does not want to do this and says so, but his boss insists. As John is working on the machine, the part which was jammed suddenly frees itself, and John's hand is pulled into the machine, causing serious injuries. The legislation does not state whether there is a right to sue for breach of the duty to switch off machines before maintenance or repair.

Julia is a journalist on the local paper who is visiting the factory to write a story about a big new order the company has just won. She witnesses John's accident. She is very upset, and decides to go outside for a breath of fresh air. She pushes open a fire door, and trips over a heap of boxes that has been piled up against the door, breaking her ankle. The safety legislation covering the factory contains a section with the heading 'Fire safety', and this section has a clause stating 'Fire doors must not be blocked or obstructed at any time'. Julia later discovers that the boxes were left there by a delivery driver who was at the wrong address; nobody at the firm had seen him arrive or knew that the boxes were there.

The legislation does not state whether there is an individual right to sue for breach of any of the duties under it, nor does it provide any other remedies for breach of these duties. Advise John and Julia whether they may have a claim for breach of statutory duty.

You should allow yourself no more than 40 minutes to complete this task.

Essay: Critically examine the rules which decide whether a claimant can succeed in a claim for breach of statutory duty.

This question should be answered in 40 minutes.

* Answer guidance is provided at the end of the chapter.

Further reading

Foste, N. (2008) 'Private law and public goals: the continuing importance of the action for breach of statutory duty' (Paper presented at the Obligations IV Conference, Singapore, 23–25 July 2008), available at: (http://works.bepress.com/neil_foster/11).
This article looks at claims that the tort of breach of statutory duty is muddled and inconsistent, and argues that in fact it still has a useful role to play in the law.

Law Commission (1969) *The Interpretation of Statutes: Report by the Two Commissions*, Scot Law Com No. 11 (NC 256).
This report looks at the problems courts face when trying to interpret statutes, and make recommendations on the approach they should take. It is about statutory interpretation in general rather than specifically in breach of statutory duty cases, but still has some useful points to make regarding just how far the courts can be said to be interpreting Parliament's intentions.

Williams, G. (1960) 'The effects of penal legislation in the law of tort', 23 MLR 233.
The late Glanville Williams was one of Britain's most highly regarded legal academics, and his writing is always entertaining and easy to read. This article contrasts common law liability with breach of statutory duty in industrial injury cases and is well worth a read.

Question and answer guidance

Problem: As we saw in this chapter, a claimant for breach of statutory duty must prove three things: that there is a right to sue; that the duty was breached; and that the damage was of a kind the statute was designed to prevent. So, taking John first, work through these elements of his potential claim. Factors in favour of there being a right to sue would be that the duty is very precise, and the legislation was clearly meant to benefit employees. However, the Act does provide another remedy for breach of the duty to switch off machines, in the form of criminal liability, so you need to explain that the courts will weigh these factors against each other and try to determine whether a claim should be possible.

If John has a right to sue, he will need to establish breach. Here is it clear what the duty is, and the degree of fault is also clear: the duty is an absolute one, so merely failing to do what the statute says is enough. Finally, the statute is clearly meant to prevent workers being injured by machines, and that is the damage John has suffered. You should also consider the possibility of defences: was John partly at fault for dealing with the machine while it was not switched off, even though he knew that was dangerous, in which case contributory negligence may apply? Or could he be said to have voluntarily taken the risk, in which case *volenti* may apply? Look back at the cases on these two defences in Chapter 3, and especially the ones involving workplace situations, and apply the rules stated there to John's situation.

Turning to Julia, you need to go through the same three elements. First, is there a claim? Again, the duty is precise and there are no other remedies, but the legislation is clearly meant to benefit employees and Julia is not one. This would tend to suggest that she will not have a right to sue under the Act; you might want to mention that she would be able to sue under the Occupiers' Liability Act 1957 instead.

Even though it looks as though Julia does not have a right to sue, you should go on to discuss the other two elements. What the duty is is very clear, and so is the standard of fault; the statute simply requires that fire doors should not be blocked or obstructed, so failing to ensure this will be enough for liability. It does not matter that the company appears not to have been at fault in any way.

Finally, was the damage of a kind that the statute sought to prevent? There is an argument that it was not, since the relevant provision was in a section headed 'Fire safety', and seems to have been intended to prevent injury and damage by fire, rather than a fall. On the other hand, Julia has suffered personal injury which is what fire safety precautions seek to prevent. The cases of *Donaghey* v. *Bolton and Paul* and *Close* v. *Steel Co.* need to be considered here.

Essay: A good way to start this essay would be to explain briefly what a claim for breach of statutory duty is, and in what kinds of circumstances it might apply. Then go on to look at the basis for the courts' approach to these cases, which is that they are seeking to work out what Parliament intended, and explain some of the criticisms that can be made of this reasoning. With this in mind, work through the rules on breach of statutory duty, and discuss the cases in each area, highlighting any problems or inconsistencies – you are being asked to 'critically examine', so simply describing the rules is not enough. You will find some useful material to help you with this in the article by Williams (1960).

Chapter 12 Trespass to the person

Key points In this chapter we will be looking at:

- The three types of trespass to the person
- How they are committed
- Defences against trespass to the person
- Limitation periods

Introduction

Trespass to the person is, at first glance, quite a strange tort. It can be committed by punching or kicking someone – but also by kissing them, touching them, cutting their hair, or simply threatening to hit them, even if the threat is never carried out. A doctor who saves someone's life may commit trespass if that person did not consent to the treatment given, and a police officer can be liable for it if they detain someone without proper cause. This is because the law protects what is often called personal integrity, or more simply a right to our own personal space. It is essentially a right to be let alone by other people, and not to have our freedom of movement restricted other than for lawful reasons. Trespass protects against infringement of this right.

Clearly, in some cases a trespass may lead to physical injury – if I walk up to you and punch you on the nose, for example, that would be a form of trespass. But because the basic right that trespass protects is simply the right to be let alone, there can be a claim for trespass even if no harm is done at all. In such cases the **damages** ordered would usually be very small, and so in practice, as you can imagine, not many people would bother to sue if there was no harm done. However, there is a category of cases in which higher damages may be won even if there is no physical injury, and these are where the **defendant** is an authority of the state (often the police). In such cases, the courts may order higher damages, to reflect the fact that state authorities should not abuse their powers.

Back in the distant past, when there was no police force, a claim in trespass would have been one of the main ways of dealing with physical violence. Today, however, the majority of such incidents are dealt with as a criminal matter, and most civil claims involving personal injury are those involving negligence. As a result, trespass has come to be mostly used in cases brought against the police or other state authorities, by people who have been wrongly detained, or mishandled during an arrest. However, in recent years, there has been a new area of growth in trespass claims from adult victims of abuse that happened while they were children. This is because of a change to the **limitation period** for claims, which we will look at later.

Types of trespass to the person

There are three different types of trespass to the person:

- assault
- battery
- false imprisonment

Although they concern different types of action, one thing that all three types of trespass have in common is that they are **actionable per se** This means that there can be a claim even if the **claimant** suffers no harm or loss at all. We will look at each type of trespass in turn.

Assault

In everyday language, to assault someone means to attack them physically – punch them on the nose perhaps, or kick them. In tort law, however, that kind of action would be called battery (which we will discuss in the next section), and assault has a different meaning. In tort law, assault is defined as an act which causes the claimant reasonably to apprehend physical violence. To put it more simply, a defendant commits assault when they do something which gives the claimant a good reason to believe that the defendant is about to use violence against them. There are therefore two elements to the tort:

assault is defined as an act which causes the claimant reasonably to apprehend physical violence

- The defendant must act.
- The action must create a reasonable expectation that immediate physical violence will be used.

The defendant's action

Obvious examples of actions that could amount to an assault would be pointing a gun at someone, raising your fist at them, or picking up a brick as if to throw it at them. But what about making threats in the form of words? If someone threatens to kill you, that clearly has the potential to make you fear violence will be used, just as raising a fist at you would. Could it then amount to a trespass? In the past, it was thought that the answer was no, but now it seems likely that words can be a trespass.

The question has not been decided in a tort case, but the criminal offence of assault is defined in a very similar way, and in *R* v. *Constanza* (1997), it was held that threats made by a stalker could be a criminal assault. In fact, in the right circumstances, even silence may be a criminal assault. In *R* v. *Ireland* (1998), the defendant was charged with criminal assault after making malicious phone calls, in which he rang the victim and then stayed silent at the end of the line. The House of Lords said this could easily make a victim fear that the caller was about to appear at the door and commit violence against them, and so it could be an assault. As the definitions of the crime and tort of assault are almost identical, it is generally believed that the same rules would apply in a civil claim for assault.

Case Summary

Where someone commits a threatening act, but at the same time uses words which make it clear that the threat will not be carried out, there is no liability. In the old case of *Tuberville* v. *Savage* (1669), the claimant and the defendant had been arguing, and the defendant reached for his sword and told the claimant 'If it were not assize time, I would not take such language from you.' Assizes were regular court sessions, held by judges who travelled from place to place, hearing cases in one town and then moving on to the next. The defendant was saying that, because the judge was in town, he would not take the risk of using his sword against that claimant. This clearly meant that the defendant was in no immediate danger, so there was no assault. A more modern example might be raising your fist at someone while saying 'I'd like to punch you, but you're not worth going to prison for.'

Case Summary

A reasonable expectation of immediate violence

The threatening act (or words) must of a kind that could give the claimant good reason to believe that the defendant is about to use physical violence against them. However, the claimant does not have to prove that they actually believed the violence was about to happen, only that, in the circumstances, it was reasonable for them to believe that. In order for the belief to be reasonable, it must be (or must appear to be) possible for the defendant to carry out the threat there and then. So, for example, it will usually be an assault to raise your fist at someone who is standing right in front of you, but not to do it from a train as it speeds past someone standing by the track, or from a fifth floor window to someone standing in the street below.

Of course, both those actions might be taken to mean 'I'll get you later', but the case of *Thomas* v. *National Union of Mineworkers* (1985) established that this is not sufficient for assault. The case arose from the 1984 miners' strike, where almost 10,000 miners across the country went on strike in protest at planned mine closures. The strike, which lasted a year, caused bitter divisions between those who joined it and those who stayed at work. The claimant was one of those who refused to join the strike, and he and other non-striking miners were brought to work each day in a special bus, so that they did not have to walk through the groups of striking miners who stood on the picket line outside. As the bus drove through each morning, the striking miners made violent gestures at those inside it. The Court recognised that this must be very intimidating for the miners on the bus but pointed out that there were police officers present, and the claimant was inside the bus and so could not actually be reached by the strikers. Therefore it was not reasonable to expect immediate physical violence and there was no assault.

Case Summary

A contrasting case is *Stephens* v. *Myers* (1830), which arose from a meeting of church officials. Mr Stephens was chairing the meeting and got into an argument with Mr Myers, who was sitting six or seven places away. The other committee members decided that Mr Myers was disrupting the meeting and should be expelled. Mr Myers was furious and lurched towards Mr Stephens, threatening to pull him out of his chair. He was held back by other committee members, and so was not able to carry out his threat. However, in this case, the Court found that there was an assault. The main difference between this case and the previous case is that in the mine worker's case, there was no possibility of the strikers using force so there was no reasonable ground to fear immediate violence, whereas in *Stephens*, Mr Myers was coming towards Mr Stephens before he was held back and so it was reasonable for Mr Stephens to fear immediate violence.

Case Summary

There can be an assault where the defendant could not act on their threat, but the claimant does not know that. If, for example, you point a gun at someone, and you know it is unloaded but they do not, that would be an assault because it is clearly reasonable for them to believe you might be about to shoot them. But if they also know the gun is unloaded, then pointing it at them would not be an assault.

You be the judge

Q: Colin is watching TV one evening when he hears a noise outside. Looking out of the window, he sees a man lying on the ground and two other men kicking him. He calls the police, and as a patrol car happens to be in the next street they arrive quickly and arrest the two attackers. As the second attacker gets into the police car, he catches sight of Colin looking out of the window and realises he must have called the police. He shakes his fist at Colin and shouts 'I'm coming back for you later! I'll break your nose so you can't stick it in other's people's business!'

Does Colin have a claim for assault?

A: No. To make a claim for assault, Colin would have to show that he had a reasonable expectation of immediate violence. As the attacker was effectively in police custody at the time the threat was made, it was not possible for him to do anything to Colin there and then, so it was not reasonable to expect immediate violence. The fact that the attacker threatened to use violence at a later time is not sufficient to amount to an assault.

Battery

Battery is defined as the intentional application of direct force to another person. There are therefore three elements to consider:

- There must be force (though as we shall see, a better word for this requirement would be contact).
- The force/contact must be direct.
- The force/contact must be intended.

There must be force

Although the traditional definition of battery uses the word force, it is a slightly misleading word here because it suggests some kind of violence. In fact, any kind of direct physical contact can amount to battery, from a touch or a kiss to a punch on the nose or a vicious kick. Cutting someone's hair or their nails could count as force, as could giving someone an injection, or performing a surgical operation on them. So can throwing something at someone, or hitting someone with an object, or stabbing them, and in the old case of *Dodwell* v. *Burford* (1670) it was held that 'unseating' someone, for example by pulling their chair out from under them, counted as direct force. Case Summary

However, clearly it would be ridiculous if every touch or kiss, let alone every haircut or operation, was considered a battery, and this is not the case. To count as battery, contact must be made without the other person's consent, and must go beyond what would be considered normal, everyday behaviour. We will look at consent as a **defence** later in this chapter, but the main point to be aware of is that it can be given explicitly, such as by signing a consent form for medical treatment, or, more often, implied by our actions. When you sit in the hairdresser's chair, for example, you are clearly giving consent for the hairdresser to touch your hair, and when a boxer steps into a ring for a fight, they are giving consent for the opponent to punch and hit them, and in fact make any kind of contact that is within the rules of the sport.

The requirement that a battery must involve contact that goes beyond normal, everyday behaviour has proved a difficult one for the courts to define. The law accepts that, unless we live on a desert island, a certain amount of physical contact with others is just part of everyday life: a bit of jostling as you get on a bus, for example, or a tap on the shoulder to attract your attention. Most of us would agree that this kind of contact is normal and acceptable, whereas punching someone or shooting at them are not, and the law agrees. However, not every kind of contact falls neatly into one group or the other, and so there are cases where the law has had to try to decide what exactly makes one type of contact a battery, and another a normal part of everyday life.

Case Summary

At one time, it was considered that contact would only be a battery if it involved some kind of 'hostile intent'. This was the view of the Court of Appeal in *Wilson* v. *Pringle* (1987), which involved a scuffle between two schoolboys. The defendant jumped at the claimant and pulled his schoolbag off his shoulder, which caused the claimant to fall over and injure his hip. The defendant's lawyers argued that this was not a battery, because it was normal behaviour among schoolboys to lark around in this way, but at first instance the claimant won his case. The Court of Appeal, however, said that for the contact to have been a battery there had to have been some element of hostility. The trial judge had not considered this, so the Court of Appeal said the case had to be retried. However, the idea of a requirement for hostility was clearly problematic, because it focuses on the defendant's motive for acting. This means that, for example, an unwanted kiss might escape liability because it was meant kindly, when it has always been clear that trespass protected against that kind of invasion of personal integrity, whether well meant or not. Similarly, if hostile intent was required it would no longer be a battery to give medical treatment without consent.

Case Summary

In more recent cases, therefore, the House of Lords has held that contact can be a battery even without any hostile intent. In *Re F* v. *West Berkshire Health Authority* (1990), they had to consider the issue of doctors giving medical treatment without the patient's consent. Clearly there would be no hostile intent here, but the House of Lords held that this did not mean that treatment without consent was not battery. Lord Goff pointed out that there were also other situations which could clearly amount to battery, even though there was no hostility, such as 'a prank that gets out of hand [or] an over-friendly slap on the back'. The test, he said, was simply whether contact fell within the category of 'physical contact which is generally acceptable in the ordinary conduct of everyday life'. If it does, there is no battery.

Unfortunately this rather leaves us where we started and it now appears that, in each new factual situation, a court will have to decide whether the contact is just an expected part of everyday life, or amounts to a trespass. If you are answering a problem question which raises this issue, and the factual situation is not one that has arisen in a known case, you should explain that the courts would look at whether the contact was part of everyday life or not, and perhaps give your view on any reasons why they might come down on one side or the other, but you are not expected to know whether or not a court would judge that particular action to be a trespass or not.

Writing and drafting

Imagine that you work for the Law Commission, and you are working on a report into how the law on trespass to the person could be clarified. One of the problems you and your colleagues have identified is that there is no clear definition of what kind of contact will amount to a battery and what will simply be considered normal everyday contact. Write a short report, beginning by explaining what the law is on this question now, and why there is a problem with it. Then consider how the law could be clarified. You might, for example, want to try to produce a clearer definition of when contact should amount to a battery. Or you could list some factors which courts should take into account when deciding whether contact should be considered a battery (should the defendant's motive be a factor, for example?). Alternatively, you might want to argue that the law should be left as it is, and the courts allowed to decide on each new factual situation. What you advise is up to you, but you should be able to give reasons for your advice, and think about how it might work in practice.

Force must be direct

Battery only applies to force (or contact) that is direct. This is probably best explained with an example: if I hit you with a brick, or I throw a brick at you and it hits you, I have used direct force on you and I could be liable for battery. If, however, I leave a pile of bricks lying around and you trip over them and hurt yourself, that is indirect force and I would not be liable for battery (though I might be liable in negligence). Direct force also requires some kind of physical contact, so pushing someone back through a doorway would be a battery, but simply standing in the doorway so they could not leave would not (though as we will see later in this chapter, it could be a false imprisonment).

The reason why direct contact is required is purely historical. Trespass is a very old tort, dating back to at least the thirteenth century. At that time, to make a civil claim you needed a document known as a writ, and these could only be issued if the facts of your case fitted very tightly defined requirements. One of the requirements for what we now know as trespass to the person was a direct action, so if a person was caused injury in an indirect way there was simply no claim. So, for example, if someone rode their horse into you, you could bring a claim, but if they left their horse loose and it ran at you, you could not. This changed in 1285, when a statute allowed writs to be issued on a case-by-case basis, if the facts were similar to cases where the traditional, fixed writs had been issued. The new, case-by-case writs became known as trespass on the case, and came to include situations where the act complained of was an indirect one. The two types of writ remained separate, and the original action for trespass kept the requirement for a direct action. Trespass on the case eventually became the basis for the tort of negligence.

The reason why direct contact is required is purely historical.

You be the judge

Q: Bill and Ben are neighbours who dislike each other intensely and are always arguing. One day Ben is pruning his apple tree when Bill comes out and says that Ben should chop the whole thing down because it blocks the light from his garden. Ben picks up a large and heavy branch and throws it at Bill. It hits him, but he is not hurt. Later, Bill's wife Daisy comes out in the garden and falls over the branch, breaking her leg.

Could Bill have a claim in trespass? Could Daisy?

Source: Pearson Education Ltd/MIXA Co., Ltd

A: Bill may have a claim in trespass, because Ben's action uses direct force against Bill, there is clearly no consent for it and it is not part of normal everyday behaviour. The fact that he is not hurt does not prevent a claim, because trespass to the person is actionable per se. Daisy, however, does not have a claim in trespass, because there was no direct force used against her.

Force must be intentional

A defendant will only be liable if the force/contact was intentional or, in other words, they meant to do what they did. So if you are standing on a bus and it comes to a sudden halt, throwing you onto another passenger's lap, there will be no battery. However, if you simply went over and sat on their lap (without being invited), that would be a battery. Similarly, if someone pushes you into someone else, you will not be liable for battery because you have not acted intentionally. The person who pushed you, however, would have committed a battery.

As you already know, trespass against the person is actionable per se, which means a defendant can be liable even if no physical harm is done. Therefore, the defendant only has to intend to take the action they did. They do not have to intend to harm the claimant. Equally, the defendant does not have to intend to use force against the claimant in particular, as long as they intended take the action they did. In *Livingstone* v. *Ministry of Defence* (1984), the defendant was a soldier, who shot his gun intending to hit a rioter. He missed and hit the claimant, who was able to sue for battery because the shooting was intentional, even though it was aimed at someone else.

Case Summary

You be the judge

Q: Andy and Lou are having a fight. Lou throws a punch at Andy, but Andy ducks, and Lou hits Vicky, who has run up behind Andy to try to stop the fight.

Could Vicky have a claim in trespass?

A: Yes. Lou intended to throw the punch, so the fact that he did not intend to hit Vicky does not prevent him being liable.

Unintentional force

There is no liability for battery if the force/contact happened because the defendant was simply careless, or did not realise it was happening. In *Letang* v. *Cooper* (1965), the claimant was on holiday in Cornwall and decided to sunbathe on a patch of grass outside the hotel, which was used as a car park. When the defendant drove into the car park in his Jaguar, he failed to see the claimant lying on the ground and accidentally ran over her legs. The claimant could not successfully sue in negligence because the three-year time limit for claims had expired, so she tried instead to claim for trespass, which had a longer limitation period. The Court of Appeal held that trespass required intentional behaviour; negligent behaviour was not enough.

Case Summary

An action that starts out unintentionally can, however, become a battery if the defendant fails to stop what they are doing once they realise they are using force against someone else. This was the situation in *Fagan* v. *Metropolitan Police Commissioner* [1969]. The defendant was reversing his car along a road, when a police officer approached him and told him to pull into the kerb. When the defendant did this, the police officer said he was not close enough and told him to move again. In doing so, he accidentally stopped his car on the police officer's foot. The officer, not surprisingly, began yelling at him to move the car, but the defendant swore at him and said he could wait. He then turned off the ignition and waited for a minute or so, before starting the car again and very slowly reversing off the police officer's foot. The Court held that there was no battery when the car ran over the police officer's foot, because there was no intention. But intention was shown once the defendant knew he was on the officer's foot but refused to move immediately.

Case Summary

The requirement for intention means that trespass is usually harder to prove than negligence. This is one of the reasons why the vast majority of claims which involve physical injury are now brought in negligence, rather than trespass.

Out and about

Over the course of a day, note down every time you are touched by another person. Think about which, if any, of these events could be considered a battery, and why (or why not).

Table 12.1 Battery and negligence compared

	Battery	Negligence
Type of action	Must be direct, e.g. throwing a brick at someone, hitting someone	Can be indirect, e.g. leaving bricks for someone to trip over
State of mind	Intention: the defendant must mean to do what they do	Failing to take reasonable care to prevent foreseeable harm
Damage required?	No. Mere touching can be enough	Yes

Law in action Other sources of compensation for assault and battery

As well as the tort system, there is an alternative source of compensation for victims of assault and battery via the criminal legal system. Assault and battery are both criminal offences as well as torts, and if the person committing them is prosecuted and convicted, their victim(s) may be able to claim compensation through the Criminal Injuries Compensation Scheme.

This awards compensation, funded by the government, to people who suffer injury as a result of violent crime. The amounts awarded are usually considerably lower than what a victim might win if they sued in tort, but the claim costs the victim nothing and is available regardless of whether the defendant has any money, since the compensation does not come from them.

Victims can also be awarded compensation directly by the court that hears their case, under the Powers of Criminal Courts (Sentencing) Act 2000. In this case the compensation does come from the offender themselves.

False imprisonment

False imprisonment is defined as depriving the claimant of freedom of movement, without any lawful justification for doing so. Therefore two elements must be proved:

- The claimant's freedom was restrained.
- The restraint was unlawful.

The claimant's freedom was restrained

The name of the tort is slightly misleading here, because it is not necessary for the claimant to be 'imprisoned' in the normal sense of being locked in a room or building. Any complete restraint on someone's freedom of movement, even for a short time, can be false imprisonment. So, for example, if someone stands in your way and prevents you from leaving a building, or even a room within a building, that can be false imprisonment. This comes back to the importance of the right to be 'let alone', which we looked at earlier. Just as the tort of battery protects against any unwanted touching, false imprisonment protects against any complete restriction on freedom of movement.

Restraint must be caused by an act

Case Summary

The imprisonment must be caused by a deliberate act, and not just by carelessness. You may remember the case of *Sayers* v. *Harlow Urban District Council* (1958), which we looked at in negligence in Chapter 3, where the claimant got trapped in a public toilet due to a faulty lock and injured herself trying to escape. As an alternative to her negligence claim, she argued the council were liable for false imprisonment, but the court rejected this claim because there was no deliberate act which caused her imprisonment.

Case Summary

In *Iqbal* v. *Prison Officers Association* (2009), the Court of Appeal suggested that liability for false imprisonment would only apply where the imprisonment was caused by the defendant's act, and not where it was caused by an omission to act. The case was brought by a prisoner against prison officers who had gone on strike. Because of the strike, he was locked in his cell all day rather than being allowed out into the common areas of the prison for three hours in the morning and two in the evening, which was the usual practice. He claimed that this amounted to false imprisonment. The Court of Appeal said that this claim offended against the general principle that there is no liability in tort for a failure to act, unless there is a specific duty to act. The prison officers had a duty to comply with their employment contracts, but this duty was owed to the prison service, not to prisoners. They had not done any act which had caused his false imprisonment, but had merely omitted to do their jobs. This in itself had not caused the claimant to be stuck in his cell; the cause of that was the prison governor's decision not to let prisoners out of their cells while there were insufficient staff due to the strike. However, Lord Justice Sullivan gave a dissenting judgment which said that the prison officers' behaviour could not reasonably be described as a 'mere omission' and that it was clear that their actions caused the governor's decision to keep the prisoners in their cells, and that the officers were aware that this would happen. There are clearly strong policy elements involved in a case like this, and it seems unlikely that it would form authority for a principle that an **omission** could never result in liability for false imprisonment.

Knowledge of the detention is not necessary

Case Summary

There can be a false imprisonment even if the claimant does not know they are being detained. In *Meering* v. *Grahame-White Aviation Co. Ltd* (1920), the claimant was employed by the defendants who suspected him of stealing paint from his workplace. They summoned him to an office to question him, and unknown to him two security guards stood outside to stop him if he tried to leave. When he later found out about the guards, he sued for false imprisonment. His employers claimed they could not be liable, because as far as he knew he was free to leave the room whenever he wanted to. The Court of Appeal disagreed. They said that with the security guards posted outside, the claimant was not free to leave, and so there was an imprisonment, whether he knew it or not. In fact, they said, the tort could even be committed where a claimant was asleep or unconscious. This view may seem a little odd, but it has been approved by the House of Lords in a modern case, *Murray* v. *Ministry of Defence* (1988), the facts of which are not important here. The reasoning behind such an apparently strange rule is simply that trespass is a tort that protects the right of freedom of movement, and if that right has been compromised there can be a claim, even if no harm has been caused. However, the House of Lords pointed out in *Murray* that in cases where the claimant was not aware that they were being detained, usually only nominal damages would be awarded. This means a very small amount of money (usually around £20), which is awarded to mark the fact that the claimant's rights have been breached, even though no harm has been done.

Restraint must be complete

Case Summary

There will only a false imprisonment if the claimant was completely prevented from moving or leaving. Blocking a particular route when another is still open is not false imprisonment. In *Bird* v. *Jones* (1845), a boat race was to be held on the Thames, and the defendant fenced off one side of the footway on Hammersmith Bridge in order to charge people to watch the race from there. The claimant regularly walked along the footpath by the river, and saw no reason why he should not do so on that day as well. When he came to the enclosure, he climbed into it, intending to walk across and climb out the other side. The defendant refused to let him do this, and said he would have to go out the way he came in, cross the road and walk across the bridge on the other side. The Court said they were not liable for false imprisonment because there was an alternative route available.

This would probably only apply, however, where it was reasonable to expect someone to use the alternative route and not, for example, if the alternative route was dangerous in some way.

Conditional detention

Imagine that you are travelling on a bus. You look up and realise that you have missed your stop, and you know it is a mile till the next one. You ask the driver to stop and let you off, but they refuse and say you have to stay on the bus until the next stop. Would this be false imprisonment? The answer would seem to be no, because it is not false imprisonment to detain someone until a reasonable condition (such as waiting for an official bus stop) is met. This was established in *Robinson* v. *Balmain Ferry Co.* (1910), where the defendant was a company which ran ferries and the claimant was going to travel on one of their boats across the harbour. The ferry company had a payment point on only one side of the harbour, which meant that passengers crossing from that side paid as they went through the turnstiles into the wharf, and passengers arriving from the other side paid as they left through the turnstiles. A notice on the wall said that a penny had to be paid on entering or leaving the wharf. Mr Robinson paid his penny on the way in, but then realised he had just missed a boat and there was a 20-minute wait for the next one. Deciding not to wait, he tried to leave, but the defendants would not let him leave until he paid a penny to exit the wharf. The Court said this was not false imprisonment. On going into the wharf, the claimant had entered into a contract to leave it by boat, or pay a penny to go back through the turnstiles, and that was a reasonable condition.

Case Summary

You be the judge

Q: **Grant and Phil are at a theme park, and decide to go on the biggest and most scary roller coaster there. They pay their money and get into the first car, but by the time all the cars are full Grant and Phil are feeling a bit nervous. The ride operator starts the ride, and the cars move up to the top of the first slope. When Grant and Phil see how high it is, they are terrified and scream to the operator to bring them back down and let them off. The ride operator refuses, and continues the ride. Grant and Phil are unable to get off until it finishes.**

Do they have a claim for false imprisonment?

A: It would appear not. Just as the claimant in *Robinson* v. *Balmain Ferry Co.* contracted to leave the wharf by boat, Grant and Phil have contracted to take the ride and get off at the end of it.

The restraint must be unlawful

There is no claim for false imprisonment where someone is detained for reasons that are allowed in law. The two most common reasons for this are where someone is under arrest, and where someone is convicted of a criminal offence and sent to prison (or held on remand before they are tried). Clearly, their freedom of movement is restricted, but there is no claim for false imprisonment purely because of this, because the law accepts that there are some situations where it is lawful to restrict this right. However, the courts do look carefully to make sure that such imprisonment is within the grounds set down by law, and there may be a claim for false imprisonment if it is not.

Lawful arrests

When a person is arrested, whether by a police officer or a private citizen, there are certain rules which must be followed in order for the arrest to be lawful. The person must usually, for example, be told that they are being arrested and what for. If these rules are not followed, the arrest is unlawful, and the person arrested may have a claim for false imprisonment. On the other hand, if the rules are followed the arrest is lawful and there is no claim for false imprisonment, even if it turns out that the person arrested has done nothing wrong (the precise rules on lawful arrests are not usually studied on a tort course, but can be found in the book *English Legal System* by Catherine Elliott and Frances Quinn (Pearson 2012).

The position of prisoners

The situation of prisoners with regard to a claim of false imprisonment has caused problems for the courts in recent years. Clearly, someone who is lawfully imprisoned cannot claim for false imprisonment on the grounds that they are prevented from leaving the prison. But can there be a claim for false imprisonment based on the conditions the prisoner is kept in?

Case Summary

This issue was raised in two cases heard together by the House of Lords: *Hague* v. *Deputy Governor of Parkhurst Prison*; *Weldon* v. *Home Office* (1991). In one case, the prisoner had been moved to a different prison and kept in isolation from other prisoners, and in the other the prisoner had been placed in a strip cell. In both cases, the claimants alleged that the prison service did not have lawful authority for these changes because they were in breach of the Prison Rules 1964, which are statutory rules detailing how prisons should be run. However, the House of Lords said there was no claim for false imprisonment, because false imprisonment was an interference with personal liberty (meaning freedom), and a convicted prisoner did not have any liberty to be interfered with. However, at the same time, the House of Lords said that if a prisoner was locked in a room by another prisoner, they could have a claim for false imprisonment against that prisoner. It would also be possible to sue an individual prison officer who locked a prisoner in a cell, knowing that they had no authority to do so.

These two examples seem to undermine the reason for the decision; either a prisoner has some liberty that can be interfered with, or they do not. And if they do have some liberty, and the conditions of their imprisonment breach the Prison Rules, their imprisonment in those conditions would be unlawful, creating a false imprisonment. It therefore seems likely that the real reason for the decision was a practical one: that the House of Lords was concerned that prison governors might be swamped with claims for false imprisonment whenever the Prison Rules were broken, perhaps even in much more trivial ways than in the cases before them. While this might seem unfair on prisoners, the House of Lords pointed out that a prisoner kept in inhumane conditions could make an application for judicial review (an action brought in **public law** to assess whether an official body has acted within the law), and if they were actually injured, they could also make a claim in negligence.

Case Summary

A more difficult issue arises where, due to a mistake, a convicted criminal is kept in prison for longer than they should be. In *R* v. *Governor of Brockhill Prison, ex parte Evans* (2000), the claimant, Ms Evans, had been convicted of several different offences and was sentenced to different lengths of time in prison for them. The sentences were ordered to run concurrently (meaning at the same time, rather than one after the other). The Criminal Justice Act 1991 provides for most prisoners to be released early, after a specified proportion of their sentence has been served, and the proportion depends on how long the original sentence was. This can make it quite complicated to calculate how long a prisoner with concurrent sentences should serve and, in an earlier case, the Divisional Court had laid down a method by which this calculation should be made.

Figure 12.1 Types of trespass to the person

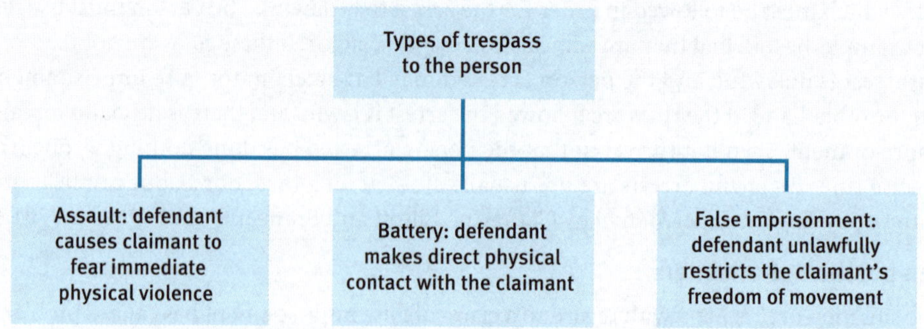

The prison governor used this to work out how long Ms Evans should be in prison, but while she was still in prison, Ms Evans went to court to challenge this method of calculating. She won that case and the Court of Appeal overruled the original decision, and stated that time spent in prison should be calculated in a different way. Calculated in this new way, Ms Evans's stay in prison should have been shorter than with the original calculation, and this meant that she should already have been released, 59 days earlier. She therefore sued the prison governor for false imprisonment during those 59 days. The House of Lords allowed her claim, even though the prison governor was following what was at the time considered to be the law, and had no lawful authority to do otherwise.

Case Summary

However, a different result was reached in the apparently similar case of *Quinland* v. *Governor of Swaledale Prison* (2002). Here the claimant had also been convicted of a number of offences, and the total of the sentences imposed for them was two years and three months. But the judge miscalculated, and said that the total was two years and six months. Fortunately someone better at maths spotted the mistake quite quickly, but the process of getting it officially corrected took some time. As a result, the claimant ended up spending six weeks longer in prison than he should have done, and sued the governor of the prison for false imprisonment during those six weeks. You might expect, given the decision in *Evans*, that the governor would be liable, but the Court of Appeal held that he was not. The Court said that in this case, it was not the governor who had made the mistake, but the court, and the governor had no authority to disobey a court order. This was undoubtedly true, but it was also true that the governor in *Evans* had no authority to calculate the claimant's time in prison other than in the way he did. Quite why the House of Lords decided otherwise is difficult to understand.

Defences

The defences which can apply in cases of trespass to the person are:

- consent;
- necessity;
- self-defence;
- statutory authority;
- lawful chastisement.

Consent

If the claimant agrees to what the defendant does, there is no trespass. In some cases consent will be given explicitly, which may be spoken or written. The most obvious example of this is that when you have an operation in hospital you will be asked to sign a consent form, to say that you agree to the planned surgery (unless the situation is an emergency and you are unconscious). In the majority of cases, though, we give consent implicitly, by our actions. If you go to the dentist for a check-up, for example, when you sit down in the chair you are implying your consent for the dentist to touch you as far as is necessary to examine your teeth.

Case Summary

An example of this defence in practice occurred in *Herd* v. *Weardale Steel Coke and Coal Co.* (1915). The claimant was a miner, who was working underground. During his shift he was asked to do some work which he considered dangerous. He refused and wanted to go back to the surface. His employers refused to let him use the lift immediately, and he had to wait 20 minutes. He sued for false imprisonment, but the court said that his employers were not liable, because by going into the mine for his shift he had consented to stay there until his shift was over.

Consent in sports

Someone who takes part in a sport consents to the kind of physical contact that is within the rules and part of the normal way the sport is played, but not to absolutely any kind of contact that may happen during the game. This means that, for example, a boxer who steps into the ring for a match cannot sue for battery just because their opponent hits them, even though this would be a battery in most other circumstances. On the other hand, if their opponent were to kiss them, without their consent, that could be a battery. Similarly, when a rugby player walks onto the pitch to take part in a match, they consent to being tackled by other players, but not to another player simply walking up and punching them on the nose.

Case Summary

In *Condon* v. *Basi* (1985), the claimant suffered a broken leg when another player tackled him in a game of football. The tackle was against the rules of the game, but it was argued that such tackles were to be expected during a match. The Court said a distinction could be drawn between contact that broke the rules but was just an error of judgement, and contact that showed a 'reckless' disregard for another player's safety. By taking part in the game, a player consented to the first kind but not the second. The claimant won, because the tackle was reckless (the case was in fact a negligence claim, but the defence applies in the same way for trespass claims).

Consent and medical treatment

Giving medical treatment which involves the application of direct force (such as an injection or an operation) without consent can be a battery, even if it is given with the best of intentions and is the right treatment for the patient. This is because, as we have seen earlier, the law recognises that we all have the right to be 'let alone' by others, and that includes the right to refuse medical treatment if we wish to.

the law recognises that we all have the right to be 'let alone' by others

Case Navigator

Case Summary

You may remember that in the negligence case of ***Chester* v. *Afshar***, which we looked at in Chapter 2, the court found that a doctor could be considered negligent where they failed to explain the full risks of surgery. In trespass, the situation is different. In *Chatterton* v. *Gerson* (1981), the defendant, a doctor, had been treating the claimant with spinal injections for a trapped nerve. She had consented to this treatment. After a while, her right leg became numb and she discovered that this was a known risk of the injections, which she had not been warned about. She sued in trespass, arguing that she could not be said to have given genuine consent when she did not know what the risks were. The Court rejected her claim. They said that as long as a doctor explains the kind of operation or treatment they plan to do, they are covered by the defence of consent, even if they do not explain all the risks involved. This effectively means that claims based on a failure to warn about potential risks will need to be brought in negligence, not trespass.

Refusal of consent

Case Summary

Where a patient is mentally competent to give their consent to medical treatment, they are entitled to refuse consent, even if that means they will suffer serious injury, or even die. In *B* v. *NHS Hospital Trust* (2002), Ms B was a 43-year-old woman, with an illness that had caused her to become completely paralysed from the neck down, and was in hospital, being kept alive by a ventilator (a machine that effectively breathes for the patient). She decided that she did not want to live any longer, and asked her doctors to switch off the ventilator that was keeping her alive. Her doctors did not want to take this step, and disagreed on whether she was mentally capable of making the decision (the illness did not affect her mind, but there were some suggestions that she might be suffering from clinical depression).

The Court was asked to decide whether, on the evidence, Ms B was mentally capable of making the decision to have the ventilator withdrawn, and if she was, whether the hospital's refusal to switch the ventilator off amounted to a trespass. The Court found that she was mentally capable, and that being the case the hospital was liable for trespass for continuing to give medical treatment, in the form of the ventilator, after they were asked to stop.

People incapable of giving consent

There are situations where a person is considered incapable of giving consent. This might be because they are in a coma after injury or illness, or are simply unconscious when medical help reaches them. In some cases, having a serious mental handicap or illness may also mean that a person is incapable of consent, but this is not always the case and the courts will look at the actual effects of the illness or handicap, using medical evidence, to see whether it does in fact mean that the person is incapable of giving meaningful consent. Where a person is judged incapable of giving consent, for any of these reasons, doctors can use the defence of necessity to give medical treatment (see below).

The limits of consent

Consent, whether explicit or implied, only applies to the specific type of contact that it was given for, and not to any other sort of contact that comes from the same person, or happens to take place at the same time. So in *Chatterton* v. *Gerson*, the case on consent to medical treatments we looked at above, the court pointed out that consent would not be a valid defence where the patient gave consent to one type of operation and the surgeon carried out a different one. If you consent to having your tonsils removed, and your tonsils are removed, you have no claim for battery. But the situation would be different if you consent to having your tonsils removed, and the surgeon takes out your appendix instead.

Case Summary

An unusual example of this principle happened in *Nash* v. *Sheen* (1953). The claimant went to the hairdressers and asked for a perm, but the hairdresser coloured her hair instead, and the colourant caused a painful skin reaction. She was able to sue for battery, because she had only consented to a perm.

Note that the issue here is not that the colourant caused harm. That was the reason why the claimant bothered to sue, but it is not the reason why she won. The reason why she won is quite simply that applying a colourant was physical contact that was not consented to, and was not something to be expected as part of normal everyday life, and that is enough to make it a battery. If the hairdresser had applied a perm as requested, and the perm had caused a skin condition, there would have been no claim for battery, because there was consent. Equally, Ms Nash would legally have had a case in battery even if the colourant had not caused a problem, although in practice most people would not bother to sue in this situation.

You be the judge

Q: Anne goes to a plastic surgeon for a facelift, and signs a consent form explaining the operation. While she is under the anaesthetic, her surgeon notices that she has a large birthmark on her shoulder and, assuming she will be pleased, removes it.

Does Anne have a case in trespass?

A: Yes. She consented to the facelift, but she did not consent to removal of the birthmark, and consent to one operation does not cover the surgeon for the other. The fact that the surgeon acted with the best of motives, and that some people might have been pleased to have the mark removed, is irrelevant.

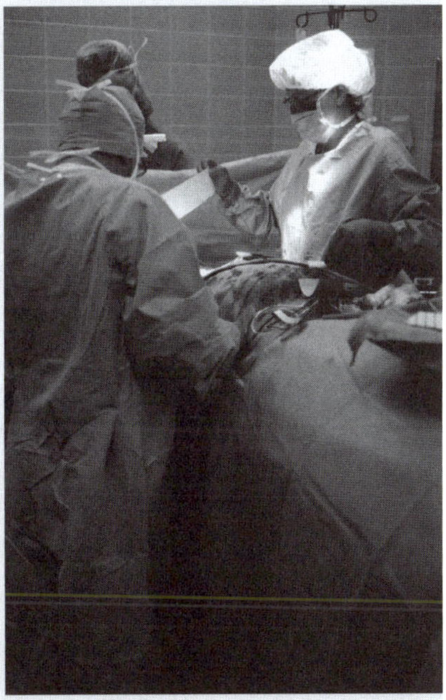

Source: Pearson Education Ltd/Photodisc

Necessity

As explained above, where a person is not competent to give consent, a doctor who gives medical treatment can use the defence of necessity instead, provided the treatment is in

Case Summary

the best interests of the patient. In *F* v. *West Berkshire Health Authority* (1990), the case concerned a 36-year-old woman, known as F in order to protect her privacy. She was severely mentally handicapped and had a mental age of about 5. She was being cared for in hospital, and was thought to have started a sexual relationship with another patient. Her mother was worried that she might become pregnant, which she believed would be a terrifying experience for her daughter. It was clear that F would be unable to use any form of contraception, and so her mother wanted to have her sterilised. The doctors wanted to make sure that they would be within the law if they did this without F's consent, and so they sought a declaration from the courts (this is an action which is brought simply to clarify what the law is on a particular matter). The House of Lords ruled that doctors would be covered by the defence of necessity where it was not practicable to communicate with the patient, and the treatment was in the patient's best interests. The test of whether the treatment was in the patient's best interests would be the ***Bolam* test**, which you may remember from negligence. The test asks whether the doctor acted in accordance with a responsible and competent body of professional opinion, or, in other words, whether other doctors, but not necessarily all doctors, would have given the treatment. In the case of *F*, the House of Lords held that the defence of necessity would apply, so the sterilisation would be lawful and not a battery (if you want to remind yourself about how the *Bolam* test works, have a look back at page 49).

Case Summary

It appears that the concept of the patient's 'best interests' need not only apply to their health. In *Re Y (Mental Incapacity: Bone Marrow Transplant)* (1996), Miss Y was a 25-year-old woman who had severe mental and physical handicaps. She was cared for in a residential home, but was regularly visited by her family and involved in important family events such as weddings. She had an older sister, who was diagnosed with a serious illness and needed a bone marrow transplant. Miss Y was found to be the best match for the transplant, but she was incapable of giving her consent to it. Her sister's doctors therefore sought a declaration on whether it would be lawful to perform the procedure without her consent. Using some fairly tortuous reasoning, the Court said that the defence of necessity would apply here. Mr Justice Connell said that Miss Y benefited from contact with her family, and especially her mother. It was clear from the evidence that she felt affection for her mother, even though she was not capable of realising that the woman who visited her was in fact her mother. He pointed out that there was a high risk of the older sister dying if the transplant did not take place, and that if this happened the effect on their mother was likely to be severe, especially as she was already in poor health herself. She would also then take on responsibility for the older daughter's young child, and these two factors would make it more difficult for her to visit Miss Y, and Miss Y would be harmed by the reduction or loss of contact with her mother. In addition, he said, the mother wanted the transplant to take place and, if it did, Miss Y's relationship with her mother would be improved. Therefore it was in Miss Y's best interests for the transplant to take place, and the defence of necessity applied.

Necessity and unborn children

The defence of necessity clearly applies to medical consent in situations where the patient cannot consent but treatment is in their best interests. But in a number of cases involving pregnant women, the courts have been asked to apply it where the woman is capable of consenting but chooses not to and treatment is in the best interests of the baby. In *Re S* (1992), the case concerned a pregnant woman, who doctors said needed to have her baby delivered by Caesarian section otherwise the child would die. The woman

Case Summary

was fully competent mentally, but refused to consent to the operation, which she said was against her religious beliefs, and her doctors sought a declaration on whether it would be lawful for them to do the Caesarian section without her consent, given that the baby's life was at stake. The Court held that the defence of necessity applied, because the baby's life was at stake.

However, in *Re MB (Medical Treatment)* (1997), the Court of Appeal said that this approach was wrong: if a pregnant patient is capable of consent to a Caesarian section but refuses it, a doctor who performs the operation will be liable for battery even if the operation is necessary to save the baby's life. However, in this case they allowed the defence of necessity to apply on the grounds that the woman was incapable of giving consent, even though she was conscious, and was not suffering from any recognised mental illness or disability. The woman had an extreme fear of needles, and although she had initially consented to a Caesarian, when she realised that it would involve needles to take blood samples and deliver the anaesthetic, she refused and said she would only have the operation if it could be done without needles. Her doctors sought a declaration that it would be lawful to do the operation, using needles where necessary, even though consent had been withdrawn. The Court found that the woman was not capable of giving valid consent. They noted that she had consented to the Caesarian, and still consented to this providing it could be done without needles. But her fear of needles was such that it dominated her thinking and made her incapable of making a rational decision. Therefore she was, at the time, suffering from an impairment to her mental powers which made her temporarily disabled and unable to consent. They said the operation was in her best interests, because she wanted a healthy child and she had accepted that a Caesarian offered the best chance of this. Therefore the defence of necessity could apply.

Case Summary

The Court of Appeal took the opportunity to confirm that the normal law on battery applies in these cases. Lady Justice Butler-Sloss said that a mentally competent patient had an absolute right to refuse medical treatment, even if doing so could lead to their own death. If that patient was a pregnant woman this rule still applied, even if the treatment was in the best interests of her unborn child, because the court could not take the child's interests into account. She commented that in several of the previous cases where Caesarians had been allowed without the woman's consent, the woman had ended up being glad at the way things had turned out, but said this fact was not relevant to the issue of whether there was a battery. However desirable it might be for the child to live, doctors could only try to persuade a woman to accept their advice; they could not lawfully go ahead and operate without her consent. The only situation in which treatment without consent was lawful was as defined in *F* v. *West Berkshire*, when the patient was incapable of giving valid consent, the treatment was necessary and doctors did no more than what was in the best interests of the patient.

Limits of the necessity defence

If there comes a point where the treatment is no longer in the patient's best interests, the defence ceases to apply. In *Airedale NHS Trust* v. *Bland* (1993), the case involved a young man, Anthony Bland, who had been seriously injured in the Hillsborough football stadium disaster that we looked at in Chapter 4. He had been crushed in the crowd, suffering severe and irreversible brain damage, and for several years had been in what the medical profession call a 'persistent vegetative state', unable to move, speak or eat, and kept alive by feeding through tubes. Doctors believed there was no hope of recovery

Case Summary

and, with the support of his parents, sought a declaration that it would be legal for them to stop feeding him through the tubes and allow him to die. The case mainly concerned whether it would be a criminal offence to withdraw treatment that was keeping someone alive, but Lord Browne-Wilkinson looked at the issue of battery as well. He said that where a patient was being given medical treatment to which they could not consent, and there came a point when it was no longer in their best interests to receive that treatment, it would be a battery to continue to give it.

Writing and drafting

You are a trainee solicitor in a high street firm. Your boss holds monthly seminars to refresh everyone's knowledge of areas of the law which they may not come across very often. This month, you have been asked to talk about the defence of necessity in trespass against the person. Prepare a short PowerPoint presentation, detailing the principles of the defence and explaining the key cases.

Reflective practice

How did you find this task? Was it easy to explain the key points? Being able to explain legal concepts to other people is a very good way to check if you have understood them yourself, so if you found this difficult you may want to read through the section thoroughly and make notes as you go. This will help you clarify the main points.

Self-defence

Despite the name, this defence applies more widely than just when a person is defending themselves. Someone who is sued for trespass against the person will have a defence if they were using reasonable force which they honestly and reasonably believed was necessary to protect themselves, or someone else, or property, or to prevent a crime. So, for example, there is no battery if someone is about to be run over and you pull them out of the way.

Reasonable force

the type and strength of force used must be balanced against the danger

How much force is 'reasonable'? This will depend on the situation, but the basic principle is that the type and strength of force used must be balanced against the danger the defendant was protecting against. So, for example, if someone is about to stab you it might be reasonable to shoot them, but it would not be reasonable to shoot someone who was about to slap you round the face. Similarly, force which might be reasonable to protect a person could be considered excessive if used to protect property.

This principle was applied in *Lane* v. *Holloway* (1968), which concerned a dispute between neighbours. Mr Lane, a retired gardener aged 64, had been drinking and got into an argument with Mr Hollway's wife, during which he called her a 'monkey-faced tart'. Hearing the argument, Mr Holloway (the defendant), who was 23, came out and said he wanted to talk to Mr Lane alone. Mr Lane hit him on the shoulder and Mr Holloway responded by punching him in the eye, causing a wound that needed 23 stitches. Mr Lane sued for battery, and Mr Holloway claimed he had been acting in self-defence. The Court rejected his defence. They accepted that he had reasonable grounds for thinking he needed to defend himself, but the force used was out of proportion to the danger and was therefore not reasonable.

Case Summary

A case where the defence did apply is *Cross* v. *Kirkby* (reported in *The Times*, 5 April 2000). Mr Kirkby was a farmer who allowed the local hunt to ride over his land when hunting foxes (this was of course before the ban on hunting). Mr Cross was among a group of hunt saboteurs who were against fox-hunting and would turn up and try to disrupt the hunt. During one hunt, Mr Kirkby tried to eject Mr Cross from his land, and in response Mr Cross jabbed him in the throat and chest with a baseball bat he was carrying and then hit him on the arm with it. Mr Kirkby grabbed the bat and hit Mr Cross with it, fracturing his skull. Mr Cross sued, and Mr Kirkby claimed he was acting in self-defence. The judge heard scientific evidence about how heavy the blow had been, which stated that it was 10 per cent heavier than a blow delivered with average force. He concluded that this amounted to excessive force, so the defence could not apply and Mr Kirkby was liable. Mr Kirkby appealed, and the Court of Appeal said the judge had not applied the right test. They recognised that in cases involving self-defence actions would often be taken in the heat of the moment, and therefore it was wrong to measure the force 'with mathematical precision'. The proper question to ask was did the defendant 'in a moment of unexpected anguish' do no more than 'what he honestly and instinctively thought was necessary?' In this case, the Court said, Mr Kirkby had only hit Mr Cross in order to bring the attack to an end, and so the defence could apply.

Case Summary

In *Ashley* v. *Chief Constable of Sussex Police* (2008), the facts of which are not important here, the House of Lords confirmed that a defendant will only be covered by self-defence if there were reasonable grounds for them to believe that they needed to use force (in other words, if a reasonable person in the same position would have thought the same). If there are no reasonable grounds, it is not enough that the defendant themselves honestly believed that there were.

Case Summary

Law in action Trespass and criminals

What happens if you wake up to find a burglar in your house, and hit them with the nearest heavy object? Or someone tries to mug you in the street, and you hit them in an attempt to stop them taking your wallet? Can they sue you for trespass to the person? This issue was addressed in section 329 of the Criminal Justice Act 2003. It provides that a person who is convicted of an imprisonable offence can only sue for trespass relating to the same incident with the permission of a court and, if permission is given, the defendant will only be liable if the force was grossly disproportionate. This is a weaker test than the normal one for self-defence, giving extra protection to victims of serious crime. The category of 'imprisonable offences' covers all serious crimes, including murder, rape, theft and burglary, and many more minor ones.

You be the judge

Q: Bill is a carpenter. He comes out of his house one morning and sees Ben trying to break into his car. He runs towards him, but Ben has already got the door open, grabs Bill's laptop, which is on the back seat, and runs away. Bill finds a heavy hammer in the toolbox he is carrying, and throws it, hitting Ben on the head.

Ben sues Bill for trespass. Does Bill have a defence?

A: Probably not. Although self-defence can apply in cases where the defendant is acting to protect property, the force used must be reasonable, and this means it must be in proportion to the harm it was seeking to prevent. It is unlikely that a court would find that the force used here was reasonable to protect property.

Statutory authority

There are a number of statutes which make it lawful to commit trespass to the person in particular circumstances. For example, the Criminal Law Act 1967 provides that no trespass is committed when a reasonable amount of force is used to lawfully arrest someone, prevent a crime or assist in the lawful detention of someone who is unlawfully at large (such as an escaped prisoner).

Lawful chastisement

The law provides that parents who exercise reasonable restraint on their children, or smack them as a punishment, have a defence against a claim for trespass to the person. However, the Children Act 2004 makes it a criminal offence to hit a child hard enough to leave a mark, and it is possible that a court might find there was no defence against a claim for battery in this circumstance.

In the past, teachers could also use the defence of lawful chastisement if they used force on a disobedient pupil, but the Education Act 1996 removed this defence.

Limitation periods

As we saw in the chapters on negligence, tort claims have to be brought within a particular period of time or the right to sue can be lost. This period is called the limitation period. Until recently, the limitation periods for negligence and trespass against the person were different. As Chapter 3 explained, negligence is covered by section 11 of the Limitation Act 1980, which provided that the normal limitation period was three years, but that the courts have discretion to extend this in suitable cases. Claims for trespass against the person, however, were covered by section 2 of the Limitation Act, which said that the limitation period was six years and could not be extended. This difference was criticised by a 2001 report from the Law Commission. They said that where a trespass against the person caused personal injury it made no sense to have completely different rules on limitation periods from those for personal injury caused by negligence.

An attempt was made to change the law in the case of *Stubbings* v. *Webb* (1993), which was brought by a woman who had been sexually abused 20 years earlier by her father and brother. Her lawyers argued that the law should be changed, because it operated unfairly in cases like hers, where the trespass had taken place when the victim was very young, and it could take years before they realised that they might have a case and summoned up the courage to sue. The House of Lords insisted at that time that the law did not allow the limitation period to be extended.

Case Summary

However, when the issue was raised again 15 years later, in *A* v. *Hoare and others* (2008), they changed their minds. In *Hoare*, the House heard six appeals together, all of them concerning sexual assaults which had taken place some years before. As you will know from studying the English legal system, a Practice Statement issued in 1966 allows the House of Lords, in appropriate cases, to change the law by not following a decision they have made in a previous case. They decided to use this power in *Hoare* and overruled *Stubbings*. The result is that cases of assault, whether sexual or otherwise, which cause personal injury (including **psychiatric injury**) are now subject to the same three-year limitation period as negligence claims, and this can be extended at a court's discretion in the same way as a negligence claim can.

Case Summary

In cases of trespass where no personal injury is caused, the limitation period is still six years, and cannot be extended. If you want to remind yourself of the rules on when a case can be extended, have a look back at page 101.

Law in action The *Hoare* case

The *Hoare* case hit the headlines in 2008, not so much because of the important change it made to the law but because the defendant, Iorworth Hoare, was already well known to the press and public. A convicted rapist, he hit the headlines when he won £7 million on the Lottery while in prison for the attempted rape of the claimant, Mrs A. The ticket had been bought while he was on day release from the prison, and there was a public outcry about the win, with many people arguing that he should not be allowed to keep the money.

Mrs A decided to sue him for trespass; this would of course have been possible at the time of the attack, but there would have been no point because Mr Hoare had little money. Under the existing time limits for trespass, her claim was too late, but as we saw above, the decision in the case changed the limitation periods on trespass in cases of deliberate assault.

However, very few newspapers reported the real legal importance of the case, which was much better represented by the other four cases heard with Mrs A's claim. These all involved claims of sexual abuse which had taken place when the (now adult) claimants were children, and they highlighted a more significant problem with the limitation periods for trespass. While it was clearly not likely that many cases like Mrs A's would occur, there were many victims of child sex abuse coming forward who had not realised that they might have a claim until long after the six-year limitation period had expired. Typically, as children they had kept silent about what was happening to them, or were not believed if they did try to expose their abusers. The abuse left them with psychiatric problems which lasted into adult life, but it was often not until they got treatment for those problems that they were made aware of the connection between the problems and the abuse. Where the claimant was a child at the time of the tort, the Limitation Act provides that limitation periods do not begin to run until they are 18 but, even so, many victims were outside the limitation period by the time they realised they might have a claim and/or summoned up courage to go to court.

Many of the claims involved abuse which had taken place in care homes or schools, and in some cases lawyers were able to present the cases as breaches of duty by the authorities running the homes or schools, and sue in negligence. This meant they could ask the courts to use their discretion to extend the limitation period. But it was very difficult to do, because lawyers essentially had to show that the authority's whole system was at fault, and this required a huge amount of investigation into how the relevant authority had worked decades earlier. And at the same time, very similar cases, involving exactly the same sort of damage, where the facts could not be squeezed to fit a negligence claim, were stuck outside the time limits for trespass. The ridiculous nature of this situation was highlighted by the case of *S* v. *W* (1995), where a woman who had been abused by her father sued him for the abuse and her mother for failing to prevent it. The abuse had happened many years before, but because her claim against her mother was in negligence, the Court used its discretion and the claim succeeded. Yet the claim against her father, who actually carried out the abuse, was in trespass so it was ruled out of time.

This situation was widely considered to be unsatisfactory and unfair on claimants, and it is in these sorts of cases that the decision in *Hoare* has really made a difference. A solicitor for one of the other claimants in *Hoare* estimated that around 6000 cases had been awaiting the result of *Hoare* and could now go ahead, and that at least the same number of victims might now be encouraged to come forward. The decision means that many more victims will get compensation, though in order to persuade a court to waive the time limit they will have to show that it is possible to have a fair hearing and that there are good reasons for the delay in bringing the claim under the normal rules of the Limitation Act (see page 101).

The other side of the situation, however, is that unlike in the case against Mr Hoare, the money will invariably come not from the abusers themselves but from local councils, who will be vicariously liable for their employees' actions. In some cases this will be paid from insurance, but not all. The irony is that calling councils to account for the past abuse of children by their employees could mean there is less money available to help protect children today. This is essentially the same problem that we looked at in Chapter 6, on negligence and public authorities: how do you provide justice for people harmed by the actions or decisions of public authorities without taking money away from the services they are there to provide?

[*Reference*: 'Lotto rapist forced to pay compensation to victim', *The Telegraph*, 31 March 2009]

Other torts that protect against physical harm

There are two other torts which are usually discussed alongside trespass to the person, because, like trespass, they are concerned with our right to be 'let alone' by other people. The first is a **common law** tort, created by the decision in *Wilkinson* v. *Downton* (1897), and the second is the statutory tort of harassment, set out in the Protection from Harassment Act 1997.

The tort in *Wilkinson* v. *Downton*

Case Summary

In *Wilkinson* v. *Downton* (1897), the claimant was a Mrs Wilkinson, who with her husband Thomas kept a pub in East London. The defendant, Mr Downton, was one of their regular customers. One day, Mr Wilkinson went to the races, leaving his wife in charge of the pub. Mr Downton, who clearly had a dubious sense of humour, decided to play what he thought was a joke on Mrs Wilkinson, and rushed into the pub saying that her husband had been seriously injured in an accident. The claimant believed him, and the shock of hearing this led her to suffer psychiatric injury later. She could not sue for assault, because she was not put in fear of immediate violence to herself, nor for battery, because there had been no physical contact. However, the judge found that there was liability in tort where someone deliberately does an act which is calculated to cause physical harm to the claimant, and physical harm is caused.

The tort has only been used in a very small number of cases since then, probably because the creation of a right to sue in negligence for psychiatric injury now covers most situations in which *Wilkinson* v. *Downton* might have been used. Some judges have doubted whether it has any place in modern law, but it has not been abolished by the courts and, as we will see, was successfully raised in a case as recently as 2006.

Elements of the tort

The elements of the tort are set out in *Wilkinson* itself, which states that it is committed where the defendant has 'wilfully done an act calculated to cause physical harm to the plaintiff [the old word for claimant] . . . and has in fact thereby caused physical harm to her'. There are therefore three elements to consider:

- a wilful act;
- physical harm must be caused;
- the act must be calculated to cause physical harm.

The tort is different from trespass against the person because the act can be indirect, and is also different from negligence because it covers intentional acts. It can therefore be seen as falling somewhere between the two.

A wilful act

'Wilful' here simply means deliberate: something the defendant meant to do rather than something that happened accidentally. It is clear from *Wilkinson* itself that words can be enough, and words were also the act complained of in *Janvier* v. *Sweeney* (1919). The claimant was engaged to a German man. The defendants wanted her to steal a letter from her employer, and they threatened that unless she did so they would tell the authorities that her fiancé was a spy. This was untrue, but coming just after the end of the First World War, when anti-German feelings were running high, it must have seemed quite likely that the authorities would put him in prison as a spy anyway. The claimant was very frightened, and she suffered a psychiatric injury as a result of the worry. The Court of Appeal held that the defendants were liable under *Wilkinson* v. *Downton*.

Case Summary

In *C* v. *D* (2006), a schoolboy claimed that his headmaster had made indecent films of him. Because the headmaster had not actually touched him, it was not possible to make a claim for battery, but he succeeded in a claim under *Wilkinson* v. *Downton*.

Case Summary

Physical harm must be caused

In *Wilkinson* itself, Mrs Wilkinson suffered both physical and psychiatric injuries, but in *Janvier*, it was accepted that 'physical harm' could comprise psychiatric injury alone. However, the tort does not allow a claim for anything less than a recognised physical or psychiatric injury. In *Wong* v. *Parkside Health NHS Trust* (2003), an employee tried to sue under *Wilkinson* v. *Downton* after suffering a campaign of harassment from three fellow workers, which caused her great distress. Lady Justice Hale said that the required damage in *Wilkinson* was 'physical harm or recognised psychiatric illness', and there could not be a claim for 'distress, inconvenience or discomfort'. This was confirmed by the House of Lords in *Wainwright* v. *Home Office* (2002), which is discussed in the next section.

Case Summary

The act must be calculated to cause physical harm

In ordinary language, this phrase seems to suggest that the defendant must have intended or meant to cause harm to the claimant. This seems at odds with the facts of *Wilkinson* itself. Mr Downton obviously made the 'joke' intentionally, but there was no evidence that in doing so he intended to make Mrs Wilkinson ill. The judge in the case, however, stated that what Mr Downton did was so likely to cause harm to Mrs Wilkinson that it was possible to 'impute' intention to him (in other words, to assume he had the intention). This was explained rather more clearly in *Wong* v. *Parkside Health NHS Trust*, the case mentioned above where an employee said she had suffered a campaign of harassment from three fellow workers. Lady Justice Hale said that:

Case Summary

> The conduct complained of has to be such that [physical or psychiatric injury] is sufficiently likely to result that the defendant cannot be heard to say that he did not 'mean' it to do so. He is taken to have meant it to do so by the combination of the likelihood of such harm being suffered as a result of his behaviour, and his deliberately engaging in that behaviour. In other words, it is not necessary to look inside the defendant's head and see whether they meant to cause harm. If they deliberately do something which is obviously very likely to cause harm, the necessary intention can be assumed.

Case Navigator

Case Summary

In ***Wainwright* v. *Home Office*** (2002), the House of Lords confirmed that the intention required is an intention to cause physical or psychiatric harm, and not just an intention to do the thing that, as it turned out, did cause the harm. Mrs Wainwright and her son Alan, who had learning difficulties, had gone to visit Mrs Wainwright's other son, Patrick, in prison. The prison had been having problems with visitors smuggling in drugs, and as part of their procedures to prevent this prison officers insisted that the Wainwrights had to take off their clothes, in separate rooms, and be searched. The Wainwrights found this procedure humiliating and upsetting, and a psychiatrist later diagnosed Alan as having post-traumatic stress disorder as a result of the experience. Mrs Wainwright did not have a recognised psychiatric injury, but said she had suffered emotional distress. They sued the Home Office, which was responsible for the Prison Service, claiming that the search was in breach of their right to privacy under the Human Rights Act 1998 (this claim is discussed at page 449) or, alternatively, that the Home Office was liable under the tort in *Wilkinson* v. *Downton* because the prison officers' actions were intended to cause distress and humiliation. The House of Lords held that there was no claim for anything less than an intention to cause psychiatric or physical injury. That being the case, Lord Hoffmann doubted whether the tort had much of a role to play in modern law, because if there was actual physical injury it would usually be easier to prove negligence than intention.

Out and about

Have a look at the case of *Wainwright* v. *Home Office*, and read the parts relating to a claim under *Wilkinson* v. *Downton*. What were the main arguments that the House of Lords used to deny the Wainwrights' claim? Do you find these arguments convincing? What arguments would you have made if you had been acting for the Wainwrights? Do you think they should have had a claim under *Wilkinson* v. *Downton*?

Statutory harassment

This tort was created by the Protection from Harassment Act 1997. Section 1 of the Act creates a criminal offence of harassment, and section 3 provides that someone who is the victim of this offence can sue in tort, which effectively means that the requirements of the criminal offence and the tort are the same. A claimant who sues under the Act may be able to claim damages for physical injury, mental distress and **economic loss**, and/or an **injunction** to prevent the harassment from happening again. Section 1 of the Act states that harassment is committed by pursuing a course of conduct which amounts to harassment, where the harasser knows or ought to know that it amounts to harassment. A 'course of conduct' is defined as behaviour that takes place on at least two occasions.

Harassment

The Act was passed primarily to deal with the problem of stalking

The Act does not define harassment, though it does say that it includes alarming someone or causing them distress, and that speech can be sufficient. The Act was passed primarily to deal with the problem of stalking, and this kind of behaviour clearly falls within the definition of harassment, but it has also been interpreted to cover other types of aggressive or hostile behaviour. In *Singh* v. *Bhakar* (2006), the claimant took part in an arranged marriage and the couple then lived with her husband's parents. Her mother-in-law treated her like a slave, making her do so much housework that her hands became infected. She also restricted the claimant's contact with her own family, made her cut her hair, which was against her religious beliefs, and forced her to wear a symbol of a different religion. After four months, the claimant left, by which time she was suffering from depression. She successfully sued for harassment.

Case Summary

In *Thomas* v. *News Group Newspapers Ltd* (2001), the case arose from an incident involving a Somali asylum seeker, who had called at a police station to ask for directions to an asylum centre in Croydon. The claimant, Ms Thomas, was a clerk at the police station, and later on she heard one of the police sergeants who had been at the front desk joking about the incident. She claimed that he said 'She found her way here 8,000 miles from Somalia, surely she can find her way back?' (which was denied by the sergeant, who said that he had in fact remarked 'She found her way here 8,000 miles from Somalia, surely she can find her way to Croydon?'). Ms Thomas felt the remark was racist and made a complaint about it. As a result, the sergeant was put in a less important job. *The Sun* newspaper got hold of the story, and ran a series of articles criticising the decision to demote the sergeant for what the paper viewed as a harmless joke that was not even heard by the asylum seeker. They identified Ms Thomas as the source of the complaint and pointed out that she was black. She began receiving racist hate mail, which left her too frightened to go to work. She sued the newspaper under the Protection from Harassment Act. The newspaper applied to have the action struck out, but the Court of Appeal held that the claimant had an arguable case and that the publication of articles in the press could amount to harassment.

Case Summary

In *Howlett* v. *Holding* (2006), the claimant, Ms Howlett, had been a local councillor, and as part of her duties had heard an application for planning permission from the defendant, Mr Holding. The application was refused and Mr Holding was so furious about this that he began a campaign against Ms Howlett, following her into shops and restaurants, and even flying a small plane over her home with a banner alleging that she

Case Summary

was a thief and unfit to hold public office. Ms Howlett sued for harassment and was granted an injunction.

Case Summary

In *Conn* v. *Sunderland* (2007), the case concerned two incidents which happened in the claimant's workplace. In the first, the claimant's foreman lost his temper and threatened to smash a window with his fist and report the claimant and two colleagues to the human resources department. Evidence was given that the two other men present were not really bothered by any of this. On the second occasion, the foreman threatened to give the claimant 'a good hiding' and said he did not care if he got the sack as a result. The claimant sued for harassment, and the Court said that it was necessary to consider whether the foreman's behaviour was serious enough to amount to the criminal offence of harassment under the Protection from Harassment Act. A defendant's behaviour might be unattractive or even unreasonable, but if it was not serious enough to justify a criminal prosecution there was no liability in tort under the Act either. In this case, the court found that the first incident was not serious enough to justify punishment as a crime. This meant that there was only one incident to consider, and that was not enough to amount to a course of conduct, so the claim failed. The Court did not consider whether the second incident amounted to harassment.

A new section 1(1A) was added to the Act under the Serious Organised Crime and Police Act 2005, designed to deal with animal rights campaigners who harass the employers and suppliers of firms involved in animal testing. It extends the Act to cover a course of conduct involving harassment of two or more people, by which the harasser intends to persuade someone not to do something they are entitled or required to do, or to do something they are not under any legal obligation to do.

Defences

Section 1(3) provides three defences. There is no claim for harassment where the defendant's behaviour:

- was for the purpose of preventing or detecting crime;
- was done to comply with the law;
- was reasonable in the circumstances.

In *Thomas* v. *News Group*, the case involving the police clerk, the racist joke and the *Sun* newspaper, the Court of Appeal suggested that the paper's coverage might be reasonable in the circumstances if the court found it to be a legitimate exercise of their right to freedom of expression under the Human Rights Act. The court would need to balance this right against the claimant's right to freedom from harassment.

Harassment at work

Case Summary

The case of *Majrowski* v. *Guy's* (2006) has widened the potential use of tort claims under the Protection from Harassment Act, because it establishes that an employer can be vicariously liable when their employees are subject to harassment from colleagues. The claimant in the case was bullied by his manager, and sued the hospital trust which employed them both, claiming that it was vicariously liable for her actions. The House of Lords confirmed that it was possible to impose vicarious liability for harassment by an employee, provided that the harassment was found to be within the course of their employement, under the normal rules on **vicarious liability.** You may remember from

Chapter 7 that employees who suffer stress at work can only sue their employers in negligence if the stress causes a recognisable psychiatric injury, and they have to meet strict requirements concerning how much the employer knew and/or did about the situation. Where the stress is caused by colleagues, it will be much easier to sue under the Protection from Harassment Act, because all that is required is a course of conduct amounting to harassment, and that the employer is liable under the usual rules of vicarious liability.

Law in action Stalkers

The Protection from Harassment Act was created in response to the problem of stalking, after a number of high-profile cases in which individuals became obsessed with someone else, and subjected them to constant and often long-term harassment. Although often associated with celebrities and obsessive fans, by the mid-1990s it was recognised that it had become a serious problem for ordinary individuals, targeted by ex-boyfriends or girlfriends, or even acquaintances who formed an obsession with them: from 1992 to 1997, one anti-stalking campaign group got more than 10,000 calls to its helpline. One of the victims who campaigned for the Act, Tracey Morgan, was stalked for eight years by a work colleague she had befriended, who followed her, phoned her, and even broke into her house and bugged it.

The civil claim added by the Act made it easier for victims to protect themselves, because they could seek an injunction to keep a stalker away. Before the Act was passed, they would usually have had to wait for the police to prosecute, which would only happen once there was enough evidence to make it likely that they could prove the case beyond reasonable doubt (and not necessarily even then). To get an injunction, the victim only has to prove their case on the usual civil standard, a **balance of probabilities**. Further protection is given by the fact that the Act also makes it a specific criminal offence to breach an injunction made under the Act.

In recent years the Act has been used against a different form of stalking, that of celebrities by paparazzi photographers. Cheryl Cole, Sienna Miller and Lily Allen have all used the Act to get injunctions against photographers, who had waited outside their homes, chased them in cars and on foot, and behaved in an intimidating way in order to get photographs of them looking upset or distressed.

Summary

- Trespass against the person protects the right of personal integrity or 'personal space'. There are three types:
  - assault
  - battery
  - false imprisonment

- They are all actionable per se, meaning a claim can arise even where the claimant suffers no harm or loss.

- Assault is committed where the defendant's action gives the claimant reasonable cause to expect immediate violence against them. The defendant's action can be a physical act, words, or even silence. It must be reasonable for the claimant to believe that the defendant could use immediate violence against them.

- Battery is committed by the intentional application of direct force to another person. 'Force' means any kind of contact that is not part of normal everyday life, and is not consented to. The force/contact must be direct, and the defendant must intend the action they take, but they need not intend to harm the claimant.
- False imprisonment is committed by unlawfully restricting someone else's freedom of movement. The claimant need not be locked up, and the tort can take place outside as well as in. There is no claim where the defendant has a lawful reason for restricting the claimant.
- There are five defences:
  - consent
  - necessity
  - self-defence
  - statutory authority
  - parental authority
- Trepass to the person which causes personal injury has a limitation period of three years, which can be extended at a court's discretion. Other cases have a limitation period of six years, which cannot be extended.
- The tort in *Wilkinson* v. *Downton* is committed by deliberately doing an act which causes physical harm, and was intended to do so. Intention can be inferred if the defendant deliberately does something which is very likely to cause harm.
- The tort of harassment under the Protection from Harassment Act 1997 is committed by a course of conduct that amounts to harassment, on at least two occasions.

Question and answer*

Problem: Gordon and Alistair are neighbours, who arrive home at the same time one evening. Gordon has just been to collect a Chinese takeaway and takes the last available parking space in the street. As they both get out of their cars, a furious Alistair raises his fist at Gordon, saying 'I'm not going to hit you this time, mate, but if you pinch my space again, you'll be sorry!' Gordon throws a box of special fried rice at Alistair. The rice hits Alistair, and Gordon runs indoors.

The following morning, Gordon is working in his garden shed when Alistair climbs over the garden fence and locks him in. Gordon has the radio on and does not hear the key turn, and because he is busy sharpening his collection of saws, he does not realise he has been locked in until his wife Sarah comes to call him for lunch and unlocks the door. There is a window in the shed, which would have been large enough for Gordon to climb through if he had broken it.

Sarah is very angry, and decides to go next door and tell Alistair what she thinks of him. As she leaves the house, she slips on a banana skin that Alistair has deliberately left on Gordon and Sarah's doorstep and hurts her leg.

Advise Gordon, Alistair and Sarah as to whether any of them have a claim in trespass.

You should allow yourself no more than 40 minutes to complete this task.

Essay: How far does the tort of trespass to the person protect people from unwanted interference with their personal integrity?

This question should be answered in 40 minutes.

* Answer guidance is provided at the end of the chapter.

Further reading

Cane, P. (2000) '*Mens rea* in tort law', 20(4) OJLS 533.
This article looks at the role of intention in tort law, and considers why it has such a relatively small role to play compared with its use in criminal law.

Conaghan, J. (1996) 'Gendered harms and the law of tort: remedying (sexual) harassment', 16 OJLS 407.
This article looks at the law on trespass to the person from a feminist perspective, and argues that it is inadequate to deal with problems specific to women, such as sexual harassment. The material here would give you an unusual and interesting angle to take in a question on problems with the law on trespass.

Trindade, F. (1982) 'Intentional torts: some thoughts on assault and battery', 2 OJLS 211.
This article takes a very detailed look at the law on assault and battery, and contains some very good and clear explanations of tricky concepts, such as the difference between direct and indirect force.

Question and answer guidance

Problem: Taking Gordon first, the first potential claim here is assault as Alistair has threatened him with violence. However, a claimant must reasonably expect immediate violence, and that is not the case here because Alistair's words make it clear he does not intend to do anything there and then; the case of *Tuberville* is relevant in this point.

Gordon might, however, be able to sue Alistair for false imprisonment. You will need to consider the cases on claimants who are imprisoned without their knowledge and who have an alternative means of exit.

Turning to Alistair, does he have a claim for battery arising from Gordon throwing the rice at him? As well as working through the requirements of the tort, you should consider whether Gordon might be able to plead self-defence.

Finally, does Sarah have a claim in trespass against Alistair? We know that he has acted intentionally, but it would seem that her claim cannot succeed because the force used was indirect. She may have a claim in negligence.

Essay: A good way to start this essay would be to explain what interference with personal integrity means. You could then work through some of the elements of the tort that highlight just how important the law considers this right to be: the fact that trespass is actionable per se, that contact need not be hostile, and that there can be false imprisonment even if the claimant does not know about it are all examples of this, and you should illustrate the points you make with relevant cases. To give the essay balance, you should also mention some of the restrictions on the protection the tort gives; the defence of necessity would be one example of this.

Visit **www.mylawchamber.co.uk/quinntort** to access tools to help you develop and test your knowledge of tort law, including practice exam questions with guidance, annotated weblinks, glossary and key case flashcards, legal newsfeed and legal updates and interactive 'You be the judge' questions.

premium mylawchamber
unrivalled support for legal education

Use Case Navigator to read in full some of the key cases referenced in this chapter with commentary and questions:

Chester* v. *Afshar [2004] 4 All ER 587
Wainwright* v. *Home Office [2003] 4 All ER 969

CASE NAVIGATOR POWERED BY LexisNexis

Chapter 13
Trespass to land

Key points In this chapter we will be looking at:

- How trespass to land is committed
- The defences to trespass to land
- The remedies for trespass to land

Introduction

In Chapter 12 we looked at the tort of trespass to the person which, as you will remember, can be committed by doing a wide variety of different things, from kissing someone to hitting them. This, as we saw, is because the law recognises that we all have a right to be 'let alone' by other people and not to have to accept unwanted physical contact, however harmless it may seem. The tort we are going to look at in this chapter, trespass to land, is based on a similar idea, except that instead of protecting against interference with our bodies it protects against interference with land. The basis of the tort is that we all have the right to keep other people and things off our land, whether or not they cause any physical harm. So, for example, if your neighbour throws a load of rubbish over into your garden, or builds a wall that is on the wrong side of the boundary between you, you may have a claim in trespass. Similarly, if someone comes into your house without your permission, trespass may give you a claim against them.

Liability for trespass to land

A **claimant** in trespass to land must show four things:

- the claim involves land;
- the land must be in the claimant's possession;
- the defendant must have interfered with the land in some way;
- the interference must be direct. This is a similar principle to the one we came across in trespass to the person, where the force or contact had to be direct.

As with trespass to the person, trespass to land is **actionable per se**, which means that there is no need for the claimant to have suffered any damage as a result of the interference. In most cases of trespass, what the claimant will be looking for is an **injunction** to stop the trespass going on. However, if the trespass has already caused some form of damage or loss, a claimant can get **damages** for that.

What counts as land?

Trespass does not apply only to land in the sense of the earth we stand on, but also to anything that is permanently attached to the surface, so a house or even just a wall would count, but not a mobile caravan. It also covers crops growing on land and anything under land. This means that, for example, someone who tunnelled under your land could be liable for trespass, even if neither end of the tunnel was on your land.

Trespass also applies to the amount of airspace above the land which is needed for the normal use and enjoyment of the land. In *Anchor Brewhouse Developments* v. *Berkley House (Docklands) Developments* (1987), the **defendants** were operating tall tower cranes. Although the cranes were on their own land, the arms of the cranes occasionally swung out over the airspace above the claimants' land. The defendants were held liable for trespass. Similarly, in *Kelsen* v. *Imperial Tobacco* (1957), the claimant successfully sued for trespass after the defendants put up an advertising sign which projected over the claimant's land by about eight inches.

Case Summary

Does that mean you could sue for aircraft flying over your land? In the vast majority of cases the answer is no. Aircraft are covered by the Civil Aviation Act 1982, which provides that there is no trespass where civilian aircraft fly over property at a height that is reasonable, given the wind, weather and all the circumstances of the case. In *Bernstein* v. *Skyviews* (1978), the defendants ran a business taking aerial photographs of homes, and selling them to the homeowners. The claimant objected to photos being taken of his house, and sued for trespass. The Court held that the defendants were protected by the Civil Aviation Act, and the fact that they were taking photographs did not alter this. But even without the Act, the Court said, there would be no trespass because the plane had flown at a height which did not affect the claimant's use of his land.

Case Summary

Land in the claimant's possession

In many cases, a claimant in trespass will be the owner of the land. However, the law also allows a claim by someone who is not the owner but who has what is called immediate and exclusive possession of the land. This is a term used in land law, which essentially means that the claimant has a legal right to be on the land, at the relevant time, and has the right to exclude others from it. For the purposes of this chapter, we can say that trespass therefore gives owners and tenants the right to sue, but not, for example, guests or lodgers.

Interference

We saw in Chapter 12 that in the tort of trespass to the person, interference with the person could be anything from a punch on the nose to a kiss. The definition of interference for trespass to land is similarly wide, and can include any of the following:

- wrongfully entering land;
- abusing a right of entry;
- remaining on land without permission;
- placing things on land.

trespass can be committed by any crossing of the boundary to someone else's property

Wrongfully entering land

This clearly covers walking or driving on to someone's land, or entering their house without permission, so includes things like walking across someone's garden without permission. However, the case of *Ellis* v. *Loftus Iron Co.* (1874) provides that trespass can be committed by any crossing of the boundary to someone else's property, however slight. For example, if you were to stand on the pavement outside someone's house and put your hand through the window, that could be a trespass, and so could putting just one foot on someone else's land.

Abusing a right of entry

A person can commit trespass if they have permission to enter land but, after entering, they go somewhere which is not included in the permission they have been given. For example, a student living in a hall of residence has implied permission to walk through the halls and corridors, go into shared kitchens and bathrooms, and their own room. But if they were to go into another student's room without permission, that would be trespass. Similarly, a shopper has implied permission to wander up and down the aisles of a supermarket, but not to go through a door marked 'Staff only'.

Abuse of right of entry also applies where someone has been allowed on to land for one purpose and, while there, they do something which is outside that purpose. For example, if you allowed a decorator into your home to paint the kitchen, and they decided to go and have a look round the bedrooms without asking you, that would be trespass. Remember that trespass is actionable per se, so just entering places where they do not have permission to be is enough to make someone liable; they do not have to do any damage while there.

Remaining on land without permission

If someone is given permission to enter land, but is then asked to leave, remaining on the land is trespass. Similarly, someone who is allowed to be on land for a certain length of time will be trespassing if they stay, without permission, once that time is up. For example, if you visit a museum, you would usually have permission to be there during normal opening hours, but if you hid and stayed there after the museum closed, that would be trespass, even though you had permission to come in.

Placing things on land

Trespass can be committed by throwing or placing something on land, which would include, for example, parking a vehicle on private land, or dropping rubbish over someone's fence. It can also cover allowing animals to stray on to someone else's land. Where trespass is committed by things on land, rather than people entering it, there is no need for boundaries to be crossed. It can be enough, for example, to plant a vine so that it grows up the defendant's wall, to pile rubbish against their fence, or to lean a bike against their shop window.

Where something is put and left on land, both the initial action and leaving the thing there are trespass, so the person in possession of the land has a continuing claim for the entire time that the thing is left there. In *Holmes* v. *Wilson* (1839), the defendants needed to support a road, and to do so they put supports on the claimant's land without getting permission. The claimant successfully sued, but the defendants did not remove the supports. The claimant sued again but, as we saw earlier, all torts have time limits after which it becomes too late to make a claim. By the time the claimant sued the second time, the time limit for a claim arising at the point when the defendants actually placed the supports there had passed, and they argued the claim was out of time. The Court disagreed: they held that this was a case of continuing trespass, and that meant that a claim existed for as long as the supports were still on the land.

Case Summary

You be the judge

Q: In which of these situations might the person described be liable for trespass?

1. **Barry is desperate to meet his favourite pop star, Tina Marina, but is unable to get tickets for her tour. Before the tour starts, a much less popular star, Jenna Marenna, is playing at the same venue; Barry gets tickets for her last show, and then finds a place to hide and camp out until Tina Marina and her entourage arrive the next day.**
2. **Shelley has an old mattress that she wants to get rid of. She can't be bothered to take it to the local tip, so she waits until after dark and then throws it into the garden of a neighbour who she knows is away on holiday.**
3. **Kate is a plumber. She is asked to install a washing machine in a customer's kitchen while the customer is out. Kate is very nosy and after finishing the job, she takes a look around the rooms upstairs, though she is very careful not to touch or disturb anything.**

Source: Pearson Education Ltd/Photodisc/Photolink

A: All three could be liable. Buying a ticket to the Jenny Marenna concert gave Barry permission to enter and be at the venue, but that permission ended once the concert was over. Shelley may be liable because she has put something on someone else's land; it does not matter that she has not set foot on the land herself. Kate could be liable because although she had permission to be in the house, that permission would only cover areas she needed to go into for the purpose for which permission was given, which was installing the washing machine.

Boundary disputes

One of the types of trespass that lawyers see most often arises from boundary disputes between neighbours. Let's say that Fred lives next door to Wilma, and she puts up a new garden fence between their two gardens. Fred believes that the fence is not on the boundary between their two gardens but a half a metre over into his garden. As we saw in the previous section, trespass can be committed by putting something on someone else's land so, if Fred is right about where the boundary lies, Wilma is trespassing on his land. In this situation, Fred may bring a case in trespass, and part of the judgment will include determining where the boundary should actually be.

Boundary disputes are a very common source of friction between neighbours and, as the Law in Action box shows, they can easily get out of hand.

Law in action Fence row couple 'lose everything'

As any high street solicitor will tell you, boundary disputes – and the legal costs that come with them – can grow out of all proportion to the size of the piece of land that the parties are fighting over. In 2009, the *Manchester Evening News* reported on the case of Mary Kendrick and John Edwards, who were faced with legal costs of tens of thousands of pounds after suing their neighbours, Stephen and Barbara Evans, over the position of a fence between their gardens.

The two sets of neighbours had been arguing over the issue since 2003, when Mr and Mrs Evans put up a fence which Ms Kendrick and Mr Edwards believed encroached onto their land by a small distance. After three years of arguing, in 2006, while their neighbours were on holiday, Ms Kendrick and Mr Edwards pulled the fence down. Ms Kendrick gave evidence that she thought doing this would 'provoke constructive discussions' about where the correct boundary between the gardens was. Mr and Mrs Evans didn't quite see it that way, and instead sued their neighbours. Despite efforts to settle, the case came to court, and the judge ruled that the fence was in the correct position, and that removing it had been unlawful. He ordered Ms Kendrick and Mr Edwards to pay for the fence to be rebuilt, and to pay nominal damages to Mr and Mrs Evans. However, he also ruled that Ms Kendrick and Mr Edwards should pay most of the legal costs of the case, which amounted to tens of thousands of pounds. The couple appealed against the costs judgment, and Ms Kendrick told the court that having to pay the costs would mean the couple 'lost everything', but although the judge expressed sympathy for them, the order was upheld.

[*Reference*: **http://menmedia.co.uk/manchestereveningnews/news/s/1093135_fence_row_couple_lose_everything**]

Interference must be direct

You may remember that in Chapter 12 we came across the rule that in trespass to the person the force used must be direct, so hitting someone with a brick could be trespass to the person but leaving a brick lying around so that they trip over it would not be. A similar distinction applies in trespass to land, where the interference with the land must be direct. Let's imagine that you live next door to someone who has a huge rose bush growing next to your fence. If they prune the roses, and throw all the branches into your garden, that would be a direct interference with your land,

the interference with the land must be direct

because the interference arises directly from their action. However, if your neighbour simply allowed the tree branches to grow over the fence and onto your land, that would be an indirect interference, and trespass would not apply. Where there is an indirect interference with land, there will often be a claim in nuisance, which we will look at in the next chapter.

A case which illustrates the distinction between direct and indirect interference is *Esso Petroleum* v. *Southport Corp* (1956). An oil tanker owned by the defendants ran aground and, in order to save the ship and the crew, the captain discharged large quantities of oil into the sea. Because of the movement of the tide at that time, the oil was swept onto the shore, polluting the claimants' land. The House of Lords held that this was not direct interference, so there was no trespass. As Lord Denning pointed out, the situation would have been different if the oil had been discharged directly onto the shore, because that would have been a direct interference.

Case Summary

Out and about

The concept of direct and indirect interference is an important one to understand, and the best way to fix it in your head is through the use of examples. For this task, try to think up 10 examples of direct interference with land, and 10 examples of indirect interference. You can take them from everyday life or, if you prefer, make them as unusual and quirky as you like – whatever you think will best help you to remember and understand the concept.

Trespass on highways

Most trespass cases concern private land, but it is also possible to trespass on public streets (usually referred to by the courts as 'the highway'). Traditionally, it was held that anyone using the highway for anything other than getting from one place to another could be trespassing. In *Hickman* v. *Maisey* (1900), the claimant owned land on which racehorses were trained. A road went across the land and the defendant, who owned a newspaper about racing, stood there watching the horses and making notes about how they were performing, so that he could write about their chances of winning races. He was found liable for trespass, because he was using the highway for something other than its proper purpose.

Case Summary

However, in *DPP* v. *Jones* (1999), the House of Lords introduced a less strict approach. The case was actually a criminal one, but it is relevant to tort because the defendants were charged with trespassory assembly under the Public Order Act 1986, and to be guilty of that offence a defendant has to have committed the tort of trespass. The defendants in the case had staged a demonstration at the side of the road beside the fence around Stonehenge. None of them had behaved in a destructive or violent way, and nobody else using the road was obstructed by them being there. Even so, the traditional view would have been that they were trespassing, because they were using the highway for something other than its ordinary purpose.

Case Summary

However, Lord Irvine said that the test for trespass on the highway was whether the defendant was using the highway for a reasonable purpose, without unreasonably obstructing people using the highway to pass by. If they were, there was no trespass. The case therefore makes clear that there is a right to do more than just pass along the highway, but what else that right includes was not decided. Lord Irvine said that in each case, it is for the trial court to decide whether the defendant's use of the highway was reasonable.

This means that if a similar case to *Hickman* were to come to court today, it may or may not be decided differently; the result would depend on whether the court thought the defendant's behaviour was reasonable.

Trespass by relation

At one time, the courts in trespass cases favoured a person who was actually in possession of land over one who had the legal right to take possession. This meant that if an owner of land was not actually in possession of land at the time a trespass happened, they had no remedy against the trespasser. The unfairness this could cause was remedied by a principle called trespass by relation. This provides that a person who has the legal right to take immediate possession of land, and who goes on to the land in order to exercise that right, is treated as though they were in possession of the land from the moment that the right to take possession existed. This means that they can sue for any trespass which occurred from that time, even if they were not actually in possession of the land.

Trespass *ab initio*

The principle of trespass *ab initio* is a very old one. It was traditionally held to mean that where someone enters land under a right granted by statute or **common law** (rather than just with the permission of the person in possession of the land), and they then do something which is an abuse of their authority, they are regarded as having been a trespasser from the moment of entry.

Case Summary

This doctrine was first defined in the *Six Carpenters Case* (1610), where the defendants went into an inn, which they were legally entitled to do, and then had some food and drink but refused to pay for it. The Court said that a wrongful act committed after lawful entry onto someone's premises could make the original entry a trespass. However, in this case the carpenters were not liable, because there had to be a wrongful act, and their refusal to pay was an **omission** to do something, not an act.

Case Summary

In *Cinnamond* v. *British Airports Authority* (1980), the defendants sued a group of six taxi drivers who had been hanging about at the airport and touting for customers. The reason why the airport authority wanted to stop this was that the airport had an official taxi rank, where fares were regulated, and the defendants were catching passengers before they got to the rank, then charging them ridiculously high fares, and in some cases refusing to give them their luggage out of the boot unless they paid up. The drivers usually got access to the airport by dropping off a passenger there, and then hanging about to see if they could pick up departing passengers. Lord Denning said that it was lawful for them to enter the airport to drop off passengers, but that they had no legal right to loiter about in the hope of picking up passengers. This was therefore a wrongful act, so trespass *ab initio* applied, and they became trespassers from the time they entered the airport.

Trespass *ab initio* and the police

As you will know if you have studied an English Legal System course, statute law gives the police a number of powers to enter people's premises without their permission. A strict application of the principle of trespass *ab initio* would mean that if, for example, police did something during a search that was not within their authority, everything else they had done during the search would also become illegal, which could mean that evidence obtained could not be used in court. However, modern cases have weakened the rule in these cases, holding that partial abuse of authority does not necessarily make everything else done during the search unlawful. In *Elias* v. *Pasmore* (1934), police officers wanted to arrest a man, and had entered the claimant's premises in order to do so. While there, they took a number of items: they had lawful authority to take some of them, but not all. It was held that they had committed trespass only with regard to the items unlawfully removed, and so their wrongful act did not mean the arrest itself was unlawful. A similar approach was taken in *Chic Fashions (West Wales) Ltd* v. *Jones* (1968), where the police searched the claimants' premises and took goods which they mistakenly believed to be stolen. This was held to be lawful, because police entering premises with a warrant have authority to remove anything which they believe has been stolen, and the Court of Appeal criticised the whole doctrine of trespass *ab initio*, saying the lawfulness of an act should be judged by whether it was lawful at the time it was carried out, not in the light of later events. It was at one time considered that this judgment meant that trespass *ab initio* was no longer good law. However, the judge who made the criticism, Lord Denning, was the very same judge who applied trespass *ab initio* in the later case of *Cinnamond* v. *British Airports Authority*, so it appears that the less strict approach may only apply in cases involving the police.

Case Summary

Law in action Squatters and the law

An obvious example of trespass occurs where squatters occupy an empty house belonging to someone else. There are no official statistics on the number of squatters, but the charity Shelter estimated in 2002 that there were at least 20,000 people squatting in the UK at any one time. People often assume that squatting must be a criminal offence, but in fact it is usually viewed by the law as a civil dispute between the owner of the property and someone who is trespassing on it. This means that if property is empty and squatters move in, the owner cannot use force to get into it if the squatters want to keep them out. Instead, the property owner has to apply for a court order to get the property back, as the film director Guy Ritchie discovered when he was forced to go to court in 2011 to evict squatters who moved into his £6 million house while it was being renovated. This can take weeks or even months and usually costs at least £1,500. However, once a court order has been issued, squatters who refuse to leave will be committing a crime.

Different rules apply if the owner was living in the property and squatters got in while they were away temporarily. In that case, the squatters would be committing a crime, and the issue can be dealt with by the police. This also applies if the owner was about to move into the property, for example where a house has been sold but there has been a gap between the previous owner moving out and the new one planning to move in. These laws were introduced specifically to protect anyone made homeless by squatters.

The term 'squatters' rights' refers to a doctrine of land law called 'adverse possession', which provides that if someone stays on someone else's land (or in their property) for at least 10 years, without the owner's permission, they can take ownership of the property. This tends to arise mostly with regard to pieces of land on the border between two neighbours – for example, if your garden fence has been 2 feet further over onto your neighbour's land than it should be for over 12 years, it may be possible to claim adverse possession of that strip of land. It can apply in squatting cases, and there have been cases of squatters being able to take over quite valuable properties, but this is rare, as property owners can usually take steps to evict squatters well within the 10-year period.

At the time of publication, the government had suggested that it might consider new laws to make squatting in any private property a crime, as is the case in Scotland. Supporters of the move argue that the lawful owner of a property should not have to suffer the distress, inconvenience and cost of going to court to evict squatters, who are taking something that does not belong to them. However, opponents argue that the vast majority of squatters are occupying properties that are derelict anyway, and that sufficient legal help already exists to help homeowners who actually live in or are about to live in the occupied property. They say that the new law would simply criminalise people who are already vulnerable, and that the government would do better to address the issues of homelessness and properties left standing empty.

The mental element

To be liable for trespass, the defendant must have intended to do the action that amounted to the trespass. In most cases of trespass this is quite clear, because of the need for a direct action. If I throw rocks on your land, for example, or if I climb in through your window, clearly I intended to do those things.

However, although the action itself must be intentional, the defendant does not have to have intended to commit a trespass, or to know that what they did would be a trespass.

You be the judge

Source: Pearson Education Ltd/Photodisc/Photolink/Kent Knudson

Q: In which of these situations might the person described be liable for trespass?

1. **Jashu and Jenny are out walking in the countryside when they get lost. In an attempt to find their way back to their car they take a short cut through a wood, not realising that it is private land belonging to Brian.**
2. **Theresa is staying at a small hotel where the guests share a bathroom. She gets up to go to the toilet in the night, but on the way back to her room she misreads the number on a door and goes into a different room instead.**
3. **John is trimming a very tall tree beside the fence which divides his garden from his neighbour's. He stretches up to reach the highest branch, loses his footing and falls into the garden next door.**

A: Jashu and Jenny may be liable because they intentionally enter Brian's land, even though they do not realise it is private. Theresa could also be liable: although she has permission to be in the hotel, that would only cover her room and any communal areas and, again, although she is acting by mistake, she intends to enter the other room. John, however, would not be liable because he does not enter the garden intentionally.

Nor do they need to have any intention to cause problems for the claimant, or have any kind of hostile purpose. Let's say, for example, that you have permission to enter a friend's garden shed to get a bike that they've offered to lend you. By mistake, you go into their next door neighbour's shed instead. That would be a trespass, because you intentionally walked into the shed, even though you did not intend to trespass because you thought it was somewhere you had permission to be. Similarly, if you were out walking in the countryside and wandered on to private land because you were lost, you would still be committing trespass because by putting one foot in front of the other and walking on to the land, you acted intentionally. By contrast, if someone pushes you on to land, or throws you there, you would not be committing trespass because you did not intend to enter.

Defences

There are three **defences** to a claim in trespass:

- licence;
- justification by law;
- necessity.

Licence

Licence essentially means permission to be on the land. Where the person in possession of the land gives someone permission for someone to be on the land, there is no trespass, even if the person with permission interferes with the land in some way, as long as they are acting within the permission they were given.

Permission can be express, meaning that someone actually tells you you have permission either verbally or in writing, or it can be implied, meaning that in the circumstances it was reasonable to assume you had permission. We looked at the circumstances when implied permission can arise in Chapter 9, on occupiers' liability, and the principles explained there also apply here.

Justification by law

Acts which would usually be a trespass will not be if they are committed in circumstances protected by the law. An example is that police officers can enter people's houses, which would usually be a trespass, if they are acting under powers given under legislation such as the Police and Criminal Evidence Act 1984, which gives them the power to enter and search a property in order to make an arrest.

Necessity

This defence applies where the defendant can show that it was necessary to enter the land. This will only apply where the necessity was a serious one, such as a need to help

Case Summary

someone in danger, to prevent a danger, or to prevent serious harm to property. An example occurred in *Cope* v. *Sharpe* (1912). The defendant was a gamekeeper, and when fire broke out on neighbouring land he was worried that it would spread to a part of his employer's land where the pheasants he was rearing nested. He went on to the neighbour's land and burnt away an area of heather, to prevent the fire from spreading. When he was sued for trespass, the Court held that he was covered by the defence of necessity because he had done what was reasonably necessary in the circumstances.

Case Summary

Necessity might also apply where the defendant is acting to protect the community in general. In *Rigby* v. *Chief Constable of Northamptonshire* (1985), the defendant successfully pleaded necessity after causing a fire by releasing CS gas into the claimant's shop, in order to try to catch a dangerous criminal who was in there.

Case Summary

However, in general, the courts are very reluctant to allow use of this defence, and it will only apply where the danger is so immediate that it can be classed as an emergency and the defendant's actions are reasonable in all the circumstances. In *Southwark Council* v. *Williams* (1971), squatters argued that it was necessary for them to occupy an empty house because they had nowhere else to go. The Court rejected this argument, and Lord Denning stated that:

> If homelessness were once admitted as a defence to trespass, no one's house would be safe. Necessity would open a door which no man could shut. It would not only be those in extreme need who would enter. There would be others who would imagine that they were in need, or invent a need, so as to gain entry.

Case Summary

A similarly restrictive approach was taken in *Monsanto* v. *Tilly* (1999). The claimants, Monsanto, are a large multinational firm which has been at the forefront of developing genetically modified food. As part of this process, they were growing genetically modified crops on test sites throughout the UK. The defendant was a member of a pressure group which considers genetically modified crops to be harmful to the environment and to public safety, and they conducted a campaign in which they entered sites where the plants were growing and uprooted part of the crop. They were sued for trespass, and claimed that they were covered by the defence of necessity because their actions were essential to protect public health and the environment. The Court of Appeal rejected this argument. They recognised that there might be circumstances where it was necessary to pull up a whole crop in order to protect others, but in this case it was clear that pulling up the crop was a symbolic gesture, designed to attract publicity to the defendants' campaign. The situation was not an emergency, and if the defendants wanted to change government policy on the issue they should do so through lawful means.

Writing and drafting

Read the case of *Monsanto* v. *Tilly* (1999). Now list, in point form, the arguments made in favour of allowing the defence of necessity in this case, and the arguments made against allowing the defence. Which arguments do you find most convincing? Why? Are there any that you find unconvincing? Why? Are there any other arguments you think should have been made on either side?

Reflective practice

Did you find it easy to pick out the arguments made in the case? Were there some arguments that were easier to follow than others? Did you feel that all the arguments were valid, even if you might have agreed more with one side than the other? Being able to identify and use the arguments made in previous cases is an essential skill for any lawyer who appears in court, so repeating this task again with other cases that you come across is very good practice.

Figure 13.1 Liability for trespass to land

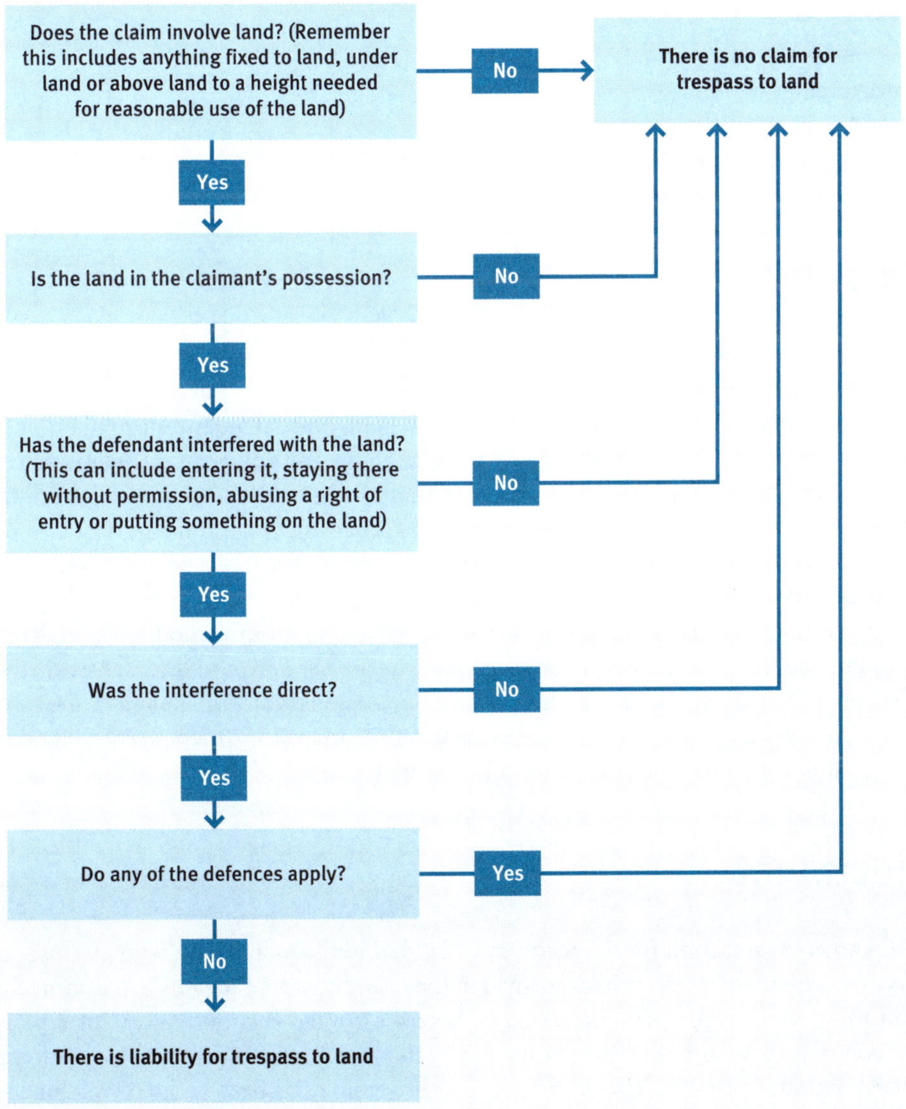

Remedies

There are two main remedies for trespass: injunctions and damages. As you know, an injunction is a court order which can be used to stop someone doing something, so if there is a continuing trespass, such as a garden fence in the wrong place, the claimant will usually be seeking an injunction to stop it. Damages may also be awarded where a trespass is continuing, or has happened in the past. If the trespass has caused harm, the damages will be calculated to compensate for this, but damages can still be ordered if no harm was done, in order to mark the fact that the claimant's rights were breached. In this situation the damages ordered are usually what are called nominal damages, meaning that they are very low because there is no real harm to comepensate for.

damages can still be ordered if no harm was done

There are also four other remedies which may be available in a trespass claim:

- re-entry;
- ejectment;
- mesne profits;
- distress damage feasant.

Re-entry

Case Summary

If a trespasser is on the defendant's land, and refusing to allow them in, the defendant can use reasonable force to enter the land. In *Hemmings* v. *Stoke Poges Golf Club* (1920), the claimant rented a cottage on the defendants' land. The defendants gave them notice to quit (a legal procedure that brings a tenancy to an end), but the claimants refused to leave. The defendants went into the cottage and removed the claimants' furniture, and when the claimants still refused to go they picked them up and carried them out. The defendants were not liable in trespass because they had used no more force than was necessary.

However, the courts are keen to prevent people taking the law into their own hands, and someone who uses excessive force against a trespasser may find themselves sued for trespass to the person. There are also statutory provisions which make it a crime to use or threaten violence in order to take possession of premises, which were designed to prevent unscrupulous landlords from mistreating tenants.

Ejectment

Also known as an action for the recovery of land, this allows a person who has lost possession of their land to get it back, provided they can show that they have an immediate right to possession. An example would be where a homeowner goes away for a period and comes back to find that their home has been taken over by squatters. In an attempt to deal with this problem, a special summary procedure has been created which allows the claimant quickly to obtain an order for possession against anyone who has occupied their land without permission.

Mesne profits

This is a claim for financial loss which the claimant has suffered through not being in possession of their land. It can include damages for wear and tear on the land or premises, for the costs of regaining possession, for any lost profits where the land or premises would usually generate an income, or for a reasonable rent. In *Inverugie Investments Ltd* v. *Hackett* (1995), the claimant had been the tenant of an apartment complex, and the defendants had ejected them unlawfully. During the time that this went on, they had run the complex, but had only managed to let out around 40 per cent of the apartments. When the claimant successfully sued for trespass, the House of Lords held that the defendant should pay damages amounting to a reasonable rent for all the apartments, not just the ones they had managed to let out.

Case Summary

Distress damage feasant

Where an object is placed or left unlawfully on the claimant's land and causes damage, the claimant can keep it until the damage is paid for. So if, for example, you kick a football into your neighbour's garden and it smashes a window, they are entitled to keep the ball until you pay for the damage to the window.

Trespass and the criminal law

It is quite common to see signs on land saying 'Trespassers will be prosecuted', but in fact these are meaningless as trespass is not a criminal offence. There is, however, an exception to this rule under the Criminal Justice and Public Order Act 1994, which introduces an offence of collective trespass aimed at preventing squatters, raves and unlawful protests.

Another example of a situation where the tort of trespass is sometimes made to look like a crime is where someone parks on private land, as the Law in Action box explains.

Law in action Trespass and parking

If you park your car on private land you may be issued with a 'ticket' that suggests you are being fined for parking illegally. Although this usually looks and sounds like the same kind of ticket you get when you park illegally on a public road (on a double yellow line, for example), in law it is not the same at all. Parking illegally on a public road is a crime and you can be fined for it. Parking on private land, however, is not a crime but a case of trespass, so the owner of the land has no right to 'fine' you for it. Legally, therefore, the 'ticket' is not a fine but a notice that they intend to take you to court, and are offering you the chance to pay the stated sum instead of going through court proceedings. This means that if you consider the sum to be unreasonable, you are quite within your rights to offer a smaller sum instead. It is then up to the landowner to decide whether to accept your offer, or take you to court.

Summary

- Trespass to land protects against interference with land.
- Land includes buildings and fixed structures, but not temporary ones.
- A claim can be made by anyone in possession of the land concerned.
- Interference with land can include entering it without permission, putting or leaving things on it, entering parts of it not covered by permission, or staying after permission has expired.
- The interference must be direct.
- The action which amounts to interference must be intentional, but an intention to trespass is not required.
- There are three defences: licence, justification by law, and necessity.

Question and answer*

Problem:

Cava is a model who recently won a TV reality show, and is rumoured to be dating a married Premier League footballer. She decides to spend her winnings on doing up her house, and employs Jake, a builder, to install a new kitchen. While Jake is working on the kitchen, Cava decides to go out shopping, leaving him alone in the house. Jake decides to have a look in her bedroom, to see if he can see any evidence of Cava's relationship with the footballer that he might be able to sell to a newspaper. He finds nothing, however, and is just coming back downstairs, without having touched or disturbed anything, when Cava walks in the front door and sees him.

Cava has come back early from her shopping trip because as soon as she got outside the door, she saw Ken, a press photographer, who was waiting in the street to take a picture of her. He was standing by her fence so as to get a good shot, and when he saw Cava he leaned so far over the fence that he fell into her front garden, crushing her favourite plants.

Thoroughly fed up, Cava decides to go and sit in the back garden and top up her tan. But when she gets out there, she finds that her next door neighbour, Carrie, is having a barbecue and so much smoke is drifting across her garden that she is forced to go back indoors.

Advise Cava as to any claims for trespass to land that she may have against Jake, Ken or Carrie.

You should allow yourself no more than 40 minutes to complete this task.

Essay:

'The tort of trespass to land protects the rights of private landowners at the expense of wider benefits to society.'

How far is this statement true?

This question should be answered in 40 minutes.

* Answer guidance is provided at the end of the chapter.

Further reading

Harlow, C. (2005) *Understanding Tort Law*, 3rd edn, Ch. 5, London: Sweet & Maxwell.

An interesting look at the development of the tort of trespass to land, and the ways the courts have used the law in different types of case.

Question and answer guidance

Problem: As always, you should take each potential claim mentioned in turn, so let's start with Cava's possible claim against Jake. Jake clearly has permission to be in the house to do the work on the kitchen, but does this permission cover him going upstairs? If not, that is trespass, and he can be liable, regardless of the fact that he did no damage and touched nothing.

In the case of Ken, we can reasonably assume that he does not have permission to be in Cava's garden. In terms of his fall into the garden, it can be argued that he did not have the necessary intention for trespass because he did not deliberately enter the land, but fell into it. However, he may still be liable, because he was already trespassing when he leaned over the hedge – remember that just putting your hand through someone's window can be trespass, and this is similar. This means, however, that he will not have to pay damages for destroying Cava's plants, because that was a result of the fall which was unintentional.

Finally, what about Cava's potential claim against Carrie? Here, there is no direct interference with land, the smoke is just drifting across, so there is no claim in trespass. However, there may be a claim in nuisance, if Cava can show that the smoke was an unreasonable interference with her use of her garden. As exam questions often combine two or more different torts, you may find it useful to come back to this question after you have read the next chapter, which deals with nuisance.

Essay: A good way to start this essay would be by explaining what the tort of trespass seeks to protect, explaining that it gives a right not to allow other people to enter or put things on land that is not theirs. You could then point out that this necessarily means that private rights are considered important, but that decided cases show that their protection is not absolute.

One initial thing to mention is that trespass to land does not apply only to landowners but to anyone in possession of land. Without going into the intricacies of land law, you can therefore point out that the tort does not protect ownership but possession of land, so it applies equally to the tenant of a rented bedsit in the same way as it does to the owner of a country estate.

You should then look at areas of the tort where the rights of the claimant come into conflict with wider social benefits. An obvious example is those cases where the defence of necessity arises, and through a critical discussion of *Cope* v. *Sharpe*, *Rigby* v. *Chief Constable of Northamptonshire*, *Southwark* v. *Williams* and *Monsanto* v. *Tilly*, you can explain how the courts have balanced the rights of a trespass claimant against arguments that trespassers have been acting for a wider social benefit. You might want to say whether you think the right balance has been struck, but remember to use arguments drawn from the cases rather than simply expressing your own opinions about issues like homelessness or GM foods.

Another issue to consider would be the cases on trespass on the highway, where you can point out the way in which the case of *DPP* v. *Jones* altered the balance between the rights of trespass claimants and the rights of people using the highway for peaceful protest.

You could also include a brief discussion of *Cinnamond* v. *BAA*, where upholding the rights of a landowner carried wider social benefits with it, in that it helped prevent unlicensed taxi drivers from cheating customers.

Finish with a conclusion that sums up what you have said, and indicates how far you think, based on the cases you have discussed, that the law's protection of landowners (and people in possession of land) is at the expense of wider social benefits.

Chapter 14
Nuisance

Key points In this chapter we will be looking at:

- ✦ How nuisance is committed
- ✦ Who can sue and be sued for nuisance
- ✦ Defences in nuisance
- ✦ Remedies in nuisance

Introduction

Let's imagine that you are a keen trumpet player, and you like to practise your trumpet whenever you feel like it. Your neighbour, however, is not a fan of trumpet music. Or at least not yours. She can hear whenever you practice, and she complains that you are disturbing her. Your view on the matter might be something like 'This is my home, and I'm entitled to play my trumpet in it whenever I like.' Her view, on the other hand, would be 'And this is my home, and I'm entitled to peace and quiet in it.' Whose right should win? This is the kind of question which the law of nuisance is designed to answer.

The principle behind nuisance law is that since we all have to coexist together, there must be give and take. We may have to put up with situations which we do not like very much, so long as they represent a reasonable balance between our rights and those of our neighbours. But where a situation goes beyond this reasonable balance, nuisance can offer a remedy. As well as disputes between neighbouring households, as in our trumpet example, it covers a wide variety of situations, from people affected by smells and fumes from factories, to homeowners bothered by aircraft noise, and buildings collapsing due to conditions on neighbouring land.

The form of nuisance which we are about to look at, and which takes up most of this chapter, is more specifically known as private nuisance. There are two other forms of nuisance, public and statutory, which we'll look at briefly at the end of this chapter.

Liability for nuisance

Nuisance is a tort that protects a claimant's right to peaceful enjoyment of their land; in other words, it protects the right not to be disturbed unreasonably by someone else. A **claimant** in nuisance must prove three things:

- ✦ there was an interference with their enjoyment of their land;
- ✦ that this interference was unreasonable; and
- ✦ that the interference caused damage to the claimant.

In addition to these three elements, the law of nuisance also includes rules about who can sue and who can be sued, which essentially depend on the parties' relationship to the land in question.

Interference with enjoyment

The law accepts that we all have a right to 'enjoyment' of the place where we live or run a business, and this basically means a right to some degree of protection against anything coming on to the land, or into a building on the land, and making life unpleasant. Obvious examples would be smells, noise, smoke, fumes or floods, but nuisance also covers invasion by more solid objects, such as tree roots or overhanging branches.

A situation that actually causes physical damage, such as a flood which damages property, will clearly amount to interference with enjoyment, but a claim can also be successful if the situation caused by the **defendant** does no physical damage but makes life seriously unpleasant or difficult for the claimant. In *Wheeler* v. *Saunders* (1995), for example, the claimant received **damages** for smells caused by their neighbour's pig farm, while in *Sturges* v. *Bridgman* (1879), a doctor successfully sued his neighbour over noise which disturbed him and his patients, and in *Schwab* v. *Costaki* (1956), the Court of Appeal allowed a claim for the emotional distress caused to neighbours of a brothel.

Case Summary

However, there are limits to the rights of enjoyment that the law will protect. There is no claim in nuisance for interference with what the law calls 'recreational facilities', such as an attractive view. This led to the perhaps surprising decision (at least to those of us who are television addicts) in ***Hunter* v. *Canary Wharf*** (1995). The claimants in the case were people living near a huge tower block which had been newly built in London's Docklands area. The building was so high that it interfered with their television reception, but the Court of Appeal ruled that this was not sufficient interference with the enjoyment of their land to allow a claim in nuisance.

Case Summary

Case Navigator

The kinds of interference that form the basis of a claim in nuisance are usually indirect. We looked at the difference between direct and indirect interference in the previous chapter on trespass, and the same sort of distinction applies here. Whereas trespass covers direct interference, such as walking on to land or throwing something on to it, nuisance claims arise from things that happen as a result of conditions or activities on the defendant's land, rather than things that the defendant actively does. So smoke or leaks of water would fall within the law of nuisance, but throwing or pouring something onto a neighbour's land would not.

Interference in nuisance also usually arises from a continuing situation rather than a one-off incident, although in *Crown River Cruises* v. *Kimbolton Fireworks* (1996), it was accepted that a one-off fireworks display could amount to a nuisance.

Case Summary

Continuing a nuisance

In many cases the nuisance will arise from a situation that the defendant has caused, such as the smell from a factory or smoke from frequent bonfires. But a defendant can also be liable for a situation which they have not caused but which arises naturally on their land and causes interference with neighbouring land. However, this will only apply if they were aware of the natural occurrence and failed to take reasonable precautions to stop it interfering with neighbouring land. This is called continuing the nuisance. An

Case Summary

example of continuing the nuisance was found in *Leakey* v. *National Trust* (1980). The defendants occupied land on which there was a large mound of earth known as Burrow Mump. After one very hot summer, they became aware that the area could be affected by landslides because the earth had become very dry, but they took no precautions against this. Sure enough a landslide happened, and it cast a large amount of earth and tree roots onto neighbouring land owned by the claimant. The defendants refused to remove this debris. The Court held that they were liable in nuisance, even though they had not actually caused the problem but only failed to prevent it. However, in situations like this, where a nuisance was not actually caused by the defendant, the Court said when deciding what the defendant should have done to deal with the problem it was reasonable to take into account the defendant's financial position, the seriousness of the risk and how far it was practical to take precautions. Lord Wilberforce stated that 'The standard ought to be to require of the occupier what is reasonable to expect of him in his individual circumstances.' Where the risk was serious, the relevant precautions were simple and/or inexpensive, and the defendant could afford to take those precautions, they might have a duty to do so. But where the risk was less serious, the precautions more difficult and/or expensive, and the defendant not well-off, there might be only a duty to share the cost with the neighbours, or even just to warn them and allow them to take the necessary precautions.

Case Summary

This principle was applied in *Holbeck Hall* v. *Scarborough Borough Council* (2000). The claimants were owners of a hotel that collapsed as a result of a landslip on neighbouring land owned by the council. The council had not caused the landslip, but they knew there was a risk of it happening because landslips had happened there before. However, these had been quite minor, and the council were not aware that a more serious landslip could occur and do such a lot of damage to the hotel. They could not have found this out without doing very expensive investigations. The Court of Appeal held that the council were not liable because they had not created the danger and they did not know it could cause such serious damage. They were not expected to have paid for expensive tests to find out what the risk was.

You be the judge

Q: Jeremy owns a large country estate on which there is a lake, one side of which borders land owned by Tarquin. The lake is naturally quite shallow, and when there is very heavy rain it tends to overflow and flood the surrounding land, including Tarquin's part. Jeremy knows this, and he has considered having some work done on the banks of the lake, but he has discovered this would cost £1,000. Jeremy could easily afford to pay this, but as he isn't using his part of the land around the lake he decides not to bother.

Can Tarquin sue Jeremy in nuisance?

A: Yes. Although Jeremy has not continued the nuisance, he was aware of it and failed to take what appear to be reasonable precautions to stop it affecting Tarquin's land.

Source: Pearson Education Ltd/Imagestate/John Foxx Collection

The interference must be unreasonable

As explained earlier, nuisance cases are a balancing act. The law accepts that as we all have to live together there must be give and take, and it acknowledges that a situation that affects one person's right to use their land as they wish to may simply be the result of their neighbour's right to do the same. In order to strike the balance between these competing rights, nuisance law uses the concept of unreasonableness. It looks at all the circumstances of the case, and only allows a claim for nuisance if, in those circumstances, the interference is considered to be unreasonable.

A good example of the way this works is *Southwark London Borough Council* v. *Mills* (1999). Here the council had converted a house into flats, and Mrs Mills lived in one of them. She sued the council, claiming that the building was poorly soundproofed and she was disturbed by noise from the other flats. The House of Lords held that the noise was perfectly normal for a residential building, and there was nothing unusual about the way the building had been converted that made it more noisy than any other apartment block. Therefore the interference with her enjoyment of her property was not unreasonable, and there was no nuisance.

Case Summary

When deciding whether the interference is unreasonable, the courts will take into account all the circumstances, but over the years they have identified the following factors as especially relevant:

- seriousness;
- locality;
- sensitivity;
- malice;
- the type of damage caused.

Seriousness

This category includes factors concerning the intensity of the interference, such as how loud the noise is, or how unpleasant the smells are. The courts will also look at how often the interference happens, how long it lasts, and when it happens. The more frequently an interference happens and the longer it lasts, the more likely it is to be unreasonable, and things that happen at particularly unsuitable times, such as noise at night, are also more likely to be considered unreasonable.

Most nuisance cases arise from situations that are ongoing, sometimes over very long periods, but even a short period can be enough if the interference is sufficiently intense. So, for example, in *Crown River Cruises* v. *Kimbolton Fireworks* (mentioned earlier), it was held that a 20-minute firework display could amount to nuisance, because for the whole 20 minutes sparks from the fireworks were falling onto the neighbouring property, which caused a fire.

Case Summary

In *Kennaway* v. *Thompson*, a case we will look at later in this chapter, Lord Lawton explained how the seriousness of an interference should be assessed:

> Nearly all of us living in these islands have to put up with a certain amount of annoyance from our neighbours. Those living in towns may be irritated by their neighbours' noisy radios or incompetent playing of musical instruments; and they in turn may be inconvenienced by the noise caused by our guests slamming car doors and chattering after a

late night party. Even in the country the lowing of a sick cow or the early morning crowing of a farmyard cock may interfere with sleep and comfort. Intervention by injunction is only justified when the irritating noise causes inconvenience beyond what other occupiers in the neighbourhood can be expected to bear.

Locality

Case Summary

Interference that would be considered reasonable in one type of area may be considered unreasonable in another. For example, a claimant in the centre of a big city cannot expect the same level of peace and quiet as someone living in the heart of the country, while animal smells are more likely to be considered unreasonable in a town than they would be in the countryside. In *Sturges* v. *Bridgman* (1879), the claimant was a doctor, who had his consulting rooms in a quiet area, where most of the other buildings were also occupied by doctors' offices. The defendant was a sweet-maker, who used heavy machinery, and the doctor held that the noise from the machines was a nuisance. The Court agreed, saying that in such a normally quiet area the noise was a nuisance, though it might not have been if it had been in a more industrial area.

Case Summary

The courts accept that the character of a particular place can change over time. This was the case in *Gillingham Borough Council* v. *Medway (Chatham) Dock Co.* (1993). The defendant company had built docks which were in use 24 hours a day. The only access to the docks was through a residential area, and this caused the residents problems with traffic noise. The council sued to try to get the traffic restricted at night, but the Court held that the fact that planning permission had been granted for the docks suggested that the character of the area had changed, from having once been primarily residential to now being mainly commercial. It found that traffic noise which might have been unreasonable when the area was mainly residential was not, however, unreasonable for a commercial area. Nevertheless, the Court stated that the fact that planning permission had been granted for an activity would not always mean that that activity could not give rise to a claim in nuisance.

Case Summary

This principle was applied in *Wheeler* v. *Saunders* (1995). The defendants had obtained planning permission to build two pig sheds, and this meant that strong smells from the pigs drifted across on to the claimant's land. The Court of Appeal confirmed that planning permission would only prevent a claim in nuisance if it meant that the character of the area had changed. In that case, it did not have this effect and so the claim could succeed.

Sensitivity

Case Summary

Traditionally, it was thought that interference would not be considered unreasonable if it causes a problem only because the claimant, or the claimant's situation, is unusually sensitive. In *Robinson* v. *Kilvert* (1889), the claimant occupied the ground floor of the defendant's premises, using it to store paper. The defendant's business, which was carried on in the basement of the same building, was making boxes. The way that these were made needed a hot, dry atmosphere, so the defendant installed a heater. This caused hot air to pass up through cracks in the floor to the claimant's workshop, and this began causing damage to one quite delicate kind of paper that he stored there. The heat was not, however, enough to cause problems for his workers, or to damage any ordinary kind of paper. He sued in nuisance, but the Court held that an interference was not unreasonable if it caused damage only to something which was exceptionally delicate. It would have been unreasonable only if it had caused problems with ordinary use of the land, in this case if the heat had been enough to damage ordinary paper, or make the claimant's workers uncomfortable.

However, if a claimant could show that the interference was sufficient to affect their ordinary enjoyment of the land, they could then claim protection for that ordinary enjoyment, *and* any extra problems caused by unusual sensitivity. In *McKinnon Industries* v. *Walker* (1951), the claimant grew orchids on land next to the defendant's factory. The factory emitted fumes and sulphur dioxide gas, which killed all the orchids. The defendant claimed that they should not be liable for the orchids, because these were delicate and difficult to grow anyway, and so the situation was unusually sensitive. However, there was evidence that the emissions from the factory would actually have killed any other flowers as well. The Court therefore found that the interference was sufficient to disturb the claimant's ordinary enjoyment of the land and, once that was established, the claimant could also claim for disturbance to more sensitive activities.

Case Summary

However, the case of *Network Rail Infrastructure Ltd* v. *Morris* (2004) suggests that the idea of abnormal sensitivity may no longer be relevant to whether interference is reasonable. Mr Morris had a recording studio, and he claimed that electromagnetic interference from a signalling system operated by Network Rail was affecting the sound of electric guitars played in his studio. Network Rail argued that this was an example of abnormal sensitivity, in that Mr Morris was carrying on an unusual business, and most businesses and homes would not have been affected by the magnetic waves that came from the signalling system. The Court of Appeal rejected this argument, though the two judges who gave reasoned judgments both had slightly different reasons for doing so (the third simply said he agreed with the other two). Lord Phillips said that the evidence showed that the interference suffered by Mr Morris was very rare, and that this by itself would suggest this was a case of abnormal sensitivity. But, he went on, the use of complex electronic equipment was a feature of modern life, and there would always be some people wanting to use equipment that caused interference, and some people wanting to use equipment that was affected by interference. The way to strike the balance was simply to decide what was reasonable, and a key part of that decision was whether Network Rail could foresee that the system would cause problems to someone in Mr Morris's position. Lord Justice Buxton agreed with this general approach, but went further and specifically stated that it was no long appropriate to consider abnormal sensitivity; the correct question was simply whether the damage was foreseeable. On the facts, the damage was not foreseeable so Mr Morris lost his case.

Case Summary

How far this judgment really changes the law is debatable. The courts may no longer wish to use the term 'abnormal sensitivity', but where harm is caused only because of some unusual aspect of the claimant's situation that will often be relevant to whether the damage was foreseeable. In *Network Rail*, for example, the signalling system did not cause problems to premises other than recording studios, and the evidence showed that the problems it did cause Mr Morris were quite rare, and for that reason Network Rail could not have been expected to foresee it.

Malice

In nuisance, a defendant is said to act with malice if they do something with a bad motive, for example to upset, annoy or inconvenience the claimant, and this can affect their liability. Behaviour that, without malice, might have been considered reasonable may be considered unreasonable if the court believes the defendant acted maliciously.

Case Summary

The case of *Christie* v. *Davey* (1893) illustrates this point. The claimant was a music teacher and held musical parties in her house. The defendant was her next door neighbour, and there had been some sort of falling out between them. After this happened, the defendant started making a habit of blowing whistles and banging trays, which could be heard on the other side of the wall between the two houses. The Court found that he had done this deliberately to disrupt the lessons and the parties. As a result, he was found liable, even though his behaviour might normally have been considered reasonable, because the fact that he was deliberately acting to cause annoyance to his neighbours made it unreasonable.

Case Summary

A similar result was reached in *Hollywood Silver Fox Farm Ltd* v. *Emmett* (1936). The claimant bred foxes on his land. He and his neighbour, the defendant, fell out, and after their disagreement the defendant told his son to shoot his gun in the air while standing close to the claimant's land, in order to frighten the female foxes and stop them breeding. The Court found that the defendant was entitled to allow guns to be shot on his own land, and in ordinary circumstances this would not be considered unreasonable. But the fact that he was doing it maliciously meant it was unreasonable, and the claimant succeeded.

Documenting the law

Neighbours at war

You might be wondering how the Court in *Christie* v. *Davey* decided that Mr Davey had acted with malice. This letter from him to Mrs Christie, which was used as evidence in the trial, gives you some idea. Mr Davey clearly had a good line in sarcasm, but if what he says is true, he does seem to have had a point!

Source: Pearson Education Ltd/Photodisc/Janis Christie

During this week we have been much disturbed by what I at first thought were the howlings of your dog, and knowing from experience that this sort of thing could not be helped, I put up with the annoyance. But, the noise recurring at a comparatively early hour this morning, I find that I have been quite mistaken, and that it is the frantic effort of someone trying to sing with piano accompaniment, and during the day we are treated by way of variety to dreadful scrapings on a violin, with accompaniments. If the accompaniments are intended to drown out the vocal shrieks or teased catgut vibrations, I can assure you that it is a failure, for they do not. I am at last compelled to complain, for I cannot carry on my profession with this constant thump, thump, scrape, scrape and shriek, shriek constantly in my ears. It may be a pleasure or a source of profit to you, but to me and mine it is a confounded nuisance and pecuniary loss and, if allowed to continue, it must most seriously affect our health and comfort. We cannot use the back part of our house without feeling great inconvenience through this constant playing, sometimes up to midnight and even beyond. Allow me to remind you of one fact, which must most surely have escaped you – that these houses are only semi-detached, so that you yourself may see how annoying it must be to your unfortunate next-door-neighbour. If it is not discontinued I shall be compelled to take very serious notice of it. It may be fine sport to you, but it is almost death to yours truly.

The type of damage

A nuisance claim does not require the defendant to have caused actual physical damage to the neighbouring land; interference with the claimant's right to peaceful enjoyment is enough. However, clearly there are cases where a nuisance can cause physical damage (such as a flood, for example), and if this happens, it will affect whether the courts find the interference to be reasonable or not. The general rule is that where the defendant has caused actual physical damage to the land or something on it, the interference will be considered unreasonable, unless the claimant or their situation is unusually sensitive. In *St Helens Smelting Co.* v. *Tipping* (1865), the claimant's land was situated in an industrial area. Fumes from the defendant's factory damaged his crops and trees, but the defendant argued that this was not unreasonable given the type of area. The Court disagreed. Locality was relevant to cases where the defendant had only disturbed the claimant's normal enjoyment of their land, but if actual damage had been caused, the defendant's behaviour was unreasonable, regardless of the locality.

Case Summary

The balancing act

When deciding whether interference is unreasonable, the courts balance the above factors against each other and look at the whole situation. This means that a factor which is decisive in one case may not be in another. An example of this is *Rushmer* v. *Polsue and Alfieri Ltd* (1906). Here the claimant was a milkman, who lived in a part of London where there were a lot of printing companies. They worked at night, which meant he could not sleep. He was the only resident in the area and the area was traditionally one where printers had their premises, so you might expect that the courts would conclude that the noise was not unreasonable for that area. But because the disturbance was so severe, they held that this outweighed the importance of the type of locality.

Case Summary

This balancing act means that the outcome of nuisance cases can be very hard to predict, as solicitor Matthew Wayman explains in the People in the Law box.

People in the law

Matthew Wayman is a solicitor at Irwin Mitchell in Sheffield, who specialises in property-related disputes including cases of nuisance.

What kinds of nuisance cases do you come across? It's a broad mix. We get cases involving smoke or noise, for example, and a lot of boundary disputes that involve an element of nuisance. It's often tagged onto other claims as well – I had one case where the clients' property backed onto a huge development site, and when the developers excavated the land, half my clients' garden ended up in the hole. We claimed for negligence, arguing that they should have carried out the excavation in a different way, but there was also a claim in nuisance, because what happened interfered with the clients' right to enjoy their property.

Source: Matthew Wayman (*text and photo*)

Most nuisance claims I deal with are between neighbours, and they're usually just ordinary householders. I work for both defendants and claimants. If you've got a boundary dispute, for example, either party could end up being the claimant, depending on who decides to take legal action first.

How would a typical nuisance case start? The first stage is an initial review – if you take a noise nuisance claim, for example, we'll look at what evidence the client has managed to collect, and if they haven't done it already, we'll contact the local authority's environmental health department, who can provide noise recording equipment and diary sheets to the homeowner, so we can get a picture of the problem. Local authorities have their own powers to deal with noise, and we encourage clients to use that route if they can, because it's a quicker option and a cheaper one. But if that doesn't do the trick, we have to consider civil legal action.

We'll recommend that a specialist surveyor for noise nuisance claims is appointed, and they'll take recordings and provide a report using data taken over a period of time, and comparing it to standards such as the World Health Organisation's guidelines on acceptable noise levels. I can then look at the report, with an expert barrister if necessary, to assess the problem and try to work out whether a court would grant an **injunction**.

What happens next? If we think there's a case, the next step is pre-action correspondence. The courts now expect the parties to try to resolve the problem themselves if possible, without involving the court. Going to court has to be seen as a measure of last resort, because it's expensive, it's stressful for the people involved, and it takes a long time. So if people can sort it out without going that far, it's much better all round. That's something I stress to clients all the time, and it does surprise some of them – some people think it's a case of you've got a problem, you issue proceedings, and two weeks later you're in court and it's dealt with. I have to explain that it can take years.

So ideally, you want to get the parties to agree a solution between themselves if you can, but that does rely on them being alive to the possibility of solving the problem, and being willing to have meetings and try mediation. I sometimes say to people, just tell me what you want to achieve. There's often a pause at the other end of the phone because, especially if they're neighbours, people can become so incensed, and the problems can run so deep, that they lose sight of what the real issue is, and they just want to have an argument, to get their day in court. But my task is to achieve their objective as quickly as possible, as cheaply as possible and going to court is very often something which doesn't meet either requirement.

If we don't get anywhere, the next stage is to issue the claim. Negotiations will often speed up then, because costs become an issue, but even so, some cases will only settle at a very late stage. I had one dispute between neighbours that went on for three years, which was eventually resolved on the day before the trial – the defendant finally gave us what we'd asked for in the first place, but by then my client had already spent £55,000 on legal fees. That's a very good example to anyone considering bringing this kind of dispute before the courts. It gets very emotional and common sense tends to go out of the window.

What kind of issues tend to come up in your nuisance cases? The main issue will often be whether the interference is reasonable or not. What the claimant is trying to prove is that their neighbour's behaviour is unreasonable, and that is a very hard question to answer, because what is reasonable to one person might not be to another. These kinds of cases are very dependent on their facts, and that means they're fraught with difficulties, because the wrong judge on the wrong day can make all the difference – if they decide your client is unduly sensitive, for example, that's that. That makes cases very hard to predict, and it's not unusual for the chance of success to be close to 50:50.

Are there any particular problems you face in these cases? The emotions attached to disputes relating to your own home can often make things difficult, and cloud a client's judgment. Part of my job is to be able to sympathise with them, but at the same time look at things objectively, try to take the emotion out of it and bring a little bit of commercial thinking to the issue. There's also the fact that people almost always underestimate how hard it can be to satisfy a judge on the merits of these kinds of cases. They always think their case is straightforward, because it's obvious to them that the other side is in the wrong, and they don't always understand why we need to prove that.

What skills and qualities do you need in your job? Time management is absolutely crucial – workloads are heavy and you're spinning a number of plates so you have to be able to manage your time effectively. Communication skills are important too because you're communicating with a variety of different people on a day-to-day basis, whether it's your client, the other side, experts, witnesses, or the court. And with the client, you're part lawyer, part counsellor – people will often talk to you in very open terms about how the problem is affecting them, so you need plenty of empathy and the ability to listen.

For this particular area of work, you also need to have an analytical eye. Property disputes are often document-heavy, and you have to have the technical expertise to be able to pick up problems quickly. You might be faced with a box of title deeds, for example, and you need to be able to read those and pick out the relevant points, because if you don't, it can rear its head two years later, and you'll have missed it.

Negotiation skills are crucial too. Property-related claims really do lend themselves to negotiation, and very often the deal which is brokered will involve matters which aren't part of the proceedings – you might have, say, a boundary dispute, but one party says OK, I'll give you that, if you give me a right of way over this area. There's no reason why that can't form part of the agreement, so it helps to think creatively as well.

There's also a degree of toughness needed for cases like the ones I run. You will have some very difficult telephone conversations with solicitors on the other side, where you're arguing your case for the benefit of your client, and it can get quite adversarial. You have to be very, very tough, because you don't want your client being pushed about – and that's not for everyone.

What's the most difficult part of the job? Probably meeking the demands of clients. With email in particular, people now expect an instant response. Expectations continue to rise and the challenge is to meet them and exceed them.

And the most satisfying part? Achieving your client's objective. If you're involved in a nuisance claim, or any property-related claim, you're dealing with something which is of huge importance to the client, not just financially but emotionally. They've come to see you because they're upset and they have a problem, and it's very satisfying to see them walk away with that problem solved, whether that means a sum of money in damages, or perhaps an undertaking from a noisy neighbour that they'll stop playing loud music. On a daily basis, that kind of thing makes a difference to people's lives, and moments like that do make it worthwhile.

Damage

In order for there to be a claim in nuisance, there has to have been some form of damage to the claimant's interests. This may take the form of actual physical damage to their land or something on it, such as the dead orchids in *McKinnon Industries* v. *Walker*, or the collapse of the hotel in *Holbeck Hall Hotel* v. *Scarborough Borough Council*. But it is not essential for there to have been actual physical damage: the distress, unpleasantness and inconvenience caused by something like bad smells or noise can be enough.

The claimant will need to show that the situation or activity actually caused the damage to them, under the normal rules of **causation** and **remoteness of damage** which we looked at in Chapter 3 (if you want to remind yourself about these, have a look back at pages 69–80 and 80–87). So in a case like *McKinnon*, for example, the claimant would usually need to bring evidence to show that the fumes from the neighbouring land actually killed the orchids. The case of *Cambridge Water Co.* v *Eastern Counties Leather* (which we will look at later) establishes that the test of remoteness in nuisance is **reasonable foreseeability**, the same as in negligence. This means that a defendant is liable for any damage that they can reasonably foresee might arise from the nuisance.

Nuisance and fault

Let's say that you own a factory which pumps out horrible smells over the land next door. If you know that this happens, and you know that it causes problems for your neighbours but you don't bother to do anything about it, should you be liable? What about if you've installed the very best smell prevention systems you can get, and the smell still leaks out? Should you be liable then? These are questions about how far the defendant in nuisance has to be at fault for a claim to succeed. Having studied negligence, you might well assume that a defendant should only be liable for interference that they could not prevent, but in nuisance the rules are a little more complicated than that.

Case Navigator

Case Summary

The latest House of Lords guidance on this subject comes from the case of ***Cambridge Water* v. *Eastern Counties Leather*** (1994), which involved the pollution of a river by chemicals from a leather processing plant (we will look at the full facts in Chapter 15 as they are more relevant there). In *Cambridge Water*, the House of Lords said that a key element of a claim for nuisance was foreseeability: a defendant could only be liable for harm that they could foresee. Where the nuisance is still going on at the time of the claim, foreseeability is obvious; the very fact that the case is being brought means that the defendant knows their behaviour may be causing a nuisance. If that behaviour is found to be an unreasonable interference with their neighbour's enjoyment of the land, and there is no **defence**, that will be enough to make the defendant liable.

Where the claimant is seeking damages for a nuisance committed in the past, the House of Lords said that a defendant who unreasonably interfered with the claimant's use of land could be liable, even if they had taken all reasonable care. However, they would not be liable for damage of a type that they could not foresee. In our examples above, therefore, the factory owner who installed the best smell prevention system possible could still be liable, but only if he could foresee the type of damage that was caused to the claimant.

Who can be sued?

Depending on the circumstances of the case, a claimant in nuisance can sue:

- the person who created the nuisance;
- the occupier of the land;
- the owner of the land.

The creator of the nuisance

Anyone who creates a nuisance can be sued for it, regardless of whether they own or occupy the land it comes from. In fact, nuisance can come from land which is not even privately owned: in *Thomas* v. *National Union of Mineworkers* (1985), it was held that striking miners picketing in the road outside a factory could be liable for nuisance.

Case Summary

The occupier of the land

In most cases, the defendant will be the occupier of the land from where the nuisance comes. An occupier need not own the land: where land (or a building) is rented, the person renting it will usually be considered the occupier, and can be sued in nuisance.

An occupier of land is liable for any nuisance that they themselves cause, or any nuisance caused by an employee, under the normal principles of **vicarious liability**, which we looked at in Chapter 8. Occupiers of land can also be liable for nuisance caused there by a third party, if the occupier knows or ought to know that there is a risk of nuisance being caused and fails to take steps to prevent it. In *Sedleigh-Denfield* v. *O'Callaghan* (1940), the defendants were an order of monks, who occupied some land where there was a large ditch. Unknown to them, the local authority had built a pipe on the land, which took water away from the ditch. The pipe had a grate to keep out leaves but it was put in the wrong place and, as a result, three years after the pipe had been laid it became completely blocked with leaves. This caused a flood on the neighbouring land, owned by the claimant. The House of Lords heard that although the defendants did not know the pipe was being built, by the time of the flood they did know it was there. Therefore, the House said, they were liable, even though they did not themselves cause the nuisance, because they knew about the risk and allowed it to continue.

Case Summary

The owner

Where land is occupied by someone who is not the owner, it is usually the occupier who would be sued, rather than the owner. However, there are three circumstances in which an owner may be held liable, even though the land is occupied by someone else:

- Where a nuisance already existed when the land was rented out, and the owners knew or ought to have known about it. If, for example, you own a flat with a leaky pipe that keeps causing floods in the flat downstairs and, knowing that, you rent your flat out, you could still be sued by the people in the flat downstairs, even though someone else is occupying the flat.
- Where the land is rented out, but the lease provides that the landlord must repair the premises, or gives them a right to enter and do repairs. This was the case in *Wringe* v. *Cohen* (1940), where the defendant owned a shop that was rented out. The defendant was responsible for keeping the shop in good repair but failed to do so and, as a result, a wall collapsed, damaging the neighbouring shop which belonged to the claimant. The defendant was held liable.

Case Summary

- Where the owner has authorised the nuisance. This would apply where the owner has specifically permitted the occupier to do the thing that is said to be the nuisance, such as, for example, burning rubbish, and also where they have permitted the occupier to

Case Summary

do something that, by its nature, inevitably creates a nuisance. This was the case in *Tetley* v. *Chitty* (1986), where the defendant landowner allowed a go-kart club to be set up on their land, and the noise from the club caused a nuisance to neighbouring residents. The defendants claimed they were not liable because they had neither caused the noise nor permitted it, but the Court disagreed. They said that the noise was an inevitable result of the activities of a go-kart club, so by allowing the club to use the land, the defendants had effectively authorised the nuisance and were liable.

Case Summary

A landowner may be found to have authorised a nuisance if they know about it and fail to take steps to prevent it. In *Lippiatt* v. *South Gloucestershire Council* (1999), the council had allowed a group of travellers to set up an unofficial camp on their land. The claimants were farmers on neighbouring land, and they claimed that the travellers had repeatedly come on to their land, causing damage, stealing and behaving aggressively. They sued the council, claiming that the council's land was the 'launching pad' for the travellers' activities, and the council's failure to prevent the problems meant they had authorised the nuisance. The council applied to have the claim struck out, but the Court of Appeal refused, and said that it was at least arguable that there was a claim in nuisance. However, in a similar case, *Hussain* v. *Lancaster City Council* (1999), the opposite result was reached. The claimants owned a small shop and flat on a housing estate owned by the council. They were subjected to continual harassment and abuse by residents of the estate, who were the council's tenants, and had complained to the council many times about this. The council had powers to evict tenants who caused these kinds of problems but they had not used them, and the claimants argued that this failure amounted to authorising the nuisance. The Court of Appeal disagreed. It said that the fact that they were the council's tenants was nothing to do with the harassment, and so the harassment could not give rise to a claim in nuisance. The distinction is not, it must be said, especially convincing.

Case Summary

Who can sue?

To sue in nuisance, a claimant has to have what is called a proprietary interest in the land affected by the nuisance. A proprietary interest in land is a legal concept which belongs to land law, but for our purposes it essentially means that the claimant has either to own the land or building or to rent it. So a property owner or a tenant can sue, but a lodger, a guest, or a relative of the owner or tenant will not be able to, even if the nuisance affects them and not the owner or tenant.

Case Summary

This position appeared, briefly, to change during the 1990s, due to the case of *Khorasandjian* v. *Bush* (1994). Here the claimant was a 16-year-old girl who had been friends with the defendant, a 21-year-old man. After their relationship broke down, he became violent and threatening towards her, making menacing phone calls to the home where she lived with her parents. Eventually he threatened to kill her, and was prosecuted and sent to prison. But the phone calls continued, and so the claimant tried suing him in nuisance. The claim succeeded, even though she had no proprietary interest in the family home. Lord Dillon said in the Court of Appeal:

> In my mind, it is ridiculous if in this present age the law is that the making of deliberately harassing and pestering telephone calls to a person is only actionable in the civil courts if the recipient happens to have the freehold or a leasehold proprietary interest in the premises in which he or she has received the calls.

This view was confirmed by the Court of Appeal in *Hunter* v. *Canary Wharf* (1995), the case we looked at earlier where residents complained about interference with television reception caused by a tower block. The Court said that there had to be a substantial link between the person whose enjoyment of land was interfered with, and the land itself. But, they said, mere occupation of a home was enough to provide this link and give the occupant a right to sue. It was no longer necessary for a claimant to have a proprietary interest in land.

Case Summary

However, the change was short-lived. *Hunter* was appealed to the House of Lords, as *Hunter* v. *Canary Wharf* (1997). The House of Lords reverted to the traditional position, and held that only claimants with a proprietary right in land could sue in nuisance. The House pointed out that since *Khorasandjian* was decided, the Protection from Harassment Act 1997 had been passed and, as we saw in Chapter 12, this creates a new tort to deal with harassment, so there was no need to adapt the law of nuisance for this purpose. They insisted that there needed to be a clear distinction between nuisance and negligence, and the way to ensure this was to maintain nuisance as a tort protecting a claimant's right to use and enjoy land, and negligence as a remedy for personal injury.

Case Summary

In addition, Lord Goff said there were practical reasons why the tort should rely on rights in land. First, he said, in many cases potential claimants and defendants often come to amicable arrangements with each other, rather than going to court. For example, those affected by nuisance might agree to it continuing if the other side paid them compensation, or agreed to limit it to particular times. If the category of potential claimants was widened, such sensible arrangements might be less likely. Secondly, without the requirement for an interest in land, it would be impossible to fix any clear limits on who could sue. The decision in *Khorasandjian* had made it plain that someone would have rights to sue if the nuisance affected the family home, but what about lodgers, au pairs or live-in employees?

The decision was regarded by some critics as a backward step. In his dissenting judgment, Lord Cooke pointed out that there was no logical reason why those who were actually enjoying the amenities of a home should not be able to sue someone who interfered with that enjoyment. He said that the decision was essentially based on policy, and since that was the case, he would have preferred the court to uphold justice than to concern itself with keeping the limits of nuisance tidy.

Certainly some of his colleagues' arguments seem overstated. The decision in *Khorasandjian* had not removed the link between the land and the claimant that distinguishes nuisance from negligence. It merely said that occupation of a home, without a proprietary interest, could be enough to establish this link. And while cases involving au pairs or lodgers could well make for more difficult decisions, they would not have been impossible ones: one obvious factor to take into account would be how much time the claimant spent on the land, and whether it could reasonably be viewed as their home. By reversing the change made in *Khorasandjian*, the House of Lords laid themselves open to criticism that they were protecting property rights, and not the right to peaceful enjoyment of the place where we live or work which, it can be argued, is really the right that nuisance seeks to protect.

However, this is an area where the law may have to change to accommodate the provisions of the Human Rights Act 1998. In *McKenna* v. *British Aluminium* (2002), over 30 claimants sued in nuisance over noise and fumes which came from the defendant's factory. Some of the claimants were children who had no proprietary interest in the land, and the defendants sought to get their claims struck out for this reason. However, the court refused to strike out the action, because there was a 'real possibility' that a court

Case Summary

hearing the case might decide that the rule on proprietary interests was in conflict with Article 8 of the Human Rights Act, which states that everyone has the right to 'respect for his private and family life, his home and correspondence'.

Case Summary

This issue was considered again in *Dobson* v. *Thames Water* (2009). The claimants sued the water company over foul smells and mosquitoes coming from the company's sewage works. Some of the claimants in the case had property rights in the affected homes but others, including children who lived there, did not. The Court of Appeal was asked to consider whether the claimants without property rights had a separate claim under Article 8, in addition to the property owners' claim in nuisance. The Court of Appeal said that this issue had ultimately to be left to the trial judge, but said that it was unlikely that there would be a separate claim because the damages awarded to the property owner would take into account the effects of the nuisance on everyone living at the property. As damages under the Human Rights Act tend to be much lower than those awarded in tort, it was unlikely that any further damages would be awarded on top of those in nuisance.

Out and about

Read the case of *Khorisandijan* v. *Bush*. In your own words, summarise the arguments made by the judges *against* allowing a nuisance claim where the claimant has no proprietary interest in land. Do you agree with these arguments? Why/why not? Would you have made any other arguments? Now look at Lord Cooke's dissenting judgment, and list the arguments he makes *in favour* of allowing a claim where the claimant has no proprietary interest in land. Do you agree with these arguments? Why/why not? Would you have made any other arguments?

This exercise will give you valuable practice in reading and understanding cases, picking out the important elements of the decision and using them as a basis for your own arguments – which is exactly what lawyers have to do when they are arguing a case. Reading original cases can seem quite difficult at first, as judges do not always make themselves as clear as they could, but if you read with a particular purpose in mind, as in this exercise, you will find it easier to focus on the arguments.

Defences

The main defences in nuisance are:

- statutory authority
- prescription

Although not actually a defence, there is also a further barrier to liability where the nuisance arises as part of the provision of a public service, such as the sewer system, and statute provides an alternative remedy to a nuisance claim. This was the case in *Marcic* v. *Thames Water Utilities Ltd* (2004). Mr Marcic lived in a house which was frequently flooded with foul water from a sewer belonging to the defendants. The problem had been going on for nine years, and was steadily getting worse. By the time Mr Marcic sued, just

Case Summary

15 minutes of heavy rain were enough to flood his house. Even though he had spent £16,000 on a new drainage system, the building was by then badly affected by damp and impossible to sell. The cause of the problem was that since the time the sewers were laid, many years before, more and more properties had been built and connected to the system and the sewers were no longer adequate to do the job. The water company were well aware of the problem, but they assigned their budget for dealing with such problems according to a strict points system, which balanced the seriousness of a problem against the cost of putting it right. Under this system, Mr Marcic's situation did not have enough points to bring him to the top of the action list. Mr Marcic sued in nuisance, and the House of Lords rejected his claim. It pointed out that the provision of sewerage services was covered by the Water Industry Act 1991, which imposed on the defendants a duty to 'provide, improve and extend such a system of public sewers . . . and so to cleanse and maintain those sewers so as to ensure that the area is and continues to be effectually drained'. The Act provides that where a company fails to perform this duty adequately, the Director General of Water Services (the independent regulator for the water industry) can make an enforcement order against them. The Act also expressly states that customers cannot use a private law claim (such as a nuisance case) to force a water company to comply with a duty under the Act which the Director General of Water Services can enforce with an enforcement order. The House of Lords therefore rejected Mr Marcic's claim, saying that allowing a nuisance claim would be inconsistent with the rules laid down in the Act. Ironically, by the time the case reached the House of Lords, the water company had actually carried out the work necessary to solve the problem, and it is tempting to suspect that Mr Marcic's decision to go to court might have helped his situation even if the actual result of the case went against him.

Statutory authority

Where a statute authorises something to be done, and doing that thing will inevitably create a nuisance, there is no liability. In *Allen* v. *Gulf Oil Refining* (1981), the defendants ran an oil refinery and residents living nearby sued in nuisance over the smells, noise and vibrations it caused. The building of the refinery was authorised by statute, but the claimants argued that although a statute had authorised the building of the refinery it did not expressly state that the defendants should operate it. The House of Lords said that this was clearly implied in the statute: Parliament would not have given the power to build a refinery unless they intended it to be used. Since the alleged nuisance was an unavoidable result of running a refinery, the defence of statutory authority succeeded and the claim failed.

Case Summary

However, in *Allen* the House of Lords pointed out that the defence could only apply where the nuisance was an inevitable result of the activity authorised by statute. Where the nuisance-making activity was authorised by statute, but the activity could have been performed without causing a nuisance, the defence would not be available. An old example of this principle can be seen in *Metropolitan Asylum District* v. *Hill* (1881). The defendant was a local authority, which had been given permission under statute to build a hospital for patients with smallpox, a serious and very contagious disease. The claimant wanted to prevent them building it in a place where it would have been a danger to the local community. The Court held that in this case, statutory authority was not a defence, because the defendants could avoid causing a nuisance by siting the hospital somewhere else.

Case Summary

Prescription

The defence of prescription gives a defendant the right to continue committing a nuisance if the nuisance has been actionable for at least 20 years and the claimant was aware of this during the relevant period. Note that it is not enough that the activity that caused the nuisance has been going on for at least 20 years; it must have been capable of creating a claim in nuisance for at least that long. If, for example, you began running a noisy factory 25 years ago but it did not become a nuisance until 15 years ago, when houses were built next door, there is no defence and the residents of the houses can sue.

Case Summary

This was the situation in *Sturges* v. *Bridgman* (1879), the case referred to earlier when a doctor's consulting room opened up next to a noisy sweetmaker's. The sweetmaker put forward the defence of prescription, because he had been making the same amount of noise for over 20 years, but the Court held this was no defence because the noise did not become a nuisance until the doctor moved in next door.

You be the judge

Q: **Giles is a farmer who has been running his farm for 30 years. Ten years ago, Linda and Robert built a house on land next door to the farm, and began to complain about the smells from the manure that Giles spreads on his fields. They decide to sue in nuisance.**

Is Giles covered by the defence of prescription?

Source: Pearson Education Ltd/Imagestate/John Foxx Collection

A: No. Although he has been running the farm and presumably causing the manure smells for over 20 years, the situation does not seem to have become a nuisance until 10 years ago.

Inapplicable defences

There are three circumstances which students often believe will provide a defence in nuisance, but which in law do not. They are:

- public benefit;
- taking reasonable care;
- coming to the nuisance.

Public benefit

What happens when a socially useful activity is alleged to cause a nuisance to those living beside it? Let's say, for example, that a particular town has had a problem with skateboarders practising in the local shopping precinct, endangering shoppers. A skate park is built, which solves that problem, but the people who live next door claim that the noise from it is a nuisance. Will the fact that there is a public interest in the park existing outweigh the nuisance to those living nearby? The traditional view was that it would not.

In *Bellew* v. *Cement Co. Ltd* (1948), the claimants sued the owners of a cement factory for nuisance. The defendants argued that it was in the public interest to keep the factory open, because its products were badly needed by the country at the time. The court held that this was no defence.

Case Summary

However, in more modern cases, the courts have taken a more flexible line. Although the fact that there is a public benefit will not stop a defendant being liable for nuisance, it may affect the remedies that the courts are willing to grant. In many cases, claimants in nuisance want an injunction to stop the nuisance happening. Where the activity causing the nuisance has a public benefit, the courts may refuse an injunction and grant damages instead, or allow only a partial injunction so that the activity does not have to stop but disruption is reduced. In *Miller* v. *Jackson* (1977), the claimants moved into a house beside a cricket club. Cricket balls were frequently hit into their garden, and they attempted to get an injunction against the club to stop play. The Court of Appeal agreed that a nuisance had been committed, and awarded damages. However, they refused to grant an injunction because the club was a benefit to the local community, and that outweighed the claimants' private interest in stopping balls being hit into their garden.

Case Summary

In *Dennis* v. *Ministry of Defence* (2003), the claimants were the owners of a country estate in Cambridgeshire, which was about two miles away from an RAF base. Training flights flew directly over the estate, causing what the claimants described as 'fearsome noise'. The Ministry of Defence claimed that it was in the country's interest for them to train fighter pilots, and that as this could not be achieved without making a certain amount of noise they should have a defence. The Court said that the Ministry were liable for the nuisance, but that the public interest here was so important that it would be wrong to grant an injunction to stop the flying. They ordered compensation instead of an injunction, stating that if society benefited from an activity it was fair that society should pay to compensate those who suffered as a result of that activity. As the Ministry of Defence is funded by taxpayers, this could be achieved by making them pay compensation to the claimants.

Case Summary

Taking reasonable care

We saw when we looked at negligence that a defendant will not be liable if they have taken reasonable care to avoid damage to the claimant. This is not the case in nuisance, though students often think it is. It may seem logical and fair that someone who has taken reasonable care and could not have done anything else to prevent a nuisance should not be liable, but remember that in nuisance the courts are not just looking at one party's behaviour. Instead, they are trying to balance the two parties' competing rights to use their land as they wish. Take, for example, a situation where Bill sets up a factory next to Bob's farm. The factory gives out horrible-smelling fumes and makes a lot of noise. If Bob sued in negligence, the court would ask whether Bill had taken reasonable steps to prevent the smells and noise. If he had, he would not be liable, even if the reasonable steps did not prevent the problem. But if Bob sued in nuisance, the question would be different. The court would look at whether the interference Bill was causing to Bob's enjoyment of his land was reasonable, and instead of asking what he could have done to avoid it they would examine the issues we looked at earlier: seriousness, locality, type of damage and so on. If, on considering these questions, they found that the interference was unreasonable, Bill could be liable even if there was nothing he could have done to prevent the nuisance.

in nuisance the courts are not just looking at one party's behaviour

'Coming to the nuisance'

We saw in Chapter 3 on negligence that a claimant cannot sue for injury or damage that they have consented to. It has been argued that a form of consent defence should also apply in nuisance, where the nuisance existed before the claimant came to the land, and by coming to a place where the nuisance was already happening, the claimant could be said to be consenting to it. This is usually referred to as 'coming to the nuisance'. The courts have, however, repeatedly rejected this argument.

Case Summary

This was the case in *Sturges* v. *Bridgman*, the case we looked at earlier, where the doctor moved in next door to the sweetmaker. The sweetmaker said his business, and the noise from it, had already existed when the doctor arrived, and so the doctor could be said to have consented to it. The court refused to accept this as a defence.

Case Summary

Case Summary

The potential defence was raised again in *Miller* v. *Jackson*, the case about the house next door to a cricket club, where the cricket club argued that they should not be liable because the claimants knew they were moving in beside a cricket club, and in *Dennis* v. *Ministry of Defence*, where the Ministry of Defence said that the airbase was there when the claimants moved into their house, and so they knew noise was likely. In both cases, the courts confirmed that 'coming to the nuisance' is not a defence.

Remedies

There are three potential remedies for nuisance:

- injunction;
- damages;
- abatement.

Injunction

An injunction is a court order to do or not do something, and because injunctions are a way of stopping a nuisance that is still ongoing, they are the main remedy in nuisance cases. An injunction is an equitable remedy, which means that the courts can refuse to issue one even if the claimant wins the case (in this situation damages will usually be given instead). Some important guidelines on when the courts should refuse an injunction were laid down in *Shelfer* v. *City of London Electric Lighting Co.* (1895). The Court said that, if the claimant has won their case, an injunction should only be refused if:

Case Summary

- the damage to the claimant's rights is small; and
- the damage is capable of being calculated in money; and
- the damage can be adequately compensated for by a small payment of money; and
- it would be oppressive to the defendant to grant an injunction.

What this effectively means is that the courts should not allow wealthy defendants, through damages, to buy the right to commit a serious nuisance. In *Shelfer* itself, the claimant had asked for an injunction because of the noise and disturbance caused by the defendant's machinery. The electricity company claimed that an injunction should not be ordered, because if they could not use the machinery many people would be deprived of electricity. Applying the four principles it had laid down, the Court rejected their argument and ordered the injunction.

However, the injunction is quite a flexible remedy because it need not necessarily stop a defendant's activity completely. The courts can issue what is called a partial injunction, which simply limits the times when the activity is performed, so the claimant suffers less from it, but the defendant does not have to stop completely. This means that the courts can use the remedy to achieve a satisfactory balancing act between the two competing rights. An example of this can be seen in *Kennaway* v. *Thompson* (1980). The claimant owned land near Lake Windermere in Cumbria. A motorboat club had been organising races and waterskiing on the lake for many years, and the claimant knew this when she bought the land and started building a house, but thought it would not cause her any disturbance. However, by the time her house was finished the club had expanded and was holding more meetings, involving more powerful and noisier boats, and making a lot more noise than she had expected. She sought an injunction to stop the club from causing excessive noise. The club argued that there was a public interest in its activities being available to those who wanted to watch or take part, but the Court said this was not a defence. However, they granted an injunction which limited, rather than completely prevented, the club's activities.

Case Summary

Damages

Where a nuisance has happened but is no longer continuing, a claimant can recover damages for the damage caused to them while the nuisance was going on. This can cover physical damage to the land, but also damage to their enjoyment of the land, such as distress, discomfort and inconvenience. Where a nuisance is still ongoing, a claimant can get an injunction to stop it and damages for the damages already caused. As we have seen in *Dennis* v. *Ministry of Defence*, the courts may also order damages instead of an injunction.

Where the damages are for physical damage to the land, it is clear that the court can simply calculate the damages by how much the damage has reduced the land's value. Calculating damages for factors such as inconvenience, distress or discomfort is more difficult. A creative approach to the problem was taken in *Bone* v. *Seale* (1975), where the claimant sued over the smells which reached his land from the defendant's pig farm. There was no actual damage to his land, so the court ordered damages of £1,000, basing their calculations on the amount that would have been awarded in a personal injury claim for loss of sense of smell.

Case Summary

However, this approach was disapproved by Lord Hoffmann in *Hunter* v. *Canary Wharf* because, he said, nuisance was a tort against land, not a tort against the person. He suggested that the correct approach was to ask what effect the problem would have on the value of the land and base the damages on that reduction.

Case Summary

Abatement

This is a form of self-help, rather than a remedy ordered by the court, and allows the claimant to take steps to end the nuisance. Let's say, for example, that your neighbour's tree overhangs your garden so much that you can't open your gate. Abatement allows

Abatement is generally only considered to be a suitable remedy for relatively minor problems

you to cut back the branches without the risk of being sued for it. It also allows entry on to the defendant's land to deal with a nuisance without liability for trespass, though the claimant must give notice that they intend to do this. If no notice is given, they will be trespassing. Abatement is generally only considered to be a suitable remedy for relatively minor problems, which would not be worth going to court over. The courts would not, for example, take kindly to someone bothered by fumes from a factory deciding to burn the place down instead of suing in nuisance.

Writing and drafting

You are a solicitor in a firm which is based in a large town. The partners are very keen to raise the profile of the firm, in order to bring in more clients, and they have agreed with the editor of the local newspaper that she will publish a series of articles written by their staff, each one giving a simple guide to an area of the law that affects the general public. You have been asked to write one on the law of nuisance. In no more than 1,000 words, write a basic guide to the law, which tells readers what nuisance is, when the law will give them a remedy for it, and what that remedy might be.

Handy tip: Remember that you are writing for an audience of non-lawyers. Keep the language simple, use examples to illustrate the points you make, and break up your text with headings so that it is easy to read, but write in continuous sentences, not note form. Stick to the basic principles of the law rather than going into great detail – your readers won't need to know the names of the cases, they just need to know whether their problem is one the law can solve.

Reflective practice

How did you find this exercise? Summarising a complete area of law in so few words is quite difficult, but it is a good test of how well you have grasped what the subject is really all about. If you found it difficult, try to analyse what part of the task made it tricky. Was it isolating the essential points? Or trying to explain them briefly and in simple terms? Or working out what exactly your audience needs to know? All of these are useful skills for lawyers, so if you think one of them needs practice, try repeating this exercise with some of the other chapters you have read.

Nuisance and the Human Rights Act 1998

As we have seen in some previous chapters, the Human Rights Act is increasingly being used as a supplement, or alternative, to traditional tort claims, and this is happening in the area of nuisance as well. The relevant provision is usually Article 8, which sets out

Figure 14.1 Liability in nuisance

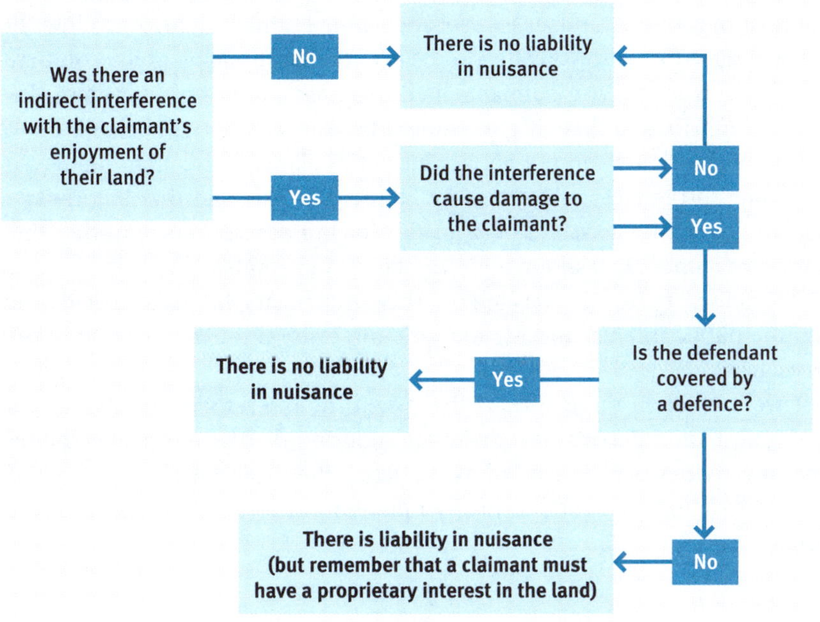

the right to respect for a person's 'private and family life, home and correspondence'. However, like most of the provisions of the Human Rights Act, it is not an absolute right and can be restricted where necessary on certain public policy grounds, including the economic well-being of the country and the rights and freedoms of others.

In other areas of tort, the Human Rights Act has offered remedies when tort law had none to offer, such as in the negligence case of *Van Colle* which we looked at in Chapter 6. It had been thought that the Human Rights Act might, in the same way, fill in some of the gaps in nuisance law, such as the lack of protection for those without proprietary rights in land. However, the first few cases under the legislation suggest that, if anything, the Act may give more protection to those who cause nuisance, and less to those affected by it, than traditional nuisance law.

Case Summary

In *Dennis* v. *Ministry of Defence*, the case we looked at earlier concerning noise from RAF training flights, the claimants made an alternative claim under the Human Rights Act, arguing that the noise breached their rights under Article 8. The Court agreed that it did breach this right. However, they said that this did not justify granting an injunction to stop the flights any more than liability in nuisance did, because 'the public interest is greater than the individual private interests [of the claimants]'. Although the Court held that the claim under the Human Rights Act would have justified compensation (if the claimants had not already got it through their nuisance claim), the emphasis on public interest over individual rights means the Act gives less protection to people suffering from nuisance than traditional principles of nuisance.

Case Summary

Article 8 also failed to help the claimant in *Marcic*, whose house, you will remember, was regularly flooded by a sewer. The claimant argued that the defendant's failure to prevent the problem breached his Article 8 rights, but the House of Lords disagreed. They referred back to a previous Article 8 case, *Hatton* v. *UK* (2003), in which residents of the area around Heathrow Airport claimed that the noise from night flights was a breach of their Article 8 rights. In *Hatton,* the European Court of Human Rights (ECHR) said that it was reasonable to assume that night flights contributed to the overall economic well-being of the country and, as we saw above, the Human Rights Act allows limits on the Article 8 right for reasons related to the economic well-being of the country. In that situation and, given that the claimants had the choice to move somewhere else if they chose to, the ECHR said the UK government had struck the right balance between the *Hatton* claimants' rights and the public interest in allowing the night flights. Applying this reasoning to the facts in *Marcic,* the House of Lords said that there was a public interest in establishing a system of priorities for building sewers, and that the system which the government had adopted in the legislation included a remedy for anyone who felt the allocation of priorities was unfair. This meant that a fair balance had been struck between the public interest and Mr Marcic's interests, and his Article 8 rights had not been breached.

What we can see in these cases is that when the interests of society are put in the balance against the interests of individuals suffering disruption to their home life by the type of activities usually classed as nuisance, the provisions of the Human Rights Act make it easy for the courts to justify upholding the public interest rather than the individual's.

A critique of nuisance law

In their book *The Wrongs of Tort* (1993), Joanne Conaghan and Wade Mansell argue that the principles of nuisance law are so vague that they allow judges to decide cases on the basis of their own prejudices and beliefs, rather than on any defined set of rules:

> Nuisance law abounds with concepts, tests and standards which are indeterminate, dictating no particular legal outcome and giving almost full reign to subjective judicial preferences. The only significant constraint is that judges must justify their decisions using the language of these wholly indeterminate concepts, tests and standards, rather than by reference to [their] subjective preferences.

They point to the fact that in deciding whether an interference is reasonable, judges have free reign to give the varying factors the weight which seems right to them, and that this will inevitably reflect a view of the world that comes with being from a particular class. Similarly, the rule that a claimant cannot claim for losses caused only because of 'abnormal sensitivity' allows a great deal of scope for judges to decide what is and is not abnormally sensitive.

Conaghan and Mansell also criticise the failure of nuisance law to protect against environmental pollution. They point out that allowing locality as a factor in deciding reasonableness effectively gives the upper hand to industry, because if you happen to live in an industrialised area nuisance law expects you to put up with the consequences. This meant that, at the time when Britain was becoming more industrialised, it was very difficult to use a claim for nuisance to deal with the effects of that industrialisation on an industry's neighbours.

Key stats Disputes between neighbours

According to 2011 research by the consumer magazine *Which?*, disputes between neighbouring households are a serious problem in the UK. Their study found that:

- Five million people were currently annoyed with their neighbours.
- Ten million had have problems with a neighbour in the past year.
- Noise was the most serious problem, affecting three in five people.
- Over 15% were forced to call the police.

Other forms of nuisance

As well as private nuisance, which we have looked at so far in this chapter, there are two other types of nuisance: statutory nuisance and public nuisance.

Statutory nuisance

Statutory nuisance is the name given to various offences under legislation covering public health and environmental issues. For example, creating excessive noise may be a statutory nuisance under the Control of Pollution Act 1974, and a building which emits smoke may be a statutory nuisance under the Clean Air Act 1956. Statutory nuisances do not involve claims in tort but are dealt with by local authorities, who can issue orders to prevent the harmful activity. In many cases, the problems the statutes are aimed at are the kind that would once have been dealt with by individual claims in nuisance, but the modern view is that these problems affect society as a whole so are better dealt with on behalf of all of us by public bodies. Statutory nuisance is therefore not considered part of tort law, and so is not discussed further in this book.

Statutory nuisances do not involve claims in tort but are dealt with by local authorities

Public nuisance

Public nuisance is not a tort, but a crime. However, it has a relationship to tort law because there are circumstances where, if a public nuisance is committed, those affected can sue in tort, which is why we will look at it in this chapter. (This also means that it does sometimes come up in problem questions.)

Despite the name, public nuisance is quite different from private nuisance. It need not have any connection with the use of land, by either the person causing the nuisance or the person affected by it, and it can just as easily arise from a single incident as a continuing situation. The leading definition of the crime of public nuisance comes from

public nuisance is quite different from private nuisance

Case Summary

the case of *Attorney-General* v. *PYA Quarries* (1957). The defendants used a blasting system in their quarry, which caused noise and vibrations and threw out dust, stones and splinters which caused problems for people living nearby. The Court of Appeal held that this could amount to a public nuisance, which it defined as any nuisance which 'materially affects the reasonable comfort and convenience of a class of her Majesty's subjects'.

This definition has been taken to cover a whole range of activities which endanger the public, or cause them inconvenience or discomfort, or prevent them exercising their rights. Examples include picketing on a road (*Thomas* v. *NUM* (1985)); blocking a canal (*Rose* v. *Miles* (1815)); obstructing a highway by queuing on it (*Lyons* v. *Gulliver* (1914)); causing noise and disrupting traffic through a badly organised music festival (*Attorney-General of Ontario* v. *Orange Productions* (1971)); and making obscene phone calls to large numbers of women (*R* v. *Johnson (Anthony Thomas)* (1996)).

The nuisance must be one which 'materially affects the reasonable comfort and convenience of a class of her Majesty's subjects', so there is no public nuisance where just one person is affected. But how many people have to be affected for them to amount to 'a class of her Majesty's subjects'? This question was examined in the *PYA Quarries* case. There were only 30 houses close to the quarry, so the quarry owners argued that the people affected were too few for it to amount to a public nuisance. The court disagreed, and said that 30 households were enough. The test, it said, was whether the nuisance was 'so widespread in its range or so indiscriminate in its effect that it would not be reasonable to expect one person to take proceedings on his own responsibility to put a stop to it, but that it should be taken in the responsibility of the community at large'. The court explained that if only two or three people were affected, that would not be enough, but the 30 households in the case were sufficient. However, they did not give any further guidance on exact numbers, and said that whether the number of people affected was enough would be a question of fact in each case. The *PYA Quarries* case also establishes that it is not necessary to prove that every member of a group or class has been affected, so long as it can be shown that a representative part of the group has been caused problems by the nuisance. A series of acts amounting to a nuisance but committed against several different individuals is not sufficient to amount to a public nuisance. In *R* v. *Rimmington* (2005), the defendant had sent over 500 packages containing racially offensive material to members of the public. Some were chosen at random, others because of the ethnic group to which they belonged. The House of Lords held that this selection of individual victims was not the same thing as a 'class of her Majesty's subjects', and so there was no public nuisance.

Case Summary

Tort claims for public nuisance

A defendant who commits public nuisance can be prosecuted for that crime, and also sued in tort by someone who is affected by the nuisance. However, not everyone affected can sue. It is only possible to make a successful claim if you can show that you have suffered 'special damage', over and above the effects of the nuisance on the rest of the group. A good example of what is meant by special damage can be seen in *Benjamin* v. *Storr* (1874). The claimant kept a coffee house in the Covent Garden area of London, and the defendant regularly left his horses and carts outside the row of shops where the coffee shop was situated, obstructing the highway and blocking out light from all the shops. The nuisance affected all the shops along the row, but the Court agreed that the defendant had suffered special damage because he was running a shop where people came to eat and drink and the smell of the horses put his customers off.

Case Summary

Table 14.1 Differences between private nuisance and public nuisance

Private nuisance	Public nuisance
Creates a claim in tort even if only one person is affected	Can only create a claim in tort if a class of people is affected *and* the claimant suffers special damage
Claimant must have an interest in land	No interest in land required
Nuisance must arise from the defendant's use of land	Can arise from activities not related to use of land

One common way in which special damage can arise is where the nuisance causes inconvenience to the rest of the affected group but, in addition, causes financial loss to the claimant. This was the case in *Tate & Lyle* v. *Greater London Council* (1983). The defendant council built some ferry terminals in the River Thames, which caused the river to get clogged up with mud. This caused problems for river users in general, but the claimants were affected more severely than most because their jetty became blocked and they had to spend a lot of money fixing the problem. The House of Lords held that this amounted to special damage.

Case Summary

Summary

- Nuisance is an unreasonable interference with someone's right to enjoyment of their land. It can include smoke, fumes, floods or smells, or more tangible problems such as tree roots. The interference is usually indirect and from a continuing situation.
- Defendants are liable for a nuisance that they have caused, or which occurs naturally, if they know about it and do not take reasonable precautions.
- In assessing whether interference is unreasonable, the courts balance all the circumstances, including factors such as seriousness, locality, sensitivity, malice and the type of damage caused.
- Damage may be physical, but need not be, and must be shown to be caused by the interference. The test for remoteness is reasonable foreseeability.
- Where a nuisance is still continuing, there is no need for proof of fault; for past nuisance, a defendant can be liable even if they took reasonable care, but only for damage of a type they could foresee.
- Liability can apply to the creator of the nuisance, the occupier of the land, or the owner of the land.
- The claimant must have a proprietary interest in the land.
- There are two defences:
  - prescription
  - statutory authority
- There are three potential remedies:
  - injunction
  - damages
  - abatement

There are two other forms of nuisance. Statutory nuisance is the term for breach of statutory rules on health and the environment, and public nuisance is a crime, defined as anything which 'materially affects the reasonable comfort and convenience of a class of her Majesty's subjects'. Where public nuisance is committed, someone suffering 'special damage' can sue in tort.

Question and answer*

Problem: Lucy owns a small factory making dog food, which has been in the same place for 22 years. Three years ago, Jeremy bought a piece of land next to the factory, and had a house built there. Smells drift across from the factory all day, and even at night when the factory is closed, which Jeremy finds very unpleasant. When he complained to Lucy, she said that she had fitted state-of-the-art systems to cut down on the smells escaping and there was nothing else she could do. She also says that they knew the factory was there when they bought the land, so they just have to put up with the smells. There are four other factories in the immediate area and no other houses.

Jeremy has employed a gardener, Rosie, to create a patio area just outside their house. Earlier this year, Lucy created an outside smoking area for her workers, which is right next door to Jeremy's garden, and clouds of smoke drift over from the factory, making it very unpleasant for Rosie when she is working. Lucy has been told about the problem, but has not taken any action. Jeremy is not affected by the smoke, because he is not at home during the day.

Advise Jeremy and Rosie.

You should allow yourself no more than 40 minutes to complete this task.

Essay: The law of nuisance seeks to balance the right of an occupier of land to enjoy that land, and their neighbour's right to do the same with theirs.

With reference to decided cases, explain how the law strikes this balance.

This question should be answered in 40 minutes.

* Answer guidance is provided at the end of the chapter.

Further reading

Campbell, D. (2000) 'Of Coase and Corn: a (sort of) defence of private nuisance', 63 MLR 197.
This very interesting article argues that the law of nuisance needs some radical reform, but that if this were to happen it could play a new and important role in protecting the environment. Not an easy read, but worth the effort.

Conaghan, J. and Mansell, W. (1993) *The Wrongs of Tort*, Ch. 6, London: Pluto Press.
The authors take a critical approach to the law of nuisance, and look at some of the social and historical views that have been behind key decisions. Full of good material for essays.

Gearty, C. (1989) 'The place of private nuisance in a modern law of torts', 48(2) CLJ 214.
Containing lots of useful information for essays, this article gives a detailed overview of the law of nuisance, highlighting problems and inconsistencies in the law.

McLaren, J.P.S. (1983) 'Nuisance law and the industrial revolution', 3 OJLS 155.
This article puts the development of nuisance law in its historical context, and shows how it has evolved in response to changing social and economic conditions.

Wightman, J. (1998) 'Nuisance – the environmental tort', 61 MLR 870.
This article is a critique of the decision in *Hunter* v. *Canary Wharf*, and argues that it has closed down any real possibility of the tort being used to regulate environmental harm.

Question and answer guidance

Problem: Taking Jeremy's claim first, you can point out that he passes the first test for a claim as he is the occupier of the property. Then you need to consider whether the smells are likely to be classed as an unreasonable interference; based on what we are told here, relevant issues will be the nature of the area, and the seriousness of the interference. Explain how the courts balance the different factors against each other. If the interference is unreasonable, does Lucy have a defence? You need to look at prescription, and also address Lucy's argument that Jeremy has 'come to the nuisance'. You should also consider whether the fact that she has taken steps to deal with the problem can make a difference – the section on fault is relevant here.

Turning to Rosie, the main issue here is that she is not an occupier of the property, so she has no right to sue – the case of *Hunter* v. *Canary Wharf* needs to be discussed here.

Essay: A good start to this essay would be to explain briefly the basic idea behind the law of nuisance, and how it seeks to strike a balance between competing rights by using the concept of unreasonable interference. You can then go on to look at the cases which indicate how the courts strike this balance, such as *Southwark Council* v. *Mills* and *Leakey* v. *National Trust*. You could also talk about the cases on location, the use of partial injunctions in cases such as *Kennaway* v. *Thompson*, and the issue of foreseeability. To give your essay some balance, it is always good to highlight any problems or inconsistencies with the way the courts handle this balance, and the material in Conaghan and Mansell (1993) would be very useful here.

Visit **www.mylawchamber.co.uk/quinntort** to access tools to help you develop and test your knowledge of tort law, including practice exam questions with guidance, annotated weblinks, glossary and key case flashcards, legal newsfeed and legal updates and interactive 'You be the judge' questions.

premium mylawchamber — unrivalled support for legal education

CASE NAVIGATOR — POWERED BY LexisNexis

Use Case Navigator to read in full some of the key cases referenced in this chapter with commentary and questions:

Cambridge Water Co. Ltd* v. *Eastern Counties Leather plc [1994] 1 All ER 53
Hunter* v. *Canary Wharf Ltd [1997] 2 All ER 426

Chapter 15
The tort in *Rylands* v. *Fletcher*

Key points In this chapter we will be looking at:

- How the tort in *Rylands* v. *Fletcher* is committed
- Defences to a claim under *Rylands* v. *Fletcher*
- The role of the tort in *Rylands* v. *Fletcher* in modern law

Introduction

These days, there are lots of ways to become famous: you can do it by winning a television talent contest, marrying a footballer, writing a book, or winning an Olympic medal, to name just a few. What you probably cannot do, however, is give your name to a whole new tort. Back in the nineteenth century, however, that is exactly what two Lancashire landowners did, when Mr Rylands and Mr Fletcher fell out over a flood caused on Mr Rylands's land by building works done on Mr Fletcher's. When the courts found that the situation was not covered by the existing laws on trespass or nuisance, they created a new tort that for some reason never acquired a proper name, and is still referred to as the tort in *Rylands* v. *Fletcher*.

At the time the tort was created, Britain was in the middle of a transformation from a mainly agricultural society, where most working people earned their living from the land, to an industrial one, where technology was advancing, and increasing numbers of factories and manufacturing plants were being built. These sometimes caused problems for neighbouring landowners, in the form of fire, floods or escapes of chemicals, and in *Rylands*, the courts created a new tort to deal with this situation, which attempted to impose **strict liability** on industrialists for any damage they did in this way, so that those who suffered the damage could get compensation regardless of whether those whose activities caused the problem were actually at fault or not.

As we will see, however, over the years elements of fault-based liability have been introduced, which to some extent weaken the original purpose, though some elements of the tort still impose strict liability.

Liability under *Rylands* v. *Fletcher*

Case Summary

The best way to understand what the tort is all about is to look at the case of *Rylands* v. *Fletcher* (1868) itself, in which all of the elements of the tort were laid down. The **defendant** was the owner of a mill and had paid another company to create a reservoir on his land, which would supply water to his mill. While the reservoir was being built, the company doing the work discovered shafts and passages from an old coal mine on the defendant's land, some of which were connected to shafts from a mine on neighbouring land which belonged to the **claimant**. The defendant did not know these shafts were there and the builders did not tell him about them. The builders could have sealed off the shafts on the defendant's land, but they failed to do this and, as a result, when the reservoir was filled the water from it burst through the shafts and flooded the claimant's mine, causing damage worth almost £1,000 (which would have been a lot of money in those days).

It was not possible to sue for trespass, because there was no direct and intentional interference with the land, and a nuisance claim was not available because the flood was an isolated incident and not a continuing state of affairs. However, the House of Lords held that the defendant was liable in tort, upholding the judgment given at first instance by Mr Justice Blackburn, who stated that:

> A person who, for his own purposes, brings on to his land and keeps there anything which is likely to do mischief if it escapes . . . is prima facie answerable for all damage which is the natural consequence of its escape.

The House of Lords also said that the thing likely to 'do mischief' must be connected to some 'non-natural use' of the land.

Although the courts claimed that the rule explained in *Rylands* had a clear foundation in previous cases, the cases they mentioned do not actually go nearly as far as *Rylands*, and it is now generally accepted that the case gave rise to a whole new tort. Unfortunately, it never got a snappy one-word name so is still referred to as 'the tort in *Rylands* v. *Fletcher*' or 'the rule in *Rylands* v. *Fletcher*'.

To succeed in a claim under the rule in *Rylands* v. *Fletcher*, four elements must be satisfied:

- There must be some 'non-natural use' of the defendant's land.
- The defendant must have brought or accumulated on the land something likely to 'do mischief', meaning cause a problem or danger, if it escapes.
- There must be an escape of the dangerous thing.
- There must be damage as a result of the escape.

A 'non-natural' use of land

The requirement for a 'non-natural' use of land means that a defendant cannot be liable under *Rylands* v. *Fletcher* if the thing that caused the problem occurred quite naturally on the land – so for example, if in *Rylands* itself the claimant's land had been

Case Summary

flooded by a river or stream there would not have been a claim. In *Giles* v. *Walker* (1890), the defendant ploughed up some woods on his land, with the result that a large crop of thistles grew there and the seeds blew onto his neighbour's land, causing problems over there. The defendant was not liable under *Rylands* because thistles grew naturally and were not brought on to the land or accumulated by him.

Case Summary

However, that does not mean that everything not occurring naturally will be a 'non-natural use'. In *Rickards* v. *Lothian* (1913), the defendant rented the upper part of a building. A tap there was turned on – it was not clear who by – and caused a flood, which damaged property stored by the claimant on the floor below. Clearly the tap and the water pipes had not occurred naturally, but the defendant was held not liable because he was making an ordinary and proper use of the building. Lord Moulton took the chance to clarify the meaning of non-natural use, saying that:

> It must be some special use bringing with it increased danger to others and [which] must not merely be the ordinary use of the land or such a use as is proper for the general benefit of the community.

Case Summary

This sounds quite straightforward, but if we think about the many technological and industrial changes that have happened since *Rylands* was decided it is perhaps not surprising that uses of land that are considered dangerous, or proper for the benefit of the community, or ordinary at one time may be looked at quite differently in another. In *Musgrove* v. *Pandelis* (1919), for example, storing a car with a tankful of petrol in a garage was seen as a non-natural use, which seems ridiculous today but would have been seen differently at a time when cars were relatively new and not widely owned and used. Similarly, in *Rainham Chemical Works* v. *Belvedere Fish Guano Co. Ltd* (1921) running a munitions factory (a factory that makes defence equipment) was judged to be a non-natural use of land, but in *Read* v. *Lyons* (1947), concerning an incident that occurred, when Britain was at war, it was not considered a non-natural use of land. Even *Rylands* itself is a product of its time: today a court would be very unlikely to consider a reservoir as dangerous, but the judges in *Rylands* may well have been influenced by the fact that, a year earlier, a reservoir had burst killing a number of people.

The modern approach to non-natural use

Case Summary

More modern cases have looked at the whole context of the use of land, including the amount of dangerous material kept there and the character of the surrounding neighbourhood. In *Mason* v. *Levy Autoparts* (1967), the defendant kept large quantities of inflammable materials on his premises and a fire started, which spread and caused damage to the claimant's land. The Court said that, in deciding whether there was a non-natural use of land, it was relevant to look at how much of the dangerous material was stored there, how it was stored, and the character of the neighbourhood. In *British Celanese* v. *Hunt* (1969), the defendants owned a factory on an industrial estate where they made electrical components. Strips of their metal foil escaped from the factory and blew onto an overhead cable, causing a power cut, which stopped production at the claimant's factory nearby. The Court held that there was no non-natural use of land, because there were no special risks attached to the storage of metal foil, the use of the land was beneficial to the community, and the factory was on an industrial estate where everyone else would also be involved in similar processes.

After cases like *Rickards* and *British Celanese*, it was generally assumed that where land was being used for industrial purposes there would be no non-natural use. However, the landmark case of ***Cambridge Water* v. *Eastern Counties Leather*** (1994) makes it clear that the courts will still find a non-natural use where what is being used or stored on the land is especially hazardous. The defendants in the case were leather manufacturers, who had been in business on the same site for many years. During the manufacturing process, they used a chemical called PCE and, over the years, huge amounts of it had been spilled and seeped through the concrete floor, polluting a borehole from which the claimants took water to supply to local homes. The pollution was only discovered in 1983, when new regulations required water companies to test for it; the defendants had stopped using PCE by then, but the damage was already done. The water company were forced to move their operations, which cost them around a million pounds. They sued the leather manufacturers under the rule in *Rylands* v. *Fletcher* and, to the surprise of the legal world, when the case reached the House of Lords it was held that storage of hazardous chemicals on industrial premises was an example of non-natural use. Lord Goff explained:

Case Summary

Case Navigator

> The mere fact that the use is common in the tanning industry cannot, in my opinion, be enough to bring the use within the exception, nor the fact that Sawston [the area where the defendant's premises were] contains a small industrial community which is worthy of encouragement or support. Indeed I feel bound to say that the storage of substantial quantities of chemicals on industrial premises should be regarded as an almost classic case of non-natural use.

Although, as we shall see later, Cambridge Water did not actually win their claim, the fact that a fairly standard industrial process was classified as a non-natural use of land meant the case was viewed as breathing new life into a tort that had been widely thought to be more or less dead. It was suggested that the rule in *Rylands* might now play an important part in protecting against industrial pollution. However, *Cambridge Water* had still not provided a clear definition of what amounted to a non-natural use of land, and the House of Lords returned to this issue again in ***Transco plc* v. *Stockport Metropolitan Borough Council*** (2003). Here the defendants owned a water pipe, which carried water from the mains supply to a block of flats. The pipe broke, through no fault of the defendants, and, over time, water seeped into a bank of earth that was supporting the claimants' gas pipe. The bank of earth collapsed, leaving the pipe without support, and the claimants had to carry out urgent and expensive repair works to prevent a gas leak. They claimed for the cost of this under *Rylands* v. *Fletcher*. The claim failed because the House of Lords said the presence of a water pipe was not an unnatural use of land, which surprised no one. However, for our purposes the usefulness of the case is that they went on to try to give a clearer definition of what non-natural use really means. Lord Bingham said that the term 'non-natural' was not really very useful, and that it might be better to think in terms of whether the defendant was an 'ordinary' user, or whether the land was being put to some 'extraordinary and unusual' use. *Rylands*, he said, should only offer a cause of action where the use of the land was extraordinary and unusual, but this would depend on the circumstances: 'a use may be extraordinary and unusual at one time or in one place, but not so at another time or in another place'. The question to be asked was whether the defendant had done something out of the ordinary, considering the time and place at which they did so.

Case Summary

Case Navigator

Case Summary

The *Transco* definition of non-natural (or extraordinary) user was applied in *LMS International* v. *Styrene Packaging and Insulation* (2005). The defendants made and stored large quantities of polystyrene, which is highly flammable, on their premises. While some of the polystyrene was being cut a spark fell onto it, causing a fire which spread to the claimants' premises. The defendants argued that they were carrying out a perfectly ordinary industrial process and so their use of the land was not non-natural, but the Technology and Construction Court held that the nature of their process created a serious risk that fire might start and spread to neighbouring premises, and this was enough to amount to a non-natural use.

As we have seen, some of the cases suggest that a further factor to be taken into account when deciding whether a use is non-natural is whether the use has some kind of benefit to the public. In both *British Celanese* and *Cambridge Water*, for example, it was argued that the industrial premises offered a public benefit by bringing jobs to the local area, while in *Rickards* it was stated that 'such a use as is proper for the general benefit of the community' was not a non-natural use. However, other cases had doubted this principle, and in *Transco* the House of Lords ruled that when considering whether a use is non-natural, it was not relevant to consider whether it was of public benefit. This again strengthens the tort as a protection against industrial pollution, since most defendants operating industrial works would be able to claim that they offered a public benefit by creating jobs, and this will no longer support their cases.

Writing and drafting

You are a trainee solicitor, and your firm has been contacted by a client who runs a chemical factory. He is being sued by the owner of neighbouring land, who claims that chemicals from your client's factory have leaked onto his land. Your boss asks you to look up the most important recent cases on non-natural user and report back to her. Read the cases of *Mason* v. *Levy*, *British Celanese* v. *Hunt*, *Cambridge Water* and *Transco* and draw up a list of bullet points to show what factors a court is likely to take into account when deciding whether your client's use of their land is non-natural.

Handy tip: Your client will ideally want to be able to show that his use of land is not a non-natural one, as this means he will not be liable under *Rylands* v. *Fletcher*. However, do not be tempted only to include points that help this argument – your boss will also need to know those factors which may count against your client, so that she can argue against them.

Something 'likely to do mischief if it escapes'

The thing that causes the problem need not be dangerous or problematic in itself, so long as it is likely to cause a problem if it escapes. In *Rylands*, for example, the water in the reservoir was not a problem in itself, it only became one because of the way it escaped into the claimant's mine shafts. Examples of dangerous things from decided cases include gas (*Batcheller* v. *Tunbridge Wells Gas Co.* (1901)); electricity (*National Telephone Co* v. *Baker* (1893)); poisonous fumes (*West* v. *Bristol Tramways Co.* (1908)); a flag pole (*Shiffman* v. *Order of St John* (1936)); tree branches (*Crowhurst* v. *Amersham*

Burial Board (1878)); and one of the chairs, complete with the person sitting in it, from a fairground 'chair-o-plane' ride (*Hale* v. *Jennings* (1938)).

Whether the thing was 'likely to do mischief' is a question of reasonable foreseeability; a defendant is not expected to guard against risks they could not possibly have known about, or which were extremely unlikely to happen. In *Transco*, Lord Bingham explained:

> I do not think the mischief or danger test should be at all easily satisfied. It must be shown that the defendant has done something which he recognised, or judged by the standards appropriate at the relevant place and time, he ought reasonably to have recognised, as giving rise to an exceptionally high risk of danger or mischief should there be an escape.

Whether the thing was 'likely to do mischief' is a question of reasonable foreseeability

In *Cambridge Water*, the case of the polluted water supply referred to above, the water company's claim failed because the leather manufacturers had no way of foreseeing that spilling chemicals on their own floor would cause pollution to the water supply, given that, among other things, the claimants' borehole was a mile away.

In most of the decided cases, the dangerous thing that the defendant has 'brought or accumulated' on the land is the same thing that escapes. However, it is possible for a claim to be allowed where the claimant has brought or accumulated something which causes something else to escape and cause a problem. An obvious example would be cases of fire, where the thing brought or accumulated is some kind of flammable material and what escapes is fire. Similarly, in *Miles* v. *Forest Rock Granite Co.* (1918), the defendants brought explosives onto their land and blew up an area of rock, which caused large boulders to fall onto the claimant's land. The claim succeeded, even though the dangerous thing they had accumulated (the explosives) was not the thing that escaped (the boulders).

Case Summary

Out and about

Try to list between 10 and 20 things that could 'cause mischief' if they escaped from someone's land – you can use everyday examples, or be as fanciful as you like. Now, read the cases on non-natural user of land, and write down what factors a court is likely to take into account when deciding whether use is natural or non-natural. Bearing these factors in mind, which of the things you have identified do you think could give rise to a claim?

An escape

The dangerous or problematic thing must 'escape' from land which the defendant owns or is in control of. This element of the tort is where strict liability still applies. As we saw earlier, when it comes to whether the hazardous thing is likely to do damage if it escapes, **reasonable foreseeability** applies, so a defendant would not be liable if they could not reasonably foresee that the thing which escapes would cause the type of damage that has been caused. But when it comes to whether there was a risk of the dangerous thing escaping at all, liability is strict. That means that a defendant can still be liable even if they could not have foreseen the escape, perhaps because the risk was very small, and even if they took all reasonable precautions to prevent the thing escaping. The reasoning behind this strict liability was explained by Lord Hobhouse in *Transco*:

> He who creates the relevant risk [by bringing or accumulating the thing that causes the harm] and has, to the exclusion of the other, the control of how he uses his land, should bear the risk. It would be unjust to deny the other a risk-based remedy and introduce a requirement of proving fault.

In other words, what the court is doing here is setting out what it sees as the correct balance between the rights of people who bring dangerous things on to their land, and the rights of those who might be affected if the dangerous thing escapes. By providing that a defendant will be liable even if they have taken reasonable care, or if a risk of escape was so small that the defendant could not be expected to see it, what they are doing is tipping the balance in favour of anyone who might be affected by the dangerous thing, on the basis that people who take the risk of bringing dangerous things on to land have to be prepared to take the consequences if they cause a problem to someone else. However, this principle is inevitably weakened by the fact that the defendant will only be liable if the damage was reasonably foreseeable, and, as we will see below, there are also **defences** which make liability less strict than it might at first appear.

The dangerous thing must go outside the defendant's land

The requirement for an escape means that the dangerous thing (or the result of it, such as fire from flammable materials) must actually go outside the borders of the defendant's land, and the damage done must also be outside those borders. This means that *Rylands* will not apply where the claimant is on the defendant's land when they are affected by the dangerous thing. In *Read* v. *Lyons* (1947), the claimant was employed to inspect munitions factories, and was visiting the defendant's factory when a shell exploded, injuring her. Because there was no evidence that the defendants were negligent, she sued under *Rylands*, but her claim failed because although shells filled with explosives were clearly a dangerous thing, the shell had not actually escaped from the defendants' land.

Case Summary

Deliberately releasing a dangerous thing

It was traditionally thought that the term 'escape' meant that the release of the dangerous thing had to be accidental. However, in *Crown River Cruises Ltd* v. *Kimbolton Fireworks Ltd* (1996) it was suggested that *Rylands* could cover intentional releases as well (in that case, letting off fireworks as part of a display), although as it turned out the defendants were held not liable under *Rylands*.

Case Summary

Damage

The tort in *Rylands* is not **actionable per se**, so the escape must cause some kind of damage. But what kind? Until recently, it was not clear whether a claim for personal injury or death could be brought under *Rylands*, but in *Transco* the House of Lords stated that this was not possible because *Rylands* was essentially a form of nuisance, and so was concerned only with claims involving land. This suggests that the damage

You be the judge

Q: Simon and Louis are next-door neighbours. Simon has a huge garden, and on Bonfire Night he puts on a big firework display, to which he invites all his neighbours including Louis. During the display, a Catherine wheel comes away from the fence that Simon has nailed it to, flies through the air and hits Louis, who is standing nearby with the rest of the guests. He is injured.

Does Louis have a case under *Rylands* v. *Fletcher?*

A: No. Although Simon has clearly brought a dangerous thing on to his land, Louis is actually on Simon's land when he is injured, so there is no escape of the dangerous thing. The answer might be different if Louis had been standing in his own garden at the time.

Source: Pearson Education Ltd/Photodisc/Life File/Jeremy Hoare

must be some form of interference with the claimant's use or enjoyment of their land, as for nuisance.

The claimant must be able to show that the damage was caused by the escape, under the normal rules of **causation** detailed in Chapter 3. As stated in *Cambridge Water* and *Transco*, the test for **remoteness of damage** is reasonable foreseeability (have a look back at pages 69–80 and 80–87 if you want to remind yourself about the rules on causation and remoteness).

Defences

There are six defences to a claim under *Rylands* v. *Fletcher*:

- consent;
- common benefit;
- contributory negligence/default of the claimant;
- act of a stranger;
- act of God;
- statutory authority.

Consent

A claimant who has consented to the dangerous thing being on the defendant's land will not have a claim under *Rylands* v. *Fletcher*. This is an application of the general defence of ***volenti***, which we have looked at in previous chapters.

Case Summary

The consent can be express, where the claimant specifically states that they are accepting the presence of the dangerous thing, but is more often implied by the claimant's behaviour. In *Peters* v. *Prince of Wales Theatre (Birmingham) Ltd* (1943), the claimant rented a shop from the defendants, who owned a theatre next door. Like most theatres, the defendants' had a sprinkler system for dealing with fires and during cold weather its pipes burst, flooding the shop next door. The claimant failed to make a case under *Rylands* v. *Fletcher*, because the sprinkler system had been in place when he rented the shop and so he was considered to have consented to it being there. This contrasts with the situation in nuisance where, as we saw in Chapter 14, 'coming to the nuisance' is not a defence.

Common benefit

This defence applies where the presence of the dangerous or problematic thing on the defendant's land is of benefit to the claimant as well as the defendant. Obvious examples would be things like shared water tanks, or gas or water pipes. In some cases, common benefit has been treated as a part of the consent defence.

Contributory negligence/default of the claimant

Contributory negligence applies in just the same way as for other torts, so if the escape of the dangerous thing is partly the claimant's own fault, **damages** may be reduced to take account of that. There is also a related defence, called default of the claimant, where the escape of the dangerous thing is entirely the fault of the claimant or, more commonly, where the claimant was using their land in a way that made them unusually vulnerable to harm. If the defence of default of the claimant applies, there is no claim. This was the case in *Eastern and South Africa Telegraph Co.* v. *Cape Town Tramways Co.* (1902). The claimants were in the business of sending messages via electric cables, and a very minor escape of electricity from the defendants' premises caused a fault in the cables, which temporarily prevented messages being sent. Their claim was rejected because the leak of electricity was not sufficient to do any permanent harm, and the Court held that the fact that the claimants' business was unusually sensitive to the effect of such a leak did not give them a claim.

Case Summary

Act of a stranger

Where the escape of the dangerous thing is caused by someone other than the defendant, who is not acting for the defendant and who the defendant has no control over, the defendant will not be liable. Despite the name of the defence, the person who causes the escape does not have to be literally a stranger; it can still apply if the defendant knows that person, provided they were not acting on the defendant's behalf.

Case Summary

The defence was applied in *Box* v. *Jubb* (1879), where the defendants' reservoir overflowed onto the claimant's land, but they were held not liable because the flooding was caused by a third person who had emptied his own reservoir into the stream which fed the defendants' reservoir. The difference between this and the facts of *Rylands* v. *Fletcher* itself is that in *Rylands* the builders who caused the flood were acting on the defendant's behalf.

In cases where the defence of act of a stranger is raised, there will usually be an alternative claim in negligence, where the claimant seeks to prove that the defendant could reasonably have foreseen the risk of a third party causing the escape and should have taken steps to prevent it.

Act of God

Despite the name, this defence does not require the intervention of any kind of god. It applies where the escape of the dangerous thing was caused purely by natural forces, in circumstances where the defendant could not reasonably have been expected to guard against it. It was applied in *Nichols* v. *Marsland* (1876), where the defendant made a dam in a natural stream on his land in order to create three artificial lakes. The whole thing was well built, and precautions against flooding would have been quite adequate for normal circumstances, but there was an extremely heavy thunderstorm – described by witnesses as the worst in living memory – which burst the banks of the lakes. Water rushed down the stream and onto the claimant's land, and swept away four bridges there. The defendant was held not liable because he could not reasonably have been expected to predict such a heavy thunderstorm, and if it had not happened the lakes would never have burst their banks.

Case Summary

However, it is now considered that the act of God defence will apply much more rarely than the *Nichols* case suggests. In *Greenock Corporation* v. *Caledonian Railway* (1917), which involved quite similar facts, the defence was held to be unavailable. The corporation had built a concrete paddling pool for children, and in the process had diverted the flow of a stream. As in *Nichols*, there was an exceptionally heavy rainstorm and the stream overflowed, flooding a nearby street and damaging the claimants' property. The House of Lords concluded that the rainfall was not sufficiently extreme to be considered an act of God, and the defence did not apply. The defence has been criticised for importing negligence principles into the strict liability aspect of *Rylands*, and it is now thought likely that it could only apply to extreme situations, such as earthquakes or hurricanes.

Case Summary

Statutory authority

Where the activity for which the defendant uses the dangerous thing is regulated by statute, the relevant Act may provide a defence to a claim regarding escape of that thing. In many cases, however, statutes do not make a clear statement about defences, and the courts will have to look closely at the wording of the Act to determine whether a defence was intended. As a general rule, there is more likely to be a defence where a statute creates a *duty* for the defendant to undertake an activity which could lead to the escape of a dangerous thing (meaning that it says they are required to do that thing), and less likely to be a defence where the statute only creates a *power* to undertake such an activity (meaning that it only says they can lawfully do that thing). In *Green* v. *Chelsea Waterworks Co.* (1894), a water pipe laid by the defendant burst, flooding the claimant's premises. The Court of Appeal held that the water company was not liable, because they were obliged by statute to provide a water supply, and the occasional burst pipe was an inevitable result of doing so. By contrast, in *Charing Cross Electricity Co.* v. *Hydraulic Co.* (1914), which featured very similar facts, the defendants had no defence, because the relevant statute gave them the power to provide a water supply, but did not oblige them to do so.

Case Summary

You be the judge

Q: Carol runs a car repair business. In her workshop she stores cylinders of oxyacetylene gas, which is used for welding and is highly flammable. Greg is a business rival of Carol's, and is furious that Carol has just won a contract with a car hire firm that he was hoping to get. He sets fire to Carol's workshop late at night, and the gas cylinders explode. The resulting fire spreads next door and burns down a shop owned by John.

Does John have a claim against Carol?

A: No. Carol is covered by the defence of act of a stranger, because the escape was caused by someone who was not acting for her and who she had no control over (remember that despite the name, the person does not actually have to be a stranger).

Source: Pearson Education Ltd/Fancy/Veer/Corbis

Figure 15.1 Liability under *Rylands* v. *Fletcher*

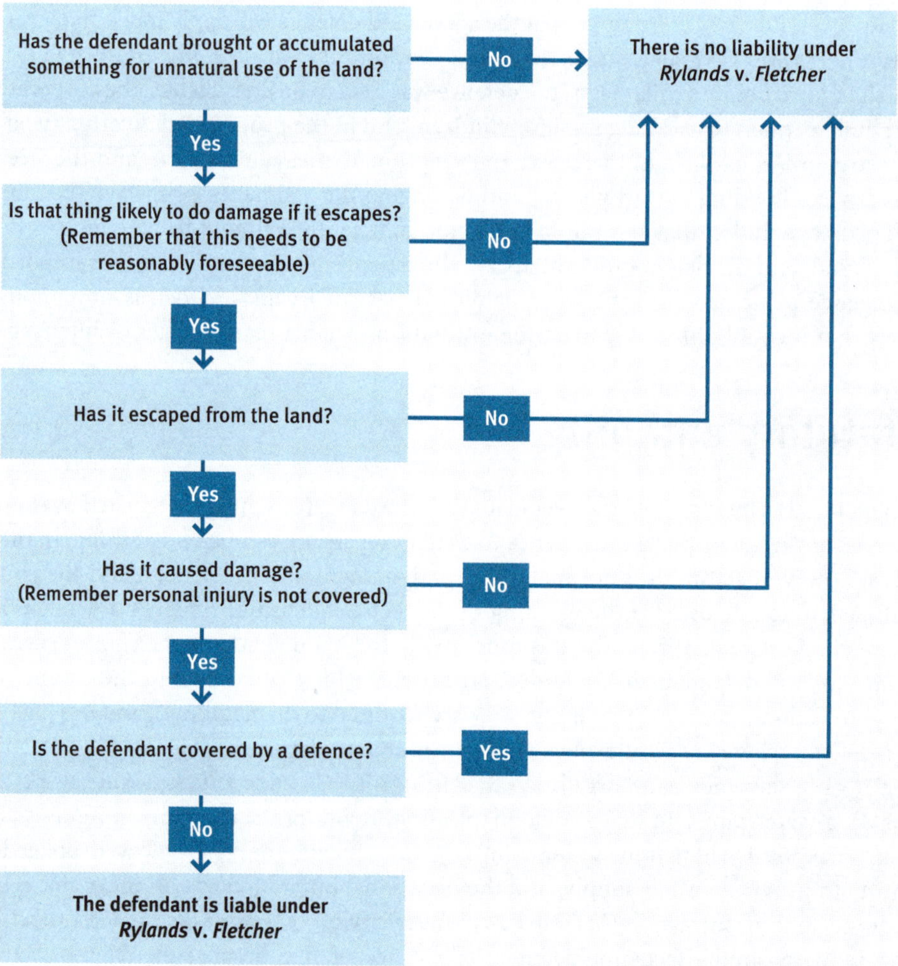

The role of *Rylands* v. *Fletcher*

As we saw earlier, *Rylands* v. *Fletcher* was decided at a time when Britain was becoming increasingly industrialised. This process brought prosperity to the country, but also brought problems in the form of pollution and industrial accidents. Against this background, the tort created in *Rylands* could have gone on to be interpreted by future courts as a wide-ranging cause of action, imposing strict liability for activities which create a risk of danger or harm, and covering not just land-based problems but also cases of personal injury. However, the increasing importance to the country of mechanised industry, and then the growth of negligence, with its emphasis on the fairness of making liability dependent on fault, meant that the strict liability approach of *Rylands* began to fall out of favour. For this reason, by the last decade of the twentieth century, it was widely thought that the tort in *Rylands* v. *Fletcher* was all but dead. When the case of *Cambridge Water* was decided, however, it was seen as bringing *Rylands* back to life, because it seemed to reactivate the idea that *Rylands* could protect against the harm caused by industry, and a flurry of academic articles argued that *Rylands* could now develop into a useful action for protecting against harm to the environment caused by industrial pollution. This has not happened though, perhaps because pollution is now largely controlled by statutory provisions, and *Rylands* remains a tort whose place in legal textbooks is much bigger than its place in the everyday practice of law.

it was widely thought that the tort in *Rylands* v. *Fletcher* was all but dead

As a result, it has been argued that the tort in *Rylands* should be abolished altogether, as has happened in the Australian legal system (see the 2004 article by Murphy, in Further reading and references sections). However, this idea was rejected in *Transco*, which is the latest House of Lords word on the subject. Their Lordships acknowledged that arguments had been made for absorbing the kinds of situations covered by *Rylands* into the much larger tort of negligence, but they said that, although *Rylands* might only be used in a very small number of cases, it still had a role to play and should be preserved. Lord Bingham stated that there was 'a category of case, however small it may be, in which it seems just to impose liability even in the absence of fault'. The categories of case which Lord Bingham chose to illustrate his point, however, seemed to confuse the issue. He mentioned the 1966 Aberfan disaster, in which a slag heap collapsed onto a village school, as an example of the kind of situation where compensation should be available even if fault could not be proved. But the tragedy of Aberfan was that it killed 144 people, 116 of them schoolchildren, rather than that it destroyed 20 houses and the school and, as the House of Lords in *Transco* had made it plain that *Ryland* should be seen as a 'sub-species of nuisance' which did not cover claims for personal injury, there would have been no claim for the most important damage the disaster caused. However, the fact remains that by allowing *Rylands* to keep breathing, rather than finally killing it off, the House of Lords is at least allowing some possibility of redress for damage caused by very hazardous activities, even where fault cannot be proved.

it has been argued that the tort in *Rylands* should be abolished altogether

Other protections against hazardous activities

Many – perhaps most – of the activities which *Rylands* could provide protection against are now regulated by statute, as governments have acknowledged the fact that technological advances bring problems as well as benefits. Some of these statutes impose strict liability for the escape of certain dangerous things, such as the Reservoirs Act 1975, regarding accumulated water, and the Nuclear Installations Acts 1965 and 1969, which cover the escape of radiation.

Summary

- The tort in *Rylands* v. *Fletcher* deals with situations where an occupier of land brings or accumulates something on to the land which is likely to cause harm if it escapes, and the thing does escape and causes damage. The thing that escapes must amount to a 'non-natural' use of the land; a defendant is not liable if the thing that caused the problem occurred quite naturally on the land.

- 'Non-natural use' has never been clearly defined, and has meant different things at different times. Modern cases suggest the courts will look at the whole context, including the amount of dangerous material and the character of the surrounding neighbourhood, and whether the land was being put to some 'extraordinary and unusual' use. The fact that the use has a public benefit does not prevent liability.

- The thing that causes the problem need not be dangerous or problematic in itself, so long as it is likely to cause a problem if it escapes. This is a question of reasonable foreseeability; a defendant is not expected to guard against risks they could not possibly have known about, or which were extremely unlikely to happen.

- Regarding the risk of the escape happening, liability is strict, so a defendant can be liable even if the risk of escape was small and they could not have expected it to happen, and even if they took all reasonable precautions to prevent the thing escaping.

- The dangerous or problematic thing must 'escape' from land which the defendant owns or is in control of; there is no liability if the claimant is on the defendant's land when they are affected by the dangerous thing.

- The escape must cause some kind of damage to the land or interference with the enjoyment of it. There is no liability for personal injury.

- There are six defences to a claim under *Rylands* v. *Fletcher*:
  - consent;
  - common benefit;
  - contributory negligence/default of the claimant;
  - act of a stranger;
  - act of God;
  - statutory authority.

Question and answer*

Problem: Anytown Council own a park through which a river flows. After a heavy rainstorm, the river bursts its banks, causing a flood, and the waters spread on to neighbouring land owned by Tom, where he lives and also runs a business breeding ornamental fish. The bottom floor of his house is flooded, causing thousands of pounds worth of damage. Some weeks later, there is an explosion in the park, and a lump of burning wood flies across onto Tom's land, setting fire to an outbuilding where he stores equipment for his business and injuring Tom who is in there at the time. It turns out that the council had been storing a huge quantity of fireworks in the park ready for a display, and Jerry, a former employee of the council, had set fire to the shed where they were stored as revenge for them sacking him.

On the other side of Tom's land is a small factory owned by Margie. She keeps drums of highly poisonous chemicals there, which are kept in a storage shed quite near the boundary with Tom's land. Margie always keeps this shed locked, as required by safety regulations, but unknown to her one of the drums has a leak and the chemical inside it seeps out and gets on to Tom's land. It contaminates his ponds and kills his fish. Margie did not know Tom bred fish.

Advise Tom as to any claims he may have against Anytown Council or Margie under the rule in *Rylands* v. *Fletcher*.

You should allow yourself no more than 40 minutes to complete this task.

Essay: Critically examine the rule in *Rylands* v. *Fletcher*.
This question should be answered in 40 minutes.

* Answer guidance is provided at the end of the chapter.

Further reading and reference

Amirthalingam, K. (2004) '*Rylands* lives', 63 CLJ 273.
This is a case note on the case of *Transco*, in which the author argues that *Rylands* v. *Fletcher* still has a place as a separate tort in modern law.

Law Commission Report No. 32 (1970) Civil Liability for Dangerous Things and Activities, London: HMSO.
This report includes recommendations for reform of the tort in *Rylands* v. *Fletcher*.

Murphy, J. (2004) 'The merits of *Rylands* v. *Fetcher*', 24(4) OJLS 643.
This interesting article looks at the Australian courts' decision to abolish the tort in *Rylands* v. *Fletcher* and expand the tort of negligence to fill the gap. The author argues against this move, and suggests that *Rylands* is still valid as a tort in its own right. Essay questions often ask whether the tort still has a role in modern law and this article will give you some useful argument to use in that kind of question.

Simpson, A. (1984) 'Legal liability for bursting reservoirs: the historical context of *Rylands* v. *Fletcher*', 13 *Journal of Legal Studies* 209 (University of Chicago Press).
This article looks at the background against which the tort was created, and why the courts decided to create a new tort at this time.

Question and answer guidance

Problem: Looking first at Tom's claim against Anytown regarding the flood, this one is quite straightforward. Liability under *Rylands* can only apply where the defendant brings on to their land or accumulates something dangerous, and not where, as here, the harm comes from a naturally occurring feature of the land.

What about Tom's claim with regard to the fire? Here you need to go through the elements of the tort and apply them to the situation. Look at the modern cases on non-natural user, and explain what the courts would look at when deciding whether the fireworks were a non-natural use. If this is a non-natural use, was it reasonably foreseeable that the fireworks would cause damage if there was an escape? Remember that reasonable foresight only applies to whether the thing was likely to be dangerous; if it was, then it does not matter whether the council could reasonably foresee that there might be an escape or not, as liability on this is strict. You might also want to mention the case of *Miles* v. *Forest Rock Granite Co.* to make the point that it does not matter that it was not the fireworks themselves that escaped but that they caused the burning wood to escape. You should also look at the type of damage caused, and point out that the council will not be liable for Tom's injury as personal injury is not covered by *Rylands*, again using authority from the cases. Don't forget to consider whether the council have a defence – is this a case of act of a stranger?

Turning to Tom's potential claim against Margie, again you need to go through the elements of the tort, using the cases to back up the points you make. A key issue here is whether it matters that Margie took what seem to be reasonable precautions to prevent the chemicals escaping – remember that under *Rylands* there is strict liability on the matter of whether the dangerous thing might escape, so this is unlikely to help her. But she can only be liable for damage of a type that she can reasonably foresee; do you think it makes a difference that she did not know that Tom kept fish? To answer this section of the question, you will need to apply the rules on remoteness of damage – have a look back at page 80 if you want to remind yourself of them.

Essay: A good way to start your essay would be to place the tort in *Rylands* in its historical context, explaining why it was created and what it was designed to do. You can then point out that its use has declined in recent years and there is some question about whether it still has a role to play.

Then work your way through the elements of the tort and, as you go, highlight any problems or weaknesses with the law. On the issue of non-natural user, for example, you could point to the lack of clarity surrounding this concept, and the way it has changed over time, which makes it difficult to predict what kinds of situation will be protected. On the issue of whether the thing was brought on to land, you can talk about the fact that reasonable foreseeability applies here and that dilutes the original concept of a strict liability tort, and on damage, you can talk about the fact that personal injury is not covered, which limits the usefulness of the tort – you might want to mention the fact that Lord Bingham in *Transco* gives the Aberfan disaster as an example of a case where the tort could be useful, yet it would not have been applicable to the worst part of the disaster. A key issue here is how far the tort is or should be a tort of strict liability, so you may want to incorporate some of the arguments for and against strict liability that we looked at on page 12 (though make sure you select those that are relevant to the kind of situations covered by *Rylands*).

You could conclude by discussing whether you think *Rylands* still has a role to play in modern law; the articles by Murphy (2004) and Amirthalingam (2004) will give you some useful arguments for this.

Visit **www.mylawchamber.co.uk/quinntort** to access tools to help you develop and test your knowledge of tort law, including practice exam questions with guidance, annotated weblinks, glossary and key case flashcards, legal newsfeed and legal updates and interactive 'You be the judge' questions.

Use Case Navigator to read in full some of the key cases referenced in this chapter with commentary and questions:

Cambridge Water Co. Ltd* v. *Eastern Counties Leather plc [1994] 1 All ER 53

Transco plc* v. *Stockport Metropolitan Borough Council [2004] 1 All ER 589

Chapter 16
Defamation: general principles

Key points In this chapter we will be looking at:

- ✦ How the tort of defamation is committed
- ✦ Who can sue and be sued for defamation

Introduction

Imagine that you are a famous actor or actress. You've just had some building work done on your home, and a few days later you read a newspaper story claiming that while the work was being done you ordered all the builders not to try to talk to you, and to face the wall whenever you walked past. This is not true, but you know that many people reading the paper will believe it and think you must be horribly arrogant. Or let's say you did some modelling when you were younger, and many years later a newspaper uses one of your old pictures to illustrate a feature on teenagers who have been given ASBOs. You have never been given an ASBO, but you think people seeing the picture will assume you have. Or you have a business selling items autographed by celebrities. One day a well-known footballer's wife happens to pass your shop, and loudly declares that your goods are fakes and her husband never signed the photograph in your window (though you know he did). Her words are reported in the papers, and you are worried that people will believe that you must be selling fakes and stop coming to your shop.

All of these are the kinds of situations that could led to a claim for defamation, and in fact they have: the first brought by Nicole Kidman, the second by actor Harry Capehorn, and the third against Victoria Beckham. Defamation protects against damage to a person's (or company's, or organisation's) reputation. It gives a claim where someone makes public an untrue statement about someone else, which could damage that person's reputation among the general public, or even just people they know.

Most defamation claims are brought over material published in newspapers, magazines or books, or broadcast on television or radio, but a claim can also be made over words spoken between individuals, written in a letter or email, or posted on a social networking site. Similarly, many defamation claims are brought by celebrities and others who are in the public eye, but the law applies to everyone and if, say, *The Sun* or the BBC said something untrue and defamatory about you or me, we could also sue for defamation.

In this chapter, we will look at liability for defamation, and in the following chapter we will examine the defences that can be used in a defamation case, the remedies claimants can be awarded, and some problems with the law.

Some background to defamation

Before we start focusing on the rules of defamation, there is some background information that is useful to know and that will help you understand the cases we will go on to look at later.

Defamation and freedom of expression

In Britain, as in most democratic societies, the law recognises a right to freedom of expression (in other words, to say whatever you want to), and this right is set down in Article 10 of the European Convention on Human Rights. However, there is no modern society where this right is completely unrestricted, in other words, where you have an absolute right to say whatever you want to regardless of any damage it might do. This is because the right to freedom of expression often conflicts with other important rights and interests, and so we have laws which aim to strike a balance between the two. For example, we have laws against revealing information that could put the country's security at risk, and against making statements that stir up racial hatred, because it is considered that protecting the country's security and preventing racial hatred are important causes, which have to be balanced against the importance of freedom of expression.

the right to freedom of expression often conflicts with other important rights and interests

The law on defamation is another example of a restriction on freedom of speech, because it means there are times when a claimant's right not to have their reputation damaged will outweigh a defendant's right to freedom of expression. In that case, the **claimant** can claim **damages** from the maker of the defamatory statement and, if necessary, an **injunction** to prevent the statement being repeated (and in rarer cases, where the claimant knows a defamatory statement is going to be made, they can get an injunction preventing it being said in the first place).

It is easy to see how an injunction prevents freedom of speech, but how do damages prevent freedom of speech, when they can come only after the damaging thing has been said? The reason why they can have this effect is simple: if a newspaper or magazine, for example, knows they may face damages if they publish a particular story, they may be less likely to do so, and so freedom of speech on that subject is being restricted by the fear of being sued. You might well think that preventing publication of information that damages someone's reputation would always be a good thing but, as we will see later, there are situations where it is in the public interest for information to be published, even though it might be untrue and damage someone's reputation. Therefore, in defamation cases, the courts will often need to balance the claimant's right to protect their reputation against the defendant's right to freedom of expression.

Procedure in defamation cases

Defamation is one of the few types of civil claim that is usually still tried by a jury. A judge can decide that a case is too complex for jury trial, but this happens only rarely. The judge's role in the case is to decide whether, in law, the statement made about the claimant is capable of being defamatory. If it is, the jury decides whether the statement is in fact defamatory. The jury also decides the damages.

The vast majority of defamation cases, however, do not go to trial at all. Most are settled out of court and, as part of the **settlement**, the **defendant** may give an apology or correction, and pay damages.

Key stats Settlements in defamation cases

Most defamation cases never reach trial and instead are settled out of court. This saves the losing side the cost of a trial, but it can still mean that the defendant has to pay hefty damages, as these recent settlements show:

- **£10,000:** Paid by *The Sun* to Lily Allen, over claims that she called Cheryl Cole 'stupid and superficial' and Victoria Beckham 'a monster'.
- **£45,000:** Paid by the BBC to the secretary general of the Muslim Council of Great Britain, after a guest on one of its programmes suggested he approved of the kidnapping of British soldiers.
- **£50,000:** Paid by *The Sun* to former *EastEnders* actor Chris Parker, after it said he had been sacked from the soap after refusing to see a psychiatrist.
- **£100,000:** Paid by the *Sunday Mirror* to a man whose photo was used by mistake to illustrate a story about a convicted rapist.
- **£550,000:** Paid by Express Newspapers to Kate and Gerry McCann, for stories implying they were responsible for the disappearance of their daughter Madeleine.

Liability for defamation

Defamation is committed by publishing a statement which lowers the reputation of the person referred to in the estimation of right-thinking members of society generally (this is known as a defamatory statement). There are three elements to the tort:

- there must be a defamatory statement;
- the statement must refer to the claimant;
- the statement must be published. As we will see, this covers not just publication in the media, but almost any communication to someone else.

However, the fact that these three elements are satisfied does not always mean that the defendant will be liable. There are a number of **defences** to defamation (which we will look at in the next chapter), which means there are situations in which defamatory statements can be published without liability. As we will see, the basis of most of these defences is that there are situations where free speech is more important than protection of reputation.

Defamatory statements

In most cases, defamation is committed by the use of words, in the form of a statement which damages the claimant's reputation. These words might be spoken out loud, broadcast on the radio or television, posted on the internet, or printed in a newspaper. They might even be part of a play or a film. But as we will see later, a 'defamatory statement' can also be committed by the use of a picture, or a piece of video.

Libel and slander

There are two types of defamation, libel and slander, and which one a claim falls under will depend on how the defamatory statement was made:

- Libel covers statements made in some kind of permanent form. In most cases, this means printed or written words, but it also covers film, pictures, statues and words or pictures on the internet. Statute provides that it also covers radio broadcasts (under the Broadcasting Act 1990) and the performance of plays (under the Theatres Act 1968), even though these both appear to be less permanent forms of expression.
- Slander applies to defamation made in a transitory form, meaning one for which there is no permanent record, such as spoken words or gestures.

The elements of the tort are the same for both libel and slander, but there is one difference between them. Merely committing a libel without a defence creates a claim; it is not necessary to prove that the defamatory statement actually caused the claimant any kind of loss. With slander however, the claimant must usually show that the defendant's statement caused them some kind of special damage, and this will almost always be financial loss. There are some exceptions to this rule, which are discussed on page 405.

Where this chapter and the next refer to defamation, whatever is said will apply to both libel and slander.

You be the judge

Q: **Which of these could create liability for slander, and which for libel?**

(a) ***The Sun*** **writes something defamatory about you.**
(b) **Someone writes something defamatory about you and posts it on Facebook.**
(c) **A reporter on BBC Radio 4 makes a defamatory remark about you.**
(d) **Someone stands up at the beginning of one of your law lectures and makes a defamatory remark about you.**

A: (a), (b) and (c) could all create liability for libel, and (d) could create liability for slander.

What does 'defamatory' mean?

Most of the original law on defamation comes from case law rather than statute, so there is no single definition of what 'defamatory' means. However, the commonly accepted definition comes from the leading tort academic, Sir Percy Winfield:

> Defamation is the publication of a statement which tends to lower the person [that the statement is about] in the estimation of right-thinking members of society generally, or which tends to make them shun or avoid that person.

This is still accurate, but a more precise definition, in line with modern cases, is the one given by academics McBride and Bagshaw in their book *Tort Law* (Longman, 2008). They say that defamation is committed by publishing a statement that would make an ordinary, reasonable person tend to:

- think less well as a person of the individual referred to; or
- think that the person referred to lacked the ability to do their job properly; or
- shun or avoid the person referred to; or
- treat the person referred to as an object of ridicule.

This definition makes it clear that the important issue is not how the defamatory statement makes the person referred to feel, or what the person making the statement meant by it. Instead, the important thing is the impression that the statement is likely to make on someone reading or hearing it; what effect will it have on their opinion of the person referred to? The person who claims they have been defamed does not have to prove that the words actually had a bad effect on anyone's view of them, only that the statement could tend to have that effect on an ordinary, reasonable listener, viewer or reader.

Defamation and truth

A statement can only give rise to a defamation claim if it is untrue. However, this gives less protection to a defendant that you might imagine, for two reasons. First, the claimant is not required to prove that the statement is untrue. If it is defamatory, the court will assume it is untrue. Secondly, if the defendant wants to claim that it is true, they must put forward the defence of justification, and *prove* that it is true. We will look at justification more fully in the next chapter, but the important thing to remember is that the defendant will not be protected just because the statement is true: they have to be able to prove it, and that is not always easy.

Some examples of defamatory statements

From what you have read so far, it will be clear that it would be defamatory to say, for example, that someone was a thief, or a paedophile, or a benefits cheat, because most ordinary, reasonable people would think less well of someone if they heard this. If a defendant makes a statement as obviously defamatory as one of these, they would usually only defend the case if they believe they can use one of the defences to defamation (for example, if they can prove that the statement is true).

In many cases, however, whether or not a statement is defamatory may not be so clear.

Case Summary

In *Cruise and Kidman* v. *Express Newspapers* (1998), the *Express on Sunday*'s magazine claimed that actress Nicole Kidman had insisted that builders working on her house should face the wall whenever she walked past. At first instance, the court found that the comment, though unpleasant, was not capable in law of being defamatory, but Ms Kidman appealed, and the Court of Appeal agreed with her that the words were capable of being defamatory. Bearing in mind that the judge at first instance would have been one who was very experienced in defamation cases, you can see the problem: if experienced judges cannot always predict what, in law, is considered defamatory, it can be very difficult for a newspaper editor, or the newspaper's lawyer, to do so. The case was eventually settled out of court, with the *Express* paying damages.

In *Jason Donovan* v. *The Face* (1998), the singer Jason Donovan sued *The Face* magazine for saying he was gay. However, he did not claim it was defamatory to say that someone was gay. Instead, he argued that he had always presented himself as being heterosexual, and that by saying he was actually gay the magazine was saying that he had lied to the public about his sexuality. The Court therefore had to consider whether an ordinary, reasonable person would think badly of a celebrity for doing this. They concluded that the allegation was defamatory.

Case Summary

In *Berkoff* v. *Burchill* (1996), the journalist Julie Burchill described actor Steven Berkoff as 'hideous-looking' and compared him to Frankenstein's monster. Usually, mere insults about someone's personal appearance would not be considered defamatory because, as we have seen, the question is not whether the statement upsets the person referred to, but whether it would make others see them in a bad light. Comments about someone's appearance would usually be less likely to do this than allegations about things they may have done, because people can see for themselves what the person looks like and form their own opinion. In this case, however, the Court said the words were capable of being defamatory, because the claimant earned his living as an actor and the statements made him an object of ridicule in that context.

Case Summary

In *Mitchell* v. *Faber & Faber* (1998), the claimant was a musician who had worked with the black rock star Jimi Hendrix during the 1960s. The defendants were the publishers of a book about Hendrix, which stated that the claimant had 'a strange contempt' for Hendrix and routinely used words like 'nigger' and 'coon' in everyday conversation. The book said that the claimant had no idea that he might offend anyone by this and did not intend any harm. The claimant sued, claiming that the book made him appear racist. The defendants argued that the book was not defamatory, because it made clear that the claimant had not intended to offend Hendrix, and that his attitude was simply typical of many people in the UK 40 years ago. The Court of Appeal rejected this argument. They said that although it was true that such attitudes were widely held at the time the book was talking about, it was necessary to consider what impression it would make on people reading it now, and therefore the words could be defamatory.

Case Summary

The 'right-thinking person' test

As we saw earlier, the test for whether a statement is defamatory is the effect it has on a 'right-thinking member of society', or in more modern terms, an ordinary, reasonable person. A statement will not be defamatory because it would make certain people with particular views think less of the person referred to, so long as it would not make the ordinary, reasonable person think less of them. This was the situation in *Byrne* v. *Deane* (1937). The claimant was a member of a golf club, where the owners illegally installed gambling machines. Someone reported them to the police, and afterwards a poem was pinned up in the club which implied that Mr Byrne had been the informant. He sued, but the Court held that the poem was not capable of being defamatory, because a right-thinking member of society would not think less well of someone for telling the police about criminal activity. The fact that some people – perhaps those who used the machines – might think badly of him was not enough.

Case Summary

Changes over time

The fact that allegedly defamatory statements are tested by their possible effect on an ordinary, reasonable person means that standards can change over time. Sixty years ago, for example, it would certainly have been defamatory to say of an unmarried woman that she had spent the night with her boyfriend. Today this would not be defamatory unless, for example, the woman had portrayed herself as being against sex outside marriage, in which case she could claim she was being presented as a hypocrite (as we saw earlier that Jason Donovan did when he was claimed to be gay).

Indirect criticisms

A statement can be defamatory even if it does not directly criticise the claimant, but instead implies a criticism. This is known as an innuendo, and here the court will look at what an ordinary reader or listener would think the statement was suggesting. In some cases, the innuendo may take the form of a deliberate hint: if a newspaper writes, for example: 'John Greedy MP says he has never taken bribes, and we all know that politicians never lie, don't we?', they are clearly implying that John Greedy is lying about taking bribes.

More often, however, the issue is that the words themselves may be factually true, but the claimant alleges that they carry a meaning or implication that is defamatory. Take, for example, a situation where John Smith has been interviewed by the police because they think he may have witnessed a murder. His local paper writes: 'John Smith has been questioned by police investigating the murder of Jane Jones.' The literal meaning is true: John was questioned by police, because he was a potential witness. But John claims the story implies he is suspected of the murder, or even that he is guilty of it, and that this is defamatory. In all these kinds of case, the court has to decide what an ordinary, reasonable person would have thought the statement meant, and whether that meaning is defamatory.

Case Summary

An example of this sort of case is *Marks & Spencer* v. *Granada TV* (1998). Granada made a television programme which said that M&S clothing was being made by child workers in Morocco. This was true, and Granada had film to prove it. However, M&S said that the programme implied that they had knowingly and deliberately used child labour to increase their own profits, when in fact they had not known that their supplier was using child workers and had stopped buying from that supplier as soon as they found out. M&S won their case.

Case Summary

Often, an innuendo will arise out of words (or words and pictures) that look quite innocent on the surface, and may have been meant quite innocently, but contain an innuendo because of external circumstances. An example of this is *Tolley* v. *J. S. Fry & Sons Ltd* (1931). Mr Tolley was a well-known and successful amateur golfer. In those days, amateur golfers did not accept any form of paid sponsorship or advertising contracts, and anyone who did so would be disapproved of. Without his knowledge, the defendants, a chocolate company, published an advert showing a cartoon of Mr Tolley holding their chocolate, with a little rhyme explaining how their chocolate was as good as his performance on the golf course. Clearly, it is not usually defamatory to suggest that someone might eat chocolate but Mr Tolley claimed that the advert would make people think he had been paid to promote the chocolate, and that as he was an amateur sportsman this would damage his reputation. The Court agreed that this innuendo was capable of being defamatory.

Case Summary

In *Dwek* v. *Macmillan Publishers* (1999), the defendants published a book which contained a photo showing the claimant sitting next to a woman who was correctly identified as a prostitute. Mr Dwek was not the subject of the book, and was not named anywhere in it, but he said that anyone seeing the picture might assume he was a client of the prostitute. The publishers argued that the words and picture were not capable of carrying this defamatory meaning, because there was no reference to the claimant, and nothing in the book that suggested he even knew the woman was a prostitute, nor had he produced any readers who had recognised him in the photo. The Court of Appeal rejected this argument, and said that, taken together, the words and photo were capable of being defamatory. It was not necessary for the claimant to prove that anyone had in fact recognised him in the photo.

The importance of context

In assessing whether a statement is capable of being defamatory, the court will look at the whole context in which it was made. In *Norman* v. *Future Publishing* (1998), the claimant was Jessie Norman, a famous opera singer, and the claim arose after she was interviewed by a classical music magazine. The magazine article was on the whole a complimentary one, and in it Ms Norman was quoted as saying, apparently in reference to her large size, that she never went through a door sideways because 'Honey, I ain't got no sideways'. She said she had never said that, and that it was defamatory because it suggested she was vulgar and undignified. The Court of Appeal found that the words were not capable of being defamatory in the context of an article that portrayed Ms Norman as a person of high standing and great dignity.

Case Summary

What about the fact that Ms Norman claimed she did not actually say the words? You may be surprised to know that in the context of defamation this is considered irrelevant. There is no liability in defamation for making a statement up and publishing it, unless the statement is defamatory. If a made-up quote is used, the person who is supposed to have said the words can sue for false attribution of ownership, under the Copyright, Designs and Patents Act 1988, but this action is taken surprisingly rarely, perhaps because it is difficult to prove that you did not say something.

Out and about

Gather together a range of newspapers (both tabloids and the more serious papers) and magazines. Bearing in mind everything you have read in this chapter so far, go through them, and see how many potentially defamatory stories and articles you can spot. Keep the examples you find, as you will use them again in an exercise in Chapter 17.

Source: Pearson Education Ltd/Photodisc/Photolink

The statement must refer to the claimant

As well as proving that the statement is defamatory, the claimant must prove that an ordinary, reasonable reader or listener would think the statement referred to him or her. Obviously, if the claimant is named in the defamatory statement, or shown in a picture that forms part of it, that is enough to establish that the statement refers to them. But a statement can also be taken to refer to someone who is not named or shown in a picture, if the details that are given would mean a reasonable person would think it was about that person. In *J'Anson* v. *Stuart* (1787), a newspaper referred to a 'swindler' who, it said had one eye and was 'well known to all persons acquainted with the name of a certain noble circumnavigator [a person who sails round the world]'. The claimant had one eye, and his name was very similar to the name of a famous admiral. He was able to show that the statement referred to him, even though his name was not mentioned.

Case Summary

Case Summary

A more modern example is *Capehorn* v. *Independent News and Media* (2006). This was the case referred to in the introduction to this chapter, involving the actor Harry Capehorn. He had done some modelling as a teenager, before his face became known on television, and an old picture from that time was used to illustrate a story on teenagers who had been given ASBOs. Normal practice when using a picture that is just there as a general illustration would be to print the words 'Posed by model', to signify that the person in the picture is not referred to in the story, but for some reason this was not done. The newspaper did not mention Mr Capehorn in the story, nor intend to suggest that he had ever had an ASBO, but he successfully claimed that anyone who recognised him in the picture might think he had. This kind of issue can be a problem for broadcasters too; for example, if a television channel was to illustrate a report on shoplifting with some general film of shoppers in a supermarket, they could be sued by anyone who was recognisable in the film, on the basis that the package as a whole is implying he or she is a shoplifter.

It is not necessary to prove that *every* reasonable reader or listener would think this, however, nor even that most would. It is enough to prove that people who knew the claimant would think the statement referred to him or her. If the claimant does that, it does not matter that the public at large might not have realised he or she was being referred to.

Unintended references

Case Summary

It is possible to be liable for defamation even where you did not intend to refer to the claimant, but to someone else, or even a fictional character. In *Newstead* v. *London Express Newspapers* (1940), *The Express* printed a story about a Harold Newstead who had been convicted of bigamy. It said he was 30 years old and lived in Camberwell. This was all true of the Harold Newstead that the newspaper intended to write about, but unknown to them there was another Harold Newstead living in Camberwell, who was not a bigamist. He successfully sued, arguing that the report could be taken to refer to him and was clearly defamatory. The newspaper would of course have had a defence if the other Harold Newstead had sued, because the story was true of him.

Case Summary

An example of defamation in a work of fiction occurred in *Hulton* v. *Jones* (1910). The defendants published a humorous story about the bad behaviour of a fictitious character called Artemus Jones, who was described as a churchwarden from Peckham, and in the story, was visiting Dieppe. Unknown to the author, there was a real Artemus Jones. He did not live in Peckham, was not a churchwarden and had never visited Dieppe, but he had previously contributed articles to the same publication, and some of his friends thought the story was about him. He sued and won his case.

This aspect of the law can seem very harsh on defendants, as there may be no way of knowing that there is another person with the same name as the one they are talking about. In a recent case, the High Court suggested that the law should take a more balanced approach, which better respects the right to freedom of expression. The case was *O'Shea* v. *Mirror Group Newspapers Ltd* (2001), and involved an advertisement carried by the newspaper for a pornographic website. The advert contained a picture of a woman, which had been published with her permission. The claimant looked very like this woman, and certain details in the advert could also have been taken to refer to her. She sued, claiming that people who knew her would think she had posed for the picture, and that this was defamatory. The Court agreed that an ordinary, reasonable reader who knew the claimant might well think the woman was her. However, they said that it was necessary to take into account the right to freedom of expression under the Human Rights Act. Requiring a newspaper to check whether every picture they might use in a defamatory context looked like someone else would place 'an impossible burden' on them, which would restrict freedom of expression to an extent that would be unreasonable. The claimant therefore lost her case.

Case Summary

There is an additional safeguard for those who make an unintended reference like those in the cases we have just looked at. They can use a special procedure set down in the Defamation Act 1996, called offer of amends, which allows them to avoid being liable for defamation if they make a prompt apology and pay damages (we will look at this in more detail in the next chapter).

Referring to a group

Where a defamatory statement refers to a class or group of people, it is not usually possible for the group as a whole, or for individual members of it, to sue for defamation unless the group is very small. So, for example, if you were to say that Mary Pipes the plumber was useless at her job, she could sue you, but if you said that all plumbers were useless at their jobs, the whole plumbing profession could not sue you, and nor could Mary or any other individual plumber.

In *Knupffer* v. *London Express Newspapers* (1944), the defendants published an article describing a group called the Young Russia party as a Fascist organisation. The group had around 2,000 members, and the claimant was one of them. He claimed that the statement defamed him personally. The House of Lords refused his claim, saying that the statement was aimed at a large group of people, and nothing in it was aimed specifically at him.

Case Summary

However, where a group is so small that the statement could be taken to refer to each and every one of them, any of them may be able to sue successfully. So while it is quite safe to say 'All lawyers are useless', it may be risking a defamation claim to say 'All the lawyers at the firm Bodgit, Snatch and Run are useless'.

There is no set number above which a class or group of people will be considered too big to be able to sue for a remark about all of them. Each case will depend on the facts and, in particular, how closely the individuals in that group can be associated with the defamatory statement. In *Riches* v. *News Group* (1986), the *News of the World* published a letter from a man which made serious allegations against the 'Banbury CID'. There were 10 members of Banbury CID and, although none of them were mentioned by name, they all successfully sued the paper for damages. (If you are wondering why the newspaper was sued and not the man who wrote the letter, the answer is that anyone who publishes a defamatory statement can be liable, even if they are only repeating what someone else has said. As the paper was more likely to be able to pay damages than the letter writer, it was sued.)

Case Summary

You be the judge

Q: **Joe Jabber is a sports journalist who writes for a newspaper. Reporting on a football match, he writes: 'There is no doubt that City should have won this match. They are a Premier League team, playing against a non-League one, yet they lost 10–0. I can only assume that their poor performance is due to the fact that they were out of their heads on drink and drugs the night before.' In fact, Joe's comment about drink and drugs is true of six of the players, but the other five had been quietly watching *Strictly Come Dancing* in their hotel rooms on the night before the match.**

Could Joe be liable for defamation?

A: Probably. It is clearly defamatory to say that someone is unable to do their job properly because they have drunk too much or taken drugs, and here the group referred to is just 11 people. They would all be known to the public, so it would be fairly easy for any of the five who did not go out drinking to claim that readers would believe the allegation referred to them. The other six would not be able to sue as Joe has the defence of justification.

The statement must be published

In ordinary language, we think of publishing information as printing it in a newspaper, magazine or book, posting it on the internet, or broadcasting it on television or radio. Many defamation cases do involve this kind of publication, but not all of them because, in law, publication has a wider meaning. A statement is considered to have been published if it has been communicated to anyone other than the claimant themselves, or the defendant's husband or wife. The reason why communication to the claimant does not cause liability is obvious; you cannot damage someone's reputation with an allegation if the only person you make the allegation to is that person. The exception for the defendant's husband or wife dates back to the old case of *Wennhak* v. *Morgan* (1888), where the Court found that there would be 'disastrous results to social life' if a statement made only between spouses could lead to liability for defamation.

Case Summary

So, what this means is that if I tell your best friend, or your mother, or even a passing stranger, that you are a thief (and this is not true), you could sue me for defamation. In practice of course, most people would not bother to go to the trouble and expense of suing over something that was told to only a few people, but in law they would have a case if they chose to bring one.

A defendant can avoid liability if they can show that it was not possible to foresee that the publication would happen. In *Huth* v. *Huth* (1915), the defendant and his wife had separated. He sent her a defamatory letter in an unsealed envelope, and it was secretly read by her butler. The Court found that the butler was not supposed to read letters addressed to the members of the household, and the defendant would have known this. Therefore the defendant could not foresee that the letter would be opened and read by someone else, and was not responsible for the publication.

Case Summary

Key stats Defamation claims

Proceedings for defamation started in the High Court during 2010:

- 27 claims for between £25,000 and £50,000.
- 47 claims for over £50,000.
- 84 claims for unspecified amounts.

[*Source*: Judicial and Court Statistics, 2010]

Publication and the internet

In recent years, the courts have been faced with the question of who can be said to be the publisher of material that appears on the internet. The person who writes the material and then posts it is clearly publishing it, whether the material appears on their own website, in a chatroom, on a messageboard or in an email. But in many cases they will not be worth suing because they are not wealthy, so just as people defamed in print may choose to sue the newspaper rather than the journalist, people defamed online have sought to make internet service providers (ISPs) liable for defamation that is posted on their servers. Two cases have established that ISPs can be liable, but only where their role in publishing the defamatory statement is comparable to that played by a book or magazine publisher, in that they have some control over what is posted.

In *Godfrey* v. *Demon Internet* (1999), the defendant ISP was found to have published material that appeared on websites that it hosted. The reasoning behind this decision was that in this situation the ISP could have been aware of the defamation and have asked the site to remove it, just as a newspaper publisher could do with one of their newspapers. By contrast, in *Bunt* v. *Tilley* (2006) an ISP was found not to have published defamatory material that appeared on a messageboard. They did not host the site which contained the board, and merely offered the system by which people sent messages to the board. The court held that this meant they were more like a telephone or postal service than a publisher, and so could not be liable for publication.

Case Summary

Case Summary

Publication by repetition

Every time a defamatory statement is repeated (by the original publisher or anyone else), that counts as a fresh claim. So it is no defence for a newspaper, for example, to claim that a defamatory statement has already been published in lots of other newspapers. If a defamatory statement is made by more than one person or organisation, the person defamed can sue all or any number of them. So if, for example, *The Sun* prints a defamatory story and the person mentioned decides not to sue, that does not stop them suing another paper that repeats the story.

People in the law

Source: Gill Phillips (*text and photo*)

Gill Phillips is a solicitor who works as Director of Editorial Legal Services for Guardian Newspapers, and deals with defamation issues for *The Guardian* and *Observer* newspapers, and *The Guardian*'s website.

Can you describe your role? As far as defamation is concerned, my job is to check what goes into the papers and the website before it's published, and to deal with any complaints that arise after publication. I work with two other full-time lawyers, and because some parts of the papers are produced through the night, there's always at least one lawyer here from 10 am to 8 pm, and outside those hours, one of us will be on call.

We're also involved in training our journalists in media law – we don't expect them to be lawyers, but they need to know enough so they know when they need to check things with us.

Do you check everything before it's published? We see everything that goes into the main section of the newspapers – the news, and the business sections, G2. On other sections, such as travel, features supplement and sport, which are less likely to cause problems, we only look at the copy if a journalist thinks there might be a legal issue with it. We also look at all web copy that is referred to us.

How often do stories present potential problems with libel? A lot of the time it's obvious that a story's fine, but we quite often need to talk to the journalist, and check what evidence they have for what they're saying. There are some words that as a lawyer you're always wary of – things like 'corrupt' or 'scam' would usually make you ask what the evidence is. And we're also very careful about suggesting that people have acted knowingly, or with a particular motive, because that's hard to prove.

Are there any particular kinds of stories that are more likely to cause a problem? The stories that are mostly likely to cause problems are those involving wealthy people such as celebrities and footballers, but also businesspeople and you have to treat every story on a case-by-case basis. Of course there are some people who are more likely to sue, but we don't think, oh, we won't get sued over that so we don't need to worry. Everyone deserves respect, and deserves not to have things written about them that aren't true, so we apply the same standards whoever the story is about.

How often would you advise against running a story because it could be libellous? It's very rare that we have to pull a story completely – I've done it about five times in 20 years. What's more likely to happen is that we'll suggest changes to make the copy more legally safe. Sometimes it's just a case of tweaking a word or two, but there are times when the story that's published ends up quite different from the original.

How do journalists react to that? It can mean some quite heated discussions – journalists tend to be fairly forceful people, and naturally, they want to defend what they've written. We have to be thorough in challenging them to make the story is legally safe, but at the same time, it's right for them to challenge us if they think we're being too cautious. Things can get heated, and in the heat of the moment, people do lose their tempers – I've been called a 'lily-livered pathetic lawyer' or words to that effect on more than one occasion! It's not an enjoyable part of the job, but it's something you know you have to do, and no one bears a grudge. In the end, we are all on the same side, though I think journalists would sometimes dispute that. A newspaper where those arguments don't happen – or for that matter one that never gets complaints – is probably not doing its job.

Often there's time pressure as well, because news is very time-sensitive, and sometimes if you don't get a story out quickly, there ends up being no point in getting it out at all, because the news is no longer topical. So in those situations you sometimes have to make some difficult decisions, and make the copy as legally safe as you can in the time you have. That may mean going out with a much softer version of the story than was originally written, but if that's better than it not being published at all, it's worth it.

How often does the company get sued for defamation? We get two or three allegations of defamation a week, but most of them are resolved without going anywhere near **litigation**. There are probably about five or six a year that end up with a writ being issued, though few of them would go to a full trial. When we get a complaint, the first thing to do is look at the article, and make a very quick decision about whether we need to take it off our website, or edit it to remove the material complained about. If we decide it's OK to leave it up, we'll always add a note that it is the subject of a complaint. Then we'll talk to the journalist, find out whether this was an unintentional defamation, or whether they meant to say what they did, because they have evidence for it.

What happens if there is evidence for what's been said? We have to decide whether we're going to fight it or not. If we think we can and should fight it, we have to think about how much that will cost. Top London solicitors can charge £500 an hour, and with a 100 per cent uplift from a **conditional fee agreement** that's £1,000 an hour, so things can get very expensive, very quickly. And there's also the fact that defamation cases are very hard to defend, because the burden of proof is all on the defendant. Even where you know the claimant has documents that would prove your case, it can be a real struggle to get them.

As a result, most cases get settled, so there's a negotiation process over what the apology will say, and most of the time, people will want damages as well, so we have to negotiate that.

Do you see any particular problems with the current law on defamation? I definitely think that the current law is far too heavily weighted in favour of claimants. As a newspaper lawyer, people might think well, she would say that. But now we have foreign claimants suing foreign newspapers over issues that don't concern the British public at all, simply because they know it's difficult to defend a claim here, so I think it's clear that things have got out of hand. And since CFAs came in, I think there have been more trivial claims, more aggressively pursued, again because they know it's going to cost us an enormous amount to fight them. There is definitely a chilling effect – the high costs of defending a libel case mean papers are thinking, could I afford to defend this? And that means they are avoiding writing about things that they should be writing about.

Defamation and damage

As we saw at the beginning of this chapter, there are two types of defamation:

- libel, which covers statements made in a permanent form;
- slander, which covers statements made in non-permanent forms such as unrecorded speech.

If someone libels you, without a defence, you will have a claim, even if the statement did not cause you any financial or other loss. The fact that the statement could damage your reputation is enough. But if someone slanders you, you will usually have to prove that the statement caused some actual damage, usually financial loss, in addition to the potential damage to your reputation. This extra damage is sometimes called 'special damage'.

However, there are four situations where a slander can create a claim even without special damage. These are where the slanderous comment suggests that:

- the claimant has committed an imprisonable offence;
- the claimant has a contagious disease, of a kind that might lead to people excluding or avoiding them. This would usually mean any kind of sexually transmitted disease, but it is arguable that if there was an epidemic of a serious disease a false claim that someone was infected could fall into this category as people might be likely to avoid them for that reason;
- that a female claimant is not 'chaste'. To suggest that someone is not chaste means to suggest that they have had sex outside marriage, and this rule dates from the Slander of Women Act 1891. As we saw earlier, today it would not usually be considered defamatory to say that a woman had sex outside marriage, so this exception has little if any practical use these days;
- that the claimant is unfit for their trade, profession or business, or any position that they hold. Examples would be saying (falsely) that someone who worked as a plumber had done a bad job on your house, or that the local mayor was corrupt.

For slander claims that do not fall into any of the categories above, the claimant will have to show that the slanderous comment caused the special damage under the usual rules of causation that we looked at in Chapter 3 (have a look back at page 69 if you want to remind yourself of them). You may remember that when an **intervening event** breaks the chain of causation the defendant will not be liable, and this issue was raised

Figure 16.1 Libel and slander

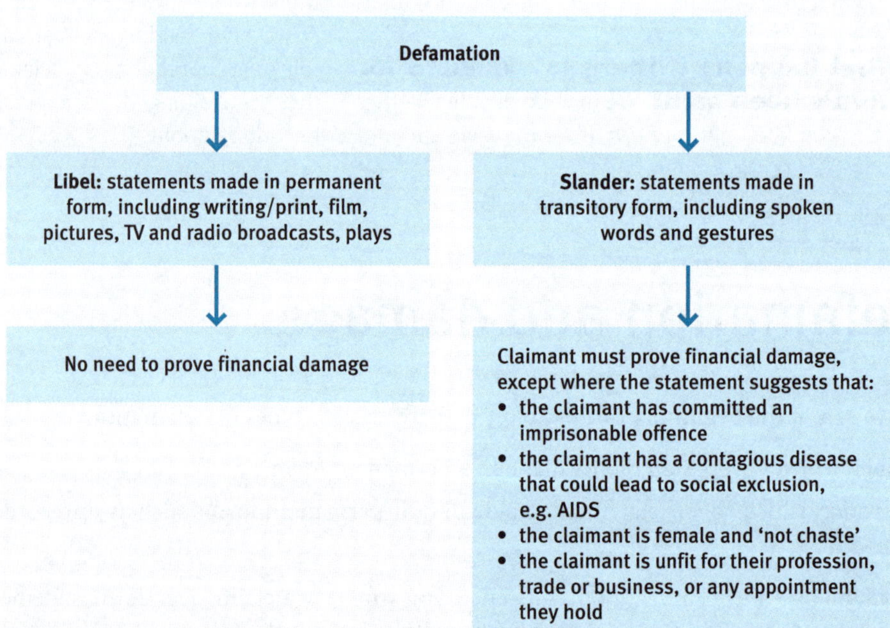

in *McManus* v. *Beckham* (2002). The defendant in the case was Victoria Beckham, and the claimant was the owner of a shop which sold autographed memorabilia. Mrs Beckham happened to walk past the shop, which was in a large shopping centre in Kent, and spotted a display of signed photographs of her husband, David Beckham. She loudly declared the autographs to be fake, and told three customers that they should not buy anything from the shop. The incident was later reported by several newspapers, and the shop owner sued Mrs Beckham for slander, claiming that her words had severely damaged his business. Mrs Beckham's lawyers argued that the claim should be struck out, because most of the damage had been done by the newspaper reports of her words rather than as a result of potential shoppers hearing what she said. They said that the newspaper reports broke the chain of causation, and therefore her words had not themselves caused the damage. The Court of Appeal rejected this argument. They said that Mrs Beckham could be liable if she realised that the 'sting' of her words (meaning the defamatory allegation that the words made) was likely to be reported in the papers, or if a reasonable person in her position would have realised this, and that the result of such reports would be damage to Mr McManus's business. They therefore refused to strike out the claim, leaving the causation issue to be tested at trial. In fact the case was eventually settled out of court.

Case Summary

Who can sue for defamation?

A claim for defamation can be brought by an individual person, or an organisation such as a company. Only living people can sue for defamation, so it is not possible to sue for damage to the reputation of, for example, a dead relative or spouse, unless the claimant can prove that the defamatory statement also affected their own reputation.

Only living people can sue for defamation

As we saw at the beginning of this chapter, the law on defamation is recognised as being a restriction on free speech, and the courts have to strike a balance between protecting free speech and allowing claimants to protect their reputations. One of the ways they have done this is to rule that certain types of public body cannot sue for defamation. In *Derbyshire County Council* v. *Times Newspapers* (1992), the council brought a claim against *The Times* over reports suggesting that the council was misusing the funds in its pension scheme. The Court of Appeal ruled that democratically elected bodies, such as local councils, were not allowed to sue for defamation. They said that there was a public interest in elected bodies being open to public criticism, and allowing them to bring defamation actions would be an unjustified restriction on the ability to express such criticism. In other words, the public interest was best served by allowing a free and open discussion of the things elected bodies do, even if that might mean that some of the criticisms were inaccurate.

Case Summary

In *Goldsmith* v. *Bhoyrul* (1998), a small political party, the Referendum Party, attempted to sue for defamation. Applying the same reasoning used in the *Derbyshire* case, Mr Justice Buckley said that political parties could not sue for defamation because the public interest required that there was free and open debate about their activities. However, it is still open to individual members of an elected body, or a political party, to sue for defamation of them personally.

Case Summary

Case Summary

In *Steel* v. *McDonald's Corp (Locus Standi)* (1999), two environmental campaigners were sued by McDonald's for distributing leaflets which made allegations about the way McDonald's sourced their ingredients and made their food. The defendants attempted to argue that, like elected bodies and political parties, large commercial companies should be prevented from suing for libel because there was a public interest in open discussion of their activities. The argument was unsuccessful, and it is still possible for a company, whether large or small, to sue for defamation.

Law in action The McLibel case

The libel case brought by McDonalds ran for two and a half years, and became known as the McLibel case. The claimants, Helen Steel and Dave Morris, were members of an environmental campaign group. The group produced a leaflet called *What's wrong with McDonald's: Everything they don't want you to know*, which accused McDonald's of exploiting children through their advertising, mistreating their staff, and damaging the environment and animal welfare in the way they sourced their ingredients. McDonald's threatened to sue five members of the group for libel if they didn't apologise and withdraw the allegations in the leaflet.

Three agreed to these demands, but Ms Steel and Mr Morris decided to fight their case. Legal aid was never available for libel cases, and no win no fee agreements were not available at that time (and would probably have been impossible to get in a case like this, where most people assumed the claimants could not win). They therefore had to represent themselves, despite having no legal expertise or experience; Helen Steel was a gardener and Dave Morris a former postman. This meant assembling their own evidence, and as many of the claims they had made involved technical matters such as the nutritional content of the company's food, and the environmental impact of their operations, this involved finding scientists and other experts from all over the world. They then had to represent themselves in court, against the very experienced (and expensive) lawyers hired by McDonald's. Expenses such as court costs were paid out of a support fund, which raised £35,000 in contributions from the general public.

Because all this was very unusual, and because McDonald's is such a well-known company, the case attracted huge publicity and became a public relations disaster for the company. The widespread coverage of the case meant that the claims that had been made against McDonald's got a much wider audience than the original leaflet could ever have reached, and there was also considerable criticism of the idea of a large, powerful corporation suing two ordinary individuals. As a way of protecting their reputation, suing began to look an increasingly unwise decision by McDonald's.

The trial became the longest in English legal history, lasting 313 days. The transcripts of the court proceedings covered 20,000 pages, 40,000 pages of written evidence were supplied, 130 witnesses were examined, and the claimants' closing speech took six weeks to deliver. Finally, on 19 June 1997, the judge delivered his verdict (unusually, the trial was heard without a jury, because McDonald's successfully argued that the issues were too technical and complex for a jury to understand).

The judge found that Ms Steel and Mr Morris had proved that their allegations that McDonald's misrepresented the nutritional value of their food, exploited children through advertising, practised poor animal welfare, and paid low wages to their staff. However, they had failed to prove their other allegations, regarding damage to rainforests, poor working conditions, and the company's foods causing serious health problems. He therefore awarded McDonald's damages of £60,000, half the amount originally claimed. McDonald's had also wanted an injunction to stop the allegations being repeated, but they decided not to pursue this and not to apply for the claimants to pay their costs (which were said to have run into millions of pounds).

The claimants then appealed against the verdict, and the Court of Appeal found that another of the allegations against McDonald's, that regular customers had an increased risk of heart disease, was true; and that another, concerning poor working conditions, was covered by the defence of fair comment (we will look at this defence in the next chapter). They reduced the damages to £40,000.

Permission to appeal to the House of Lords on the remaining allegations was refused, and so the claimants brought a case before the European Court of Human Rights (*Steel and Morris* v. *UK* (2005)). They alleged that Britain's libel laws infringed the Article 6 right to a fair hearing because legal aid was not available. The ECHR agreed, pointing out that the fact that the claimants had to do everything themselves, while McDonald's had access to lawyers, gave McDonald's an unfair advantage, and meant that the claimants were denied the chance to present their case effectively.

The claimants also argued that English libel law breached the Article 10 right to freedom of expression. They said that campaigning groups such as theirs needed to be able to speak freely, and requiring them to prove their allegations were true placed an unacceptable restriction on their freedom of speech. In addition, they argued that large corporations should not be allowed to sue for defamation (in the same way as councils are not), because there was a public interest in free speech about, and criticism of, their activities. The ECHR rejected the idea that large corporations should not be able to sue, pointing out that there was also a public interest in protecting the commercial success of companies, not only for their shareholders and customers, but for the economic well-being of society. They also said it was not an excessive restriction on freedom of speech to expect those who make allegations to prove them. However, they said that if a country's laws did provide this sort of protection for the reputation of large corporations, they had to provide some way of allowing claimants a fair chance of defending themselves in court. For this reason, they found that the UK had breached Article 10 because of the lack of legal aid, rather than because of any problems with the law on defamation itself.

The verdict suggests that the government now has a responsibility to provide legal aid in defamation cases involving ordinary individuals being sued by large organisations. However, these cases rarely arise and as there has not been another since the verdict has not been tested.

After the original court case ended, Ms Steel and Mr Morris said they had no intention of paying the £40,000 damages ordered by the court, and the damages remain unpaid.

[*References*: 'McLibel: Longest case in English history', **http://news.bbc.co.uk/1/hi/uk/4266741.stm**; 'McLibel Two win legal aid case', *The Guardian*, 15 Feb 2005]

Who can be sued?

Liability in defamation is not for making the defamatory statement but for publishing it. This means that it is not only the person who says or writes the defamatory words who can be liable but anyone who plays a role in making them public. If a defamatory statement appears in a newspaper, for example, the person defamed can sue the writer, the company that owns the newspaper, the printers, the company that distributes the paper to sellers, and even the shop that sells it. In practice, however, most claimants will sue the company that owns the newspaper (or magazine, radio or television station). This is because the individual writer is not usually worth suing because they could not afford to pay the damages, and printers, distributors and sellers are usually covered by the defence of innocent dissemination, which we will look at on page 430.

The fact that liability attaches to publishing the words, rather than saying or writing them in the first place, means that repeating someone else's words, or passing on rumours, can be defamation just as if you had been the person who first said the words. The fact that you make it clear that the words are someone else's does not prevent you being liable, whether or not the person defamed chooses to sue the maker of the statement as well.

repeating someone else's words, or passing on rumours, can be defamation

You be the judge

Q: **Terry Star is a singer who has been a member of a very successful boy band for over ten years. The band has just split up, and Terry does an interview with a national newspaper in which he says that the split was caused by another band member, Joe Flakey, who had such a serious drug problem that he could no longer remember the words to any of the band's songs. The newspaper story says: 'Terry claims that his fellow band member was so stoned he couldn't recall the lyrics to even the band's biggest hits. Joe Flakey refused to comment on the allegations.'**

In fact the claims are untrue; Joe doesn't have a drug problem, and is perfectly able to sing every song the band has ever recorded. Does Joe have a case against the newspaper?

A: Yes. The fact that the words quoted were originally Terry's does not stop the newspaper being liable, because they have published them. Terry can also be sued because he published the words by communicating them to the newspaper.

Summary

- Defamation is committed by publishing a statement which lowers the reputation of the person referred to.
- There are two types: libel applies to statements in permanent form, slander to statements in temporary form.
- The claimant must prove:
  - the statement complained of was defamatory;
  - the statement referred to the claimant;
  - the statement was published.
- A statement will be defamatory if it 'tends to lower the person in the estimation of right-thinking members of society', or exposes the person to 'hatred, contempt or ridicule'. This can include indirect criticisms (innuendoes).
- The claimant need not be named; the statement will be taken to refer to them if a reasonable person would think it did. It is not possible to defame a class of people, unless it is so small that the statement could be taken to refer to every individual member.
- In libel, there is no need to prove damage, but in slander damage must be proved, except for claims that the claimant
  - has committed an imprisonable offence;
  - has certain contagious diseases;
  - is female and 'not chaste';
  - is unfit for their trade, profession or business.
- The maker of the statement, and if printed, the owners, distributors and printers of the publication can be sued;
- Only living people can sue. Companies and organisations can sue, but not democratically elected bodies or political parties.

Question and answer

Exam questions on defamation invariably include some consideration of the defences available. As defences are covered in Chapter 17, the questions there are designed to test your knowledge of the material in both this chapter and that one.

Further reading

Harlow, C. (2005) *Understanding Tort Law*, 3rd edn, Ch. 7, London: Sweet & Maxwell.
A very clear and easy to read examination of the problems with the law of defamation, and in particular the restrictions it places on freedom of expression.

Loveland, I. (1994) 'Defamation of government: taking lessons from America', 14 *Legal Studies* 206.
This article looks at the case of *Derbyshire* v. *The Times*, and argues that the decision is both too narrow and too wide. It compares the English approach to political criticism with that in the USA, which will give you some useful material for essays regarding defamation and freedom of expression.

Milo, D. (2008) *Defamation and Freedom of Speech*, Oxford: Oxford University Press.
A very useful book to look at if you are writing an essay on defamation, this one looks at the clash between the competing rights of reputation and freedom of expression.

Robertson, G. and Nicol, A. (2008) *Media Law*, 5th edn, London: Penguin.
A clear and detailed look at the law on defamation and the problems with it, written in a readable and entertaining style with lots of real-life examples.

Rubenstein, M., ed. (1972) *Wicked, Wicked Libels*, London: Taylor & Francis.
A collection of individual essays written by contributors who are or were involved in libel law on a practical basis, including lawyers, publishers and a successful claimant. A good read that will give you a real insight into how this area of the law works in practice, though bear in mind that some information about the law may be out of date.

Visit www.mylawchamber.co.uk/quinntort to access tools to help you develop and test your knowledge of tort law, including practice exam questions with guidance, annotated weblinks, glossary and key case flashcards, legal newsfeed and legal updates and interactive 'You be the judge' questions.

premium mylawchamber unrivalled support for legal education

Chapter 17 Defamation: defences, remedies and problems

Key points In this chapter we will be looking at:

- Defences to a defamation claim
- Remedies for defamation
- Problems with the law on defamation

Introduction

In the previous chapter we looked at the kinds of statements that can create liability for defamation and saw that, essentially, anything which damages someone's reputation can fall into this category. However, when you read newspapers, magazines and websites, you will come across statements all the time that have the potential to damage reputations: television reviews that say a particular actor was wooden, for example, or gossip websites that accuse celebrities of having affairs, or newspapers suggesting that a certain politician is useless at his or her job. Why would anyone publish this kind of material when **damages** for defamation can run into tens of thousands of pounds?

Sometimes the answer will be that the publisher does not think the subject of the remark will sue, perhaps because they cannot afford it, or they feel that doing so will just attract attention to the story, but in most cases the reason why publishers take what looks like a risk is that they believe they are covered by one of the nine **defences** that apply to defamation, which means that they can make a defamatory statement without being liable. These defences are a key part of how the tort operates in practice, and the main subject of this chapter.

We will also look at the remedies available to a **claimant** who wins a defamation action, and then go on to find out about some of the criticisms that are frequently made of defamation law and the way it works in practice.

Defences to a defamation claim

There are nine defences available to a claim of defamation, and a **defendant** who can successfully argue any one of them will avoid liability, even if it is clear that they have published a defamatory statement which refers to the claimant.

The general defence of consent, or ***volenti***, explained in Chapter 3, applies to defamation claims, and protects a defendant where the claimant has agreed to the defamatory information being published. In practice, this is rare, and the most important defences are specific to defamation. They are:

- justification;
- absolute privilege;
- qualified privilege;
- the *Reynolds* defence;
- neutral reportage;
- honest comment;
- innocent dissemination;
- offer of amends.

Justification

If a defamatory statement is true, and the defendant can prove that, they will have a defence. It is not necessary to prove that every single detail is true so long as, taken as a whole, the statement is accurate. An example of this principle can be seen in *Alexander* v *North Eastern Railway Co.* (1865). The claimant had been convicted of a criminal offence, and the defendants said that he had been offered a choice of paying a fine, or going to prison for three weeks. In fact, the potential prison sentence was only two weeks. The defendants successfully pleaded justification.

Case Summary

Where a statement contains two or more allegations about the claimant, section 5 of the Defamation Act 1952 applies. It provides that the defence of justification can still be used even if the defendant cannot prove that all the allegations are true, so long as the unproven statements do not cause significantly more damage to the claimant's reputation than has already been caused by the statements that are proved true. In *Gecas* v. *Scottish Television* (1992), Scottish Television (STV) was sued over a programme about war crimes. The claimant, Mr Gecas, was a Lithuanian man, who had been the head of a special police division during the Second World War. At the time the programme was made, he was running a bed and breakfast in Edinburgh. The programme accused him of being involved in the murder of thousands of Jews in Lithuania and Belarus during the war and stated, among other things, that he had personally 'finished off' Jews who had been thrown into communal burial pits but were still alive. STV were able to prove that he had been involved in the killings, but not the specific allegation about killing people in the burial pits. They were able to rely on the defence of justification because, the judge said, the claim about the burial pits did not materially injure Mr Gecas's reputation, given the other allegations that had been proved about him.

Case Summary

Absolute privilege

This defence is another way in which the law attempts to balance free speech against protection of reputation. It recognises that there are some situations where free speech is so important that it completely outweighs any potential damage to someone's reputation. Absolute privilege therefore makes it impossible to sue over defamatory statements made in any of the following circumstances:

- Any statement made in Parliament by a member of the House of Commons or House of Lords, or any report published by either House.
- Any report published by either House of Parliament, or made by either House and republished in full by someone else.
- Any statement made by one officer of state to another, in the course of the officer's duty. There is no set definition of the term 'officer of state', but it is accepted that it covers government ministers and secretaries of state. It is not clear which politicians below those ranks would be covered.
- Statements made by officials of the EU, as part of that role.
- Statements made during judicial proceedings by a judge, jury member, witness, lawyer or one of the parties in a case.
- Fair, accurate and contemporaneous media reports of judicial proceedings held in public. Fair, accurate and contemporaneous simply means that the report provides a balanced view of the proceedings, without misrepresenting anything and is published as soon as possible after the statement is made.
- Any statement made by one spouse to another.

Absolute privilege means that, in any of the above situations, the person described can say anything about anyone, true or not, and cannot be sued for defamation. In a court case, for example, people will often make serious allegations about each other, which may or may not turn out to be true. Clearly, it would be impossible for justice to be done if they could be sued for defamation if the allegations could not be proved true. Similarly, it is in the public interest for court proceedings to be fully reported, and this could not happen if the media could be sued for repeating what is said in court.

> if an MP makes a defamatory statement about someone in Parliament, absolute privilege applies

Absolute privilege covers only the people and situations described on the list above. It does not cover anyone else who repeats the statement if they are not in one of the categories on the list. For example, if an MP makes a defamatory statement about someone in Parliament, absolute privilege applies and the MP cannot be sued for defamation. But if the MP repeats that statement outside Parliament, absolute privilege does not apply and they may be sued if they do not have another defence. Similarly, absolute privilege would not apply if a newspaper reported comments made in Parliament, though in this case the defence of qualified privilege (see below) will usually apply.

You be the judge

Source: Pearson Education Ltd/Photodisc/Daisuke Morita

Q: Billy Bloggs has been charged with attempting to murder his Auntie Mary. In court, she says: 'I saw him put poison in my tea, so I didn't drink it. If I had, I would have been dead. He was after my money, he always has been.' The local newspaper reports the accusation as part of a report of the whole trial, which is published the same day as Auntie Mary gives her evidence. However, the accusation is not true, and when the case continues the next day Billy is acquitted.

Can Billy sue Auntie Mary for defamation? Can he sue the newspaper?

A: Billy can't sue Auntie Mary, because she made her statement in court, and so she is covered by absolute privilege. Fair, accurate and contemporaneous reports of court proceedings are also covered by absolute privilege, so he can't sue the newspaper either.

Qualified privilege

Like absolute privilege, qualified privilege protects statements made in circumstances where protecting free speech is considered to be more important than protecting reputation. Qualified privilege applies in a wider range of situations than absolute privilege does, but it is subject to one important limitation: the protection of the defence is lost if the statement is made 'with malice'. We will look at precisely what this means at the end of this section, but for now, a simple explanation is that a statement will be made 'with malice' if it was made with some kind of improper motive, such as to injure the reputation of the person mentioned, rather than to promote the purpose of the defence, which is to allow free expression on important matters.

Qualified privilege applies in a wider range of situations than absolute privilege does

Some of the situations in which qualified privilege applies have been set down in statute, while others are covered by **common law** privilege, which as you know means they have been created by judicial decisions. We will look first at the qualified privilege situations set out in statute, and then at the common law situations.

Qualified privilege under statute

Section 15 of the Defamation Act 1996 lists the types of statement that are covered by statutory qualified privilege. The defence only covers information which is 'of public concern', and the publication of that information must be 'for the public benefit'. This means that if someone was to make a comment about, for example, a celebrity's private life, in one of the situations listed in the Act, the defence would be unlikely to cover this unless it related to a matter of public interest.

The situations in which the defence applies are divided into two groups. The first group, listed in Schedule 1 of the Act, are statements which the Act describes as having 'qualified privilege without explanation or contradiction'. This means that if a defamatory statement is made in any of the situations listed in Schedule 1, the maker of the statement cannot be sued for defamation unless the statement was made with malice.

The statements protected under Schedule 1 include:

- Fair and accurate reports of parliamentary proceedings anywhere in the world.
- Fair and accurate reports of court proceedings, public inquiries, proceedings of international organisations or conferences, if held in public, anywhere in the world.
- Fair and accurate copies of or extracts from any register or other document required by law to be open to public inspection, or any material published by a government, legislature, international organisation or international conference, anywhere in the world.
- Notices or advertisements published by or on the authority of a court, or a judge or officer of a court, anywhere in the world.

The second group of situations, listed in Schedule II, is described as 'privileged subject to explanation or contradiction'. This means that if a person makes a defamatory statement in one of the situations listed in Schedule II, without malice, they cannot normally be sued for defamation. However, if the person defamed seeks to put their side of the story, and the publisher of the statement does not give them a reasonable chance to do so, the protection of qualified privilege will be lost. So if, for example, a newspaper reports, without malice, that a local politician was accused of fraud at a public meeting (one of the situations covered by Schedule II), the politician cannot normally sue for defamation because qualified privilege will apply. But if the politician writes to the newspaper to give their side of the story, and asks the paper to publish the letter, the paper will lose the protection of qualified privilege if it refuses to do so.

The list in Schedule II is a long one, but for our purposes here the most important types of statement it protects are those made as part of:

- general meetings of any UK public companies;
- public sittings of tribunals, boards and committees acting under powers given to them by statute;
- decisions by associations dealing with the arts, sciences, religion, charity, trade, industry and sports;
- proceedings of public meetings held in any EU state.

Case Summary

In *McCartan Turkington Breen* v. *Times Newspapers* (2000), the House of Lords considered whether a press conference could count as a public meeting. The conference had been called by a committee which was trying to clear the name of Private Lee Clegg, a British soldier who had been convicted of murder after killing a man while on duty in Northern Ireland. A *Times* journalist attended the press conference, and used information obtained from it to write a story criticising the firm of solicitors who had represented Private Clegg at his trial. The solicitors firm then sued the paper for defamation. *The Times* claimed that they were covered by qualified privilege, because a press conference was a public meeting. The solicitors firm argued that a press conference could not be considered public, because it was not open to anyone who wanted to attend but only to members of the press who had been invited. The House of Lords, however, agreed with *The Times*. They said that the starting point for their decision was the importance of free expression, and it was largely through the media that the public was kept informed about important issues. If those who organise a meeting issue a general invitation to the press, they are indicating that they want or intend the information given at the meeting to be reported to the wider public, and therefore a press conference was effectively a public meeting.

Qualified privilege under common law

The situations described above are all set down in the Defamation Act 1996. But the defence of qualified privilege existed before this Act was passed, and so it also applies in a number of situations which have been developed through common law in cases that have come before the courts.

The traditional definition of when common law qualified privilege will apply comes from the case of *Adam* v. *Ward* (1917). The claimant, an MP, made false accusations in the House of Commons about a major general in the army. Because he was speaking in Parliament, he was protected by absolute privilege. The Army investigated the allegations and found them to be false, and wrote to the major general telling him this. The letter contained defamatory allegations about the MP, but the House of Lords held that it was protected by qualified privilege. Lord Atkinson said that qualified privilege applied to occasions where 'the person who makes a communication has an interest or duty, legal, social or moral, to make it to the person to whom it is made, and the person to whom it is made has a corresponding interest or duty to receive it'. He went on to say that 'reciprocity is essential'. This means that it is not enough for the person making the statement to have a duty or interest in doing that; they will only be protected by the defence if they communicate the statement to someone who has a legal, social or moral interest or duty to receive it.

Case Summary

In *Downtex* v. *Flatley* (2003), the claimant and defendant had entered into a business contract, but later had a dispute about it in which each of them claimed the other owed them money. The defendant, Mr Flatley, received an anonymous letter saying that Downtex were in financial difficulties; it was never proved where this letter came from. He then wrote to several other companies who supplied goods to Downtex, suggesting that Downtex might be unable to pay any money it owed them. This was untrue and defamatory of the company, but Mr Flatley claimed he was covered by qualified privilege because there was a mutual interest in companies who might be affected by Downtex's financial difficulties finding out about those difficulties. The Court of Appeal rejected this argument, saying that there was no reciprocity of interest. Although other suppliers might well be interested in this information, Mr Flatley had no duty to tell them about Downtex's alleged financial problems.

Case Summary

Whether each party has a sufficient duty/interest to give/receive the information will be a matter of fact in each case. However, decided cases have established that such duties will usually exist in the following situations.

Statements made in self-defence

If someone publishes defamatory remarks about you, any statement you make to defend yourself against their allegation will be covered by qualified privilege. This means that you cannot be sued if your defence of yourself contains defamatory remarks about them. This was the situation in *Osborn* v. *Thomas Boulter & Son* (1930). The claimant ran a pub, and was supplied with beer by the defendants. He wrote to them complaining that their beer was weak, and they wrote back saying that he must be watering it down before serving it to his customers. He sued them for defamation, but his claim was dismissed because the brewery were defending themselves against the allegations he had made.

Case Summary

This case, by the way, is an example of a situation in which the defendant was sued even though the defamatory allegation was only published to one other person, namely the secretary who typed the letter.

Information given to the police where a crime is suspected

Case Summary

In *Croucher* v. *Inglis* (1889), it was stated that where a person suspects a crime has been committed, they have a duty to tell the police. It is equally clear that the police have a duty to receive such information. Qualified privilege should also apply wherever someone knows of or suspects serious wrongdoing and reports it to the appropriate authorities.

Communications between officers of a company

Case Summary

Where one employee of a company tells another something which affects the interests of the company, the communication will be privileged. In *Watt* v. *Longsdon* (1930), the defendant was a director of a company that the claimant worked for. While the claimant was working abroad, the defendant received a letter from someone the claimant was working with accusing him of sexual misconduct and claiming that he was a drunk, a thief and a liar. None of this was true, but the defendant did not know that. He showed the letter to the other directors of the company, and to the claimant's wife. The court held that when the defendant showed the letter to the other directors, he was covered by qualified privilege, because he had a duty to make his fellow directors aware of the allegations and they clearly had an interest in hearing them as, if true, they could damage the business. However, he was not covered by qualified privilege when he showed the letter to the claimant's wife. She may have had an interest in receiving the information, but he did not have a duty to show it to her.

Malice

Case Summary

As we saw at the beginning of this section, a defendant who fits into any of the situations described above will only be protected by qualified privilege if they act without malice. This applies to both statutory and common law qualified privilege. Malice is yet another word that has one meaning in ordinary language, and another in law. (In fact it has two, as malice is also used in another defence, honest comment, in a slightly different way. But we will look at that later.) In everyday language, to do something with malice means to do it with spite, in order to hurt or offend someone. In the defence of qualified privilege, malice can have this meaning, but it also goes further than that. In *Horrocks* v. *Lowe* (1975), the House of Lords explained that someone would be acting with malice if they 'abused the privileged occasion'. Lord Diplock explained:

> in all cases of qualified privilege there is some special reason of public policy why the law accords immunity from suit – the existence of some public or private duty, whether legal or moral, on the part of the maker of the defamatory statement which justifies his communicating it or of some interest of his own which he is entitled to protect by doing so. If he uses the occasion for some other reason he loses the protection of the privilege.

As we saw at the beginning of this section, the reason why qualified privilege applies in certain situations is because it is in the public interest to have free discussion of the kind of issues raised in those situations. Therefore, where a person makes a statement with the purpose of promoting free discussion of important issues they will be covered.

But if they make a defamatory statement for another motive, they may be considered to have 'abused the occasion'. This motive might be personal spite, as in the everyday meaning of malice, but it need not be.

Take, for example, a public meeting of a large British company, a situation which is covered by statutory qualified privilege. At the meeting, one director, John, accuses another, Jane, of fraud. The reason for allowing such meetings to be covered by qualified privilege is so that there is free and open discussion of the way such companies are run, since this ultimately affects the health of the British economy, and is therefore important to everyone in society. If John is making his allegation so that the issue can be discussed publicly, in order to deal with a potential problem for the company, he is acting within the purpose of the defence and will be covered by it. But what if he secretly hates Jane and wants to damage her reputation? In this case, John's reason for making the accusation is his own personal spite towards Jane, so he is acting with malice and will not be protected by qualified privilege. Or what if he has nothing against Jane personally, but wants her sacked so he can have her job? Or he knows that the new boss of the company does not like women directors, and so he speaks out against Jane in order to make himself popular with the new boss? He may not be motivated by personal spite in these situations, but in legal terms he has acted with malice, because he is misusing the privileged occasion for a purpose other than the one for which the law makes the occasion privileged.

Case Summary

In *Angel* v. *HH Bushell* (1968), the claimant and defendant had started to do business together, but then had a disagreement. The defendant wrote to someone who they both knew, saying that the claimant 'did not know normal business ethics'. He claimed qualified privilege, but the Court rejected the defence because he was clearly motivated by his anger at the defendant rather than any duty to tell the other person what had happened.

Case Summary

In *Lillie and Reed* v. *Newcastle City Council* (2002), the claimants were nursery nurses, who were accused in an official report of abusing the children they looked after. The report had been prepared by a Review Team employed by the local council. The accusations were completely false, and the nurses sued. The Court agreed that there was a public interest in publishing allegations of child abuse and said such reports would usually be covered by qualified privilege. But in this case, they found, the Review Team had decided that the nurses were guilty, and had deliberately presented a false picture of the evidence and said things that they must have known were not true, in order to try to prove this. The trial judge found that they had acted with malice and so were not protected by qualified privilege.

Proving malice

Of course, it is not possible for judges or juries to look inside the defendant's mind in order to discover why they acted as they did. Instead, they must judge the defendant's motive from what they said or did. If it is clear that the defendant did not, or could not, have believed the accusation was true, that can be evidence that they acted from an improper motive, since there is no public interest in free discussion of information you know is not true. Equally, an honest belief that the words were true may be evidence that the defendant did not have an improper motive. But the key issue is whether the defendant was misusing the occasion for a bad motive, and so a defendant may be found to have acted with malice even when they did believe their words were true, if the reason for saying them was still an improper one.

Where malice is alleged, the judge decides whether there is sufficient evidence of malice to put the question before the jury and, if there is, it is then up to the jury to decide whether the defendant was motivated by malice. Other possible signs of malice, mentioned in *Horrocks* v. *Lowe*, were if the defendant's accusations were worse than was actually necessary to perform what they claim is their duty, or if there is evidence of dislike or spite from previous relations between the parties. A jury will consider these, together with their own view of the defendant's explanation for their actions, to decide whether they think there was malice.

The *Reynolds* defence

In the past, the common law defence of qualified privilege provided little protection for the media because it covered only the person who had a duty to make, or interest in making, a statement and not anyone else who repeated it. So, for example, if you tell the police that you suspect your next-door neighbour might be dealing drugs, your neighbour cannot sue you even if the allegation is not true, because you have a duty to tell the police and they have a duty to receive the information. But if the police tell the local newspaper, and it publishes your allegations, your neighbour could sue the newspaper, because the newspaper has no duty to publish what you told the police.

Case Summary

This situation was addressed in the case of *Reynolds* v. *Times Newspapers* (1999), where the House of Lords adapted qualified privilege to create a new defence which protects the media where it has acted responsibly in reporting matters of public interest. This form of qualified privilege is known as the *Reynolds* defence, after the case in which it was created. It is sometimes still referred to as a form of qualified privilege, but in *Loutchansky* v. *Times Newspapers* (2002) the Court of Appeal stated that it was a new defence, separate from qualified privilege and with its own rules.

The *Reynolds* case arose from a news story published in *The Times* about the former Irish prime minister, Albert Reynolds, and the circumstances leading up to his resignation. Mr Reynolds claimed the story suggested that he had deliberately misled the Irish parliament, which was undoubtedly defamatory. *The Times* put forward the defence of qualified privilege, arguing that it should apply to all discussion of matters of public interest, because the media had a duty to report such matters, and the public had an interest in being informed about them.

The House of Lords refused to go that far in extending the defence, but they agreed that it was important that information on matters of public interest should be freely available. However, they pointed out that allowing people to defend their reputations against false allegations was also in the public interest. In the case of politicians, for example, it was important for the public to make informed choices about the people they might vote for. But that meant not only knowing who was bad, but also who was good. Therefore, it was in the public interest for people to know if allegations were false.

The House of Lords therefore sought to strike a balance, by extending privilege to cover defamatory information which is published fairly and responsibly and in the public interest, even if it turns out not to be true. In deciding whether the *Reynolds* defence applies, the courts must balance a number of different factors, covering the importance of the subject and the behaviour of the media in reporting it. These factors, listed in *Reynolds*, are:

- *The seriousness of the allegation.* The more serious the allegation, the greater the care the press must show in handling it. On the other hand, if an allegation is not especially serious, it may be of insufficient public interest to be covered by the defence.

- *The nature of the information, and the extent to which it is the subject of public concern.* Only information of serious public interest will be covered and not, for example, trivial gossip about celebrities.
- *The source of the information.* Important issues here will include whether the informants had direct knowledge of the events or not, whether they were being paid for their stories, and whether they had their own 'axes to grind'.
- *The steps taken by the journalist to check the information.* This is essentially a test of whether the journalist has acted responsibly. There are no hard and fast rules on what the journalist has to do but steps such as checking the story with more than one source will count in favour of applying the defence.
- *The status of the information.* This factor concerns how authoritative the source of the information is. If an allegation has already been the subject of an authoritative investigation, for example, there would seem to be good reason why the public should be told about it. The Court of Appeal also mentioned government press releases, reports by the chairmen of public companies, and the speeches of university vice-chancellors as examples of sources with authority. In effect, if someone in some kind of authority puts about a defamatory allegation, there is likely to be a public interest in it being published, so that it can be either acted on, or refuted if it is not true.
- *The urgency of the matter.* This factor takes account of the fact that, as the Court of Appeal put it, 'news is a perishable commodity', and needs to be published quickly in order to make the maximum impact. Although the need to publish quickly will not excuse publishers from failing to make basic checks or attempt to get the other side of the story, the courts should take into account the fact that waiting too long can make it pointless to publish at all.
- *Whether the claimant was asked to comment on the story.* The claimant must usually have been given a fair chance to give a reasoned answer to the allegations. However, if a claimant refuses to answer, or the publisher genuinely cannot contact them in time, the defence may still apply. This is why, at the end of a potentially defamatory article, you often read phrases like 'Joe Bloggs refused to comment' or 'Jane Bloggs was unavailable for comment'.
- *Whether the article included the claimant's side of the story, at least in general terms.* The way in which the claimant's side of the story is presented will be important here; there is obviously a big difference in the protection the press can expect to get for stating the claimant's view and allowing it to speak for itself and, for example, quoting it in a context which suggests it is not to be believed. Again, the press will not be disadvantaged by this factor if the reason for not putting the other side of the story is that the claimant refused to give it.
- *The tone of the article.* A story raising queries or suggesting an investigation may, the House of Lords implied, be more likely to be protected than one which presented all the allegations as a matter of fact, or sensationalised them.
- *The circumstances of publication, including the timing.* This last factor allows the court to take into account other factors which seem relevant to the issue of whether the publisher has behaved responsibly.

The court said in *Reynolds* that the factors on the list are not necessarily the only ones which might be looked at. Other factors might also be taken into account, and the weight given to different factors would also vary from case to case. In *Jameel* v. *Wall Street Journal*, which we will look at below, the court made it clear that the *Reynolds* factors are guidelines to use when deciding whether the media has behaved responsibly. They are not a set of tests that defendants have to pass, and the *Reynolds* defence can apply even if a defendant has not fulfilled all the criteria, as long as overall they have behaved fairly and responsibly.

In *Reynolds* the House of Lords also stated that in weighing up these factors the courts should have regard to the importance of freedom of expression, and should be slow to conclude that a publication was not in the public interest, especially where information was already in the field of public discussion. This potentially gives the media a high degree of protection for important stories which are fairly handled. Ironically, in the *Reynolds* case itself, *The Times* lost. The House of Lords agreed that the subject was one of legitimate public concern. On the other hand, the allegation made was a serious one, yet the paper had not mentioned Mr Reynolds's explanation for the events concerned, even though this was available to them. As a result, they found that the story was not covered by qualified privilege.

The *Reynolds* defence in practice

Case Summary

The *Reynolds* defence has since been raised in a number of important cases, though not always successfully. In *Bonnick* v. *Morris* (2002), a newspaper published a story about a state-owned Jamaican company, JCTC, entering into two contracts with another company, Prolacto. The claimant was employed by JCTC but had left just after the second contract was agreed. The newspaper reported that the contracts were unusually advantageous to Prolacto, and that the claimant had left JCTC just after making the second contract. The claimant argued that this was defamatory, because it implied that he had acted improperly in arranging the contract and that was why he had had to leave. The newspaper pointed out that it had approached JCTC for comments, but it had refused to say anything, and they had also spoken to the claimant, who had explained that there was nothing suspicious about the contracts and that they had no connection with his leaving the company. The Court agreed that the article was defamatory, but said it was covered by qualified privilege because the subject was a matter of public interest, the paper had acted responsibly, particularly given that the story was not one which was obviously defamatory. This was a straightforward application of the purpose behind the *Reynolds* defence: to protect discussion of matters of public interest, where in all the circumstances the media was justified in going ahead and publishing what they did, when they did.

Case Summary

A high-profile case in which the defence was not successful is *Grobbelaar* v. *News Group Newspapers* (2001). The footballer Bruce Grobbelaar sued *The Sun* over reports that he had been paid to fix the results of matches he played in. The paper had been given a tip-off that Mr Grobbelaar had been involved in match fixing. They arranged for the person who supplied the tip-off to tape a conversation in which Mr Grobbelaar accepted money to fix a match, and admitted to doing so in the past. The resulting story took up several pages, with headlines screaming 'World exclusive – Grobbelaar took bribes to fix games' and 'I saved goal by mistake and lost £125,000'.

Before the case came to court, Mr Grobbelaar was charged with two criminal offences related to match fixing but was acquitted. *The Sun* pleaded qualified privilege, and the Court of Appeal applied the *Reynolds* factors (at this stage the *Reynolds* defence was still considered a type of qualified privilege). They held that the defence did not apply. Among the factors which the Court said led to this decision were that the main witness against the claimant was thoroughly unreliable, the newspaper had evidence from a world-class goalkeeper that suggested Mr Grobbelaar's performance on the pitch showed no signs of match fixing, and that there was no real urgency for the paper to publish when they did. But the main factor was the tone and weight of the story, which appeared over several pages for seven days and seemed to be suggesting Mr Grobbelaar was definitely guilty, rather than, for example, raising questions or asking for an investigation. However, the result of the case was less of a disappointment for the paper; although Mr Grobbelaar won, the House of Lords reduced the £85,000 damages ordered by the jury to £1, in recognition of the fact that, although it could not be proved that he fixed matches, he had admitted that he took bribes.

Case Summary

In *Loutchansky* v. *Times Newspapers* (2002), a story in *The Times* accused Russian businessman Grigori Loutchansky of being involved in serious crime. The paper claimed qualified privilege because, it said, the subject was one of public concern and the story was based on authoritative sources, including reports by the CIA and British intelligence services. *The Times* initially lost but appealed, and the case was sent back to the original judge to reconsider. Second time round, the judge still found against the newspaper. Summarising the *Reynolds* defence, he said the question was whether the paper had behaved responsibly in publishing the articles. He agreed that the matter was one of public concern, but said that the allegations made were very serious and potentially very damaging to Mr Loutchansky's reputation, and therefore demanded a high degree of care on the paper's part before publishing them. This standard had not been met: some of the sources were unsafe, while the allegations were vague and the paper had not made enough effort to check them. The paper had tried to contact Mr Loutchansky but, the judge said, they should have tried harder, and although the story stated that Mr Loutchansky had repeatedly denied the allegations, this bare statement did not amount to giving his side of the story.

Case Summary

In *Gillian McKeith* v. *News Group Newspapers* (2005), the television nutritionist Gillian McKeith sued *The Sun* over a story which claimed her nutritional qualifications were bogus because she got her degree via a correspondence course with a small American college. The paper put forward the *Reynolds* defence, but the Court held that it could not apply. Although the issue was of public concern, given that the claimant was offering nutritional advice to the public, there was no public interest that required *The Sun* to tell its readers that Ms McKeith's degree was 'worthless' when its reporters admitted knowing that it took two years of work to get the qualification. In addition, they had not put their allegations to Ms McKeith for comment.

Writing and drafting

You are the legal adviser to a firm which publishes local newspapers. One of the papers has a story about a local councillor, who they claim has been taking bribes from local firms in return for helping them to win valuable contracts with the council. You think the story may be covered by the *Reynolds* defence. Draw up a short list of questions you would want to ask the journalist who wrote it, in order to work out whether the defence will apply.

Neutral reportage

This is a relatively new defence, which developed out of the *Reynolds* defence. The defence applies to reports about a matter of public interest, where any defamatory allegations are reported in a completely neutral manner, without suggesting that they are or may be true. In these cases, the courts have held that it is not necessary to fulfil all the *Reynolds* criteria, and may not even be necessary to take steps to check that the allegations are true.

Case Navigator

Case Summary

The defence of neutral reportage has its origins in ***Jameel* v. *Wall Street Journal*** (2006), though in this case it was not yet recognised as a separate defence. The claimant was a wealthy Saudi Arabian businessman, who had been mentioned in a story in the *Wall Street Journal*. The story said that several prominent Saudi citizens, including Mr Jameel, had had their bank accounts monitored by the Saudi government at the request of the United States government. The paper said this was done to make sure they were not giving money to terrorist groups, either knowingly or unknowingly. Mr Jameel said the article was defamatory, because it suggested he might be involved in funding terrorism. The paper put forward the *Reynolds* defence, but it could not meet all the *Reynolds* criteria. However, the House of Lords said that the defence could still apply, because the criteria were only ever intended to be used as guidelines for judging whether a story should be protected by the defence; they were not specific tests that the media had to pass. In this case, the story was presented in a balanced way, without suggesting that there was reason to suspect Mr Jameel of involvement in terrorism, and it was a matter of great public interest. This was exactly the kind of reporting that the *Reynolds* defence was designed to protect.

Case Summary

This idea that a balanced report on a matter of public interest could be protected even when the *Reynolds* criteria were not met then began to develop in a new and separate defence of neutral reportage. In *Roberts* v. *Gable* (2007), the Court of Appeal explained how the neutral reportage defence works and when it will apply. Lord Justice Ward said that there were nine points which had to be considered when deciding whether a report or article should be covered by neutral reportage:

- The information must be in the public interest.
- The story, taken as a whole, must have the effect of reporting the fact that the defamatory allegations were made, rather than suggesting that they might be true.
- The protection is lost if the journalist adopts the allegations as their own, or fails to report in a fair and neutral way.
- The test of whether the story was neutral reportage is an objective one, and all the circumstances surrounding the research, the way the information was reported and the purpose of the report would be relevant.
- The publication must meet the standards of responsible journalism, and in deciding this the *Reynolds* criteria would be relevant, adjusted as necessary for the special nature of reportage.
- The seriousness of the allegations is relevant, and the more serious the allegations, the more important it would be for the journalist to try to verify whether they were true. But the question to be asked is whether the public has a right to know that the allegations were being made. If the answer is yes, the report could be protected, even if the allegations were serious ones in terms of harm to the claimant's reputation.
- The defence will not necessarily fail because the journalist did not take steps to ensure the information was accurate.

- It is not necessary that the claimant is a public figure or prominent person.
- The urgency of the story is relevant, and it is accepted that public interest could decline with time. Decisions which had to be made in a hurry to meet deadlines would be treated more sympathetically than those made when there was time to reflect.

In *Roberts* v. *Gable*, the case concerned a report in the anti-fascist newspaper *Searchlight* about a feud between different groups in the British National Party. It said that the two sides were each making allegations about threats of violence, and a theft. The claimants were among those named in the article, and had not been given a chance to comment on the allegations reported in it. In fact, no real attempt had been made to check that the allegations were true. The Court of Appeal held that *Searchlight* was protected by the neutral reportage defence, because they had simply reported that the dispute existed and that each side was making accusations against the other. They had not suggested that the allegations were true.

Case Summary

A case where the neutral reportage defence was rejected is *Galloway* v. *Daily Telegraph* (2006), where the *Telegraph* reported accusations that MP George Galloway had taken money from the dictator Saddam Hussein. The paper claimed it was presenting neutral reportage of allegations against a public figure, which the public had a right to know about. This argument was rejected by the judge. He said that the paper had not merely reported neutrally the fact that the allegations had been made, but had 'embraced the allegations with relish and fervour'. They had, for example, used the headline 'Damning new evidence' which suggested that the evidence pointed to Mr Galloway's guilt. They had made no attempt to check the allegations, and although they had spoken to Mr Galloway they had not told him that the story they were working on would suggest that he had acted for personal gain, so he had not had a chance to reply to that allegation.

Who can use the *Reynolds* and neutral reportage defences?

Case Summary

Both these defences were originally created in cases involving media reports, and were described in terms of protecting free speech by the media. However, in *Seaga* v. *Harper* (2008), the **Privy Council** said that there was no reason why the *Reynolds* defence could not be used to cover any case where the subject of the defamatory remarks was a matter of public interest, and the author/speaker had been responsible and, where appropriate, followed the *Reynolds* guidelines. The case itself involved verbal remarks made by a politician about a deputy police commissioner. Although the Privy Council said the defence could apply to material published in this way, on the facts the defence failed because the politician had not taken sufficient care to check that what he was saying was true. The neutral reportage defence was not mentioned in the case, but there seems no reason why it too could not apply to statements other than press reports.

Honest comment

Case Summary

This defence was traditionally known as fair comment, but in the recent case of *Joseph* v. *Spiller* (2010) the Supreme Court held that it should be renamed honest comment the better to reflect the nature of the defence. This defence is designed to uphold freedom of speech, by protecting fair and honest commentary about matters of public interest. The defendant must prove five elements:

- The subject was a matter of public interest.
- The words are a comment, and not a statement of fact.
- The comment is honest.
- The facts on which the comment is based are true, or subject to privilege.
- The comment was made without malice.

A matter of public interest

Case Summary

In *London Artists* v. *Littler* (1969), Lord Denning defined matters of public interest as anything that was 'such as to affect the public at large, so that they may legitimately be interested in, or concerned at, what is going on'. The definition is therefore quite wide, but there is no set classification of which subjects are or are not matters of public interest, and in each case it is up to the judge to decide whether the subject is one of public interest. However, as a general rule, comments about local or national government, trade unions, the police, and people involved in public affairs will usually be matters of public interest. The defence is also considered to apply to reviews of books, plays, art, film, television or restaurants.

A comment and not a statement of fact

This may seem a very clear distinction, but it is not always as clear as you might imagine. If I say 'Jack Dodgy was convicted of theft in 1997' I am clearly intending to make a statement of fact. But what if I say 'Jack Dodgy is fit and healthy, and has been offered numerous jobs. But he has never done a day's work in his life, and has lived off benefits since he was 16. In my view, that makes him a thief.' Assuming that the information about Jack being offered jobs and never taking one is true, is my calling him a thief a statement of fact, or a comment? You could argue that I am stating as a fact that his behaviour amounts to a theft, but you could also argue that I'm merely stating my opinion of his behaviour, and that is a comment. You can see, therefore, that this issue is not always straightforward.

Case Summary

In *Burstein* v. *Associated Newspapers* (2007), the cases concerned a review in the *London Evening Standard* of an opera about suicide bombers. The reviewer said 'I found the tone depressingly anti-American, and the idea that there is anything heroic about suicide bombers is, frankly, a grievous insult.' The composer of the opera sued, claiming that the review was suggesting, as a fact, that he, the composer, sympathised with terrorist causes, and viewed suicide bombers as heroic. The Court of Appeal threw the case out, saying that it was very clear that the review was a comment and not a statement of fact. Even if it did imply something about the composer's beliefs, that did not mean it ceased to become a comment. The facts referred to were true, and the opinion the reviewer formed from those facts were ones which could be honestly held.

Case Summary

In *Keays* v. *Guardian Newspapers* (2003), *The Guardian* published an article about the claimant, who was known to the public because she had had an affair with a senior politician, and had had his child. Ms Keays had for a long time refused to talk to the press, but she had recently changed her mind and decided to publish her story. *The Guardian*'s article questioned her motives for doing this. The judge held that this must be a comment and not a statement of fact, as *The Guardian*'s journalists could not know as a fact what was on Ms Keays's mind.

Case Summary

In *Galloway* v. *Daily Telegraph* (2006), the case we looked at above where the *Telegraph* claimed that the MP George Galloway had received money from Saddam Hussein, the *Telegraph* also pleaded honest comment, but the court said the stories were clearly meant as allegations of fact. They pointed to a headline stating 'Damning new evidence', and said that by using the word 'damning' the paper was suggesting that Mr Galloway was, as a matter of fact, guilty of taking the money.

Case Summary

In *British Chiropractic Association* v. *Singh* (2010), the British Chiropractic Association (BCA) sued science journalist Simon Singh over a story in *The Guardian*, which said that BCA members' claims about the medical problems their treatments could treat were made 'without a jot of evidence', and that the BCA 'happily promotes bogus treatments'. The BCA argued that the words were intended as a statement of fact, and therefore could not be covered by the honest comment defence. The Court of Appeal disagreed. They pointed out that in the evidence supplied to the court, Mr Singh had set out his reasons for believing that there was no reliable evidence that the treatments worked, while the BCA in their evidence had been able to make an equally detailed case arguing that there was evidence that the treatments worked. This showed, they said, that the original article had not been intended as a statement of fact, but as an evaluation of the available evidence about the treatments. The word 'bogus' was used to emphasise Mr Singh's opinion of the evidence, rather than a factual assertion. That made the article a statement of opinion, not fact, and so the defence was available. The Court of Appeal case was purely to decide whether honest comment was available (not to try the libel claim itself) and the effect of the decision was that, had the case gone to trial, Mr Singh would have been able to argue the honest comment defence. Whether it would have succeeded must remain a mystery as the BCA dropped their claim after the Court of Appeal decision on honest comment.

The comment must be honest

In the past it was held that the comment had to be 'fair', which suggested it had to be balanced and justified by the facts. In recent cases, however, the courts have stressed that what is required is not fairness but honesty. A comment will be considered honest if it is an honest expression of the defendant's views, even if it is very rude and unpleasant, and regardless of whether the judge or jury would agree with it. As Lord Nicholls explained in the *Reynolds* case:

> the basis of our public life is that the crank, the enthusiast, may say what he honestly thinks as much as the reasonable person . . . The true test is whether the opinion, however exaggerated, obstinate or prejudiced, was honestly held by the person expressing it.

Of course, neither the judge nor the jury can see inside the defendant's head, so honesty is judged on the basis of whether the statement expresses an opinion which a reasonable person could honestly have formed from the facts of the situation. In *Cornwell* v. *Sunday People* (1983), the actress and singer Charlotte Cornwell sued the *Sunday People* newspaper over a review written by its television critic. The review said, among other things, that Ms Cornwell was ugly, and that her bottom was too big. Her lawyers argued that as she was clearly of perfectly normal weight and appearance, this was not an opinion that the reviewer could honestly have held. Ms Cornwell won her case.

Case Summary

Facts must be true

Even if the words used are comment, they will often be based on one or more facts. If we take the case of *Burstein*, for example, on the review of the opera about suicide bombers, the comment that the reviewer made was based on the fact that the opera was about suicide bombers. Similarly, in *Keays*, the comment about Ms Keays's motives for publishing her story was based in the fact that she had published her story. Where a comment is based on facts, the defence of honest comment can only apply if the facts are true, or are subject to the defence of privilege (either qualified or absolute). In *David Soul* v. *Matthew Wright* (2001), Mr Wright reviewed a play that David Soul was appearing in, and described it as 'without doubt the worst West End show'. A review would normally be covered by honest comment, but Mr Wright was not able to use the defence because he had not actually been to see the show, so his claims about what he had seen were not true. However, where a comment is based on more than one fact, and only some of them can be proved true, the defence will not necessarily fail. The Defamation Act 1996 provides in section 6 that where only some of the allegations can be proved, the defence can stand as long as what is said is fair comment when the facts that are proved are taken into account.

Case Summary

Where a comment is based on facts, the courts have traditionally held that the factual basis for the comment has to be made clear when the comment is made. In *Telnikoff* v. *Matusevitch* (1991), the defendant wrote a letter to *The Daily Telegraph*, which was about an earlier article that had appeared in the paper, and claimed that this article was racist and anti-Semitic. The *Telegraph* published the letter, and the author of the original article sued. The defendant argued honest comment, and wanted to use parts of the original article to back up his defence by showing that his letter was honest comment given what the article had said. But the House of Lords said he could not do this, because he had not quoted those parts of the article in his letter, which meant that readers could not judge what he said on that basis; they would only be influenced by what was actually in the letter.

Case Summary

This rule now appears to have been relaxed in the recent case of *Joseph* v. *Spiller* (2010), which was the first defamation case to be heard by the Supreme Court. The claimants were a Motown tribute band called the Gillettes, who had a contract with the defendant, a booking agency. The contract included a 're-engagement clause', which stated that if the Gillettes were asked to perform again within a year at any of the venues the agency had booked for them that booking had to be arranged through the agency, which would then receive a fee. The Gillettes were booked by a restaurant in Leeds, which really liked the band, but took against the boss of the booking agency, Mr Spiller, and did not wish to deal with him again. So when the restaurant booked the Gillettes to appear again they made the booking directly with the band. When Mr Spiller learned of the booking he wrote to the band, complaining that they had breached their contract. They emailed back, dismissing the complaint and saying, among other things, that the contract was just a formality and 'holds no water in legal terms'. Mr Spiller responded by posting a notice on the company's website, which said they would not be accepting further bookings for the Gillettes because the band were not professional enough and had been unable to abide by the terms of their contract. It said that Mr Joseph, who ran the Gillettes had advised the agency that 'the terms and conditions of . . . contracts hold no water in legal terms', and suggested that this meant it would be unwise for anyone to book them as they might not meet their commitments.

Case Summary

Mr Spiller argued that the notice was fair comment, and that the facts it was based on were the email that said the contract held no water and the fact that the Gillettes had breached their contract by accepting a direct booking from the Leeds restaurant. The claimants argued that the defence could not apply, because the notice had not specified what the breach of contract related to, and had misquoted their email by suggesting that they considered 'contracts' generally not to be legally binding when what they had said was specific to the contract with the agency. This, they argued, meant the facts on which the comments were based were not sufficiently clear. The Supreme Court rejected this argument. Giving the leading judgment, Lord Phillips said that it was necessary to 'identify in general terms what it is that has led the commentator to make the comment, so that the reader can understand what the comment is about'. But it was not necessary to detail the facts so specifically as to allow the reader to judge whether the comment was accurate. Part of the reason for making this change, Lord Phillips said, was that the internet had made it possible for people to make public comment about others in a way that did not exist when the defence of fair comment was developed. It would often be impossible for readers to assess these comments without detailed information about the facts, and if fair comment was only to apply where readers were able to do this the defence of fair comment would lose much of its point.

Applying this approach to the *Spiller* case, the Court held that the defendant was entitled to plead the defence of honest comment. The two facts relied on as the basis of the comment were the email and the breach of contract. The Supreme Court said the email did show a careless disregard for the band's contractual obligations, which was what the website notice had alleged, and the misquoting did not appear to make much difference to that. In addition, it was sufficient that the notice had referred to a breach of contract; they did not have to go into detail about what the breach was.

Note that this was an interim hearing to decide whether the defendant could plead fair comment, and not a full trial of the case, so we do not know whether the defence will actually succeed.

Made without malice

You will remember that we looked at malice in connection with the defence of qualified privilege, and saw that its meaning there was different and wider than the normal everyday meaning of malice. Like qualified privilege, honest comment is unavailable as a defence if the defendant has acted with malice. But just to make things a bit more complicated, it appears that malice has a slightly different meaning for the purposes of honest comment. It had been thought that malice could be defined in the same way for both defences, but in *Cheng* v. *Tse Wai Chun* (2000) Lord Nicholls said this was not the case. He said that in the defence of honest comment (then known as fair comment), a defendant will be said to have acted with malice if they did not honestly believe what they said was true. If they do believe what they say is true, then there is no malice, even if the defendant was in fact motivated by 'spite, animosity, intent to injure, intent to arouse controversy or other motivation'. This meant, he said, that 'critics need [not] be mealy-mouthed in denouncing what they disagree with.'

Case Summary

Take, for example, a situation where Anil, a journalist, writes a review of a restaurant run by a chef, Gordon, who he cannot stand. His review says that the food was terrible and the service even worse. His dislike of Gordon may mean that he takes great pleasure in giving the restaurant a bad review, but as long as the views expressed are his genuine opinion of the meal and the venue, he can still be covered by honest comment. If, on the other hand, he thinks the meal he ate for the review is fine but decides to be rude about it anyway, out of spite, his review would not, in law, be covered by honest comment because he did not genuinely hold the opinion he expressed. As with malice in qualified privilege, the jury will have to judge whether the defendant honestly believed their words were true by looking at all the circumstances of the case.

You be the judge

Q: **Sam Square-Eyes is the TV critic for a national newspaper. He writes a review of a new comedy, which says: 'This was the most unfunny thing I've ever seen. The script is pathetic, and the acting is beyond awful. Everyone in the cast is bad, but the worst by far is Susie Stunna, the former Page 3 girl who now thinks she can act. Then again, what can you expect from someone who takes part in drunken orgies with footballers?'**

Is Sam's review covered by honest comment?

A: No. The first two sentences are clearly comment, and as long as Sam genuinely believes what he is saying to be true, and is not acting with malice, they will be covered by the defence. However, the last sentence is a statement of fact, and would not be covered by this defence. It might be covered by the defence of justification if Sam can prove it is true.

Source: Pearson Education Ltd/Comstock Images

Innocent dissemination

As we saw earlier, a claimant in defamation can sue not only the maker of the defamatory statement but also anyone involved in making it public. This can appear quite unfair on printers, distributors and sellers, who may have had no real say in what appears in the publications they work with. The defence of innocent dissemination exists to protect them.

The defence is set out in section 1 of the Defamation Act 1996. It is available to anyone who:

- is not the author, editor or publisher of the defamatory statement; and
- took reasonable care in relation to its publication; and
- did not know and had no reason to believe that what they did caused or contributed to publication of a defamatory statement.

Case Summary

The defence was tested in *Godfrey* v. *Demon Internet* (1999). The defendant was an internet service provider, and the defamatory statement was part of a message posted to an internet newsgroup by an unknown person (which is why Mr Godfrey chose to sue Demon instead of the person making the statement). Mr Godfrey had asked Demon to remove the defamatory message but they had failed to do so. They claimed they were covered by innocent dissemination, because they were not the publisher and had no reason to believe they had contributed to the publication of a defamatory statement. The Court agreed that, for the purposes of the defence, they were not the publishers of the statement. However, they lost the protection of the defence because they had not taken down the statement once they knew it was there, so they could not show that they had taken reasonable care.

It is important to understand that the fact that an organisation is not 'the publisher' for the purposes of this defence does not mean that the information was not published by them. You will remember that in the previous chapter we looked at the fact that one of the requirements for a defamation claim is that the statement has to have been published, meaning communicated to someone other than the claimant and the defendant's spouse. In *Godfrey* v. *Demon*, the defendants put forward an alternative argument, claiming that they could not be said to have published the defamatory statement, because they had only stored it on their server. The court rejected this view. They said that booksellers and libraries had been successfully sued for publishing defamatory material contained in books they stocked, and this was the same as an internet service provider storing material on its server, from where it was published every time a user read it on the internet. For the purposes of the basic requirements of defamation, they had published the material, but for the purposes of innocent dissemination, they were not the publisher.

Case Summary

You be the judge

Q: Simon Single used to go out with a glamour model called Carol Cutie, before she was famous. Simon finds out that Carol has written a book about her life in which she says he cheated on her with both of her sisters. This is not true. Simon wants to prevent the book from being sold, so he writes to the three biggest booksellers in the UK and tells them that the book contains defamatory material about him. They ignore his letters. After the book comes out, Simon sues Carol, and the firm that publishes her book. Can he also sue the three booksellers?

A: Yes. The booksellers have published the defamatory statement, so they are liable. They would not be covered by the defence of innocent dissemination, because they were warned about the presence of defamatory material but did not take reasonable precautions to prevent its publication.

Offer of amends

The offer of amends procedure was designed as a way to avoid long and costly defamation trials by allowing the defendant to put right the damage to the claimant's reputation at an early stage. Set out in the Defamation Act 1996, it works in two different ways: as a defence; and as a way to reduce the cost of damages if the claimant wins.

The procedure can only act as a defence if the defendant did not know or have reason to believe that the statement complained of was false and defamatory and was likely to be understood as referring to the claimant. It therefore applies mostly to cases where someone has been defamed by accident, such as where a story was true of one person but not of another person with the same name. The defendant makes a written offer to publish an apology or correction and pay damages, and the claimant can choose whether or not to accept the offer. If they say no, and the case goes to trial, the court will consider whether the offer was reasonable and made within a reasonable time. If it was, the defendant will have a defence.

If the defendant did know that the story was false, defamatory and likely to be taken as referring to the claimant, they cannot use the offer of amends procedure as a defence but they can use it to try to reduce their damages if they are found liable. If they make an offer of amends which is refused, and the claimant then wins the case, the court will usually reduce the damages by a significant amount, to show approval of the fact that the defendant tried to put right the damage. This happened in *Nail* v. *HarperCollins and News Group* (2004). HarperCollins had published a book about the actor Jimmy Nail, which made allegations about his sexual behaviour, and the *News of the World* published details from the book. Mr Nail sued, claiming damages of £70,000–£100,000. The defendants made an offer of amends, with damages of £37,500, which Mr Nail rejected. He won his case, but the judge awarded only £30,000, and said that defendants who tried to make amends were entitled to expect that the court would recognise that effort by reducing the damages. The Court of Appeal approved that view.

Case Summary

If the claimant accepts the offer, the parties can agree the details of the apology and the amount of damages between themselves. If they cannot agree, the court can decide these issues for them. Once an offer of amends is accepted, the proceedings come to an end.

If a defendant wants to use this procedure, they have to make the offer before putting forward any other defence. It is not possible to start off claiming a defence, and then make an offer of amends later if you realise your defence might fail. This is because the offer of amends procedure is designed to allow defendants to put things right quickly, rather than to give them an escape route if they do not think they can win their case.

Out and about

For the previous chapter you did an exercise in which you looked for defamatory statements in newspapers and magazines. You may have been surprised at how many you found, but in practice defamatory material is published every day. Sometimes this is simply because the publisher believes the subject will not sue but, as we have seen in this chapter, it is often because they believe they are covered by a defence. So this time, go through the material again and consider whether, in each case, one or more defences apply.

Writing and drafting

In the Out and About exercise you found examples of defamatory material which may be covered by a defence. Choose one of the stories that you found and, basing your arguments on case law, draft an explanation of which defence should apply, and why.

This exercise will help you focus on the case law and look at how it applies to a new set of facts. This is the same skill that you use in tackling problem questions, and the same skill that lawyers have to use when they argue a case.

Remedies for defamation

The main remedies for defamation are:

- damages
- injunctions

Damages

Damages for defamation are calculated to compensate for the damage to the claimant's reputation. In some cases there may be an actual financial loss as well, for example, if the defamation causes loss of business. But as we saw earlier, a claim can succeed without any financial loss, and so damages will often be purely for the damage to reputation. Defamation is unusual among torts in that both the verdict and the damages are decided by a jury. This, along with the obvious difficulty of calculating what damage to reputation is worth, means they can be unpredictable and in the past there was concern that juries were awarding damages that were unreasonably high. In a few cases damages had run into millions, and this was seen as undesirable given that in personal injury cases damages usually only reach these levels when the claimant has been very seriously disabled and will need lifelong care.

To deal with this problem, section 8 of the Courts and Legal Services Act 1990 gave the Court of Appeal a power to overturn a jury decision on damages, and instead award 'such sum as appears to be proper'. The power was used in *John* v. *Mirror Group Newspapers* (1996), an appeal by the Mirror Group in a case brought by Elton John. He had successfully sued them over an untrue story claiming that he was hooked on a bizarre diet which was a form of the eating disorder bulimia nervosa, and was awarded £350,000. The Court of Appeal reduced the damages to £75,000, and also gave guidance for judges in future cases. They said that judges should help juries to value the damage to a claimant's reputation by telling them about the levels of damages typically ordered in personal injury cases. They might, for example, point out that someone who is paralysed in an accident would typically get around £125,000, while a lost arm is 'worth' £45,000, and a lost eye £20,000. The jury could then compare the impact of these sorts of injuries with the impact on the claimant of the damage to their reputation.

Case Summary

Since the Elton John case, the Court of Appeal has continued to take steps to keep defamation damages at what they consider to be a more sensible level. In *McCartan Turkington Breen* v. *The Times*, for example (the case we looked at earlier on whether a press conference was a public meeting), an award of £145,000 was reduced to £75,000.

Injunction

A claimant may also seek an **injunction**, either to stop a defamatory statement being published again, or to prevent one being published in the first place. Cases where a claimant seeks to prevent publication in the first place usually involve the media. What usually happens is that the claimant finds out that someone is planning to publish a story, which they claim is defamatory, perhaps because they or someone they know have been questioned by journalists or the paper has sought to get their side of the story. In

if the claimant can silence the story for a while it may become less newsworthy

this situation publication is usually about to happen, so if the claimant wants to stop it they cannot wait for a full trial. They can, however, apply for an **interim injunction**, which is issued without a full trial of the issues and is designed as a temporary measure until a full trial can be held. However, in a case involving the media, interim injunctions can in practice have a much stronger effect, because if the claimant can silence the story for a while, it may become less newsworthy and so never be published at all. This clearly has serious implications for free speech, since it means that a claimant who can get an injunction can effectively prevent criticism of themselves and their activities without giving the media a chance to argue their case properly.

Case Summary

For this reason, the courts have always been reluctant to grant interim injunctions in defamation cases; in *Bonnard* v. *Perryman* (1891) it was stated that they should only do so in the clearest cases, where it was obvious that any reasonable jury would say the statement concerned was defamatory. This traditional protection has now been strengthened by section 12 of the Human Rights Act 1998. It states that in cases affecting freedom of expression (which could be any defamation case), interim injunctions should not be granted unless the court is satisfied that if the case does go to trial the claimant is likely to be able to establish that publication should not be allowed. In addition, the Human Rights Act provides that when considering requests for injunctions on journalistic material a court should consider:

- the importance of freedom of expression;
- the extent to which material is already, or is about to be, available to the public;
- the extent to which publication would be in the public interest;
- any relevant privacy code (this refers to the codes of practice issued by various bodies in the media industry).

The result is that interim injunctions are likely to be granted only where the claimant can convince the court that the defendant is planning to publish defamatory material which is obviously untrue, and where there is no arguable defence, or a defence put forward is unlikely to succeed.

Writing and drafting

You are the lawyer for a national newspaper group. One of the papers wants to run the following story, and asks you to check it for libel.

Judge took bribes from gangster ring

The truth about last month's sensational acquittal of the so-called Heavy Boys Gang on charges of money laundering, kidnap and theft can now be revealed: Judge Colin Crooked, who heard the trial, was bribed by the gang. For a payment of £1 million, he agreed to rule that vital evidence should be kept from the jury. Half the money was paid when the trial started, and the rest when the jury acquitted the gang.

An ex-member of the gang told our reporter: 'We found out that the judge had money problems, so two members of the gang contacted him, and he said he was willing to do a deal. The money was paid into a secret bank account, as the judge requested.' Shortly after the trial, Judge Crooked bought a yacht, costing £500,000.

Judge Crooked was widely criticised for ruling that evidence from the kidnap victim should not be put before the jury because she was only 4 years old and her evidence could not be relied on. Although it is unusual for children this young to testify in a criminal case, their evidence can be given if the judge allows it.

You see immediately that the story is potentially defamatory.

1. List any defences that might protect the newspaper.
2. Draft a list of questions you would need to ask the editor and/or the reporters who worked on the story, to decide whether any defence(s) could apply.
3. Consider whether there are any changes that could be made to the article, to make it more likely to be protected by a defence.

Reflective practice

If you can, take a few minutes to think about how this exercise went. What did you find difficult? Was it easy to recognise the possible defences? Did you need to refer back to the text, or did the rules for each defence stick in your mind? How easy (or difficult) was it to apply the law to the situation you were asked to deal with? Is there anything you would do differently if you did a similar exercise?

Time limits

As we have seen in previous chapters, all torts have time limits after which it becomes too late to make a claim. The limitation period for defamation actions is one year, but section 32A of the Limitation Act 1980 provides that the courts have a discretion to extend this. In deciding whether to grant an extension, the courts have to decide whether the disadvantage to the claimant if the time period is not extended is greater than the disadvantage to the defendant if it is extended. In other words, is it more unfair on the claimant to refuse an extension than it is unfair on the defendant to grant one? In making this decision, they should take into account all the circumstances, including the length and reason for the delay, and the impact of that delay on the availability of evidence.

Problems with the law on defamation

As we have seen throughout this chapter, defamation law is supposed to strike a balance between protection for reputation and protection for free speech. Our laws on defamation, and the way they operate, have been widely criticised as failing to strike the right balance, especially compared with the laws in other countries. The following are some of the areas that have been criticised. The government has recently published a draft bill which aims to reform the law on defamation, and goes some way to meeting some of these criticisms; we will look at its provisions at the end of this section.

Costs and the 'chilling effect'

The costs of a defamation case are higher in the English courts than anywhere else in the world. A study by Oxford University looked at costs across 12 European countries, and found that the cost of even a relatively simple defamation case here is 14 times higher than in France, 35 times higher than in Sweden and 266 times higher than in Germany. It is very common for the legal costs to be much higher than any damages paid if the claimant wins.

In most cases the losing party must pay the other side's costs, so unless a defendant believes they have an extremely strong case there is huge pressure on them to **settle**. What is less often realised outside legal circles is that even if you win a civil case you will not necessarily get all your costs back. The claimant can ask the court to look at the costs you are claiming and decide whether they are reasonable, and it is quite common to find that the court orders the losing party to pay only perhaps 90 per cent of the costs that the defendants have paid to their lawyers. Given that a defamation case can cost hundreds of thousands of pounds to defend, even a defendant who has a very strong case may be put off fighting by the knowledge that, even if they win, it could cost them tens of thousands of pounds. Freedom of speech campaigners say that this situation creates a 'freezing effect' on the media, making them more likely to avoid writing about certain subjects, people or organisations altogether; to pull out of a story if a libel claim is threatened; or to agree a quick settlement rather than defending a case.

According to the Oxford study into comparative costs across Europe (Programme in Comparative Media Law and Policy 2008), this situation has been made worse by the introduction of **conditional fee agreements**. Usually known as 'no win, no fee' arrangements, they allow a solicitor to take on a case and charge an extra fee (known as the 'success fee') if they win and nothing if they lose. According to the Oxford study, in defamation cases it is routine for solicitors to charge a 100 per cent success fee, effectively doubling the cost of the case. This way of paying for cases was originally introduced as a way of ensuring that people who were not well off could still have access to justice, and it does ensure that, provided their case is strong enough to persuade a law firm to take it, even people who are not wealthy can make a claim for defamation. However, in defamation it has caused problems. As we saw above, in most cases, the losing party in a case pays the other's costs and their own. The usual way for no win, no fee claimants to protect against this liability is to take out insurance, but there is no rule that they have to do this. Nor is it usually possible to prevent a claim being brought on a no win, no fee basis where the claimant clearly could not pay the defendant's costs if they lost and has no insurance. This means that claimants on no win, no fee deals can effectively hold a defendant (usually a media organisation) to ransom: the defendant faces the risk that if they defend a case, they will at best still end up having to pay their own costs if they win, and if they lose may face a bill for double the claimant's costs as well as their own. This means there is no financial incentive for them to defend a case, even if they believe they can win.

> claimants on no win, no fee deals can effectively hold a defendant to ransom

Case Summary

This was the situation in *Musa King* v. *Daily Telegraph* (2004), where the claimant sued over claims in the *Telegraph* that he was associated with Al Qaeda. He had no money and would clearly not have been able to pay the *Telegraph*'s costs if he had lost, but had secured a no win, no fee arrangement with a 100 per cent success fee. The maximum damages likely to be payable if the claimant had won would have been around £150,000, but the costs were likely to be around £1 million. Even if the paper had won their case, they would have ended up paying their own costs of around £400,000. They tried to get the Court to protect them from this situation, but although Lord Justice Brooke agreed that the arrangement did create a 'a chilling effect on a newspaper exercising its right of freedom of expression', he said that Parliament had created the no win, no fee system and the courts could not interfere with it. The *Telegraph* was forced to settle the case for £50,000.

Nor is the problem confined to cases where the claimant is poor. Although CFAs were introduced to help poorer claimants get access to justice, they can be used by anyone, no matter how rich (Cherie Blair, Heather Mills and footballer Marco Materazzi have all used them in defamation claims, for example). Where a wealthy claimant uses a CFA, the defendant risks having to pay a success fee which effectively doubles the claimant's costs, plus their own costs, if they lose. The Oxford study concludes that in these cases, too, media organisations often settle cases rather than take the risk of defending them or, more worryingly, actively avoid criticism, even if true, of people and organisations who are known to be likely to sue.

Key stats Defamation costs and damages compared across Europe

A study by Oxford University asked lawyers in 12 European countries to look at the facts of two typical libel cases, one fairly complex and the other simpler, and asked them how much the trial would cost in their system and what level of damages were likely to be awarded if the claimant won. In both cases, costs were significantly higher in English cases than in any of the other countries, and damages in England were the second highest. The tables below are for the less complex case.

Defamation costs and damages compared in 12 European countries

	Costs £	Likely damages £
Belgium	28,000	7,000
Bulgaria	600	400
Cyprus	4,000	21,000
England and Wales (with a CFA)	666,000	50,000
England and Wales (without a CFA)	360,000	
France	14,000	1,500
Germany	2,500	7,000
Ireland	87,000	26,500
Italy	107,000	8,500
Malta	500	8,500
Romania	4,000	2,000
Spain	2,000	5,000
Sweden	19,000	5,000

[*Source*: Based on information from *A Comparative Study of Costs in Defamation Proceedings Across Europe (2008)*, by the Programme in Comparative Media Law and Policy, Centre for Socio-Legal Studies, University of Oxford]

What the claimant must prove

In English law the claimant needs only to prove that the statement was defamatory, referred to them, and was published. If they do this the defendant can be liable, even if there was no real fault on their part, for example because they believed the material was true, or because they did not realise the statement could be taken to refer to someone other than the person they meant. By contrast, in many other jurisdictions it is harder to prove a defamation case. In the USA, for example, a claimant has to prove that the statement is false, and has to prove that the defendant was at fault. If the claimant is not a public figure, they must prove that the defendant was careless, but if they are a public figure, they face a harder test, and must show that the defendant knew the statement was false, or had 'serious doubts' about whether it was false or not.

In recent years we have seen some moves by the English courts to rebalance the law, for example in the case of *O'Shea* v. *Mirror Group Newspapers Ltd* (2001), where the court said that the media should not be expected to go to unreasonable lengths to ensure that they did not accidentally show a picture that looked like someone else. The *Reynolds* defence also focuses on whether the defendant was actually at fault, and provides protection where the defendant has acted responsibly even if the material published turned out to be untrue. However, it is still easier to succeed in a defamation claim here than in any comparable legal system.

Liability for comment

As far as free speech is concerned, the freedom to express an opinion is just as important as the freedom to publish factual information. Recognising this, the defence of honest comment gives some protection for statements which are comments rather than factual allegations but, as we saw earlier, the defendant still has to show that the comment was honest and made without malice. This contrasts with the law in the USA, and some European countries, where much more of a distinction is made between comment and allegations of fact. In the USA, the Supreme Court has said, in *Milkovich* v. *Lorain Journal* (1990), that statements of opinion about matters of public concern, which do not contain any false factual allegation, cannot be the basis of a defamation action. In some states, the courts have gone further and found that there can be no defamation claim for any kind of comment which does not contain a factual allegation.

Protection for matters of public interest

As we saw earlier, in *Reynolds* v. *Times Newspapers*, *The Times* argued that the defence of qualified privilege should cover all media coverage of matters of public interest. This, it is argued, would promote free speech because the media would be free to write about important issues even if they involved someone wealthy and powerful who might be likely to sue. The courts refused to go this far, but in recent years we have seen a move towards more protection for matters of public interest. The *Reynolds* defence itself is an example of this, as is the ban on claims by elected organisations and political parties, and of course the traditional defences of absolute and qualified privilege also give some protection to coverage of public interest matters.

Even so, the protection in English law for matters of public interest is often compared unfavourably to that in US law. As we saw above, in the US, a claim made by a public figure regarding a matter of public interest can only succeed if the claimant can prove that the defendant published the material knowing it was untrue, or regardless of having serious doubts about whether it was true. The category of 'public official' includes all politicians, local and national, but also candidates for public office, appointed public officials and a wide range of government employees.

This rule, introduced in the case of *New York Times* v. *Sullivan* (1964), is strictly applied by the courts, and the case also established that the judge in each case should scrutinise the jury's findings so as to make sure that freedom of expression is adequately respected. In the *New York Times* case itself, this led to the judge finding that the jury could not properly find that the paper knew the material was false, or doubted its truth, even though there was evidence that at least one person at the paper thought it was false, and material in their own archives showed that it was false.

The *New York Times* rule means that it is very difficult for public officials of any kind to prevent full and frank discussion of their activities by threatening to sue or actually making a claim, and according to one study the result is that in cases where the rule applies only around 10 per cent of claimants succeed (Franklin 1980).

Of course, the other side of giving greater protection to allegations about public figures is that there will be times when untrue material is published and the public official is left without any means of clearing their name. The argument in favour of the US approach is that those occasions are a price worth paying to make sure the media is not frightened away from publishing material which the public has an interest in knowing about.

Law in action Libel tourism

In recent years, London has been nicknamed 'the libel capital of the world', as more and more claimants from abroad bring libel cases here, even if the defamatory statements were made in newspapers or magazines that are primarily published in a different country. Known as 'libel tourism', this is happening because, as we have seen, Britain's defamation laws are among the strictest in the world. Compared to most other countries, our laws give far more protection to reputation than to freedom of speech, which makes it easier for a claimant to win here than in most other countries. In addition, the cost of a libel action is much higher here than elsewhere, so there is pressure on defendants to settle a claim, even if there is a chance they could have won it, rather than risk the cost of going to court. As a result, claimants from abroad are increasingly bringing their cases in the UK courts rather than at home,

Source: Pearson Education Ltd/Pearson Education Asia Ltd/Coleman Yuen

simply because they are more likely to get a settlement or win.

A further cause of libel tourism is that the UK courts impose very few restrictions in cases from abroad. To be able to sue in the UK, claimants from abroad have to show only two things:

- They have a reputation in this country. This effectively means little more than that a number of people in this country know who they are.
- The defamatory statement was circulated here. The arrival of the internet means the second requirement is also very easy to satisfy, since material published all over the world can be downloaded here.

This means that cases are being accepted even where, in common-sense terms, there is no real link to the UK. In *Mardas* v. *New York Times* (2008), for example, the claimant was a Greek citizen suing two American newspapers. One of the papers did not publish the article in its UK edition, the other sold only 177 copies in the UK and only 31 people in the UK read the article on the internet. Mr Mardas did not pursue a similar claim in the US courts. Similarly, in *Mahfouz* v. *Ehrenfeld* (2004), a Saudi Arabian billionaire sued an American academic in London over a book which was not published in the UK but was only available if bought from America via the internet. Only 23 copies were bought by UK buyers. By contrast, defamation claims in the US can be heard only if the publication was 'expressly aimed' at readers/listeners in that country.

The UK courts have been criticised for allowing libel tourism, which effectively means that claimants can bypass the laws in their own countries and avoid any protection for free speech that those laws may give. In response, some US states have passed new laws, providing that libel judgments won in the UK are unenforceable. Free speech campaigners are now concerned that the libel tourism trend is spreading beyond claims against the media. Mark Stephens, a media lawyer who frequently acts for defendants in libel cases, told *The Times* in November 2009 that threats of libel action in London are regularly made against human rights and anti-corruption organisations by those they criticise: 'We have threats against just about every reputable organisation you can think of, from Human Rights Watch to Greenpeace', he said. 'The organisations know that even if they are right they may still be sued, and the cost of defending themselves [in London] will be huge.'

[*Reference*: 'World's libel tourists flock to UK courts', *The Times*, 1 November 2009]

Proposals for reform

Given the criticisms above, it is not surprising that many calls have been made for reform of the law on defamation. One of the most high-profile recent sets of recommendations came in 2009, from the Libel Reform Campaign, which campaigns to protect free speech. It said England's libel laws were causing serious problems for the media and authors, and preventing them from doing their job properly. In their report, *Free Speech is Not For Sale*, the Libel Reform Campaign said:

> English libel law imposes unnecessary and disproportionate restrictions on free speech, sending a chilling effect through the publishing and journalism sectors in the UK. This effect now reaches around the world, because of so-called 'libel tourism', where foreign cases are heard in London. The law was designed to serve the rich and powerful, and does not reflect the interests of a modern democratic society.

The report suggest that a major overhaul of the law is needed. Their recommendations include:

- Capping libel damages at £10,000 and make an apology the chief remedy, to counter the problem that English law is more about making money than protecting reputation.

- Shifting the burden of proof so claimants have to demonstrate damage, thereby removing the anomaly that the defendant is guilty until proved innocent.
- Tackling 'libel tourism' by preventing cases being heard in London unless 10 per cent of copies of the offending publication are circulated in England.
- Stopping large and medium-sized companies from being able to launch libel actions unless they can prove that the publication was malicious, and caused financial damage to the business.
- Establishing a libel tribunal, along the lines of employment tribunals, as an alternative to expensive court trials.
- Reducing the prohibitive cost of defending libel actions by capping costs and making success fees non-recoverable.
- Strengthening the public interest defence, and expanding the definition of honest comment.

The drive for reform was further strengthened in 2010, when the Supreme Court took the opportunity of hearing their first defamation case, *Joseph* v. *Spiller*, to criticise the current law and suggest some reforms. Giving the leading judgment, Lord Phillips suggested that there might be a case for widening the scope of the honest comment defence by removing the requirement for the comment to be on a matter of public interest, and making the key test whether the claimant honestly held the opinion, rather than whether a reasonable person could have done so. He also suggested that the time had come to stop using juries in defamation cases, which would save time and therefore reduce costs.

In response to these and other criticisms, in March 2011 the government published a draft bill on reform of the law of defamation. Its main provisions are:

- A claimant would be required to prove that the defamatory statement has caused or is likely to cause substantial damage to his or her reputation. As you know, currently a claimant need only show that the statement fits within the definition of defamatory, so this should mean that only quite serious libels can create a claim.
- There would be a single publication rule for material published online. Currently material on the internet is considered to be published every single time someone downloads it, which means that material left in online archives can lead to claims years after the original story was published and is a serious problem for publications that keep old material online.
- There would be a new defence of responsible publication on a matter of public interest, which would clarify and strengthen the current *Reynolds* defence. It would essentially mean that if a story covers a subject that is in the public interest, and the media have behaved reasonably in how they went about researching and writing the story, they will have a defence, even if what they say turns out to be untrue. This should provide increased protection for important stories, though how well it works would depend on exactly how it ends up being defined.
- Honest comment and justification would be replaced with clearer, statutory defences of 'honest opinion' and 'truth'.
- Juries would no longer be used in the majority of cases, which would speed up proceedings and help cut costs.

Consultations on the bill were still going on at the time this book was published. Apart from the provision on juries, the bill does not address the issue of costs, but a separate bill, the Legal Aid, Sentencing and Punishment of Offenders Bill looks likely to reform the law on conditional fee agreements by providing that a winning claimant can no longer claim the success fee or uplift from the defendants. This would mean defendants might be more easily able to defend claims; on the other hand, it will make it much harder, if not impossible, for people who are not extremely wealthy to sue for defamation.

Summary

- There are nine defences to defamation. The general defence of consent applies but is rarely used; the others are specific to defamation.
- Justification applies when the defendant can prove the statement is substantially true.
- Absolute privilege applies to statements made in Parliament or parliamentary reports; between officers of state; between spouses; in judical proceedings and in fair, accurate and contemporaneous court reports.
- Qualified privilege arises by statute and under common law. In both cases statements must be made without malice. Statutory qualified privilege applies to statements made in circumstances listed in Schedule 1 of the Defamation Act 1996, which are in two categories. Common law qualified privilege applies where one party has a legal, social or moral duty to communicate information to another, and that party has a duty to receive it.
- The *Reynolds* defence applies to serious, responsible coverage of subjects of public interest.
- Neutral reportage applies to coverage of subjects of public interest, reported neutrally.
- Honest comment applies where the defendant can prove the statement was honest comment on a matter of public interest. The comment must be made without malice.
- Innocent dissemination protects printers and distributors, where they have no reason to believe material published was defamatory.
- Offer of amends allows a defence where the defendant offers an apology and damages. If not accepted, and the client wins, damages will be reduced.
- There are two remedies, damages and injunctions. Juries decide damages, but the Court of Appeal can decrease or increase them. Injunctions may be given to prevent initial publication, or prevent repetition. The Human Rights Act puts restrictions on the use of injunctions to prevent initial publication.
- The limitation period is one year, but the courts have discretion to extend this.
- Problems with defamation include costs and the ‘chilling effect’; what the claimant must prove; liability for comment; lack of protection for matters of public interest.
- The government is currently consulting on reform of the law of defamation.

Question and answer*

Problem: Jeremy and Kate are reporters on a local paper. Jeremy goes to see a production of *Hamlet* at the local theatre in order to write a review of it. When the curtain opens, he is surprised to see that the actor playing Hamlet is Michael, a former friend of Jeremy's, who he fell out with after Michael stole his girlfriend. In his review, he writes 'The actor playing Hamlet forgot his lines nine times. He was so pathetically bad that he was an embarrassment to watch. A poodle would have played the part better.'

As he leaves the theatre, Jeremy spots Angela, who he recognises as a local GP. He sees a man go up to her and shout 'How dare you show your face in public! My wife Zuleika would still be alive if it wasn't for you! Everyone in this town knows you are a drunk, and that's why you can't do your job!' The man walks off, and Angela runs to her car and drives away. Jeremy tries to contact Angela the next day, but she refuses to take his calls. The manager of the medical centre where she works tells Jeremy that none of the GPs there have alcohol problems. Jeremy writes a story for the paper that says:

> *A GP from the Smalltown Medical Centre has been accused by a grieving husband of causing the death of a patient. Leaving the theatre on Friday night, she was accosted by an Asian man in his 30s, who shouted: 'How dare you show your face in public! My wife Zuleika would still be alive if it wasn't for you! Everyone in this town knows you are a drunk, and that's why you can't do your job!' The GP, who was visibly upset, fled the scene in her pink Rolls Royce. She was unavailable to comment on the allegations, but the manager of the Smalltown Medical Centre said: 'None of the GPs here have a problem with alcohol. The man who made these ridiculous accusations is either a liar or a lunatic.'*

Kate is sent to report on a court case in which the defendant, Gordon Goody, is accusing of attacking another man. Kate reports that the alleged victim said in court: 'He came at me with a knife, and said he would kill me.' As she leaves the court, the victim's mother comes up to her and tells her that everyone on their estate knows Gordon is a bad lot, and that her son is not the first person he has attacked. Kate reports this as well. After her report is published, the victim breaks down in court and admits that he made the whole thing up. Gordon is acquitted.

Can Jeremy or Kate be sued over the stories they have written? Consider any defences they may be able to use.

You should allow yourself no more than 40 minutes to complete this task.

Essay: 'The law of defamation must strike a balance between protecting reputation, and upholding the right to free speech'.

How well does the English law of defamation balance these two competing interests?

This question should be answered in 40 minutes.

* Answer guidance is provided at the end of the chapter.

Further reading and references

Franklin, M.A. (1980) 'Winners, losers and why? A study of defamation litigation', American Bar Foundation Res. J 455.
This is the article referred to on page 439, which looks at why the *New York Times* rule means that it is very difficult for public officials of any kind in the USA to prevent full and frank discussion of their activities by threatening to sue, or actually making a claim.

Gibbons, T. (1996) 'Defamation reconsidered', 16(4) OJLS 587.
Written in response to the Defamation Act 1996, this interesting article argues that changing the rules of the tort is not the best way to deal with the problems it contains. The author suggests that a better approach would be to look again at the basis for protecting a right to reputation, and provide a remedy for unsubstantiated allegations, rather than focusing on protection of reputation.

Libel Reform Campaign (2009) *Free Speech is Not for Sale*, available at libelreform.org
This is the report by the pressure group Libel Reform Campaign, which suggests radical reforms of the laws on defamation. It is very useful if you need to do an essay on problems with defamation law.

McNamara, L. (2007) *Reputation and Defamation*, Oxford: Oxford University Press.
This book looks at what reputation actually is, and why the law should protect it. The author argues that the current law does not protect reputation very well, and suggests an alternative approach. Worth reading if you are writing an essay on problems with defamation.

Programme in Comparative Media Law and Policy (2008) *A Comparative Study of Defamation Costs in Europe*, Centre for Socio-Legal Studies, University of Oxford.
This study compares the costs of defamation actions across Europe, and explains some of the reasons why costs are so high in this country.

Question and answer guidance

Problem: Taking Jeremy's theatre review first, his comments appear to be potentially defamatory, but we know that reviews like this are often covered by the defence of honest comment, so you need to apply the elements of that defence to what Jeremy wrote. Particular issues will be whether all of it can be considered comment, what facts it was based on, and whether Jeremy was acting with malice.

The story about the GP is also clearly defamatory, but a key issue here is who could sue? Jeremy has not mentioned Angela by name, but might she still have a claim? And could any of the other GPs at the centre also claim? Possible defences that you should consider include justification, qualified privilege and the *Reynolds* defence; these do not necessarily apply but you should consider whether they do and if not, why not.

There is also one another person who might be able to sue Jeremy over this story: the man who accused Angela of being responsible for the death of his wife. This is because Jeremy has repeated the allegation by the manager of the medical centre that the man is a liar. Consider whether he might have a claim, and whether any defences would apply.

Regarding Kate's court report, the possible claimant here is Gordon. You will need to consider the defence of absolute privilege; is Kate covered by this for either or both of the accusations she reports?

Essay: A good way to start this essay would be to explain that the primary purpose of defamation is to protect reputation, but that because English law considers freedom of expression to be an important right, the protection given to reputation is restricted by a number of measures which protect free speech. You could then list some of these: they include the restrictions on claims by public authorities and political parties; the defences of fair comment, privilege (both kinds), the *Reynolds* defence and neutral reportage; and the restrictions on injunctions preventing publication.

Then go on to discuss each of these issues, highlighting cases which show how – and how well or badly – the courts strike this balance, and bringing in some of the criticisms you read about at the end of this chapter. If you have time, you could also mention the procedural factors that affect free speech, in particular the issue of costs.

You could conclude your essay by looking at some of the proposals for reform, and saying whether you think these would result in a better balance between protection of reputation and free speech.

Visit **www.mylawchamber.co.uk/quinntort** to access tools to help you develop and test your knowledge of tort law, including practice exam questions with guidance, annotated weblinks, glossary and key case flashcards, legal newsfeed and legal updates and interactive 'You be the judge' questions.

premium mylawchamber
unrivalled support for legal education

Use Case Navigator to read in full some of the key cases referenced in this chapter with commentary and questions:

Jameel and another* v. *Wall Street Journal Europe SPRL [2006] 4 All ER 1279

CASE NAVIGATOR
POWERED BY LexisNexis

Chapter 18
Privacy and confidentiality

Key points In this chapter we will be looking at:

- The background to privacy protection in tort
- How the tort of breach of confidence/ misuse of private information is committed
- Remedies for breach of confidence/misuse of private information

Introduction

When Catherine Zeta Jones married Michael Douglas on 18 November 2000, they planned a day to remember. The lavish ceremony and reception at New York's Plaza Hotel cost £1.5 million, the cake was six foot tall, and the 350 guests included Sean Connery, Stephen Spielberg, Tom Jones, Meg Ryan and Russell Crowe. It was a wedding that would go down in showbusiness history – but what the happy couple didn't plan on was it playing a starring role in law textbooks as well. Unknown to them, a photographer sneaked into the wedding and managed to get a series of shots, which were sold to *Hello!* magazine. The couple were furious, not least because they had a lucrative deal giving a rival magazine exclusive rights to pictures of the day, and so they sued *Hello!* The result was a legal battle which ran for several years, gave the world such memorable quotes as Ms Zeta Jones's 'A million pounds isn't a lot of money to us', and kicked off what has become the modern law on privacy.

Even though the couple didn't actually win their claim for what they called breach of privacy, the case was the first in a stream of similar claims against the media, which quickly carved out a new form of privacy protection. The result is that today celebrities routinely take or threaten legal action if the media publishes information or photos that they would rather were kept private – yet, as we will see, there is still officially no tort of 'breach of privacy' in English law. Instead, this modern privacy law has been created by combining a much older tort, breach of confidence, with the provisions of the Human Rights Act 1998. Its rules are still emerging, along with heated debate about whether it is a necessary protection against press intrusion, or an unjustified curb on press freedom.

Privacy protection: the background

The tort of breach of confidence started taking shape during the nineteenth century, and one of the earliest cases is *Prince Albert* v. *Strange* (1849). The case centred around some drawings which Queen Victoria and her husband Prince Albert had made of each other, for their own amusement. Unauthorised copies of them were made by someone on the staff of a printer, from whom the Royal couple had ordered some prints, and found their way into the hands of Mr Strange, who wanted to put them into a public exhibition. The drawings were quite innocent, but the Royal family regarded them as private so Prince Albert went to court to try to prevent them being made public.

Case Summary

The Court granted an **injunction**, basing their decision partly on the fact that Prince Albert owned what we would now call the copyright to the pictures, but also on the fact that the way the drawings had been obtained must have amounted to 'a breach of trust, confidence or contract'. In other words, Prince Albert had given the drawings to the printer in the expectation that they would not be passed on, and this trust, or confidence, had been broken.

Over the years, the tort began to develop its own rules, and these were defined in *Coco* v. *A. N. Clark* (1969), the facts of which are not important here. The three elements of the tort were stated to be:

Case Summary

- the information disclosed or about to be disclosed 'has the necessary quality of confidence' (or in other words, is information that would be considered private rather than public); and
- the information was obtained in circumstances which imposed 'an obligation of confidence'; and
- the **defendant** has made or intends to make unauthorised use of the information.

The tort of breach of confidence was therefore committed when someone disclosed private information, in circumstances where doing so would be breaking a duty of confidentiality to the owner or subject of the information. By the 1960s, the typical case would involve a defendant leaking their employer's trade secrets to a rival company, or leaking government information to the press. But then came a case which broadened the tort in a very important way. *Argyll* v. *Argyll* (1967) was brought by the Duchess of Argyll, who successfully prevented her ex-husband, the Duke, from publishing details of their stormy marriage, on the grounds that married couples owed each other a duty of confidentiality. This was the first time that breach of confidence had been used to protect private information of a more personal kind.

Case Summary

The expansion of breach of confidence

At this stage, breach of confidence claims had only succeeded where there was a pre-existing relationship between the parties which suggested that they owed each other a duty of confidentiality. This meant that a claim could be brought, for example, between spouses, or employers and employees, or as in Prince Albert's case, where there was a contractual relationship. But if there was no pre-existing relationship, there could be no breach of confidence. This obviously limited the circumstances in which the tort could be used. Over the years, however, this requirement was chipped away, until in

Case Summary

Attorney-General v. *Guardian Newspapers (No. 2)* (1990), where the then government tried unsuccessfully to prevent publication of a book about spies, Lord Goff stated that a pre-existing relationship was no longer required. Instead, he said, a duty of confidence would arise 'when confidential information comes to the knowledge of a person . . . in circumstances where he has notice, or is held to have agreed, that the information is confidential, with the effect that it would be just in all the circumstances that he should be precluded from disclosing the information to others'.

This meant that a breach of confidence could be found, for example, where obviously private information was stolen, or where someone found a private diary or letter in the street and made some unauthorised use of the information in it. This considerably widened the potential usage of the breach of confidence action, and was an important step towards the later opening up of the law. But the action could still be used only in fairly limited circumstances, and was certainly not considered to be a complete protection for personal privacy.

Calls for a privacy law

From the late 1980s the press began to publish increasingly sensational stories about things that celebrities and public figures would have preferred to stay private. This coincided with the rise of the 'paparazzi', freelance photographers who specialise in taking unauthorised photos of celebrities and selling them to the highest bidder(s). As the money paid for such pictures began to rise and rise, especially if they showed celebrities in embarrassing situations, some paparazzi began using increasingly intrusive methods to get the most sought-after shots, including harassing and following celebrities, chasing them in their cars, or using long distance lenses to take pictures from places where they could not be seen. Their best-known target was Princess Diana, who, by the time of her divorce from Prince Charles, was constantly stalked by photographers, and was being chased by paparazzi when she was killed in a car crash.

This increasingly intrusive coverage led to calls for the then government to pass a law to protect privacy. The idea was that such a law would state exactly what the press could and could not do, in terms of how they went about gathering news and pictures, and what they were allowed to publish. However, then as now, there were also opposing voices, who held that privacy laws would prevent the press from exposing wrongdoing. As a result, during the 1980s and 1990s, both Conservative and Labour governments had decided against creating a specific statute on privacy.

By 1998, however, it was widely thought that we would get a privacy law anyway. This was because the Human Rights Act, passed that year, provides a right to privacy in Article 8 of the European convention on Human Rights (ECHR), which states that: 'Everyone has the right to respect for his private and family life, his home and his correspondence.' Would this mean that the courts would now recognise a specific right to privacy? And if they did, how was this right to be balanced against the media's right to freedom of expression, which was protected in Article 10 of the ECHR? It was not long before those who had most to gain from a right to privacy began to put these questions before the courts.

Law in action The price of privacy

One reason for the increasingly intrusive coverage of celebrities and public figures since the 1980s is simply the amount of money that can be made. If a celebrity is big news, even a shot of them doing something ordinary, like popping out to the shops, can earn a paparazzo photographer several thousands of pounds, while pictures that reveal newsworthy information, or show aspects of a celebrity's private life, are worth very much more. The first photos that revealed that Princess Diana was in a relationship with Dodi Fayed sold for £250,000, and the same price was paid for shots of Britney Spears attacking a photographer's car with an umbrella, and pictures of Angelina Jolie and Brad Pitt on holiday during the early days of their relationship. A photographer who managed to get the first shots of Gwyneth Paltrow out with her new baby sold them for around £500,000.

Naturally, newspapers and magazines only pay these prices because using the pictures boosts their sales, and so their profits. The right celebrity on the cover can boost sales by as much as a third, and higher sales mean the publication can usually earn more from adverts as well. With the top-selling UK celebrity magazines together worth around £300 million, the financial stakes are high.

By contrast, the **damages** awarded in privacy cases are relatively small: Catherine Zeta Jones and Michael Douglas, for example, won under £15,000. **Settlements** tend to be higher: Sienna Miller, for example, won a £37,000 settlement from a picture agency in 2008, and in the same year Elizabeth Hurley accepted £58,000 from two agencies who had taken pictures of her on her honeymoon. However, even these figures can still be lower than the rewards to be gained from publishing photos that the reading public wants to see.

Source: Pearson Education Ltd/Blend Images/TIPS Images

[*References*: http://news.bbc.co.uk/1/hi/entertainment/7402442.stm; http://www.guardian.co.uk/media/2008/nov/22/privacy-policy]

The current law on privacy

Case Summary

Case Navigator

Given the title of this chapter, you might be surprised to know that there is still no specific tort of breach of privacy in English law. This was stated categorically by the Court of Appeal in ***Wainwright* v. *Home Office*** (2002), and confirmed by the most recent House of Lords judgment on the subject, *Campbell* v. *Mirror Group Newspapers* (2004), which we will look at later in this chapter. *Wainwright* differs from the other cases in which breach of privacy has been claimed, in that it does not deal with the publication of private information but with an alleged physical breach of personal privacy. The **claimants** were a mother and son, who had gone to visit Mrs Wainwright's other son in prison. They were strip-searched, apparently to make sure they were not carrying drugs into the prison, and found the procedure so humiliating and stressful that Mrs Wainwright became very distressed, and her son Alan developed post-traumatic stress disorder. They sued the Home Office for, among other things, invasion of privacy under the Human Rights Act. The Court rejected this claim. They said that there was no general right to privacy, only existing torts which protected particular aspects of privacy, such as breach of confidence which protected private information, and trespass which protected the privacy of a person's body, home and property.

However, since the Human Rights Act was passed the courts have extended and manipulated the tort of breach of confidence so that now, while we do not officially have a tort of privacy, the breach of confidence action has developed a new form. Now usually referred by the courts as a claim for misuse of private information, this form of action has become a tort of privacy in all but name.

The *Douglas* case

Case Summary

As explained above, the first major case to test whether the Human Rights Act created a new law of privacy was *Douglas* v. *Hello! Ltd* (2001), in which Michael Douglas and Catherine Zeta Jones sued *Hello!* over the unauthorised pictures of their wedding. They claimed for both breach of confidence and breach of their right to privacy under the Human Rights Act.

As we saw above, the tort of breach of confidence has three elements: the information used must be private; it must be obtained in circumstances where it is clear that there is 'an obligation of confidence'; and there must be an unauthorised use of it. In this case, the Court said, *Hello!* must have known there was an obligation of confidence because the couple had taken extreme precautions to prevent unauthorised pictures being taken, even banning invited guests from bringing their own cameras. For the same reason, it was clear that *Hello!*'s use of them was unauthorised.

However, *Hello!* argued that the pictures could not be considered private information, because the couple had agreed to sell pictures of the wedding to another magazine, *OK* (which happens to be *Hello!*'s main rival). *Hello!* said the claim was not about wanting to keep the day entirely private, but protecting a lucrative deal with *OK* and this meant they could not succeed in a claim for breach of confidence. In the High Court, Mr Justice Lindsay disagreed. He said that the very fact that rights to the pictures could be sold was what gave them the necessary element of confidentiality. It made them a valuable commercial asset, just like a trade secret, and the law of confidentiality had always protected such assets. The Douglases won their claim for breach of confidence.

But what about the claim for breach of privacy? This was first discussed by the Court of Appeal, in an interim hearing to decide whether to impose an injunction banning *Hello!* from publishing the pictures. One of the judges there said that there was a right to privacy, while the other two sat on the fence, saying that there was no need to decide on the issue because the existing law of confidentiality offered protection in this situation. As we saw above, when the case came to a full trial, Mr Justice Lindsay agreed with this conclusion, and because the couple won their case on breach of confidence there was no need to pursue the privacy claim.

This meant that the judiciary had not said yes to a tort of privacy, but had not ruled out creating a law of privacy either, if it could be shown that one was needed. As a result, the *Douglas* case became a springboard for a series of other claims in which celebrities and other public figures attempted to use the breach of confidence action to protect their personal privacy. Among them were footballer Gary Flitcroft, who tried to prevent details of his extramarital affairs being published, TV presenter Jamie Theakston, who tried to suppress coverage of his visit to a brothel, and model and campaigner Heather Mills, who

> the *Douglas* case became a springboard for a series of other claims

wanted to prevent the press from revealing the location of her new house. But it was a case brought by supermodel Naomi Campbell in which the new type of confidentiality action, misuse of private information, was first defined by the House of Lords.

The *Campbell* case and misuse of private information

Case Summary

Campbell v. *Mirror Group* (2004) was brought by Ms Campbell after the *Daily Mirror* published a series of stories about her treatment for drug addiction. The stories included the fact that she was attending meetings of Narcotics Anonymous (NA), and details of the way in which NA was helping her to deal with her addiction. There were also photos of her leaving an NA meeting. The photos had been taken secretly by a press photographer who was hiding nearby, and it was thought that the information had been supplied either by someone who knew Ms Campbell or another member of the NA group. Ms Campbell had for some time had a high profile in the media, which she encouraged, and she had frequently claimed that, unlike many other models, she did not have a drug problem.

An early attempt to sue for invasion of privacy was abandoned, and Ms Campbell framed her case specifically in terms of breach of confidence. She accepted that the press had a right to publish the fact that she was a drug addict, given that she had denied this in the past. However, she said that publishing details of the treatment that she was receiving, and pictures of her at the place where she was receiving it, was a breach of confidence. This, she claimed, was because these details were clearly the kind of information that any reasonable person must realise was obtained confidentially, just as any detailed information about a person's medical treatment would be.

The House of Lords, by a majority, upheld her claim, and took the opportunity to explain the current relationship between breach of confidence and invasion of privacy. Lord Nicholls confirmed that, as stated in *Wainwright*, 'there is no over-arching, all-embracing cause of action for "invasion of privacy"'. However, he said, protection of various aspects of privacy was a fast developing area of the law, which had been spurred on by the Human Rights Act 1998. The position was now that an examination of the rights to privacy under Article 8, and freedom of expression under Article 10, had to be included in any breach of confidence claim.

Lord Nicholls said that the action for breach of confidence had 'changed its nature' once the requirement for a pre-existing confidential relationship was removed (this was the development referred to in *Attorney-General* v. *Guardian Newspapers (No. 2)* (1990), which we looked at earlier). As a result, he said, the law now imposed a duty of confidence 'whenever a person receives information he knows or ought to know is fairly and reasonably to be regarded as confidential'. This, he said, effectively means there is a duty of confidence whenever a person receives information that is private, and the essence of the tort is now 'misuse of private information'. In addition, he said the time had come to recognise that 'the values enshrined in Articles 8 and 10 are now part of the cause of action for breach of confidence'.

Lord Hoffmann agreed, and said that the claim for breach of confidence was now focused on 'the right to control the dissemination of information about one's private life and the right to the esteem and respect of other people'. The *Campbell* case lays down the basic shape of the tort of misuse of private information and, since then, later cases have further developed the law.

Liability for misuse of private information

The situation now is that the traditional tort of breach of confidence still exists, and would still be used in cases of, for example, a defendant leaking information about a trade secret. But there is also a second, newer tort, created in *Campbell*, called misuse of private information. It is this tort that is used in the steady stream of claims brought by celebrities over the past few years, which you will have read about in the newspapers. These are often referred to in the media as 'privacy claims' but the correct name for the tort they are claiming in is 'misuse of private information'.

Case Summary

In *Campbell*, the House of Lords held that in cases involving 'misuse of private information', a two-stage test should be applied (in place of the three-stage test from *Coco* v. *Clark*, which was used for traditional breach of confidence actions). The court should ask:

- did the claimant have a reasonable expectation of privacy with respect to the information disclosed?; and if they did,
- is the person's right to privacy under Article 8 of the European Convention on Human Rights more important, in the circumstances, than someone's else's right to freedom of expression under Article 10? (This is usually, though not always, the media's right.)

Reasonable expectation of privacy

In deciding whether the claimant had a reasonable expectation of privacy, the courts take account of a wide range of factors. In *Murray* v. *Express Newspapers* (we will look at the facts of this case later), the Court of Appeal said:

> As we see it, the question whether there is a reasonable expectation of privacy is a broad one, which takes account of all the circumstances of the case. They include the attributes of the claimant, the nature of the activity in which the claimant was engaged, the place at which it was happening, the nature and purpose of the intrusion, the absence of consent and whether it was known or could be inferred, the effect on the claimant and the circumstances in which and the purposes for which the information came into the hands of the publisher.

Not all these factors have yet been closely examined, but the decided cases do shed light on some of them.

Effects on the claimant

Case Summary

In *Campbell*, a key issue was the effect that the revelations could have had on Ms Campbell, and in looking at this the courts took into account the fact that she was recovering from drug addiction and this, they concluded, made her especially vulnerable. Lord Hope suggested that the courts ask: 'whether disclosure of the information about the individual ("A") would give substantial offence to A, assuming that A was placed in similar circumstances and was a person of ordinary sensibilities . . . The mind that has to be examined is that not of the reader in general but of the person who is affected by the publicity.'

The story complained of in *Campbell* detailed how often Ms Campbell went to NA meetings, and what was likely to happen there; the pictures, which were taken secretly, showed her outside the door of the hall where the meeting was held. Ms Campbell had previously, on several occasions, denied having a drug problem; in fact she had specifically stated that drug abuse was a big problem in the modelling industry, but she was not one of those involved. It was agreed by both sides that publication of the basic facts of Ms Campbell's drug problem, and the fact that she was attending Narcotics Anonymous, was not a breach of confidence because it corrected a false image she had previously presented. However, the majority of the judges agreed that the precise details of her treatment should be protected. This was for two reasons. First, giving details of the kind of things that would happen at NA meetings, and how frequently Ms Campbell attended them, was essentially the same thing as revealing details of someone's medical treatment, and revealing that kind of information had always been seen as a breach of confidence. Secondly, publishing the details of her treatment could have a harmful effect on Ms Campbell's efforts to beat her addiction, and this too meant she had a reasonable expectation of privacy.

This approach was also applied, though with the opposite result, in *Terry* v. *Person Unknown* (2010), where the footballer John Terry attempted to get an injunction preventing publication of any stories about the fact that he was having an affair with the ex-girlfriend of another England team member. In refusing to continue the injunction Mr Terry had obtained, Mr Justice Tugendhat said that the personality and circumstances of the claimant were relevant: 'the less sensitive the information is considered by the applicant to be, and the more robust the personality of the applicant . . . the less a court may find a need to interfere with freedom of expression by means of an injunction'. In this case, he judged that the information was not especially intrusive, and that John Terry appeared to have 'a very robust personality, as one might expect of a leading professional sportsman'. There was no real suggestion that he was likely to be caused personal distress by the revelations, and it appeared that the real reason for the action was to protect his commercial interests.

Case Summary

You be the judge

Q: Terry Lovey is a famous actor. He gets a call from a reporter, Nicki Nosey, who says she has information that Terry is being treated for a sexually transmitted disease, and she wants a comment from him as her paper is going to publish the story. Terry decides to go to court to stop the story being published. Does he have a legitimate expectation of privacy for the information?

A: Yes. The case of *Campbell* makes it clear that information about a person's medical treatment is covered by a legitimate expectation of privacy.

The nature of the activity

In *The Author of a Blog* v. *Times Newspapers Limited* (2009), the Court ruled that an anonymous blogger did not have a legitimate expectation of privacy regarding his identity. The claimant was a serving police constable, who writes a blog about his police work under the pseudonym 'Night Jack'. *The Times* had worked out his real name from things he had said in the blog, and he sought an interim injunction preventing them

Case Summary

from publishing any information that would or might lead to his identification, claiming this was misuse of private information. In considering whether he had a reasonable expectation of privacy, Mr Justice Eady said that the fact that bloggers may take steps to disguise their identity was not sufficient reason to prevent those who work it out from revealing it. Blogging was a public not a private activity and there was no reasonable expectation of privacy.

Sexual activity

It now seems clear that where a story or pictures concern someone involved in sexual activity, there will be a legitimate expectation of privacy, providing the activity involves consenting adults. In *Jagger* v. *Darling* (2005), the model Elizabeth Jagger was awarded an injunction preventing further publication of CCTV images, which showed her and her boyfriend 'engaging in sexual activities' inside the closed door of a nightclub. The Court said this was a situation where there was clearly a legitimate expectation of privacy.

This approach was backed up in *Mosley* v. *News Group Newspapers* (2008). The claimant was Max Mosley, the President of the FIA, which runs Formula 1 motor racing. He had been secretly filmed at a sado-masochistic orgy with five prostitutes, and the *News of the World* published the story. Mr Justice Eady upheld Mr Mosley's claim for misuse of private information, stating that public figures were entitled to a personal life, and people's sex lives were 'essentially their own business'. He said that there would usually be a reasonable expectation of privacy with regard to sexual activity, especially if it was on private property and between consenting adults, regardless of whether some of them were paid to join in.

However, although there will usually be a reasonable expectation of privacy with regard to details about sexual activity, the same does not necessarily apply to merely revealing that two people are in a sexual relationship with each other. In *Terry* v. *Person Unknown* (2010), the case we looked at earlier where footballer John Terry sought a permanent injunction preventing publication of any stories about the fact that he was having an affair, Mr Justice Tugendhat said there was a difference between publishing intrusive details and/or photographs concerning a sexual relationship, and merely publishing the fact that the relationship was going on. He said that if John Terry could have shown that there was a real threat that intrusive details or pictures might be published, he would have been entitled to an injunction preventing that publication because he would be likely to have been able to prove at trial that the publication was misuse of private information. But the fact that there might be publication of the fact that the relationship existed was not sufficient to justify an injunction.

Nature of the intrusion

A number of cases have been very clear about the fact that photographs, especially if taken covertly, will be considered more intrusive than words alone. In *Douglas*, the court said that this applied even if words could have conveyed exactly the same information, and there might not have been a breach of confidence if *Hello!* had merely reported on the wedding, rather than actually publishing pictures of it.

However, this does not mean that pictures will always be covered by a reasonable expectation of privacy. In *Campbell*, the House of Lords said that this depends on what information they convey and the context in which they were taken. Baroness Hale said that there was no expectation of privacy with regard to pictures of someone, famous or not, going about their ordinary business in a public place, or as she put it, 'popping out for a pint of milk'. Such pictures could only ever convey trivial information, such as what the person chose to wear when doing the shopping, and trivial information was not protected by the law of confidence.

However, in the case of the pictures of Ms Campbell leaving her NA meeting the situation was different. Although the pictures were taken on a public street, the situation was such that their publication could add to the potential harm to Ms Campbell, by making her think she was being followed by photographers and betrayed by whoever told them where the meeting was. This might discourage her from continuing with the meetings. That suggested there was a legitimate expectation of privacy and the pictures should not have been used.

Case Summary

The principle that there is no expectation of privacy regarding pictures of people doing ordinary things in public places was applied in *Sir Elton John* v. *Associated Newspapers* (2006). The case involved pictures of Elton John, taken when he had just arrived home, which showed him walking from his car with his driver. He complained that it invaded his privacy because it appeared to show that his baldness was returning (Sir Elton famously had a hair transplant many years ago). He attempted to get an injunction preventing the *Daily Mail* from publishing the photos, but his application was refused. Mr Justice Eady said that the pictures did not convey any kind of private information. They were in the same category as a shot of someone 'popping out for a pint of milk', which Baroness Hale had said created no expectation of privacy.

Children and photographs

Case Summary

It appears that children may have a reasonable expectation of privacy in situations where an adult might not. As we saw in *Campbell* and then in the *Elton John* case, there is no expectation of privacy where an adult is photographed going about their ordinary business in a public place. However, in *Murray* v. *Express Newspapers plc and Another* (2008), the Court of Appeal held that it was arguable that a child had a reasonable expectation of privacy which could be breached by a photographer taking pictures of them in a public place, for publication, when the photographer knew that this would be objected to by the child's parents.

The child in question was David Murray, the 19-month-old son of a Mr and Mrs Murray, the latter better known as J.K. Rowling. The family, including David in his buggy, were photographed by a hidden photographer using a long lens when they were walking along a street in Edinburgh. The picture was published in the *Sunday Express* magazine. On David's behalf, Mr and Mrs Murray sued the *Sunday Express* and Big Picture, the agency whose photographer took the picture of David.

The claim was initially struck out on the grounds that there was no basis for a claim of privacy. The *Sunday Express* then settled with the Murrays but the agency, Big Picture, did not. Mr and Mrs Murray appealed against the **striking out**, and the Court of Appeal upheld their appeal. The original judge had said that routine acts such as a visit to a shop or a ride on a bus could not involve any reasonable expectation of privacy, but the Court of Appeal disagreed. It would always depend on circumstances and the position of a child might be different from that of an adult. There was no guarantee of privacy just because the claimant was a child, and the courts would need to balance the right to privacy against the right to freedom of expression, but it was at least arguable that David had a reasonable expectation of privacy and so the action should not be struck out. They went on to say that in principle the courts should protect children from intrusive media attention, at least to the extent of holding that there could be a reasonable expectation that a child would not be targeted for photographs taken for publication, without consent, and which the photographer knew would be objected to.

It is important to note that this was a striking-out action and not a full trial. The case establishes that a child in David's situation *may* have a reasonable expectation of privacy, but until the claim goes to a full trial it remains to be seen whether, on the facts, he *did* have an expectation of privacy. The Court of Appeal's finding also emphasised that David's parents had always tried to keep him out of the public eye; it is not clear whether the situation might be different if the claimants were parents who had happily used their children for publicity purposes but then objected to particular photographs or disclosures.

Sources of information

Case Summary

The way in which information was obtained is also relevant, as it has always been in the traditional breach of confidence action. In *Loreena McKennitt* v. *Niema Ash and Purple Inc Press* (2006) the claimant, Ms McKennitt, was a very successful Canadian folk singer and the defendant, Ms Ash, had been a close friend of hers. The case arose because Ms Ash wrote a book about going on tour with Ms McKennitt. It discussed, among other things, Ms McKennitt's personal and sexual relationships; her personal feelings, including her reaction to the death of her fiancé some years earlier; her health and diet; her emotional vulnerability; and details of a dispute between her, Ms Ash, and Ms Ash's business partner concerning a property purchase. In the book, Ms Ash referred to her very close friendship with Ms McKennitt, and said that it was because of this close relationship that she was able to present such a revealing portrait of the singer. In the High Court, Mr Justice Eady said that the fact that they had a close friendship was a reason why Ms McKennitt had a reasonable expectation that conversations between them, about personal matters, would stay private. He ordered an injunction banning further publication, along with £5,000 damages. This finding was supported by the Court of Appeal.

Information in the public domain

In the traditional tort of breach of confidence, there was a **defence** where the material complained of was already completely or substantially 'in the public domain', meaning where a substantial number of people already knew about it. This idea appears to apply also in the misuse of private information action, except that rather than treating it as a defence the courts look at how far the information was already known when they are deciding whether the claimant had a legitimate expectation of privacy. In *HRH Prince of Wales* v. *Associated Newspapers* (2006), the case was brought by Prince Charles after the *Mail on Sunday* published extracts from journals he had written. For many years, the Prince had kept diaries, reporting on his thoughts and views as he went about his official engagements. He routinely sent copies to between 20 and 70 friends and acquaintances, and the newspaper said this meant their content was already in the public domain. The court disagreed, saying they were only ever circulated privately, to specific people, and this did not amount to being in the public domain. Quoting from the judgment in *Douglas* v. *Hello!*, Mr Justice Blackburne said:

Case Summary

Information will be confidential if it is available to one person (or a group of people) and not generally available to others, provided that the person (or group) who possesses the information does not intend that it should become available to others.

Partial revelations

Case Summary

What is the position where parts of a story are in the public domain, but someone wants to publish even more revealing information on the same subject? This was one of the issues in *Loreena McKennitt* v. *Niema Ash*, the case of the Canadian folk singer and the book written by her friend (or, by then, ex-friend). Ms McKennitt's fiancé had died in a sailing accident some years earlier, and the book gave a detailed picture of how devastated she had been by his death. Ms McKennitt said she had a legitimate expectation of privacy for this information. But she had in the past given interviews about her fiancé's death, as part of a campaign to prevent similar accidents, and Ms Ash claimed that this meant the matter was in the public domain. The Court disagreed. It said that where a case involved personal information, the fact that the information had been revealed to one group of readers did not mean that fresh revelations to different groups could not cause grief or distress. For this kind of information, protection should only be lost where the information is so generally accessible that it can no longer be considered confidential.

Law in action The phone hacking scandal

During 2011 privacy laws were more in the news than ever, owing to the discovery that reporters at the *News of the World* had routinely hacked into the voicemails of celebrities and people in the public eye in order to get private information. This had the potential to create liability in both the traditional tort of breach of confidence, since the information was obtained in circumstances where it was clearly confidential, and in misuse of private information, because there is obviously a reasonable expectation of privacy for anyone's voicemails.

When it was revealed that among the phones hacked was that of Milly Dowler, a young girl who was missing for several days before it was discovered that she had been murdered, and the mother of Sarah Payne, whose daughter was murdered by a paedophile, there was a public outcry, which eventually resulted in the *News of the World* being closed. The company which owned the paper, News International, settled claims with a number of celebrities, and paid the Dowler family £3 million in settlement of their claim, but there are at least 90 other claims in progress and one law firm has estimated that there may have been as many as 6,000 victims.

Source: Pearson Education Ltd/Photodisc/Steve Cole

[*References*: http://www.bbc.co.uk/news/uk-16682663; http://www.guardian.co.uk/uk/2011/jul/04/milly-dowler-voicemail-hacked-news-of-world; http://www.bbc.co.uk/news/uk-16216085]

Privacy v. freedom of expression

As explained above, working out whether the claimant has a legitimate expectation of privacy is only the first part of the two-part test set out in *Campbell*. If there is no legitimate expectation of privacy, that is the end of the claim. If there is a legitimate expectation of privacy, the court must then balance the claimant's right to privacy against the defendant's right to freedom of expression. Exactly what factors they take into account varies from case to case, but essentially, what the courts are asking is whether there is a public interest in publishing the information, which might outweigh the claimant's right to privacy.

Case Summary

In *Campbell*, the House of Lords approached the issue by taking apart the various elements of the material published, and asking which parts were in the public interest and which were not. Ms Campbell had in the past gone out of her way to deny that she had a drug problem, and their Lordships said it was in the public interest to know that she had been lying about this. Therefore, with regard to the information that she was a drug addict, and was receiving treatment, the paper's freedom of expression outweighed her right to privacy and they were within the law to publish that information.

However, there was not such a strong public interest in knowing the details of her treatment, such as where and how often she attended meetings, and what happened at them. In addition, the photos were particularly intrusive, given that they were taken secretly when Ms Campbell was at the door of a Narcotics Anonymous meeting. Therefore, with regard to the photos and the detailed information about treatment, Ms Campbell's right to privacy outweighed the paper's right to freedom of expression.

Contributing to a public debate

Case Summary

One factor which can tip the scales in favour of publication is where the material complained of is relevant to some kind of important debate or discussion which is going on in the news and the country at large. This was the situation in *Rio Ferdinand* v. *MGN Newspapers* (2011), where the footballer Rio Ferdinand sued over a story about an affair he had had. In balancing Mr Ferdinand's right to privacy against the newspaper's right to freedom of expression, Mr Justice Nicol looked first at the effect of the story itself, and found that it did not 'excessively intrude . . . into the claimant's private life'. A picture used to illustrate it merely showed Mr Ferdinand and the woman concerned in a hotel room, fully clothed and not even kissing, and was clearly taken by someone else who was openly in the room so there was no serious intrusion there either. On the other side of the scales, however, there was a genuine public interest in publishing the story, because Rio Ferdinand had recently been appointed captain of the England football team and there had been some debate about his suitability for this post, given that the England captain was seen as a role model for young boys and that in the past Rio Ferdinand had had a 'wild image' and had admitted to being unfaithful to his then partner, now his wife. The story from which the case arose clearly contributed to this debate, especially as Mr Ferdinand had made deliberate attempts to portray himself as a reformed character. Therefore, on balance, the judge concluded 'the balancing exercise favours the Defendant's right of freedom of expression over the Claimant's right of privacy'.

Case Summary

In *The Author of a Blog* v. *Times Newspapers Limited* (2009), the case of the anonymous blog by a police officer (see page 453), *The Times* argued that there was a public interest in revealing the blogger's identity, given that his blog was breaking police conduct regulations by revealing information gained during police investigations. In addition, the public was entitled to know the blogger's identity in order to assess how far they should believe what they read was true. The claimant argued that the public interest was in his favour, because he was contributing to a debate of general interest. In addition, if he was identified he would be disciplined and this would affect his right to freedom of expression. Mr Justice Eady said that it was not the Court's job to protect the claimant from disciplinary action. If the claimant was contributing to a debate of general interest, then the story about him in *The Times* would be doing the same. He therefore refused to order an injunction, on the grounds that even if at trial it was found that the claimant did have a right to privacy regarding his identity, this was likely to be outweighed by the public interest in a police officer having made these communications.

Public interest and celebrities

The courts have been very clear that there is a distinction between 'the public interest' and 'things the public are interested in'. This means that there will not, as a rule, be a public interest in publishing stories about the sex lives, eating habits or other activities of celebrities, unless they raise an issue which it is in the public interest to know about. In *Mosley* v. *News Group Newspapers* (2008), the case involving the President of Formula 1 motor racing and his sado-masochistic orgy, the paper claimed that the orgy had had a 'Nazi theme'. They said there was a public interest in knowing that a man in the claimant's public position was indulging in sado-masochistic sex with prostitutes, and doing so within a Nazi-themed setting. Mr Justice Eady found that, on the facts, there was no truth in the allegations of Nazi overtones. That being the case, he said that there was no public interest in revealing the fact that someone in the claimant's position was taking part in sado-masochistic orgies which did not go so far as to break any criminal law. If the claimant had been involved in mocking the Holocaust in such a way as to call into question his role in an organisation to which he was accountable, the defence could apply, but here there was no evidence of this.

Case Summary

Correcting a false picture

One situation where there may be a public interest in publishing stories about the personal lives of celebrities is where a celebrity has presented a particular image to the public, and the confidential information shows this image to be false. As we saw earlier, in *Campbell* the House of Lords held that there was a public interest in the *Mirror* revealing that Naomi Campbell was a drug addict, given that she had frequently said that many models had problems with drugs, but that she did not.

Case Summary

This reasoning was also applied in *Beckham* v. *News of the World* (2005), where David and Victoria Beckham were refused an injunction to stop their ex-nanny revealing details about the state of their marriage. The newspaper said that there was a public interest defence in the revelations, because the couple presented themselves as blissfully happily married, and the nanny's stories about blazing rows between them contradicted this. The case was eventually settled out of court.

Case Summary

As we saw earlier, in *Rio Ferdinand* v. *MGN Ltd* (2011) the Court accepted that it was in the public interest to publish a story about Mr Ferdinand's extramarital affair because he had taken deliberate steps to present himself as a 'family man', who had been unfaithful to his partner in the past but was now reformed. An additional factor was that, as captain of the England football team, he was supposed to be a role model.

Case Summary

Similarly, in *Mosley*, Mr Justice Eady confirmed that publication might have been in the public interest if the information corrected a false image put about by the claimant. This might be the case, for example, if he had promoted himself as someone who was opposed to sex outside marriage. But that was not the situation here, so there was no public interest in publishing the story.

Case Summary

However, this approach will only apply where the story involves serious misbehaviour, and not to more trivial claims about a celebrity not living up to their public image. In *McKennitt*, the author claimed Ms McKennitt presented herself as holding certain personal values, but these were not always reflected in her behaviour. She said her book corrected this false impression. However, Mr Justice Eady rejected this argument. He said that while revelations of serious misbehaviour by a celebrity might be justified in the public interest, relatively trivial matters would not: 'the mere fact that a celebrity falls short from time to time, like everyone else, could not possibly justify exposure, in the supposed public interest, of every peccadillo or foible cropping up in everyday life'.

The Princess Caroline case

Case Summary

The way the courts balance the competing rights of privacy and freedom of expression in cases involving the media is also influenced by a key case from the European Court of Human Rights, *Von Hannover* v. *Germany* (2004) brought by Princess Caroline of Monaco. The daughter of Prince Rainier and the late Princess Grace of Monaco, Princess Caroline was frequently featured in the British press during her teens and 20s, and was sometimes spoken of as a possible wife for Prince Charles, despite never having shown the slightest inclination to take up that post. In recent years, she has not appeared so often in newspapers here, but the media in some other European countries are fascinated by her, and report obsessively on her life and relationships. The Princess tried to sue certain newspapers in the German courts, complaining that she was constantly being followed and photographed by paparazzi, even when she was going about normal activities such as shopping or taking her children to school. The German courts refused her claim, saying that as a public figure she had to accept that the public had a legitimate interest in knowing about even her ordinary daily life.

Princess Caroline then took her case to the European Court of Human Rights (ECHR), claiming that German law did not protect her right to privacy under Article 8 of the European Convention on Human Rights (the treaty which the Human Rights Act puts into English law). The ECHR upheld her claim. They said that the key question when balancing the rights of privacy and freedom of expression was whether the material published contributed to 'a debate of general interest'. If it did, the right of freedom of expression was more likely to win out, but if it did not, the right of privacy was likely to have more importance. In this case, it said, the pictures made no real contribution to a debate of general interest. There was no legitimate public interest in seeing pictures of Princess Caroline when she was not performing her official role, so her right of privacy should take priority over the media's right to freedom of expression.

You might wonder at this point why Elton John lost the case referred to earlier, given that he was just going about his daily business like Princess Caroline and that pictures of him walking to his house from his car would not seem to contribute anything to a debate of public interest. In the *Elton John* case, Mr Justice Eady said that the difference between the two cases was that the Princess was so constantly followed and photographed that the photographers' behaviour amounted to harassment, and this was not the case for Elton John. Yet if you read the ECHR's judgment, it is very difficult to agree with this interpretation. The Princess did complain of being harassed, and the Court does refer to this with disapproval, but the reasons given for the Court's decision are more concerned with the publication of the pictures than the way in which they were obtained.

A better explanation may be that the Court of Appeal was bound by precedent to follow the decision of the House of Lords in *Campbell*. There, as we saw, the judgment included the principle that there was no protection against the revelation of trivial information or pictures of people going about their ordinary business. If a case on the subject were to go before the Supreme Court now, however, they might well fall into line with the ECHR's view that even such ordinary information and pictures should be protected, unless there is something about them that informs public debate on an important subject. Not doing this would mean that the claimant in such a case could potentially bring a claim before the ECHR, for failure to apply the Human Rights Act.

The right to tell

Privacy cases often involve weighing the claimant's right to privacy against the media's right to freedom of expression. But where a story involves two people, there may be a different clash of interests to consider: the party wanting to tell the story, against the party wanting to keep it secret. Let's say, for example, that Susie, a model, gets involved in a relationship with a politician who she does not know is married. She thinks the relationship is serious, but when the press find out about the affair the politician dumps Susie by text message and seeks an injunction to prevent publication of his name or any details that would identify him. Susie wants to put her side of the story, and 'name and shame' the politician for treating her so badly, but the injunction would prevent her from doing that. The courts therefore have to weigh up Susie's right to freedom of expression regarding her own story, with the politician's right to protect his privacy by preventing the story from being published.

This issue arose – in a quite different context – in *McKennitt*, the case we looked at above where the defendant, Ms Ash, had written a book about the claimant, Ms McKennitt, a well-known folk singer. Part of Ms Ash's claim was that the story was not just Ms McKennitt's but hers as well, and that her right to freedom of expression meant she should be free to tell it. The Court therefore had to weigh Ms Ash's right to freedom of expression with regard to telling the story of her friendship with Ms McKennitt, against Ms McKennitt's right to privacy in wanting to keep parts of what was also her story private. The Court found that if a person wants to publish information about their relationship with someone else, and that information is of a kind that would normally create an expectation of privacy, the material published has to be shaped in such a way as to protect the other person's privacy. Mr Justice Eady commented that: 'It does not follow that, because one can reveal one's own private life, that one can also expose confidential matters in respect of which others are entitled to protection if their consent is not forthcoming.'

Case Summary

The conduct of the defendant may also be relevant in deciding the balance between their freedom of expression and the claimant's privacy. In *CC* v. *AB* (2006), the claimant was a well-known figure in the sporting world. He had had an affair with a married woman and her husband had found out. The husband wanted to tell the story to the press, and the claimant applied for an injunction to prevent this. The Court agreed to keep the names of the parties secret, since revealing them would obviously have made any injunction pointless. The judge granted the injunction and said he was influenced in his decision by the fact that the defendant clearly wanted revenge on the claimant, and

Case Summary

had in fact behaved threateningly to him. He also took into account the fact that the defendant's wife was said to be very distressed by the thought of publicity, and said that she and their children also had rights to privacy which should be protected, even though it was the claimant who had put that privacy at risk by having the affair.

Out and about

Gather together a selection of celebrity magazines and tabloid newspapers. Using what you have read about the tests for misuse of private information, go through them, picking out any stories which you think could give rise to a successful claim.

Remedies

There are two remedies for a privacy claim, injunction and damages. In most cases, a claimant will prefer to get an injunction before publication so that they can stop the material ever being seen by the public. Damages are a lesser remedy because they cannot undo the damage, and in privacy cases they are relatively low.

Injunctions

The main remedy for breach of confidence is an injunction. Claimants can apply for an injunction to prevent publication in the first place, or to prevent further publication if the material has already been published. In either case, the injunction may be an interim one, which is designed to put the situation on hold until the issue is tried, or a permanent one, which is issued if a claimant proves their case at trial. In some cases an **interim injunction** will be issued before trial and then, if the claimant wins, it becomes a permanent one.

If a court imposes an injunction preventing publication, that injunction applies to all media organisations which know about the injunction and not just the newspaper named in the case.

Restrictions on injunctions

When considering either type of injunction in a case involving the media, the Human Rights Act makes it clear that the courts must take into account the potential effect on press freedom. Section 12 of the Act states that if a court is asked to give any order which could affect freedom of expression, with regard to journalistic material, they must:

- take into account the importance of the right to freedom of expression;
- consider the extent to which the material concerned is already in the public domain;
- consider any public interest in publication.

This essentially means that a court has to consider whether there may be a defence even at the stage of an application for an interim injunction and not just later at trial.

Where the material has not yet been published, and the claimant is asking for an injunction to prevent publication, section 12 also provides that an injunction should only be granted where the claimant can show that they are 'likely' to prove a breach of confidence if the case goes to trial. In *Cream Holdings* v. *Banerjee* (2004), the House of Lords said this would usually mean that the injunction should only be ordered if the claimant could prove that it was more likely than not that they would win at trial. However, an injunction might be granted in exceptional situations where the claimant could not prove they were more likely than not to win, but where the consequences of disclosing the information would be especially serious for them.

Injunction or damages?

An injunction to prevent publication before the case has been fully tried is a serious restriction on press freedom. Therefore, a claimant seeking such an injunction to prevent publication before trial must also prove that, if they win their case, their loss could not be equally well compensated by damages. This is not usually difficult with confidentiality cases involving secret information, since no amount of money can make the information secret again. But there are cases where monetary compensation may be sufficient, and there an injunction will be refused. In *Douglas*, the case about Catherine Zeta Jones's wedding, the court refused to stop the publication of the wedding pictures in *Hello!* The harm done by *Hello!* was that it had compromised their right to sell pictures of themselves, and this was something that money could compensate for, so it was not appropriate to order an injunction.

Injunctions in practice

In media cases, an interim injunction will often be all the claimant needs, because if they can keep the issue out of the news for long enough the story may become stale and then will not be covered anyway. This means a claimant who gets an injunction can effectively kill a story without needing to prove their case at trial. The problems this can cause for the media are made worse by the fact that injunctions can be issued at very short notice. Judges will do this over the telephone, even at night, and it is not unusual for an injunction to be ordered just before a paper goes to press or even after printing has started.

> a claimant who gets an injunction can effectively kill a story

The Human Rights Act aims to offer some protection in this situation. It provides that interim injunctions preventing publication should not be made unless the journalist is present or the claimant has taken steps to notify them, but in practice this provision is quite easy to get round. In *Douglas* v. *Hello!*, for example, the initial temporary injunction was granted late at night, over the telephone, even though the only step *OK* had taken to contact *Hello!* was to ring their offices. Not surprisingly, the only person there at that time was a security guard. New guidelines for the courts, issued after the controversy over so-called super injunctions, may address the problem in the future (see the Law in Action box on super injunctions).

On the other hand, if the media can successfully fight off an interim injunction the claimant may not bother taking the matter to trial, because to do so would only give even more publicity to the information.

Law in action Super injunctions

You will probably have read or heard about 'super injunctions', which have been the subject of much press coverage during the last couple of years. The press frequently uses the term to mean any injunction granted to prevent press revelations about a celebrity, but in fact the term super injunction really refers to a particular type of injunction where the terms are so wide that the order not only bans any publication of the details of the story and the identities of those involved in it but also prevents the press from even mentioning that the injunction exists. This means that not only is the public prevented from reading the story, but also prevented from even knowing that someone is trying gag the press.

This is clearly a huge restriction on press freedom, and not surprisingly this type of injunction became very controversial. It was widely reported that the courts were issuing these injunctions very frequently, but this appears to have been exaggerated. There are no comprehensive records showing how many have been granted, but research by *The Daily Telegraph* ('Courts issue 80 gagging orders in six years', 13 May 2011) suggests that there have probably been around 12 genuine super injunctions between 2000 and 2011 (the 80 orders referred to in the headline was the total of injunctions in privacy cases). Even so, given the draconian nature of the injunctions, it is hard to believe that even one case a year demands quite such wide protection.

A much more frequently used order, which also has serious implications for media freedom, is the anonymised injunction. In this type of injunction, the name of the claimant is kept secret (in the name of the case they will be referred to by randomly-chosen initials), which again means that the press cannot report that that particular person has tried to suppress publication of information about them, though in this case they can report the existence of the injunction and the basics of the story, as long as they do not identify the claimant. There are known to have been at least 25 anonymised injunctions granted between January 2010 and July 2011. This is potentially a serious curb on press freedom – but, on the other hand, it can be argued that if the press are allowed to report the claimant's name, there would be little point in them applying for the injunction in the first place, since at the very least it could be reported that there was something that person wanted to hide.

In response to growing concern about what was perceived to be the increased use of super and anonymised injunctions, the **Master of the Rolls**, Lord Neuberger, conducted an investigation into the use of these two types of order. It confirmed that genuine super injunctions are now rarely granted, and in fact rarely applied for, but that they had been granted too readily in the past. The report issued new guidelines for the use of super and anonymised injunctions, stating that they should be granted 'only when they are strictly necessary'. Where an anonymised injunction was granted, the court should give a reasoned judgment stating why anonymity was granted. In addition, the media should be informed about applications for injunctions, so that they had a chance to put a case against any order.

In practice, the power of the internet means that neither super injunctions nor anonymised ones are necessarily as powerful as they appear to be in theory. The first high profile super injunction to hit the press came in 2009, in the *Trafigura* case, where *The Guardian* was prevented from publishing a report which claimed that an oil company, Trafigura, had been dumping toxic waste in the Ivory Coast. When an MP raised a question in Parliament about the report, the terms of the injunction meant *The Guardian* could not even publish a story about the parliamentary question, so the newspaper reported that there had been a question in Parliament that they could not report, nor could they say who had asked it, or which minister might answer it. This led to an outbreak of speculation on the social media site Twitter on what the question was about and very quickly it became known that it concerned Trafigura, and the full text of the question was published on Twitter after a human rights activist found it on a government website. The super injunction became pointless, and Trafigura agreed that the injunction could be lifted.

A similar, but more absurd, situation arose from the case of *CTB* v. *Newsgroup Newspapers* (2011) which, even if you do not recognise the name of the case, you will certainly have heard about. The claimant in the case was a well-known footballer, who obtained an injunction banning reporting of his name in connection with a story about an alleged affair with the *Big Brother* contestant Imogen Thomas. The injunction was anonymised, so the press reported that Ms Thomas had had an affair with a footballer but that they were unable to name him. This led to a nationwide guessing game, played out on Twitter and internet messageboards, and before very long, anyone who wanted to know the identity of the player could find it online in a matter of seconds.

Eventually, MP John Hemming named the footballer in the House of Commons, where he was covered by Parliamentary privilege. The press then began to report what the MP had said, and by that evening, the-secret-that-wasn't-a-secret was out. Despite this, at the time of going to press, the injunction remained in place.

[*References*: 'Courts issue 80 gagging orders in six years', *Daily Telegraph*, 13 May 2011; Report of the Committee on Super Injunctions: Super Injunctions, Anonymised Injunctions and Open Justice, available at **http://www.guardian.co.uk/law/interactive/2011/may/20/superinjunctions_neuberger.report;** 'Injunction fails to stop footballer affair reporting', *Press Gazette*, 24 May 2011]

Damages

Although most breach of confidence cases concern claimants who are trying to get an injunction to prevent publication, there are also cases where confidential information is published before the claimants have a chance to try to prevent it. In this situation, they can go to court to try to get damages (and if necessary an injunction against further publication). However, damages in this type of claim are not especially high, compared, for example to those in defamation actions. In *Campbell* v. *MGN* (2004), for example, Naomi Campbell was awarded £3,500, while Catherine Zeta Jones and Michael Douglas received damages of £14,600. This must have seemed like small change to them, given that when asked during the trial how important the deal with *OK* was to them, Ms Zeta Jones famously said 'A million pounds isn't a lot of money to us.'

damages in this type of claim are not especially high

Law in action Settlements

As we have seen, the claim for misuse of private information is quite a new one, and there are only a handful of decided cases. However, that is only part of the picture. As you already know, the majority of tort claims do not end up in a court hearing but are settled beforehand, and this is also true for breach of confidence/misuse of private information claims.

In celebrity cases in particular, settlements have distinct advantages for both sides. For the celebrity, a full court case will often mean that the matter they want to keep private is even more widely exposed. If they settle a case they avoid this problem, and at the same time usually achieve some protection for their privacy, because they have shown the media that they are someone who will sue if necessary. Within the media, it is well known that some celebrities are more likely to sue than others, and there is no doubt that they tend to be treated more carefully as a result.

Some celebrities have taken this approach a little further, and actually used the terms of a settlement to negotiate ongoing protection for their privacy. For example, actress Sienna Miller settled with a picture agency in 2008 over what she regarded as intrusive photos. As part of the settlement, she insisted that the agency undertake not to allow its photographers to follow her, put her under surveillance, or take pictures of her at home, in buildings not open to the public, or anywhere where she had a reasonable expectation of privacy. She agreed that she would not have an expectation of privacy when entering or exiting a bar, restaurant or nightclub, on a public highway, or when attending a 'red carpet' event such as a film premiere, so the agency was free to photograph her in those situations.

For the media, the advantage of a settlement is quite simply that it avoids establishing any precedents. The law on privacy has developed very quickly over the past few years, and nobody quite knows how far it will go. The last thing that the media want is for a case to go to trial and reach the higher courts, then end up establishing a definite precedent that would restrict what they can do.

For example, as we saw earlier, the Princess Caroline case suggests that public figures have a legitimate expectation of privacy even when going about the most harmless everyday activities. So far (and this may even have changed by the time you read this book), the English courts have not followed this principle, but instead have taken the view expressed by the House of Lords in *Campbell* that there is no expectation of privacy for celebrities 'popping out for a pint of milk'. But *Campbell* was decided before the Princess Caroline case, and EU law dictates that the next time a case on this issue reaches the Supreme Court they will need to make sure their decision is in line with the approach taken by the ECHR. If the Supreme Court does that, and rules that there is a legitimate expectation of privacy for ordinary activities, that will mean that the media will be taking the risk of being sued every time they photograph a celebrity without their consent when they are walking down the street, on holiday, or leaving a nightclub, unless the picture contributes to an important public debate, or the press have another defence. Since such pictures have become a staple ingredient of tabloid newspapers, and almost the entire content of some celebrity magazines, it is not difficult to see why the media would prefer to keep these issues away from the courts.

[*References*: **http://www.guardian.co.uk/media/2008/nov/21/sienna-miller-big-pictures-privacy; http://www.lawgazette.co.uk/gazette-in-practice/legal-updates/media-law-23**]

Writing and drafting

You are the in-house lawyer for a large newspaper company. The editor of one of your newspapers wants to run the following story.

Pure lies: we expose Penny's drink problem

She claims to be a role model for a healthy lifestyle, but now *The News* can reveal that actress Penny Pure has been battling a drink problem for over three years. As a paid spokesperson for a chain of health clubs, Penny has often been interviewed in magazines about her eating and drink habits. This is what she told Healthy Bodies magazine just last month: 'I cut out alcohol from my diet years ago, and I feel so much healthier for it. I pity people who need a drink to enjoy themselves – I'd rather go for a nice run.'

Yet just last week, our photographer caught Penny leaving a meeting of Alcoholics Anonymous. A source within the group told us: 'She's been coming for three years now. She comes to a meeting about twice a week, and she's treated just like the rest of us. She's not a celebrity here, she's just Penny, an alcoholic. She stands up and talks about how she's feeling, and whether she's had a drink that day. Last week she was in a terrible state, crying and saying that she'd never beat this problem.'

It's thought that Penny's problems started after her boyfriend, actor Jeremy Gorgeous, was killed by a runaway camel on the set of his last film, *Just Deserts*. Since then, Penny has campaigned for better safety standards in the film industry, telling BBC News in 2005: 'I was devastated by Jeremy's death, and I want to make sure nothing like this ever happens again. It's the only way I can get over my loss.' Yet it seems the campaign hasn't helped her deal with her feelings. A close friend told us: 'She puts on a brave face in public, but behind closed doors she's cried herself to sleep every night since he died. She has pictures of him in every room, and kisses them all before she goes to bed at night. And she has a toy camel that she kicks around the floor. It's very sad.'

The newspaper wants to run the following photos: Penny leaving an Alcoholics Anonymous meeting; Penny jogging in a park near her home; Penny out shopping with her 5-year-old niece.

Using your knowledge of the cases in this chapter, draft the advice you would give on whether the paper would be at risk of a claim for misuse of private information if they published this story and the pictures that go with it. If you think they would be at risk of a claim, consider whether you can suggest any changes to the story, or the selection of pictures, which would make it possible to publish safely.

Reflective practice

If you can, take a few minutes to think about how this exercise went. How did you go about spotting any problem areas in the story? Did you find it easy to work out how the law applied to the story? What, if anything, did you find difficult about the task? What might you do differently another time?

Alternative protection against invasion of privacy

People, famous or otherwise, who believe their privacy has been invaded by magazines and newspapers have an alternative to court action in the form of a complaint to the Press Complaints Commission (PCC). The PCC is an independent body, which operates a Code of Practice that all national and local magazines and newspapers should abide by. The Code includes the following provisions on privacy:

- Everyone is entitled to respect for his or her private and family life, home, health and correspondence, including digital communications.
- It is unacceptable to photograph people in private places without their consent (private places are defined as places where there is a reasonable expectation of privacy, and this may include public property as well as private).
- Editors may not use the fame, notoriety or position of a parent or guardian as sole justification for publishing details of a child's private life.
- The press should not publish material acquired by using hidden cameras or listening devices, intercepting phone calls or emails, or unauthorised removal of documents or photos.

Unlike going to court, complaining to the PCC is free. If the PCC agrees that the Code has been breached, it aims to resolve complaints by agreement, which may include the paper or magazine publishing an apology or correction. If agreement cannot be achieved, the PCC

Unlike going to court, complaining to the PCC is free.

can insist on a report of its decision being published. It cannot, however, fine the publication, or get financial compensation for the complainant. Currently one in five complaints to the PCC concerns some kind of alleged invasion of privacy.

Writing and drafting

You work for the Law Commission. The government has asked the Commission to consider whether it would be a good idea to pass a new Act, which would define the law on protection of privacy. Present the arguments for and against such a law, and give your conclusion on whether such as a statute would be an improvement on the current situation.

Handy tip: You will find useful material for putting together your arguments in the articles recommended in the Further reading section at the end of this chapter.

Summary

- There is no actual tort of invasion of privacy, but in recent years the courts have taken the tort of breach of confidence and extended and manipulated it to create a new tort, misuse of private information, which protects against publication of private information and pictures.
- The case of *Campbell* v. *MGN* established a two-part test for misuse of private information:
  - did the claimant have a reasonable expectation of privacy with respect to the information disclosed?; and if they did,
  - is their right to privacy more important, in the circumstances, than someone else's right to freedom of expression under Article 10?
- Whether there is a reasonable expectation of privacy depends on a number of factors, including the attributes of the claimant, the nature of the activity in which the claimant was engaged, the place at which it was happening, the nature and purpose of the intrusion, the absence of consent and whether it was known or could be inferred, the effect on the claimant and the circumstances in which and the purposes for which the information came into the hands of the publisher.
- The courts must balance the competing rights to privacy and freedom of expression, and relevant issues include how far the information was a matter of public interest, or contributes to debate of general interest, the conduct of the defendant, and whose story it is to tell.
- The two main remedies are injunction and damages. There are restrictions on the use of injunctions in press cases.

Question and answer*

Problem: Geeta Gossip is the editor of a Sunday newspaper. She gets a phone call from the ex-girlfriend of a well-known pop star, Ricky Rocker, who has become known for his campaigns against drugs. He has always claimed that many pop stars have drug problems, but that he had never touched any kind of drug. The ex-girlfriend says she is willing to give an interview about the fact that Ricky frequently took drugs when they were together. She says he never took drugs in public, but would often smoke cannabis when they were at home alone.

Later that day, Geeta gets a call from a freelance photographer, who says he has photographs of a well-known politician kissing a man who is not her husband. The photos were taken without the couple's knowledge; some are taken through the window of the man's house, while the others show them in the street outside. The politician has recently been campaigning for tighter privacy laws that would prevent the press from reporting allegations about the private lives of public figures.

Can Geeta publish the allegations about Ricky's drug taking? Can she publish the photographs of the politician? Discuss these questions with reference to the tort of misuse of private information (there is no need to consider defamation).

You should allow yourself no more than 40 minutes to complete this task.

Essay: Does English law include a tort of invasion of privacy?

This question should be answered in 40 minutes.

* Answer guidance is provided at the end of the chapter.

Further reading

Aplin, T. (2007) 'The development of the action for breach of confidence in a post-HRA era', *Intellectual Property Quarterly* 19.
A detailed look at the way the tort of breach of confidence has been transformed to provide wider protection for individual privacy.

Eady, Mr Justice (2009) Speech at the University of Hertfordshire (available online at http://www.judiciary.gov.uk/NR/rdonlyres/1D20B7A7-62FB-461D-BA12-2437CB8CF61A/0/justiceeadyunivofhertfordshire101109.pdf)
Mr Justice Eady is the judge who has decided most of the key cases on privacy, and played a key role in developing the law. In this speech he talks about how and why the law developed as it did, and the importance of striking the right balance between privacy and freedom of expression. Well worth reading.

Phillips, G. (2010) 'Wayne Rooney's infidelity exposes law's misogyny', *The Guardian*, 13 September (available online at http://www.guardian.co.uk/media/2010/sep/13/wayne-rooney-infidelity-law-misogyny)
In this very interesting newspaper article, the in-house lawyer for Guardian Newspapers argues that the protection given by the courts to sexual matters is sexist, allowing men to cover up their infidelity and treating the women involved as mere objects.

Phillipson, G. (2003) 'Transforming breach of confidence? Towards a common law right of privacy under the Human Rights Act', 66 MLR 7266.
This article looks at some of the early cases on privacy, and examines the principles behind them.

Robertson, G. and Nicol, A. (2008) *Media Law*, 5th edn, London: Penguin.
A very clear and detailed look at the law on privacy and the problems with it, written in a readable and entertaining style with lots of real-life examples.

Rozenberg, J. (2004) *Privacy and the Press*, Oxford: Oxford University Press.
Joshua Rozenberg is a lawyer and journalist, who has been legal correspondent for the BBC and *The Daily Telegraph*. This book gives a clear and very well-written overview of the law of privacy (though bear in mind it may be a few years out of date, given that privacy law has been moving so quickly), with lots of real-life examples. A very good read.

Rozenberg, J. (2011) 'Mr Justice Eady on balancing acts', *Index on Censorship*, 12 June (available online at http://www.indexoncensorship.org/2011/06/mr-justice-eady-on-balancing-acts/#)
An interview with the judge who heard most of the key cases on privacy, and played a key role in developing the principles on misuse of private information. He talks about the background to the law, and how judges balance the rights to privacy and freedom of expression.

Question and answer guidance

Problem: Starting with the allegations against Ricky, you need to consider, first, whether he had a legitimate expectation of privacy regarding his drug habit. Relevant issues will be the nature of the activity exposed, and here you need to discuss *Campbell*, and the source of the information, where *McKennitt* is relevant because the information was only known about because of a close relationship. Then discuss the balancing act that a court would conduct, between the media's right to freedom of expression and Ricky's right to privacy. Does it make a difference that Ricky has portrayed himself as anti-drugs?

Regarding the photos of the politician, again you need to assess whether there was a reasonable expectation of privacy, and the key issue here would be the fact that there are photos as well as words, how they are obtained and what they show – look at the cases of *Campbell* and *Mosley* for some guidance on this. Then discuss how the courts might balance the right to freedom of expression against privacy. Do you think the politician's campaign for strong privacy laws might be relevant? Have a look at the *Rio Ferdinand* case and see if there are any possible parallels there.

Essay: You could start this essay by explaining that there is officially no tort of invasion of privacy, but that the courts have extended and manipulated the tort of breach of confidence over the past few years, so that today we have something which looks very like a tort of privacy and appears to do the same job. Explain why the official view is that there is no tort of privacy, referring to the *Wainwright* case, and then go on to look at how the tort of misuse of private information works to protect privacy, using cases to back up the points you make.

You should also look at the limitations the tort has put on protection of privacy, by highlighting when a claimant will not have a reasonable expectation of privacy, and when the right to freedom of expression will outweigh the right to privacy, again drawing on the cases to make your points.

A good way to conclude the essay would be by discussing where any of these limitations mean that English law gives insufficient protection against invasions of privacy, or whether you feel the correct balance is being struck.

Visit **www.mylawchamber.co.uk/quinntort** to access tools to help you develop and test your knowledge of tort law, including practice exam questions with guidance, annotated weblinks, glossary and key case flashcards, legal newsfeed and legal updates and interactive 'You be the judge' questions.

Use Case Navigator to read in full some of the key cases referenced in this chapter with commentary and questions:

Wainwright* v. *Home Office [2003] 4 All ER 969

Chapter 19
Deceit

Key points In this chapter we will be looking at:

- How the tort of deceit is committed
- How damages for deceit are calculated
- Differences between negligent misstatement and deceit

Introduction

No one really knows exactly how long human beings have been involved in making deals with each other. But what we can probably guess is that from the very earliest days of swapping one thing for another, or buying goods or services with money, there were people who were not honest about their side of the bargain, who lied about what the other person was getting, or what it was worth, or what it could be used for. So, not surprisingly, laws to deal with this kind of behaviour have existed for a very long time, and the tort of deceit is one of them. It was first recognised over two hundred years ago in the case of *Pasley* v. *Freeman* (1789), though similar claims have existed since at least the fourteenth century.

In *Pasley* v. *Freeman*, the **claimant**, Mr Pasley, was a merchant, and a Mr Falch wanted to buy some goods from him on credit. Knowing that Mr Freeman knew Mr Falch, Mr Pasley asked him whether he thought Mr Falch could be relied on to pay for the goods. Mr Freeman knew that in fact there was a good chance Mr Falch would not pay up at all, but he told Mr Pasley that Mr Falch was financially sound. Sure enough Mr Falch failed to pay for the goods, and Mr Pasley sued Mr Freeman, on the grounds that his untrue statement about Mr Falch had caused Mr Pasley to lose money. His claim succeeded and is seen as the beginning of the modern tort of deceit, which allows a claim where the **defendant** has told a lie, either knowing it not to be true or not caring whether it was true or not, with the intention of encouraging the claimant to do something, and the claimant suffers loss as a result.

Originally, the law would often have been used in disputes between individuals – many early cases concerned horse sellers, who have been described as the forerunners of today's used car salesmen, and might be sued, for example, for saying that a horse was young and healthy when it was actually old and worn out. Today, although the law of deceit can still apply in disputes between individuals about goods bought and sold, in practice consumer protection measures such as the Sale of Goods Act 1979 are of more importance. However, deceit remains an important tort in commercial disputes between companies, and in the insurance industry it is sometimes used against people who make false claims on their policies. In recent years, as we will see later, it has been extended, with some controversy, into a new area with a successful claim against a woman who lied to her partner about who was the father of her child.

Elements of the tort

A claimant in deceit must prove six things:

- that the defendant made a false statement, in other words, that they lied;
- that the statement was one of fact, in that the defendant was suggesting something was factually true rather than just giving an opinion;
- that the defendant knew the statement was untrue, or at least did not genuinely believe it was true;
- that the defendant intended the claimant, or a group of people which included the claimant, to act on the statement;
- that the claimant acted on the statement;
- that acting on the statement caused damage to the claimant.

The false statement

In many deceit cases, the statement will be made in words, whether spoken or written. Let's say I'm trying to sell you a car. If I tell you that it has never failed to start in the five years I have owned it, when in fact I have often had to get the bus to work because the car refuses to start in cold or damp weather, that would clearly be a false statement. We would probably more commonly call it a lie.

a false statement can be made even if no words are spoken or written

However, a false statement can be made even if no words are spoken or written, if the defendant effectively tells a lie by the way he or she acts (for this reason, cases sometimes use the term 'representation' rather than statement, but it means the same thing). An example of a false statement made without using words occurred in *R* v. *Barnard* (1837). The defendant lived in Oxford, where at the time it was common for students to wear academic gowns and mortar boards. A local bookshop offered discounts to students, and Mr Barnard dressed up in a mortar board and gown so that he would look like a student and be given the discount. Although he did not at any point say 'I am a student', this was held to be a false representation. Similarly, in *Legh* v. *Legh* (1930), it was held that a man who had agreed to pay his wife half his income would be making a false representation if he then sent her £30,000, when his income was £80,000. Even without words, he would be falsely implying that his income was £60,000.

Case Summary

Case Summary

Keeping silent

What would be the position if, as in the example above, I sold you a car that had problems starting and, rather than lying about it, I simply did not mention the problem? In terms of deceit, merely keeping silent would not lead to liability; there must usually be some kind of statement or representation, whether by words or conduct. So if I merely kept silent about the problem, with the car example, you would not have a case against me in deceit (though you might have a claim in contract law).

merely keeping silent would not lead to liability

However, there are four situations where keeping silent can contribute to liability for deceit:

Half-truths

A statement or conduct which only tells part of the truth can be a false representation, if leaving out certain details means that what you do say is misleading. So, to take the car example again, if you asked me 'Does the car have any defects?' and I said 'The brakes, the clutch and the steering all work perfectly, it's an absolute bargain', I would be giving you a false representation of the car's condition, because leaving out the information about the starting problem makes the rest of my answer misleading.

Deliberate concealment

Case Summary

Actively concealing information can amount to a false representation. In *Gordon* v. *Selico Ltd* (1986), a landlord who deliberately covered up dry rot in a flat when he showed it to a potential tenant was held to have made a false representation.

Statutory requirements

In some circumstances, there is a statutory duty to reveal particular information, and failure to do so can amount to a false representation. For example, under the Companies Act 2006 certain information must be included in a company prospectus (a document companies produce for people considering buying shares in them). If a company failed to provide certain information and, in doing so, gave a false picture, they could be liable for deceit.

Changing situations

Case Summary

If a representation is true when it is made, but the situation changes, making it untrue, a defendant who stays silent about the change may be liable in deceit. In *Incledon* v. *Watson* (1862), the defendant owned a school, which he wanted to sell to the claimant. At the start of their negotiations, he said that the school had a particular number of pupils, which was true at the time. As the negotiations went on, and before the claimant agreed to buy, the number of pupils went down, making the school potentially less profitable, but the defendant did not mention this to the claimant. His silence was held to be a false representation.

You be the judge

Q: Daisy owns a flat, which she wants to sell. It has a very bad damp problem, and she is worried that this might put buyers off. Donald comes round to view the flat, and does not notice the signs of damp, so Daisy does not mention the problem. Donald buys the flat, and then discovers the damp problem.

Could Daisy be liable for deceit?

A: No. Silence alone cannot make her liable for deceit. She could, however, have been liable if she had tried to cover up the problem, or if Donald had asked her if there was any damp and she had lied.

Source: Pearson Education Ltd/Photodisc/Greg Kuchik

A statement of fact

The lie that the defendant tells, whether in words or by their behaviour, has to be about a matter of fact. So, for example, if the seller of a racehorse were to say, untruthfully, 'He is the son of a Grand National winner', that would be a false statement of fact, because it is a matter of fact whether the horse's father won the Grand National or not. But if he were to say 'This horse will win the Grand National one day', that is not a matter of fact, because he cannot possibly know whether it is true or not. It is just a statement of the seller's opinion. There could be liability in deceit for the first statement, but not the second.

However, the distinction is not always clear-cut, and may depend on what the defendant could have known. In *Bisset* v. *Wilkinson* (1927), the defendant was selling some land to the claimant, who intended to use it as a sheep farm. The defendant said he thought the land would support 2,000 sheep, but in fact it was not nearly big enough for this number. His statement sounds like a statement of fact, but the Court took into account the fact that the defendant was not a sheep farmer and the land had never been used for sheep. In that context, what he was giving was just a statement of opinion (or more accurately perhaps, a guess) and not a statement of fact.

Case Summary

The other side of this is that the courts will be more ready to find that there is a statement of fact where a defendant makes what could look like a statement of opinion in a situation where they have more knowledge than the claimant about whether the statement is true or not. In that situation, the courts have held that the defendant is not just saying 'I believe that this is true' but also 'There is good reason to believe this is true'. In *Smith* v. *Land and House Property Corporation* (1884), the claimant bought a hotel from the defendant. The defendant had said that the hotel was let to 'a most desirable tenant', but in fact the tenant had not paid his rent for some time. Although the question of whether someone was a 'desirable tenant' or not could be seen as a matter of opinion, in this case the court held it was a statement of fact, because the landlord was in a better position than the buyer to know what was going on with the tenant.

Case Summary

Promises and intentions

Promises about the future and statements of intention are not usually considered to be statements of fact. So if I ask you to invest in my company, and tell you it will make you £10,000 a year for the rest of your life, that is generally viewed as a statement of opinion, not of fact, and would not create liability for deceit. However, statements about the future and a defendant's intention can be viewed as statements of fact if they can be taken to mean that the defendant is saying a certain factual situation does or will exist. In *Edgington* v. *Fitzmaurice* (1885), the directors of a company tried to attract people to invest in the firm by saying that the money invested would be used to finish off company buildings, buy equipment, and generally develop the company into a money-making business. In fact, the company was in debt, and the defendants actually planned to use the money invested to pay some of what was owed. The defendants argued that what they had said was merely a statement of intention, not of fact. However, Lord Justice Bowen rejected this idea, and said that 'the state of a man's mind is as much a fact as the state of his digestion'. In other words, the defendants had been stating as a fact that, when they said it, they were intending to spend the money on developing the company. This was not true and so they could be liable.

Case Summary

Case Summary

However, a defendant will not be liable if they state an intention which, at the time, they honestly hold, and then later change their mind. This was the situation in *Wales* v. *Wadham* (1977). The defendant, Mrs Wadham, had been married to Mr Wales, who left her. She frequently said that she would never marry again, and he believed this when he gave her a generous financial settlement. She later met a Mr Wadham, changed her mind, and married him. The difference between the two cases was that, at the time she made the statement, Mrs Wadham honestly believed she would never marry again. In *Edgington*, on the other hand, the defendants were stating as a fact that they had plans to invest the money in the business, when they knew they had no such plans.

Writing and drafting

You have a car that you want to sell. It is in reasonably good condition, but there is a problem with the brakes. Write a short advert to put in your local paper, which will get people interested in buying the car, without making you liable for deceit.

Knowledge that the statement was false

As its name suggests, the tort of deceit is all about dishonesty, so clearly there is no claim for a deceit where someone made a statement that they had no idea was untrue, even if that statement causes a loss to the claimant. Nor will the courts allow a claim for deceit where a false statement was only made through carelessness or stupidity. It must be shown that the defendant either:

- knew the representation was false, or
- did not honestly believe it was true, or
- was reckless about whether it was true or false. In this context, to be reckless means not to care whether the representation was true or not.

Case Summary

This very important principle was established in *Derry* v. *Peek* (1889). The defendants were directors of a tram company, who issued a brochure for potential investors that said that they were going to be running steam-driven trams. They needed a permit to do this, and they did not have the permit at the time they made the statement, but they honestly believed there would be no problem getting it. In fact, they were not able to get the permit, so they could not run the trams and investors lost money. The House of Lords held that where a defendant honestly believed they were telling the truth, as the defendants here did, there was no liability for deceit. This applies even if the defendants have been careless in not making sure that what they said was true.

Intention that the claimant should act

To be liable for deceit, the defendant must have intended for the claimant to act on the false statement. Clearly, the courts cannot look inside the defendant's head to see what they intended, so they have to judge what was intended from the defendant's behaviour, and the circumstances. We saw earlier, for example, that companies wanting to attract investors will often publish a prospectus with information about the company and its prospects. The prospectus will highlight projects that the company is involved in, and perhaps new products or services that it hopes to offer, and clearly the idea is that this information should encourage potential investors to act on what they read in the document by buying shares. In this situation, then, it would be clear that the company intended people to act on their statements. But if a director of a company made the same kinds of statements about the company to someone they happened to meet at a party, it would be harder to show that the director intended that person to act on their words. They might have intended that, but they might just have been making conversation, so the court will need to look at all the circumstances. In this case, for example, it might be relevant to ask whether the claimant had ever bought shares, or expressed an interest in doing so, and, if so, whether the defendant knew that.

The false representation does not have to be made to the claimant, as long as the defendant intends the claimant, or a group of people which includes the claimant, to act on it. In *Langridge* v. *Levy* (1837), the defendant sold a defective gun to a man, who mentioned that it was for his son. The seller knew there was a problem with the gun, but he told the buyer that it was in good condition. Because of the defect, the man's son was injured while using it, and he was able to claim for deceit.

Case Summary

Disputes over meaning

As we saw in the chapter on defamation, the same statement can have more than one possible meaning, and one meaning can be true while the other is not. If the claimant thinks that a statement means one thing, which is false, and the defendant says they meant something else, which is true, which meaning does the defendant have to have intended the claimant to act on? This was the question in *Smith* v. *Chadwick* (1884). The defendants issued a company prospectus which said that 'the present value of the turnover or output of the entire works is over £1,000,000 per annum'. This could have been taken to mean that the business was capable of making that amount of money (which was true), but it could equally have been taken to mean that the business had actually made that amount in a particular year (which was not true). The claimants said that they had believed the defendants were saying the business had actually made that sum, and that was what they had acted on. The court held that in order for the defendants to be liable, the claimants had to show that the defendants had intended them to act on the false meaning, or had deliberately made use of the fact that there were two possible meanings to deceive the claimants. If the defendants had not realised that there was another meaning than the true one, or if they had not intended any possible untrue meaning to influence the claimant, they were not liable.

Case Summary

Acting on the statement

The claimant must show that the false statement influenced them to act as they did. Take, for example, a situation where I tell you that a pair of shoes I want to sell you are by a well-known designer, and this is a lie. If what I have said about the designer makes you more likely to buy the shoes, you have acted on my false representation. But if you do not have the slightest interest in designer labels, and just buy the shoes because you think they are nice, you have not acted on my representation and you have no claim in deceit.

Case Summary

This was the situation in *Smith* v. *Chadwick*, the case we looked at above, where the claimants bought shares in a company because of what they read in the prospectus. Another part of their claim was that they had bought the shares because it said in the company prospectus that a particular person was a director of the company, when in fact he was not. However, the claimants admitted that they had never heard of this person before they read the prospectus, and so the Court found that the claim made about him could not have played any part in their decision to buy the shares.

Case Summary

However, the false representation does not have to be the only reason why the claimant acted, as long as it is one of them. This was established in *Edgington* v. *Fitzmaurice*, the case we looked at earlier, where the company directors lied about their intentions by saying they planned to build up the company when in fact they wanted money to pay their debts. Mr Edgington had mistakenly believed that if he invested he would get a charge over company property, which meant that if the company went bust he would have some legal protection for his money. This was not true, and was his own mistake, not caused by anything the defendants had said. He admitted that had he known he would not get a charge on company property he would not have invested. That being the case, could he still claim that acting on the lie about the directors' intentions for the business had caused his loss, rather than his own mistake? The Court of Appeal said he could. The false statement did not have to be his only reason for acting, as long as it influenced him to act as he did.

Case Summary

Nor is it necessary for the claimant to prove that they would definitely not have acted as they did if the false representation had not been made. In *Downs* v. *Chappell* (1997), the claimants bought a bookshop business from the defendant. They were an older couple, who had recently given up running a newsagent's shop because it was too much for them, and were looking for a small business that would support them until they retired. The defendant showed them a set of accounts which showed that the shop was making a very good and growing profit, and they bought it. In fact, although the business was making a profit, the accounts had greatly exaggerated the amount it was making. The evidence was that the claimants would probably have bought the shop even if they had been shown accurate accounts, but the Court of Appeal allowed a claim for deceit because it was clear that the false representation the defendant made had played a substantial part in the decision to buy. They said that the situation would have been different if, for example, the claimants had asked an expert to check the accounts and discovered that they were incorrect, but gone ahead anyway. In that case the accounts would not have played a role in their decision and so they could not have been said to have acted on the false statement.

You be the judge

Q: **Amanda is an expert on rare books. She finds a very early edition of what was her favourite book as a child, *Alice in Wonderland*, at a book fair. The seller tells her it is worth £500, although he knows that it is actually worth less. However, Amanda has been doing a lot of research into children's books lately, and she believes that this edition is actually worth about £750. She buys it. She later has it valued, and finds it is worth only £200.**

Does Amanda have a case in deceit?

A: No. Amanda did not buy the book because the seller told her it was worth £500, she bought it because she thought it was worth £750. Therefore she was not acting on the false statement.

Damage to the claimant

The claimant must be caused damage as a result of acting on the false statement. In most deceit cases, this will be financial loss, but **damages** can be given for any kind of loss which results from the false representation. This includes personal injury, as we saw in *Langridge* v. *Levy*, the case of the faulty shotgun, and in *Shelley* v. *Paddock* (1979), damages were awarded for mental distress where the claimant was induced to buy a property in Spain because of false representations by the defendant and it turned out that the house was not his to sell. As we will see in the Law in Action box, Claims about paternity, on page 480, damages have also been ordered – controversially – for the distress of a man who was told he was the biological father of a child who was actually someone else's.

Case Summary

The claimant must show that the loss or damage was caused by them acting on the false representation. As we saw in Chapter 3, when assessing **causation** the courts will ask not only whether the tort was the factual cause of the loss, but whether the loss is too remote from the defendant's behaviour to make the defendant liable. In negligence and most other torts, a defendant will only be liable for losses which were **reasonably foreseeable**. However, in deceit, the test for whether a loss is too remote is not reasonable foreseeability, but the **direct consequence test**. Using this test, the defendant will be liable for any loss or damage which directly flows from the claimant acting on the false representation, even if the defendant could not have foreseen that loss or damage. This test is clearly harder on the defendant than the reasonable foreseeability test, and the courts have made it clear that this is to mark the fact that someone committing deceit has deliberately behaved badly, in contrast with someone committing negligence who may simply have been careless. In *Smith New Court Securities* v. *Scrimgeour Vickers*, the facts of which we will look at below, Lord Steyn said the reason for imposing the direct consequence test was that:

> First it serves a deterrent purpose in discouraging fraud . . . in the battle against fraud civil remedies can play a useful and beneficial role. Second, as between fraudster and the innocent party, moral considerations militate in favour of requiring the fraudster to bear the risk of the misfortunes caused by his fraud.

Calculating damages for deceit

The way the direct consequence test works can be seen in *Smith New Court Securities* v. *Scrimgeour Vickers* (1997). The claimant was persuaded to buy 28 million shares in a company called Ferranti, at the price of 82p each, after the defendant falsely stated that there were other buyers who wanted them. The shares were in fact only worth 78p each at that time. Unknown to the defendant, Ferranti itself had been the victim of a major fraud, and when this fraud was made public, the shares dropped to 44p each. The claimant successfully sued the defendant for deceit, and the defendant argued that the damages should be the difference between the value of the shares at 78p and the value if they had been worth 82p. The House of Lords disagreed. They said that the fraud on Ferranti had already happened when the defendant made the false representation, even though neither the defendant nor the claimant knew that. The claimant bought the shares because of what the defendant had said, and therefore as a direct result of the false representation, the claimant ended up with 28 million shares which were only worth 44p each. Therefore, the defendant had to pay damages equal to the difference between 28 million shares at 82p, and 28 million shares at 44p.

Case Summary

Writing and drafting

You are a trainee solicitor in a high street firm. Your boss has just seen a client who she thinks may have a claim in deceit, but such claims do not come up very often in a small firm and she wants to remind herself of the rules of the tort. Prepare a memo, detailing the rules of the tort, and giving brief details of the key cases.

Law in action Claims about paternity

As you will have seen by now, most deceit claims involve business transactions of some kind. However, in recent years there have been attempts to use the tort in a completely different situation, where women have lied to men about who is the father of their children. In England, this issue was raised in *A* v. *B* (2007), where the claimant sued his former girlfriend after discovering that the son he thought was his was actually fathered by someone she had had an affair with. He did not find this out until the little boy was 5 years old. He sued for deceit. His girlfriend had not known for sure that the boy was not his, but she had had unprotected sex with the other man at the relevant time. Mr A knew that there had been at least a one-night stand with someone else, and so had asked her whether he was the father of the child. She repeatedly said yes. As we saw above, to be liable for deceit, a defendant must either know they are making an untrue statement, or be reckless as to whether it was true or not. The court held that in this case, the fact that the defendant did not know whether she was telling the truth when she said Mr A was the father, but ignored the possibility that it was not true, was clearly enough to establish recklessness. Mr A successfully claimed damages for the distress caused by finding out that the child, who he loved as his own, was not in fact his.

A similar case in Australia, *Magill* v. *Magill* (2006), failed on the facts, but the High Court of Australia made it clear that it had no policy objection to deceit being used in this kind of case.

The decision in *A* v. *B* (2007) was a controversial one, which was widely reported in the press. While some argued that men in Mr A's situation had a right to know the truth, it was also suggested that the case effectively meant women had a legal duty to 'spill the beans' if they had doubts about who had fathered their child, and that this could lead to many more families breaking up, with consequent harm to the child, even if the doubts proved to be wrong. Mr A was also criticised for taking the case to court, because of the effect this would have on the child who, like Mr A, was an innocent victim. The main question raised was whether this was an area where an action that was designed for commercial disputes was really appropriate, even though in the case of *A* v. *B* it proved quite straightforward to frame the facts into a claim for deceit.

Source: Pearson Education Ltd/Nick Koudis/Photodisc

Claimants at fault

In most of the torts we have looked at so far, the **defence** of **contributory negligence** applies, and will reduce the damages payable where the damage or loss was partly the claimant's own fault. This is not the case in deceit. As we saw above, the courts take very seriously the fact that a defendant has deliberately been dishonest, and so a defendant can still be liable even if the claimant's own carelessness contributed to their loss. In *Standard Chartered Bank* v. *Pakistan National Shipping Corporation* (2002), the claimants paid money in a deal which they had been induced to make by the defendants' false representation. However, due to their own negligent research, they thought they could get the money back, and there was evidence that they would not have paid it if they had known that that would not be possible. The defendants argued that this amounted to contributory negligence; in other words, if the claimants had been more careful, they would never have paid the money. The House of Lords rejected this argument. Lord Hoffmann said:

Case Summary

> It is said here that [the claimants] would not have paid if they had . . . not mistakenly and negligently thought that they could obtain reimbursement. In my opinion, the law takes no account of these other reasons for payment. This rule seems to me based upon sound policy. It would not seem just that a fraudulent defendant's liability should be reduced on the grounds that, for whatever reason, the victim should not have made the payment which the defendant successfully induced him to make.

Deceit and negligent misstatement

Case Navigator

In Chapter 5 we looked at claims for **negligent misstatement**, as developed from the case of ***Hedley Byrne* v. *Heller***. As you will have noticed by now, this kind of claim looks quite similar to one in deceit, since they are both based on liability for statements which induce someone to act in a way that ends up causing loss or damage to them. When *Hedley Byrne* was decided, it was seen as a way of providing more protection to claimants than the tort of deceit did. This was because in deceit the requirement that the defendant must know that their representation was untrue, or not care whether it was true or not, could be very difficult to prove. In addition, this requirement meant that defendants who believed that what they said was correct, but had not bothered to check, even if the statement might be a very important one, would not be liable. Under *Hedley Byrne*, however, they could be.

However, in practice the two types of action offer different advantages to claimants. Although a claimant in deceit must prove knowledge or recklessness, there need not be a special relationship between the parties, as there must be in negligent misstatement. Nor does the claimant have to show it was reasonable for them to have acted on the defendant's statement, as they do in negligent misstatement. They only have to show that the statement played a significant role in their decision.

> deceit has two very strong advantages for claimants

In addition, deceit has two very strong advantages for claimants who can prove their case. The first advantage is that contributory negligence is not a defence, so even if the claimants themselves have been careless or stupid in acting on the representation they can still win their case. This would not usually be the situation in negligent misstatement, because, first, this might make it unreasonable to have relied on the statement, and secondly, the defence of contributory negligence is available. The second big advantage is that the test for remoteness, the direct consequence test, is much more generous to claimants than the reasonable foreseeability test used in negligent misstatement. For example, we saw in *Smith New Court Securities* v. *Scrimgeour Vickers* that the claimant was allowed to claim for the effects of a fraud that neither party knew about when the false representation was made. This meant that they could claim for the difference between 28 million shares costing 82p and 28 million shares costing 44p. If the reasonable foreseeability test was applied, however, the fact that the defendant could not have known about the previous fraud would mean that it would be ignored when calculating damages. In that case, the claimant would only have been able to get the difference between the price of the shares at 82p and the price of 78p, which was what they were actually worth when he bought them. When you are talking about 28 million shares, that makes a big difference.

Table 19.1 Differences between negligent misstatement and deceit

	Negligent misstatement under *Hedley Byrne* v. *Heller*	**Deceit**
Special relationship between the parties required	Yes	No
Must be reasonable for the claimant to rely on the statement	Yes	No
Defendant's state of mind	Negligence	Knowledge/recklessness
Test of remoteness	Reasonable foreseeability	Direct consequence
Contributory negligence available as defence	Yes	No

Summary

- The tort of deceit compensates for loss caused by false statements made knowingly or recklessly.
- The statement can be written, spoken or in the form of conduct. Silence is not sufficient but there can be liability for half-truths, deliberate concealment, failure to mention a change in situation or where there is a statutory duty to reveal information.
- The false statement must be a factual one, and not a statement of opinion. A statement of intention may count if it falsely suggests an intention the defendant did not have.
- The defendant must know the statement is false, or be indifferent as to whether it is true.
- The defendant must intend the claimant to act on the statement, but the statement need not be made to the claimant. If a statement has more than one possible meaning, the defendant is only liable if they intended the claimant to act on an untrue meaning.
- The claimant must act on the statement, but it need not be the only reason for acting.
- The claimant must be caused damage, and the defendant is liable for all damage which flows directly from the claimant's reliance on the false representation. Damages can be claimed for financial loss, property damage, personal injury and mental distress.

Question and answer*

Problem: Karen is the owner of a garage, which she is trying to sell to Mark. Karen has 20 years of experience in her business, while Mark has never been involved in the motor industry in any way. During their negotiations, Karen tells Mark 'You could earn about £100,000 a year from this business.' Mark assumes that she means the business currently makes profits of £100,000, but in fact it makes around £50,000 a year, and Karen knows this. The accounts for the business show the real profit, but Mark does not ask to see them.

Mark knows that Karen is very popular with her customers, and he makes it clear to Karen that he is not interested in buying the garage if his new business will be in competition with any new business she might set up. Karen says 'You won't need to worry about competition from me, I'm going to set up a new place in Bigtown', which is a town 100 miles away. Before the sale is completed, he finds out from a friend that Karen has established a new business in Bigtown, but she has also set up another branch of it half a mile away from the old garage that he is buying. By now he is so excited about starting his business that he decides to go ahead with the deal anyway. Lots of the garage's old customers go to Karen's new business and, by the end of the first year, Mark's business has made only around £20,000.

Advise Mark as to whether he has a claim against Karen in deceit.

You should allow yourself no more than 40 minutes to complete this task.

Essay: Given the introduction of claims for negligent misstatement, in *Hedley Byrne* v. *Heller*, what role does the tort of deceit play in modern law?

This question should be answered in 40 minutes.

* Answer guidance is provided at the end of the chapter.

Further reading

Keeton, R.E. (1937) 'Fraud: statements of intention', 15 *Texas Law Review* 409.
This article looks at the principles behind the tort of deceit. It includes some discussion of American cases, but makes some useful arguments which apply to English law as well.

Treitel, G. (1969) 'Damages for deceit', 32 MLR 556.
This article looks at how damages for deceit are calculated, and compares this with the calculation of damages for breach of contract.

Question and answer guidance

Problem: There are two statements here which could potentially lead to liability for deceit, so take each one in turn and work through the elements of the tort.

Starting with the claim that Mark 'could earn about £100,000 a year', consider whether this is a statement of fact, or of opinion; the fact that Karen knows the garage business, and her business, is relevant here. You should also point out that she would have to be deliberately making a false statement or reckless as to whether it was true, in order to be liable; as she knows the garage only makes £50,000 this will depend on whether she meant the £100,000 claim to be a statement of opinion, or she was lying about a statement of fact. Karen's statement has two possible meanings, one false and one true, so you need to consider what she actually intended Mark to act on. We do not have any evidence either way on this, but you can discuss the case of *Smith* v. *Chadwick*, and explain how the judgment there applies to this situation: if Karen does not realise there is a possible false meaning to her statement, or had not intended any false meaning to influence Mark, she will not be liable. Consider too whether it makes any difference that Mark was offered the chance to see the accounts, but didn't bother to look at them.

Turning to the second statement, about Karen moving to another town, you need to consider whether this is a false statement – it is factually true, but does what she leaves out make the statement misleading, and what difference does this make? Then look at whether it is a statement of fact; the case of *Edgington* v. *Fitzmaurice* is relevant here. Could Karen have meant what she said at the time but later changed her mind, and if so, does that make a difference? Consider too whether Mark could be said to have relied on Karen's statement, remembering that it need not be the only reason for him buying the garage.

Essay: This question requires you to show a knowledge of both deceit and negligent misstatement (which is covered in Chapter 5), and the differences between them. You could start your answer with a brief outline of each tort, and point out that although they deal with similar situations there are important differences between them, which mean that deceit still has a role to play in modern law.

Then work through some of the key differences between the torts (you'll find these in Table 19.1 on page 482), and explain why these justify a need for both torts.

For example, negligent misstatement will only apply where there is a special relationship between the parties, and the reason for this, as explained in cases like *Esso* v. *Mardon*, is that it is the special relationship that justifies requiring the defendant to take reasonable care in giving advice. But where we are talking about deliberate or reckless dishonesty, it is fair to be stricter on defendants and impose liability without the need for a special relationship. You can explain that for this reason the fact that the defendant intended the claimant to rely on their false statement is enough.

Similarly, the fact that in deceit a claimant does not have to show it was reasonable for them to have acted on the defendant's statement, as they do in negligent misstatement, means a defendant can be liable even when the claimant could have avoided the problem by taking basic precautions. There is an argument that this is fair in cases where the defendant has deliberately set out to be dishonest; you might want to use Lord Hoffmann's quote from *Standard Chartered Bank* to back up this point.

You should also discuss the different rules on causation, and the fact that the direct consequence test is much more generous to claimants than the reasonable foreseeability test used in negligent misstatement. You can use the case of *Smith New Court Securities* v. *Scrimgeour Vickers* to show the difference this can make in practice and point out that, again, the stricter approach is taken because deceit deals with deliberate or reckless dishonesty.

Visit **www.mylawchamber.co.uk/quinntort** to access tools to help you develop and test your knowledge of tort law, including practice exam questions with guidance, annotated weblinks, glossary and key case flashcards, legal newsfeed and legal updates and interactive 'You be the judge' questions.

premium mylawchamber
unrivalled support for legal education

CASE NAVIGATOR
POWERED BY LexisNexis

Use Case Navigator to read in full some of the key cases referenced in this chapter with commentary and questions:

Hedley Byrne & Co. Ltd* v. *Heller & Partners Ltd [1963] 2 All ER 575

Chapter 20 Liability for animals

Key points In this chapter we will be looking at:

- Liability under common law for damage or injury caused by animals
- Liability under the Animals Act 1971
- How the Act classifies different species
- Defences under the Act

Introduction

The cases that we have looked at so far all have one thing in common: the damage or injury has been caused by people, whether individuals acting alone, or in groups such as companies. But can you get compensation if damage or injury is caused by an animal? If a cow strays into your garden and tramples your runner beans, you clearly cannot sue it for trespass, any more than you can sue a poodle if it bites you, but in these situations, as you might guess, the law imposes liability on the owner of the animal, or the person in control of it at the time the damage was done – but only in certain circumstances. This type of liability is the subject of this chapter.

Liability for damage caused by animals can arise in two different ways. The first is that damage caused by animals comes within the scope of several **common law** torts, as in the example of the trespassing cow above. In these types of situation the normal rules associated with those torts apply, as we will see below. The second source of liability is the Animals Act 1971, which provides specific statutory rules about damage caused by animals and is the main subject of this chapter.

You will probably also have heard of the Dangerous Dogs Act 1991, which among other things makes it an offence to possess certain types of dog. This Act imposes criminal liability, and so is not relevant to the issues discussed in this chapter.

Liability for animals at common law

In theory, almost any tort could be committed as a result of something done by an animal – the renowned tort academics Winfield and Jolowicz point out, for example, that a person could be liable in defamation for training a parrot to make defamatory remarks about someone in public (*Winfield and Jolowicz on Tort,* Sweet & Maxwell, 2010). However, the torts most likely to be committed in connection with animals are negligence, nuisance, and trespass against the person.

a person could be liable in defamation for training a parrot to make defamatory remarks

Negligence

Aside from the specific forms of action provided in the Animals Act, negligence is the most likely form of tort claim for damage caused by animals. In such cases, the situation will be that the animal has caused damage, and the owner or controller of it is claimed to have been negligent in failing to prevent the damage. The normal rules of the tort apply, so the owner or controller of an animal will be liable for personal injury or property damage if it was **reasonably foreseeable** that the animal might cause that kind of damage, and the owner or controller failed to take reasonable steps to prevent that happening. This was the case in *Draper* v. *Hodder* (1972), where the **claimant** was a child who had been savaged by a pack of Jack Russell dogs who lived next door. Their owner was an experienced dog breeder, and although the dogs had never attacked anyone before, they did have a habit of running next door in a pack. Expert evidence was given that, as a breed, Jack Russells have a tendency to attack moving people or objects when they are travelling in a pack. The Court held that because the owner had a lot of experience with Jack Russells, he could be expected to know about that tendency and, as he admitted knowing that the dogs were in the habit of running next door, he should have fenced them in. It was therefore foreseeable that someone might be injured by the dogs, and by not fencing them in, the owner had breached his **duty of care** in negligence.

Case Summary

Nuisance

Animals can be a source of noise, smells and general disruption, and where this affects neighbouring land there may be a claim against the owners/controllers in nuisance, following the normal rules of the tort. In *Leeman* v. *Montagu* (1936), for example, the noise made by cockerels from about 2 am every morning was held to be a nuisance, as was the smell of pigs in *Wheeler* v. *JJ Saunders* (1996).

Case Summary

Trespass to the person

As we saw in Chapter 12, trespass to the person includes both assault, meaning to put someone in fear of violence, and battery, which means to intentionally apply force to another person without their consent. Both of these can be committed using an animal: threatening someone with a snarling dog can lead to liability for assault just as inciting a dog to bite someone could constitute a battery

threatening someone with a gun would, while inciting a dog to bite someone could constitute a battery. The normal rules and **defences** apply.

However, remember that for assault and battery the behaviour has to be intentional, so these torts only cover situations where the owner or controller of the animal deliberately uses or encourages it to threaten or attack someone. If the owner simply failed to take precautions to prevent the animal attacking someone, the correct claim would be negligence.

The Animals Act 1971

the Act divides animals into two different groups: dangerous species and non-dangerous species

The basic principle behind the Animals Act 1971 is that any liability imposed on the owners or keepers of animals should be related to the degree of risk they have caused or allowed to arise, though how far it has achieved this is a matter of debate. For this reason, the Act divides animals into two different groups: dangerous species and non-dangerous species. Where someone owns or keeps an animal classified as a dangerous species, the Act imposes **strict liability** for any damage caused by the animal, which means the owner/keeper can be liable, even if there was nothing they could have done to prevent the damage. The thinking behind this is that if you choose to keep an animal from a dangerous species, you must accept the risk that it might cause harm. Where someone owns or keeps an animal from a non-dangerous species, however, they will only be liable in certain circumstances and, as we will see later on, the rules on this form of liability require the courts to assess how far the owner/keeper was actually at fault for what happened.

Under the Animals Act, camels are classified as dangerous and dogs as non-dangerous.

One area of the Act which sometimes causes confusion is that the way it classifies different species as dangerous or non-dangerous does not necessarily correspond to the way most of us would decide whether a species was dangerous or not. Under the Animals Act, camels are classified as dangerous and dogs as non-dangerous. However, if you take care to refer to the definitions under the Act when looking at cases involving animals, rather than relying on your own common-sense idea of whether a species is dangerous or not, the distinction is quite straightforward to apply.

Who is liable under the Act?

The Act imposes liability on the 'keeper' of the animal. In many cases this will be the owner, but it need not be. Section 6(3) specifies that a person will be considered to be the 'keeper' of a particular animal if:

(a) he owns the animal or has it in his possession; or

(b) he is the head of a household in which a member under the age of 16 owns the animal or has it in his possession.

Section 6(3)(b) covers cases where the animal is owned or kept by a child, and essentially makes their parent or guardian liable for the damage done.

Liability for dangerous animals

As mentioned earlier, the Act classifies animals into dangerous and non-dangerous species, each with different rules on liability. Section 6(2) of the Act defines dangerous species as:

(a) a species not commonly domesticated in the British Isles; and

(b) whose fully grown animals normally have such characteristics that they are likely, unless restrained, to cause severe damage or that any damage that they may cause is likely to be severe.

To be classified as a dangerous animal, therefore, the animal must belong to a species that is not usually kept as pets or working animals in this country. That means that as well as foreign animals, such as lions and tigers, it includes wild animals that are native to this country, such as foxes and wildcats. The fact that an animal is often kept as a pet or a working animal in other countries is irrelevant: camels, for example, are widely domesticated in Arab countries, but under English law they still come under the category of dangerous animals.

If an animal species is one that is commonly domesticated in this country, it will be classified as non-dangerous. If it is not one that is commonly domesticated in this country, there is a second question to ask, stated in section 6(2)(b). This requires that the species must either be likely to cause severe damage if not restrained, or must be the kind of species that may be unlikely to cause damage but, if they did, would probably cause serious damage.

The first part of section 6(2)(b) is fairly straightforward, and refers to any species which could obviously be dangerous if it escaped from its enclosure or cage; obvious examples would be lions or tigers. But what about the second part of section 6(2)(b): species which are unlikely to cause damage, but which would cause serious damage if they did? An example of this kind of species was given in *Behrens* v. *Bertram Mills Circus* (1957), where the claimants were injured when a frightened elephant, belonging to the circus, ran off and knocked over the kiosk they were working in, injuring them. The circus argued that the elephant was tame and well-trained, and had not actually attacked the claimants. However, the Court held that although that particular elephant was not aggressive or violent, and was therefore not likely to cause serious damage if unrestrained, the sheer size of any elephant meant that if it did cause damage, the damage was likely to be serious, and so it was classified as a dangerous animal. The case was decided under common law, before the Animals Act was passed, but the distinction under the Act works in the same way, and it is likely that any very large animal would fall into this category because its size alone means any damage done is likely to be severe.

Case Summary

There are two things to remember here: first, that to be classified as a dangerous animal, a species must fulfil *both* section 6(2)(a) and (b), and secondly, that the classification applies to species and not particular animals. If the species as a whole falls within the definition of dangerous, it does not matter that the particular animal is trained not to be dangerous.

Out and about

Try to think of at least 20 species of animal that would be classified as dangerous under the Animals Act 1971. Are there any that surprise you?

Figure 20.1 Dangerous and non-dangerous animals

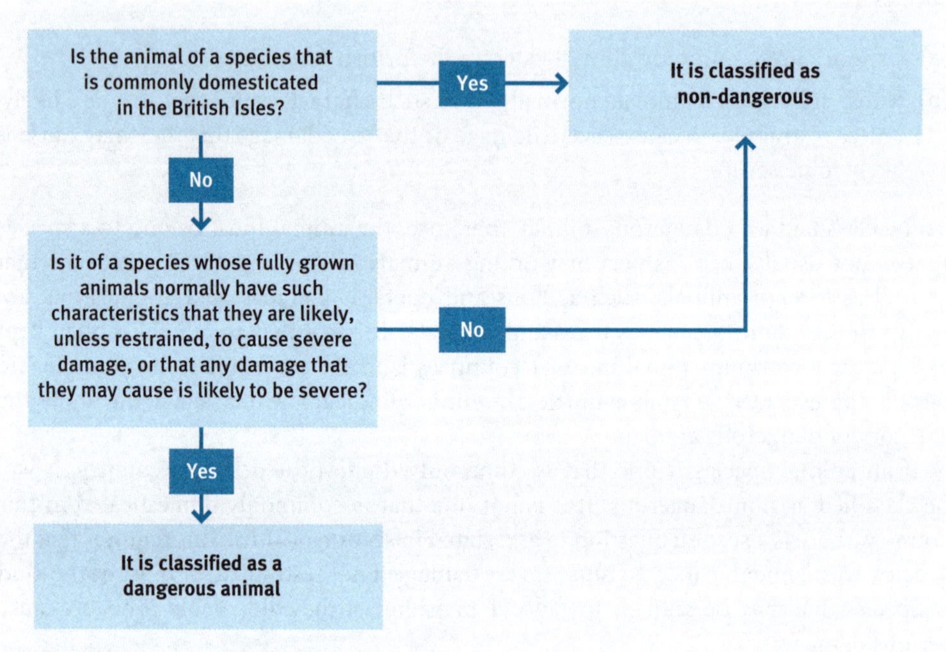

Strict liability

If an animal falls within the definition of a dangerous species, strict liability applies to any harm it causes. Section 2(1) provides that

> Where any damage is caused by an animal which belongs to a dangerous species, any person who is a keeper of the animal is liable for the damage, except as otherwise provided by this Act.

The reference to 'as otherwise provided' refers to the fact that the Act lays down three defences (see below). However, if a **defendant** cannot claim one of these, liability is strict, which means that it does not matter whether the animal's keeper was at fault, or whether they did their best to prevent the damage. If they are the keeper of the animal that caused the damage, and they have no defence, they will be liable. As we saw earlier, the thinking behind this is that keeping a dangerous species of animal is a risky activity, and anyone who chooses to do it must take responsibility for the risk.

Note that although the animal has to be one which makes it likely that the damage done will be severe, it is not necessary that the damage done is actually severe, in order for liability to arise. If a tiger were to get loose from a circus, get into someone's garden and dig up all their plants, for example, the keeper of the tiger would be strictly liable for the damage done, because the tiger would be classified as a dangerous species. Once that classification is made, it does not matter that the damage is not related to the dangerous characteristics of the animal.

Case Summary

Nor does the animal have to be vicious in any way: in *Behrens* v. *Bertram Mills Circus*, the case of the runaway elephant, Mr Justice Devlin commented that if an escaped tiger got into someone's house in the night and jumped on to their bed, and the unfortunate homeowner suffered a heart attack at the shock of waking up to find a tiger lying on their chest, the owner would be liable, even if the tiger was just being friendly.

You be the judge

Q: John has a pet lion called Susan, who has lived with him since she was a cub. He has trained her never to attack or even chase anyone, and she has never done so. Recently, someone left open the back gate to John's garden and Susan wandered out. She got out into the road and caused a car accident in which Peter was injured. Peter wants to make a claim under the Animals Act 1971. Would Susan be classified as a dangerous or non-dangerous animal?

A: Susan would be classified as a dangerous animal, since lions are not commonly domesticated in this country, and as a species lions are likely to cause damage if not restrained. As we saw in *Behrens* v. *Bertram Mills Circus*, it does not matter that Susan herself is not likely to attack anyone because she is trained, nor does it matter that the damage was not caused by her attacking anyone.

Writing and drafting

Read again the 'You be the judge' problem above. Now imagine you are a trainee solicitor and John is your client. He is being sued by Peter and you need to advise him about his liability. He insists that Susan is no more dangerous than a cat, and he cannot understand why you say a court would classify her as a dangerous animal. Write a letter to him, explaining in simple terms why the case would be judged under section 2(1) of the Act.

Liability for non-dangerous animals

All species which do not fall within the category of dangerous, as explained above, are classed as non-dangerous, and liability for these animals is covered by the provisions of section 2(2) of the Act. Again, it is the species which is classified as dangerous, not the individual animal. Damage or injury caused by a dog, for example, no matter how vicious, will always be judged under section 2(2), because dogs are commonly domesticated in this country and therefore do not fit the legal definition of dangerous.

Remember that there are two parts to the definition of dangerous and to be classified as dangerous the species must fit both of them. So a species that fits the first part because it is not commonly domesticated in this country, but not the second part, will be classified as non-dangerous.

You be the judge

Q: Which of these animals would be classified as dangerous under the Animals Act 1971, and which would be considered non-dangerous?

- **(a) A large pit bull terrier which has already bitten two people.**
- **(b) A cat.**
- **(c) A bear that has been kept as a pet and trained to be obedient and gentle.**
- **(d) An elephant.**

Source: Pearson Education Ltd/Digital Stock

A: (c) and (d) would be considered dangerous. Neither of them are commonly domesticated in this country, even though elephants are used as working animals in other parts of the world. As a species, bears are known to attack people and so would be considered to be likely to cause damage if unrestrained. Elephants are generally not aggressive towards people, but their size alone means that if they did cause damage it is likely to be severe. The pit bull terrier and the cat would both be considered non-dangerous, because they are species that are commonly domesticated in this country. In ordinary language, we would of course describe this particular pit bull terrier as dangerous, but under the Act it still falls within the definition of non-dangerous species. The fact that it is known to have attacked would however be relevant when deciding the keeper's liability under section 2(2) of the Act.

Elements of liability for non-dangerous animals

As we saw earlier, where an accident involves an animal classified as dangerous, the claimant need only prove that the animal caused the damage and, as long as there is no defence, the keeper is liable. With non-dangerous animals, however, the situation is different, and a claimant must satisfy three tests in order to establish that the keeper is liable. These are set out in section 2(2), which provides that the keeper of a non-dangerous animal will only be liable for damage caused by it if each of the following three requirements is satisfied:

(a) The damage is of a kind which the animal, unless restrained, was likely to cause, or which, if caused by the animal, was likely to be severe; and

(b) the likelihood of the damage or of its being severe was due to characteristics of the animal which are not normally so found in animals of the same species or are not normally found except at particular times or in particular circumstances; and

(c) those characteristics were known to that keeper or were at any time known to a person who at that time had charge of the animal as the keeper's servant or, where that keeper is the head of a household, were known to another keeper of the animal who is a member of that household and under the age of sixteen.

In this section we can see again the attempt to link liability with the degree of risk taken, as the rules above are clearly designed to make sure that the keeper of a non-dangerous animal is not liable unless they knew there was a risk. Even so, as with section (2)(1), liability is technically strict, so if the situation satisfies all three of the tests above, and the keeper has no defence, he or she will be liable, even if they did their best to prevent the damage. As we will see, there are questions about whether recent interpretations of the Act push strict liability too far.

All three of the requirements must be satisfied, so it is sensible to work through them in turn when considering whether someone has incurred liability under the Act.

The kind of damage

Section 2(2)(a) requires that the damage caused has to be of a kind that the animal was likely to cause or, if the animal was not likely to cause that kind of damage, the damage it could cause was likely to be severe. In *Curtis* v. *Betts* (1990), a bull mastiff attacked and injured the claimant when he went up to talk to it as it was being loaded into its owner's car to go off on a journey. In that case section 2(2)(a) was easily satisfied, as a bull mastiff is a big dog with a powerful bite.

Case Summary

The characteristics of the animal

Section 2(2)(b) provides two different sources of liability. The first ('characteristics of the animal which are not normally so found in animals of the same species') is fairly straightforward, and means that the particular animal concerned must have permanent or habitual characteristics which you would not usually expect in that sort of animal. For example, in *Kite* v. *Napp* (1982) a dog which had the peculiar habit of attacking people who were carrying handbags was held to fall within this category.

Case Summary

The characteristic does not necessarily have to be a tendency to attack, however; it only has to be a characteristic which is present in that particular animal and not normally in others of the same species, and is likely to make any damage severe. In *Wallace* v. *Newton* (1982) the claimant worked with horses, and was injured while she was looking after the defendant's horse. The horse was known to be nervous, and while being loaded onto a trailer it jumped forward and injured the claimant's arm. The Court held that the horse did not need to have a tendency to attack people; section 2(2)(b) could be satisfied by the fact that the horse had a tendency to behave in a particular way when nervous, which was not found in most horses, and which could clearly cause severe damage or injury.

Case Summary

The second limb ('characteristics . . . which are not normally found except at particular times or in particular circumstances') deals with temporary characteristics of an animal, which make it behave in a dangerous way in certain situations even if it is not normal for them to do so most of the time. This part of the Act has caused problems for the courts, because it is badly drafted and has two potential meanings. First, it could mean characteristics which are normal to that type of animal, but only in certain situations. An example would be that it is quite normal for a female dog with puppies to attack anyone she thinks is threatening them, even though attacking people would not be normal behaviour for a dog at any other time. The second possible meaning is that the section refers to characteristics which are not normal for that type of animal, but exist in the particular animal concerned and only arise at particular times or in particular circumstances. This might include, for example, a dog which was docile with people it knows but had a tendency to attack strangers.

The difference between these two possible interpretations is very important. If the second interpretation is preferred, keepers would only be liable if they knew that their animal had abnormal characteristics, but if the first interpretation is the right one, keepers could be liable even if their animals were behaving as any other animal would in the circumstances. Remember that if these tests are satisfied, strict liability is imposed, so a keeper is liable even if they have taken reasonable care. The first interpretation therefore exposes animal owners and keepers to potentially very wide liability.

Which interpretation?

Until 2003 it was not clear which interpretation was correct, and in four Court of Appeal decisions two had favoured one interpretation and two the other. We need only look at two of them to see the effects of the two different interpretations. In *Curtis* v. *Betts*, the case we looked at above where the child was attacked by a bull mastiff, the dog was not normally vicious and had always been friendly with the young claimant, but was said to have attacked him because he approached it when it was being put into the owner's car. The dog saw this as its territory, and there was evidence that it was normal for such dogs to attack when defending their territory though not at other times. The Court adopted the first interpretation of section 2(2)(b), that the dangerous characteristic can be one that is quite normal for that kind of animal but only in certain circumstances, and the owner was liable.

Case Summary

In *Breeden* v. *Lampard* (unreported, 21 March 1985), however, the Court of Appeal favoured the second interpretation, that the dangerous characteristic must be one which is abnormal. The claimant was involved in a fox hunt, and when he got near the defendant's horse it kicked out and injured his leg. Evidence was given that it was quite normal for horses to kick out when they were approached too closely or too quickly, and Lord Justice Lloyd stated that:

Case Summary

> If liability is based on the possession of some abnormal characteristic known to the owner, then I cannot see any sense in imposing liability when the animal is behaving in a perfectly normal way for all animals of that species in those circumstances, even though it would not be normal for those animals to behave that way in other circumstances.

The defendant was therefore not liable.

So which is the correct interpretation? The matter was resolved – though not without causing controversy – by the decision in *Mirvahedy* v. *Henley* (2003), where the House of Lords opted for the first interpretation, holding that the dangerous characteristic does not need to be an abnormal one, and keepers can be liable even if the characteristic which causes damage is perfectly normal in that species in that situation. The claimant in the case was seriously injured when his car collided with a horse owned by the defendants. The horse had been kept, with three others, in a field with an electric fence and a wooden fence. On the night in question, something (it was never discovered what) had frightened them, and they stampeded their way out of the field and ended up on the busy road where the accident happened. Evidence was given that although it was not generally normal for horses to behave in this way, it was normal for them to do so when they had been badly frightened. Therefore the behaviour which caused the damage could be described as 'characteristics . . . which are not normally found except at particular times or in particular circumstances', falling within section 2(2)(b). The defendants were therefore liable for the damage.

Case Summary

It was suggested in *Mirvahedy* that section 2(2)(b) should not apply, because it would be wrong to impose strict liability on an owner for behaviour which was quite normal. The defendants' lawyers argued that the Act was only ever intended to impose strict liability where an animal had unusual characteristics, either all the time or at certain times, that posed a risk to others. The House of Lords rejected this view, stating that section 2(2)(b) also imposed strict liability in situations where an owner knew that the animal had characteristics which were perfectly normal for its breed and only arose in certain circumstances, but which could make the animal dangerous in those circumstances. Lord Nicholls gave the example of a dog owner who knows that bitches with puppies are likely to bite, and said it was just as reasonable to expect them to accept liability for injuries caused when their dog has puppies as it is to expect an owner of a dog known to be generally vicious to accept liability for any injury it causes. The decision has proved very controversial and led to calls for a change in the law – see the Law in Action box, below.

The characteristic must be dangerous

A characteristic found in an animal will only create liability if that characteristic is a dangerous one. In *McKenny* v. *Foster* (2008), the defendant's cow had recently been separated from her 7-month-old calf. She was in a properly enclosed and gated field, and had shown no signs of distress when the calf was taken away. Shortly afterwards, she somehow managed to escape by climbing a 6-barred gate and crossing a 12-foot cattle grid. The latter is a device used to stop animals escaping, which consists of metal bars across a dip in the road with gaps between the bars that are wide enough for animals' feet to slip through, which puts them off walking on the grid. The cow in the case was thought to have either jumped clear over the grid or somehow picked her way across on the bars. She then strayed on to a busy road, and was hit by a car driven by the claimant. The claimant's partner and another passenger died in the crash, and the farmer was sued. Expert evidence showed that what had caused the cow to act in this way had to be extreme agitation and distress at being separated from her calf, but that it was not in any way normal for a cow separated from a calf to act as this one had done. The Court of Appeal stressed that for a characteristic of the animal to lead to liability, it had to be both dangerous and to have caused the damage or injury. It was accepted that the cow's maternal instinct to want to be with her calf was a perfectly normal characteristic of a cow separated from her calf. But it was not this instinct in itself which was dangerous or had caused the damage, so this characteristic was not enough to impose liability. The characteristic which was dangerous and had caused the damage was this particular cow's extreme agitation at being separated from her calf, and this was not normal in any circumstances nor was it known to the defendant, so there was no liability.

Case Summary

Characteristics and damage

As we saw above, liability for animals classified as non-dangerous has two parts. First, section 2(2)(a) requires that the damage caused has to be of a kind that the animal was likely to cause, or if the animal was not likely to cause that kind of damage, the damage it could cause was likely to be severe. And, secondly, section 2(2)(b) states that the likelihood of the damage or of its being severe must be due to characteristics of the animal which are not normally so found in animals of the same species or are not normally found except at particular times or in particular circumstances. These two parts do not operate independently of each other; there must be a link between the the argument made under section 2(2)(a) and that made under section 2(2)(b).

This is best explained by the case of *Clark* v. *Bowlt* (2006). The case involved a horse, called Chance, which was being ridden along a public road. As the claimant drove slowly past in his car, Chance veered out from the verge; the rider could not control the horse and it hit the claimant's car. At first instance, it was found that section 2(2)(a) was satisfied

Case Summary

because Chance weighed 600 lbs, and so it was clear that if she caused damage it was likely to be severe, while section 2(2)(b) was satisfied because in particular circumstances, such as when they were frightened, horses had the characteristic of ignoring their rider and moving where they wanted to. The Court of Appeal rejected this view, stating that it was not possible to use one characteristic for the first test and a different one for the second. If it was the weight of the horse that satisfied the test of whether damage was likely to be severe, then weight had to be the characteristic used for section 2(2)(b) as well. As Chance was not abnormally heavy, and the weights of horses do not vary according to times or circumstances, the section 2(2)(b) test was not satisfied. The claim therefore failed.

Law in action The fallout from *Mirvahedy* v. *Henley*

The decision in *Mirvahedy* v. *Henley* came as something of a shock to those who owned or worked with horses. Before the case, it was assumed that a keeper would only be liable where they knew their animal had some abnormal characteristic which made it dangerous, but the *Mirvahedy* decision means that the keeper of an animal can face strict liability even where the animal has behaved perfectly normally in the circumstances. This meant that animal owners and keepers were much more likely to be found liable for accidents, and has become a particular problem for businesses which keep horses, who have to take out insurance against accidents caused by these animals. Because the risk of being found liable had increased, insurance premiums went up by as much as 200 per cent, which meant a riding school, for example, could be faced with a bill of £6,000 a year, when they had previously been paying £2,000. It was claimed that smaller stables and schools might even be forced out of business by the extra costs, and that it was unfair to impose liability on animal keepers who had taken every reasonable precaution. There have been several attempts to change the law and provide protection for keepers who have taken reasonable care, though none has so far succeeded.

Source: Pearson Education Ltd/Corbis

On the other side of the debate, however, the Association of Personal Injury Lawyers has pointed out that allowing keepers to avoid liability would inevitably mean less protection for the victims of accidents.

The knowledge of the keeper

Section 2(2)(c) essentially means that the keeper of the animal will not be liable unless they were aware of the characteristics that meant the animal might be dangerous, or unless an employee or a child for whom the keeper is responsible knew about these characteristics. Again, this is because the Act is only intended to impose strict liability in circumstances where it was reasonable to expect an owner to take extra care.

Writing and drafting

You are a trainee in a firm of solicitors, which has recently opened a branch in a country town and expects to take on new local clients there. Your boss asks you to give a brief talk to your colleagues on the provisions of the Animals Act 1971. Prepare a PowerPoint presentation on the Act that will give them a good overview of the way it works.

Handy tip: Remember that in this task you will be talking to fellow lawyers, so you should include a useful amount of detail, with reference to decided cases where these are necessary to show how the provisions of the Act apply in practice.

Law in action Danger at work

One of the most common areas for claims under the Animals Act is from workers who have to go into people's homes and gardens in the course of their work and who are attacked by pet dogs. The Communications Workers Union estimates that 5,000 postal workers and 400 telecoms engineers are injured by dogs every year. Although in many cases they will be able to sue the dog owner for compensation, the number of attacks suggests this is not enough of a threat to make dog owners keep their pets under control, and so in 2008 the CWU launched its 'Bite Back' campaign, to try to get more serious criminal penalties for the owners of aggressive dogs. So far the changes they want have not been made.

Defences

The Animals Act provides three defences, which can be used to escape liability for damage done by both dangerous and non-dangerous animals.

Section 5(1) states that a defendant will not be liable for damage done by an animal which is wholly the fault of the person who suffers it. In *Nelmes* v. *Chief Constable of Avon and Somerset* (1993), the defence was held to apply where the claimant had kicked a dog which then bit him. Note that this section does not provide a defence where the claimant was only partly to blame for the damage, so it does not operate like the defence of contributory negligence although it sounds similar.

Case Summary

Section 5(2) provides that the owner or keeper of an animal will not be liable for damage done by that animal if the person who suffers the damage voluntarily accepts the risk of it. In *Cummings* v. *Granger* (1977), the claimant was bitten by an Alsatian, which was used as a guard dog in the defendant's scrapyard. The claimant had gone to the yard late at night with her boyfriend, who knew the defendant and had a key. There was a sign saying 'Beware of the Dog', and the claimant admitted that she had seen it. The Court of Appeal held that she knew of the risk and decided to take it; therefore the defendant was covered by section 5(2).

Case Summary

Section 5(3) says that a defendant will not be liable for damage caused by an animal to a trespasser on the premises where the animal is kept, provided that:

- either the animal was not kept there for the protection of persons or property; or
- the animal was kept there for the protection of persons or property, but it was not unreasonable to keep it for that reason.

This effectively means that there is a defence where a trespasser is injured by an animal that is not a guard dog, or where the animal is a guard dog and it is reasonable for the defendant to keep one. The provision actually applies to all animals, not just dogs, but clearly it is most likely to be applied to dogs.

This was accepted as offering an alternative defence in *Cummings* v. *Granger*, since the fact that the scrapyard was in an area that made it likely to be a target for thieves made it reasonable to keep a guard dog there.

Trespassing livestock

The Animals Act also covers liability for livestock which stray on to someone else's land. Livestock is defined by section 11, and includes cattle, horses, donkeys, hinnies (a horse-donkey cross), mules, sheep, goats, poultry and deer (but not wild deer).

Section 4 provides that where livestock belonging to one party stray on to land belonging to someone else, and cause damage to the land or property, the person owning the animals will be liable. This section only covers personal injury or damage to property belonging to the landowner or occupier. Where straying livestock cause damage or injury to someone else, that person would only be able to claim damages if they had a case under section 2 of the Animals Act 1971, or in a common law tort.

The owner of straying livestock is also liable for any costs incurred by the landowner or occupier in keeping the livestock before it is returned to its owner, so if a local farmer's sheep wander on to your land, and you end up having to feed them for a while before they come to collect them, you can claim for the cost. Liability for both damage and expenses is strict, so the owner of the livestock will be liable regardless of whether they knew that the livestock were liable to stray, and regardless of whether they took precautions to stop them straying, unless they have a defence.

Defences covering straying livestock

The defences under section 5(1) and 5(2), described above, also apply to straying livestock, as does the defence of **contributory negligence**. However, it is important to note that it is not possible to use section 5(1) to argue that damage is wholly the fault of the claimant because they did not fence off their own land (and therefore prevent other people's livestock from getting in). This is because there is traditionally no duty in law to fence off your land. This does not apply, however, where the claimant or someone else had a 'duty to fence' the claimant's land, for example under the contract for renting the land.

There is also an additional defence, in section 5(5), which provides that the owner of straying livestock will not be liable where the livestock had strayed from a highway, and their presence there was a reasonable use of the highway.

You be the judge

Q: **Sharon lives next door to Andy, who keeps goats. Knowing that the goats will escape if they can, Andy has put up a high fence between the two gardens, but one day the goats manage to get over the fence and eat all the clothes hanging on Sharon's washing line. Does Sharon have a claim under the Animals Act 1971?**

A: Yes. Sharon can claim under the provisions on straying livestock contained in section 4. This imposes strict liability, so the fact that Andy has taken reasonable precautions will not prevent him being liable.

Remedies

As well as the usual remedy of **damages**, section 4 allows an extra remedy to landowners or occupiers when livestock stray on to their land. The landowner/occupier can keep the livestock until any damage is paid for, though they must notify the police and, if known, the livestock owner within 48 hours. They must feed the livestock while they are kept, but the cost of this can be reclaimed from the owner. If the livestock owner offers to pay for the damage, the livestock must be given back, but if, after 14 days, no such offer has been made, or the owner has not been identified, the landowner/occupier can sell the livestock. They can then keep the cost of feeding the animals, any costs associated with the sale and the cost of the damage done; anything extra must be returned to the owner if identified.

Animals on the highway

Section 8 provides that where animals stray from unfenced land on to a highway, liability will be decided using the ordinary rules of negligence. The reason why this provision was needed was to change the common law that existed before the Act was passed, which held that animal owners were not liable for damage caused by their animals straying on to roads. This rule had been put in place when there were many more animals and many fewer vehicles, and had become out of step with modern problems.

The Act provides for one exception. If the animals wander on to the highway from land that is unfenced, the act of leaving them on that land will not in itself incur liability, as long as the land is common land, or is situated in an area where fencing is not customary, or is a town or village green, and the owner had a right to place the animals there.

Special liability for dogs

Two sections of the Animals Act make special provision for the situation of dogs who are or may be about to injure or kill livestock. Section 3 provides that where a dog kills or injures livestock, the keeper of the dog will be liable for the damage, unless they are covered by a defence. The relevant defences are:

- contributory negligence;
- the defence defined in section 5(1) of the Animals Act, covering fault of the claimant (see above);
- the defence defined in section 5(2) of the Animals Act, covering voluntary assumption of risk (see above);
- a specific defence detailed in section 5(4) of the Animals Act, which states that a dog owner will not be liable where his or her dog kills or injures livestock which have strayed into land occupied by the dog owner, or where the dog's presence on the land was authorised by the occupier.

Section 9(3) deals with the issue of dogs 'worrying' livestock, a traditional term which covers not just attacking or injuring livestock, but also chasing them or being off a lead and not under close control in a field where sheep are. Section 9(3) provides that it is lawful for a person to kill or injure a dog which is worrying, or is about to worry livestock, where there is no other reasonable means of preventing it from doing so. It is also lawful to kill a dog which has been worrying livestock, is still in the vicinity of the livestock, is not under the control of any person, and there are no practical means of discovering who owns it. In both cases, the person killing the dog must also show that they were entitled to act to protect the livestock (which will usually mean being the owner of the livestock or the land it was on, or being authorised by the land or livestock owner). They must also notify the police within 48 hours.

Remoteness of damage

As with any tort, the claimant must prove that the animal concerned actually caused the damage, both factually and legally. As you will remember, there are two possible tests of legal **causation**, or **remoteness of damage**: the **direct consequence test** and the reasonable foreseeability test. The Act does not specifically state which test should apply, but as liability is strict it is generally assumed it is the direct consequence test.

Summary

- The owner or keeper of an animal can be liable under common law, or under the Animals Act 1971.
- The Animals Act 1971 divides animals into two different groups: dangerous species and non-dangerous species.
- The person liable is the owner, the person in possession of the animal, or if that person is under 16, the head of their household.
- Dangerous animals are defined as species not commonly domesticated in this country, which have characteristics that mean they are likely to cause severe damage unless restrained, or any damage they may cause is likely to be severe.
- Keepers of a dangerous animal are strictly liable for damage or injury, unless covered by a defence.

- All species which do not fall within the category of dangerous, as explained above, are classed as non-dangerous.
- The keeper of a non-dangerous animal will be liable for damage caused by it if:
  - the damage is of a kind which the animal, unless restrained, was likely to cause, or which, if caused, was likely to be severe; and
  - the likelihood of the damage or of its being severe was due to characteristics of the animal not normally found in that species or not normally found except at particular times or in particular circumstances; and
  - those characteristics were known to the keeper, a person in charge of the animal as the keeper's employee or to someone under 16 in the keeper's household.
- The Act provides three defences:
  - fault of the person suffering damage;
  - voluntary acceptance of the risk;
  - damage caused to trespasser where the animal is not kept for protection, or it was reasonable to keep it for protection.
- The Act provides for strict liability where livestock trespass on to neighbouring land, subject to defences.
- Liability for animals on the highway is decided by the normal rules of negligence.
- Where a dog kills or injures livestock, the keeper of the dog will be liable for the damage, unless they are covered by a defence.
- It is lawful for a person to kill or injure a dog which
  - is worrying or about to worry livestock, where there is no other reasonable means of preventing it from doing so; or
  - which has been worrying livestock, is still in the vicinity of the livestock, is not under the control of any person, and there are no practical means of discovering who owns it.
- The claimant must prove that the animal concerned actually caused the damage, both factually and legally. The test for remoteness of damage is assumed to be the direct consequence test.

Question and answer*

Problem: Terry takes his daughter Susie to the circus and, when they get there, Susie is very excited to find that they have ringside seats. The first act involves a team of horses, but in the middle of the routine there is a loud noise in the street outside. One of the horses, Champion, is frightened by the noise and runs straight towards Terry, injuring him.

The noise outside turns out to have been caused by animal rights protestors and, during the commotion, no one notices that one of them has let out the circus's lion, which is kept in a secure cage. The lion has been trained to be gentle around people, but it is very big. Startled by all the noise, it runs away and because it is not looking where it is going it bumps into Jaspal, who is walking down the street, and knocks him over, breaking his ankle.

Advise Terry and Jaspal about any claims they may have against the circus, under the Animals Act 1971.

You should allow yourself no more than 40 minutes to complete this task.

Essay: To what extent is it true that the Animals Act 1971 imposes strict liability?

This question should be answered in 40 minutes.

* Answer guidance is provided at the end of the chapter.

Further reading

Howarth, D. (2003) 'The HOL and the Animals Act: closing the stable door'. 62 CLJ 548.
A detailed look at the case of *Mirvahedy* v. *Henley*, and the problems with the Animals Act.

Law Commission Report 13 (1967) *Civil Liability for Animals*, London: HMSO.
This report looks at the state of the law before the Animals Act was passed, and highlights some of the problems the Act was designed to solve. The report's proposals formed the basis of the 1971 Act.

Animals Act 1971 (Amendment) (Research Paper 08/25), Library of the House of Commons (available online at www.parliament.uk/briefing-papers/RP08-25.pdf)
This briefing paper is about the proposed amendments to the Animals Act, which were prepared in response to the criticisms of the Act made after *Mirvahedy* v. *Henley*. It contains lots of useful background material on the Act and the problems with it.

Question and answer guidance

Problem: Starting with Terry's claim, the first thing to consider is whether you are dealing with a dangerous or non-dangerous species. In this case it is straightforward, as horses are commonly domesticated in this country, so it is classified as a non-dangerous species. You therefore need to consider the three elements of liability under section 2(2) of the Act. Work through each element, mentioning cases where they are relevant to the problem. Remember that you do not necessarily need to know whether the circus would be liable, only how the courts would apply the law in this situation. So, for example, you do not need to know whether running away at the sound of a loud noise is normal behaviour for a horse, but you should be able to apply the decision in *Mirvahedy*, and explain that the circus can be liable even if this was normal behaviour for a horse startled by a sudden noise. Similarly, we are not told whether the circus knows whether Champion was likely to behave as he did when startled, but you can explain that they will only be liable if they did know about any characteristic that would cause this behaviour. Remember that if they fit the conditions for liability, then liability is strict, so it does not matter that the noise was the fault of the animal rights protestors.

Turning to Jaspal, again you need to consider which type of species the lion is, and here we are dealing with a dangerous species. You should explain that this means strict liability applies, unless there is a defence, so the fact that the circus kept the lion in a secure cage will not help them avoid liability. Point out too that it is the characteristics of the species that are important, not those of the particular animal, so the fact that the lion is trained to be gentle with people does not change anything. Nor does the fact that Jaspal's injury is not caused by the lion attacking him or being vicious in any way. The only way that the circus can avoid liability is if they have a defence; you should briefly look at what the defences are and explain that none of them apply here.

Essay: At the beginning of your answer, you should define what strict liability is – the concept that means that someone who breaches a particular legal provision can be liable even if they took care and could not have prevented the breach, though they may be covered by defences.

You could begin looking at the Act by explaining that the thinking behind the Act is that people's liability for animals should reflect the degree of risk they are causing and that, as a result, animals are classified into non-dangerous and dangerous animals. Explain that strict liability in its pure form only applies to dangerous animals, and the reasoning for that. You should also point out that there are defences available even for claims involving dangerous animals.

You should then go on to explain how liability for non-dangerous animals can arise under the Act, referring to the fact that damage must be of a kind which was likely to happen if the animal was not restrained, or was likely to be severe (section 2(2)(a)); that damage must be due to the peculiar characteristics of the animal (section 2(2)(b)); and that the keeper or a member of their household must have knowledge of the characteristic (2(2)(c)). In explaining each requirement, you should assess how far it fits in with the concept of strict liability, and use cases to illustrate your points. The first requirement, about the type or severity of damage, for example, is clearly an aspect of strict liability, because liability does not rely on anything the keeper does or does not do, it is merely about the existence of a risk. If that risk exists, the requirements of section 2(2)(a) are fulfilled. When discussing the second requirement, the animal's characteristics, you should talk about the argument made in *Miravedy* v. *Henley*, that this section should not impose strict liability for normal animal behaviour, and the conclusion that the House of Lords came to in that case. With regard to the third requirement, knowledge, you could argue that this in a sense reduces the possible harshness of strict liability, because a defendant cannot be liable unless he knows of a risk, and if you know of a risk, you should take precautions to prevent it. In this sense, therefore, it could be argued that is not possible to be liable without a degree of fault. You should also discuss the fact that there are defences which allow defendants to escape liability, and you should explain what these are.

Your conclusion should sum up how far the Act imposes strict liability and, based on what you have said, whether you think it is correct to do so to the extent it does.

Chapter 21
Remedies

Key points In this chapter we will be looking at:

- The remedies that are available to a claimant who wins their case, namely damages and injunctions
- The different types of damages, and when they are awarded
- How damages are calculated
- How injunctions work and when they are awarded

Introduction

Over the past 20 chapters, we have looked mostly at the issue of liability in tort: what has to happen in order for a **claimant** to win their case. In this chapter, we look at what happens once the case has been won: what can the claimant get to compensate for the loss or damage, or in some cases, prevent loss or damage happening or happening again?

The two main remedies in tort cases are **damages**, which are an award of money, and **injunctions**, which are court orders preventing the **defendant** from doing something, such as publishing confidential material in a privacy case, or, in rarer cases, ordering them to do a particular thing. There are also some remedies which are specific to particular torts, and these have already been discussed in the relevant chapters.

Damages

There are two main types of damages awarded in tort cases:

- *Non-compensatory damages*: these come in three types, each of which performs a different function.
- *Compensatory damages*: these are by far the most common type of remedy in tort. They are called compensatory because they are an amount of money which is calculated to compensate the claimant by putting them back in the position they would have been in if the tort had never been committed.

Non-compensatory damages

The three types of non-compensatory damages are:

- nominal
- contemptuous
- exemplary

Nominal damages

These are awarded where the defendant has breached the claimant's legal rights, but no real damage has been done. In *Watkins* v. *Secretary of State for the Home Department* (2006), the House of Lords held that nominal damages are only appropriate for claims involving torts that are **actionable per se**, such as trespass. The court will award a very small amount, usually around £2, and the claimant may have to pay their own costs.

Case Summary

You might wonder why anyone would bother going to court in a case where nominal damages are likely to be awarded. One reason is that the court verdict does establish that the tort alleged has been committed, and so can be used to clarify matters over which the parties have been in dispute. For example, disputes between neighbours often concern where the boundary between their land lies: if one neighbour builds a fence where they believe the boundary is, but the other neighbour thinks the fence is too far over and therefore on their land, they may make a claim in trespass. In this situation they will not necessarily be looking for damages, but simply want to establish where the boundary lies; if they win, the court verdict is stating that the land concerned is theirs. Considering that these claims often involve just a few metres of land, and that such a case could easily cost £50,000 or more, this might not necessarily be seen as a sensible use of court time or the parties' money, but as any lawyer who deals with them will tell you, neighbour disputes often go beyond what might usually be considered reasonable.

Contemptuous damages

Contemptuous damages are used in rare cases where the court recognises that the claimant's legal rights have been breached, but has reason to believe that the case should never have been brought and wishes to show its disapproval of the claim. In such cases, the claimant will be awarded a very small amount (often the lowest coin in circulation at the time, so currently 1p), and will usually have to pay their own costs. The main use of contemptuous damages is in defamation cases, where the material complained of is defamatory, but because of the claimant's own bad behaviour the damage to their reputation is minimal. The Law in Action box about the *Grobbelaar* case looks at an example of this.

The main use of contemptuous damages is in defamation cases

Law in action The *Grobbelaar* case

An example of a case where contemptuous damages were ordered is *Grobbelaar* v. *News Group* (2001), which we looked at in defamation. As you may remember, the goalkeeper Bruce Grobbelaar sued over claims that he had taken bribes to fix the results of football matches by letting in goals on purpose. Although Mr Grobbelaar admitted taking bribes, the newspaper could not prove that he had ever actually tried to fix a match, and an attempt to use the qualified privilege defence failed, so he won his case. Mr Grobbelaar initially won £85,000, but when the case was appealed to the House of Lords, it reduced the damages to just £1, on the grounds that a substantial award of damages should not be made to someone who had flagrantly breached their moral and legal obligations.

Source: Pearson Education Ltd/Image Source

[*References*: **http://www.publications.parliament.uk/pa/ld200102/ldjudgmt/jd021024/grobb-3.htm; http://www.telegraph.co.uk/news/uknews/1411194/1-libel-damages-for-goalkeeper-with-no-reputation-to-lose.html**]

Exemplary damages

Also known as punitive damages, these are awarded where the court believes the defendant has behaved particularly badly, and wants to show its disapproval of their conduct by imposing damages that are high enough to punish the defendant, and to deter others from doing the same thing. Exemplary damages are controversial, because punishing wrongdoing is usually seen as the role of criminal law. This raises questions about whether a civil court is really the right place to hand out punishment, given that the case needs only to be proved on a **balance of probabilities**, whereas the criminal law demands proof beyond reasonable doubt before punishment can be ordered.

Case Summary

Because of these doubts, the higher courts have laid down strict rules about when exemplary damages may be ordered. In *Rookes* v. *Barnard* (1964), the House of Lords stated that they should only be used in three types of case:

- *Conduct calculated to make a profit:* These are cases, usually in defamation, where the defendant has been prepared to commit a tort because they knew doing so would make them a lot of money. An example would be publishing a story about a celebrity which was known to be untrue and defamatory, because it would increase sales by enough to make it worth taking the chance of being sued.
- *Oppressive, arbitrary or unconstitutional conduct by government servants:* This category covers cases where people who work for the government in some way, such as police officers or local government officials, misuse their powers. A common example would be where the police have wrongfully arrested someone, in a situation where the court feels it needs to highlight how badly they have behaved towards that person.
- *Statutory authorisation:* Exemplary damages may also be ordered where a statute expressly provides for them. Very few statutes do this.

In *Watkins* v. *Secretary of State for the Home Department* the House of Lords stated that exemplary damages may not be used in cases involving torts actionable per se.

Case Summary

The categories above refer to particular types of behaviour, rather than to specific torts. In *AB* v. *South West Water* (1993) a further restriction on the use of exemplary damages was suggested, when the Court said that they could not be applied in any tort where they had not applied before *Rookes* v. *Barnard* was decided. The judgment was criticised as being irrational, because it meant that the availability of exemplary damages depended entirely on what cases had happened to come before the courts before. In *Kuddus* v. *Chief Constable of Leicestershire Constabulary* (2001), the House of Lords accepted this criticism and said that the list of torts in which exemplary damages could be used was not closed. The claim in the case was for misfeasance in public office, and the defence argued that exemplary damages could not be applied because they had not been applied in a misfeasance case before *Rookes* v. *Barnard* was decided. Misfeasance in public office is a tort involving misconduct by public servants, and the alleged behaviour clearly fitted into the second category listed in *Rookes* v. *Barnard*, so the House held that exemplary damages could be ordered. The issue was the type of behaviour committed, not the name of the tort under which the claim was brought.

Case Summary

Case Summary

Where exemplary damages are ordered, this may be in addition to compensatory damages that are calculated to compensate for the specific loss the claimant has suffered.

Compensatory damages

Compensatory damages are the main form of remedy in tort cases and, as we saw above, they are designed to put the claimant in the position they would have been in if the tort had never been committed. This is sometimes known by the Latin phrase '***restitutio in integrum***'.

The claimant is expected to take reasonable steps to limit their own losses, and the defendant will not be liable for losses that are caused only by the claimant's failure to take such reasonable steps. So if, for example, the defendant has caused a flood which damages the claimant's property, and there are simple steps which the claimant could take to minimise the damage (such as moving items upstairs, or notifying the defendant so the source of the leak can be found), the claimant would usually be expected to take such steps. They could not simply let the damage go on getting worse and expect the defendant to pay for all of the loss. However, the courts recognise that as the damage is not the claimant's fault in the first place, they should not be expected to make unreasonably difficult efforts to reduce the loss, only to take reasonable steps. In *Ronan* v. *J. Sainsbury plc* (2006), the claimant was injured while working for Sainsbury's at the age of 19. He went on to start a career in banking, as he had planned, but eventually had to leave his job as a result of the effects of his injury. He decided to make a career change and went to university, and when the case came to court, after he had finished his degree, he claimed for loss of earnings during the three years he was studying. There was evidence that his health had improved during his time at university, to the extent that he could have gone back to his old job in banking, and Sainsbury's therefore argued that he should have limited his loss by giving up university and going back to his old job. The Court disagreed: the decision to change career had been caused by his accident, and it was unreasonable to expect him to change again and go back to his old job.

The claimant is expected to take reasonable steps to limit their own losses

Case Summary

Calculating compensatory damages

Calculating compensatory damages is usually straightforward in cases where the only damage is a financial loss which has already happened. In claims for deceit or **negligent misstatement**, for example, the court can simply work out how much money the claimant has lost, and make the defendant repay that. Similarly, where there is damage to property, the court can just calculate the costs involved in making good that damage. As well as the cost of replacing the item at current market prices, this can include other losses related to the damage: for example, if your car is damaged in an accident for which someone else is at fault, your claim might include the cost of a hire car while it is repaired (in practice of course this will usually be something your insurance company provides, but they would then seek to recover those costs from the **tortfeasor**).

However, the compensatory principle is also applied to cases where the damage is not, or not only, financial, such as claims for personal injury. Here, the idea is the same – to find a sum of money that, as far as money can, compensates directly for the damage done – but the calculations are more complex, because the courts have to attach a financial value to things like pain and suffering and the inability to do things the person could have done before they were injured. In addition, in many personal injury cases the courts have to consider future as well as past losses. Will the claimant's medical condition become worse, or might they in time recover, either partly or fully? Will they be able to go back to work and, if not, what might this cost them over what would have been their working lifetime? For these reasons, calculating damages for personal injury can be quite complicated. As part of the process, such damages are divided into two types: pecuniary, and non-pecuniary.

Pecuniary damages

These are damages which seek to compensate for actual financial loss, such as earnings lost through being unable to work, or the cost of care for claimants who have been severely injured and can no longer look after themselves on a day-to-day basis. Money already spent before the trial will obviously be known, but the courts may also have to work out how much claimants should be given to compensate for their future needs.

Medical and other expenses

The claimant can get back any reasonable expenses they have paid, or will have to pay in the future, as a result of the injury. Most people in this country get their medical care paid for by the NHS, and in this case they cannot claim for those costs, and will in fact have an amount deducted for the living expenses (including food and other bills) that they save while in hospital. However, a claimant can choose to have private medical care if they want to, and the costs of this can be claimed back from the defendant (if you were wondering why all accident victims don't take this option, remember that you would only get the costs of private care back if you won your case and, at the stage of needing hospital care, you would not usually be certain of doing that).

If a claimant needs care other than medical treatment (such as help with washing and dressing, or in very serious cases, full-time nursing care), either at the time of the accident or for the rest of their lives, they can claim back the costs of this. In many cases, care is actually provided by a family member. The case of *Donnelly* v. *Joyce* (1974), where the claimant was a child and his mother had to give up work to look after him, establishes that if the person providing care is caused financial loss by doing so, the claimant can get that amount back in damages as well, because it is their need for care which has caused the loss. In *Hunt* v. *Severs* (1994) it was explained that the money is given to the claimant in trust for the person providing care, which means given on their behalf.

Case Summary

Case Summary

However, where the person providing the care is actually the tortfeasor, any loss of earnings they suffer through providing the care cannot be claimed back. This might sound fairly unlikely to happen in any case, but not if we look at the case of *Hunt* v. *Severs*, where this principle was laid down. The claimant in the case was paralysed in an accident which happened while she was a pillion passenger on a motorbike, driven by her then boyfriend. Her boyfriend gave up work to care for her and they were later married. She sued him for negligently causing the accident, which may seem odd until you remember that in road accident cases it is not the driver who pays damages but their insurance company. So in practice the claimant was not really suing her boyfriend, but instead claiming her legal rights against the insurance company which he had paid to provide him with cover. She won the case, and was awarded damages for her injuries and her own loss of earnings, but the Court refused to allow a claim for the defendant's own loss of earnings through taking care of her. It said that there could be no grounds for making the defendant pay the claimant a sum which the claimant would then be obliged to give back to him. This rather oddly suggests that both parties would have been better off if the defendant had not done the right thing and taken care of her.

Case Summary

Loss of earnings

In many cases, a large element of the claim will be loss of earnings. To calculate this, the court has to consider how much the claimant could have expected to earn in their lifetime if they had never been injured, and whether they are now unable to earn at all, or might be able to go back to work but in a lower paid job. This process requires the courts to guess what might or might not have happened to the claimant regardless of the accident: for example, someone who at the time of their accident was working as a junior reporter on the local paper might have stayed in a similar job throughout their life and earned much the same, allowing for inflation; or might have been made redundant in two years time, had to take a completely different job and ended up earning much less; or might have gone on to get a job on a national newspaper and earned four or five times as much as they used to. This part of the process also requires that the courts assess the medical evidence about whether and how much the claimant's condition is likely to improve or worsen as time goes on, which is not always possible to predict with certainty.

The idea is that the court should be able to come up with a lump sum which, once invested, will produce an income that compensates for the losses caused by the defendant, no more and no less. They do this using a three-step process:

1. *Calculating the difference between the claimant's income before the accident, and afterwards.* This is called the net annual loss. In some cases the claimant may be so badly injured that they can no longer work, while others may be able to work, but at lower pay than before if they can no longer do the same job or work the same hours. In assessing this figure, the court cannot simply assume that the claimant would have gone on earning the same salary had the accident not happened: there might, for example, have been a good chance that they would have been promoted to a better-paid position. This process therefore involves some guesswork. The figure that the court comes up with at the end of this process is known as the multiplicand.
2. *Working out how long the loss is likely to continue.* Medical evidence will be needed to assess whether the condition is likely to last for the claimant's lifetime, or might at some point improve. The court then takes the number of years that the condition is expected to last, and reduces it to take account of what are called 'the vicissitudes of life'. This means taking into account the fact that, even without the accident, the claimant might not necessarily have remained healthy and able to work and/or have

lived to a normal lifespan. Now the court has before it the annual income that the claimant needs, and the number of years they are likely to need it for. However, simply to multiply one by the other would mean overcompensating the claimant, because of the way investments work. If a claimant needs £10,000 a year for 10 years, that would suggest a lump sum of £100,000. However, to get an income of £10,000 a year, the claimant does not actually need £100,000, because the idea is that they should invest the money, so that it makes more money over the 10 years. What they need is a lump sum that, if invested so that it produces a particular rate of return, will give them a yearly income of £10,000 for 10 years, and this may be considerably less than £100,000. So the court works out how much this should be, assuming a rate of return laid down by the Lord Chancellor under the Damages Act 1996. This is currently 2.5 per cent, which is calculated to reflect the rate that can be achieved through long-term, low-risk investments. The number reached at the end of this process is called the multiplier.

3. *Calculating the lump sum needed.* The court then multiplies the multiplier by the multiplicand, to reach the lump sum which should be awarded to the claimant. In some cases this lump sum is now being replaced by a series of payments over time, and we will look at how this works later in the chapter.

Where the claimant is a child and was not earning anything before the accident, the court uses a figure based on the average wage that would be earned during the early years of work as the multiplicand, and applies a low figure for the multiplier, based on the assumption that the 'vicissitudes of life' mean that the child may never have become a wage earner.

Law in action £4.3 million damages for a reckless tackle

The difficulty of assessing damages for future earnings can be seen on a larger than usual scale in the case of *Collett* v. *Smith and Middlesbrough Football Company* (2008), which hit the news when it was heard by the Court of Appeal. It involved a young footballer, Ben Collett, whose career was ended by a reckless tackle and who won record damages of £4.3 million. Mr Collett, who was 18 at the time of the accident, had been playing in Manchester United's Youth Academy, and had been given a one-year professional contract. He was making his first appearance for Manchester United reserves, when he was tackled by a Middlesbrough player, Gary Smith, and his leg was broken in two places. The injury meant that he would not be able to play professional football again, and he successfully sued both Middlesbrough and Gary Smith.

Source: Ingram Publishing

In assessing the damages, the courts had to look at what Mr Collett could have been expected to earn had he not been injured, and this meant looking at what kind of career he could be expected to have as a professional footballer; clearly his income would be very different if he ended up spending his career in the Npower League Two, than if he went on to gain a regular place with a Premier League team. The Manchester United manager, Sir Alex Ferguson, was called to give evidence, and said that 'I thought the boy showed fantastic focus, a great attitude to work hard, and they are qualities to give any player an outstanding chance in the game.' This and other evidence about his previous performance led the courts to conclude that Mr Collett had been on course to spend most, perhaps all of his career in the Premier League, and could have expected to earn millions of pounds. He was therefore awarded record damages of £4.3 million.

However, experts in sports law questioned this conclusion, pointing out that of Mr Collett's 10 teammates in the 2003 FA Youth Cup Final, fewer than half were playing for Premier League clubs by 2008. Sports lawyer Ian Blackshaw, quoted in *The Times* (12 August 2008), said: 'Just because someone has come through the academy and has started to play, it doesn't necessarily follow that the next 10 years will be brilliant, and that has to be reflected in the level of damages.'

[*Reference*: **http://www.independent.co.uk/news/uk/home-news/the-16343million-football-career-that-never-was-891508.html**]

Calculating lost years

As we have seen, the courts take into account how long a person could normally be expected to live, bearing in mind the 'vicissitudes of life', to calculate how long the claimant will need their income for. But what happens if the claimant is expected to live for fewer years than normal, because of the damage done by the defendant? In such a case it would clearly be unfair simply to reduce the amount of damages because the income would not be needed for so long, when this was the defendant's fault and therefore should not benefit them. In *Pickett* v. *British Rail Engineering* (1980) it was decided that the correct approach was to use the claimant's predicted life expectancy if the accident had not happened, but reduce it by the amount that they would have spent on supporting themselves during that time. This means, for example, that if a claimant would have been expected to live a normal lifespan and retire at 65, but because of the accident is only likely to live to 30, they can still claim loss of earnings for the period between ages 30 and 65, but with an amount deducted to represent what it would have cost them to support themselves during those years.

Case Summary

Non-pecuniary damages

These are damages which are designed to compensate for losses other than directly financial ones. Damages generally fall into three groups:

- for the injury itself;
- for pain and suffering;
- for loss of amenity, which means the inability to do everything the claimant could do before the injury happened.

The injury

This is the most straightforward element, as the courts can consult guidelines from the Judicial Studies Board, which set out the range of appropriate damages for particular types of injury. So, for example, loss of one arm is considered to be 'worth' £65,000–£100,000, while being paralysed from the neck down (tetraplegia) would usually attract an award of £220,000–£275,000.

Out and about

Get a copy of the Judicial Studies Board *Guidelines for the Assessment of General Damages in Personal Injury Cases* from your library. Use it to work out how much the following claimants might get in damages for their injuries alone.

(a) Jake is in a car crash. He suffers a broken leg, a fractured cheekbone and scarring to his face.

(b) Paola slips on some spilt juice in a supermarket. She breaks her wrist and sprains her ankle.

(c) Ivan falls from some scaffolding at work, and is paralysed from the neck down.

(d) Carola suffers damage to her scalp when a hairdresser negligently uses a straightening solution on her hair. A large patch of hair falls out and medical evidence suggests it will not grow back.

(e) Nigel gets his arm caught in a machine at work, and it has to be amputated below the elbow.

Pain and suffering

The same category of injury may cause different amounts of pain and suffering, so the courts will individually assess this, based on medical evidence. The claimant can get damages for pain and suffering caused by the original injury, and any operations needed to treat it. Because the damages awarded are designed to reflect what the individual claimant has actually experienced, a claimant who has been unconscious since the injury occurred does not receive any damages for pain and suffering, on the grounds that they cannot feel them (*Wise* v. *Kaye* (1962)).

Loss of amenity

This category of damages reflects that fact that an injury may rob a claimant of the ability to live life in the same way as they did before. Depending on the extent of the injury, it might include, for example, damages for losing specific physical capabilities, such as the ability to hear or see; for having their sex life and/or prospects of marriage damaged; or for losing the ability to do a specific activity which the claimant had previously enjoyed, such as sport, playing with their children, or taking part in a particular hobby.

Case Summary

Unlike pain and suffering, damages for loss of amenity are available to a claimant who has been unconscious since the injury. This was established in *West* v. *Shepherd* (1964), where the claimant, a 41-year-old woman, was severely injured in a car accident. She was paralysed from the neck down, had little or no ability to communicate, and it was not clear whether she was aware of her surroundings. The defence argued that there should be no claim for loss of amenity if she was not aware of this loss, but the House of Lords rejected this argument and said she should be able to claim for loss of amenity, because that loss was a fact, even if she was not aware of it.

Case Summary

In 1999, the Law Commission argued that damages for non-pecuniary loss in personal injury cases were too low to properly compensate claimants (Law Commission Report 257, 1999). In *Heil* v. *Rankin* (2000), the Court of Appeal agreed that this was true of the most serious cases, and said damages in these cases should rise, though not those in less serious claims.

Deductions

As we have seen, the idea of compensatory damages is to give the claimant exactly the amount they need to make good their loss: no less, but also no more. That means that if a claimant receives other money as a result of their injury (such as social security benefits, or sick pay from their employer) that amount may be deducted from their damages, so that they are not compensated twice.

Social Security benefits

The Social Security (Recovery of Benefits) Act (1997) provides that where a claimant has received certain social security benefits during the five years after the accident or until the damages are ordered (whichever is earlier), these must be deducted from their compensation and paid back to the state. However, the benefits can only be set off against the corresponding category of damages so, for example, if the claimant has received benefits covering the cost of care, this amount can only be deducted from the element of their damages which relates to paying for care. To see how this works, take a claimant who has received £7,000 in income support and £3,000 in attendance allowance and is then awarded £10,000 for loss of earnings and £2,000 for the cost of care. The £7,000 in income support is set off against the £10,000 for loss of earnings, and the £3,000 attendance allowance (which is given to help pay for care) is set off against the £2,000 awarded by the court for care costs. This leaves the claimant with £3,000, because the outstanding £1,000 attendance allowance cannot be set off against the £10,000 awarded for loss of earnings. In addition, deductions for social security benefits cannot be made from the part of the award given for pain and suffering.

benefits can only be set off against the corresponding category of damages

Sick pay

In *Hussain* v. *New Taplow Paper Mills* (1988), the House of Lords stated that sick pay from an employer was the equivalent of a salary and so should be deducted from damages, unless the terms of the employment contract required the sick pay to be paid back to the employer out of damages.

Insurance payouts

Some people take out insurance to protect themselves if they are unable to work through accident or illness. This insurance may pay either a lump sum or a replacement for income over a particular period, and therefore replaces salary in very much the same way as sick pay does. However, in *Parry* v. *Cleaver* (1970) the House of Lords stated that these payments should not be deducted from tort damages, because to do so would discourage people from taking out insurance, which they considered a sensible step, and would also provide an unjustified benefit to defendants. The same rule applies to payments made by charities, and to disability pensions paid by employers.

Case Summary

The rule was criticised by the Law Commission in 1997 on the grounds that it over-compensates victims, which is a waste of resources and against the principles of tort law. The Commission argued that deducting the payments from damages would not discourage people from taking out insurance, because most people do so in order to protect against income loss generally (for example, by redundancy), and not just loss as the result of a tort, so they would still want the cover. This argument, however, ignores the fact that this type of insurance is often very expensive, and a claimant who has been paying for such insurance would effectively be cheated of the benefits they have paid for while the courts hand a bonus to defendants who have done nothing to deserve it.

Writing and drafting

You are a solicitor in a firm which specialises in personal injury. Write an advice sheet for clients, explaining how their compensation will be calculated and what may be deducted from it.

Handy tip: Remember you are writing for ordinary people, not lawyers, so keep your language clear and simple, and think about what your clients will want to know. This is a good way to test whether you have really understood a subject.

Compensation and death

So far we have looked at the way in which the law compensates injured victims of tort, aiming to put them back in the position they would have been in had the tort not been committed, at least as far as money can do so. But what happens if a tort ends up killing the victim? Clearly there can be no compensation for the victim, but in many cases their death will have an impact, both financial and emotional, on their close family. Do they have a claim against the tortfeasor? Before 1934 the answer was generally no. If someone died as a result of a tort their claim against the tortfeasor died with them – which could mean that a tortfeasor would be better off if they killed someone than if they injured them. This was also the case if someone was the victim of a tort, but died of unrelated causes before the case was decided.

However, there are now two ways in which a tortfeasor can be sued even though their victim has died:

- Under the Law Reform (Miscellaneous Provisions) Act 1934, whoever inherits the victim's estate also inherits their claim against the tortfeasor.
- Under the Fatal Accidents Act 1976, dependants of a victim who dies as a result of a tort have their own claim against the tortfeasor.

These provisions both apply to all the torts covered in this book, except defamation, where the claim comes to an end if either party dies.

Claims under the Law Reform (Miscellaneous Provisions) Act 1934

The 1934 Act provides that if the victim of a tort dies, their estate inherits the right to sue the tortfeasor. Their estate is the legal name given to all the money and property the person leaves behind and, in practice, this means that whoever inherits this also inherits the right to sue the tortfeasor.

As far as losses relating to the time between the injury and the death are concerned, the estate's claim is the same one as would have been brought by the victim if they had lived, so any compensatory damage would reflect the loss that would have been caused to them between the time the tort caused them injury or loss and the time they died. To see how this works, we can take the example of someone who is injured in a car accident and from that time is unable to work. Six months later, they die. Their estate (or the person inheriting it) can sue the person who caused the accident for the victim's lost earnings between the time of the accident and the time they died, as well as for any expenses incurred as a result of the accident and any non-pecuniary losses such as pain and suffering (see page 512). However, the estate cannot claim for losses arising after the death (such as loss of earnings for years that the victim could have been expected to live if the accident had not happened), nor for the death itself. This is because the Fatal Accidents Act 1976 provides dependants of the dead person with a claim on their own behalf for losses arising from the death (which we will look at below).

The claim provided for under the Law Reform (Miscellaneous Provisions) Act 1934 applies both where the tort caused the victim's death, and where the victim of a tort dies of unrelated causes before the case is decided. However, if the death was caused by the tortfeasor, then any losses or gains to the estate which are caused by the death are ignored when calculating the damages. So if, for example, the victim was receiving a pension which stops on their death, the defendant would not be expected to compensate this loss. On the other hand, if the victim was insured, and the death resulted in a payout from the insurance, this will not be deducted from the damages. The only exception to this rule is that where the death was caused by the tortfeasor the estate can claim funeral expenses.

Claims under the Fatal Accidents Act 1976

Where a tort causes someone's death, there can be a huge financial impact on their family, as well as an emotional one. The Fatal Accidents Act addresses this issue, providing close relatives who were financially dependent on the victim with a right to sue the tortfeasor. Section 1(3) of the Act defines dependants as including spouses and former spouses, children, parents, uncles and aunts, siblings, and other close relatives. If the victim was living with a partner but not married to them, they have to have been living together immediately before the death and for at least two years, and to have been living 'as the husband or wife of the deceased' during that time, in order to have a claim. In order for their claim to exist, they have to be able to show that the tortfeasor caused the death, and that the dead person would have had a claim against the tortfeasor. This means that if the tortfeasor would have had a **defence** against the victim, that defence will also apply to the dependant's claim.

In practice, most claims under the Act involve spouses and/or children of the dead person. The Act allows a claim for loss of support, which essentially means the financial losses which have been caused to the dependant(s) by the fact that the victim is no longer there to look after them. This includes claims where the relatives were financially dependent on the victim's income, and also where they were dependent on that person's services, so in *Berry* v. *Humm* (1915) it was established that a man whose wife did not have a job outside the home can sue for the loss of her 'housekeeping services' (this case was decided under earlier law, but remains valid today and, we can assume, would apply equally where a woman went out to work and her husband looked after the home). Similarly, in *Hay* v. *Hughes* (1975), children were able to sue for the loss of their mother's services, with the compensation being judged on the cost of a housekeeper (and again, the same should apply if a stay-at-home dad were killed as the result of a tort).

Case Summary

Case Summary

The Act also allows a second category of claim, which gives a set payment of £10,000 as compensation for the mental distress of the bereavement itself. This is only available to the dead person's spouse, or the parents if the person was not married.

You be the judge

Q: **Erik is injured in an accident at work. He has severe head injuries and, after six months, he dies. His wife, Freya, inherited his estate. She is suing his employer. If she wins, which of these can she claim?**

(a) Damages for Erik's pain and suffering.
(b) Loss of Erik's earnings for the six months before he died.
(c) The cost of Erik's treatment in a private hospital for the six months before he died.

A: Freya can claim all of these. Because she has inherited Erik's estate, the Law Reform (Miscellaneous Provisions) Act 1934 provides that she also inherits the claim that he would have had against his employer, so she can claim damages for his pain and suffering, lost earnings and hospital treatment, just as he would have been able to.

Law in action Are bereavement damages high enough?

In 2007, researchers at the University of Warwick published an interesting study on bereavement damages, which suggested that the methods courts used to calculate such damages meant that the amounts ordered did not come close to compensating claimants for the loss suffered. As we have seen, the calculations tend to look mainly at the economic value of the dead person to the family, and the Warwick researchers found that this approach could not take into account the level of unhappiness caused by the death of a close relative. They proposed a new approach, which would examine the effect on mental well-being of particular life events, including bereavement.

The researchers used the British Household Panel Survey, which is a yearly survey of the same 5,000 households, chosen to represent a cross-section of British society. Among other things, it asks people about significant events that have happened over the past year, and also includes questions which are designed to measure mental well-being. The survey can therefore be used to measure the effect on mental well-being in those who mention that they have suffered a bereavement. In addition, it asks about changes to household income which, when cross-referenced to the mental well-being data, can measure the effect of particular amounts of money on mental well-being. By putting these two pieces of information together, the researchers came up with a set of sums which they said would be a true reflection of the emotional impact of bereavement, and the amount of money needed to compensate for that impact. So far, however, the legal system has shown no interest in adopting this method of calculation.

[*Reference*: Oswald, A.J. and Powdthayee, N. (2007) 'Death, happiness and the calculation of compensatory damages'. Working Paper, University of Warwick, Department of Economics, Coventry]

Death of the defendant

The law prior to 1934 also meant that if a defendant died before the case was decided, the claim died with them and the victim would be left without any means of getting compensation. This was also changed under the Law Reform (Miscellaneous Provisions) Act 1934. Now, if a defendant dies before a case is decided, the victim of their tort can sue whoever inherits their estate, using exactly the same claim as they would have used against the defendant who has died.

Aggravated damages

In rare cases, the courts will award an amount over and above that which would usually be calculated to compensate the claimant's losses because there are factors about the defendant's behaviour which mean that the claimant has suffered more than would usually be expected. These are called aggravated damages. They are usually considered as compensatory, because they are triggered by the effect of the defendant's action on the claimant, even if they are extra to the normal amount that would be considered adequate compensation.

Case Summary

In *Rowlands* v. *Chief Constable of Merseyside* (2006), the claimant was awarded aggravated damages when she sued the police for false arrest. She had been handcuffed in front of her children, and when she asked for the cuffs to be loosened because they were causing severe pain a police officer deliberately pulled them, increasing the pain. The Court awarded aggravated damages in recognition of the extreme humiliation and distress caused by the police officer's treatment of her. This was over and above the distress that would normally be caused by a false arrest.

How damages are paid

Traditionally, damages have been paid as a lump sum and the whole amount is given after the case has been decided, covering both past and future losses. As we saw earlier, with regard to future losses the idea is that the sum awarded for these would be invested so as to provide an income for as long as necessary (in some cases a claimant's whole life). However, there were a number of problems with this approach:

- Personal injury cases can take a long time to come to trial and the claimant and their family may suffer serious financial problems in the meantime, through losing income and possibly having to pay for care and/or special adaptations at home. As well as being a hardship in itself, this can put pressure on the claimant to accept even an obviously unfair offer from the defendant, in order to get some money when they most need it.
- Calculating the lump sum means estimating how long the claimant is likely to live. If they live longer than the court calculates, there is a chance the money will run out. This leaves the claimant dependent on state benefits, which is both undesirable for them and means the defendant has escaped paying the full cost of their actions.
- If the claimant's choice of investment gives a lower rate of return than expected, or if they fail to invest the money, it will run out more quickly than predicted and the claimant will be under-compensated.
- Inflation can mean that an income which, 20 years before, was judged to meet the claimant's needs, might no longer do so.
- A one-off payment has to be based on medical experts' predictions of the long-term effects of the claimant's injuries. If they get this wrong, and the claimants suffers further problems that were not predicted, the compensation may not reflect the true extent of their pain and suffering or loss of amenity, and/or they may face increased care costs or a lower income, which are not covered by the compensation they were given. One example is cases of skull fractures, which can lead to severe epilepsy developing later in life. As it will not be clear at the time of trial whether this is going to happen, it is impossible for the court to compensate for it.

In recognition of these issues, there are three alternatives to a one-off lump sum payment:

- interim payments;
- periodical payments;
- provisional damages.

Interim payments

The Senior Courts Act 1981 allows the courts to order an interim payment before a case comes to trial (or is **settled**), where the defendant admits liability but the parties are in dispute about how much the damages should be. This can be a useful provision in cases where the claimant has already suffered financial loss and cannot easily wait until the case is decided or settled. The court can only make such an order where the defendant is insured, is a public body or can be shown to have the resources to make an interim payment.

Periodical payments

These are designed to meet the problems of lump sums running out, for any of the reasons discussed above. The claimant will usually get a lump sum to cover losses incurred up until the case is decided, but for future losses they get a regular income for as long as the condition lasts (as periodical payments are mainly used in cases of very serious injury, this will usually be many years and often the claimant's whole lifetime). Rather than attempting to work out how long the claimant will live, the court simply calculates how much should be paid and how often, and it is then up to the defendant to work out how to cover this amount for as long as may be necessary.

In the past, this kind of arrangement (which was more often known as a structured settlement) was only available where both parties consented to it, but the Courts Act 2003 now gives courts the power to decide that damages for future loss should be wholly or partly in the form of periodical payments, regardless of whether the parties agree. They can only do this where they can be reasonably certain that the payments will continue for as long as necessary, which essentially means that the defendant must be a public authority, or an insurance company within the Financial Services Compensation Scheme, which provides cover if an insurance company goes bust.

The Damages (Variation of Periodical Payments) Order 2005 provides that the amount of the periodical payment can be varied in the future, if the claimant's condition becomes worse or better. This can only happen if the possibility of a change was foreseen at the time of the trial, as the provision for variation must be included in the original order.

Provisional damages

The provision for varying periodical payments is one way of addressing the problem of changes in a claimant's condition. A second way, which can be used with traditional lump sum damages, is provided in the Senior Courts Act 1981. Section 32A allows courts to award provisional damages in cases where there is a known chance that the claimant may suffer a 'serious deterioration' in the condition caused by the tort. To use this provision, the claimant must ask for it at the time of trial. The court awards damages based on the claimant's medical condition at that time, and then, if the condition does get worse, the claimant can go back to court to get the damages increased to reflect this. The damages can only be increased once. In practice, claimants have not proved to be very keen on provisional damages, because they can usually get slightly higher damages at the original trial if they do not ask for provisional damages. In addition, the courts have interpreted the phrase 'serious deterioration' quite restrictively. In *Willson* v. *Ministry of Defence* (1991), the claimant had an ankle injury, which might later have led to arthritis. The Court said that this would not be considered a 'serious deterioration' and so provisional damages were not appropriate. To qualify, the deterioration that might happen would need to be a new event, rather than just an ordinary progression of the condition or illness.

Case Summary

Injunctions

An injunction is a court order, which either requires the defendant to do something, or requires them not to do something, or to stop doing something they are already doing. Injunctions are what is called equitable remedies and, for historical reasons, this means that they are applied in a different way to damages. A defendant who wins their case will automatically be entitled to damages (though there may of course be argument about how much the damages should be). With injunctions, however, the claimant does not have the same right. They can ask for an injunction instead of or as well as damages, but the court has a discretion on whether to say yes, and will usually try to balance the rights of both parties in making the decision (you can see how they do this in the case of *Redland Bricks*, below).

Prohibitory and mandatory injunctions

Most injunctions tell a defendant not to do something, or to stop doing something that they are already doing. These are called **prohibitory injunctions**, and they are most often used in defamation and privacy cases, to prevent publication or republication, and in torts where the problem is a continuing one, such as trespass and nuisance. In a nuisance case, for example, a landowner who is allowing smells, fumes or dust to drift on to a neighbour's property might be given a prohibitory injunction ordering them to stop doing so.

An injunction which tells a defendant to do something (rather than not do something) is called a **mandatory injunction**. These are usually given where the defendant has committed a tort which causes a problem for the claimant, and the injunction will require them to take specified actions to resolve the problem. For example, let's say that your neighbour is having some major building work done, which causes your house to become unstable. A court might make a mandatory injunction requiring your neighbour to do whatever was necessary on their side to restore the support to your house.

However, mandatory injunctions are seen as being more troublesome to defendants than prohibitory ones, and so they are not granted easily. In *Redland Bricks Ltd* v. *Morris* (1970), the House of Lords stated that mandatory injunctions should only be granted where damages would not be adequate to compensate for the harm done. The defendant in the case had been digging on their own land, and this had caused subsidence on the claimant's land. The claimants had been awarded damages for the problems already

Case Summary

Documenting the law

An application for an injunction

This is the application form that a claimant who wants an injunction must complete:

Application for Injunction
(General Form)

Name of court	Claim No.
Claimant's Name and Ref.	
Defendant's Name and Ref.	

Notes on completion

Tick which boxes apply and specify the legislation where appropriate

(1) Enter the full name of the person making the application

(2) Enter the full name of the person the injunction is to be directed to

(3) Set out any proposed orders requiring acts to be done. Delete if no mandatory order is sought.

(4) Set out here the proposed terms of the injunction order (if the defendant is a limited company delete the wording in brackets and insert 'whether by its servants, agents, officers or otherwise').

(5) Set out here any further terms asked for including provision for costs

(6) Enter the names of all persons who have sworn affidavits or signed statements in support of this application

(7) Enter the names and addresses of all persons upon whom it is intended to serve this application

(8) Enter the full name and address for service and delete as required

☐ By application in pending proceedings

☐ Under Statutory provision ______________________

☐ This application is made under Part 8 of the Civil Procedure Rules

Seal

This application raises issues under the Human Rights Act 1998 ☐ Yes ☐ No

The Claimant(1)

applies to the court for an injunction order in the following terms:

The Defendant(2)

must(3)

The Defendant

be forbidden (whether by himself or by instructing or encouraging or permitting any other person)(4)

And that(5)

The grounds of this application are set out in the written evidence of(6) sworn (signed) on

This written evidence is served with this application.

This application is to be served upon(7)

This application is filed by(8)

(the Solicitors for) the Claimant (Applicant/Petitioner) whose address for service is

Signed Dated

* Name and address of the person application is directed to

This section to be completed by the court

To*

of

This application will be heard by the (District) Judge

at

on the day of 20 at o'clock

If you do not attend at the time shown the court may make an injunction order in your absence

If you do not fully understand this application you should go to a Solicitor, Legal Advice Centre or a Citizens' Advice Bureau

The court office at

is open between 10am and 4pm Mon - Fri. When corresponding with the court, please address all forms and letters to the Court Manager and quote the claim number.

N16A General form of application for injunction (04.07) HMCS

Source: Available at **http://hmctsformfinder.justice.gov.uk/courtfinder/forms/n16a_e0407.pdf**

Documenting the law

An injunction

This is a copy of an injunction:

PF39CH
Order for an Injunction (Intended action)

[IN THE HIGH COURT OF JUSTICE] Claim No.........
[... ....] DIVISION]
] DISTRICT REGISTRY
[ ] COUNTY COURT
BEFORE the Honourable Mr Justice/Master/District Judge

.................20.........

IN AN INTENDED ACTION BETWEEN

Between

Intended Claimant

and

Intended Defendant

ORDER FOR AN INJUNCTION BEFORE THE ISSUE OF A CLAIM FORM

IMPORTANT:-
NOTICE TO THE INTENDED DEFENDANT ("the Defendant")

(1) This Order [prohibits you from doing] [obliges you to do] the acts set out in this Order. You should read it all carefully. You are advised to consult a solicitor as soon as possible. You have a right to ask the Court to vary or discharge this Order.

(2) If you disobey this Order you may be found guilty of Contempt of Court and [any of your directors] may be sent to prison or fined [and you may be fined] or your assets may be seized.

Include the words in square brackets in the case of a corporate defendant. This notice is not a substitute for the indorsement of a penal notice

An Application was made on the by Counsel for .... (who is to be the Claimant in a Claim against............) to the Judge who heard the Application supported by the Witness Statements / affidavits listed in schedule 1 to this order, and accepted the undertakings in Schedule 2 at the end of this Order.
IT IS ORDERED that up to and including [.......(*date*) the ("the Return Date")] [trial of the intended action]:-

The Defendant must/must not (*body of injunction*)

SUBSTITUTED SERVICE/SERVICE OUT OF THE JURISDICTION

1) The Claimant may issue and serve the Claim Form on the Defendant at.......(*address*) by....... (*date*).
2) If the Defendant wishes to defend the Claim he must acknowledge service within ....days of being served with the Claim Form.

VARIATION OR DISCHARGE OF THIS ORDER

The Defendant may apply to the Court at any time to vary or discharge this Order but if he wishes to do so he must first inform the Claimant's solicitors [in writing].

NAME AND ADDRESS OF CLAIMANT'S SOLICITORS

The Claimant's solicitors are:- (*name, address and telephone number*)

INTERPRETATION OF THIS ORDER

1) In this Order the words "he" "him" or "his" include "she" or "her" and "it" or "its".
2) Where there are two or more Defendants then (unless the contrary appears)
   (a) References to "the Defendant" mean both or all of them;
   (b) An Order requiring "the Defendant" to do or not to do anything requires each Defendant to do or not to do it;
   (c) A requirement relating to service of this Order or of any legal proceedings on "the Defendant" means on each of them.

THE EFFECT OF THIS ORDER

1) A Defendant who is an individual who is ordered not to do something must not do it himself or in any other way. He must not do it through others acting on his behalf or on his instructions or with his encouragement.
2) A Defendant which is a corporation and which is ordered not to do something must not do it itself or by its directors, officers, employees, or agents or in any other way.

SERVICE OF THIS ORDER

This Order shall be served by the Claimant on ....

SCHEDULE 1.

witness statements/Affidavits

The Claimant relied on the following Witness Statements / Affidavits:

1)
2)

SCHEDULE 2.

Undertakings given to the Court by the Claimant

1. To pay any damages which the Defendants (or any other party served with or notified of this Order) shall sustain which the Court considers the Claimant should pay.
2. If made without notice to any other party to serve on the Defendant Application Notice, evidence in support this Order as soon as practicable.
3. If made before filing the Application Notice to file and pay the appropriate fee on this or the next working day.
4. To issue a Claim Form and pay the appropriate fee on this or the next working day and to serve the Claim Form on the Defendant as soon as practicable.
5. To file a Witness Statement [substantially in the terms of the draft Witness Statement produced to the Court and initialled by the Judge] [confirming the substance of what was said to the Court by the Claimant's Counsel/Solicitors]

Source: Available at **http://hmctsformfinder.justice.gov.uk/HMCTS/GetForm.do?court_forms_id=841**

caused and a mandatory injunction requiring the defendants to restore support to their land. Because this work would have cost more than the total value of the claimant's land, the defendants appealed, and the House of Lords agreed than an injunction was not appropriate. They said that where, as here, the defendants have acted wrongly but not unreasonably, the cost of carrying out the order could be a reason to refuse it. However, if a defendant had acted unreasonably, and particularly if they had in some way tried to get an advantage over the claimant or the court, the fact that the work might be very expensive should not prevent an injunction being given.

Interim and final injunctions

Injunctions given at the end of a trial, which are intended to be the final resolution of the dispute, are called **final injunctions**. Injunctions can also be given at an earlier stage, before the case goes to a full trial, where the claimant wants to prevent harm occurring, and these are called **interim** or **interlocutory injunctions**. For example, as we saw in Chapter 16, celebrities often seek an interim injunction as soon as they find out that the press is about to publish details of something they would prefer to keep private.

Interlocutory or interim injunctions are relatively rare, for the obvious reason that it is considered preferable to try a case, giving both sides a fair hearing, before imposing a remedy. They will not be granted unless the court is satisfied that, if the tort happens and the case comes to trial, damages would not be an adequate remedy.

In *American Cyanamid* v. *Ethicon* (1975), the House of Lords set down further guidelines for when such injunctions should be granted. There should, they said, be a serious question to be tried, and the balance of convenience between the parties should be in favour of the injunction. This means that the court will weigh up the problems caused for the claimant if the injunction is not granted, against the problems caused for the defendant if it is granted. The claimant may be required to agree to pay the defendant's costs if the case does come to trial and the defendant wins, and to pay damages for any loss caused by the injunction itself.

Case Summary

Where the injunction requested is designed to prevent publication, usually in defamation or privacy cases, an extra set of restrictions are imposed by the Human Rights Act 1998 in order to protect the right to freedom of expression. Section 12(3) provides that interim injunctions preventing publication should not be granted unless the court is satisfied that the claimant is likely to be able to prove their case at trial, and that in deciding whether an injunction should be granted the courts should take into account the right to freedom of expression. In *Cream Holdings Ltd* v. *Banerjee* (2004), the House of Lords held that this meant that unless the party seeking the injunction could establish that it was more likely than not that they would win at trial, the courts should be 'exceedingly slow' to grant the order; however, there might be some cases where it was appropriate to grant the order even without such a strong case, such as where the consquences of publication were especially serious, or where time factors meant the court needed to impose a 'holding injunction' in order to consider the application for an interim injunction.

Case Summary

Refusing an injunction

As we saw above, injunctions are an equitable remedy, which means the courts have discretion to refuse a winning claimant an injunction, and order the defendant to pay

Case Summary

damages instead (usually at the defendant's request). In *Shelfer* v. *City of London Electric Lighting Co.* (1895), it was held that courts would only usually be justified in refusing an injunction and ordering damages instead where the harm done to the claimant was small and could be compensated adequately by damages, and where an injunction would be oppressive to the defendant.

Case Summary

An example of the way in which the courts approach this question can be seen in *Regan* v. *Paul Properties* (2006). The defendant was constructing a new building near the claimant's home. Part of the planned building would have reduced the light coming into the claimant's living room, which would have cut the value of his home by around £5,000. He had complained about this from an early stage, but the defendant went ahead anyway. Mr Regan eventually sued, and asked for an injunction to force changes to the defendant's plans, which would avoid the light problem. However, because much of the building work had been done by the time the case came to court, these changes would have cost the defendant around £175,000. They therefore argued that an injunction would be oppressive and, following *Shelfer*, damages should be given instead. The Court of Appeal disagreed. They said that the extent of the light blockage could not be adequately compensated for by money, and also pointed out that despite the fact that the claimant had complained at an early stage, and made it clear that he wanted to keep the light in his property, and did not want damages instead, the defendant had pressed on with the building work. It was their behaviour that had made the costs so high, and so it was not oppressive to allow an injunction.

Summary

- The main remedy in tort is damages. These can be compensatory or non-compensatory. Compensatory damages are the most common remedy in tort and are calculated to compensate the claimant by putting them back in the position they would have been in if the tort had never been committed. Non-compensatory damages come in three types: nominal, contemptuous and exemplary, each performing a different function.

- Compensatory damages include pecuniary damages, which compensate for financial loss such as expenses and loss of earnings, and non-pecuniary damages, which compensate for other losses such as pain and suffering. Damages for loss of earnings are calculated using a three-step process, which aims to calculate a lump sum which, if invested, will replace the income the claimant could have earned.

- If a claimant receives other money as a result of the tort, such as sick pay or welfare benefits, that may be deducted from compensation so that the claimant is not overcompensated. Insurance payouts are not deducted.

- If the victim of a tort dies, their estate inherits their claim under the Law Reform (Miscellaneous Provisions) Act 1934, and under the Fatal Accidents Act 1976 dependants of a victim who dies as a result of a tort have their own claim against the tortfeasor.

- Damages were traditionally paid as a lump sum at the end of a trial, but this caused a number of problems for claimants. These have to some extent been addressed by the use of interim payments, periodical payments, and provisional damages.

- The other main remedy in tort is an injunction. This is a court order which requires the defendant to do something (called a mandatory injunction), or not to do something or to stop doing something they are already doing (a prohibitory injunction).
- Injunctions are equitable remedies, and for historical reasons this means that a court has discretion to refuse an injunction and award damages instead. This is usually done where the harm done to the claimant was small, and could be compensated adequately by damages, and where an injunction would be oppressive to the defendant.
- An injunction can be final, given at the end of a case to resolve the dispute, or interim/interlocutory, given before the case goes to a full trial where the claimant wants to prevent harm occurring. There are restrictions on when interim injunctions can be granted.

Question and answer*

Problem: Lucy Loveliness is a top model. This year she won a contract with a major fashion house called Style Fashions, and starred in a series of high-profile ads with two other very well-known models. Lucy has just spent the money she earned from the campaign on a very expensive new house. On her first morning there, she goes out to pick up the newspapers, and finds that one of them has published a story claiming that 'one of the top models in the Style Fashions campaign has been dating a drug dealer', saying that the drug dealer bought the model her new house with money from his drug empire and she willingly accepted it. The story is not true, and the editor of the paper knows this, but he also knows that such a compelling story will raise sales of the paper.

Lucy gets home and is very upset to find that a fan, who has read the story in the paper and worked out her address, is standing in her front garden shouting 'Lucy, I love you, leave the drug dealer and marry me.' She shouts at him and he runs away.

Determined to enjoy her new house, despite all the upset, Lucy goes out into the back garden. She has only been there for five minutes when her next-door neighbour starts practising on his drums. The noise is deafening and, to Lucy's dismay, it turns out that her neighbour practises every day, for four hours. She complains, but he says that as he was there first she will just have to put up with it. After a month of this, she decides something has to be done.

Advise Lucy as to any claims she may have, and what remedies should could expect if she wins each case.

You should allow yourself no more than 40 minutes to complete this task.

Essay: Damages in tort are intended to put the claimant in the position they would have been in if the tort had never been committed. How far does the law do this?

This question should be answered in 40 minutes.

* Answer guidance is provided at the end of the chapter.

Further reading and references

Judicial Studies *Board (2006) Guidelines for the Assessment of General Damages in Personal Injury Cases*, Oxford: Oxford University Press.
These are the guidelines used by judges in personal injury cases, and which detail a range of different levels of damages for different types of injury. This is an interesting book to look through as it gives you a real perspective on the kinds of sums that the tort system deals with.

Law Commission Report 247 (1997) *Aggravated, Exemplary and Restitutionary Damages*, London: The Stationery Office.
This report looks at the policy basis for damages which seek in some way to punish the wrongdoer, and argues that the law needs clarification and reform.

Law Commission Consultation Paper 147 (1999) *Damages for Personal Injury: Collateral Benefits*, London: The Stationery Office.
This looks at the issue of when deductions should be made from claimants' damages, because of other money they have received as a result of the tort such as sick pay or insurance payouts.

Law Commission Report 257 (1999) *Damages for Personal Injury: Non-pecuniary Loss*, London: The Stationery Office.
This report looks at damages for pain and suffering and loss of amenity, examining problems with the law and considering suggestions for reform.

Law Commission Report 263 (1999) *Claims for Wrongful Death*, London: The Stationery Office.
This report looks at the compensation available under the Fatal Accidents Act 1976, and recommends reforms aimed at bringing the law into line with modern society.

Lewis, R. (2001) 'Increasing the price of pain: damages, the Law Commission and *Heil* v. *Rankin*', 64 MLR 100.
A very interesting article, written in response to the decision in *Heil* v. *Rankin* that damages for pain and suffering and loss of amenity should be increased. The author argues that this category of damages is a major cause of high costs, inefficiency and injustice in personal injury cases, and suggests that increasing them is a mistake. The article is full of useful background on how personal injury cases really work in practice.

Lewis, R. (2006) 'The politics and economics of tort law: judicially imposed periodical payments', 69(3) MLR 418.
This article looks at the provisions of the Damages Act on periodical payments, the effect they are likely to have on the negotiating process in personal injury claims, and the wider economic and political context.

Question and answer guidance

Problem: Remedies rarely come up as the sole subject of a problem question, so this question tests your knowledge of some of the torts we have looked at in previous chapters, as well as the remedies that may be available for them. In the first paragraph, the claim is clearly defamation, and the main issue you need to consider is whether the statement can be said to refer to Lucy, given that she is not actually named. Then consider what kind of remedy she might get.

In the second paragraph the claim is trespass and you can point out that this is committed merely by being on someone's land without their permission. However, given that the fan does not appear to have done any damage, what kind of damages do you think Lucy might get?

Finally, the claim against the neighbour would be in nuisance, so you need to explain how a court would decide whether the neighbour was liable. Lucy will obviously want to get an injunction to stop the music being played, so you need to look at how the courts will approach this, and what principles they will use to decide whether to grant an injunction or give damages instead.

Essay: A good way to start this essay would be to explain that a key principle of tort law is to compensate victims for losses or harm caused to them, and perhaps contrast this with criminal law where the aim is to punish those who have done wrong, or contract where the aim is to protect an expected gain. You can then explain that this is why tort damages seek, as far as possible, to put the claimant in the position they would have been in if the tort was never committed.

You could then give some examples of how the law attempts to do this, by talking about how damages are calculated – in loss of earnings claims, for example, you can show that the courts go to considerable lengths to work out how to compensate for future earnings. Then go on to look at some of the ways in which tort law fails to put people back in the position they would have been in had the tort not been committed. You can point out that there are some situations where money simply cannot do this – it cannot, for example, reverse an injury, or make private information that has been published secret again. There are also practical problems with lump sum payments, and you can explain how these have been addressed.

If you have time, you could widen your answer and look at some of the rules of tort law which make it impossible to restore the claimant to their pre-tort position – you could, for example, consider the **reasonable foreseeability test**, which means a defendant will not be liable for losses they could not foresee. A claimant still has those losses, so if they cannot claim for them they cannot be put back into their pre-tort position.

Glossary

Note: Glossary terms are highlighted in the text in **black bold**.

Actionable per se If a tort is actionable per se, the claimant only has to prove that the tort has been committed. They do not have to have suffered any damage, injury or loss. Trespass to land and to the person are the best-known examples of torts actionable per se.

Balance of probabilities The standard of proof in tort cases (and all civil cases). The claimant has to prove that it is more likely than not that the defendant committed the tort and caused the damage or loss. This contrasts with the stricter standard of proof in criminal cases, where the prosecution must prove their case beyond reasonable doubt.

***Bolam* test** A test used in negligence cases where the negligence involves some kind of professional work or service. To decide whether the defendant has breached their duty of care, the court will ask whether they have taken reasonable care, but often there is disagreement within the relevant industry or profession as to what amounts to reasonable care. In *Bolam* v. *Friern Hospital Management Committee* (1957) it was held that the question to ask is whether the defendant acted in accordance with a practice accepted as proper 'by a responsible body of medical men skilled in that particular art'. In other words, if there are other doctors who think that what the defendant did was correct, the defendant can be said to have taken reasonable care. The test is now also used outside medical cases, in any situation where there is a difference of opinion between professionals or industry experts as to what is a reasonable standard of care.

Burden of proof To have the burden of proof means to be the party who has to prove their case. In a tort case, it is the claimant who must prove that the defendant committed the tort, rather than the defendant having to prove that they did not.

'But for' test A claimant in tort must show that the defendant's behaviour caused their damage, injury or loss. The main test used to prove causation, it asks whether the loss, damage or injury would have happened but for the tort, or in other words, would the loss, damage or injury have happened if the tort had not happened.

***Caparo* test** The basic test for a duty of care in negligence, which the courts use when they are faced with a new factual situation in which it is not clear whether the defendant owes a duty of care to the claimant. It asks whether the damage was reasonably foreseeable, whether there was proximity between the claimant and the defendant, and whether it is fair, just and reasonable to impose a duty.

Causation Where a tort requires the defendant to have caused damage (or where a tort is actionable per se but the claimant has suffered damage and wants to claim for it), the claimant must show that the defendant actually caused the damage. The rules of causation set out how that is to be done.

Claimant The party who brings a case in tort, meaning the person who alleges that the tort has been done to them. They can be an individual person, a company or an organisation.

Clinical negligence The name given to negligence involving medical treatment, such as operations which go wrong.

Common law Created by the decisions made in cases which come before the higher courts. These decisions set rules and principles, so that similar cases which come afterwards are decided in the same way. Most of the law of tort has been created in this way.

Conditional fee agreement An arrangement between lawyers and clients, under which the client pays the solicitor nothing if they lose their case, but if they win, must pay a success fee or uplift over and above the normal fee. Also known as a 'no win, no fee' agreement.

Contributory negligence A general defence, available in most torts, which means that where the tort or the damage it causes is partly the claimant's own fault, the damages which would otherwise have been ordered can be reduced to reflect this.

Damages An amount of money awarded to a claimant who wins their case.

Defence A set of rules which, if they apply to the situation in the case, mean that a defendant can avoid liability even though they have committed a tort, or pay lower damages than they otherwise would.

Defendant The party who is alleged to have committed a tort and who is sued by the claimant. They can be an individual person, a company or an organisation.

Direct consequence test One of two tests used to decide on remoteness of damage (see below). Where this test applies, a defendant will be liable for all loss or damage that arises directly from the tort regardless of how unusual or unpredictable it might be.

Duty of care The concept is one of the ways in which the law draws the boundaries of the tort of negligence. A defendant can only be liable in negligence if they owe a duty of care to the claimant, or to an identifiable group or category of people to which the claimant belongs. The basic test is the *Caparo* test (see above), although other tests are used in, for example, cases involving pure economic loss or psychiatric injury.

Economic loss The term used when a claimant has lost money as a result of the defendant's tort, but the loss has not been caused by a personal injury or damage to the claimant's property. It is sometimes known as pure economic loss to distinguish it from financial losses that do arise out of personal injury or property damage, such as loss of earnings after an accident, or the cost of hiring a car if yours is damaged in a crash. In negligence, economic loss is subject to special rules on when there will be a duty of care.

Eggshell skull rule A rule which means that if a claimant has some kind of pre-existing weakness which makes the damage done by the defendant worse, the defendant must take the claimant as they find them and pay for the extra damage as well.

Ex turpi causa non oritur actio The Latin name for the defence of illegality (see below), meaning 'no action may be based on an illegal cause'.

Final injunction One given at the end of a trial and intended to be a final resolution to the dispute.

Floodgates The 'floodgates' argument or issue is often referred to by both judges and academics writing about tort. It refers to the suggestion that if the courts decide to extend liability in a particular situation a huge number of similar claims might be brought. That has three possible implications. First, that the court system may be overwhelmed with claims. Secondly, that insurance costs may go up, and thirdly, that the change may place too much of a burden on those who would be sued, and make it harder for them to predict whether they were likely to be sued. The floodgates argument is therefore used to justify decisions or principles which restrict the situations in which a defendant will be liable. Liability for psychiatric injury in negligence is an example of an area where the floodgates argument has been used.

Illegality A defence which applies where the damage or injury to the claimant is connected with the fact that they have committed an illegal act, sometimes known as *ex turpi causa non oritur actio* (see above). The basic reason for the defence is public policy: many people would find it offensive if, for example, someone who steals your car could sue you for negligence because the brakes were not working and they crashed and hurt themselves.

Implied term A term which the law states will be part of a particular type of contract, regardless of whether the parties agree that it should be there, or whether it is written down anywhere. An example is that, under the Sale of Goods Act 1979, if you buy something from someone there is an implied term in the contract between you that the thing you buy will be 'of satisfactory quality'.

Injunction A court order which requires a defendant to do something, or not to do something, or to stop doing something they are already doing.

Interim injunction An order granted before a claim has gone through a full trial, usually because there is an urgent need to prevent something happening or happening again. A common example is in privacy cases, where a claimant finds out that the press is about to publish private information about them and seeks an interim injunction to prevent this happening, rather than allowing it to go ahead and then suing for damages, which cannot undo the damage that they believe publication would do.

Interlocutory injunction Another name for an interim injunction.

Intervening act Where a tort requires the defendant to have caused damage (or where a tort is actionable per se but the claimant has suffered damage and wants to claim for it), the claimant must show that the defendant actually caused the damage. Sometimes something else happens after the tort, which contributes to the damage in such a way that this event, rather than the tort, can be said to have caused part of the damage. This is known as an intervening act, and a defendant will not be liable for any damage caused by it. Sometimes known as *novus actus interveniens* (see below).

Joint liability Meaning two or more defendants are liable for the same tortious incident. It can arise in two ways: vicarious liability (see below) and common design. Common design applies where the same wrongful act is committed by two or more people together, with a joint purpose. In cases of joint liability, the claimant can sue one, some or all of the defendants (usually depending on who is most likely to be able to pay), but can only be compensated for up to the total value of the loss, whether they get that all from one defendant or it is split between some or all of them. They cannot sue one defendant for the total loss and then sue another for more money.

Latent damage Damage which is caused by a tort but which does not appear or is not visible at the time when the tort happens. Special rules can allow a claimant to get compensation for latent damage even if it does not appear until after the normal limitation period has expired.

Limitation period A time limit, after which a claim cannot usually be brought. The time limits for most common torts are set out in the Limitation Act 1980. The Act also gives the courts discretion to extend time limits in some situations.

Litigation The name given to the process of bringing a case to court. A series of hearings on a related subject, sometimes with different claimants, may be referred to using this term; the 'Lloyd's litigation', for example, refers to a series of cases brought by claimants who had lost money by getting involved with the insurance organisation Lloyd's.

Mandatory injunction A court order requiring someone to do something. For example, if your neighbour was having some major building work done which caused your house to become unstable, a court might make a mandatory injunction requiring your neighbour to do whatever was necessary on their side to restore the support to your house.

Master of the Rolls The head of the civil justice system in England and Wales, and the leading judge in the Civil Division of the Court of Appeal, presiding over the most important or sensitive cases.

Negligent misstatement The name given to a negligence action in which the claimant has suffered pure economic loss, and brings their claim under the rules developed in the case of *Hedley Byrne* v. *Heller* (1963).

Neighbour principle This comes from the case of *Donoghue* v. *Stevenson* (1932) and is considered to be the foundation of the tort of negligence. The principle was created by Lord Atkin, who said that 'You must take care to avoid acts or omissions which you can reasonably foresee would be likely to injure your neighbour.' He went on to explain that, by neighbour, he meant 'persons who are so closely and directly affected by my act that I ought to have them in contemplation as being so affected when I am directing my mind to the acts or omissions which are called into question'.

Neighbour test This comes from the neighbour principle (see above), and asks whether a claimant could reasonably foresee that their behaviour was likely to cause harm or loss to their neighbour, as defined in the neighbour principle.

Nervous shock A term that is sometimes used to refer to psychiatric injury or illness. When used in negligence cases it is misleading as it suggests that a claimant can get damages for being shocked or distressed, when in fact they can only claim if they have a medically recognised psychiatric injury or illness, such as depression or post-traumatic stress syndrome.

No fault A term used when a defendant can be liable without a claimant having to prove that there was anything the defendant did wrong, or anything they could have done to prevent the harm suffered by the claimant. For example, in New Zealand there is no-fault liability for personal injury caused by certain types of accident, which means that a claimant has to prove that they have been injured and that the defendant caused that injury but need not prove that the defendant was negligent.

Non-delegable duty If an individual or organisation has a non-delegable duty, they can delegate the performance of that duty but not the legal liability for it. In other words, they can ask (and usually pay) someone else to do what the duty requires, but if the duty is not done, or not done properly, the party who has the duty can be sued. An example of a non-delegable duty is an employer's duty to take reasonable precautions for the safety of their employees. If an employer asks another company to service its lifts, for example, and this work is done poorly with the result that an employee is injured, the employer will be liable.

Novus actus interveniens The Latin name for an intervening act (see above).

Omission A failure to act. For example, if I break into your house, that is an act. But if I go in to feed your cats while you are on holiday and then don't lock the door when I leave, that is an omission. As a general rule, negligence imposes liability for acts and not omissions, but there are some situations where a defendant can be liable for an omission.

Out-of-court settlement The name given to the situation where the parties to a case agree a solution between them, rather than going to court and having the court decide who wins and, if it is the claimant, what remedy they should get. Most tort cases are settled, with only a tiny minority actually going to court. The settlement usually comes after a process of negotiation between the parties and may happen quite soon after a claim is made or as late as the same day the court hearing is due to be held.

Part 36 offers During the time between a claim being issued and the date set for a court hearing, the parties will usually try to negotiate a settlement. As part of this process either side can make an offer, which means suggesting an amount of damages which they will be willing to pay or accept as a final settlement. Under part 36 of the Civil Procedure Rules, which are the set of rules that govern the way civil cases are run, if one side makes a realistic offer and the other side turns it down and the case goes to trial, the existence of the offer can make a difference to the costs awarded. This is known as a part 36 offer. From a claimant's point of view, part 36 means that if they turn down an offer, and then win their case but are awarded damages equal to or less than the offer, the court can decide that the claimant should pay their own costs and those of the defendant from the date at which the offer expired (instead of the defendant paying both sets of costs as they usually would). This can be a frightening prospect for claimants, and it is well known in the personal injury world that insurers use part 36 offers as a bullying tactic to put pressure on claimants to settle.

Primary victim A term used in negligence cases involving psychiatric injury, covering a claimant who has either suffered physical injury as well as psychiatric injury, or was at risk of physical injury but in fact suffered psychiatric injury only. A primary victim can claim for their psychiatric injury under exactly the same rules as they can claim for their physical injury. See also Secondary victim.

Privy Council More correctly known as the Judicial Committee of the Privy Council, it started out in the days of the British Empire and acted as a final court of appeal for cases from countries in the Empire. Today it still has that role for many countries which are or were part of the Commonwealth, overseas territories of the UK and Crown dependencies.

Prohibitory injunction A court order requiring someone not to do something, or to stop doing something. For example, in a privacy case a newspaper might be ordered not to publish private information, or in a nuisance case a noisy neighbour might be ordered to stop an activity which makes an unreasonable amount of noise.

Psychiatric injury An illness or injury which affects the mind, rather than the body, such as depression or post-traumatic stress disorder.

Public law The branch of law which deals with the relationship between citizens and the state. It contains rules about what the state can and cannot do, and provides remedies where, among other things, the state or one of its organisations or officers has done something which they do not have the legal right to do.

Reasonable foreseeability test One of two tests used to decide on remoteness of damage (see below). In torts where the test applies, a defendant will only be liable for a type of damage that they could reasonably foresee and, if they could foresee the type of damage, they will be liable for all damage of that type, even if they could not foresee how serious it would be.

Remoteness of damage A legal test which decides whether the defendant's carelessness is sufficiently closely related to the damage to make it fair for them to pay compensation.

Res ipsa loquitur Latin for 'The facts speak for themselves', this refers to a legal principle which applies in negligence cases where the circumstances are that harm could not possibly have arisen unless there was negligence. In this situation, a court will be prepared to infer that there was negligence, unless the defendant has evidence to refute this.

Restitutio in integrum The principle behind damages in tort, which seek to restore the claimant to the position they would have been in if the tort had never happened. Latin for 'Restoration to the uninjured state'.

Secondary victim A term used in negligence cases involving psychiatric injury, covering someone who suffered psychiatric injury as a result of the tort but neither suffered physical injury nor was at risk of physical injury. It includes, for example, people who witness accidents, or are involved in helping to rescue people from accidents. Secondary victims can only claim for their psychiatric injury in very limited circumstances.

Settle To settle a case means to agree a solution without going to court. Most tort cases end this way.

Settlement See Out-of-court settlement.

Several liability Arises where two or more tortfeasors act independently of each other, but the result of their acts is damage to the claimant. The claimant can sue one of the tortfeasors for the full amount of the claim or can sue one or more of them at once for the full amount of the claim. Once a claimant has received the total amount that is relevant to the damage, whether from one or more of the defendants, they cannot receive any more (so a claimant could not, for example, recover damages twice by suing two different defendants for the full amount each).

Striking-out application Made by a defendant where a case raises a question of law (such as, 'Is there a duty of care in this situation?'). When the application is heard, the defendant argues that even if the facts of what the claimant says are true, this does not give them a legal claim against the defendant. The court conducts a preliminary examination of the case, in which it assumes that the facts alleged by the claimant are true and from there decides whether they give rise to an arguable case in law – so in a striking out application for a duty of care case, they are deciding whether, on the facts before them, the defendant may owe a duty of care to the claimant. If the court decides that there is no possibility that a duty of care could exist in that situation, the case can be dismissed (struck out) without a full trial. If the court finds that there is an arguable case for a duty of care, the striking-out application is dismissed and the case can proceed to a full trial.

Strict liability A defendant can be liable purely by committing the acts or omissions which make up the tort, regardless of whether there was anything they could have done to prevent the damage. Under the Consumer Protection Act, for example, a manufacturer can be liable for damage caused by a defective product, even if they had taken reasonable precautions to prevent the defect arising.

Tortfeasor An old-fashioned name for the person or organisation that commits a tort.

Vicarious liability An employer is liable where a tort is committed by an employee in the course of their employment.

Volenti non fit injuria Usually known as *volenti*, this is a defence which applies where the claimant has consented to the risk which results in damage or loss to them. Latin for 'No injury can be done to a willing person'.

Index